FROMME

MAUI

1st Edition

By Jeanne Cooper

FROMMER'S STAR RATINGS SYSTEM

Every hotel, restaurant, and attraction listed in this guide has been ranked for quality and value. Here's what the stars mean:

★ Recommended
★★ Highly Recommended
★★★ A must! Don't miss!

AN IMPORTANT NOTE

The world is a dynamic place. Hotels change ownership, restaurants hike their prices, museums alter their opening hours, and buses and trains change their routings. And all of this can occur in the several months after our authors have visited, inspected, and written about these hotels, restaurants, museums, and transportation services. Though we have made valiant efforts to keep all our information fresh and up-to-date, some few changes can inevitably occur in the periods before a revised edition of this guidebook is published. So please bear with us if a tiny number of the details in this book have changed. Please also note that we have no responsibility or liability for any inaccuracy or errors or omissions, or for inconvenience, loss, damage, or expenses suffered by anyone as a result of assertions in this guide.

PREVIOUS PAGE: **Enjoying the sunset in Maui.**
CURRENT PAGE: **Four Seasons Lanai Manele Golf Course.**

CONTENTS

Aerial view of Maui.

A LOOK AT MAUI

For a magnificent introduction to the Hawaiian Islands, Maui hits the mark. It's a bucket-list destination, ticking off pretty much all the boxes of quintessential Hawaiian sights and experiences. Ethereal white-sand beaches? Check. Amazing outdoor adventures against a stunning backdrop of mossy valleys and volcanic peaks? Check. Farm-to-table food, funky little surf towns, and glamourous pampering at luxe resorts? Check, check, and check. Maui deftly walks a high wire, where the rich and famous serenely coexist with surfer dudes and farmers and fat green turtles lazing on world-class beaches. On Maui, eye-popping natural wonders are just a turn in the road away, from the lush green forests and coastal towns along the Road to Hana to the harsh, windswept summit of Haleakala mountain. Maui County also includes the smaller islands of Molokai and Lanai, both with their own cinematic beauty and singularly fascinating sights.

A beautiful black-sand beach on the Road to Hana.

UPCOUNTRY MAUI

A starry night sky overlooks the observatories at Haleakala, the island's 10,023-foot-high mountain and world's largest dormant volcano. See p. 161.

A hula dancer at the Feast at Lele, in Lahaina, one of Maui's most popular luau, a mix of traditional Hawaiian entertainment and delicious regional foods. See p. 33.

Waimoku Falls in a tropical rain forest along the Road to Hana. See p. 210.

The historic K. Matsui Store in the town of Makawao, Maui's Upcountry capital and home to the island's paniolo (Hawaii's cattle-driving cowboys). See p. 151.

Hikers overlooking the volcanic landscape in Haleakala National Park. See p. 161.

Riding horseback along Sliding Sands Trail, which descends to the valley floor of the dusty volcanic crater of Haleakala. See p. 157.

The lovely red-sand beach at Kaihalulu is tucked away in a hidden cove on the Road to Hana. See p. 161.

The bloom of an orange-pink pincushion protea, common in Maui.

WEST MAUI

Diners at Aloha Mixed Plate, a popular beach-side barbecue restaurant in Lahaina. See p. 99.

Budding young surfers at surf camp on Maui's Kaanapali Beach. See p. 180.

The colorful low-rise streetscape of Lahaina, a former missionary town and once the center of the global whaling industry. See p. 135.

Picasso triggerfish at Black Rock, Kaanapali Beach. See p. 180.

ABOVE: A Hawaiian stilt foraging in a salt marsh on Maui.
BELOW: Explosive breach of a humpback whale off Lahaina. See p. 213.

ix

A high-rise view of resorts along Kaanapali Beach. See p. 180.

An artisan in traditional Polynesian garb handcarves wooden keepsakes at the Old Lahaina Luau. See p. 234.

The historic banyan tree in Lahaina Town's Courthouse Square was planted in 1873 and is now 50 feet tall. See p. 137.

Aerial drone photo of stand-up paddleboarder off Wailea Beach. See p. 182.

Christmas is celebrated in Maui with the arrival of Santa Claus by outrigger canoe at Wailea Beach.

Green sea turtle swimming off the shores of Maui.

Wailea Seaside Chapel, the charming white wedding chapel at the Grand Wailea hotel. See p. 72.

Couple paddleboarding off the rugged coastline of Wailea. See p. 190.

The beautiful crescent curve of Wailea Beach. See p. 182.

LANAI

The lush hillsides of Maunalei Gulch. See p. 307

ABOVE: A sumptuous deck at the Four Seasons Resort Lanai. See p. 287. BELOW: You can see the rusted wreck of an old U.S. Navy ship on Lanai's Shipwreck Beach. See p. 302.

Pele's Deli, in the center of the quaint old plantation town of Lanai City. See p. 282 and 296.

The historic Kaunolu Village site, a 200-year-old royal residential compound, holds the ruins of 86 house platforms and 35 stone shelters. See p. 300.

The Garden of the Gods, on Lanai's North Shore, was so named for its rugged volcanic landscape of rust-red boulders and rocks. See p. 297.

Outrigger canoe team paddling on a voyage from Oahu to Molokai. See p. 270.

Simple white church in the former leprosy colony on Molokai. See p. 260.

Halawa Valley waterfall. See p. 265.

Molokai's mossy, broad-shouldered slopes are the world's tallest sea cliffs. See p. 241.

Sliced Molokai purple sweet potato, an island staple. See p. 255.

Trees canopy a red-dirt road in the Molokai Forest Preserve. See p. 263.

THE BEST OF MAUI

A nyone who has been to Maui has heard or seen the Hawaiian expression *Maui no ka 'oi:* "Maui is indeed the best." Many who've been to the Valley Isle agree, returning year after year or even relocating to Maui, enthralled by its staggeringly beautiful scenery and brilliant sunsets, its balmy weather, the annual display of humpback whales frolicking in its waters, and the year-round genuine aloha of its diverse people, inspired by Native Hawaiian traditions of hospitality and cooperation.

Here are some of the natural and cultural treasures to experience on Maui, along with highlights of its always-expanding options for adventure, dining, and family fun. Since Maui County includes **Lanai** and **Molokai** (as well as uninhabited Kahoolawe), I've included top picks from those islands, too.

THE best BEACHES

- **Kaanapali Beach** (West Maui): If you don't approve of the high-rise hotels and condos lining this sandy strand, just turn your back on them. The views of Lanai and Molokai and the scarlet-orange sunsets between them make it easy to gaze on the water instead—especially in winter, when humpback whales spout just a few hundred yards out. The snorkeling around Black Rock (Puu Kekaa) also may lure you in. There's great people-watching on its boardwalk, too. See p. 180.
- **"Big Beach"/Makena State Park** (South Maui): South of Wailea's more manicured, resort-lined beaches, by a 360-foot cinder cone near the end of the road, lies this wild child, known variably as Makena Beach, Big Beach, or Oneloa ("Long Sand"). More than a half-mile long and 100 feet wide, it's a sun worshipper's paradise—just leave its powerful shorebreak to the experts. See p. 183.
- **Hookipa Beach** (North Shore): Pause on the road to Hana to watch the windsurfers and kitesurfers harnessing the wind and waves in an exhilarating offshore display; then head to its eastern end to admire the hauled-out *honu*—Hawaii's green sea turtle—from a respectful distance. See p. 184.

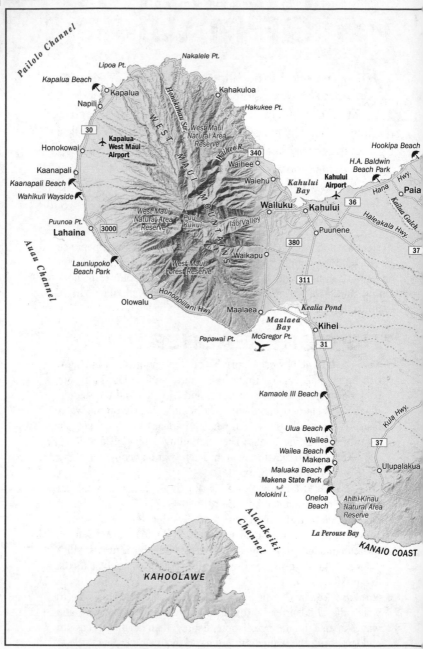

Pailolo Channel

Nakalele Pt.

Lipoa Pt.

Kapalua Beach
Kapalua

Napili

Kahakuloa

Hakukee Pt.

30

Honokowai

Kaanapali

Kaanapali Beach

Wahikuli Wayside

Honoapiilani St.

WEST MAUI MOUNTAINS

West Maui Natural Area Reserve

Wailee R.

340

Waihee

Waiehu

Kahului Bay

Kahului Airport

Hookipa Beach

H.A. Baldwin Beach Park

Hana Hwy.

Kailua Gulch

Paia

Kapalua-West Maui Airport

Puunoa Pt.

Lahaina

3000

West Maui Natural Area Reserve

Puu Kukui

Iao Valley

Wailuku

Kahului

36

Haleakala Hwy.

Puunene

380

37

Auau Channel

Launiupoko Beach Park

West Maui Forest Reserve

Waikapu

311

Olowalu

Honoapiilani Hwy.

Maalaea

Kealia Pond

Maalaea Bay

Kihei

Papawai Pt.

McGregor Pt.

31

Kamaole III Beach

Ulua Beach
Wailea

Wailea Beach
Makena

Maluaka Beach
Makena State Park

Molokini I.

Oneloa Beach

Ahihi-Kinau Natural Area Reserve

La Perouse Bay

KANAIO COAST

Kula Hwy.

37

Ulupalakua

Alalakeiki Channel

KAHOOLAWE

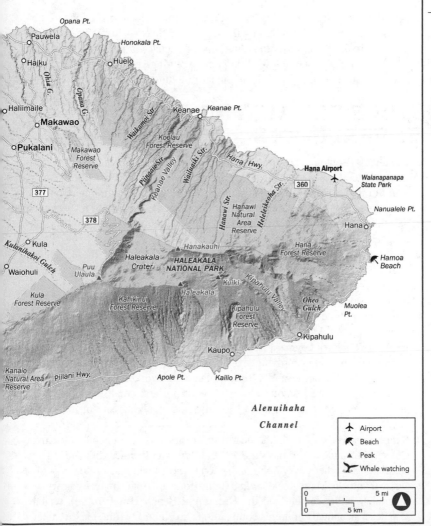

PACIFIC

OCEAN

Opana Pt.

Pauwela

Honokala Pt.

Haiku   Huelo

Olili G.

Opana G.

Haliimaile

Keanae   Keanae Pt.

Makawao

Koolau
Forest Reserve

Pukalani

Makawao
Forest
Reserve

Waikamoi Str.

Piinaue Str.

Keanae Valley

Wailuaiki Str.

Hana Hwy.

Hana Airport

377

360

Waianapanapa
State Park

378

Hanawi Str.

Heleleikeoha Str.

Hanawi
Natural
Area
Reserve

Nanualele Pt.

Hana

Kula

Kulanihakoi Gulch

Hanakauhi

Hana
Forest Reserve

Hamoa
Beach

Haleakala
Crater

HALEAKALA
NATIONAL PARK

Waiohuli

Puu
Ulaula

Kuiki

Kipahulu Valley

Muolea
Pt.

Kula
Forest Reserve

Kahikinui
Forest Reserve

Haleakala

Kipahulu
Forest
Reserve

Ohea
Gulch

Kipahulu

Kaupo

Kanaio
Natural Area
Reserve

Piilani Hwy.

Apole Pt.   Kailio Pt.

Alenuihaha

Channel

✈ Airport
🏄 Beach
▲ Peak
🐋 Whale watching

0   5 mi

0   5 km

o **Waianapanapa State Park** (East Maui): On the dramatic Hana coast, jet-black sand contrasts with the azure sea, whose strength has carved out sea arches. Caves with cultural significance dot the shoreline, and a cliffside trail leads through an ancient *hala* forest. Plan to picnic or camp here. See p. 184.

o **Papohaku Beach Park** (Molokai): The currents are too strong for swimming, but the light-blond strand of sand, nearly 300 feet wide and stretching for some 3 miles—one of Hawaii's longest beaches—is great for picnicking, walking, and watching sunsets, with Oahu shimmering in the distance. See p. 246.

o **Hulopoe Beach** (Lanai): This large sprawl of soft golden sand is one of the prettiest in the state. Bordered by the regal Four Seasons resort on one side and lava-rock tide pools on the other, this protected marine preserve offers prime swimming, snorkeling, tide-pool exploring, picnicking, camping, and the chance to spy on resident spinner dolphins. See p. 293.

THE best AUTHENTIC EXPERIENCES

o **Eat Local:** People in Hawaii love food. Want to get a local talking? Ask for her favorite place to get poke or saimin or shave ice, not to mention *malasadas* or mochi. Maui County's islands offer excellent fine-dining opportunities (see "The best Restaurants"), but they also have plenty of respectable hole-in-the-wall joints and beloved institutions that have hung around for decades.

o **Paddle an Outrigger Canoe:** The first humans to inhabit these islands arrived via outrigger sailing canoes, and the modern six-person canoe remains a potent metaphor for the collaboration. Learn the Hawaiian lore of the *wa'a* ("vah-ah") and spot a swimming turtle or two while paddling; it's often a complimentary resort experience. See a list of providers beginning on p. 190.

o **Explore Lahaina's Layered History:** A seat of Hawaiian royalty, a riotous rest stop for whalers, a proving ground for Christian missionaries, a gathering place for Japanese and Chinese plantation workers—Lahaina brims with historic homes, unique places of worship, and small but intriguing museums, easily visited as part of a self-guided walking tour or individually. See p. 135.

o **Experience Hula:** Called "the heartbeat of the Hawaiian people" by King David Kalakaua, hula has a deep cultural significance beyond "The Hukilau" and other perky *hapa haole* songs most mainland visitors associate with it. On Maui, local *halau* (hula troupes) perform **free shows** at several shopping centers and the **Kaanapali Beach Hotel** (p. 52), which also hosts an annual children's competition, **Na Keiki O Hula,** in November (see p. 53). The **Old Lahaina Luau** (p. 234) is the real deal, showcasing

Hawaiian dance and storytelling nightly on a gracious beachfront stage. On Molokai, reverent dancers celebrate the birth of hula during the 3-day **Ka Hula Piko** festival (p. 281) held in late spring.

o **Listen to Slack Key Guitar:** Just as much as the ukulele, the style of guitar tuning and picking introduced by *paniolo* (cowboy) is a signature sound of Hawaii. Although many restaurants and hotel bars offer free performances, Maui's long-running **Masters of Slack Key Guitar** weekly concert series (p. 235) in Napili attracts virtuosos who share their melodic music and stories behind their songs with genial host George Kahumoku, Jr.

o **Trek to Kalaupapa** (Molokai): The only access to this hauntingly beautiful and remote place is by foot, mule, or nine-seater plane. Hikers can descend the 26 switchbacks on the sea cliff's narrow 3-mile trail to **Kalaupapa National Park** (p. 260), a once-in-a-lifetime adventure. After you've reached the peninsula, you'll board **a tour bus** (p. 266)—your transport back to a time when islanders with Hansen's disease (leprosy) were exiled to Molokai and Father Damien and other selfless souls sacrificed their lives to their care.

THE best OUTDOOR ADVENTURES

o **Witness the Whales:** From December to April, humpback whales cruise Hawaiian waters. You can see these gentle giants from almost any shore; simply scan the horizon for a spout. Hear them, too, by ducking your head below the surface and listening for their otherworldly music. The shallower channels between South Maui and Kahoolawe and between West Maui and Lanai offer the best bets for seeing the massive marine mammals up close. Try **Trilogy** (p. 187) for a first-class catamaran ride, or, if you're adventurous, climb into an outrigger canoe with **Hawaiian Paddle Sports** (p. 189).

o **Snorkel in a Submerged Crater:** You'll have to take a boat or high-speed raft to get there, but the crescent wall of Molokini, half a mile wide and extending some 300 feet below the ocean, provides shelter for a shallow reef with a phenomenal array of colorful fish. Get there early and in comfort with **Kai Kanani** (p. 187) or **Trilogy** (p. 187).

o **Visit a Volcanic Summit:** All of the Hawaiian Islands were formed by shield volcanoes, and all are now extinct—except on the southernmost islands of Maui and Hawaii. On Maui, **Haleakala** ("House of the Sun") has been dormant for at least several centuries, but you can sense its impressive force by driving up to its 10,023-foot summit in Haleakala National Park and hiking into the vast crater (p. 154).

o **Get Misted by Waterfalls:** Waterfalls thundering down into sparkling pools are some of Hawaii's most beautiful natural wonders. On Maui, the Road to Hana offers numerous viewing opportunities, beginning with **Twin Falls** (p. 165). Drive past Hana to the **Kipahulu District** (p. 175) of

THE welcoming LEI

A lei is aloha turned tangible, communicating "hello," "goodbye," "congratulations," and "I love you" in a single strand of fragrant flowers. Leis are the perfect symbol for the islands: Their fragrance and beauty are enjoyed in the moment, but the aloha they embody lasts long after they've faded.

Traditionally, Hawaiians made leis out of flowers, shells, ferns, leaves, nuts, and even seaweed. Some were twisted, some braided, and some strung. Then, as now, they were worn to commemorate special occasions, honor a loved one, or complement a hula dancer's costume. Each island has a representative lei: Maui's is the **rose,** called roselani or lokelani ("heavenly rose").

Leis are available not only from florists, but also at the airport, supermarkets, and large drug stores. You can arrange in advance to have a lei-greeter meet you as you deplane; **Greeters of Hawaii** (www.greetersofhawaii.com; ✆ **800/366-8559**) serves Kahului. In addition, many hotels offer family-friendly workshops on stringing your own lei, typically with sturdy purple orchids or, for kids, paper petals. Visitors to Molokai can make an appointment to create a more fragrant lei with pink and white blossoms they'll gather themselves at **Molokai Plumerias** (p. 256).

Haleakala National Park to ogle the multiple cascades of **Oheo Gulch** and follow the **Pipiwai Trail** (p. 175) through bamboo forest to the 400-foot wonder of **Waimoku Falls.**

o **Four-Wheel It on Lanai** (Lanai): Off-roading is a way of life on barely paved Lanai. Rugged trails lead to deserted beaches, abandoned villages, sacred sites, and valleys filled with wild game. Unsure about driving yourself? **Rabaca's Limousine Service and Island Tours** (p. 289) will take you to remote areas in comfortable vehicles with friendly guides.

THE best HOTELS

o **Fairmont Kea Lani** (Wailea): This Wailea resort offers a quiet beachfront locale, massive suites, residential-sized villas, a plethora of pools, an expert spa with a thoughtful wellness program, and excellent dining, from the fresh poke bowls in the marketplace to the gourmet take on plantation fare at **Ko** (p. 116). Sunsets are mesmerizing, especially when accompanied by an artisan cocktail in the resort's **Luana Lounge.** See p. 238.

o **Four Seasons Resorts** (Wailea and Lanai): The vast **Four Seasons Resort Maui at Wailea** (p. 71) and the more intimate **Four Seasons Resort Lanai** (p. 291) have very different styles in architecture and decor, but both share a commitment to service and unique experiences for all ages that is hard to beat. Dining is pricey but impeccable.

o **Hotel Wailea** (Wailea): A rare adults-only oasis on this family-friendly island, this Relais & Chateaux boutique hotel radiates style and serenity from its hilltop garden setting. It offers beach shuttle service, but it may be hard to pull yourself away from the daybeds and artisan cocktails at the pool. See p. 73.

o **Montage Kapalua Bay** (Kapalua): The luxurious residential villas, uncrowded tiered and infinity pools, and unparalleled spa seem hidden from public view here—and that's a big part of its quiet appeal, along with easy access to sandy beaches and snorkeling coves. See p. 59.

o **Travaasa Hana** (Hana): Nestled in the center of quaint Hana town, this 66-acre resort wraps around Kauiki Head, the dramatic point where Queen Kaahumanu was born. You'll feel like royalty in one of the Sea Ranch Cottages here. Floor-to-ceiling sliding doors open to spacious lanais, some with private hot tubs. You'll be far from shopping malls and sports bars, but black- and gold-sand beaches are a short walk or shuttle ride away. Immerse yourself in the resort's long list of Hawaiian cultural activities or just soak in the tranquility. See p. 81.

o **Wailea Beach Resort** (Wailea): A $100-million transformation of this Marriott property added more of what Wailea is known for—high style, high-end restaurants, and higher prices—but also a unique, fun-loving esprit all of its own, from playful lawn sculptures to elaborate pools and its own food truck. See p. 73.

THE best RESTAURANTS

o **Kaana Kitchen** (Andaz Maui, Wailea): Treat Chef Isaac Bancaco's grid menu like a gourmet bingo card; every combination is a winner. Start off with a hand-mixed cocktail and the ahi tataki: ruby-red tuna, heirloom tomato, and fresh burrata sprinkled with black salt and nasturtium petals. The $45 breakfast buffet grants you access to the kitchen's novel chilled countertops, stocked with every delicacy and fresh juice you can imagine. See p. 70.

o **Mama's Fish House** (Paia): Overlooking Kuau Cove on Maui's North Shore, this restaurant is a South Pacific fantasy. Every nook is decorated with some fanciful artifact of salt-kissed adventure. The menu lists the anglers who reeled in the day's catch; you can order ono "caught by Keith Nakamura along the 40-fathom ledge near Hana" or deepwater ahi seared with coconut and lime. The Tahitian Pearl dessert is almost too stunning to eat. See p. 125.

o **Tin Roof** (Kahului) and **Lineage** (Wailea): Celebrity chef Sheldon Simeon won the hearts of *Top Chef* fans not once, but twice. Now he's done the same for Maui diners. He and his wife, Janice, first opened **Tin Roof** (p. 91), a humble to-go lunch spot in an industrial Kahului strip mall, with a fun, Filipino-inspired menu (including an Instagram-worthy chocolate bibingka cupcake). In 2018, they added the chic but equally whimsical **Lineage** (p. 116) in the Shops at Wailea, with snacks, small plates, and family-sized dishes on a dinner-only menu inspired by Sheldon's roots in Hilo.

o **Merriman's** (Kapalua): Chef Peter Merriman, one of the founders of Hawaii Regional Cuisine, oversees a locally inspired culinary empire that includes the more casual **Monkeypod Kitchen** in Wailea and Whalers Village (p. 118). The farm-to-table menu at his elegant Kapalua outpost (p. 108) almost matches the breathtaking island, ocean, and beach views from its perch on a rocky point.

o **Japengo** (Kaanapali): The sunset views are dazzling from this promontory at the Hyatt Regency Maui, but so is the artful sushi and innovative Japanese fusion dishes incorporating fresh island ingredients. Despite stiff competition, it's justifiably a perennial favorite in local polling. See p. 102.

THE best OF MAUI FOR KIDS

o **Spend a Day at the Beach**: Maui is abundant in beachgoing options, but those with small kids will especially appreciate beaches with gentler drop-offs, calmer waters, and facilities like restrooms and picnic tables. Kihei's **Kamaole Beach III** (p. 181), aka **Kam-3,** has all this plus a children's playground—great for when water conditions are a bit rough. In West Maui, **Kapalua Beach** (p. 178) on the Kapalua Resort offers a protected cove with plenty of shade and beach rentals (the kids can try their hand at stand-up paddling), while **Launiupoko Beach Park** (p. 181) south of Lahaina has a natural wading pool formed by boulders that shields little ones from the surf.

o **Tour or Even Sleep at the Aquarium** (Maalaea): The inviting touch pools and vast shark-filled tanks at the **Maui Ocean Center** are great for daytime visits. Kids can book a sleepover, staying up into the wee hours to watch glowing jellies and other nocturnal animals. See p. 149.

o **Zip Over a Tropical Farm**: The beginner's dual zipline at **Maui Tropical Plantation** is perfect for pint-sized adventurers and their parents, who can enjoy a narrated tram ride through the fields and orchards of this scenic compound at the base of the West Maui Mountains. See p. 132.

o **Play in a Fantasy Pool:** When the surf has kicked up, it's great to have a ready alternative. Every Maui resort has a noteworthy pool, but the lazy river, grottoes, and other fun features of the fantasy pool at the **Grand Wailea** (p. 72) are over the top. Kids will find thrills on the towering slide at the **Wailea Beach Resort** (p. 73) and the pirate ship at the **Westin Kaanapali Ocean Resort Villas** (p. 48).

MAUI IN CONTEXT

Since the Polynesians navigated their way across the Pacific to the Hawaiian Islands a millennium ago, Hawaii's chain of floating emeralds has bedazzled travelers from around the globe. All of the islands are spectacular in their own way, but people on Maui—including the legions of loyal visitors to the Valley Isle—are fond of saying *Maui no ka 'oi:* Maui is the best.

The Hawaiian Islands bask in the warm waters of the Pacific, blessed by a tropical sun and cooled by gentle tradewinds—creating what might be the most ideal climate imaginable. Mother Nature has carved out verdant valleys, hung brilliant rainbows in the sky, and trimmed the islands with sandy beaches in a spectrum of colors. Maui is also blessed by dazzling sunsets that cast their glow on the neighboring islands of Kahoolawe, Lanai, and Molokai. All are part of Maui County, sharing historic ties and, in some cases, now-friendly rivalries.

Here, the indigenous Hawaiian culture embodies "aloha spirit," an easy-going generosity that takes the shape of flower leis freely given, monumental feasts shared with friends and family, and hypnotic melodies played late into the balmy night. The polyglot cultures that arrived on Maui and the rest of Hawaii during the plantation era have adopted this spirit as theirs, too, and adapted the feasts to include a panoply of ethnic cuisines found nowhere else.

Visitors are drawn to Maui not only for its incredible beauty, but also for its opportunities for adventure. Go on, gaze into that immense volcanic crater, swim in a sea of rainbow-colored fish, tee off on a championship golf course, hike through a rainforest to hidden waterfalls, and kayak into the deep end of the ocean, where whales leap out of the water for reasons still mysterious. Looking for rest and relaxation? You'll discover that life moves at an unhurried pace here. Extra doses of sun and sea allow both body and mind to recharge.

Maui is a sensory experience that will remain with you long after your lei's heady perfume fades. Years later, a sweet fragrance, the sun's warmth on your face, or the sound of the ocean breeze will deliver you back to the time you spent on the Valley Isle.

THE FIRST HAWAIIANS

Throughout the Middle Ages, while Western sailors clung to the edges of continents for fear of falling off the earth's edge, Polynesian voyagers crisscrossed the planet's largest ocean. The first people to colonize Hawaii were unsurpassed navigators. Using the stars, birds, currents, and wind as guides, they sailed double-hulled canoes across thousands of miles, zeroing in on tiny islands in the center of the Pacific. They packed their vessels with food, plants, medicine, tools, and animals: everything necessary for building a new life on a distant shore. Over a span of an estimated 800 years, the great Polynesian migration connected a vast triangle of islands stretching from Aotearoa (New Zealand) to Hawaii to Easter Island and encompassing the many diverse archipelagos in between. Historians surmise that Hawaii's first wave of settlers came via the Marquesas Islands as early as 500 A.D., although archaeological records better document the second human wave of settlers from the Society Island, beginning around 1000 A.D.

Over the centuries, a distinctly Hawaiian culture arose. The voyagers became farmers and fishermen, as skilled on land as they had been at sea; they built highly productive fish ponds, aqueducts to irrigate terraced *kalo lo'i* (taro patches), and 3-acre *heiau* (temples) with 50-foot-high rock walls. Farmers cultivated more than 400 varieties of *kalo,* or taro, their staple food; 300 types of sweet potato; and 40 different bananas. Each variety served a different need—some were drought-resistant, others medicinal, and others good for babies. Hawaiian women pounded the bark of mulberry trees to fine layers and then inked it with bamboo stamps to create intricately patterned *kapa* cloth—some of the finest in all of Polynesia. Each of the Hawaiian Islands was its own kingdom, governed by *ali'i* (high-ranking chiefs) who drew their authority from an established caste system and *kapu* (taboos). Those who broke the *kapu* could be sacrificed.

The ancient Hawaiian creation chant, the *Kumulipo,* depicts a universe that began when heat and light emerged out of darkness, followed by the first life form: a coral polyp. The 2,000-line epic poem is a grand genealogy, describing how all species are interrelated, from gently waving seaweeds to mighty human warriors. It is the basis for the Hawaiian concept of *kuleana,* a word that simultaneously refers to privilege and responsibility. To this day, Native Hawaiians view the care of their natural resources as a familial duty and honor.

WESTERN CONTACT
Cook's Ill-Fated Voyage

In the dawn hours of January 18, 1778, Captain James Cook of the HMS *Resolution* spotted an unfamiliar set of islands, which he later named for his benefactor, the Earl of Sandwich. The 50-year-old sea captain was already famous in Britain for "discovering" much of the South Pacific. Now on his third great voyage of exploration, Cook had set sail from Tahiti northward across uncharted waters. He was searching for the mythical Northwest Passage that was said to link the Pacific and Atlantic oceans. On his way, he stumbled upon Hawaii (aka the Sandwich Isles) quite by chance.

Cook stayed just a couple of weeks after landing at Waimea, Kauai, on January 20, before sailing to the Pacific Northwest and Alaska, but the wheels of a terrible fortune were already set in motion. With the arrival of the *Resolution,* Stone Age Hawaii entered the age of iron. Sailors swapped nails and munitions for fresh water, pigs, and the affections of Hawaiian women. Tragically, the foreigners also brought with them syphilis, measles, and other diseases that decimated the Hawaiian people. Captain Cook estimated the native population at 400,000 in 1778. (Later historians claim it could have been as high as 900,000.) By the time Christian missionaries arrived 42 years later, the number of Native Hawaiians had plummeted to just 150,000.

Cook returned to the islands later that year, catching sight of Maui on November 26, 1778, but high surf prevented him from landing. Instead, he continued on to the island of Hawaii, where his initial visit on January 17, 1779, was well-received. A second, 2 months later, was not. In a skirmish over a stolen boat, Cook was killed by a blow to the head. His British countrymen sailed home, leaving Hawaii forever altered. The islands were now on the sea charts, and traders on the fur route between Canada and China stopped here to get fresh water. More trade—and more disastrous liaisons—ensued.

Two more sea captains left indelible marks on the islands. The first was American John Kendrick, who in 1791 filled his ship with fragrant Hawaiian sandalwood and sailed to China. By 1825, Hawaii's sandalwood groves were gone, and many of those who had been forced to harvest them were dead from their labors. The second was Englishman George Vancouver, who in 1793 left behind cows and sheep that ventured out to graze in the islands' native forest and hastened the spread of invasive species. King Kamehameha I sent for cowboys from Mexico and Spain to round up the wild livestock, thus beginning the islands' *paniolo* (cowboy) tradition.

King Kamehameha I was an ambitious *ali'i* who used Western guns to unite the islands under single rule, a years-long effort that included a bloody battle in 1790 in Maui's now-tranquil Iao Valley. After his death in 1819, the tightly woven Hawaiian society began to unravel. One of his successors, Queen Kaahumanu, abolished the *kapu* system, opening the door for religion of another form.

Staying to Do Well

In April 1820, New England missionaries bent on converting Hawaiians arrived on Hawaii Island, and by 1821 had set to work on Maui, initially in Lahaina. The newcomers clothed the natives, banned them from dancing the hula, and nearly dismantled the ancient culture. The churchgoers tried to keep sailors and whalers out of the bawdy houses, where whiskey flowed and the virtue of native women was never safe. To their credit, the missionaries created a 12-letter alphabet for the Hawaiian language (now 13, including the glottal stop, or *'okina*). They also taught reading and writing—opening the oldest school west of the Rockies in Lahaina, Maui, where they also operated Hawaii's first printing press—and began recording the islands' history, which until that time had been preserved solely in memorized chants, or *oli*. Hawaiians quickly added Western-style singing (*mele*) and musical composition to their creative repertoire.

Children of some missionaries became business leaders and politicians, often marrying Hawaiians and receiving royal grants of land, causing one wag to remark that the missionaries "came to do good and stayed to do well." In 1848, King Kamehameha III enacted the Great Mahele (division). Intended to guarantee Native Hawaiians rights to their land, it ultimately enabled foreigners to take ownership of vast tracts of land. Within two generations, more than 80% of all private land was in *haole* (foreign) hands. Businessmen planted acre after acre of sugarcane and imported waves of immigrants to work the fields: Chinese starting in 1852, Japanese in 1868, and Portuguese in 1878, among other nationalities.

King David Kalakaua was elected to the throne in 1874. This popular "Merrie Monarch" built Iolani Palace in 1882, threw extravagant parties, and lifted the prohibitions on hula and other native arts. For this, he was much loved. He proclaimed, "hula is the language of the heart and, therefore, the heartbeat of the Hawaiian people." He also gave Pearl Harbor to the United States; it became the westernmost bastion of the U.S. Navy. While visiting chilly San Francisco in 1891, King Kalakaua caught a cold and died in the royal suite of the Palace Hotel. His sister, Queen Liliuokalani, assumed the throne.

The Overthrow

For years, a group of American sugar plantation owners and missionary descendants had been machinating against the monarchy. On January 17,

WHO IS hawaiian IN HAWAII?

Only *kanaka maoli* (Native Hawaiians) are truly Hawaiian. The sugar and pineapple plantations brought so many different people to Hawaii that the state is now a remarkable potpourri of ethnic groups: Native Hawaiians were joined by **European Americans, Japanese, Chinese, Filipinos, Koreans, Portuguese, Puerto Ricans, Samoans, Tongans, Tahitians,** and other **Asian and Pacific Islanders.**

Add to that a sprinkling of **Vietnamese, African Americans, American Indians, South Americans,** and **Europeans** of every stripe. Many people retained the traditions of their homeland, and many more blended their cultures into something new. That is the genesis of Hawaiian Pidgin, local cuisine, and holidays and celebrations unique to these Islands.

1893, with the support of the U.S. minister to Hawaii and the Marines, the conspirators imprisoned Queen Liliuokalani in her own palace. To avoid bloodshed, she abdicated the throne, trusting that the United States government would right the wrong. As the Queen waited in vain, she penned the sorrowful lyric "Aloha Oe," Hawaii's song of farewell.

U.S. President Grover Cleveland's attempt to restore the monarchy was thwarted by Congress. Sanford Dole, a powerful sugar-plantation owner, appointed himself president of the newly declared Republic of Hawaii. His fellow sugarcane planters, known as the Big Five, controlled banking, shipping, hardware, and every other facet of economic life in the Islands. In 1898, through annexation, Hawaii became an American territory ruled by Dole.

Oahu's central Ewa Plain soon filled with row crops; the Dole family planted pineapple on its sprawling acreage. On Maui, Alexander & Baldwin, founded by sons of missionaries in 1870, started with a 560-acre sugarcane farm and quickly added more cane fields, sugar mills, and pineapple plantations to create a vast empire. Planters imported more contract laborers from Puerto Rico (1900), Korea (1903), and the Philippines (1907–31). Many of the new immigrants stayed on to establish families and become a part of the islands. Meanwhile, Native Hawaiians became a landless minority. Their language was banned in schools and their cultural practices devalued.

For nearly a century in Hawaii, sugar was king, generously subsidized by the U.S. government. Sugar is a thirsty crop, and plantation owners oversaw the construction of flumes and aqueducts that channeled mountain streams down to parched plains, where waving fields of cane soon grew. The waters that once fed taro patches dried up. The sugar planters dominated the territory's economy, shaped its social fabric, and kept the islands in a colonial-plantation era with bosses and field hands. But the workers eventually went on strike for higher wages and improved working conditions, and the planters found themselves unable to compete with cheap third-world labor costs.

Tourism Takes Hold

Tourism in Hawaii began in the 1860s. Kilauea volcano was one of the world's prime attractions for adventure travelers. In 1865 a grass structure known as Volcano House was built on the rim of Halemaumau Crater to shelter visitors; it was Hawaii's first hotel. The visitor industry blossomed as the plantation era peaked and waned.

In 1901 W. C. Peacock built the elegant Beaux-Arts Moana Hotel on Waikiki Beach, and W. C. Weedon convinced Honolulu businessmen to bankroll his plan to advertise Hawaii in San Francisco. Armed with a stereopticon and tinted photos of Waikiki, Weedon sailed off in 1902 for 6 months of lecture tours to introduce "those remarkable people and the beautiful lands of Hawaii." He drew packed houses. A tourism promotion bureau was formed in 1903, and about 2,000 visitors came to Hawaii that year. In 1916, the summit of Haleakala became part of one of the first national parks—then called

SPEAKING hawaiian

Nearly everyone in Hawaii speaks English, though many people now also speak at least some 'olelo Hawaii, the native language of these islands. Most roads, towns, and beaches possess vowel-heavy Hawaiian names, so it will serve you well to practice pronunciation before landing in Kahului or perambulating in Pa'ia.

The Hawaiian alphabet has only 12 traditional letters: 7 consonants (h, k, l, m, n, p, and w, the latter sometimes pronounced like v) and 5 vowels (a, e, i, o, and u)—but those vowels are liberally used! Usually they are "short," pronounced: ah, eh, ee, oh, and oo. For example, wahine (woman) is wah-hee-nay. Combinations of vowels typically produce diphthongs: ei is pronounced ay, ai and ae something like eye, au and ao something like the ow in how, iu like you, and so on.

When two vowels appear consecutively, they're often separated by an 'okina, a diacritical mark shaped like a single open quotation mark that represents a glottal stop, or slight pause. Appearing only before or between vowels, it's considered a consonant and recognized as a 13th letter. You'll also see a kahako, or macron (line) over a vowel indicating stress. Observing these rules, you can tell that Pa'ia, the popular surf town on Maui's North Shore, is pronounced PAH-ee-ah and the lovely state park in Hana, Wai'anapanapa, is pronounced Why-AH-nah-pah-nah-pah.

Incorporate aloha (hello, goodbye, love) and mahalo (thank you) into your vocabulary. If you've just arrived, you're a malihini (newcomer). Someone who's been here a long time is a kama'aina (child of the land). When you finish a job or your meal, you are pau (finished). On Friday, it's pau hana, work finished. You eat pupu (appetizers) when you go pau hana.

Note: For typographical reasons, Hawaiian punctuation marks are generally not included in this edition, but you will see them on road signs, menus, and publications throughout Hawaii.

Hawaii National Park and including Mauna Loa and Kileaua on the Big Island.

The steamship was Hawaii's tourism lifeline. It took 4½ days to sail from San Francisco to Honolulu. Streamers, leis, and pomp welcomed each Matson liner at downtown's Aloha Tower. Well-heeled visitors brought trunks, servants, and Rolls-Royces and stayed for months. Scheduled interisland air service and airplane sightseeing tours began in 1929, by what would eventually become Hawaiian Airlines, but visitors rarely explored neighbor islands like Maui. Instead, Oahu's population amused visitors with personal tours, floral parades, and hula shows.

Beginning in 1935 and running for the next 40 years, Webley Edwards's weekly live radio show, "Hawaii Calls," planted the sounds of Waikiki—surf, sliding steel guitar, sweet Hawaiian harmonies, drumbeats—in the hearts of millions of listeners in the United States, Australia, and Canada.

By 1936, visitors could fly to Honolulu from San Francisco on the *Hawaii Clipper,* a seven-passenger Pan American Martin M-130 flying boat, for $360 one-way. The flight took 21 hours, 33 minutes. Modern tourism was born, with five flying boats providing daily service. The 1941 visitor count was a brisk 31,846 through December 6.

World War II & Statehood

On December 7, 1941, Japanese Zeros came out of the rising sun to bomb American warships based at Pearl Harbor and airfields across Oahu. This was the "day of infamy" that plunged the United States into World War II.

The attack brought immediate changes to the islands, including Maui, where a small Japanese sub fired a shell at Kahului (today the site of the Maui Beach Hotel). Martial law was declared, stripping the Big Five cartel of its absolute power in a single day. Prominent Japanese Americans (or those deemed otherwise "suspect") were interned, along with German nationals. Hawaii was "blacked out" at night, Waikiki Beach was strung with barbed wire, and Aloha Tower was painted in camouflage. Only young men bound for the Pacific came to Hawaii during the war years; many came back to graves in a cemetery called Punchbowl. Young Japanese American men eventually formed one of the war's most decorated battalions.

The postwar years saw the beginnings of Hawaii's faux culture. The authentic traditions had long been suppressed, and into the void flowed a consumable brand of aloha. Harry Yee invented the Blue Hawaii cocktail and dropped in a tiny Japanese parasol. Vic Bergeron created the mai tai, a drink made of rum and fresh lime juice, and opened Trader Vic's, America's first themed restaurant featuring the art, decor, and food of Polynesia. Arthur Godfrey picked up a ukulele and began singing *hapa-haole* tunes on early TV shows.

In 1946, Maui's first resort hotel opened in remote Hana, hosting a San Francisco minor league baseball team that helped spread the fame of "Heavenly Hana." In 1955, Henry J. Kaiser built the Hilton Hawaiian Village at the edge of Waikiki, and the 11-story high-rise Princess Kaiulani Hotel opened on a site not far away, where the real princess once played. Hawaii greeted 109,000 visitors that year.

In 1959, the Territory of Hawaii became the 50th state of the United States. That year also saw the arrival of the first jet airliners, which brought 250,000 tourists to the state. By 1962, the opening of the Royal Lahaina hotel marked the debut of Maui's first full-fledged resort, Kaanapali Beach, offering golf and glamorous lodgings along what had been a quiet shoreline.

By the 1980s, Hawaii's annual visitor count surpassed 6 million. Fantasy mega resorts bloomed on Maui and other neighbor islands like giant artificial flowers, swelling the luxury market with ever-swankier accommodations. Hawaii's tourist industry—the bastion of the state's economy—has survived worldwide recessions, airline-industry hiccups, and increased competition from overseas. Year after year, the Hawaiian Islands continue to be ranked among the top visitor destinations in the world, with Maui singled out for its beaches and beauty.

MAUI TODAY
A Cultural Renaissance

Despite the ever-increasing influx of foreign people and customs, Native Hawaiian culture is experiencing a rebirth. It began in earnest in 1976, when members of the Polynesian Voyaging Society launched *Hokule'a*, a double-hulled canoe of the sort that hadn't been seen on these shores in centuries. In their craft, named for ancient Hawaiians' guiding star, "Star of Gladness" (Arcturus to Westerners), the daring crew sailed 2,500 miles to Tahiti without modern instruments, relying instead on ancient navigational techniques. Most historians at that time discounted Polynesian wayfinding methods as rudimentary; the prevailing theory was that Pacific Islanders had discovered Hawaii by accident, not intention. The success of modern voyagers sparked a fire in the hearts of indigenous islanders across the Pacific, who reclaimed their identity as a sophisticated, powerful people with unique wisdom to offer the world. Maui's voyaging society, founded in 1975, proudly launched its own 62-foot sailing canoe, *Mo'okiha O Pi'ilani*, in 2014.

The Hawaiian language has found new life, too. In 1984, a group of educators and parents recognized that, with fewer than 50 children fluent in Hawaiian, the language was dangerously close to extinction. They started a preschool where *keiki* (children) learned lessons purely in Hawaiian. They overcame numerous bureaucratic obstacles (including a law still on the books forbidding instruction in Hawaiian) to establish Hawaiian-language-immersion programs across the state that run from preschool through post-graduate education. In 2001, Maui celebrated the high school graduation of its first class of students to be in such a program from kindergarten on. Native Hawaiian cultural advisors, grounded in both the language and traditions of their forebears, have become de rigueur for most large hotels and resorts.

Hula—which never fully disappeared despite the missionaries' best efforts—is thriving. At the Big Island's annual Merrie Monarch Festival in Hilo, which commemorates King Kalakaua, hula *halau* (troupes) from Hawaii and beyond gather to demonstrate their skill and artistry. Fans of the ancient dance form are glued to the live broadcast (or live stream, watched from around the globe) of what is known as the Olympics of hula; Maui's dancers have taken top honors many times. Maui also hosts two long-running hula competitions: one for child soloists, Hula O Na Keiki, and a sort of all-stars contest for adults, Ku Mai Ka Hula. *Kumu hula* (hula teachers) have safeguarded many Hawaiian cultural practices as part of their art: the making of *kapa*, the collection and cultivation of native herbs, and the observation of *kuleana*, an individual's responsibility to the community.

In Maui County, visitors are welcome to share in that *kuleana* by, among other volunteer opportunities, restoring fish ponds on Maui and Molokai, removing invasive plants in Haleakala National Park, joining nonprofit groups reforesting Kahoolawe, counting whales from Maui's shoreline, or caring for cats at sanctuaries on Lanai and Molokai, which protects endangered native and migratory birds. You can also help safeguard this fragile environment by using reef-friendly sunscreen, packing a reusable water bottle, and refraining from littering. Sharing the aloha that you receive, with a smile, a wave, or friendly conversation, will help preserve Hawaii's unique culture, but is also its own reward.

DINING ON MAUI
The Gang of 12

In the early days of Hawaii's tourism industry, the food wasn't anything to write home about. Continental cuisine ruled fine-dining kitchens. Meats and produce arrived much the same way visitors did: jet-lagged after a long journey from a far-off land. Island chefs struggled to revive limp iceberg lettuce and frozen cocktail shrimp—often letting outstanding ocean views make up for uninspired dishes. In 1991, 12 chefs—including Maui's Bev Gannon, Roger Dikon, Mark Ellman, and Amy Ferguson—staged a revolt. They partnered with local farmers, ditched the dictatorship of imported foods, and brought sun-ripened mango, crisp organic greens, and freshly caught *uku* (snapper) to the table. Coining the name **Hawaii Regional Cuisine (HRC),** they gave the world a taste of what happens when passionate, classically trained cooks have their way with ripe Pacific flavors.

Nearly 3 decades later, the movement to unite local farms and kitchens has only grown more vibrant. Many of the HRC heavyweights continue to keep things hot in island kitchens. On Maui, Gannon and Ellman still run several popular restaurants apiece (including her **Gannon's** and **Haliimaile General Store** and his **Frida's** and **Mala Ocean Tavern**), while HRC cofounders Peter Merriman and Roy Yamaguchi also have outposts of their culinary empires here (**Merriman's** and **Monkeypod Kitchen** from the former, **Roy's** and **Humble Market Kitchin** from the latter).

They aren't, by any means, the sole source of good eats on Maui, however. *Top Chef* fan favorite Sheldon Simeon celebrates his Filipino roots and local cuisine at his simple **Tin Roof** lunch counter in Kahului and chic **Lineage** restaurant in Wailea. Francophiles will delight in the classic French cooking at **Gerard's** on Maui. High-quality sushi can be found from humble spots in Central Maui to gourmet resort restaurants such as *Iron Chef* Matsuhara Morimoto's **Morimoto Maui** in Wailea and D.K. Kodama's **Sansei** in Kapalua. Hyper-fresh "farm to table" cuisine is now just par for the course at popular oceanfront restaurants in Lahaina and Kaanapali, as well in as more moderately priced dining rooms in Kahului and Kihei.

Plate Lunches, Shave Ice & Food Trucks

Haute cuisine is alive and well on Maui, but equally important in the culinary pageant are good-value plate lunches, shave ice, and food trucks.

The **plate lunch,** like Hawaiian Pidgin, is a gift of the plantation era. You find plate lunches of various kinds served in to-go eateries across the state. They usually consist of some protein—fried mahi-mahi, say, or teriyaki beef, shoyu chicken, or chicken or pork cutlets served katsu-style (breaded, fried, and slathered in tangy sauce)—accompanied by "two scoops rice," macaroni salad, and a few leaves of green, typically julienned cabbage. Chili water and soy sauce are the condiments of choice. Like **saimin**—the local version of noodles in broth topped with scrambled eggs, green onions, and sometimes pork—the plate lunch is Hawaii's version of comfort food.

Because this is Hawaii, at least a few fingerfuls of **poi**—steamed, pounded taro (the traditional Hawaiian staple crop)—are a must. Mix it with salty *kalua* pork (pork cooked in a Polynesian underground oven known as an *imu*) or *lomi* salmon (salted salmon with tomatoes and green onions). Other tasty Hawaiian foods include **poke** (pronounced *po-kay*), a popular appetizer made of cubed raw fish seasoned with onions, seaweed, and roasted *kukui* nuts); **laulau,** pork, chicken, or fish steamed in *ti* leaves; **squid luau,** cooked in coconut milk and taro tops (such a popular dish that its name became synonymous with a feast); **haupia,** creamy coconut pudding; and **kulolo,** a steamed pudding of coconut, brown sugar, and taro.

For a sweet snack, the prevailing choice is **shave ice.** On hot, humid days, long lines of shave-ice lovers gather for heaps of finely shaved ice topped with sweet tropical syrups. Sweet-sour *li hing mui* is a favorite, and gourmet flavors include calamansi lime and red velvet cupcake. Aficionados order shave ice with ice cream and sweetened adzuki beans on the bottom or sweetened condensed milk on top. A fun challenge is to determine your favorite shave ice on Maui: Is it from **Ululani's, Surfing Monkey, Island Cream,** or another roadside stand?

the stars ON MAUI

Although Hawaii's iconic landscapes have served as a backdrop for numerous films and TV shows, including the modern reboots of *Jurassic Park, Magnum PI,* and *Hawaii Five-O,* Maui tends to attract Hollywood celebrities more for vacations or part-time residence, rather than for work. Among the few films shot here, *Just Go With It* has Adam Sandler and Jennifer Aniston luxuriating at the Grand Wailea's pool and passing through the lobby of the Mana Kai on Maui, while the classic *Papillon* features several scenes filmed in Hana, including Steve McQueen's cliff-jumping escape.

Movie stars who have called Maui home include Clint Eastwood, Woody Harrelson, Owen Wilson, and Oprah Winfrey, whose Ulupalakua farm on the slopes of Haleakala is famed for its enviable, 4-mile private "driveway" to Kihei. They're joined by just as many stars from the music pantheon: Mick Fleetwood, Sammy Hagar, the late George Harrison, Kris Kristofferson, Willie Nelson, and Steven Tyler, among them. Locals allow celebs to live their lives like any other visitor or resident, so you'll earn street cred by doing the same.

WHEN TO GO

Most visitors come to the Hawaiian Islands when the weather is lousy else-where. Thus, Maui's **high season**—when prices are up and resorts are often booked to capacity—is generally from mid-December to March or mid-April. In particular, the last 2 weeks of December, first week of January, and the week in mid-February beginning Presidents' Day are prime time for travel to Maui. Spring break is also jam-packed with families taking advantage of the school holiday.

If you're planning a trip during peak season, make hotel and rental car reservations as early as possible, expect crowds, and prepare to pay top dollar. The winter months tend to be a little rainier and cooler. But there's a perk to traveling during this time: Hawaiian humpback whales are here, too.

The **off-season,** when the best rates are available and the islands are less crowded, is late spring (mid-Apr to early June) and fall (Sept to mid-Dec), although holidays and special events during those periods may drive up prices briefly.

If you plan to travel in **summer** (mid-June to Aug), don't expect to see the fantastic bargains of spring and fall—this is prime time for family travel. But you'll often find much better deals on packages, airfare, and accommodations than in the winter months.

Climate

Because Hawaii lies at the edge of the tropical zone, its islands technically have only two seasons, both of them warm. There's a dry season that corresponds to **summer** (Apr–Oct) and a rainy season in **winter** (Nov–Mar). It rains every day somewhere in the islands at any time of the year, but the rainy season can bring enough gray weather to spoil your sunbathing opportunities. Fortunately, it seldom rains in one spot for more than 3 days straight.

The **year-round temperature** doesn't vary much. At the beach, the average daytime high in summer is 85°F (29°C), while the average daytime high in winter is 78°F (26°C); nighttime lows are usually about 10° cooler. But how warm it is on any given day really depends on *where* you are on the island.

Each island has a **leeward** side (the side sheltered from the wind) and a **windward** side (the side that gets the wind's full force). The leeward sides (the west and south) are usually hot and dry, while the windward sides (east and north) are generally cooler and moist. When you want arid, sunbaked, desert-like weather, go leeward. When you want lush, wet, rainforest weather, go windward.

Hawaii also has a wide range of **microclimates,** thanks to interior valleys, coastal plains, and mountain peaks. The often chilly, lunar landscape of the summit of Haleakala, which can see snow in winter, lies in sharp contrast to the warm, arid scrubland of Wailea and the humid rainforest of Kipahulu at its

Hey, No Smoking in Hawaii

Well, not *totally* no smoking, but Hawaii has one of the toughest laws against smoking in the U.S. The Hawaii Smoke-Free Law prohibits smoking in public buildings, including airports, shopping malls, grocery stores, retail shops, buses, movie theaters, banks, convention facilities, and all government buildings and facilities. There is no smoking in restaurants, bars, or nightclubs. Most B&Bs prohibit smoking indoors, and most hotels and resorts are smoke-free even in public areas. Also, there is no smoking within 20 feet of a doorway, window, or ventilation intake (so no hanging around outside a bar to smoke—you must go 20 ft. away). On Maui, smoking is also banned at all county community center and recreation facilities, including beach parks and the Waiehu Golf Course; for a complete list of parks, see **www.mauicounty.gov/ parks**. Adults may not smoke in vehicles when children 17 and under are riding with them.

base. The locals say if you don't like the weather, just drive a few miles down the road—it's sure to be different!

Holidays

When Hawaii observes holidays (especially those over a long weekend), travel between the islands increases, inter-island airline seats are fully booked, rental cars are at a premium, and hotels and restaurants are busier.

Federal offices are closed on all federal holidays, and state and county offices observe all of them except Columbus Day (known here as Discoverers' Day). Federal holidays in 2020 include New Year's Day (Jan 1); Martin Luther King, Jr., Day (Jan 20); Presidents' Day (Feb 17); Memorial Day (May 25); Independence Day (July 4, but observed July 3); Labor Day (Sept 7); Columbus Day (Oct 12); Veterans Day (Nov 11); Thanksgiving (Nov 26); and Christmas (Dec 25).

State and county offices are also closed on local holidays, including Prince Kuhio Day (Mar 26), honoring the birthday of Hawaii's first delegate to the U.S. Congress; King Kamehameha Day (June 11), a statewide holiday commemorating Kamehameha the Great, who united the islands and ruled from 1795 to 1819; and Admission Day (Aug 16), which honors the admittance of Hawaii as the 50th state on August 21, 1959.

Maui County Calendar of Events

Please note that, as with any schedule of upcoming events, the following information is subject to change; always confirm the details before you plan your trip around an event. Unless otherwise noted, events are on Maui.

JANUARY

PGA Tournament of Champions, Kapalua Resort. Top PGA golfers compete for the $8.75-million purse. Go to www.pgatour.com/ toc or call © **808/665-9160.** Early January.

Ka Molokai Makahiki, Mitchell Pauole Center, Kaunakakai, Molokai. Makahiki, a traditional time of peace in ancient Hawaii, is re-created with performances by Hawaiian music groups and *halau* (hula schools), sporting competitions, crafts, and food. It's a wonderful chance to experience ancient Hawaii. Ceremonial games start at 7:30am. Go to www.visitmolokai.com/wp/events-molokai-events-calendar or call ✆ **800/800-6367** or 808/553-3876. Late January.

FEBRUARY

Maui Whale Festival, Kalama Park, Kihei. A month-long celebration of Hawaii's massive marine visitors, with a film festival, benefit gala, harbor party, whale-watches with experts, and the "great whale count." Go to www.mauiwhalefestival.org or call ✆ **808/249-8811.** Throughout February.

Chinese New Year, multiple locations. In 2020, lion dancers will be snaking their way around the state on January 25, the start of the Chinese Year of the Rat. On Maui, lion dancers perform at the historic Wo Hing Temple on Front Street. See visitlahaina.com/events or call ✆ **888/310-1117** or 808/667-9175.

MARCH

Whale & Ocean Arts Festival, Lahaina. The entire town of Lahaina celebrates the annual migration of Pacific humpback whales with this weekend festival in Banyan Tree Park. Artists offer their best ocean-themed art for sale, while Hawaiian musicians and hula troupes entertain. Enjoy marine-related activities, games, and a touch-pool exhibit for kids. Get details at http://visitlahaina.com/events or call ✆ **888/310-1117** or 808/667-9175. Early March.

Four Seasons Maui Wine & Food Classic, Wailea. Celebrity chefs and world-renowned vintners pair up for wine dinners, tastings, workshops, and an oceanfront gala over the 3-day event. See www.fourseasons.com/mauiclassic or call ✆ **808/874-8000**.

Prince Kuhio Day Celebrations, Lahaina and Wailuku. March 26 is a state holiday, marking the birth of Jonah Kuhio Kalanianaole, who was born on this day in 1871, elected to Congress in 1902, and helped create the Hawaiian Homesteads program. Hawaiian music, a royal procession, oratory, and a taro cook-off are part of the festivities at Paukukalo Homestead in Wailuku. Lahaina also offers music and children's activities in Banyan Tree Park on the weekend closest to the holiday. See www.gohawaii.com/islands/maui/events. Late March.

Celebration of the Arts, Ritz-Carlton Kapalua. Contemporary and traditional Hawaiian artists give free hands-on lessons during this 3-day festival, which also features song contests and rousing debates on what it means to be Hawaiian. Go to https://kapaluacelebrationofthearts.com or call ✆ **808/669-6200.** Easter weekend (mid-March through late April.)

APRIL

Maui County Ag Fest, Waikapu. Maui celebrates its farmers and their fresh bounty at this well-attended event. Kids enjoy barnyard games while parents duck into the Grand Taste tent to sample top chefs' collaborations with local farmers. Go to https://mauiagfest.org or call ✆ **808/243-2290.** First Saturday in April.

Buddha Day, Lahaina Jodo Mission, Lahaina. Each spring this historic mission holds a flower festival pageant honoring the birth of Buddha. Call ✆ **808/661-4304.** First Sunday in April.

Daylight Saving Time

Most of the United States observes daylight saving time, which lasts from 2am on the second Sunday in March to 2am on the first Sunday in November. **Hawaii does not observe daylight saving time.** So, when daylight saving time is in effect in most of the U.S., Hawaii is 3 hours behind the West Coast and 6 hours behind the East Coast. When the U.S. reverts to standard time in November, Hawaii is 2 hours behind the West Coast and 5 hours behind the East Coast.

East Maui Taro Festival, Hana. Taro, a Hawaiian food staple, is celebrated through music, hula, arts, crafts, and, of course, taro-inspired feasts on a Saturday. Go to www.tarofestival.org or call 𝓒 **808/264-1553.** April.

MAY

Outrigger Canoe Season, statewide. From May to September, canoe paddlers across the state participate in outrigger canoe races nearly every weekend. Go to www.ocpaddler.com for this year's schedule of events.

Lei Day Celebrations, Central Maui. May Day (May 1) is Lei Day in Hawaii, Hale Hoi-keike (Bailey House Museum) in Wailuku hosts an all-day Lei Day Heritage Festival with hula, lei-making, poi pounding, and other crafts. That night, the Maui Arts & Cultural Center in Kahului usually hosts a Hawaiian music concert with top artists. See www.mauimuseum.org and www.mauiarts.org, or call 𝓒 **808/244-3326** (museum) or 808/242-2787 (arts center). May 1.

Maui Matsuri, Kahului. This 3-day festival celebrating Japanese and Okinawan culture kicks off at Queen Kaahumanu Center on a Friday with live entertainment. A week later, a grassy knoll at the UH Maui campus turns into a Japanese village for 2 days with food stalls, all-ages activities, crafts, and entertainment. For details, see www.mauimatsuri.com or call 𝓒 **808/283-9999.** Mid- to late May.

Molokai Ka Hula Piko Festival, Mitchell Pauole Center, Kaunakakai, Molokai. This 3-day hula celebration occurs on the island where the Hawaiian dance was born and features performances by hula schools, musicians, and singers from across Hawaii, as well as local food and Hawaiian crafts: quilting, woodworking, and featherwork. Go to www.kahulapiko.com or call 𝓒 **800/800-6367** or 808/553-3876. Late May to early June.

JUNE

Obon Season, all islands. This colorful Buddhist ceremony honoring the souls of the dead kicks off in June. Synchronized dancers (you can join in) circle a tower where taiko drummers play, and food booths sell Japanese treats late into the night. Each weekend a different Buddhist temple hosts the Bon dance. Go to www.gohawaii.com/events for a statewide schedule. June–August.

Waa Kiakahi, Kaanapali Beach Resort. A fleet of traditional Hawaiian sailing canoes arrives on Kaanapali Beach on a Friday afternoon with a special welcome ceremony, followed by canoe rides and tours on Saturday and a departure ceremony on Sunday. See www.kanaapaliresort.com/calendar or call 𝓒 **808/661-3271.**

Maui Windsurfing Race Series, Kanaha Beach Park, Kahului. This series of four 1-day windsurfing slalom races takes place at Kanaha Beach Park, west of Kahului Airport in Central Maui. Go to http://uswindsurfing.org/maui-slalom-series or call **Hi-Tech Maui** at 𝓒 **808/877-2111.** June–August.

Kapalua Wine & Food Festival, Kapalua. Big-time oenophiles and food experts gather at the Ritz-Carlton, Kapalua, for 4 days of formal tastings, panel discussions, and samplings of new releases. The seafood finale ranks among the state's best feasts. Go to http://kapaluawineandfoodfestival.com or call 𝓒 **800/KAPALUA** (527-2582). Early June.

King Kamehameha Celebration, all islands. This state holiday (officially June 11, but celebrated on different dates on each island) features a massive floral parade, *ho'olaulea* (party), and much more. Maui: http://visitlahaina.com/events or 𝓒 **808/667-9194.** Molokai: 𝓒 **808/553-3876.** Mid-June.

Maui Film Festival, Wailea Resort. Sundance, Cannes, Tribeca and...Maui! Hawaii is home to a major film festival, where movies are screened under the stars at a posh Wailea golf course. Five days of premiere screenings, celebrity awards, and lavish parties. Go to www.mauifilmfestival.com or call 𝓒 **808/579-9244.** Mid-June.

Molokai Holokai Hoolaulea, Kapalua, Maui, and Kamalo, Molokai. This 2-day paddling festival incorporates two races for outrigger canoes, stand-up paddleboards, prone boards, and other watercraft. The first day sends paddlers from Maui's D.T. Fleming Beach across the Pailolo Challenge to Molokai; the second offers 1- to 10-mile contests for all ages along Molokai's South Shore fringing reef. For details, see www.molokai holokai.com.

JULY

Fourth of July Fireworks, Lahaina. Front Street is the viewing spot for official fireworks launched from an offshore barge around 8pm, but expect to see smaller, often impromptu displays elsewhere, too. Get details at http://visitlahaina.com/events. July 4.

Makawao Parade & Rodeo, Makawao. The annual 3-day parade and rodeo has been a highlight of this upcountry cowboy town for more than 60 years. Good fun! Go to www. makawaorodeo.net or call ℰ **808/572-9565.** On or around July 4.

Lanai Pineapple Festival, Lanai City, Lanai. The local pineapple is long gone, but this day-long festival celebrates the island's plantation legacy, including a pineapple-eating contest, a pineapple-cooking contest, arts and crafts, food, music, and fireworks. Go to www.lanaipineapplefestival.com or call ℰ **808/565-7600.** Early July.

Molokai 2 Oahu Paddleboard World Championships, starts on Molokai and finishes on Oahu. Some 200 international participants journey to Molokai to compete in this 32-mile race, considered to be the world championship of long-distance paddleboarding. The race begins at Kaluakoi Beach on Molokai at 7:30am and finishes at Maunalua Bay on Oahu around 12:30pm. Go to www.molokai2oahu.com or call ℰ **760/944-3854.** Late July.

AUGUST

Neil Pryde Hawaii State Championship, Kanaha Beach Park, Kahului. Top windsurfers compete in the final race of the series. Go to http://uswindsurfing.org/maui-slalom-series

or call **Hi-Tech Maui** at ℰ **808/877-2111.** Late July or early August.

Run to the Sun, Kahului to Haleakala National Park. Restarted in 2019 after a 10-year pause, this iconic endurance event by Valley Isle Road Runners involves a climb of 10,000 feet over 36 miles and several climate changes; both individual runners and relay teams compete. See www.facebook. com/runtothesunmaui or call ℰ **808/222-2484.** Mid-August.

SEPTEMBER

Aloha Festivals, various locations. Parades and other events celebrate Hawaiian culture and friendliness throughout the state. The parades with flower-decked horses are particularly eye-catching; Maui's version takes place in Lahaina and Hana, and Molokai's in Kaunakakai. Also on Maui, the Ritz-Carlton, Kapalua, hosts the annual Richard Hoopii Falsetto contest, the Queen Kaahumanu Center presents a day of music and hula, and Lahaina hosts a 2-day weekend festival with live entertainment and arts and crafts; the first week of October Hana follows its parade with a week of special events of every stripe. On Lanai, a 1-day festival in Dole Park includes Hawaiian music, hula, children's activities, and contests; **Expeditions Ferry** provides a special late ferry for purchasers of the $5 Aloha Festivals ribbon. Go to www.alohafestivals.com or call ℰ **808/923-2030.** September through early October.

Maui Breadfruit Festival, Maui Nui Botanical Garden, Kahului. Cooking demonstrations, tastings, cultural activities, and live entertainment help spread the word about breadfruit, a traditional food source in Polynesia. See www.mnbg.org/LaUlu.html or call ℰ **808/249-2728.**

Ku Mai Ka Hula, Maui Arts & Cultural Center, Kahului. Now in its 15th year, the island's only adult hula competition features men and women from award-winning (troupes) in solo and group events, including senior divisions. At the start of the MACC's fall season, the half-day event also includes arts, crafts, and food. See www.mauiarts.org or www. facebook.com/KuMaiKaHula or call ☏ **808/ 242-2787.** Early September.

Hana Relay, Kahului to Hana. If you're not on one of the teams running 52 miles along the twisting, narrow road to Hana, you'll want to avoid driving it this Saturday. Runners have a blast, though, with a big party in Hana at the end; the Valley Isle Road Runners event sells out every year. See www.virr. org or call ☏ **808/222-2484.** First Saturday after Labor Day.

Na Wahine O Ke Kai, Hale O Lono Harbor, Molokai, to Waikiki, Oahu. The finale to the outrigger canoe season, this exciting race starts at sunrise on the South Shore of Molokai and travels 40 miles across the channel to end in triumphant festivities at the Hilton Hawaiian Village. For details, visit www. nawahineokekai.com. Late September.

Kapalua Open, Kapalua Resort. This USTA–sanctioned event features the largest tennis purse for a tournament in the state. Registration includes a tennis tourney, dinner, raffle, and T-shirt (and trophy if you've got the skills!). Go to www.golfatkapalua.com/kapalua_tennis_open or call ☏ **808/662-7730.** Labor Day weekend.

Maui Ukulele Festival, Maui Arts & Cultural Center, Kahului. Part of a statewide festival, the 15th incarnation of Maui's version features a free concert from 1 to 5pm with a large lineup of virtuosos, including names like Jake Shimabukuro. A morning workshop, food booths, and ukulele door prizes are also part of the fun. Get the details at www. ukulelefestivalhawaii.org. Late September.

OCTOBER

Maui County Fair, War Memorial Complex, Wailuku. Now in its 96th year, the oldest county fair in Hawaii features a parade, amusement rides, live entertainment, and exhibits over 4 days. Go to www.mauifair.com or call ☏ **808/280-6889.** Early October.

Maui Marathon, Kahului to Kaanapali. Maui's only qualifier for the Boston Marathon starts at 5am in Kahului; runners (ages 16 and up) have 8 hours to make it to the finish

in Kaanapali. Shorter events—5K, 10K, and half-marathon—take place the same day. Valley Isle Road Runners organizes shuttles between the start and finish. Go to www. mauimarathon.com or call ☏ **808/222-2484.** Mid-October.

Hawaii Food & Wine Festival, Kaanapali Beach Resort. Cofounded by Alan Wong and Roy Yamaguchi (two of the state's most celebrated chefs), this 3-week gourmet bonanza takes place on Oahu, Maui, and Hawaii Island, including wine and spirit tastings, cooking demos, field trips, and glitzy galas. Maui's 3-day weekend of events is hosted by several Kaanapali hotels and its resort association. See www.hawaiifood andwinefestival.com or call ☏ **808/738-6245.** Late October.

NOVEMBER

Hula O Na Keiki/Hawaiian Festival of Arts and Crafts, Kaanapali Beach Resort. Held jointly, these two popular events include the children's hula competition Hula O Na Keiki, featuring boys and girls ages 5 to 17 dancing as soloists and couples in modern and ancient styles, and 3 days of arts and crafts workshops, vendors, and live entertainment. Find details at www.kbhmaui.com/hawaii-culture/hula-o-na-keiki or call ☏ **808/ 661-0111.**

Na Mele O Maui, Maui Arts & Cultural Center, Kahului. A traditional Hawaiian song competition for children in kindergarten through 12th grade, sponsored by Kaanapali Beach Resort but staged in Kahului. Free admission. Go to www.mauiarts.org or call ☏ **808/242-7469.** Late November or early December.

Maui Jim Maui Invitational Basketball Tournament, Lahaina Civic Center, Lahaina. Elite college teams (such as five-time winner the Duke Blue Devils) battle for the ball in this intimate annual preseason tournament. Go to www.mauiinvitational.com. Thanksgiving weekend.

DECEMBER

Festival of Lights, all islands. On Maui, kids can play in a "snow zone" and make holiday crafts beneath the Lahaina Banyan tree, glowing with thousands of twinkle lights. Molokai celebrates with a host of activities in Kaunakakai. Call ☏ **808/667-9175** on Maui; ☏ **808/553-4482** on Molokai. Early through late December.

First Light, Maui Arts & Cultural Center, Kahului. The Maui Film Festival screens Academy Award contenders over the holidays. Go to www.mauifilmfestival.com or call ☏ **808/579-9244.** Mid- to late December.

SUGGESTED ITINERARIES

The lay of the land on Hawaii's second-largest island runs the gamut from sun-kissed golden beaches and fragrant rainforests to the frigid, windswept summit of Haleakala. Maui is a splendid natural playground with plenty to see and do, and the following itineraries are designed to help you make the most of your trip as you navigate the island. But they also provide plenty of opportunities to do nothing but pause, refresh, and replenish against a backdrop of unparalleled scenic beauty.

Even if you have few ambitions beyond digging your toes in the white sand, we highly recommend signing up for a **tour** or **outdoor activity** while you're here. For details on the attractions and activities recommended below, go to chapters 4 and 5.

ONE WEEK ON MAUI: THE HIGHLIGHTS

You'll need at least a week to savor Maui's best experiences. I recommend splitting your vacation between East and West Maui, starting with hot and sunny beaches and ending in the rejuvenating rainforest. We've designed this itinerary assuming you'll stay in West Maui for the first 3 days, but it works just as well if you stay in Wailea or Kihei. To minimize driving, move your headquarters to lush East Maui on day 4. *Note:* Spend your final night in Kihei, Paia, or Kahului for the most convenient access to the airport the next day.

Day 1: Arrive & Explore West Maui ★★★

Upon arrival, fuel up in Kahului at **Tin Roof**, **Da Kitchen,** or **Maui Fresh Streatery** (see "Where to Eat," p. 89) before heading to your hotel. Check in and then go for a reviving dip at one of West Maui's prime beaches (p. 178). Meander around the historic old town of **Lahaina** (p. 135). Because you were savvy enough to book reservations for the **Old Lahaina Luau** (p. 234) a month in advance, you can immerse yourself in Hawaiian culture as the sun drops into the sea.

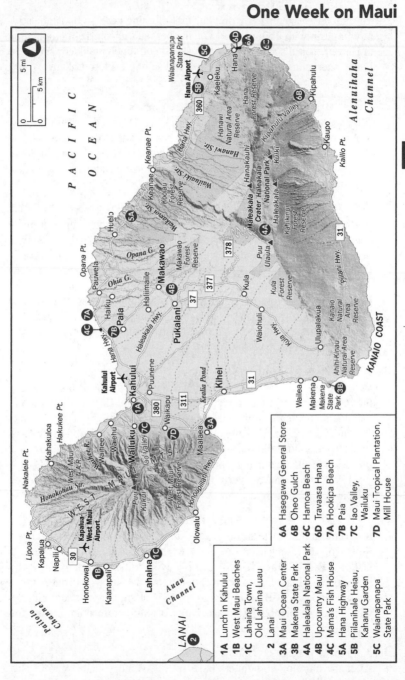

1A Lunch in Kahului
1B West Maui Beaches
1C Lahaina Town, Old Lahaina Luau
2 Lanai
3A Maui Ocean Center
3B Makena State Park
4A Haleakala National Park
4B Upcountry Maui
4C Mama's Fish House
5A Hana Highway
5B Piilanihale Heiau, Kahanu Garden
5C Waianapanapa State Park
6A Hasegawa General Store
6B Oheo Gulch
6C Hamoa Beach
6D Travaasa Hana
7A Hookipa Beach
7B Paia
7C Iao Valley, Wailuku
7D Maui Tropical Plantation, Mill House

Day 2: Sail to Lanai ★★★

You'll likely wake up early on your first morning here, so book an early-morning trip with **Trilogy** (p. 187), the best sailing/snorkeling operation in Hawaii. You'll spend the day (breakfast and lunch included) sailing to Lanai, snorkeling, touring the island, and sailing back to Lahaina. You'll have the afternoon free to shop or nap.

Day 3: Sunbathe in South Maui ★★★

Take a drive out to **Makena State Park** (p. 183) and soak in the raw beauty of this wild shore. On the way, pay a visit to the sharks and sea turtles at the **Maui Ocean Center** in Maalaea (p. 149). Linger in South Maui to enjoy the sunset and feast at one of the area's terrific restaurants (recommendations start on p. 110).

Day 4: Ascend a 10,000-Foot Volcano ★★★

Venture up to the 10,023-foot summit of **Haleakala,** the island's dormant volcano. Witnessing the sunrise here can be phenomenal (as well as mind-numbingly cold and crowded). Aim for a little later and hike in **Haleakala National Park** (p. 154), an awe-inspiring experience any time of day. On your way back down the mountain, stop and tour **Upcountry Maui** (p. 151), particularly the communities of **Kula** and **Makawao.** Plan for a sunset dinner in Kuau at **Mama's Fish House** (p. 125). Stay at the **Inn at Mama's Fish House** (p. 79) or lodgings in Paia (recommendations start on p. 78).

Day 5: Drive the Hana Highway ★★★

Pack a lunch and spend the entire day driving the scenic **Hana Highway** (p. 161). Pull over often to take photos, smell the flowers, and jump in the mountain-stream pools. Yield to all those speeding by, and breathe in Hawaii. Take a hike along the black sands of **Waianapanapa State Park** (p. 169) or admire the majesty of **Piilanihale Heiau** amid the tropical profusion of the National Tropical Botanical Garden's **Kahanu Garden** (p. 169). Spend the night in **Hana** (hotel recommendations start on p. 81).

Day 6: Explore Heavenly Hana ★★★

In the morning, stock up on snacks and drinks at **Hasegawa General Store** (p. 161), and head out early to the Kipahulu end of Haleakala National Park at **Oheo Gulch** (p. 174). Hike to the waterfalls and swim in the pools (if conditions permit) before the day-trippers arrive. Stretch out on the beach at **Hamoa Beach** (p. 185) or soothe your sore muscles with a spa treatment at **Travaasa Hana** (p. 81) before splurging on dinner there.

Day 7: Sightsee & Shop ★★★

After the morning commuters have set off, wend your back to Central Maui on the Hana Highway, stopping at any attractions you skipped on the way. Ogle turtles or windsurfers (or both) at **Hookipa Beach** (p. 202) before checking out the boutiques in **Paia** (recommendations start on p. 230), where you also can find a tasty lunch (recommendations start on p. 123). Explore the verdant gardens and waterfalls on the short walk through **Iao Valley** (p. 134) near the quaint town of Wailuku, where shoppers can also find one-of-a-kind souvenirs and antiques (see p. 225) and pick up treats at **Home Maid Bakery** (p. 89) for tomorrow's plane ride home. Sample the wares at Waikapu's **Maui Tropical Plantation** (p. 91), where you can enjoy a last island farm-sourced dinner at its **Mill House** restaurant (p. 91).

ONE WEEK ON MAUI WITH KIDS

Although some parents may enjoy taking their children on the long and winding road to Hana and overnighting in rural East Maui, this itinerary assumes that they'd prefer to plant themselves in a child-friendly condo or hotel resort—preferably one with a pool and close to the beach—and do day-trip activities from there. This itinerary is based in West Maui, but you can follow a similar agenda in South Maui, or uproot yourself midweek to minimize driving time between the two.

Day 1: Arrive & Refresh in West Maui ★★
Upon arrival, refuel with a bargain **lunch in Kahului** (see suggestions beginning on p. 89) before stopping at **Costco** (p. 89) for groceries or snacks and drinks for the week. Check in to your lodgings and revive with a dip in the pool, whether it's an elaborate fantasy pool at an upscale resort like the **Hyatt Regency Maui** (p. 50), **Sheraton Maui** (p. 51), or **Westin Kaanapali Ocean Resort Villas** (p. 48), or a simpler affair at a more affordable condo in Kahana or Napili (see suggestions beginning on p. 53). Since the kids are likely to fall asleep early tonight, keep dinner plans simple—either at your hotel or takeout pizza from one of West Maui's excellent pizzerias (see suggestions beginning on p. 93).

Day 2: Sail, Snorkel & Sightsee ★★★
Everyone likely will wake up early on your first morning here, so reserve an early-morning trip with **Trilogy** (p. 187), a premium outfitter. You'll spend the day (breakfast and lunch included) sailing to Lanai, snorkeling, and playing at the beach, before cruising back to Lahaina; in winter (Dec–Mar), the journey doubles as a whale-watching trip, and dolphins may pop up from the waves anytime. You'll have the afternoon free to explore the shops or sample shave ice in Lahaina, along with ogling the many trunks and shady branches of the massive **Banyan Tree** (p. 137) in the town's historic center. Enjoy dinner at your condo or in one of Lahaina's many casual, lively restaurants.

Day 3: Spend a Day at the Beach ★★

A day at the beach is about as kid-pleasing as you get, so slap on your reef-safe sunscreen, stake your towel or beach chair within view of the kids, and let them frolic in the water at the nearest beach with good conditions (see descriptions beginning on p. 177). For current conditions at West Maui's two beaches with lifeguards, **Hanakaoo** (p. 181) and **D.T. Fleming Park** (p. 178), visit **hawaiibeachsafety.com/maui**. If you're hanging out at Kaanapali Beach, follow the boardwalk to the food court or other casual dining options at **Whalers Village** (p. 104). If you're checking out one of the beaches near the tony Kapalua Resort, find affordable lunch fare at the Honolua General Store. If it's a Tuesday night, head to **Napili Kai Beach Resort** (p. 53) for its long-running *keiki* (children's) hula and Polynesian dance show, including a Hawaiian craft fair, from 5:30 to 6:30pm ($10 adults, $5 6–12). Stay for dinner at the resort's island-themed **Sea House Restaurant** (p. 105), which has a $7 children's menu.

Day 4: Meet Marine Life & Zipline on a Farm ★★★

In the morning, perhaps after a make-your-own pancake breakfast at **Slappy Cakes** (p. 107), head to **Maui Ocean Center** in Maalaea (p. 149). Allow several hours to enjoy the fascinating exhibits and interactive presentations in its shallow reef, turtle lagoon, tidepool, and massive aquarium (starring black-tip reef sharks). You can have lunch here, but the food and ambience are better at your next stop, **Maui Tropical Plantation** in Waikapu (p. 132). Enjoy a farm-fresh meal with views of the plantation fields under the beautiful West Maui Mountains. Take the 45-minute narrated **tram tour** through the 60-acre farm and around its scenic lagoon, sampling tropical fruits and learning how to husk a coconut along the way. Adventurous children as young as 5 also can enjoy an aerial view of the scenery on the five introductory-level ziplines—all dual, so mom or dad can zip side by side if desired.

Day 5: Ascend a 10,000-Foot Volcano ★★★

Don't worry about trying to witness a chilly sunrise atop 10,023-foot **Haleakala** with the family, but do take time to venture up the dormant volcano with some fun stretch-your-legs and snack breaks on the way. Book a casual, 30-minute walking tour of **Surfing Goat Dairy** in Kula (p. 152) to learn how the cheese-making dairy works. You can also pet some of the goats, take snaps of them gamboling on a surfboard playground, and buy lunch, treats, and goat-milk gelato while you're there. There are no food concessions inside **Haleakala National Park** (p. 154), where you'll stop to amble along the nature trail in **Hosmer Grove** (p. 159) before reaching **Haleakala Visitors Center.** If you're properly prepared with hats, sunglasses, light jackets, and refillable water bottles, head as far down the lunar **Sliding Sands Trail** (p. 157) as you think the little ones can realistically ascend later. Drive a little farther to the actual summit and its observatories at **Puu Ulaula** and point out the rare silversword plants that can take 30 years to bloom On your return, stop in the cowboy town of Makawao for a pastry at **T. Komoda Bakery** (p. 121) and then follow Baldwin Avenue downslope and take a short detour east to check for turtles at the east end of **Hookipa Beach Park** (p. 184); be sure to look but don't touch. Have dinner at one of **Paia**'s casual, multicultural restaurants or cafes (suggestions begin on p. 123).

Day 6: Ride the Waves & Savor Shave Ice ★★

Maui has many small **surf breaks** perfect for beginners and a number of protected bays ideal for learning to **stand-up paddle (SUP)**; sign up for a lesson from one of the providers listed in "Beaches and Outdoor Activities" (beginning on p. 179), and rent a board to practice your skills afterward. Most large resort hotels and several private outfitters (see p. 190) also offer **outrigger canoe** experiences, in which up to five family members can join a steersman in paddling Hawaiian-style (and perhaps even spot whales in season). You can frolic in the water for free at **Kamaole Beach Park III** in Kihei (p. 181), which offers a playground and picnic tables as well as a sandy beach. Kihei also is loaded with moderately priced restaurants (suggestions begin on p. 110); save room for a distinctively local-style dessert at **Ululani's Hawaiian Shave Ice** (p. 96).

Day 7: Celebrate at a Luau ★★★

On your last full day, head back to a favorite beach or explore a new one (beach descriptions begin on p. 177). Or take a short hike to see a waterfall, with a drive to lush **Iao Valley** (p. 134). Reward yourself afterward with a *malasada* (Portuguese doughnut) from Home Maid Bakery in Wailuku. Celebrate your last night on Maui at a family-friendly luau like the **Old Lahaina Luau** (p. 234) or the **Drums of the Pacific Luau** at the Hyatt Regency Maui Resort & Spa (p. 50); book well in advance.

FIVE NIGHTS ON MAUI FOR ROMANCE

Whether you're on a romantic getaway, a honeymoon, or a milestone anniversary trip, Maui sets a stunning stage for memorable bonding experiences with your significant other. To keep expenses down, this itinerary includes only 5 nights, but by all means extend your stay if you can—sometimes there's nothing more idyllic than just relaxing with the one you love on the Valley Isle. *Note:* Make reservations well in advance for all lodging, sit-down restaurants, and paid activities mentioned here.

Day 1: Experience Aloha ★★★

After your flight lands in Kahului, your first day begins with a short but scenic drive to Paia to check in to intimate **Inn at Mama's Fish House** (p. 79), part of its namesake restaurant's compound on a sandy cove where you can dip your toes in the water under swaying palms. Refresh in your adults-only suite before an early dinner at famed **Mama's Fish House** (p. 125), also overlooking the cove. Even though it's just a few steps from your room (meaning no one has to be designated driver), you'll want to allow plenty of time to soak in the restaurant's traditional Hawaiian hospitality and savor its exquisitely plated, locally sourced island fare. Plus, you'll also be making an early start in the morning— good to do while you're still adjusting to the time difference.

Day 2: Head off to Hana ★★★

Grab a healthy breakfast and picnic fare at nearby **Kuau Store** (p. 164) before beating the crowds on the scenic **Hana Highway** (p. 161). Pull over often to take photos of waterfalls, explore nature trails, and sample the wares at roadside stands. Take turns driving, yield to all those speeding by, and breathe in Hawaii. Stretch your legs before sunset on the black sands of **Waianapanapa State Park** (p. 184) before spending the night at in a luxurious bungalow at serene **Travaasa Hana, Maui** (p. 81), where you'll also have an elegant dinner at its **Preserve Kitchen + Bar** (p. 127), ideally with live Hawaiian music and hula in its lounge afterwards. Or book a cozy and more affordable oceanfront studio at **Hana Kai Maui** (p. 84), where lush rainforest meets the black sand of Hana Bay.

Day 3: Hike to Waterfalls & Hit the Beach ★★

After breakfast—whether a simple beachfront affair at the **Barefoot Cafe** (p. 127) or something more gourmet at **Preserve Kitchen + Bar** (p. 127)—take another scenic (but shorter) drive to the lush **Kipahulu District** (p. 156) of Haleakala National Park, where you'll dip into the tiered pools of **Oheo Gulch** if conditions permit. Hike the **Pipiwai Trail** (p. 175) through lush forest, where towering stalks of bamboo act as nature's wind chimes, to 400-foot **Waimoku Falls** (p. 210). On your return, stop for a roadside barbecue lunch at **Huli Huli Chicken at Koki Beach** (p. 128), then backtrack slightly to relax at dreamy **Hamoa Beach** (p. 185) before dinner at Preserve or a food stand.

Day 4: Drive to a Sunnyside Oasis ★★★

Hana may have been too misty or rainy for sunbathing, but that's just more incentive for snuggling. You can do both in South Maui, where you'll spend your last 2 nights. Since you're seeking romance, head there from Hana via narrow, winding **Piilani Highway** across the sere southern flanks of Haleakala. You may feel as if you're the only souls alive all the way to Upcountry Maui, where you can stop for lunch at a cozy bistro in **Kula** or **Makawao** (dining suggestions begin on p. 120) before descending through former sugarcane fields. In the afternoon, check in at one of Wailea's luxury oases known for cossetting couples. In fall, the **Four Seasons Maui Resort at Wailea** (p. 71) offers special classes and activities for couples, from sushi-making to stargazing and sunset photography. Couples feel special year-round at the adults-only, hillside retreat of **Hotel Wailea** (p. 73), thanks to spacious suites, daybed cabanas by the pool, beautiful garden paths, and the option of a private chef's dinner in a treehouse. Enjoy a sunset walk on the beach before **dinner and drinks** at one of Wailea's top-notch restaurants, including the Four Seasons' lively lobby lounge (more suggestions begin on p. 113).

Day 5: End a Leisurely Day at a Luau ★★★

On your last full day, enjoy time at one of Wailea's **outstanding beaches** (suggestions begin on p. 182) or on the broad sand of rugged **Makena State Park** (p. 183); you can also take a **private kayak tour** from Makena Landing with **Hawaiian Paddle Sports** (p. 189). In the afternoon, snooze by the pool in a private cabana, or experience even deeper relaxation with a spa treatment and island-inspired rain showers at **Willow Stream Spa** in the **Fairmont Kea Lani** (p. 70). End your day with Maui's most romantic luau, the **Feast at Lele** (p. 234), featuring private tables with waiter service, chef-prepared cuisine with open bar, and expert Polynesian dancers who perform on the beach as the sun sets behind them.

ONE WEEK ON MAUI FOR FOODIES

Decades ago, a special night out in Hawaii meant surf and turf—the seafood frozen and the steak from the mainland. But thanks to the Hawaii Regional Cuisine movement (p. 17), founded in 1991, island farmers and ranchers now work with ambitious chefs to provide a dazzling variety of fresh ingredients, from tropical fruits grown near the shore to Upcountry Maui's cool-weather produce, beef, and lamb. Although many chefs are classically trained, more and more draw from the island's multicultural heritage and their own families' roots to create unique menus you'll find nowhere else. This itinerary samples some of the most distinctive food experiences Maui has to offer at every price range, paired with some exceptional scenery and a few days at the beach.

Day 1: Savor Local Flavor ★★★

Upon arrival, fuel up in Kahului like the locals do. Enjoy Filipino-inspired fare at *Top Chef* favorite Sheldon Simeon's **Tin Roof** (p. 91), an abundant plate lunch or loco moco (burger, eggs, rice, and gravy) at **Da Kitchen** (p. 90), or the ethnic cuisine of the week at the **Maui Fresh Streatery food truck** (p. 89). Save room for a hot *malasada* (Portuguese doughnut) or freshly made peanut butter mochi (sweet rice flour treats) at **Home Maid Bakery** in Wailuku before checking in at the **Inn at Mama's Fish House** in Paia (p. 79) or nearby lodgings (suggestions begin on p. 78). You'll have made reservations well in advance for dinner at **Mama's Fish House** (p. 122), where you can splurge on exquisitely plated seafood along with gracious Hawaiian hospitality in a gorgeous beachfront setting.

Day 2: Drive the Road to Hana ★★★

After rising early, as most do on their first day here, pick up fresh-pressed juice, organic coffee, and a breakfast wrap at the natural food deli in the **Kuau Store** (p. 126) before hitting the **road to Hana** (p. 161). Along the way, you can take a prearranged farm tour by the cascades of **Twin Falls** (p. 165), sample fresh banana bread from **Aunty Sandy's** on the scenic **Keanae Peninsula** (p. 166), stop for artisan coconut ice cream at **Coconut Glen's** in Nahiku (p. 92), and pick up preserves and fresh tropical fruit at the **Hana Farms** farmstand just outside Hana (p 169). Stroll among the collection of breadfruit cultivars at oceanfront **Kahanu Garden** (p. 168) before dining on Hana-grown produce and other Maui ingredients on the lanai at the **Preserve Kitchen + Bar** (p. 127) at **Travaasa Hana** (p. 81); overnight there or at a vacation rental (suggestions begin on p. 81).

Day 3: Take an Upcountry Farm Tour ★★★

If you leave early enough in the morning, you can drive the rugged southern slopes of Haleakala leading to Upcountry Maui and ogle the pools at **Oheo Gulch** (p. 174) along the way. Or simply retrace your route back to Twin Falls and head up the wriggling roads from there to Haliimaile, where you'll have lunch at **Haliimaile General Store** (p. 119), the rustic flagship of Hawaii Regional Cuisine cofounder Bev Gannon. You'll need reservations for a tour of one of two farms in Kula after lunch: **Surfing Goat Dairy** (p. 152), which makes more than 30 kinds of cheese plus gelato and truffles, or the 80-acre **Ocean Organic Vodka** organic farm & distillery (p. 152), which uses deep ocean water from Hawaii Island and heritage sugarcane to produce Ocean Organic Vodka. (The views of the West Maui Mountains from here are intoxicating, too.) Head down the mountain to check in to your condo or hotel in South Maui (suggestions begin on p. 60) in time for sunset dinner, perhaps at **Humble Market Kitchin** (p. 115). Chef Roy Yamaguchi, another renowned Hawaii Regional Cuisine cofounder, pays tribute to his island roots at this outpost in the impressively renovated **Wailea Beach Resort** (p. 73).

Day 4: Soak Up the Sun & Shave Ice ★★★

You've earned **a day at the beach** now, and South Maui offers plenty of options (suggestions begin on p. 217). Speaking of options, you'll have a tough time choosing from the many flavors and toppings of **Ululani's Hawaiian Shave Ice** (p. 96) when you want to cool off; be sure to add a scoop of locally made Roselani's haupia (coconut pudding) ice cream to the bottom. For lunch, try one of Kihei's affordable, farm-sourced casual restaurants like **Nalu's South Shore Grill** (p. 112) or **Three's** (p. 112). You'll be splurging tonight on either elegant sushi and Japanese cuisine at **Morimoto Maui** (p. 113) or an innovative chef's table dinner at **Kaana Kitchen** (p. 70), both at the chic **Andaz Maui** in Wailea (p. 70).

Day 5: Explore Plantation Heritage ★★

After a morning snorkel, perhaps as part of a boat trip with **Kai Kanani** to Molokini (p. 187), head to lushly landscaped **Maui Tropical Plantation** (p. 132) in Waikapu for lunch at the creative **Mill House,** which sources ingredients from the fields and orchards surrounding it. The quirky sculptures of former sugarcane plantation machinery may inspire you to stop at the **Alexander & Baldwin Sugar Museum** (p. 131) in Puunene on the way back. The backbreaking labor by workers from a variety of Asian, European, Pacific Islander, and other ethnicities helped create Hawaii's iconic plate lunch. For dinner, sample gourmet interpretations of dishes brought to the islands by these laborers at Chef Tylun Pang's **Ko** (the Hawaiian name for sugarcane) at **Fairmont Kea Lani** (p. 70) or Chef Sheldon Simeon's playful **Lineage** (p. 116) in the Shops at Wailea.

Day 6: Go West ★★★

Head to West Maui for a day at the beach in Kaanapali or Kapalua (suggestions begin on p. 180), stopping in Olowalu along the way to pick up sandwiches and handheld coconut pies at **Leoda's Kitchen and Pie Shop** (p. 100). For dinner, marvel at the multi-island views as well as the pioneering farm-to-table cuisine at **Merriman's** in Kapalua (p. 108), or go more casual, and a little easier on your budget, at **Leilani's** (p. 103) in Whalers Village, which also relies on island farmers and fishermen for its island/American menu.

Day 7: Feast at a Gourmet Luau ★★★

After walking off some of the decadent calories on the **Wailea Beach Path** (p. 182) and going for one last swim in the pool or beach, it's time to celebrate your last night on Maui. You've made reservations well in advance for the **Feast at Lele** in Lahaina (p. 94), an upscale luau where the private table service includes multiple courses highlighting the cuisine of the cultures represented onstage: Maori (New Zealand), Samoan, Tongan, and Hawaiian. The excellent wine list, craft beer, and cocktails will also inspire you to toast your culinary journey.

FOUR DAYS ON MOLOKAI

You can make a day trip to Molokai if you're truly short on time, but that's a lot of time to spend in airports and in a car or tour bus to see a few highlights. This itinerary assumes that you stay 3 nights, beginning with a mid-morning nine-seater flight from Maui's main airport in Kahului to Molokai's main airport in Hoolehua. You could also depart from Honolulu, which offers flights on 42-passenger turboprops as well as on smaller prop planes, and wait to start your Maui vacation after the Molokai visit. Either way, the contrasts between Maui or Oahu with low-key, untrammeled Molokai will be striking. *Tip:* Start your itinerary on a weekday for more opportunities to shop, dine, and sightsee.

Day 1: Get a Taste of the Island ★★

After picking up your rental car (a must) at the airport, drive a few minutes to the post office in Hoolehua to **"Post-a-Nut"** (p. 259), i.e., decorate and mail a coconut to friends or family. Afterward, head to nearby **Purdy's Macadamia Nut Farm** (p. 259) for an engaging tour with tasty samples in an orchard planted more than a century ago. Stop by **Kualapuu Cookhouse** (p. 255) for a hearty lunch or **Coffees of Hawaii** (p. 258) for a pick-me-up and coffee tasting before heading downhill. Enjoy the views of the **Molokai Plumerias** orchard (p. 256), typically in bloom March to October, en route to **Kaunakakai** (p. 256). Cruise its **quaint stores** (p. 278) and peek into modern **St. Damien Church** (p. 257) to see artwork honoring the man whose sacrifices will inspire Day 2 of your trip, before checking into your (preferably air-conditioned) room at **Hotel Molokai** (p. 249) 2 miles east of town. Enjoy sunset over the ocean and an island-sourced dinner at **Hiro's Ohana Grill** (p. 253) onsite, but save room for the late-night bread run at **Kanemitsu Bakery** (p. 255). Order the delicious sweet bread with cream cheese and jam, and save any leftovers you don't consume on the spot for breakfast the next day.

Day 2: Tour Kalaupapa ★★★

Whether you're hiking, taking the short flight, or riding the mules down to **Kalaupapa National Historical Park** (p. 260), you will need to be 16 years or older, and have made reservations in advance—up to a month or more for the **Molokai Mule Ride** (p. 267). But the effort and expense are worth it to explore this otherwise inaccessible, always impressive site of natural beauty and tragic history, where two Catholic saints, **Father Damien** and **Mother Marianne Cope** (p. 257), helped care for those cruelly exiled here in the late 19th century after they contracted leprosy (today known as Hansen's disease). After your return "topside" in late afternoon, admire the view from the **Kalaupapa Lookout** in **Palaau State Park** (p. 258) and take the short trail to the park's **Phallic Rock**, a legendary source of fertility. Have dinner and drinks at lively **Paddlers' Restaurant and Bar** (p. 253) in Kaunakakai before calling it an early night.

Day 3: Hike into the Past ★★★

Head into town early to rent snorkel gear at **Molokai Fish & Dive** (p. 268) and buy picnic fare at the **Store House** (p. 255) or other convenient food outlet (see "Where to Eat on Molokai," p. 253), before starting your scenic, shore-hugging drive to the lush East End and historic **Halawa Valley** (p. 264). Make reservations several weeks in advance for a **cultural tour** (p. 265) with the Solatorio family, which includes a hike past ancient Hawaiian heritage sites to the gorgeous, 250-foot **Mooula Falls.** You'll picnic here and, in safe conditions, take a dip in its cool waters. On your way home, admire the twin beaches of **Halawa Beach Park** (p. 270), but save your swimming for **Sandy** and **Kumimi** beaches (p. 270–271); if the water is calm, you can snorkel at the latter. Stop at the two churches St. Damien built outside of Kalaupapa: the picturesque **Our Lady of Seven Sorrows** (p. 264) and tiny **St. Joseph** (p. 264), which has a touching lei-draped, lava-rock statue of Damien by its little cemetery. If it's Thursday, head back to **Kualapuu Cookhouse** for live music and the prime-rib special; otherwise, enjoy local entertainment by the pool at Hotel Molokai and one last dinner at **Hiro's Ohana Grill** before your return flight the next day.

TWO DAYS ON LANAI

The smallest of all the Hawaiian Islands, this former pineapple plantation makes a fun day trip from Maui, particularly on **Trilogy's Discover Lanai tour** (p. 188), which includes snorkeling at Hulopoe Bay, an optional (but recommended) van tour of Lanai City, and barbecue lunch. But it's well worth spending at least 2 days and 1 night on Lanai to appreciate its surprising variety of experiences and landscapes, not to mention Laani City's small-town charm or the splurge-worthy dining at the Four Seasons resort. This itinerary includes ferry service from Maui, which you should book well in advance—but you can also begin or end the journey with a short flight to or from Honolulu. *Note:* Shuttle service is fast and inexpensive enough (typically $10 a ride) that it's not worth it to rent a car for a short trip (assuming any are available), unless you're a party of more than two.

Day 1: Explore Beaches, Backroads & Boutiques ★★★

After taking the morning ferry from Lahaina to Manele Bay, perhaps accompanied by spinner dolphins during the 45-minute crossing, buckle up for the wide-ranging 3½-hour tour in a roomy Suburban with **Rabaca's Limousine Service** (p. 289). Your driver will navigate the rugged roads to the otherworldly rock formations of Keahiakawelo (**"Garden of the Gods,"** p. 297), remote **Shipwreck Beach** (p. 302), the restored **Ka Lanakila** church and other plantation-era vestiges in abandoned **Keomoku village** (p.300), among other photo-ready sites. Afterwards, drop off your bags at the rustic-chic **Hotel Lanai** (p. 292); renovated in 2018, the plantation-era inn has just 10 rooms, so book well in advance. Enjoy a late, homestyle lunch at one of Lanai City's mom-and-pop restaurants and cafes (recommendations begin on p. 293). All are close to **Dole Park,** a broad open space lined with towering pines. Take time to peruse the intriguing boutiques and art galleries (see "Shopping," p. 307) on the town's perimeter before savoring an inventive, island-inspired dinner at handsomely renovated **Lanai City Bar & Grille** (p. 294) back at the

Hotel Lanai. The hotel's bar and patio is also a social hub for island residents, especially when live music is offered and the firepits are ablaze. Or pay for a shuttle to the Four Seasons Resort Lanai to dine like a Hollywood celebrity—or a Silicon Valley tycoon, since Larry Ellison owns the resort as well as most of Lanai—at **Nobu** (p. 293). This farflung outpost of the sumptuous sushi and Japanese fusion restaurant chain founded by chef Nobu Matsuhisa includes a few Lanai-only specialties.

Day 2: Discover Fish, Fields, Forest, & Felines ★★★

After an early complimentary breakfast at Hotel Lanai or coffee and a pastry in town, check out of your room but ask to stow your bags to maximize the rest of your time on Lanai. If you've brought snorkel gear with you, take a Rabaca's shuttle (book the day before) down to **Hulopoe Beach** (p. 293). This marine preserve generally offers safe swimming and terrific snorkeling, with abundant fish and frequent visits by spinner dolphins. The tidepools hold a bevy of fascinating critters, too. Afterwards, hike the 1-mile Kapihaa Trail past heritage sites along Manele Bay and climb to the **Puu Pehe** or Sweetheart Rock lookout (p. 307) before a pricey but delicious poolside lunch at **Malibu Farm** (p. 295) at the Four Seasons, above Hulopoe Bay. If you'd prefer a guided experience in Lanai's pristine waters, you can opt instead for a 3-hour **snorkeling tour** with Lanai Ocean Sports (p. 302), which includes lunch; book well in advance. In the early afternoon, shuttle back to the innovative, indoor-outdoor **Lanai Cat Sanctuary** (p. 298) to nuzzle with some of the hundreds of friendly felines, learn about the shelter's efforts to protect native and migratory birds, and enjoy refreshments in its ocean-view cat cafe. If you're not a fan of furballs, check out the ziplines, spa, or other amenities of the **Koele Wellness Center** (p. 290), expected to open by late 2019. One benefit of all the shuttling: You'll have time to treasure the serenity of the former Dole plantation's now-fallow pineapple fields and forested **Mount Lanaihale,** the tallest peak on the island at 3,379 feet. Return to the hotel to retrieve your bags and shuttle down to the harbor for the 4:30pm ferry (the most popular return time) or grab a casual early dinner in town before the final ferry departs at 6:45pm.

WHERE TO STAY
ON MAUI

Although room rates are higher here in general than on other Hawaiian Islands, Maui has accommodations to fit every taste and budget, especially if you're willing to venture away from the pricey beachfront resorts. Luxury oceanfront suites that appeal to honeymooners and well-heeled travelers, moderately priced ocean-view condos that will sleep a family of four, rustic rainforest cabins for adventurous sorts—each offers a unique perspective for a Valley Isle vacation.

When planning your trip to Maui, remember: The high season, when rooms fill up quickly and rates vault skyward, runs from mid-December to March. A second high season, when rates are high but reservations are somewhat easier to get, is summer (late June to early Sept). The off-seasons, with fewer tourists and cheaper rates, are April to early June and late September to mid-December.

When it comes to booking a stay outside of a traditional hotel, be aware that Airbnb, VRBO, and other home-sharing and vacation rental online platforms have changed the landscape considerably. Condo properties in resort areas, which don't need special permits to serve short-term guests, now may be listed with one set of rates on a property management company's website, and another on VRBO or Airbnb, or all three. In residential areas, the county now more strictly regulates home shares and vacation rentals, as well as bed-and-breakfasts (which can also no longer offer hot breakfasts cooked in house). The rules were largely designed to limit the impact on housing prices and quality of life in quiet neighborhoods, but may mean a favorite haunt from years past is no longer in business.

I've tried to honor that intent by including only permitted properties below; the law requires such lodgings outside designated resort areas to post their permit and tax ID numbers online. Still, some 16,000 units outside these residential zones don't require special permits, so you should never have a problem finding a legitimate rental somewhere.

Wherever you stay, a hefty combination of 14.416% in county and state accommodations and excise taxes should be tacked on to your final bill (if it's not, your host likely does not have the proper

price CATEGORIES

These categories reflect the reality of high demand for lodgings on Maui, and the adage that "you get what you pay for." The truly cheap accommodations often have major downsides, so it's worth spending a little more for clean, comfortable, and convenient lodgings—or an unforgettable, romantic splurge.

Price categories are assigned by the most common room rates, typically the lowest for that lodging.

Very Expensive	$450 and up
Expensive	$350–$450
Moderate	$200–$350
Inexpensive	Under $200

permits). If you're staying at an upscale hotel or resort, expect to pay a daily "resort fee" ($20–$35 a day) in addition to your room rate; those fees are noted in descriptions below and are meant to cover phone, Internet, and resort facilities use, but are really just a dodge to advertise lower rates than your final bill will show.

All hotel rooms are nonsmoking, but some properties may have designated outdoor areas for smokers. Unless noted in the fine print below, parking is free and rooms include air-conditioning. All pools listed below are outdoors; not all are heated. References to "cleaning fees" below are for one-time, post-checkout cleaning of condos and vacation rentals, not daily services.

CENTRAL MAUI

Kahului

MODERATE

Marriott Courtyard ★ Business travelers and vacationers looking to save on airport drive time will find a comfortable night's sleep here. The hotel has soundproofed walls that adequately muffle noise from the neighboring airport. Spacious rooms are attractively furnished, featuring contemporary, island-inspired artwork. Suites come with full kitchens—super-convenient considering the lobby has a 24-hour market, and several grocery stores are a 5-minute drive away. The palm-fringed pool deck is nice at night when it's lit by the glow of the firepit.

532 Keolani Pl., Kahului. www.marriott.com/kahului. © **808/871-1800.** 138 units. $279–$299 double; $349–$469 suite; $409–$529 1-bedroom; $520–$618 2-bedroom. Parking $12. Free airport shuttle. **Amenities:** Deli-style restaurant; fitness center; Jacuzzi; coin-operated laundry; 24-hr. market; pool; free Wi-Fi.

INEXPENSIVE

Maui Beach Hotel ★ Off busy Kaahumanu Avenue but backing up onto a small beach, this budget hotel is managed by Aqua Aston Hospitality, which specializes in sprucing up older properties and adding services to make them more appealing yet still affordable. Here, fourposter bed frames with pineapple finials and matching dark wood furniture, framed Hawaiiana prints, and flatscreen TVs with Blu-Ray DVD players elevate otherwise basic rooms with wall-unit air-conditioners and motel-style bathrooms. A la carte breakfast and Sunday brunch and dinner buffets in the open-air, second-floor **Rainbow Terrace** restaurant also provide good value if you don't have time to venture off-property, which includes a few tempting oceanview hammocks.

170 W. Kaahumanu Ave., Kahului. www.mauibeachhotel.com. © **866/970-4168** (reservations only) or 808/877-0051. 150 units. Doubles from $169–$179. Daily amenity fee $15. Parking $5. **Amenities:** Restaurant; lounge; free airport shuttle (6am–9pm); ATM; laundry room; pool; free Wi-Fi.

Maui Seaside ★   As if frozen in time, this harborside hotel looks much the same as it might have in the 1970s, with rattan furniture, aloha print bedspreads, and faux-leather booth seating in **Tante's,** the attached restaurant (7am–2pm daily). But it doesn't feel musty: The vintage decor has been updated and the aloha look is now trendy. Rooms in the two-story building face the pool and Kahului Harbor with its sandy beach, where canoe clubs launch their paddling practice.

100 W. Kaahumanu Ave., Kahului. www.mauiseasidehotel.com. © **800/560-5552** or 808/877-3311. 180 units. Double $159–$184. Some rates include breakfast. Children under 12 stay free in parent's room using existing bedding. Extra person $15. Parking $10. **Amenities:** Restaurant; laundry room; pool; free Wi-Fi.

Wailuku
MODERATE
Old Wailuku Inn at Ulupono ★★   Innkeepers Janice and Thomas Fairbanks and their daughter Shelly offer genuine Hawaiian hospitality at this lovingly restored 1928 estate hidden down a sleepy side street in old Wailuku town. Rooms in both the inn and the three-bedroom Vagabond House are decorated with native ohia wood or marble floors, high ceilings, and traditional Hawaiian quilts—most with king-size beds. Each room has a private, luxurious bathroom stocked with plush towels and Aveda toiletries and either

WHAT YOU'LL really PAY

The prices quoted here are for two sample dates, one in early June (during low season) and one in February (high season); holiday weekends and rack rates, the maximum that hotels charge, may be higher. Be sure to check the hotel's website, as many prices fluctuate frequently by demand as well as season, and special packages that include breakfast, activities, and/or rental cars, or require advance purchase, may offer good value. Many hotels offer small discounts for seniors, AAA (automobile club) members, active military, and state residents.

During the off-season (Sept to early Dec and Mar to early June), you will find the best deals, although holiday weekends and the week before or after Easter will see spikes.

When comparing rates, expect to pay more for a one-bedroom condo apartment than you would for just a hotel room; factor in savings on meals, even if it's just reheating leftovers or simple breakfasts.

Note: Quoted discount rates almost never include breakfast, hotel tax, or any applicable resort fees.

a claw-foot tub, a whirlpool tub, or a deluxe multihead shower. You'll want to linger in the fragrant gardens and curl up with a book on the enclosed lanai. Your hosts pull out all the stops at breakfast, serving tropical fruits and pastries beginning at 7am and Belgian waffles, five-cheese frittatas, and Molokai sweet-potato pancakes at 8am. The inn is located in Wailuku's historic center, so you'll hear a bit of road noise if the air-conditioning isn't on, but it's just a 5-minute walk from Hale Hoikeike (Bailey House Museum), Market Street's antique shops, and several good restaurants. Iao Valley is a 5-minute drive away.

2199 Kahookele St. (at High St., across from the Wailuku School), Wailuku. www.maui inn.com. © **800/305-4899** or 808/244-5897. 10 units. $185–$280 double, includes full breakfast. Check for online specials. 2-night minimum. **Amenities:** Jacuzzi; free Wi-Fi.

INEXPENSIVE

Backpackers should head to Wailuku's **Banana Bungalow Maui** ★, a funky Happy Valley hostel at 310 N. Market St. (www.mauihostel.com; © **800/846-7835** or 808/244-5090), with dorm rooms (four to six beds, some for women-only) for $47 and private rooms with shared bathrooms for $106 single, $119, $142 triple. This "party hostel" with a Friday night keg of beer also provides many other free amenities not often found in hostel-type accommodations, such as airport shuttle, daily tours across Maui, high-speed Internet access, make-your-own pancake breakfast, and a barbecue grill and Jacuzzi out back. Dorm-style accommodations ($38) and private rooms ($79–$99) are also available in old Wailuku at the **Northshore Hostel,** 2080 W. Vineyard St. (www.northshorehostel.com; © **866/946-7835** or 808/986-8095). Lodgings are on the open-air second floor (no elevator); breakfast, Wi-Fi, and limited airport and area shuttle are included. *Note:* Neither has air-conditioning, so rooms can be warm and humid, especially in summer. Solo travelers might not feel safe in old Wailuku after dark.

WEST MAUI

Lahaina

VERY EXPENSIVE

Puunoa Beach Estates ★★   If you're taking a family to Maui, consider these gorgeous townhouses in an exclusive 3-acre enclave on a white-sand beach. Of the 10 on site, four individually owned and decorated two-bedroom, two-bath units and one three-bedroom unit (1,700 sq. ft. and up) are available for rent through Classic Resorts. All have private beachfront lanai, hardwood floors, marble bathrooms, and modern kitchens. Prices are high, but the amenity list has everything you should want for a first-class vacation rental in a dream location. It's within walking distance of the center of Lahaina, but the residential location makes you feel miles away. *Bonus:* Unlike some condos, these include daily maid service and no resort fees.

45 Kai Pail Place, Lahaina. www.puunoabeachestates.com. © **866/504-9465** or 808/661-3339. 10 units. $909–$1,058 2-bedroom (sleeps 4), $969–$1,457 3-bedroom (sleeps 6). 5- to 7-night minimum. **Amenities:** Concierge; fitness center; outdoor pool; sauna; complimentary snorkeling equipment; video library; whirlpool; free Wi-Fi.

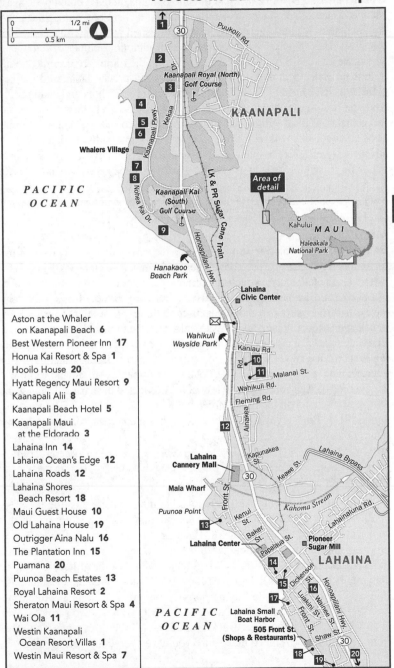

0 — 1/2 mi
0 — 0.5 km

1

(30)

Puukolii Rd.

Kaanapali Royal (North) Golf Course
3

KAANAPALI

2

Kekaa

Kaanapali Pkwy.

4

5

6

Whalers Village

7

8

Nohea Kai Dr.

PACIFIC OCEAN

Kaanapali Kai (South) Golf Course

9

Lk & PR Sugar Cane Train

Area of detail

Kahului   M A U I

Haleakala National Park

Honoapiilani Hwy.

Hanakaoo Beach Park

Lahaina Civic Center

Wahikuli Wayside Park

Kaniau Rd.

Rd.

10

11

Malanai St.

Wahikuli Rd.

Fleming Rd.

Ainakea

12

Kapunakea St.

Lahaina Bypass

Lahaina Cannery Mall

(30)

Keawe St.

Mala Wharf

Kahoma Stream

Lahainaluna Rd.

Puunoa Point

Front St.

Kenui St.

Baker St.

13

Lahaina Center

Papalaua St.

Pioneer Sugar Mill

LAHAINA

14

15

Dickenson St.

16

Wainee St.

Honoapiilani Hwy.

17

Luakini St.

Front St.

PACIFIC OCEAN

Lahaina Small Boat Harbor

505 Front St.
(Shops & Restaurants)

Shaw St.

(30)

18

19

20

Aston at the Whaler
  on Kaanapali Beach **6**
Best Western Pioneer Inn **17**
Honua Kai Resort & Spa **1**
Hooilo House **20**
Hyatt Regency Maui Resort **9**
Kaanapali Alii **8**
Kaanapali Beach Hotel **5**
Kaanapali Maui
  at the Eldorado **3**
Lahaina Inn **14**
Lahaina Ocean's Edge **12**
Lahaina Roads **12**
Lahaina Shores
  Beach Resort **18**
Maui Guest House **10**
Old Lahaina House **19**
Outrigger Aina Nalu **16**
The Plantation Inn **15**
Puamana **20**
Puunoa Beach Estates **13**
Royal Lahaina Resort **2**
Sheraton Maui Resort & Spa **4**
Wai Ola **11**
Westin Kaanapali
  Ocean Resort Villas **1**
Westin Maui Resort & Spa **7**

4

WHERE TO STAY ON MAUI | West Maui

43

EXPENSIVE

Hooilo House ★ Located just outside Lahaina, about a mile up the West Maui Mountains from Launiupoko Beach Park, this six-bedroom, solar-powered bed-and-breakfast is constructed and furnished with materials and furniture from Bali, but the views are all Maui, including cloud-topped Lanai across the channel. The atmosphere is relaxing, the rooms are decorated with traditional Bali doors and custom beds, there's a private lanai, and the big bathrooms have huge tubs and outdoor showers. The Kohola and Nalu rooms have the best ocean views; all come with flatscreen TVs, mini-fridges, and individual A/C plus ceiling fans. The property also has a small swimming pool. Continental breakfast includes vegan breads and muffins (gluten-free by advance request), cereal, granola, hard-boiled eggs, and tropical fruit, including some picked from the house orchard (mango, papaya, banana, and more.)

138 Awaiku St., Lahaina. www.hooilohouse.com. ✆ **808/667-6669.** 6 units. $359–$399 double. Rates include continental breakfast. 3-night minimum. **Amenities:** Pool; free Wi-Fi.

MODERATE

Best Western Pioneer Inn ★ This once-rowdy home away from home for sailors now seems respectable—even charming. The circa-1901 hotel is a two-story plantation-style structure with big verandas that overlook the streets of Lahaina and the harbor, which is just 50 feet away. Simply furnished rooms have smallish bathrooms, mounted air-conditioners (not silent, but they do muffle the outdoor noise), and private balconies. Note that all rooms are up a flight of stairs. The quietest units face the garden courtyard—an outdoor dining area shaded by an enormous *hala* tree—but for people-watching from your veranda, get a room that overlooks Front Street. I recommend room no. 31, over the banyan court, with a view of the ocean and the harbor. If you want a front-row seat for all the Front Street action, book no. 36 or 49. The **Pioneer Inn Grill & Bar** serves a good breakfast and great cheap drinks at happy hour.

658 Wharf St. (in front of Lahaina Pier), Lahaina. www.pioneerinnmaui.com. ✆ **800/457-5457** or 808/661-3636. 34 units. $197–$319 double. Free parking (across the street). **Amenities:** Restaurant; bar w/live music; outdoor pool; free Wi-Fi.

Lahaina Inn ★ If you like old hotels that have genuine historic touches, you'll love this place. A ship's figurehead announces this historic inn in the center of Maui's old whaling town. Each tiny, antiques-stuffed room has a private bathroom, air-conditioning, and two rocking chairs on a lanai overlooking Lahaina's action. Rooms 7 and 8 have views of the glittering Pacific. Downstairs is **Lahaina Grill,** one of the island's most celebrated restaurants. You won't need a car while staying here—shopping, restaurants, and marine activities are immediately outside your door—but you will need earplugs; this is an urban area, and garbage trucks rumble past in the early morning. The front desk closes at 7pm, so make sure you have everything you need before they leave for the day. Guests have beach, pool, and tennis privileges at the inn's sister property, the Royal Lahaina Resort in Kaanapali.

127 Lahainaluna Rd. (off Front St.), Lahaina. www.lahainainn.com. © **808/661-0577.** 12 units. $135–$225 double; from $195–$239 suite. Next-door parking $15 per day. **Amenities:** Restaurant; privileges at Royal Lahaina Resort; free Wi-Fi.

Lahaina Roads ★   Oceanfront condos aren't usually tailored to slim budgets, but you're in luck here. Named for the Mala Wharf roadstead where a string of pretty boats anchor offshore, this condominium complex offers small, reasonably priced, individually owned units in an older building located in the quiet part of Lahaina, away from the noisy, crowded downtown area but just down the street from Lahaina Cannery Mall, Old Lahaina Luau, several terrific restaurants, and Puunoa ("Baby") Beach. One- and two-bedroom units benefit from full kitchens, oceanfront lanais, and a heated seaside pool. The drawbacks: Bedrooms face the road, which can make nights noisy, and some units lack air-conditioning (it can be boiling hot in Lahaina). You'll also find units for rent on VRBO; the contact info below is for the professional management of seven of the 17 units.

1403 Front St. (1 block north of Lahaina Cannery Mall), Lahaina. Book with Chase'N Rainbows: www.westmauicondos.com/resorts/lahaina-roads. © **877/611-6022** or 808/359-2636. 17 units. $165–$255 1-bedroom; $245–$410 2-bedroom. Cleaning fee from $200. 5-night minimum. **Amenities:** Pool; free Wi-Fi.

Lahaina Shores Beach Resort ★   First there's the location, right on the beach; second there's the location, away from the hustle and bustle of downtown Lahaina; and third there's the location, next door to the 505 Front St. restaurants and shops. This seven-story condominium project (of studios and one-bedroom units) resembles an old plantation home, with arched colonnades at the entry and an open-air, beachfront lobby. From the moment you step into the airy units (from 550 to 1,430 sq. ft.), you'll feel like you are home. The units all have full kitchens, large lanai, and ocean or mountain views; daily maid service is included, and parking is free. Ask for an oceanfront unit for that terrific view of the water with the island of Lanai in the distance. *Note:* You'll find lower rates on VRBO, but check the fine print

---

BAREFOOT ETIQUETTE

In Hawaii, it is traditional and customary to remove your shoes before entering anyone's home. The same is true for most vacation rentals and bed-and-breakfast facilities. Most hosts post signs or will politely ask you to remove your shoes before entering the house or condo. Not only does this keep the place clean, but you'll also be amazed at how relaxing it is to walk around barefoot. If this custom is unpleasant to you, this kind of stay may not be for you.

closely for one-time cleaning fees and other charges that bring them more in line with the ones below managed by Classic Resorts.

475 Front St., Lahaina. www.lahainashores.com. © **866/934-9176** or 808/661-4835. 199 units. $248–$418 studio double; $305–$585 1-bedroom double; from $424 1-bedroom penthouse double. Rollaway bed $20. **Amenities:** Concierge; pool; free Wi-Fi; tennis courts (across the street); whirlpool.

Maui Guest House ★★

This is one of Lahaina's great bed-and-breakfast deals. Tanna Swanson offers guests many extras at her renovated home, tucked away in a residential Lahaina neighborhood (please be respectful of neighbors). For starters, each of the five private rooms has a full-size Jacuzzi (seriously!), noiseless air-conditioning, and gorgeous stained-glass windows depicting reef fish, flowers, and other Hawaiian scenes. Guests also have access to the saltwater pool; large, fully stocked kitchen; and a 30-foot sundeck for sunbathing, stargazing, and whale-watching. Swanson's home is 1 mile from downtown Lahaina and Kaanapali's beaches. Tennis courts are nearby, and Wahikuli Wayside Park beach is about a block away. *Note:* Four of the rooms can accommodate a twin bed in addition to the queen, by request, but children must be at least 12 to stay here (because of the hot tub in the room). Full payment is due 60 days in advance.

1620 Ainakea Rd. (off Fleming Rd.), Lahaina. www.mauiguesthouse.com. © **800/621-8942** or 808/661-8085. 5 rooms. $199 double, includes continental breakfast. **Amenities:** Concierge; saltwater pool; watersports equipment; laundry facilities; free Wi-Fi.

Outrigger Aina Nalu ★

This lushly landscaped condo complex sprawls over 9 acres on a relatively quiet side street—a rarity in downtown Lahaina. The good-size units—only some of which are managed by Outrigger—are tastefully decorated with modern tropical accents; all have kitchens or kitchenettes, laundry facilities, air-conditioning (a must in Lahaina), and bathrooms with large granite showers (but no tubs). Both pools are appealing places to retreat during the midday heat—particularly the infinity pool deck with its bright red cabanas and pavilion for poolside picnics. All of the historic whaling town's excitement—restaurants, shops, galleries, marine activities, and the small sandy cove at 505 Front St.—is within a 10-minute stroll. *Note:* Rates for some two-bedroom, two-bath units near the pool may be $150 higher than similar units. You'll see Aina Nalu units on VRBO with potentially lower rates and cleaning fees, but the daily parking fee ($20) is the same.

660 Wainee St. (btw. Dickenson and Prison sts.), Lahaina. www.outriggerainanalu condo.com. © **866/253-9743** or 808/667-9766. 197 units. $159–$289 studio; $159–$299 1-bedroom; $189–$499 2-bedroom. 2-night minimum. Cleaning fee $175–$225. Parking $20. **Amenities:** Concierge; grills; whirlpool; 2 pools; free Wi-Fi.

The Plantation Inn ★★

Tucked away behind **Gerard's,** Maui's award-winning French restaurant (p. 94), this romantic inn was built in 1987 but looks as if it has been here since the days of Hawaiian royalty—an artful deception. The 14 rooms and four suites are tastefully furnished with vintage touches: fourposter beds, hardwood floors, French doors, and Hawaiian quilts. All units are blissfully quiet, and some have lanais overlooking Lahaina Town. Two extras seal this inn's appeal: the daily complimentary gourmet breakfast (courtesy of Gerard's), served poolside, and a super-convenient location—in the heart of Lahaina—that makes most driving unnecessary (although parking is free when you must).

174 Lahainaluna Rd. (btw. Wainee and Luakini sts., 1 block from Hwy. 30), Lahaina. www.theplantationinn.com. *(C)* **800/433-6815** or 808/667-9225. 18 units. $175–$253 double; $275–$300 suite. Extra person $40. Rates include full breakfast and $50 credit at Gerard's; free self-parking. Check website for deals. **Amenities:** Restaurant and bar; concierge; whirlpool; coin-operated laundry; large outdoor pool; free Wi-Fi.

Puamana ★★ These 30 acres of townhouses set right on the water are ideal for those who want to be able to retreat from the crowds and cacophony of downtown Lahaina into the serene quiet of an elegant neighborhood. Private and peaceful are apt descriptions for this complex: Each unit is a privately owned individual home, with no neighbors above or below. Most are exquisitely decorated, and all come with full kitchen, lanai, barbecue, and at least two bathrooms. Puamana was once a private estate in the 1920s, part of the sugar plantations that dominated Lahaina; the plantation manager's house has been converted into a clubhouse with an oceanfront lanai, library, card room, sauna, table-tennis tables, and office. *Note:* Rates for garden-view units are significantly lower—sometimes by several hundreds of dollars a night—than those for oceanfront units. The contact info below is for just one of the management companies offering rentals here, but you'll also find units here through VRBO and other rental agencies.

Pualima Pl. at Front St., Lahaina. www.vacation-maui.com. *(C)* **800/676-4112** or 808/661-3484. 40 units. $195–$445 1-bedroom; $225–$725 2-bedroom; $385–$695 3-bedroom. Cleaning fee $248–$280. Parking $10 per day. 3-night minimum. **Amenities:** Jacuzzi; 3 pools (1 for adults only); tennis court; free Wi-Fi.

INEXPENSIVE

In addition to the following choices, consider value-priced **Old Lahaina House ★** (www.oldlahaina.com; *(C)* **800/847-0761** or 808/667-4663), which features four somewhat dated but comfy twin- and king-bedded doubles for just $159 to $209. All units have air-conditioning, refrigerator, coffee pot, Wi-Fi, and access to the pool and outdoor kitchen. It's at 407 Ilikahi St., about a 2-minute walk to the water just across Front Street.

Lahaina Ocean's Edge ★ Here's a small apartment complex located right on the water. You can take a 10-minute stroll from this quiet neighborhood to the closest beach, or walk 20 minutes to the center of Lahaina town. The units are small (400 sq. ft.) but clean and have full kitchens, a separate bedroom, and views of the ocean (from most units); some have air-conditioning, lanais, and sitting areas. In the middle of the complex is a tropical garden. I recommend the Ocean Front Queen units, which have private balconies or lanais with tremendous views, as well as air-conditioning. Families will like the Ohana Suite, the only two-bedroom unit (800 sq. ft.). *Note:* Some units require access by stairs.

1415 Front St., Lahaina. www.makaiinn.net. ✆ **808/662-3200.** 18 units. $179–$219 rooms; $249–$299 suite. Extra person $15. **Amenities:** Laundry room; free Wi-Fi.

Wai Ola ★   Just two blocks from the beach, in a quiet residential development behind a tall concrete wall, lies this lovely, adults-only retreat, with shade trees, sitting areas, gardens, a pool, an ocean mural, and a range of accommodations. You can book a small studio, a couple of suites inside the home, a separate honeymoon cottage, a one-bedroom apartment, or the entire 5,000-square-foot house. Hosts Kim and Jim Wicker will gladly provide any information you need to make your vacation fabulous. Every unit has a welcome fruit basket when you arrive, plus coffee beans for the coffeemaker. Kim often surprises her guests with "a little something" from her kitchen, like cheesecake or heavenly brownies. You'll also find a deck, barbecue facilities, and an outdoor wet bar on the property; a great beach and tennis courts are nearby.

1565 Kuuipo St., Lahaina. www.waiola.com. ✆ **800/492-4652** or 808/661-7901. 4 units. $169–$179 studio; $179–$199 suite; $209–$219 1-bedroom honeymoon cottage. No children allowed. **Amenities:** Jacuzzi; pool; free Wi-Fi; free use of watersports equipment.

Kaanapali
VERY EXPENSIVE
Kaanapali Alii ★   This luxurious oceanfront condo complex sits on 8 landscaped acres in the center of Kaanapali Beach. Units are individually owned and decorated—some are considerably fancier than others. Both one- (1,500-sq.-ft.) and two-bedroom (1,900-sq.-ft.) units come with the comforts of home: spacious living areas, gourmet kitchens, washer/dryers, lanais, and two full bathrooms. Resortlike extras include bell service, daily housekeeping, and a complimentary kids' club (summer only). Views from each unit vary dramatically; if watching the sun sink into the ocean is important to you, request a central unit on floor six or higher. Mountain-view units shouldn't be disregarded, though. They're cooler throughout the day, and the West Maui Mountains are arrestingly beautiful—particularly on full-moon nights. Other amenities include a swimming pool, a kiddie pool, barbecues and picnic areas, and tennis courts. You can even take yoga classes on the lawn.

50 Nohea Kai Dr., Lahaina. www.kaanapalialii.com. ✆ **866/664-6410** or 808/667-1400. 264 units. 1-bedroom $465–$695; 2-bedroom $680–$1,050. 5-night minimum. Check for online specials. Free parking. **Amenities:** Babysitting; concierge; fitness center; fitness and yoga classes; 36-hole golf course; kids' club (June–Aug); 2 outdoor pools; 3 lighted tennis courts; watersports equipment; free Wi-Fi.

The Westin Kaanapali Ocean Resort Villas ★★   In contrast to the hotel-style Westin (see below), this elegant condo complex is so enormous it has two separate lobbies. The 26 acres fronting serene **Kahekili Beach** function as a small town, with two grocery stores, three pools (yes, that's a life-size pirate ship in the kids' pool), three restaurants (hit the sports bar **Pailolo Bar & Grill** during a game), a Hawaiian cultural advisor, the luxurious **Spa Helani** (the 80-min. Polynesian ritual is unforgettable), and a high-energy gym with its own steam rooms, saunas, and lockers. Managed by Westin, the individually owned units (from studios to two-bedrooms) are outfitted with Westin's trademark Heavenly beds, huge soaking tubs with jets, and upscale kitchens. Despite its seemingly massive footprint, the resort has accrued awards for its eco-friendly practices. One fun example: On July 4th, the resort ditches the usual fireworks display (which spreads ash on the fragile coral reefs) and opts instead to celebrate with "flower-works," dropping 60,000 orchids on the property. The lucky guest who finds the rose amid the orchids gets a free spa treatment or snorkel cruise. *Tip:* Ask for some leeway with the 4pm check-in and 10am checkout times.

6 Kai Ala Dr., Kaanapali Resort. www.westinkaanapali.com. © **866/716-8112** or 808/ 667-3200. 1,021 units. Studio from $399; 1-bedroom from $559; 2-bedroom from $829. Extra person $89. Valet $20, self-parking $15. **Amenities:** 3 restaurants; 2 bars; babysitting; children's program; concierge; 36-hole golf course; 2 fitness centers; 6 outdoor pools (including children's pool w/pirate ship); 4 whirlpools; room service; shuttle service; spa; tennis courts; free Wi-Fi.

EXPENSIVE

Aston at the Whaler on Kaanapali Beach ★   In the heart of Kaanapali, right on the world-famous beach, lies this oasis of elegance, privacy, and luxury. The relaxing atmosphere strikes you as soon as you enter the open-air lobby, where light reflects off the dazzling koi in the meditative lily pond. No expense has been spared on these gorgeous accommodations; every unit, from studio (640 sq. ft.) to two-bedroom (up to 1,952 sq. ft.), has a full kitchen, marble bathroom, 10-foot beamed ceilings, and blue-tiled lanai—and spectacular views of Kaanapali's gentle waves or the humpback peaks of the West Maui Mountains. Next door is Whalers Village, with numerous restaurants, bars, and shops; Kaanapali Golf Club's 36 holes are across the street. *Note:* Contact info and rates below are for units managed by Aqua Aston Hospitality; you'll find additional units listed on www.thewhaler.com, VRBO, and other platforms.

2481 Kaanapali Pkwy. (next to Whalers Village), Lahaina. www.astonhotels.com. © **888/ 671-5310** or 808/661-4861. 360 units. Studio double $265–$359; 1-bedroom (1 or 2 baths, sleeps up to 4) $339–$565; 2-bedroom (2 baths, sleeps up to 6) $569–$1,079. Check website for specials. Daily resort fee $20. Parking $12 per day. **Amenities:** Concierge; refurbished fitness room; Jacuzzi; outdoor pool; Hina Mana Salon & Spa; tennis courts; free Wi-Fi.

Honua Kai Resort & Spa ★★   This North Kaanapali Beach resort is a favorite with residents and locals alike. The property sits on 38 acres bordering Kahekili Beach, immediately north of busier, flashier Kaanapali Beach. The resort's upscale yet relaxed atmosphere takes a cue from its natural surroundings. Island-inspired artwork in the lobby gives way to colorful koi ponds, artfully landscaped grounds, and meandering swimming pools (including a fun family zone with pirate ship). Luxe accommodations range from spacious 590-square-foot studios to vast 2,800-square-foot three-bedroom units, with top-of-the-line appliances, lanai, and ocean views. The resort's sociable restaurant, **Duke's Beach House** (p. 103), offers an "onolicious" breakfast and live music. Stock up on organic snacks, gelato, and local coffee at **Aina Gourmet Market** in the lobby, which also offers delicious takeout fare. Ho'ola Spa boasts the island's only therapeutic Himalayan salt room and uses organic, made-in-Hawaii products in its treatments. *Note:* The development of the luxury townhome development Luana Garden Villas on the mountain side of Honua Kai is reflected in lower rates for those units facing the construction versus other "resort" and ocean views.

130 Kai Malina Pkwy., North Kaanapali Beach. www.honuakai.com. ℂ **855/718-5789** or 808/662-2800. 600 units. Studio (king bed plus sofabed, sleeps up to 4) $269–$495; 1-bedroom (sleeps up to 4) $309–$583; 2-bedroom (sleeps up to 6) $434–$736; 3-bedroom (sleeps up to 8) $1,083–$1,970. Daily $29 resort fee. **Amenities:** Restaurant; deli; bar; nearby 36-hole golf course; 5 whirlpools; 5 pools; nearby tennis courts; watersports equipment rentals; free Wi-Fi.

Hyatt Regency Maui Resort & Spa ★★　You'll almost feel like royalty when you walk into this palatial resort with exotic parrots and South African penguins in the lobby. The southernmost property on Kaanapali Beach, it covers some 40 acres with nine manmade waterfalls, abundant Asian and Pacific artwork, and a waterpark pool with a swim-up grotto bar, rope bridge, and 150-foot lava-tube slide that keeps kids occupied for hours. Spread out among three towers, the resort's ample rooms have huge marble bathrooms, feather-soft platform beds, and private lanais with eye-popping views of the Pacific or the West Maui Mountains. Two Regency Club floors offer a private concierge, complimentary breakfast, sunset cocktails, and snacks—not a bad choice for families looking to save on meals. Daily activities range from sushi-making classes at **Japengo,** the resort's superb Japanese restaurant (p. 102), to stargazing on the rooftop. Camp Hyatt offers pint-size guests weekly scavenger hunts, penguin-feeding opportunities, and access to a game room. The oceanfront **Kamaha'o, Marilyn Monroe Spa,** a 20,000-square-foot wellness retreat, boasts 15 treatment rooms, sauna and steam rooms, and a huge menu of celebrity-inspired body treatments. Book your treatment before you leave home—this place is popular. The onsite **Drums of the Pacific Luau** ($123–$158 adults, $76 ages 6 to 12; www.drumsofthepacificmaui.com; ℂ **808/867-4727**) entertains with hula specific to Kaanapali and features some intriguing options on its sprawling buffet.

200 Nohea Kai Dr., Lahaina. https://maui.regency.hyatt.com. ℂ **808/661-1234.** 806 rooms; 31 suites. Double (queen or king) $255–$551; Regency Club double $415–$641; suite $555–$1,081. Daily $32 resort fee. Extra person $75 ($125 in Regency Club rooms). Children 18 and under stay free in parent's room using existing bedding. Packages available. Valet parking $32; self-parking $22. **Amenities:** 5 restaurants; 3 bars; luaus; babysitting; children's program; wildlife and star-gazing tours; concierge; club floor; 36-hole golf course; health club and classes; whirlpool; half-acre outdoor pool; room service; shuttle service; spa; 6 tennis courts; watersports equipment rentals; free Wi-Fi.

Sheraton Maui Resort and Spa ★★   The Sheraton occupies the nicest spot on Kaanapali Beach, built into the side of Puu Kekaa, the dramatic lava rock point at the beach's north end. The sand has been disappearing as of late, but the snorkeling is still great around the base of the point, also known as Black Rock. At sunset, cliff divers blow a conch shell before diving into the sea from the torch-lit promontory. The resort's prime location, ample amenities, and great service make this an ideal place to stay. Rooms feature Hawaiian-inspired decor, private lanais, and Sheraton's trademark Sweet Sleeper beds, which live up to their name. The Ohana (family) suites accommodate all ages with two double beds plus a *pune'e* (sleeping chaise). The lagoonlike pool is refreshing but can't beat a sea full of actual fish and turtles just steps away. Activities ranging from outrigger canoe to hula and ukulele lessons will immerse you in Hawaiian culture; at night the **Maui Nui Luau** has the usual exciting fire-knife dance finale. Treatments at the elegant **Spa at Black Rock**—especially those catering to couples—are exquisite. Fans of **Hank's Haute Dogs** on Oahu will find their favorite gourmet dogs here, as well as more formal restaurants serving island and Japanese cuisine, while DJs spin tunes from 10pm to midnight on weekends at the **Black Rock Lounge.** Rooms (and spectacular suites) perched on the point include access to the Na Hoku club lounge with free breakfast and evening appetizers.

2605 Kaanapali Pkwy., Lahaina. www.sheraton-maui.com. © **866/627-8114** or 808/661-0031. 508 units. Doubles $288–$509; suites $589–$859. Extra person $89. Children 17 and under stay free in parent's room using existing bedding. Daily $25 resort fee. Valet parking $30 (free 1st day); self-parking $22. **Amenities:** 5 restaurants; poolside bar; weekly luau; club lounge; babysitting; children's program (at Westin Maui Resort & Spa); lobby and poolside concierge; 36-hole golf course; fitness center; whirlpool; lagoon-style pool; room service; shuttle service; spa; 3 tennis courts; watersports equipment/rentals; free Wi-Fi.

Westin Maui Resort & Spa ★★   The fantasy begins in the lobby, where waterfalls spill into a pool stocked with flamingos and black swans. The lavish grounds wind around an 87,000-square-foot water wonderland with five pools and an extra-speedy, 128-foot-long waterslide. After enjoying the pool action (often rather noisy from the sound ricocheting off the hotel wings), hit the beach for snorkeling, stand-up paddling, kayaking, or parasailing (in season)—the sky truly is the limit. Recharge at **Relish Burger Bistro**, the poolside restaurant, but save your appetite for **Wailele Polynesian Luau**, the resort's 3-hour luau experience ($115–$145; www.westinmauiluau.com) that's heavy on the fire-knife dancing. (*Note:* Kids can get an all-day dining pass for $20.) Stroll two doors down to shop at Whalers Village; when you're ready to drop, your Westin Heavenly Bed offers no fewer than five different pillows and a divine mattress. If you need further revivifying, hit the **Heavenly Spa** for a Hualani fruit scrub and *lomilomi* massage. In keeping with Westin's wellness theme, the hotel also offers a "mind and body" studio for yoga and meditation classes and a 2,000-square-foot fitness center, with loaner workout clothes at the ready, courtesy of New Balance.

2365 Kaanapali Pkwy., Lahaina. www.westinmaui.com. ℂ **866/627-8413** or 808/667-2525. 759 units. Double $290–$689; suite $691–$1,339. Extra person $89. Children 18 and under stay free in parent's room. Daily $30 resort fee. Valet parking $35, self-parking $30. **Amenities:** 3 restaurants; 3 bars; babysitting; bike rentals; children's program; concierge; 36-hole golf course; fitness center; 5 pools and whirlpools; room service; spa; tennis courts; watersports equipment rentals; free Wi-Fi.

MODERATE

Another option to consider, in addition to those below, is the **Royal Lahaina Resort** (27800 Kekaa Dr., Lahaina; www.royallahaina.com; ℂ **800/222-5642** or 808/201-2926). But skip the overpriced (and sometimes overbooked) hotel rooms in the 12-story tower and stay instead in one of the roomy 132 cottages tucked among the well-manicured grounds. You can book a cottage room (350 sq. ft.) for two people for $285 garden view, $385 ocean view; or a two-bedroom cottage suite for up to eight people for $689, with no resort fee (daily valet parking $20, self-parking $15).

Kaanapali Beach Hotel ★★ It's older and less high-tech than its upscale neighbors, but the Kaanapali Beach Hotel has an irresistible local style and a real Hawaiian warmth that's missing from many other Maui properties. Depending on your taste, you'll find this property's giant carved tikis, whale-shaped pool, and somewhat dated decor kitschy or refreshingly unpretentious. Instead of African parrots and Asian artwork, the lobby is adorned with traditional Hawaiian hula implements and weapons—many created by the staff during their annual Makahiki celebration. Three low-rise buildings border Kaanapali Beach; the beachfront units are mere steps from the water. The large-ish, motel-like rooms are decorated with wicker and rattan furniture, historic photos, and Hawaiian-style bedspreads. Hula and live music create a festive atmosphere every night in the courtyard. During the day, the expert watermen and women at Hale Huaka'i (the resort's water activity center) will teach you surf or paddle. Dry off and head to Hale Ho'okipa, the new cultural center, to practice throwing a fish net or playing the bamboo nose flute. The staff serenades you during a morning welcome reception and a farewell lei ceremony. *Note:* This is the rare hotel that permits smoking—but only on the lanais of designated rooms, about 40, all on the 6th (top) floor of its Lanai and Kauai wings, and only when sliding doors to the rooms are shut.

2525 Kaanapali Pkwy., Lahaina. www.kbhmaui.com. ℂ **800/262-8450** or 808/661-0011. 432 units. Double $205–$350; suite $340–$360. Extra person $40. Packages available,. Valet parking $18; self-parking $14. **Amenities:** 2 restaurants; pool bar; babysitting; family activities; concierge; 36-hole golf course nearby; cultural center; pool; spa and salon services; access to tennis courts; watersports equipment rentals; free Wi-Fi.

Kaanapali Maui at the Eldorado ★ It may have been one of Kaanapali's first properties in the late 1960s, but this 10-acre condo complex still manages to feel new. Developed in an era when real estate was abundant and contractors built to last, each spacious, individually owned unit has a full kitchen, washer/dryer, central air-conditioning, and outstanding ocean and mountain views. Studios are a roomy 660 square feet, with a king or queen bed plus a sofabed; larger units in the two-story (no elevator) buildings are a great choice for active families. It's set on Kaanapali Golf Course, not on the beach, but guests have exclusive use of a beachfront pavilion on North Kaanapali, aka Kahekili Beach. It's a quick trip by car or golf cart. You're also within walking distance of excellent and affordable restaurants at Whalers Village or the Fairway Shops—a real bonus in otherwise pricey Kaanapali. *Note:* Contact info and prices below are for the 87 units managed by Outrigger; other units may be rented via VRBO or different platforms. Grocery service and daily housekeeping are optional; the daily resort and condo fees totaling $32 and onetime cleaning fees ($150–$250) sadly are not.

2661 Kekaa Dr., Lahaina. www.outrigger.com. © **303/369-7777** (reservations) or 808/661-0021. 204 units. Studio $145–$199; 1-bedroom $169–$389; 2-bedroom $299–$439. 2-night minimum. Packages available. Daily $17 resort fee. Daily $15 condo fee. $150–$250 cleaning fee. **Amenities:** Beach pavilion; concierge; 36-hole golf course; 3 pools; free Wi-Fi.

Honokowai, Kahana & Napili

EXPENSIVE

Napili Kai Beach Resort ★★★ This small resort nestled on Napili's white sandy cove feels like a well-kept secret. For 50-plus years, the staff here has been welcoming return guests for a taste of unspoiled paradise. The weekly mai tai and golf putting parties are blasts from the past, but the modern conveniences in each unit and startling ocean views will focus you on the splendid here and now. From the three buildings on the point (Puna, Puna 2, and Lani), you can gaze from your bed at the ocean, which looks like an infinity pool starting at the edge of your lanai. All units (aside from eight hotel rooms) have full kitchens, washer/dryers, flatscreen TVs, ultra-comfortable king-size beds, and private lanais separated by attractive shoji screens. Hawaiian cultural activities include *poi* pounding and *lauhala* weaving workshops and weekly authentic *keiki* (children's) hula shows and slack-key-guitar concerts, the latter led by Grammy award–winning musician George Kahumoku. Kids 12 and under eat for free at the resort's **Sea House** restaurant, which also has great happy-hour specials (p. 105). As cozy as the rooms are, you'll probably spend most of your time on the beach or in the protected bay paddling past lazy sea turtles. *Note:* There's no resort fee. The lower rates listed below apply most of the year; the higher rates are for the Christmas/New Year's period.

5900 Honoapiilani Rd. (at north end of Napili, next to Kapalua), Lahaina. www.napilikai. com. © **800/367-5030** or 808/669-6271. 162 units. Hotel room double $335–$435; studio $410–$705; 1-bedroom $690–$995; 2-bedroom $975–$1,575; 3-bedroom $1,155–$1,755. Packages available. **Amenities:** Restaurant; bar; babysitting; children's activities at holidays; concierge; 24-hr. fitness room; 2 18-hole putting greens; discounted rates at nearby golf courses; 4 pools; free Kapalua shuttle; tennis courts nearby (and free use of rackets); free use of watersports equipment; free Wi-Fi.

MODERATE

In addition to the choices below, consider one of the individually owned, low-rise units at **Polynesian Shores** ★, 3975 Lower Honoapiilani Rd. (near Kahana), Lahaina (www.polynesianshores.com; ✆ **800/433-6284** or 808/669-6065). Every unit (from $159 for one bedroom, from $220 for two bedrooms, $395 for three bedrooms) has floor-to-ceiling sliding-glass doors that open onto a private lanai with an ocean view. There's great snorkeling off the beach out front.

Another option is **Hoyochi Nikko** ★, 3901 Lower Honoapiilani Rd. (in Honokowai), Lahaina, which has 17 older (but well-maintained) one-bedroom units (and a few one-bedrooms with a separate loft) sharing 180 feet of oceanfront. You'll find units on VRBO and a number of other websites, including that of Maui Lodging Properties (www.mauilodging.com; ✆ **808/669-0089**), which offers rates of $200 to $260, 4-night minimum, plus cleaning fees of $135 to $165.

Aston at Papakea Resort ★   Just a mile north from Kaanapali lie these low-rise buildings, surrounded by manicured, landscaped grounds and ocean views galore. Palm trees and tropical plants dot the property, a 12-hole putting green wraps around each of two kidney-shaped pools, and a footbridge arches over a lily pond brimming with carp. Each pool has its own private cabana with sauna, Jacuzzi, and barbecue grills; a poolside shop rents snorkel gear for exploring the offshore reefs. All units have dishwashers, big lanais, washer/dryers, and air-conditioning. The studios have pull-down beds to save space during the day. *Note:* When comparing rates, be sure to factor in the daily resort fee ($17) and one-time cleaning fee ($89).

3543 Lower Honoapiilani Rd. (in Honokowai), Lahaina. www.astonhotels.com. ✆ **888/671-5309** or 808/669-4848. 364 units. Studio $153–$342; 1-bedroom (sleeps up to 4) $185; 2-bedroom (sleeps up to 6) $242–$482. Daily resort fee $17. Cleaning fee $89. **Amenities:** 2 whirlpool spas; 2 pools; 3 lighted tennis courts; pickleball; watersports equipment rentals; yoga classes; free Wi-Fi.

Honokeana Cove ★★   These large, secluded units—cozily set around an oceanfront pool in a lush tropical setting—have fabulous views of Honokeana Cove. The beach here isn't sandy (it's composed of smooth round rocks), but the water just offshore is excellent for snorkeling (turtles have been spotted here) and for whale-watching in winter. The well-appointed units all come with full kitchens and lanai; some have air-conditioning, but ceiling fans and tradewinds also cool units nicely. Amenities include barbecues, deck chairs, and tiki torches lit every evening. The management holds weekly *pupu* (appetizers) parties so you can meet the other guests. All in all, a well-priced option in an expensive neighborhood.

5255 Lower Honoapiilani Rd. (in Napili), Lahaina. www.honokeana-cove.net. ✆ **800/237-4948** or 808/669-6441. 33 units. 1-bedroom (1 bath; sleeps four) $188–$251; 1-bedroom plus loft (1 or 2 baths; sleeps four or five) $198–$279; 2-bedroom (2 or 2½ baths; sleeps four) $276–$426; 3-bedroom (2 or 2½ baths; sleeps 6 or 7) $393–$624. Extra person $15. 3- to 5-night minimum; 7- to 14-night minimum over Christmas/New Year's. **Amenities:** Concierge; heated pool; barbecues; coin laundry facilities; free Wi-Fi.

Hotels & Restaurants from Kapalua to Honokowai

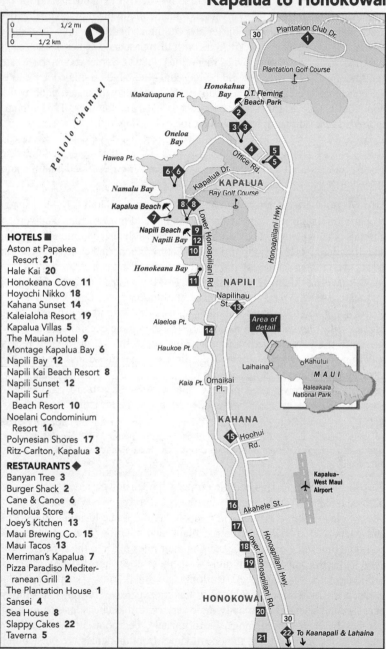

HOTELS ■

Aston at Papakea
  Resort **21**
Hale Kai **20**
Honokeana Cove **11**
Hoyochi Nikko **18**
Kahana Sunset **14**
Kaleialoha Resort **19**
Kapalua Villas **5**
The Mauian Hotel **9**
Montage Kapalua Bay **6**
Napili Bay **12**
Napili Kai Beach Resort **8**
Napili Sunset **12**
Napili Surf
  Beach Resort **10**
Noelani Condominium
  Resort **16**
Polynesian Shores **17**
Ritz-Carlton, Kapalua **3**

RESTAURANTS ◆

Banyan Tree **3**
Burger Shack **2**
Cane & Canoe **6**
Honolua Store **4**
Joey's Kitchen **13**
Maui Brewing Co. **15**
Maui Tacos **13**
Merriman's Kapalua **7**
Pizza Paradiso Mediter-
  ranean Grill **2**
The Plantation House **1**
Sansei **4**
Sea House **8**
Slappy Cakes **22**
Taverna **5**

Kahana Sunset ★ Set in the crook of a sharp bend on Lower Honoapiilani Road is a series of three-story wooden condos, stair-stepping down a hill to a secluded beach on Keonenui Bay—a strip of golden sand all but unknown, even to locals. Decor varies dramatically in the individually owned units, many of which feature master and children's bedrooms up a short flight of stairs. All units have full kitchens with dishwashers, washer/dryers, cable TV, and expansive lanais with marvelous views. Some rooms have air-conditioning, while most rely on ceiling fans—suitable on this cooler end of the coastline. The center of the property features a small heated pool, whirlpool, and barbecue grills. This complex is ideal for families: The units are roomy and the adjoining beach is safe for swimming.

4909 Lower Honoapiilani Hwy. (at the northern end of Kahana), Lahaina. www.kahana sunset.com. © **800/669-1488** or 808/669-8700. 79 units. 1-bedroom $189–$370; 2-bedroom $315–$590. 3- to 5-night minimum. **Amenities:** Secluded beach; barbecues; concierge; 2 pools (including kiddie pool); free Wi-Fi.

The Mauian Hotel ★★ Perched above beautiful Napili Bay, this vintage property offers a blend of old-time hospitality and modern flair. The verdant grounds burst with tropical color; the pool deck is shaded by umbrellas by day and lit with tiki torches at night. Rooms feature Indonesian-style furniture and lanais overlooking the grassy lawn and glittering Pacific. The 38 studios (360 sq. ft.) have full kitchens and either king or queen beds with Tempur-Pedic mattresses. As with the six hotel rooms, the studios have no phones or TVs—encouraging you to unplug—though you'll find a TV and an extensive DVD library in the *ohana* (family) room. Guests gather there each morning for coffee, fresh fruit, and pastries before heading out to snorkel or try their luck at stand-up paddling in the supremely calm bay. Live music and free mai tais attract guests to the weekly "aloha party" by the pool, where they share *pupu* (appetizers) and travel tales. Nightly sunsets off the beach are spectacular—particularly during winter when whale spouts dot the horizon.

5441 Lower Honoapiilani Rd. (in Napili), Lahaina. www.mauian.com. © **808/669-6205**. 44 units. Double $219–$249; studio $239–$400. Extra person $20. **Amenities:** Coin-operated laundry; continental breakfast, outdoor pool; shuffleboard courts; free limited Wi-Fi.

Napili Sunset ★ This humble property hidden down a side street consists of three buildings, two facing spectacular Napili Bay and one across the street. At first glance, they don't look like much, but the prime location, low prices, and friendly staff make up for the plain-Jane exterior. The one- and two-bedroom units are beachfront, meaning their rates fall into the expensive category. Upstairs units have bathtubs, while those downstairs have direct access to the sand. Across the street, overlooking a small, kidney-shaped pool and gardens, the more economical studios feature expansive showers and Murphy beds. All units benefit from daily maid service, full kitchens, and ceiling fans (studios have air-conditioning). Unfortunately, bedrooms in the beachfront buildings face the road, but the ocean views from the lanais are outstanding.

The strip of grassy lawn adjoining the beach is an added perk—especially when the sandy real estate is crowded. Several good restaurants are within walking distance, along with Kapalua's tennis courts and golf courses. The beach—one of Maui's best—can get a little crowded because the public beach access is through this property.

46 Hui Rd. (in Napili), Lahaina. www.napilisunset.com. © **808/669-8083.** 43 units. Studio $239; 1-bedroom $389; 2-bedroom $629. **Amenities:** Daily maid service; barbecues; coin-operated laundry; heated pool; free Wi-Fi.

Napili Surf Beach Resort ★   This well-maintained, superbly landscaped condo complex has a great location on Napili Beach—one reason its high season rates fall into the expensive category. The well-furnished, extensively renovated units (all with full kitchens and portable air conditioners in living rooms) offer free daily maid service, a rarity in condo properties. Management encourages socializing: In addition to weekly mai tai parties and coffee socials, the resort hosts annual shuffleboard and golf tournaments, as well as get-togethers on July 4th, Thanksgiving, Christmas, and New Year's. Facilities include three shuffleboard courts and three gas barbecue grills. *Note*: The management also lists units on Airbnb.

50 Napili Place (off Lower Honoapiilani Rd., in Napili), Lahaina. www.napilisurf.com. © **800/541-4547** or 808/669-8002. 53 units, some with shower only. Studio double (sleeps up to 3) $239–$408; 1-bedroom double (sleeps up to 4) $350–$472. Extra person $15. **Amenities:** 2 heated pools, barbecues; laundry facilities; shuffleboard; free Wi-Fi.

Noelani Condominium Resort ★★   This oceanfront condo is a great value, whether you stay in a studio or a three-bedroom unit (ideal for large families). Though it's on the water, there's no sandy beach here (despite the photos posted on the website)—but right next door is a sandy cove at the Pohaku Beach Park (good for surfing, not as great for swimming); better beaches are a 5-minute drive away. Bright splashes of teal help offset the somewhat dated dark rattan furniture in the units, which feature full kitchens with older but clean appliances, daily maid service, panoramic views of passing whales during winter, and sunsets year-round; one-, two-, and three-bedrooms have washer/dryers. In the Orchid building's deluxe studios, you can see the ocean from your bed. Units in the Anthurium Building boast oceanfront lanais just 20 feet from the water (the nicest are on the ground floor), but the bedrooms face the road. Guests are invited to lei-making and weekly mai tai parties in the poolside cabana and have access to a teeny-tiny gym with a million-dollar view. With no cleaning fee, this place is a real deal.

4095 Lower Honoapiilani Rd. (in Kahana), Lahaina. www.noelani-condo-resort.com. © **800/367-6030** or 808/669-8374. 40 units. Studio $170–$250; 1-bedroom $215–$295; 2-bedroom $335–$430; 3-bedroom $370–$515. Extra person $20. Children under 18 stay free in parent's room. Packages available. Rates include continental breakfast on 1st morning. 3-night minimum. **Amenities:** Concierge; fitness center; oceanfront whirlpool; barbecue grills; laundry center (for studios); 2 pools (1 heated); DVD library; free Wi-Fi.

INEXPENSIVE

Keep in mind that high-season rates may put the following options into the moderate category, although they remain good value even then.

Hale Kai ★   This small two-story condo complex is ideally located, right on the beach and next door to a county park—a great location for those traveling with kids. Shops, restaurants, and ocean activities are all within a 6-mile radius. The units are older but in excellent shape; they come with well-equipped kitchens (with dishwasher, disposal, microwave, and blender) and louvered windows that open to the tradewinds. Lots of guests clamor for the oceanfront pool units, but I find the park-view units cooler, and they still have ocean views (upstairs units also have cathedral ceilings). This place fills up fast, so book early; repeat guests make up most of the clientele.

3691 Lower Honoapiilani Rd. (in Honokowai), Lahaina. www.halekai.com. ℂ **800/446-7307** or 808/669-6333. 40 units. 1-bedroom double $108–$215; 2-bedroom (1 or 2 baths, sleeps up to 6) $158–$295; 3-bedroom (2 baths, sleeps up to 6) $261–$450. Extra person $10. 5-night minimum. **Amenities:** Concierge; pool; free Wi-Fi.

Kaleialoha ★   This condo complex for the budget minded has one-bedroom units with a sofabed in the living room, which allows you to comfortably sleep four, and a solar-heated pool with a great sunset barbecue area. All of the island-style units feature fully equipped kitchens, with everything from dishwashers to washer/dryers, and large private lanais; some have air-conditioning. There's great ocean swimming just off the rock wall (a sandy beach is nearby); a protective reef mows waves down and allows even timid swimmers to relax. *Note:* Contact and rates info below is for a management company currently representing 16 units in three price categories; you may find units listed elsewhere.

3785 Lower Honoapiilani Rd. (in Honokowai), Lahaina, HI 96761. www.mauicondosoceanfront.com. ℂ **800/222-8688** or 808/669-8197. 18 units. 1-bedroom double $139–$285. 7-night minimum over Christmas/New Year's. Extra person $15. Cleaning fee $145. Damage insurance $29. **Amenities:** Concierge; heated pool; free Wi-Fi.

Napili Bay ★   This small two-story condo complex sits on the southern edge of picturesque Napili Bay. Fall asleep to the sound of the surf and wake to birdsong. Individually owned studio apartments are compact (400 sq. ft.), with king- or queen-size beds in the oceanfront living room (rather than facing the road like so many on this strip). You'll find a stocked kitchen, beach and snorkeling equipment, and a lanai with front-row seats for the sunset. You won't find a pool on the property or air-conditioning in the rooms, but louvered windows and ceiling fans keep the units fairly cool—and why waste time in a pool when you're steps away from one of the island's calmest and prettiest bays? *Note:* Contact and rates info below are for one of the property managers; you'll also find units on VRBO and other rental sites.

33 Hui Dr. (off Lower Honoapiilani Hwy., in Napili), Lahaina. www.alohacondos.com/maui/napili-bay-resort. ℂ **877/877-5758.** 28 units. Double $109–$289. Cleaning fee $130. Reservation fee $25. Minimum stays may apply. **Amenities:** Barbecue; laundry facilities; free Wi-Fi.

Kapalua

VERY EXPENSIVE

Montage Kapalua Bay ★★★   Built on the site of the old Kapalua Bay Hotel, this 24-acre compound offers just 50 impeccably furnished rental residences, from one-bedroom to four-bedroom (1,250–4,050 sq. ft.). The low density—and astronomical prices—means there's never a crush at the terraced Sunset Pool with gorgeous Lanai and Molokai views, or the more intimate infinity-edged Beach Club Pool, or anywhere else on the beautifully landscaped grounds. It's hard to leave the cocoon of the roomy villas, which offer gourmet kitchens, high-end linens and robes, spa-like bathrooms, and lanais or balconies with massive daybeds. Still, you don't want to miss the chance to "talk story" with cultural advisor Silla Kaina over lei-making, ukulele classes, or another of the free Hawaiian-themed activities. (Look for Kaina's portrait by local artist Pegge Hopper, supplementing the series she did for the Kapalua Bay Hotel.) The 30,000-sq.-ft., two-story **Spa Montage Kapalua Bay** includes a vast fitness center with a raft of weekly classes, infinity-edge pool, and well-stocked boutique. The open-air restaurant **Cane & Canoe** (p. 107) epitomizes most of the culinary offerings at the resort: expensive, not particularly exciting, but satisfying enough and graciously served. An in-room poke-making cooking class (among others) with Executive Chef Chris Damskey, however, is an exceptional experience, as is renting the Cliff House overlooking Namalu Bay for a private meal. *Note:* It's hard to believe at this price level, but room rates do not include the $48 daily resort fee.

1 Bay Dr., Kapalua. www.montagehotels/kapaluabay. ℰ **808/662-6200.** 50 units. 1-bedroom (sleeps 4) $701–$1,495; 2-bedroom $998–$1,845; 3-bedroom $1,381–$2,425; 4-bedroom $2,401–$4,825. Daily $48 resort fee. Valet parking $30. **Amenities:** Concierge; 3 restaurants; 2 bars; 2 pools; fitness center; luxury spa; beach services; children's and teen programs; business center; market; resort shuttle; in-room laundry; free Wi-Fi.

Ritz-Carlton Kapalua ★★★   This Ritz is a complete universe, one of those resorts where you can happily sit by the ocean with a book for 2 whole weeks and never leave the grounds. It rises proudly on a knoll, in a singularly spectacular setting between the rainforest and the sea. During construction, the burial sites of hundreds of ancient Hawaiians were discovered in the sand, so the hotel was moved inland to avoid disrupting the graves. The setback gives the hotel a commanding view of Molokai.

Today, Hawaiian cultural advisor Clifford Nae'ole helps guide resort developments and hosts the Ritz's signature events, such as the Celebration of the Arts—a weeklong indigenous arts and cultural festival. The resplendent accommodations feature dark wood floors, plush beds, marble bathrooms, and private lanais overlooking the landscaped grounds and mostly undeveloped coast. The Ritz offers one of the best club lounges in the state, serving gourmet coffee and pastries, a lunch buffet, cookies in the afternoon, hot appetizers and drinks at sunset, and assorted goodies throughout the day. Additional amenities include several superior restaurants; a 10,000-square-foot, three-tiered pool; and the 17,500-square-foot **Waihua Spa,** with steam rooms, saunas, and whirlpools surrounded by lava-rock walls. Make sure to visit **Jean-Michel Cousteau's Ambassadors of the Environment center** and explore the captivating activities for adults and kids. (You can even feed the resident pot-bellied pigs.) A bit of a hike from the resort proper, **D. T. Fleming Beach** is beautiful but tends to be windier and rougher than the bays immediately south; a 5-minute shuttle ride delivers you to calmer Oneloa or Kapalua.

1 Ritz-Carlton Dr., Kapalua. www.ritzcarlton.com/en/hotels/kapalua-maui. © **808/669-6200.** 463 units. Double $449–$654; club-level double $1,045–$1,170; suite $837–$1,165; 2-bedroom suite $1,237–$1,685; club-level suite $1,545–$1,570. Extra person $50 (club level $100). Daily $35 resort fee. Valet parking $30; self-parking $22. **Amenities:** 4 restaurants; 4 bars; babysitting; basketball courts; bike rentals; children's program; club floor; concierge; cultural-history tours; fitness room with classes; 2 championship golf courses and golf academy; hiking trails; outdoor 3-tiered pool; room service; shuttle service; luxury spa; tennis complex; watersports equipment rentals; free Wi-Fi.

MODERATE

Kapalua Villas ★★★ The stately townhouses populating the oceanfront cliffs and fairways of this idyllic coast are a (relative) bargain, particularly if you're traveling with a group. Several of the island's best restaurants (Sansei and Merriman's Kapalua) are within walking distance or a quick shuttle trip, and you're granted signing privileges and a discount at the nearby championship golf courses. Outrigger manages many of the individually owned one-, two-, and three-bedroom units, which feature full kitchens, upscale furnishings, queen-size sofa beds, and large, private lanais. You'll enjoy the spaciousness—even the one-bedrooms exceed 1,200 square feet. Of the three complexes (Golf, Ridge, and Bay Villas), the Bay units are the nicest, positioned on the windswept bluff overlooking Molokai on the horizon. In the winter, oceanfront villas let you whale-watch without leaving your living room.

200 Village Rd., Kapalua. www.kapaluavillasmaui.com. © **800/367-2742** or 808/665-9170. 1-bedroom $225–$359; 2-bedroom $285–$425; 3-bedroom $395–$1,099. Daily $35 resort fee. $250–$325 cleaning fee. **Amenities:** Restaurants and beaches nearby; concierge; in-room laundry; golf; tennis; 9 outdoor pools; resort shuttle; free Wi-Fi.

SOUTH MAUI

You'll find an overwhelming number of vacation rental homes and condos in South Maui listed on websites such as VRBO, Airbnb, and even Hotels.com. Sometimes it's helpful to turn to an on-island booking agency that requires its units to meet certain standards and can easily help you if anything goes wrong during your stay. Among many others, **Condominium Rentals Hawaii** (www.crhmaui.com; © **800/367-5242**) offers affordable, quality properties in Kihei, Wailea, and Maalaea, some of which are detailed below.

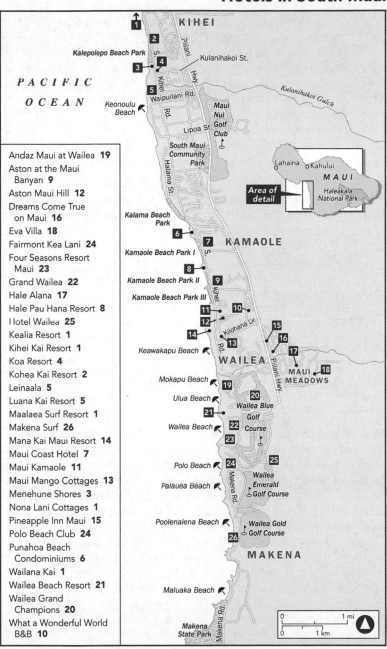

Andaz Maui at Wailea **19**
Aston at the Maui Banyan **9**
Aston Maui Hill **12**
Dreams Come True on Maui **16**
Eva Villa **18**
Fairmont Kea Lani **24**
Four Seasons Resort Maui **23**
Grand Wailea **22**
Hale Alana **17**
Hale Pau Hana Resort **8**
Hotel Wailea **25**
Kealia Resort **1**
Kihei Kai Resort **1**
Koa Resort **4**
Kohea Kai Resort **2**
Leinaala **5**
Luana Kai Resort **5**
Maalaea Surf Resort **1**
Makena Surf **26**
Mana Kai Maui Resort **14**
Maui Coast Hotel **7**
Maui Kamaole **11**
Maui Mango Cottages **13**
Menehune Shores **3**
Nona Lani Cottages **1**
Pineapple Inn Maui **15**
Polo Beach Club **24**
Punahoa Beach Condominiums **6**
Wailana Kai **1**
Wailea Beach Resort **21**
Wailea Grand Champions **20**
What a Wonderful World B&B **10**

4

WHERE TO STAY ON MAUI | South Maui

Kihei

MODERATE

In addition to the following properties, consider the **Aston at the Maui Banyan** (www.aquaaston.com; ✆ **877/997-6667** or 808/924-2924), a condo property across the street from Kamaole Beach Park II, with two tennis courts and a pool onsite. The large one- to three-bedroom units are very nicely done and feature full kitchens, air-conditioning, and washer/dryers. Rates run from $169 to $390 for hotel rooms, $199 for one-bedroom units and $269 to $475 for two-bedroom units—be sure to ask about packages.

Note: During high season, some of the listings in this category fall into the expensive category ($350–$450), but they're still available at moderate rates ($200–$350) for much of the year, and sometimes for even less than that.

Aston Maui Hill ★ This condo complex with Mediterranean-style stucco buildings, red-tile roofs, and three-stories-tall arches marks the border between Kihei and Wailea—an excellent launching pad for your vacation. Managed by the respected Aqua Aston chain, Maui Hill combines the amenities of a hotel—24-hour front desk, concierge, pool, hot tub, tennis courts, putting green, and more—with the convenience of a condo (and no resort or cleaning fees!). Units are spacious, with ample kitchens, air-conditioning (welcome in this climate), washer/dryers, queen-size sofa beds, and roomy lanais—most with ocean views. (For prime views, seek out units #35 and #36.) Two of South Maui's best beaches are across the street; restaurants, shops, and golf courses are nearby. Check the website for significant discounts.

2881 S. Kihei Rd. (across from Kamaole Park III, btw. Keonekai St. and Kilohana Dr.), Kihei. www.astonmauihill.com. ✆ **855/945-4044** or 808/879-6321. 140 units. 1-bedroom $229–$280; 2-bedroom $302–$395; 3-bedroom $451–$560. Weekly rates discounted. **Amenities:** Concierge; putting green; pool; whirlpool; tennis courts; free Wi-Fi.

Eva Villa ★ At the top of the Maui Meadows neighborhood above Wailea, Rick and Dale Pounds have done much to make their affordable B&B one of Maui's classiest. The hillside location offers respite from the shoreline's heat—and yet it's just a few minutes' drive to the beaches, shopping, and restaurants of both Kihei and Wailea. The tastefully designed cottage has a decent-size kitchen and living room, smallish bedroom, washer/dryer, and a sweet outdoor shower. The poolside studio is a single, long room with a huge kitchen and barstool seating. The suite next door has two bedrooms and a kitchenette. You aren't forced to be social here; continental breakfast (fresh fruit, juice, muffins, coffee) comes stocked in your kitchen. And with just three units, the luxurious pool deck is rarely ever crowded.

815 Kumulani Dr., Kihei. www.mauibnb.com. ✆ **808/874-6407.** 3 units. Double $155–$225. Rates include continental breakfast. Cleaning fee $115. Extra person $20. 5- to 7- night minimum. No credit cards. **Amenities:** Heated outdoor pool; free Wi-Fi.

Hale Alana ★ This three-bedroom, three-bathroom Polynesian-style vacation home in the residential neighborhood of Maui Meadows (a 5-min. drive from the nearest good beach) is a great value for a large family or three couples traveling together. The master bedrooms have California-king-size beds, walk-in closets, and dual sinks and showerheads; the third bedroom has two double beds and a large closet. Skylights and an interior lava-rock wall add to the tropical environment, cooled by ceiling fans and air-conditioning. The deck has panoramic views, plus tables and chairs, a pool, hot tub, and a barbecue grill.

490 Mikioi Place (in Maui Meadows), Kihei, HI 96753. www.halealana.com or www.beachbreeze.com. ⓒ **855/283-2231** or 808/283-2231.1 unit. $540–$650 3-bedroom (sleeps up to 7). Cleaning fee $350. 7-night minimum. **Amenities:** Pool; whirlpool; free Wi-Fi.

Hale Pau Hana Resort ★ Located on the sandy shores of Kamaole Beach Park, but separated from the white-sand beach by a velvet-green manicured lawn with a heated saline pool, this is a great condo resort for families. Each of the large units has a private lanai, a terrific ocean view, and a complete kitchen; one-bedrooms in the high-rise wing have two baths. The management goes above and beyond, personally greeting each guest and acting as your own concierge service. Guests can mingle at the free morning coffee hour Monday through Saturday, or at the bring-your-own *pupu* parties held twice a week at sunset. The location is in the heart of Kihei, close to shopping, restaurants, and activities.

2480 S. Kihei Rd., Kihei. www.hphresort.com. ⓒ **800/367-6036** or 808/879-2715. 79 units. 1-bedroom $317–$434; 2-bedroom $427–$490. Extra person $15–$25. 4- to 7-night minimum. **Amenities:** Concierge; saltwater pool; barbecues; laundry room; free Wi-Fi.

Kohea Kai Resort ★★ Across the street from windswept Sugar Beach in North Kihei, this cheery boutique property welcomes all, and caters especially to gay and lesbian travelers (many who started coming here when it was still an LGBT-focused resort known as Maui Sunseeker). When you book a standard room, studio, or suite, expect bright decor, comfy California king–size beds, air-conditioning (wall mount), and spacious ocean- or mountain-view lanais. Suites have full kitchens or kitchenettes. The three penthouse suites are fabulous—especially #622, a three-bedroom suite (all king beds) with private two-person hot tub. Rates include a full hot breakfast. Chat with fellow guests over eggs and bagels or in the rooftop hot tub, where you can take in the panoramic view of Maalaea Bay and the West Maui Mountains. Maui's best beaches are a short drive away; the owners supply beach chairs and coolers.

551 S. Kihei Rd., Kihei. www.koheakai.com. ⓒ **808/879-1261.** 26 units. Double $256–$400; studio suite $306–$470; 1-bedroom suite $356–$500; penthouse suites $489–$900. Resort fee $25. Extra person $45. Rates include breakfast. **Amenities:** Concierge; 2 whirlpools (rooftop hot tub is clothing-optional); pool; free parking; free Wi-Fi.

Maalaea Surf Resort ★ Despite its name, this little-known beachfront retreat isn't in Maalaea, nor is it a resort. Rather, it's a collection of charming condos spread out across 5 acres at the far north end of Kihei. The four-unit townhouses with double-hipped roofs all have ocean views, big kitchens (with dishwashers), cable TV, and central air-conditioning—a nice perk in summer. Sugar Beach, the adjacent salt-and-pepper stretch of sand, extends 3-plus miles to Maalaea. Often windy, it's not the best for swimming, but it's unmatched for sunsets (and whale-watching in winter). This is a decent headquarters for adventurers who want to explore the entire island.

12 S. Kihei Rd. (at N. Kihei Rd. and Route 311), Kihei. www.maalaeasurfresort.com. ℂ 800/423-7953 or 808/879-1267. 34 units. 1-bedroom $230–$395; 2-bedroom $305–$560; 5–7-night minimum. **Amenities:** Concierge; 2 pools; barbecues; shuffleboard; 2 tennis courts; free Wi-Fi.

Mana Kai Maui Resort ★ Even the views outside the elevator are astounding at this eight-story hotel/condo, which practically has its toes in the sand of beautiful Keawakapu Beach. Every unit in the 1973 building is oceanfront (though many lack views). Most, if not all, have been renovated with contemporary, island-inspired furnishings. The north-facing hotel rooms, which account for half of the units, have no lanais and at 210 sq. ft. are small enough to be filled by their king-size beds and kitchenettes. The one- and two-bedroom condos have full kitchens, sitting areas, and small lanais that overlook the glittering Pacific and several islands on the horizon; the ones with the best views also have air-conditioning. There's a surf shack on-site, along with a gourmet grocery/deli, oceanfront restaurant, and yoga studio. *Fun fact:* The lobby's iconic turtle mural appears in the film *Just Go With It.*

2960 S. Kihei Rd., Kihei. www.manakaimaui.com. ℂ 800/525-2025 or 808/879-1561. 98 units. Hotel room double $196–$290; 1-bedroom $315–$735; 2-bedroom $400–$835. **Amenities:** Restaurant; bar; barbecues; concierge; laundry facilities; daily maid service; pool; watersports equipment rentals; free Wi-Fi.

Maui Coast Hotel ★ The chief advantage of Kihei's sole hotel is location, location, location. It's less than a block from sandy, sun-kissed Kamaole Beach Park I and within walking distance of South Kihei Road's bars, restaurants, and shopping. Another plus: nightly entertainment at the popular pool bar. Guest rooms are smallish, with sitting areas, sofabeds, huge flatscreen TVs, central air, and private garden lanais—no ocean views, though. Throughout the solar-powered hotel, you'll find wonderful paintings by local artist Avi Kiriaty. Book the less-expensive "deluxe room" over the somewhat cramped "one-bedroom suite," unless you absolutely need the extra privacy. The **ami ami** restaurant serves reasonably priced local and organic dishes.

2259 S. Kihei Rd., Kihei. www.mauicoasthotel.com. ℂ 808/874-6284. 265 units. Double $260–$502; suite $276–$518; 1-bedroom $292–$522. Children 17 and under stay free in parent's room using existing bedding. Daily resort fee $25. Extra person charge $30. Packages available. **Amenities:** 2 restaurants; pool bar w/entertainment; free use of bicycles; concierge; rental car desk; fitness center; laundry facilities; pool (plus children's pool); 2 whirlpools; room service; 2 lighted tennis courts; free Wi-Fi.

Maui Kamaole ★   Directly opposite Kamaole Beach Park III's sandy beach, enormous lawn, and playground, this comfortable condo complex is ideal for families. Convenience is key here in the center of Kihei's beach and shopping zone, a short walk to the boat ramp, too. Each roomy, privately owned and furnished unit comes with an all-electric kitchen, central air, two bathrooms, and two private lanais. The one-bedroom units—which easily can accommodate four—are a terrific deal, especially during low season. (In the peak season, higher rates, three mandatory fees, and local taxes mean the final tab runs nearly $525 a night!) They're all on the ground floor, opening onto a grassy lawn. The attractively landscaped property runs perpendicular to the shoreline, and some buildings (indicated by room numbers that start with E, F, K, L, and M) are quite a trek from the beach. Families with small children should seek out units beginning with A, B, G, or H, which are nearest to the beach but off the road. C units are close to both beach and pool.

2777 S. Kihei Rd., Kihei. www.mauikamaole.com. ⓒ **844/430-0606.** 316 units (not all in rental pool). 1-bedroom $190–$353; 2-bedroom $246–$485. $40 booking fee. Damage insurance $35. Cleaning fee $125–$150. **Amenities:** 2 pools; 2 whirlpools; 2 tennis courts; free Wi-Fi.

Maui Mango Cottages ★★   Why stay in a condo when you can feel at home in one of these two beautifully updated, vintage cottages? They're shaded by mature mango trees on a 1-acre lot and lie within a short walk to swimmable Keawakapu Beach (and close to Wailea's 1½-mile beach path)—so take advantage of the complimentary beach chairs, coolers, and boogie boards. Both cottages have fully equipped kitchens, washer-dryers, air-conditioning, three parking spaces, and decks with tables, chairs, and barbecues; kids can run around the large yard while parents make dinner or drink their morning coffee. Cottage 1 is great for families, with one king bedroom and another with three twin beds, a great room, office, and bathroom with island-style private outdoor shower. Plantation-style Cottage 2 is ideal for two couples or larger families, offering two king bedrooms and one with two twin beds, living room, and 1½ small but modern baths. Friendly owners Charlie and Yvonne, who have three boys of their own, chose furnishings with just the right mix of comfort and sturdiness, with fun marine- and beach-themed prints serving as colorful accents to soft pastel walls and neutral upholstery. *Note:* The website will direct you to VRBO for booking; that platform charges a varying service fee tied to the room rate plus a refundable damage deposit of $295.

45 Kilohana Dr., Kihei. www.mauimangocottages.com. 2 units. Cottage 1 (sleeps 4–5) $195–$395; cottage 2 (sleeps 6) $395–$445. Cleaning fee $150. VRBO service fee $116–$268. 5-night minimum. **Amenities:** Barbecues; free Wi-Fi.

Pineapple Inn Maui ★★   Enjoy a resort vacation at a fraction of the price at this oasis in residential Maui Meadows, luxuriously landscaped with tall coconut palms, pink hibiscus the size of dinner plates, a lily pond, and—best of all—a saltwater pool that's lit at night. The four guest rooms in the two-story "inn" are equally immaculate: Each has upscale furnishings, a private lanai with a serene ocean view, and a kitchenette that your hosts, Mark and Steve, stock with pastries, bagels, oatmeal, juice, and coffee upon arrival. The bright and airy cottage (two bedrooms, one bath; sleeps 4) is one of the island's best deals. Landscaped for maximum privacy, it has a full kitchen, dark wood floors, central air, beautiful artwork, and a private barbecue area. Guests are invited to stargaze from the communal hot tub and make use of the fully equipped outdoor kitchen. Shopping, beaches, restaurants, and golf are minutes away, and you can borrow snorkeling equipment, beach chairs, umbrellas, boogie boards, and a cooler to take on your outdoor adventures.

3170 Akala Dr., Kihei. www.pineappleinnmaui.com. © **808/298-4403**. 5 units. Double $169–$219; cottage $235–$295. 3-night minimum for rooms, 6-night minimum for cottage. Rates include breakfast. **Amenities:** Saltwater pool; watersports equipment; free Wi-Fi.

Punahoa Beach Condominiums ★★ This small, four-story oceanfront condo complex sits on a large grassy lawn between the Charley Young surf break and Kamaole I Beach—an ideal headquarters for active sunseekers. Each of the 13 units boasts a lanai with a marvelous view of the Pacific and islands on the horizon, and are stocked with beach towels, beach chairs, and umbrellas. All are individually owned and decorated, so the aesthetic varies widely. (The website features photos of each.) Studios feature queen-size Murphy beds, full bathrooms, and compact, full-service kitchens. The three one-bedroom penthouses—the only units with air-conditioning—are the sweetest option. Shopping and restaurants are all within walking distance. Rooms go quickly in winter, so reserve early; rates also dip for the first 2 weeks in July.

2142 Ililli Rd. (off S. Kihei Rd., 300 ft. from Kamaole Beach I), Kihei. www.punahoabeach. com. © **800/564-4380,** © 808/879-2720. 13 units. Studio $142–$247; 1-bedroom double $179–$329; 1-bedroom penthouse $244–$354; 2-bedroom double $249–$345. Extra person $15. Cleaning fee $125–$150. Booking fee $35. 5-night minimum. **Amenities:** Barbecues; coin-operated laundry; free Wi-Fi.

INEXPENSIVE

In addition to the choices below, also check out **Luana Kai Resort** ★, 940 S. Kihei Rd., Kihei (www.luanakai.com; © **808/879-1268**). This older condo complex with swimming pool, hot tub, and two tennis courts has 113 units ($129–$209 one-bedroom, $159–$269 two-bedroom, $259–$309 three-bedroom; 4- to 7-night minimum; $75–$150 cleaning fee). All have full kitchens, laundry, and free Wi-Fi; air-conditioning is in select rooms and requires additional payment of $25–$30 a night depending on unit size. The three-story building does not have elevators.

Kihei Kai Resort ★, 61 N. Kihei Rd (www.kiheikai.com; © **808/891-0780**), fronts 4-mile-long Sugar Beach with individually decorated one-bedroom apartments ($143–$232 double, plus $120 cleaning fee and $79 reservation fee) that are ideal for families. All have full kitchens, air-conditioning and free Wi-Fi; facilities include a pool and coin laundry.

You may spot some of the 10 units of two-story **Wailana Kai** ★, 34 Wailana Place, Kihei, on VRBO and other rental websites. A block from Sugar Beach on a quiet cul-de-sac, these one-bedroom units with full kitchens benefit from concrete soundproof walls, a pool, and barbecue; some have ocean views. Rates typically start at $150 with cleaning fees around $110.

Dreams Come True on Maui ★   This bed-and-breakfast (where "you are never just renting a room") was a dream come true for hosts Tom Croly and Denise McKinnon, who, after several years of vacationing in Maui, opened this three-unit property in 2002. They offer a stand-alone cottage and two private suites in their house on a half-acre in the Maui Meadows neighborhood, just a 5- to 10-minute drive from the shopping, restaurants, golf courses, and beaches of Kihei and Wailea. The adults-only suites offer a private entrance and lanai, kitchenette, 42-inch TV, air-conditioning, and use of laundry facilities. Continental breakfasts are offered room-service style: Choose from the menu of freshly baked pastries, mangoes right off the tree, and other treats. Hang your order on your door, and in the morning it'll be delivered at your chosen time. Rooms are a bit tight, but you're free to use the oceanview deck, living room, and outdoor cooking area. The one-bedroom cottage has ocean views from several rooms, vaulted ceilings in the living room, wraparound decks, and marble in the kitchen and bathroom. Suites and units have air-conditioning, but tradewinds tend to cool them naturally. Tom is on duty as a personal concierge, doling out beach equipment and suggestions for where to snorkel, shop, or eat dinner.

3259 Akala Dr., Kihei. www.dreamscometrueonmaui.com. ✆ **877/782-9628** or 808/879-7099. 3 units. Suites (4-night minimum; no children under 12) $125–$149; cottage (6-night minimum) $169–$199. $125 cleaning fee; extra person $15. Continental breakfast included with suites. **Amenities:** Concierge; free Wi-Fi.

Kealia Resort ★   This oceanfront property at the northernmost end of Kihei isn't a resort, but it *is* worth a second look. From the outside, the older building might seem shabby, but on the inside the privately owned units shine—and rates are good, even with all the fees. Avoid the lower-priced studios facing noisy Kihei Road. Instead, go for one of the oceanfront units (such as no. 203, which hangs over the pool). All have full kitchens, washer/dryers, and private lanais with truly spectacular views of 3-plus-mile-long Sugar Beach. Twice a week the management hosts social events for guests to mingle: Wednesday *pupu* parties and Friday morning coffee-and-doughnut get-togethers. *Tip:* Ask for some leeway with the 10am checkout time.

191 N. Kihei Rd., Kihei. www.kealiaresort.com. ✆ **800/265-0686** or 808/879-0952 51 units. Studio $140–$160; 1-bedroom $185–$245; 2-bedroom $245–$295. Kids under 13 stay free in parent's room. Extra person $10. Cleaning fee $89–$131. Booking fee $25. Damage insurance $40. 4- to 10-night minimum. **Amenities:** Pool; barbecues; free Wi-Fi.

Koa Resort ★   Located just across the street from the ocean (but with views mostly blocked by another property), Koa Resort comprises five two-story wooden buildings on more than 5½ acres of landscaped grounds. There's plenty of room for families, who can enjoy the tennis courts, pool, and putting green. The spacious, privately owned one-, two-, and three-bedroom units are decorated with care, and kitchens come fully equipped. All feature large lanai, ceiling fans, and washer/dryers; some have air-conditioning. For maximum peace and quiet, ask for a unit in Building 2, far from Kihei Road. Bars, restaurants, and a golf course are nearby. *Note:* Contact info and rates below are for the three units managed by Bello Realty; you'll find many others on VRBO and similar sites.

811 S. Kihei Rd. (btw. Kulanihakoi St. and Namauu Place), Kihei. www.bellomaui.com. ℰ **800/541-3060** or 808/879-3328. 54 units, some with shower only. 1-bedroom $115–$145; 2-bedroom (available through VRBO) $150–$300; 3-bedroom $200–$350. **Amenities:** 18-hole putting green; heated pool, whirlpool, 2 tennis courts; free Wi-Fi.

Leinaala ★

From Kihei Road, you can't see Leinaala amid the jumble of buildings, but this oceanfront boutique condo offers excellent accommodations at affordable prices. The building is set back from the water, with a county park—an oasis of green grass and tennis courts—in between. A golf course is nearby. The units are compact but filled with everything you need: a full kitchen, sofabed, and oceanview lanai. (Hideaway beds are available if you need one.) *Note:* Contact info below is for one manager of five units; you'll find more units listed on VRBO and other sites.

998 S. Kihei Rd., Kihei. www.rentalsmaui.com. ℰ **800/808-8138.** 24 units. 1-bedroom double $139–$220; 2-bedroom $210–$295. Booking fee $50. Cleaning fee $115–$140. 3-night minimum. **Amenities:** Pool; free Wi-Fi.

Menehune Shores ★

Though the property shows its age in some places, units are generally well-maintained and have ocean views and lanai. The kitchens are fully equipped, the individually owned units have washer/dryers, and the oceanfront location guarantees a steady breeze that keeps rooms cool; not all units have air-conditioning. The horseshoe-shaped building sits in front of the ancient Hawaiian fishponds of Kalepolepo. Some Hawaiians still fish them using traditional throw nets, but generally the pond serves as protection from the ocean waves, making it safe for children (and those unsure of their ability) to swim in the relatively calm waters. Amenities include a heated pool, shuffleboard courts, and a whale-watching platform on the roof garden.

760 S. Kihei Rd. (btw. Kaonoulu and Hoonani sts.), Kihei. www.menehunereservations. com. ℰ **808/879-3428**. 64 units. 1-bedroom double $180–$230; 2-bedroom $210–$290; 3-bedroom $300–$380. Cleaning fee $130–$170. Booking fee $60. Credit card processing fee 3%. Booking fee $60. 3-night minimum. **Amenities:** Restaurant; bar; gas grills; heated pool; shuffleboard; free Wi-Fi.

Nona Lani Cottages ★

Family-owned since the 1970s, this oceanside retreat is one of North Kihei's sweetest deals. Eight tiny vintage cottages are tucked among the coconut palms and plumeria trees, a stone's throw from Sugar Beach; some have ocean views across the road. Inside is everything you'll need: a compact kitchen, a separate bedroom with a queen-size bed, air-conditioning, and a cozy lanai—not to mention updated cabinetry and travertine tile floors. The three suites in the main house are stuffy; stick to the cottages. The charming grounds include a barbecue area and outdoor *hale* for weddings or parties—but no pool or spa. Your hosts, the Kong family, don't offer daily maid service, but they do make fresh flower leis—buy one and fill your cottage with fragrance. Wi-Fi is spotty here.

455 S. Kihei Rd. (just south of Hwy. 31), Kihei. www.nonalanicottages.com. © **808/879-2497.** 11 units. Suites $183–$235; cottage $248–$340. Extra person $25. 2–4-night minimum. Cleaning fee $40 studio, $75 cottage. **Amenities:** Barbecues; coin-operated laundry; on-site wedding coordinator; free Wi-Fi.

What a Wonderful World B&B ★ Repeat guests adore hostess Eva Tantillo, whose years of experience in the travel industry shows in thoughtful touches around her lovely property. Every unit is air-conditioned and lovingly furnished with hardwood floors, Hawaiian quilts, luxurious slate showers, and "tea kitchens"—a dining area with small fridge, sink, prep space, dishes, glasses, and cutlery. The Guava Suite is smallest and a little dark. The largest suites, Papaya and Mango, are light-filled and offer a spacious living room, bathroom, and separate bedroom. Eva serves continental breakfast on the lanai, with views of the ocean, West Maui Mountains, and Haleakala. You're also welcome to use the full kitchen or barbecue. For movie nights, the common area has a gigantic TV and a fancy popcorn maker. This elegant B&B is centrally located in a residential Kihei neighborhood, about a half-mile from Kamaole III Beach Park and 5 minutes from Wailea's golf courses, shopping, and restaurants. *Bonus:* No minimum stay or cleaning fee; cash discount.

2828 Umalu Place (off Keonakai St., near Hwy. 31), Kihei. www.amauibedandbreakfast. com. © **808/879-9103.** 4 units. Double $160–$225. Rates include breakfast. Children under 12 stay free in parent's room. **Amenities:** Beach equipment; barbecue; laundry facilities; free Wi-Fi.

Wailea

Great weather, lush landscaping, multimillion-dollar resort hotels, golf courses, luxury homes, 2 miles of golden shoreline—Wailea has it all, so expect to pay accordingly. Golfers should note that guests at all Wailea resorts enjoy special privileges at the Wailea Golf Club's three 18-hole championship courses: Blue, Gold, and Emerald.

Keep in mind that condos may offer the best value, in terms of space and kitchen facilities, although they lack the fantasy pools and destination restaurants of the resorts. Among other rental companies, **Destination Residences Hawaii** (www.destinationhotels.com; © **800/367-5246** or 808/495-4546) offers a wide selection of luxury rentals at eight properties in Wailea and Makena, as well as options in Lahaina and Kaanapali. Guests receive a lei greeting and Tesla X shuttle within the resort, among other perks. Be aware that nightly rates exclude an 8.85% service fee as well as the 14.441% in local taxes, which makes the units even pricier. Nevertheless, you can find base rates in low season starting as little as $212 a night for a one-bedroom, two-bath, fairway-view unit at **Wailea Grand Champions.**

Tip: The **Polo Beach Club** condominiums are bit older, but often larger and closer to the beach than newer developments. expect to pay $1,000 a night or more in high season for a two-bedroom, two-bath unit sleeping 6, and $560–$645 in low season with advance purchase ($942–$1,085 otherwise), plus the service and taxes.

VERY EXPENSIVE

Andaz Maui at Wailea ★★★   The Andaz continues to garner rave reviews—small wonder, considering its prime beachfront locale, chic decor, apothecary-style spa, and phenomenal restaurants, including one by superstar chef Masaharu Morimoto. Foodies should look no further: Not only is the **Morimoto Maui** sushi bar a must, but the resort's other restaurant, **Kaana Kitchen,** might be *even better.* Before you eat, though, you'll want to freshen up in your room. Accommodations here aren't the island's largest, but they ramp up the style quotient with crisp white linens, warm wood furniture, and midcentury accents. Wrap yourself in a plush robe and nosh on the complimentary minibar snacks from the sanctuary of your private lanai. Wander past the tiered infinity pools (which look best at night, when lit in a shifting palette of colors). Then hit gorgeous **Mokapu Beach** out front to snorkel, kayak, or paddle an outrigger canoe. This resort is a dynamic blend of modern and ancient values. Visit with the resident artist in the lobby gallery, or learn to braid *ti*-leaf leis or make coconut-fiber cordage. Whatever you do, don't miss the **Awili Spa,** where you can mix your own massage oil and body scrubs. Fitness classes and outrigger canoe excursions are complimentary, and you even have a free GoPro to use for the duration of your stay. If you splurge on one of the two-, three-, or four-bedroom villas, you'll have an entire wall that opens to the Pacific, a private plunge pool, and a luxurious kitchen to call your own.

3550 Wailea Alanui Dr., Wailea. https://maui.andaz.hyatt.com. ℂ **808/573-1234.** 198 units. Double $489–$749; 1-bedroom suite $769–$1,629; call for villa prices. Resort fee $45. Valet parking $30. **Amenities:** 3 restaurants, 24-hr. market; 3 bars; concierge; 24-hr. fitness center; use of Wailea Golf Club's 3 18-hole golf courses; 4 cascading infinity pools; 24-hr. room service; shuttle; luxury spa with pool; watersports-equipment rentals; free fitness classes and excursions; free minibar; free Wi-Fi.

Fairmont Kea Lani Maui ★★★   At first blush, this blinding-white complex of Arabian turrets looks a tad out of place—but once you enter the orchid-filled lobby and see the big blue Pacific outside, there's no doubt you're in Hawaii. For the price of a regular room at the neighboring resorts, you get an entire suite here. Each unit in the all-suites hotel has a kitchenette with granite countertop, living room with sofabed (great for families), spacious bedroom, marble bathroom (head immediately for the deep soaking tub), and large lanai with views of the pools, lawns, and Pacific Ocean. The two-story beachfront villas are perfect for families or couples traveling together: Each of the 37 units has two or three bedrooms, a high-end kitchen, washer/dryer, and private plunge pool just steps from the white sand. They come stocked with complimentary snacks and drinks; breakfast buffet is included and you can order room service, fixings to barbecue yourself, or a meal prepared by a chef onsite (free valet parking is another perk). **Polo Beach** is public, but feels private and secluded. Huge murals and artifacts decorate the resort's manicured property, which is home to two top restaurants (**Ko,** p. 116, and **Nick's Fishmarket,** 114), a fun lounge with great cocktails and craft beer, an excellent bakery and gourmet deli, and the **Willow Stream Spa.** Escape into this heavenly retreat to experience the rain showers, steam rooms, and warm lava-stone foot beds. Youngsters can build volcanoes in the kids' club or practice swimming with a mono-fin in "Mermaid University," while the entire family can get into rhythm paddling a Hawaiian outrigger canoe.

4100 Wailea Alanui Dr., Wailea. www.fairmont.com/kealani. (℃) **866/540-4456** or 808/875-4100. 450 units. Suites $560–$1,309; villas $1,218–$2,419. $40 resort fee. Valet parking $35; free self-parking. **Amenities:** 4 restaurants; gourmet bakery & deli; 3 bars; babysitting; children's program; concierge; 24-hr. fitness center; use of Wailea Golf Club's 3 18-hole courses; 2 large family pools; adults-only pool; 140-ft. water slide and swim-up bar, 24-hr. room service; luxury spa and salon; use of Wailea Tennis Center's 11 courts; watersports-equipment rentals; free Wi-Fi.

Four Seasons Resort Maui at Wailea ★★★

Words fail to describe how luxurious you'll feel rubbing elbows with celebrities in this über-elegant yet relaxed atmosphere. Perched above Wailea Beach's golden sand, the Four Seasons inhabits its own world, where poolside attendants anticipate your needs: cucumber slices for your eyes? Mango smoothie sampler? Or perhaps your sunglasses need polishing? The adults-only infinity pool with underwater music, private cabanas, and a swim-up bar is what all pools aspire to be. The roughly 600-sq.-ft. guest rooms feature dream-inducing beds, deep marble bathtubs, walk-in showers big enough for two, and furnished lanais, most with superlative ocean views. If you get stuck with a North Tower room over the parking lot, ask politely to be moved. The sublime spa offers an incredible array of body treatments ranging from traditional Hawaiian to craniosacral and Ayurvedic massage. (As nice as the spa facility is, treatments in the oceanside thatched *hale* are even more idyllic.) The resort's restaurants, **Spago, Ferraro's,** and **DUO,** are great; the lively lobby lounge has delicious sushi, craft cocktails, and sunset hula. Finally, this might be the island's most kid-friendly resort: Perks include milk and cookies on arrival, toddler-proofing for your room (everything from furniture bumpers to toilet-seat locks), *keiki* menus in all restaurants, a high-tech game room, and the unmatched, complimentary Kids for all Seasons program from 9am to 5pm. In "Couples Season" (Sept–mid-Dec), a variety of unique activities (some complimentary) allow adult guests to sharpen skills like photography or cooking, as well as learn new ones, like celestial navigation. As you admire Kahoolawe across the channel, be grateful for the resort employees who use their precious vacation time to help reforest it. No resort fee. *Tip:* Wedding parties should book #798 or #301—stunning suites with room for entertaining.

3900 Wailea Alanui Dr., Wailea. www.fourseasons.com/maui. ⓒ **800/311-0630** or 808/874-8000. 380 units. Double $655–$1,220; club floor $1,640–$1,970; suite $1,350–$2,850. Children 17 and under stay free in parent's room. Packages available. Valet parking $34. **Amenities:** 3 restaurants, 4 bars w/nightly entertainment; babysitting; free use of bicycles; free children's program; concierge; concierge-level rooms; putting green; use of Wailea Golf Club's 3 18-hole courses; fitness center with classes; 3 outdoor pools; room service; resort shuttle; luxury spa and salon; 2 on-site tennis courts; use of Wailea Tennis Center's 11 courts; watersports equipment rentals; free Wi-Fi ($20 for premium).

Grand Wailea ★★   Built by a Japanese multimillionaire at the pinnacle of Hawaii's fling with fantasy megaresorts, the Grand Wailea is the grand prize in Hawaii vacation contests and the dream of many honeymooners—but it's better suited to families and couples who like some hustle and bustle. No expense was spared during construction: Some $30 million worth of original artwork decorates the grounds, much of it created expressly for the hotel by Hawaii artists and sculptors. More than 10,000 tropical plants beautify the lobby alone, and rocks hewn from the base of Mount Fuji adorn the Japanese garden. **Humuhumunukunukuapuaa,** the excellent, Hawaiian-themed restaurant (named for the state fish, and nicknamed **Humu**), floats atop an artificial lagoon, and light filters majestically through the stained-glass walls of the wedding chapel. Guest rooms come with lavish, oversize bathrooms and plush bedding. But for kids, all that matters is the resort's unrivaled pool: an aquatic playground with nine separate swimming pools connected by slides, waterfalls, caves, rapids, a Tarzan swing, a swim-up bar, a baby beach, a lazy river, and a water elevator that shuttles swimmers back to the top. If this doesn't sate them, an actual beach made of real golden sand awaits just past the resort hammocks. The Grand is also home to Hawaii's largest and most resplendent spa: a 50,000-square-foot marble paradise with mineral soaking tubs, thundering waterfall showers, Japanese furo baths, Swiss jet showers, and many other luxe features, but large and lively groups can make it less tranquil than other spas.

Those looking for more room and a bit more privacy should try the **Villas at Hoolei,** adjoining the Grand Wailea Resort, with shuttle service between the two. The 3,200- to 4,000-square-foot, three-bedroom, three-and-a-half-bath, two-story villas have it all: elevators, gourmet kitchens, two-level covered lanai with gas grill and refrigerator, and access to all resort services and amenities.

3850 Wailea Alanui Dr., Wailea. www.grandwailea.com. ⓒ **800/888-6100** or 808/875-1234. 780 units. Double $499–$969; suite $1,339–$3,759; Napua Club Room $939–$1,059; Hoolei Villas from $1,495–$2,195. Extra person $50 ($100 in Napua Tower). Daily resort fee $40. Valet parking $35. **Amenities:** 6 restaurants; 4 bars; art and garden tours; babysitting; children's program; concierge; concierge-level rooms; use of Wailea Golf Club's three 18-hole courses; fitness center and classes; 5 whirlpools (including one atop an artificial volcano); adults-only outdoor pool; 2,000-ft.-long pool with a swim/ride through grottoes; room service; scuba-diving clinics; shuttle service to Wailea; Hawaii's largest luxury spa and salon; racquetball court; use of Wailea Tennis Center's 11 courts; watersports-equipment rentals; free Wi-Fi.

Hotel Wailea ★★★　This stylish boutique hotel is one of a kind in Wailea: Not only is it Hawaii's only Relais & Châteaux property, it's an adults-only, hillside haven, with just 72 suites on 15 acres. Compared with the flashier resorts at the coastline, it's small, secluded, and serene—an oasis for honeymooners. The pool and cabanas with sprawling daybeds are swank, with free cocktails by the firepit from 5 to 6pm and mixology classes every Sunday morning. The verdant grounds and koi ponds have been transformed into a meditative garden. Large suites are outfitted with modern luxuries: wide-planked wood floors, Hawaiian *kapa*-inspired prints on plush king-size platform beds, deep soaking tubs, and daybeds on the lanai. Tidy kitchenettes feature Nespresso machines, two-burner Wolf stoves, and Sub-Zero refrigerators. Hotel staff will load up a free tote bag with towels and water and chauffeur you throughout Wailea in Tesla Model X cars. It's a 3-minute shuttle to the beach, and the hotel's kiosk at Wailea Beach can supply you with umbrellas and chairs. Take advantage of the free outrigger canoe trip offered on Wednesdays. This isn't a place that nickel-and-dimes guests, and employees come to know you on a first-name basis. Definitely plan to indulge at the hotel's restaurant; the name, concept, and management have changed several times in recent years but the food and the views are always top-notch. ***Brides-and grooms-to-be, take note:*** The lawn and gazebo at the hotel's entrance is a fairy-tale venue for weddings and receptions, and the private-dining, ocean-view *hale* in the resort's orchard is ultra-romantic.

555 Kaukahi St., Wailea. www.hotelwailea.com. ℂ **866/970-4167** or 808/874-0500. 72 units. Suites $529–$819. 2-person max occupancy; ages 16 and older. Daily $40 resort fee. Packages available. **Amenities:** Restaurant; 2 bars; concierge; fitness center; heated pool; whirlpool; room service; free shuttle service; beach services; free mixology classes and canoe trips; organic garden and orchard; signing privileges at nearby Grand Wailea; spa; free Wi-Fi.

Wailea Beach Resort & Spa ★★★　Airy and comfortable, this spectacularly renovated resort managed by Marriott accentuates rather than overwhelms its sublime environment. Eight buildings, all low-rise except for an eight-story tower, unfold along 22 luxurious acres of lawns and gardens punctuated by coconut palms and Instagram-worthy sculptures and seating. You'll want to spend your entire vacation beneath the cabanas at the two large, exquisite infinity pools. Unless you're age 12 or under—then your parents will have to drag you away from the adventure pool with its four slick slides and animal sculptures that spit water. The resort is ideally positioned on a grassy slope between Wailea and Ulua beaches, so there's plenty of sandy real estate to explore, too. Rainy day? Watch a movie on a 90-foot screen while reclining on pillowy beanbag chairs in the new cinema. Rooms have tile or wood floors, modern furnishings, and lanais with views of the picturesque coastline. The small **Mandara Spa** offers an array of treatments (from massages to body wraps and rejuvenating facials) in a very Zen atmosphere. Just downstairs is celebrated restaurateur Roy Yamaguchi's casual restaurant, **Humble Market Kitchin** (p. 115); a little secret is that the in-house restaurant, **Kapa**, has wonderful island-themed food and views, too. Kids can fuel up on shave ice and poke at the **Mo Bettah Food Truck.** Adults will enjoy cocktails at the **Whale's Tale Beach Bar,** which also serves light breakfast and lunch fare, at the resort's southern border by Wailea Beach.

3700 Wailea Alanui Dr., Wailea. www.waileamarriott.com. ✆ **808/879-1922.** 547 units. Doubles $451–$890; suites $659–$2,639. Packages available. Extra person $40. Daily $35 resort fee. Valet parking $40, self-parking $30. **Amenities:** 2 restaurants; 2 bars; cafe; children's program; food truck; family game center; luau, babysitting; concierge; use of Wailea Golf Club's 3 18-hole golf courses; fitness center; 3 heated pools (1 adults-only and 1 kids-only); room service; spa; use of Wailea Tennis Center's 11 courts; free watersports-equipment and bike rentals; free Wi-Fi in lobby ($15–$19 in room).

Makena

Since the Makena Beach & Golf Resort was turned into a private club with luxury condos (to the dismay of many who liked to brunch or golf there), the only opportunities to stay on this more rugged, remote end of South Maui are in vacation-rental homes and condos, such as those at the older but gracious **Makena Surf** ★★, 4850 Makena Alanui, Kihei. Its low-rise buildings overlook sandy, secluded **Poolenalena Beach** (also known as Paipu Beach), with cobblestoned paths winding through lush gardens.

Among other management companies with units here, **Destination Residences Hawaii** (www.destinationhotels.com; ✆ **800/367-5246** or 808/495-4546) rents roomy, individually owned two-bedroom/two-bath and three-bedroom/three-bath oceanfront units. The former run $1,460 in high season and $586–$671 in low season with advance purchase ($985–$1,128 otherwise)—not counting the 8.85% service fee as well as the 14.441% in local taxes. You'll also find 32 condos and eight rental homes in Makena on VRBO at varying, but typically very expensive ($500-plus), nightly rates.

UPCOUNTRY MAUI

Makawao
EXPENSIVE

Lumeria ★★★ Halfway between Paia and Makawao on the slopes of Haleakala, a historic women's college (the oldest wooden building on Maui, built in 1910) has been lovingly restored as a boutique resort. Nestled into six landscaped acres are two dozen guest rooms, a resplendent lobby, yoga studio, spa, meditation garden, and farm-to-table restaurant. A small but dazzling pool overlooks a valley full of waving sugarcane as hammocks sway in the ironwood trees. Views of the West Maui Mountains and distant shores are stunning. The crystals, sacred artwork, and *objets d'art* tucked into every corner contribute to the charmed ambience of this serene retreat. Rooms are small—nearly filled by their plush fourposter beds—but luxuriously appointed with organic Italian linens, Japanese *tansu* cabinets, and showers with river-rock floors; ceiling fans and the higher elevation keep them cool. A stay

Upcountry Hotels & Restaurants

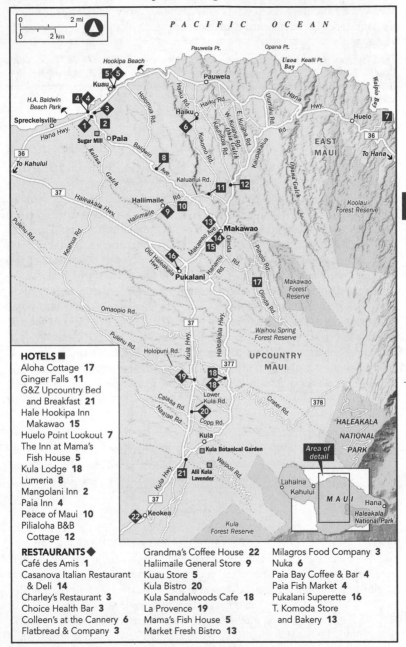

HOTELS ■
Aloha Cottage **17**
Ginger Falls **11**
G&Z Upcountry Bed
  and Breakfast **21**
Hale Hookipa Inn
  Makawao **15**
Huelo Point Lookout **7**
The Inn at Mama's
  Fish House **5**
Kula Lodge **18**
Lumeria **8**
Mangolani Inn **2**
Paia Inn **4**
Peace of Maui **10**
Pilialoha B&B
  Cottage **12**

RESTAURANTS ◆
Café des Amis **1**
Casanova Italian Restaurant
  & Deli **14**
Charley's Restaurant **3**
Choice Health Bar **3**
Colleen's at the Cannery **6**
Flatbread & Company **3**

Grandma's Coffee House **22**
Haliimaile General Store **9**
Kuau Store **5**
Kula Bistro **20**
Kula Sandalwoods Cafe **18**
La Provence **19**
Mama's Fish House **5**
Market Fresh Bistro **13**

Milagros Food Company **3**
Nuka **6**
Paia Bay Coffee & Bar **4**
Paia Fish Market **4**
Pukalani Superette **16**
T. Komoda Store
  and Bakery **13**

includes access to daily yoga, meditation, horticulture, and aromatherapy classes, as well as breakfast for two at the chic, semi-private restaurant, **Wooden Crate.** Baldwin Beach is only 2½ miles away; the staff will set you up with stand-up paddleboard equipment or pack a picnic for an excursion to Hana.

1813 Baldwin Ave., Makawao. www.lumeriamaui.com. (C) **808/579-8877.** 25 units. Double $369–$539. Rates include organic breakfast. Resort fee $25. **Amenities:** Restaurant; spa; concierge; 2 whirlpools (1 saltwater); pool; watersports equipment rental; yoga and aromatherapy class; free Wi-Fi.

MODERATE

Aloha Cottage ★★ If getting away from it all is your goal, this exotic retreat in the eucalyptus forest above Makawao might be your place. On 5 luxuriously landscaped acres sits the octagonal Aloha Cottage and Thai Tree House, both reminiscent of something you'd see in Southeast Asia. The interior of the 590-square-foot cottage is lavishly furnished with vaulted ceilings, teak floors, Oriental rugs, and intricate Balinese carvings. (Whenever you glance at your reflection in the magnificent bathroom mirror, you'll feel like royalty.) Both the Cottage and Tree House feature granite counters, a gas stove, and teak cabinetry that makes cooking a pleasure. Olinda Road is a winding, narrow track that ascends through the trees above Makawao—coming and going from here is an adventure unto itself. After a day of exploring Maui, it's a sweet relief to enjoy a home-cooked dinner on the lanai, soak in the outdoor tub built for two, and retire to the king-size cherrywood bed where you can stare through the skylight at the stars. *Note:* The property was for sale at press time, but was continuing to honor reservations.

1879 Olinda Rd., Makawao. www.alohacottage.com. (C) **808/573-8555.** 2 units. Cottage $279; tree house $259. 4-night minimum. Discounts for weekly stays. $125 cleaning fee. Not suitable for children under 10. **Amenities:** Outdoor tub; barbecue; laundry facilities; free Wi-Fi.

INEXPENSIVE

Ginger Falls ★★ This cozy, romantic, intimate cottage, hidden on 2½ acres in Maliko Gulch, overlooks a stream with bamboo, sweet-smelling ginger, and banana trees; after extended rain, there may even be a waterfall. It's perfect for honeymooners, lovers, and fans of Hawaiiana art. The moment you step into this 400-square-foot, contemporary, casual-chic cottage (with an additional 156-sq.-ft. screened deck), you will be delighted at the carefully placed memorabilia (ukulele tile, canoe paddle, and the like) found throughout. The cottage has a full kitchen with everything you could possibly want to cook with, including breakfast for your first morning. The Hawaiian theme carries into the living room, where a cabinet painted with a tropical design houses a VCR and stereo. The comfy queen bed opens to the living area. The screened porch has a table, chairs, and a couch—perfect for curling up with a good book. There's also a barbecue outside, plus all the beach toys you could want to borrow. Host Bob is a ceramic artist (with his creations throughout the cottage), and his wife, Sonny, manages Dolphin Galleries, from where she has selected the best of the best artwork for the cottage.

355 Kaluanui Rd., Makawao. www.wildgingerfalls.com. ℂ **808/573-1173.** 1 unit. $195–$205 double. 3- to 5-night minimum. Cleaning fee for stays Dec 20–Jan 5 $75. **Amenities:** Gas grill, hot tub, laundry, free Wi-Fi.

Hale Hookipa Inn Makawao ★★ Cherie Attix restored this historic 1924 plantation-style home to its original charm, filling it with Hawaiian artwork, antique furniture (a giant oak armoire, wrought-iron bed frame, and vintage shutters repurposed as a headboard), and a generous dose of love. Although its residential neighborhood is unprepossessing, it's a 5-minute walk from the shops and restaurants of Makawao, a 15-minute drive from beaches, and an hour's drive from the top of Haleakala. The three pretty guest rooms have separate outside entrances and private bathrooms—two with claw-foot tubs. The Kona Wing is a two-bedroom suite with use of the kitchen. In addition to a daily continental breakfast, Cherie offers guests fresh eggs from her hens. Unlike many B&B operators, she allows 1-night stays— perfect for hikers wanting a head start on Haleakala in the morning—for the small surcharge of $15. Best of all: She sponsors a terrific "volunteer on vacation" program. Lend a hand at one of the dozen local organizations listed on her website and she'll knock 5% off of your stay at Hale Hookipa.

32 Pakani Place, Makawao. www.maui-bed-and-breakfast.com. ℂ **877/572-6698** or 808/572-6698. 4 units. Double $150–$190. Rates include continental breakfast. $15 surcharge for 1-night stays. No children under 9. **Amenities:** Tropical fruit orchard; voluntourism program; free Wi-Fi.

Kula

This cool, remote, upcountry community offers million-dollar views and a location convenient to Haleakala National Park. Here you'll find true peace and quiet about a 30- to 40-minute drive away from the beach. Those planning a sunset or sunrise visit to Haleakala might want to consider staying at **Kula Lodge** ★, 15200 Haleakala Hwy., Kula (www.kulalodge.com; ℂ **808/878-1535**). Less than a mile from the start of twisting, turning Highway 378, which

---

A Private Cottage

If you'd like your own private cottage, consider **Peace of Maui** ★, 1290 Haliimaile Rd. (just outside of Haliimaile town), Makawao (www.peaceofmaui. com; ℂ **808/572-5045**). The well-built cottage offers a full kitchen, two bedrooms, a living room with two queen-sized futon sofas, a daybed, and a large deck with gas barbecue and views of the ocean and West Maui mountains. If those views grow tiresome, there's a flatscreen TV with cable in every room. Granola, oatmeal, and tropical fruit are placed in your pantry each night. Rates are the same year-round: $250 a night, 3-night minimum, plus a $75 cleaning fee. The owners also have more basic rooms in the adjacent lodge (with shared bathroom and kitchen facilities) for $115 per night double ($95 single).

ascends to the summit, it offers dazzling views, a serviceable restaurant open for three meals a day, and five rustic cottages, all with electric fireplaces (needed up here) and some with lofts ($200–$275). The adjacent Kula Marketplace, which offers local and international artisan wares, and painter Curtis Wilson Cost's gallery are worth a stop here even if you aren't staying the night.

INEXPENSIVE

G&Z Upcountry Bed and Breakfast ★★ Former state tourism director Marsha Wienert has a keen sense of what makes upcountry Maui special, and thankfully she and husband John have decided to share some of that with visitors. Their B&B unit sits on a half acre next to their 6-acre farm, which grows tropical fruit, coffee, and vegetables; with its own entrance, this is really a fully equipped apartment. The eat-in kitchen features up-to-date stainless-steel appliances and a gleaming wood floor; the modern bath has a large walk-in shower; and the light-filled living room includes a queen sofabed and large flatscreen TV (there's another in the bedroom with a king bed). Better yet, you can watch the sunset from the large lawn, framed by jacaranda and avocado trees. During the day, go for a hike in **Haleakala National Park** (p. 154), within a 45-minute drive, or stroll through the blooming fields at **Alii Kula Lavender** farm (p. 153), 5 minutes away. The Wienerts deliver fresh fruit, scones or breads, coffee, and tea to your room for breakfast.

60 Kekaulike Ave., Kula. www.gandzmaui.com. © **808/224-6824.** 1 unit. Double $149. Rates include continental breakfast. $25 extra person. Up to two adults and two children 18 or younger can stay here. No cleaning fee or minimum-night requirements. **Amenities:** Barbecue; free Wi-Fi.

EAST MAUI
Paia & Kuau

This former sugar town was reborn as a haven for hippies and surfers. Today the vibe is more sophisticated and artsy, but you'll still see board shorts and beards aplenty.

EXPENSIVE

Paia Inn ★★ Embedded in colorful Paia town, this vibrant boutique inn offers a stylish introduction to Maui's North Shore. The inn comprises several vintage buildings that get progressively closer to the turquoise waters of Paia Bay. The owner's impeccable style seeps into every corner of the inn, from the organic Malie bath products in the travertine-tiled showers to the antique Balinese drawers repurposed as sink cabinets. Note that the rooms in the main building are on the small side and hang right over Hana Highway's restaurants, surf shops, and cafes. The one- and two-bedroom suites in the next buildings are spacious, secluded retreats where you'll feel immediately at home. Couples will appreciate #10, which has a private outdoor shower and a fourposter daybed. But it can't rival the three-bedroom beach house nestled up against the golden, sandy beach. Idyllic in every way, this miniature mansion is outfitted with a Viking stove, Jacuzzi, gorgeous artwork, and a huge outdoor living room. It's exclusive enough to attract celebrities, who've made it their Maui headquarters. In the courtyard behind the lobby, the **Paia Inn Café** serves outstanding brunch. Massages are available in the upstairs spa rooms.

93 Hana Hwy., Paia. www.paiainn.com. © **800/721-4000** or 808/579-6000. 17 units. Double from $189; 1-bedroom suite from $399; 2-bedroom suite from $499; 3-bedroom beach house from $1,000. **Amenities:** Restaurant, beach access; concierge; day spa; laundry services; free parking; free use of watersports equipment; free Wi-Fi.

MODERATE

The Inn at Mama's Fish House ★★★
The Gaudí-esque architect responsible for Mama's Fish House and its gracious interpretation of Old Polynesia also worked his magic on a handful of private suites and cottages next door. Amid the coconuts on a pocket-sized beach, the Inn at Mama's features large private lanais with barbecues; imaginative Hawaiian artwork; fresh flowers tucked into large, fluffy bath towels; terrific toiletries; free laundry; and an easy stroll to **Mama's Fish House,** what many consider to be the finest restaurant on Maui. Each unit is unique; the luxury junior suites are especially classy, with deep soaking tubs and travertine showers. One- and two-bedroom cottages sit amid the tropical garden's red ginger, while a few two-bedroom units face the ocean. The solid, upscale furnishings define casual elegance, with a few splashes of coral, teal, and other tropical color among neutral upholstery and dark woven chairs and side tables. Although restaurant guests stroll about the property until 10pm, privacy is assured in your cottage's large enclosed lanai. In the morning, you'll be greeted with a tray of fresh fruit and banana bread. The inn sits on a small, sandy beach known simply as Mama's. It's better for exploring tide pools than for swimming—though Baldwin Beach is a short drive away and the thrills of Hookipa are right next door. Keep in mind that this is the windward side of the island—it's often windy and rainy. You'll be perfectly situated here for a trip to Hana.

799 Poho Place (off Hana Hwy. in Kuau), Paia. www.innatmamas.com. © **800/860-4852** or 808/579-9764. 12 units. Garden studio $275; 1-bedroom $300–$850; junior suite $425; 2-bedroom cottage $395–$850. **Amenities:** Beach; barbecue; free laundry; free Wi-Fi.

Mangolani Inn ★★
A mile from the beach, and within walking distance of Paia's boutiques and cafes, this laidback compound off busy Baldwin Avenue is full of surprises. Mango trees offer shade and privacy in the large yard, where guests have the use of hammocks, hot tub, barbecue, and picnic tables, along with beach gear and laundry. Adventurous travelers will want to perch in the treehouse, built into a mango tree, with a king-sized bed and full-size sofabed; guests share a bath and kitchen with the adjacent four-bedroom house, an air-conditioned sanctuary with tile floors, granite counters, and a

spacious covered lanai. The house can be combined with the treehouse to sleep up to 10. Downstairs is a studio, also air-conditioned and similarly stylishly remodeled, with touches like a leather couch, bamboo trim, walk-in stone-tiled shower, and vessel sink.

325 Baldwin Ave., Paia. www.mauipaia.com. ✆ **808/579-3000**. 3 units. Studio $250–$350; treehouse $260–$360; $80 cleaning fee; 5-night minimum. 4-bedroom house $1,000–$1,400 weekly; cleaning fee $250. House with treehouse $1,250–$1,750 weekly; cleaning fee $300. **Amenities:** Barbecue; hammocks; hot tub; laundry facilities; watersports gear; free Wi-Fi.

Haiku

This former pineapple-plantation village offers vacation rentals and B&Bs in a quiet, pastoral setting about 10 minutes from the beach.

MODERATE

Pilialoha B&B Cottage ★   In the heart of Haiku, this country cottage is set on a large lot with towering eucalyptus trees and some 200 varieties of roses blooming in the garden. Tastefully appointed in green and white, this simple cottage is somewhat dated, but is private, clean, and spacious. The kitchen and closets are extremely well-equipped—you'll find everything you need, from a rice cooker to beach towels, coolers, yoga mats, and fleece jackets for Haleakala sunrise trips. Your hosts, Machiko and Bill Heyde, live on-site and are happy to offer sightseeing suggestions. If you mention to Machiko that you're heading up the mountain, she'll likely send you off with a thermos of coffee and her homemade bread. Suitable for one or two people, the cottage is minutes from the restaurants and shopping of Haiku and Makawao and a short drive from Paia's beaches. In the winter months when Haiku weather can be cool and rainy, the gas fireplace is a welcome amenity.

2512 Kaupakalua Rd. (½-mile from Kokomo intersection), Haiku. www.pilialoha.com. ✆ **808/572-1440**. 1 unit. $175 double. 3-night minimum. **Amenities:** Watersports equipment; laundry facilities; free Wi-Fi.

Huelo

About 15 to 20 minutes past Haiku, the largely unknown community of Huelo (which hopes to keep it that way) appeals to those who appreciate places still largely untouched by "progress."

MODERATE

Huelo Point Lookout ★★   "Romantic hideaway" may be a cliché, but it's an apt characterization for this unique, enchanting enclave on a remote promontory off the Hana Highway. It includes a two-bedroom house with loft and three cottages tucked among tall coconut palms and sharing a large free-form garden pool. All units have a private hot tub, kitchen or kitchenette, colorful tropical decor, and intoxicating views; cottages also have beautiful outdoor showers. Haleakala Cottage is a studio with a Cal-king bed, three lanais (garden and mountain scenery), and a full kitchen. The Rainbow Honeymoon Lookout just has a fridge, sink, and dishwasher in its kitchenette, but it boasts ocean and Haleakala views, as well as four lanais, two within sight of waterfalls. View junkies will want to rent the Lookout House, to gaze at a huge stretch of the Hana Coast—sometimes with whales spouting just off the point—as well as admire the vast greenery lining gullies and ridges. The house comes with a full kitchen, of course, and 2½ bathrooms; renting just the top floor is also an option. Heated towel racks make misty mornings especially delicious.

222 Door of Faith Rd., Haiku. https://maui-vacationrentals.com. © **808/201-1714**. 4 units. Cottages double $250–$385; top floor of house (1-bedroom, 1½ bath) $395–$450; house (2-bedroom with loft, 2½ bath, sleeps 4) $3,150–$4,158 weekly. Cottages and top floor 3-night minimum. House 7-night minimum. Extra person $30. **Amenities:** Pool; private hot tubs; barbecues; laundry facilities.

AT THE END OF THE ROAD IN EAST MAUI: HANA

Note: To locate the following accommodations, see the "Hana" map on p. 171.

Very Expensive

Travaasa Hana ★★★   Ahhh . . . arriving at Travaasa (formerly the Hotel Hana-Maui) is like letting out a deep sigh. The atmosphere is so relaxing you'll forget everything beyond this remote seaside sanctuary. Nestled in the center of rustic Hana town, the 66-acre resort wraps around Kauiki Head, the dramatic point where Queen Kaahumanu was born. All of the accommodations here are wonderful, but the Ocean Bungalows (adults only, except over the holidays) are downright heavenly. These duplex cottages face the craggy shoreline, where horses graze above the rolling surf. Floor-to-ceiling sliding doors open to spacious lanais. Book your stay here a la carte or all-inclusive; the latter includes three meals a day and a $175 resort credit per person per day—go ahead, indulge yourself in one Hawaii's nicest spas. Whichever you choose, your room will be stocked with luxurious necessities: plush beds with organic linens, bamboo floors, giant soaking tubs, complimentary bottled water, fair-trade coffee, homemade banana bread, and irresistibly scented bath products. You'll be far from shopping malls and sports bars, but stunning beaches in various hues are just a short walk or shuttle ride away. The genuinely hospitable staff—often related to each other, and the second or third generation in their families to work here—will set you up with numerous activities, many at no charge. Try stand-up paddling in Hana Bay, practice your archer's aim, take a tour of a nearby tropical fruit farm, or learn to throw a traditional Hawaiian fishing net. (I never quite mastered it, but shook off my failure with a delicious bask in one of the heated pools with a serene view.) Rooms have no TVs (the Club Room has a giant one), but there are nightly talk-story sessions around the fire; if live Hawaiian music and hula in the lounge are on tap while you're staying here, don't miss it. This is luxury in its purest form. *Tip:* Stay 3 nights or more and fly for free from Kahului to Hana Airport.

5031 Hana Hwy., Hana. www.travaasa.com/hana. ℂ **888/820-1043.** 66 units. A la carte: suites $575–$625, bungalows $970–$1,325. All-inclusive: suites $1,085, bungalows $1,335–$1,835. Discounts for single occupancy. Daily resort fee $26. **Amenities:** Restaurant; bar; concierge; fitness center/fitness classes; complimentary clubs and use of the 3-hole practice golf courses; 2 heated pools; laundry facilities; limited room service; luxury spa; tennis courts; free Wi-Fi.

Moderate

Bamboo Inn ★   This oceanfront, solar-powered "inn" is really just three exquisite suites, all with private lanais overlooking Waikaloa Beach's jet-black sand. The sumptuous accommodations include beds with ocean views, separate living rooms, and either a full kitchen or kitchenette. Naia, the largest unit, sleeps four and has a deep soaking tub on the lanai; the romantic first-floor Honu Suite has a queen bed, hot tub for two on its oceanview deck, and a private outdoor shower. The rooms and grounds are decorated with artifacts collected by your friendly and knowledgeable host, John Romain, during travels across Asia and Polynesia. Carved Balinese doors, Samoan tapa cloths, coconut wood floors, and a thatched-roof gazebo add a rich, authentic elegance to a naturally lovely location. Waikaloa isn't great for swimming, but it's an incredible spot to watch the sunrise. All of Hana is within easy walking distance.

4869 Uakea Rd., Hana. www.bambooinn.com. ℂ **808/248-7718.** 3 units. $210–$285 double. 2-night minimum. Extra person $15. **Amenities:** Beach, beach equipment; barbecue; free Wi-Fi (but only in outdoor gazebo).

Ekena ★   Just one glance at the 360-degree view, and you can see why hosts Robin and Gaylord gave up their careers on the mainland and moved here. This 8½-acre piece of paradise in rural Hana boasts ocean and rainforest vistas; the floor-to-ceiling glass doors in the spacious Hawaiian-style pole house bring the outside in. The elegant two-story vacation rental is exquisitely furnished, from the comfortable U-shaped couch that invites you to relax and take in the view to the top-of-the-line mattress on the king-size bed. The fully equipped kitchen has everything you should need to cook a gourmet meal; each bedroom has a master bath with oversize tub. Only one floor (and one two-bedroom unit) is rented at any given time to ensure privacy. The grounds are impeccably groomed and dotted with tropical plants and fruit trees. Hiking trails into the rainforest start right on the property, and beaches and waterfalls are just minutes away. Robin places fresh flowers in every room and makes sure you're comfortable; after that, she's available to answer questions, but she also respects your privacy. *Note:* No cellphone signal here—plan to go into town or bring a calling card.

290 Kalo Rd., off Hana Hwy., Hana. www.ekenamaui.com. ℂ **808/248-7047.** 2 units. 1-bedroom (sleeps 2) $275–$400; 2-bedroom (sleeps 4) $350–$475. 3-night minimum. No children 13 and under. **Amenities:** Free Wi-Fi.

Hamoa Bay House & Bungalow ★★   This Eden-like property has two units: a bungalow and a house. Romance blooms in the 600-square-foot Balinese-style treetop bungalow, a gorgeous one-room studio with a beckoning bamboo bed, full kitchen, and a hot tub that hangs over the garden. The screened lanai and area downstairs function as separate rooms, giving you ample space. The house is just as spacious and appealingly decorated, with a large master bedroom and small second bedroom. Well set apart from one another, both the house and bungalow have private outdoor lava-rock showers and access to tropical fruit trees (mmm, papayas) and flowers. The property is on Hana Highway, just a 10-minute walk from Hamoa Beach.

6463 Hana Hwy., between two entrances to Haneoo Rd., 2 miles south of Hana. www.hamoabay.com. ℂ **808/248-7884.** 2 units. Bungalow $285–$310 (sleeps up to 2); house $325–$420 (sleeps up to 4). 3-night minimum. **Amenities:** Beach nearby; barbecue; hammock; beach equipment; barbecue; outdoor shower; whirlpool; free Wi-Fi.

Hamoa Beach House ★   Just around the bend from famed Hamoa Beach, this enormous three-bedroom, two-bathroom '70s-era house is a great option for families or big parties. The rich woods, earthy tones, and rattan furnishings imbue the spacious interior with a cozy, nostalgic feeling. The living room has cathedral ceilings, two-story-tall windows that open up to the ocean, and when you need other visual distraction, cable TV and a DVD player. The upstairs bedrooms have vaulted ceilings, outdoor lanais facing the ocean, and a total of four king-size beds. A sweet little library is stocked with beach reading. Beneath the coconut palms outside, you'll find hammocks, a barbecue grill, a hot tub, and an outdoor shower—everything you need to enjoy Hana to the fullest.

487 Haneoo Rd., Hana. www.hamoabeachhouse.com. ℂ **808/248-8277.** 1 unit. $595–$625 for 6-person occupancy, $50 per extra person (sleeps up to 8). 3-night minimum (2 nights available with $150 cleaning fee). **Amenities:** Beach nearby; beach equipment; barbecue; outdoor shower; whirlpool; free Wi-Fi.

Hana Guest Houses ★★   Three miles south of Hana Town lies the glorious compound of Malanai, named for the gentle breezes that cool its leafy, fragrant gardens and two handsomely restored, plantation-style cottages with ocean views. Hale Manu ("Bird House") offers two bedrooms with vintage rattan furniture; a modern bathroom with a fun mix of bamboo trim, stone floors, shiplap walls, and tiled shower/tub; an airy great room (living, dining, and kitchen) with soaring beamed cupola ceiling; and a large deck with recliners and outdoor dining furniture. Hale Ulu Lulu ("Breadfruit-Shaded House"), built in the 1900s to house managers of the Hana Sugar Plantation, sports a mix of charming antique details (claw-foot tub, beadboard cabinets) and contemporary luxuries (Brazilian mahogany floors, granite and koa kitchen counters). Both come with stacked washer-dryers, gas BBQs, and beach gear. Hamoa Beach and Waioka Pool (an oceanfront swimming hole also known as Venus Pool) are within a 15-minute walk or brief drive.

6776 Hana Hwy., Hana. https://hanaguesthouses.com. © **808/248-8706.** 2 units. 1-bedroom (sleeps 2, adults only) $285–$300; 2-bedroom (sleeps up to 4; up to 2 children 12 and older allowed) $285–$300 double, $25 per extra person. 3-night minimum. Discounts for weekly stays. **Amenities:** Beach gear; laundry facilities; free Wi-Fi.

Hana Kai Maui Resort ★★ "Condo complex" might not mesh with your idea of getting away from it all in Hana, but Hana Kai is truly special. Set on Hana Bay, the individually owned units feature many hotel-like extras, such as organic bath products and fresh tropical bouquets. Studios and one- and two-bedroom units have kitchens and private lanais—but the corner units with wraparound ocean views are worth angling for. Gorgeously appointed Kaahumanu (#5) has a daybed on the lanai that you may never want to leave. For couples, Popolana (#2) is small but sweet, with woven bamboo walls and a Murphy bed that no one ever puts up. And why would you? You can lie in it and stare out to sea or, at daybreak, watch the sun rise straight out of the ocean. No air-conditioning or TVs—but they're not necessary here. *Note:* Sound can carry here, so bring earplugs if you're a light sleeper.

1533 Uakea Rd., Hana. www.hanakaimaui.com. © **800/346-2772** or 808/248-8426. 18 units. Studio $235–$305; 1-bedroom $265–$355; 2-bedroom $425–$475. $20 reservation fee. Extra person $15. 2-night minimum for oceanfront units. Children 6 and under stay free in parent's room. **Amenities:** Black-sand beach; beach equipment; barbecue; daily housekeeping; laundry facilities; free Wi-Fi.

INEXPENSIVE

Hana Inn ★ This is as close to a hostel as you can get in Hana, but in a beautifully renovated rambling house on a lushly landscaped 1-acre lot with views of Hana Bay. Formerly known as Joe's Place, the house was originally built in 1923, completely rebuilt in in 1982, and then lovingly restored in 2018 by new owner Gabby Franklin and family, who replaced virtually every fixture and piece of furniture. The seven bedrooms—only one with private bathroom—are still somewhat spartan, but have comfy new beds and attractive wood floors. The shared baths are clean and modern, too. Upstairs rooms nos. 5 and 6 have views of the bay (a 4-min. walk away) as well as king beds; families will want to book no. 7, which can sleep up to six with two double beds and two singles (including a bunk with one of each); it has its own bathroom across the hall. All guests are welcome to use the large, updated living room with HD-TV and cable, as well as the older but functional kitchen, outfitted with pots and pans.

4870 Uakea Rd., Hana. www.joesrentals.com. © **808/248-7033.** 8 units, 7 with shared bathroom. Single with shared bathroom $89–$119 (extra person $20 for up to 3 people); room with four beds with shared bathroom (up to 4 people included in rate) $116–$146, $20 per extra person for up to 6 people; queen room with private bathroom $116–$136 (single or double).

WHERE TO EAT

D ining on Maui has never been more memorable: Farm-to-table has become a byword as homegrown and mainland-transplanted chefs make the most of the Valley Isle's incredible bounty of produce, seafood, and grass-fed beef. Both simple lunch counters and fine-dining resort restaurants draw on those ingredients to celebrate, refine, or reimagine dishes reflecting the island's multicultural heritage: Hawaiian, Asian, American, and European. Don't miss the chance to veer from your comfort zone to try something new that you may never see back home.

Small farms provide a rainbow array of tropical fruits and heirloom vegetables, from sunrise papayas to purple sweet potatoes. Chefs have their picks of fresh ahi (tuna), mahimahi (dorado) and ono (wahoo), not to mention several hues of snapper—onaga (ruby), opakapaka (pink), ehu (red), and uku (gray)—seasonal catches, and shellfish raised in deep-water ocean farms and freshwater ponds on Kauai and Hawaii Island. Maui coffee makes a delicious rub for ranch-raised beef from Maui Cattle Company, which also sources lamb from its collective of ranches on the uplands of Haleakala and Kahakuloa and the misty pastures of Hana.

While time-honored institutions such as **Mama's Fish House** and **Haliimaile General Store** continue to delight visitors and well-heeled residents, a newer crop of chefs has inspired colleagues across the island to raise their game. At **Ka'ana Kitchen,** Chef Isaac Bancaco nearly outshines his celebrity neighbor, "Iron Chef" Masaharu Morimoto, who brought a high-octane Japanese fusion cuisine to Andaz Maui in Wailea. Both are outstanding; make time for each if you can swing it. On West Maui, Chef Gerard Reversade continues to plate up perfect French cuisine at **Gerard's.** *Top Chef* star Sheldon Simeon explores his Filipino roots and Hilo upbringing with playful pizzazz at his latest sensation, **Lineage,** in the Shops at Wailea.

Of course, the impact on your wallet may be equally memorable. Luckily, you don't *have* to spend a fortune to eat well here. Here are a few tips on saving money on food:

o Maui has a number of **budget eateries,** including Simeon's **Tin Roof** and chef Les Tomita's **Da Kitchen,** which specialize in

PRICE CATEGORIES

The restaurant reviews below are listed according to geographic areas and pricing. Pricing is based on the cost of the majority of the entrees (generally a dinner entree, unless noted).

Very Expensive	$45 and up
Expensive	$30–$45
Moderate	$15–$30
Inexpensive	under $15

expert versions of island comfort food. Both are reviewed below; also check the "Inexpensive" category for each region covered below.

○ Choose lodging with **self-catering kitchen facilities** so you aren't spending all your money on dining out.

○ You can get more for your money by visiting pricier restaurants at **lunch,** when menu items are generally cheaper, or at **happy hour,** when two "small plate" appetizers can equal the size of a dinner entree, at half the cost.

○ Keep in mind that many restaurants serve **portions equivalent to two meals** on the mainland; pop that doggie bag of tasty leftovers in your fridge or mini-fridge for the next day's lunch or dinner.

○ **Food trucks, convenience stores,** and even **gas stations** often have inexpensive, homemade fare very much worth sampling, including hearty plate lunches, *musubi* (burrito-sized sushi), and peanut butter mochi (pounded rice confectiona). For the lowdown on eating local, see "Plate Lunches & More: Local Foods," below.

PRACTICAL MATTERS: MAUI'S RESTAURANT SCENE

Dining on Maui tends to be casual—don't wear your bathing suit, but an aloha shirt with nice shorts and shoes will do in most restaurants.

Hours

People eat early on Maui. Many local residents get up before the sun, and tend to eat dinner around 6 or 7pm. Visitors generally are jet-lagged and happy to go to dinner around sunset. Most restaurants on Maui close early and don't take reservations after 8:30pm (unless noted). Some restaurants are now offering late-night happy hours, starting at 9 or 10pm, which allows kitchen staff and other night owls to dine out, too.

Prices, Taxes & Tipping

Prices in Maui are higher than you're probably used to paying at home. But remember, you are on an isolated island—it costs more to import food here, which makes meals more expensive. Budget a little extra for dining out.

Most price ranges listed in this chapter are just the cost of the entree; obviously, if you also order an appetizer, salad, or dessert, the bill will be higher.

Expect to see Hawaii's general excise tax (4.25%) to be added to your bill. Tipping is the standard custom in Hawaii (just like the mainland United States), and you'll want to reward good service with a 15 to 20% tip, based on your total bill (minus the tax).

Reservations

Reservations are generally not necessary unless otherwise noted in the reviews below, but all bets are off during peak holiday periods, especially in winter. Make reservations for dinner in advance so you won't have to wait for a seat. **OpenTable.com** allows online reservations for some 100 restaurants and luaus, so take advantage of that before you travel.

If you want to get a good seat at **sunset,** be sure to make reservations. Restaurants fill up for sunset, which varies from 5:30 to 6:30pm, depending on the time of year.

PLATE LUNCHES & MORE: LOCAL FOOD

Hawaii has a classification of food seen nowhere else on the planet: "local food." Its broad umbrella includes plate lunches and poke, shave ice and saimin, bento lunches and *manapua*—cultural hybrids all.

Reflecting a polyglot population of many ethnicities, Hawaii's idiosyncratic dining scene is eminently inclusive. Consider surfer chic: Barefoot in the sand, in a swimsuit, you chow down on a **plate lunch** ordered from a lunch wagon, consisting of a filling protein (teriyaki beef, shoyu chicken, garlic shrimp, etc.), "two scoops rice," macaroni salad (often larded with tuna or potato), and a few leaves of green, typically julienned cabbage. It's washed down with a soft drink, often a sugary, island-made juice blend, in a paper cup or straight out of the can. Like **saimin**—the local version of noodles in salty broth topped with egg, green onions, and char siu pork—the plate lunch is Hawaii's comfort food.

ORDERING FRESH fish

The **Monterey Bay Aquarium website** (www.montereybayaquarium.org) offers lots of information on sustainable fish choices, plus free downloadable pocket guides and smartphone apps. Click on "Save the Oceans" to get started.

Most restaurants on Maui are honest and want to give you the freshest of the

daily catch, but some are not so honest. Be sure to ask your server:

- ○ When was the fresh catch caught?
- ○ Where was it caught? (If it was not caught in Hawaii waters, it is not fresh.)
- ○ Has the fish ever been frozen? (Some restaurants think "fresh frozen" is the same thing as "fresh fish." Do not eat at restaurants that think this way.)

But it was only a matter of time before the humble plate lunch became a culinary icon in Hawaii. These days, even the most chichi restaurant has a version of this modest island symbol (not at plate-lunch prices, of course), while vendors selling the real thing—carb-driven meals served from wagons—have queues that never end.

Other **Hawaiian foods** include those from before and after Western contact, such as *laulau* (pork, chicken, or fish steamed in ti leaves), kalua pork (pork cooked in a Polynesian underground oven known here as an *imu*), squid luau (actually octopus, cooked in coconut milk and taro tops), poke (cubed raw fish seasoned with onions, seaweed, sesame oil, soy sauce and the occasional sprinkling of roasted kukui nuts), haupia (creamy coconut pudding), and *kulolo* (steamed pudding of coconut, brown sugar, and taro).

Cooked, pounded, and moistened taro is the source of **poi**—an easily digestible, nourishing carbohydrate source for babies; a condiment to be mixed with any fish; and a repository of deep cultural associations for Native Hawaiians, who believe a stillborn ancestor became taro to feed those who came after him. You don't have to like it (and if you have the runny luau version, thinned to keep costs down, you probably won't), but it's worth trying a dollop on lomi salmon (salted salmon with tomatoes and green onions) to understand its culinary appeal. Whatever you do, please don't mock it publicly—locals already know most visitors aren't fans. Plus, prices are often high, thanks to the shortage of cheap land, water, and labor for the intensive taro-growing process.

Japanese immigrants contributed a popular to-go meal available throughout Hawaii: the **bento.** This compact, boxed assortment of picnic fare usually consists of neatly arranged sections of rice, pickled vegetables, and fried chicken, beef, or pork. Increasingly, however, the bento is becoming more health-conscious, as in macrobiotic or vegetarian brown rice bentos (the same is true for today's plate lunches). A derivative of the modest box lunch Japanese laborers brought to work in sugarcane and pineapple fields, bentos are dispensed everywhere, from department stores to corner delis and supermarkets.

What the Heck Is a *Pupu*?

If you're not old enough to remember the '60s craze for tiki bars and pupu platters, you might not know that pupu (pronounced *poo-poo*) means "appetizer." Although it may sound unappetizing to English speakers (and believe me, locals have heard your jokes), Maui menus are big on *pupu*, which range from small bites to generous helpings.

Also from the plantations comes **manapua,** a steamed, doughy sphere filled with tasty fillings of sweetened pork or sweet beans— Hawaii's version of the Chinese char siu bao. In the old days, the "manapua man" would make his rounds with bamboo containers balanced on a rod over his shoulders. Today you'll find white or whole-wheat manapua containing chicken, vegetables, curry, and other savory fillings.

For dessert or a snack, the prevailing choice is **shave ice,** Hawaii's version of a snow cone. Particularly on hot, humid days, long lines of shave-ice lovers gather for heaps of finely shaved ice—much fluffier than that in a mainland snow cone—topped with sweet tropical syrups. The fast-melting mounds, which require prompt, efficient consumption, are quite the ritual for sweet tooths. Aficionados order shave ice with ice cream and chewy rice mochi balls at the bottom and sweetened adzuki beans or coconut cream on top.

CENTRAL MAUI

Kahului and Wailuku have a few tasty finds. Minutes outside of the airport in a windy dirt lot across from Costco, you'll find an array of **food trucks** dishing out everything from pork belly sandwiches to poke (seasoned raw fish). Only a few blocks west is the island's best food truck, culinary educator Kyle Kawakami's **Maui Fresh Streatery ★★** (137 E. Kaahumanu Ave., Kahului; www.mauifreshstreatery.com; ✆ **808/344-7929**), which changes menu themes regularly. One of the most popular is Kawakami's Korean-inspired lineup: boneless fried chicken with spicy gochujang sauce, fries with Maui beef kalbi and kim chi mayo, and crispy pork belly.

Before or after a flight, be sure to budget time to swing by **Home Maid Bakery ★★** (1005 Lower Main St., Wailuku; https://homemaidbakery.com; ✆ **808/244-7015**) for a mouthwatering welcome treat or *omiyage* (the Japanese tradition of giving specialty foods as gifts). Founded in 1960, the bakery offers a huge variety of delectable treats, including mochi (rice flour), doughnuts (Portuguese-style doughnut holes), *manju* (Japanese-inspired turnovers with sweet bean or fruit fillings) and *ensemada* (Filipino sweet rolls). Equally impressive in this quiet town are the bakery hours, 5am to 9pm daily.

Kahului

In addition to the restaurants below, diners seeking Hawaiian specialties will want to visit **Poi by the Pound ★** (430 Kele St.; www.poibythepound.com; ✆ **808/283-9381**) for kalua pork (complemented by fresh poi), pork and butterfish laulau, squid luau, and spicy or shoyu poke ($8 to $24). It's open Monday to Saturday 9am to 10pm, till 5pm Sunday.

MODERATE

Bistro Casanova ★ MEDITERRANEAN Hungry and marooned in Kahului? Head to this Mediterranean bistro only a mile from the airport for hearty salads, traditional Italian pastas, fresh fish, or a giant bowl of paella ($34, serving two). The casual but classy restaurant fills with business lunchers at noon. It's more relaxed at dinner (unless there's a big show at the nearby Maui Arts & Cultural Center—then it will be hopping). It offers a private room for big parties and a full bar for *pau hana* (after work) drinks.

33 Lono Ave., Kahului. www.casanovamaui.com. ✆ **808/873-3650.** Main courses $14–$20 lunch, $14–$42 dinner. Mon–Sat lunch 11am–2:30pm, tapas 3–5pm, happy hour 4–6pm, dinner 5–9pm.

Da Kitchen ★★ LOCAL/ISLAND CUISINE For a fast infusion of island style, head straight from the airport to this surprisingly attractive, airy cafe in a strip mall, the more polished sit-down version of its original Kihei food counter. Executive chef and co-owner Les Tomita has won an avid local following for enormous portions of island favorites such as chicken *katsu* (breaded cutlet), kalua pork, and saimin, as well as juicy burgers, salads, and fish and chips, all made with fresh, high-quality ingredients—lean beef, hormone-free chicken, and homemade sauces among them. Look for the chalkboard specials and slake your thirst with a li hing mui lemonade or craft beer. If there's a wait to be seated, the host will take your cellphone number and text you when your table is ready; thanks to speedy service, the line moves quickly.

425 Koloa St., Kahului. http://dakitchen.com. ℂ **808/871-7782.** Lunch and dinner main courses $16–$31. Mon–Sat 11am–9pm.

INEXPENSIVE

Ten minutes from the airport on Hwy. 31, **Queen Kaahumanu Center** (275 Kaahumanu Ave.; www.queenkaahumanucenter.com)—the structure that looks like a white *Star Wars* umbrella—has a very popular food court. Favorites include **Ramen Ya** for a steaming bowl of noodles, and **HiTea,** for bubble teas and smoothies. Outside of the food court, but still in the shopping center, are **Koho's Bar & Grill,** dishing out burgers and plate lunches; and **Starbucks.** There's also a branch of **Maui Tacos** (p. 106). When you leave Kaahumanu Center, take a moment to gaze at the West Maui Mountains to your left from the parking lot.

Down to Earth ★ ORGANIC HEALTH FOOD Stop in here for a vegetarian snack or bag full of local organic produce. During mango season, this large, full-service natural-foods store carries as many as three different locally grown varieties of the fruit—worth their weight in gold. The deli includes creative salads, lasagna, chili, curries, and dozens of tasty dishes—including gluten-free and vegan options. Deli attendants can whip up a faux Reuben sandwich or tasty meatless burger for you. The upstairs dining area is plain but convenient, with easy parking in the store's lot.

305 Dairy Rd., Kahului. www.downtoearth.org. ℂ **808/877-2661.** Self-serve hot buffet, salad bar, and deli; food sold by the pound; average $7–$12 for a plate; sandwiches $6–$11. Mon–Sat 6am–10pm; Sun 7am–9pm (deli closes 1 hr. before store).

Restaurant Matsu ★ JAPANESE/LOCAL Customers have come from Hana (more than 50 miles away) just for Matsu's California rolls, while regulars line up for the cold saimin (julienned cucumber, egg, Chinese-style sweet pork, and red ginger on noodles) and the bento plates (various assemblages of chicken, teriyaki beef, fish, and rice). The *nigiri* sushi items are popular, especially among the don't-dally lunch crowd. The *katsu* pork and chicken, breaded and deep fried, are other specialties of this casual Formica-style diner. Try the tempura *udon,* steaming mounds of wide noodles swimming in homemade broth and topped with condiments. The daily specials are a changing lineup of home-cooked classics: oxtail soup, roast pork with gravy, teriyaki ahi, miso butterfish, and breaded mahimahi.

161 Alamaha St., Kahului. ☏ **808/871-0822.** Most items under $14. Mon–Fri 10am–3pm; Wed–Fri 5–7pm and 5–8pm; Sat 10am–2pm.

Tin Roof ★★★ FILIPINO/PLATE LUNCH Celebrity chef Sheldon Simeon won the hearts of *Top Chef* fans not just once, but twice, and Maui residents couldn't adore him more. After launching **Star Noodle** (p. 101) into fame, he and his wife, Janice, opened their own business—a humble to-go spot at the very back of an industrial strip mall in Kahului. The menu, inspired by his Filipino roots, is so much fun: buy a 50-cent "dime bag" of house-made furikake to sprinkle on your mochiko chicken. Add a 6-minute egg to your pork belly bowl. You'll want to Instagram yourself eating the chocolate b'day cake bibingka, covered in party-colored sprinkles. Drinks include Maui Brewing Company's root beer and Valley Isle kombucha. For even more inventive evening fare, visit his newer sit-down restaurant in Wailea, **Lineage** (p. 116).

360 Papa Pl. (but facing Dairy Road), Kahului. www.tinroofmaui.com. ☏ **808/868-0753.** Most items under $9, chef specials $14. Mon–Sat 10am–2pm.

Wailuku & Waikapu
MODERATE

A Saigon Cafe ★ VIETNAMESE It's hard to say which is better at this beloved neighborhood restaurant—the delicious Vietnamese cuisine or the hilarious waiters who make wisecracks while taking your order. Whatever you order—the steamed opakapaka with ginger and garlic, one of a dozen soups, the catfish simmering in a clay pot, or the fragrant lemongrass curry—you'll notice the freshness of the flavors. Owner Jennifer Nguyen grows many of her own vegetables and herbs and even sprouts her own mung beans. Try the Buddha rolls dunked in spicy peanut sauce and the Vietnamese "burritos." You make the latter tableside—tricky at first, but fun.

1792 Main St., Wailuku. www.asaigoncafe.com. ☏ **808/243-9560.** Main courses $6–$31. Mon–Sat 10am–9:30pm; Sun 10am–8:30pm. Heading into Wailuku from Kahului, go over the bridge and take the 1st right onto Central Ave.; then take the 1st right on Nani St. At the next stop sign, look for the building with the neon sign that says OPEN.

Mill House ★★★ ISLAND FUSION Awe-inspiring views of the West Maui Mountains, lush lakeside gardens, and sugar-mill-machinery-turned-sculptures create the scenic backdrop for the signature restaurant of **Maui Tropical Plantation**, already a destination-worthy attraction for its ziplines, train ride, and boutique shops (see p. 132). Maui Culinary Academy graduate Taylor Ponte trained with renowned chefs Alan Wong and Jeff Scheer before assuming the role as executive chef here, where his larder includes produce from on-site Kumu Farms, Oprah's Farm (yes, *that* Oprah), and other local growers as well as beef from cattle grazing on native grasses on the slopes above the restaurant. Ponte's dishes reflect Italian, Hawaiian, and Asian origins enlivened by local ingredients and a creative sensibility (e.g., taro-leaf

MAUI'S best ICE CREAMS

Given the warm days and ready supply of tropical ingredients, it should be no surprise that locally made ice cream is a popular treat on Maui. What may surprise you is just how delicious, and varied, the offerings are.

o **Roselani Tropics Ice Cream,** Maui's best made-from-scratch, old-fashioned ice cream that's widely available, got its start in 1932, when Manuel Nobriga began making his rich, smooth ice cream at the Maui Soda & Ice Works plant in Wailuku. His granddaughter Cathy Nobriga Kim has expanded his ice cream line to 32 flavors, divided among seven labeled "gourmet" (16% butterfat), including chocolate macadamia nut, Hawaiian vanilla bean and Kona coffee varieties, and 25 labeled "premium" (12% butterfat), such as haupia (coconut pudding), banana mac crunch, and matcha green tea. Mix the haupia or vanilla with one of Roselani's three tangy sherbets—guava, lilikoi (passionfruit), or orange—for a decadent Maui version of a Dreamsicle. You'll spot it in local grocery stores and on many a restaurant and cafe menu (including at **Ululani's Shave Ice,** p. 96); for a list of outlets, visit http://roselani.com/locations/maui.

o **Island Cream Co.** (in the Lahaina Gateway Center, 305 Keawe St., Lahaina, www/islandcreamco.com; 𝄞 **808/298-0916**) offers a unique blend of ice cream and gelato, with a large daily rotating selection from more than 40 flavors. Sweet potato pie, Maui French toast, and haupia pineapple are among the unique varieties of "island cream," as it's called here, while sorbets come in another 20 or so flavors, including tropical specialties like strawberry guava, pineapple ginger, and blood orange. The selection of flavors for shave ice is dizzying, too: Try one over a scoop of ice cream with strawberry-mango puree, boba balls, and sweetened condensed milk "snowcap"—a fun concoction known as a Sploshy. Island Cream is open 11am to 9pm daily.

o Sampling the original wares of **Coconut Glen's** (1200 Hana Hwy., Nahiku; http://coconutglens.com; 𝄞 **808/248-4876**) may require the most effort: It's 37 miles east of Paia near mile marker 27.5 along the Road to Hana (see p. 169). But the vegan, organic ice cream ($7 a scoop, cash only) is a welcome reward after all the waits at one-lane bridges and road-hugging curves on the Hana Highway. The original coconut is delicious, but you can also ask for a sample of the handful of other daily flavors: banana rum raisin, lilikoi, and chili chocolate chipotle are some favorites. You'll need to eat it in your car or stand under the trees at this tiny stand on a busy day.

o Unknown to many, **Surfing Monkey Shave Ice** (https://surfingmonkey shaveice.com; two locations: 1881 S. Kihei Rd., Kihei, 𝄞 **808/359-9282**; and the Shops at Wailea, 3750 Wailea Alanui Dr., 𝄞 **808/359-9282**) serves five varieties of Coconut Glen's ice cream, along with 10 Roselani flavors, for $6 a scoop ($8 double). Try them on their own or with a shave ice made with all-natural syrups. The Kihei stand is open 10:30am to 9pm daily, the Wailea shop 11am to 9pm daily. For more shave ice outlets carrying Coconut Glen's and Roselani, see also **Ululani's Hawaiian Shave Ice**, p. 96.

risotto with bone marrow; gnocchi with shiitake, zucchini, and fried quinoa). Burgers, fish sandwiches, and the pricey steak ($55) come in more straight-forward but no less tasty preparations. Don't skip the cocktail menu featuring cold-pressed sugarcane and local elixirs. Happy hour brings craft beer for $5, a half-dozen plates (including the burger, two chicken bao buns, and squash pizza with runny egg and truffled brie) for $10, and Koloa rum cocktails for $8 to $12. Foodies will want to book a seat at the weekly **Chef's Table** ($150), a communal, multi-course meal with conversation with chefs, live music, sparkling wine, and gratuity included in the cost. Coffee comes from **Mill House Roasting Co.**, which also has an onsite cafe with locally made pastries (open daily 8am–4pm).

1670 Honoapiilani Hwy., Waikapu. www.millhousemaui.com. © **808/270-0333**. Main courses $12–$55. Daily 11am–9pm; happy hour 2–5pm.

INEXPENSIVE

Sam Sato's ★ NOODLES/PLATE LUNCH Hidden away in Wailuku's industrial area, this humble, family-owned eatery dates back to 1933. It's one of Maui's last ma-and-pa eateries, and everything on the menu is under $10. Sit at the cafeteria-like counter and strike up a conversation with your neighbor. Try your dry mein (al dente noodles served with slices of char siu pork, bean sprouts, green onions, and broth on the side) with a side order of grilled teriyaki meat sticks. On the way out, stock up on Sam Sato's other famous specialty: baked *manju*, flaky pastries filled with sweetened lima or adzuki beans. This small restaurant fills up quickly, but service is fast; you'll see a lot aficionados picking up takeout orders, too.

At the Millyard, 1750 Wili Pa Loop, Wailuku. © **808/244-7124**. Plate lunches $8–$9. Mon–Sat 7am–2pm; 7am–4pm bakery and preordered takeout items.

WEST MAUI

The West and South Coasts of Maui are where most of the island's visitors stay, so these oceanside communities offer a range of restaurants, from Maui's best-known chefs to small mom-and-pop cafes. You will find eateries with romantic atmosphere, breathtaking views, and yummy food. You will also find an increase in prices, especially inside resorts. Ocean-view restaurants often command a premium too; consider those more affordable spots with mountain views or terraces under the stars.

Lahaina

VERY EXPENSIVE

Lahaina Grill ★★ NEW AMERICAN This classy restaurant has been collecting accolades for its perfectly executed island cuisine, gracious service, and great wine list since 1990. The striking decor—splashy artwork by local painter Jan Kasprzycki, pressed-tin ceilings, and warm lighting—creates an appealing atmosphere. Despite lacking an ocean view, the bar is among the busiest in town and often features special pricing. The menu hasn't strayed much over the years; fans will still find their favorites: the prawn- and scallop-stuffed blue-corn panko-crusted chile relleno appetizer ($29), the aromatic Kona coffee–roasted rack of lamb ($55), and the memorable triple berry pie ($17). If you're planning a special event or a large party, you can book a private room and design your own menu with the chef.

127 Lahainaluna Rd., Lahaina. www.lahainagrill.com. © **808/667-5117.** Reservations required. Main courses $35–$62. Daily 5–9pm. Bar daily 6–10pm (closing earlier on slow nights).

EXPENSIVE

The Feast at Lele ★★★ POLYNESIAN   Even those who think they've seen all the luaus they need have been won over by the Feast at Lele, while first-timers—especially couples looking for a romantic evening—will definitely be wowed. The Feast at Lele (the ancient name for Lahaina) stands out from other luaus as the gourmet choice, thanks not only to the cuisine of Pacific'O Executive Chef Adrian Aina but also to the unique, intimate ambience and high-quality performances (from the producers of the equally renowned Old Lahaina Luau). Although most luau seating is communal, guests here sit at elegant private tables in the sand behind Pacific'O, facing a small stage and the island of Lanai. Instead of watery mass-made mai tais, the complimentary beverages include expert cocktails, fine wine, and craft beer. As the sun dips into the sea behind them, chanting dancers regale you with stories of Polynesia. Their stories and dances progress from Hawaii to Aotearoa (New Zealand), Tahiti, and Samoa, while diners feast on each island nation's culinary specialties. During the opening hula, you might sample Hawaiian fish with mango sauce, *imu*-roasted kalua pig, and *sous vide* lomi salmon with local tomatoes and black sea salt. While watching the exciting Maori *haka,* you might find braised short ribs in a kiwi soy *jus* and a medley of *kumara* (sweet potato) and stewed mushrooms on your plate. Pace yourself; each of the four savory courses includes three dishes. Then there's dessert—typically vanilla coconut cake with caramelized pineapple and coconut haupia pudding with island fruit—accompanied by a fantastic fire-knife dance (an art form invented in San Francisco but perfected and popularized by Samoans). Book well ahead during peak travel periods.

505 Front St., Lahaina. www.feastatlele.com. © **866/244-5353** or 808/667-5353. Reservations required. Set 5-course menu (includes all beverages) $135 adults, $99 children 2–12. Apr 1–Sept 30 daily 6:30pm seating (to 9:30pm); Oct 1–Mar 31 daily 5:30pm seating (to 8:30pm).

Gerard's ★★★ FRENCH   Chef Gerard Reversade has called Hawaii home for nearly 4 decades, but his accent remains firmly French. His charming residence-turned-restaurant beneath the Plantation Inn in Lahaina is equally authentic. Chilled cucumber soup transcends simplicity with goat cheese and fresh dill. The roasted opakapaka served with fennel fondue and spiked with hints of orange, star anise, and ginger is stellar, as are the scallops

Restaurants in Lahaina & Kaanapali

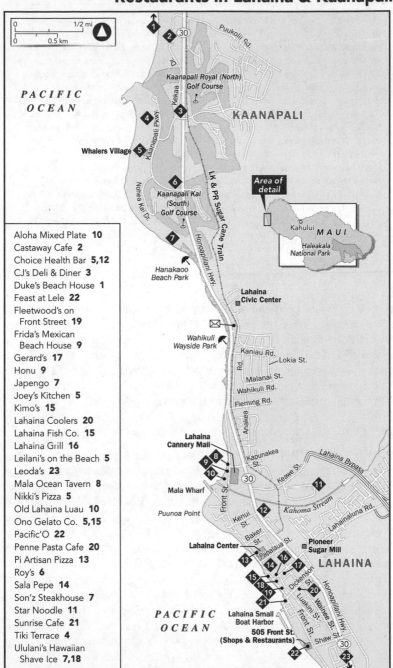

Aloha Mixed Plate **10**
Castaway Cafe **2**
Choice Health Bar **5,12**
CJ's Deli & Diner **3**
Duke's Beach House **1**
Feast at Lele **22**
Fleetwood's on
  Front Street **19**
Frida's Mexican
  Beach House **9**
Gerard's **17**
Honu **9**
Japengo **7**
Joey's Kitchen **5**
Kimo's **15**
Lahaina Coolers **20**
Lahaina Fish Co. **15**
Lahaina Grill **16**
Leilani's on the Beach **5**
Leoda's **23**
Mala Ocean Tavern **8**
Nikki's Pizza **5**
Old Lahaina Luau **10**
Ono Gelato Co. **5,15**
Pacific'O **22**
Penne Pasta Cafe **20**
Pi Artisan Pizza **13**
Roy's **6**
Sala Pepe **14**
Son'z Steakhouse **7**
Star Noodle **11**
Sunrise Cafe **21**
Tiki Terrace **4**
Ululani's Hawaiian
  Shave Ice **7,18**

David and Ululani Yamashiro are near-religious about shave ice. At their multiple shops around Maui (www.ululani shawaiianshaveice.com. ℰ **808/877-3700**), these shave-ice wizards take the uniquely Hawaiian dessert to new heights. It starts with the water: Pure, filtered water is frozen, shaved to feather lightness, and patted into shape. This mini snowdrift is then doused with your choice of syrup—any three flavors, from calamansi lime to lychee to red velvet cake. David makes his own gourmet syrups with local fruit purees and a dash of cane sugar. The passionfruit is perfectly tangy, the coconut is free of cloying artificial sweetness, and the electric green kiwi is studded with real seeds. Add a "snowcap" of sweetened condensed milk, and the resulting confection tastes like the fluffiest, most flavorful ice cream ever. Locals order theirs with chewy mochi morsels, sweet adzuki beans at the bottom, or tart *li hing mui* powder sprinkled on top. The Wailuku location also has *manapua* (steamed buns) and chow fun noodles; all are open daily. **Kaanapali:** In Hyatt Regency Maui, 200 Nohea Kai Dr., 10am–5:30pm; **Lahaina:** 790 Front St., 10:30am–9pm; **Kihei:** 61 S. Kihei Rd.,10:30am–6:30pm; **Wailuku:** In Safeway, 58 Maui Lani Pkwy, Ste. 5000, 10:30am–6pm; **Kahului:** 333 Dairy Rd., 10:30am–6pm; **Paia:** 115 Hana Hwy., 10:30am–8pm.

5

West Maui

WHERE TO EAT

au gratin and rack of lamb. Don't miss the venison ragout (with Jamaican pepper, chestnuts, pearl onions, and pasta) if you spot it on the menu; you'll not only enjoy a savory dish but also be doing your part to help remove invasive axis deer from the islands. Chef Reversade is every bit as much of a baker as a chef, and the savory dishes that incorporate pastry—such as the shiitake and oyster mushroom appetizer—are delights. The dessert menu ($12) has a half-dozen excellent offerings, including a marvelous *millefeuille* with Tahitian vanilla ice cream, plus housemade sorbets.

At the Plantation Inn, 174 Lahainaluna Rd., Lahaina. www.gerardsmaui.com. ℰ **808/661-8939.** Reservations recommended. Main courses $39–$58. Daily 6–8pm.

Pacific'O ★ PACIFIC RIM   You can't get any closer to the ocean than these tables overlooking the beach at 505 Front Street. Start with flash-fried oysters and wakame seaweed salad or lobster ravioli. Move on to saffron beet risotto studded with seared shrimp and chunks of seafood. Vegetarians will delight in the Portobello mushrooms with quinoa and cilantro pesto. (The kitchen sources ingredients from its own O'o Farm up in Kula.) This is a superb and relatively affordable lunch spot. Indulge in ginger-crusted fish ($23) or smoked pork sandwich ($14) and a glass of spicy Syrah while watching the ships sail by. At night, the rear lawn leading to the beach transforms into a dramatic setting for the excellent **Feast at Lele** luau (p. 234). **Sunday brunch** is also a delight, featuring organic eggs Benedict (choice of pork belly, ahi, or crab), avocado kimchee toast, and a gourmet "loco moco"—the local gutbuster usually made with two scoops of rice, hamburger patty, fried egg, and gravy. The Pacific'O version ($17) features caramelized Maui onion gravy, an organic poached egg, and a choice of Kauai grass-fed beef or house-made sausage; the rice is fried like tater tots. Plan for a post-meal nap.

505 Front St., Lahaina. www.pacificomaui.com. © **808/667-4341**. Reservations recommended. Main courses $14–$23 lunch, $29–$46 dinner; $13–$22 Sun brunch. Daily 11.30am–4pm and 5:30–9:30pm; Sun brunch 9:30am–2pm.

MODERATE

Fleetwood's on Front Street ★ AMERICAN   Rock & Roll Hall of Famer Mick Fleetwood ventured into the restaurant business with commendable results. His snazzy eatery occupies the top two floors of a lovingly restored three-story building on Front Street. For dinner, best bets include the locally grown salads, fresh fish entrees, or the Lahaina burger (Kauai grass-fed beef, aged cheddar, smoked bacon, and tomato jam). At lunch, served only on the rooftop, the menu features salads and casual fare such as Maui beer-battered fish and chips, a fried chipotle chicken sandwich, and fresh-catch fish tacos. Although the food may not be particularly exciting, the atmosphere is outstanding: The dining room's cozy booths and wraparound bar evoke an older, more sophisticated era, while the rooftop offers spectacular view and the frequent live entertainment is top shelf. *Tip:* Nightly at 6pm, local musicians offer a short, free performance, ranging from bagpipes to Hawaiian chanting. Mick and his celebrity friends often pop in to play a set. When it rains, the upstairs seating is closed.

744 Front St., Lahaina. www.fleetwoodsonfrontst.com. © **808/669-6425**. Reservations recommended. Main courses $15–$22 lunch, $29–$49 dinner. Daily 11am–2pm (rooftop only) and 5–10pm.

Frida's Mexican Beach House ★ MEXICAN   Mark Ellman, longtime Maui restaurateur who also founded Maui Tacos, runs three restaurants in a row on the beautiful seashore fronting Mala Wharf. Frida's features Mexican-inspired cuisine served on bright pottery in a breezy dining room accented with pretty tiles and wrought-iron chandeliers. Sip one of 40 tequilas at the open-air bar. Rib-eye mojo de ajo and grilled Spanish octopus with tomatillo salsa and fresh guacamole are delicious, especially on the romantic oceanfront lanai; save room for churros, artfully arrayed like a plumeria blossom.

1287 Front St., Lahaina. www.fridasmaui.com. © **808/661-1287**. Reservations recommended. Main courses $16–$40. Mon–Fri 11am–3pm and 4:30–9pm; Sat–Sun 9am–3pm and 4:30–9pm; daily 3–4:30pm happy hour.

Honu ★★ PIZZA/SEAFOOD   Snag an oceanfront table where the gentle tide nearly tickles your toes and spy on the green sea turtles for whom restaurateur Mark Ellman named his restaurant, the second in a trio that includes Mala Ocean Tavern and Frida's. Honu's diverse menu is guaranteed to please everyone in your party, from the fried oyster sandwiches and authentic Neapolitan pizzas to the wok-fried Dungeness crab. The Middle Eastern kale salad will turn doubters into believers: Finely chopped kale is massaged with preserved lemon vinaigrette and tossed with bittersweet walnuts, rich and salty pecorino shavings, sweet slivers of chewy dates, and pomegranate seeds that burst on the tongue. Gluten-free and *keiki* (children's) menus are available, along with an extensive offering of draft beers, single malt scotches, and handcrafted cocktails.

1295 Front St., Lahaina. www.honumaui.com. ℂ **808/667-9390.** Reservations recommended. Main courses $17–$48. Daily 11am–3pm and 4:30–9pm; 3–4:30pm happy hour.

Kimo's ★ STEAK/SEAFOOD   Founded in 1977, Kimo's has a loyal following that keeps it from falling into the faceless morass of waterfront restaurants serving surf and turf with great sunset views. Part of the TS Restaurants chain, it's a formula that works—not only because of its oceanfront patio **Lanai Bar** and upstairs dining room, but also because of its good value. Burgers and sandwiches are affordable and consistent, and the seasonal fresh catch—whether grilled, coconut-crusted, or lobster-topped—is a solid choice. The waistline-defying hula pie (macadamia nut ice cream in a chocolate-wafer crust with fudge and whipped cream) originated here. Four can share it easily.

845 Front St., Lahaina. www.kimosmaui.com. ℂ **808/661-4811.** Reservations recommended for dinner. Main courses $14–$20 lunch, $25–$49 dinner. Restaurant daily 11am–3:30pm and 4:45–10pm; chef's tasting menu (happy hour) 4:45–5:30pm. Bar daily 11am–midnight.

Lahaina Coolers ★ AMERICAN/INTERNATIONAL   The huge marlin hanging above the bar and persimmon-colored walls set a cheery tone at this casual indoor/outdoor restaurant. On Sunday, breakfast is served until 1pm. The huevos rancheros come in a sizzling cast-iron skillet heaped with kalua pork, and you have your choice of eggs Benedict: classic; Cajun, with seared fish and salsa; and the "Local," with kalua pork on Hawaiian sweet bread. The lunch menu includes Evil Jungle Pasta, chicken spiked with peppery Thai peanut sauce over linguine, and a variety of wraps and sandwiches. Prices increase at dinner, when the focus is on pasta and fresh seafood, but are still a fraction of what you'd pay at most Front Street establishments.

180 Dickenson St., Lahaina. www.lahainacoolers.com. ℂ **808/661-7082.** Main courses $8–$15 breakfast, $13–$17 lunch, $18–$33 dinner. Daily 8am–1am (dinner served till midnight).

Lahaina Fish Co. ★ SEAFOOD   The open-air dining room is literally over the water, with flickering torches after sunset and a relatively affordable seafood-focused menu—especially at lunch, when you can dine oceanside on burgers with Maui Cattle Co. beef, turkey, shrimp, or taro/lentil, or fresh seafood—perhaps fish tacos, ahi poke tostadas, or the catch of the day. Bonus: Mai tais are $6.50 from noon to 5pm. Chef Keith Salvador becomes more creative with dinner preparations, such as wok-fried ahi in a teriyaki mochiko batter with seaweed salad and kimchee or a seafood quinoa paella that includes Maui smoked venison chorizo as well as herb-rubbed island fish, tiger shrimp, and scallops. *Tip:* The Outlets of Maui offers 3 hours of free parking with validation.

831 Front St., Lahaina. www.lahainafishcompany.com. ℂ **808/661-3472.** Main courses $15–$21 lunch, $27–$39 dinner. Daily 11am–9:30pm.

Mala Ocean Tavern ★★ AMERICAN/INTERNATIONAL   Brighter and classier than "tavern" suggests, Mark Ellman's tiny restaurant overlooking Mala Wharf in Lahaina is perfect. The oceanfront seating lets diners peer down on sea turtles foraging in the surf. The bartenders know their business, and the complimentary edamame guacamole alerts your taste buds that something delicious is about to happen. The multicultural menu offers health-conscious and hedonistic options, from the *gado gado* (a vegan Indonesian rice dish heaped with sugar-snap peas and coconut peanut sauce), stir-fries, and Greek-style pita wraps to hearty pastas (including a vegetarian mushroom Bolognese) and braised pork shank with mashed purple Molokai sweet potatoes. The daily brunch is among Maui's tastiest, with local organic eggs served in Benedicts, chilaquiles, huevos rancheros, and spicy Israeli *shakshuka*. *Note:* Brunch and lunch are moderately priced, but many dinner entrees fall under the expensive category. Night owls will appreciate the late-night happy hour from 10pm to midnight daily.

1307 Front St., Lahaina. www.malaoceantavern.com. ☎ **808/667-9394.** Main courses $10–$17 brunch, $15–$23 lunch, $22–$49 dinner. Daily 9am–2pm, 11am–2pm, and 4:30–10pm. Early happy hour 2–4:30pm; late-night happy hour 10pm–midnight.

Pi Artisan Pizza ★ PIZZA   Perhaps the best reason to visit the Outlets of Maui shopping center is this gourmet pizzeria, which prides itself on fast service and fresh, local ingredients as well as its 800-degree *kiawe* (mesquite) wood-burning oven. The seared ahi tataki with fresh arugula and miso wasabi aioli is one of its most outstanding signature pizzas, but classics like pepperoni and mushroom also show pizzaz with housemade mozzarella, savory sauces, fresh herbs, and ample toppings. Other options include pastas, sandwiches, and salads. *Note:* Gluten-free crusts are available for an extra $2. The *keiki* menu (pizza or spaghetti with fountain drink) is also a deal at $6.

900 Front St., Lahaina. http://pi808.com. ☎ **808/667-0791.** Main courses $11–$21; pizza $10–$18. Daily 11:30am–9:30pm; happy hour 3–5pm.

Sala Pepe ★★ ITALIAN   The dinner-only menu at this small Italian bistro changes to reflect what's in season, but the quality stays consistent. The married owners (husband Michele is from Milan, wife Qiana is from Brooklyn) put a ton of love into their handcut pastas and pizza pies. Don't be surprised to see top chefs from nearby restaurants dining here on their day off. Daily specials include heavenly ravioli *fatti in casa* with short-rib ragu, or sopressata piccante pizza. Everything is written on the chalkboard in Italian—if you can't understand it, don't worry. It all translates as delicious.

In Old Lahaina Center, 878 Front St., Lahaina. www.salepepemaui.com. ☎ **808/667-7667.** Main courses $14–$43. Mon–Sat 5–10pm.

INEXPENSIVE

Aloha Mixed Plate ★ PLATE LUNCH/BEACHSIDE GRILL   This veteran beachfront eatery offers a mix of its longtime favorites—fresh-made chow fun noodles, Korean kalbi ribs, and seared fresh-catch sandwiches—and newer, inventive dishes like a roasted beet salad with grilled pineapple, local greens, mascarpone, and *ume* (Chinese plum) vinaigrette. Some of the ingredients, like the smoky beets and meltingly good short ribs, are roasted in the traditional Hawaiian *imu* (underground oven) at the Old Lahaina Luau grounds next door. Breakfast features Hoaloha Bake Shop sweet rolls in its egg Benedicts, taro hash with kalua ham and eggs, and a delightfully fluffy soufflé pancake. At the bar, try the Sassy Wahine (Hornitos tequila, mango purée, lime and orange juice, strawberry swirl, and *li hing mui* rim) or the Jala-Pina margarita, which blends Hornitos with a shrub of jalapeno, pineapple, and lime.

1285 Front St., Lahaina. www.alohamixedplate.com. © **808/661-3322.** Main courses $10–$19. Daily 8am–10pm; happy hour 3–5pm.

Choice Health Bar ★★ GOURMET DELI/CAFE   This health-conscious juice bar and cafe is where the beautiful people in Lahaina come to fuel up. After a taxing morning of standup paddling past sea turtles, re-energize here with a smoothie, cold-pressed juice, or one of a half-dozen açai bowls, like the "green buzz," featuring berries, banana, spirulina, coconut water, goji, bee pollen, and honey. Daily lunch specials include raw pizza on seed crusts with rosemary-cashew chèvre and healthy plates with tasty lemon-flax kale salad, coconut-garlic quinoa, vegan soup, and dessert. It also has locations in Whaler's Village in Kaanapali and Paia.

1087 Limahana Place (off of Honoapiilani Hwy.), Lahaina. www.choicehealthbar.com. © **808/661-7711.** Breakfast and lunch main courses $10–$14. Mon–Sat 8am–5pm; Sun 9am–2pm.

Leoda's Kitchen and Pie Shop ★★ SANDWICHES/BAKERY   As you approach the counter, you'll see why the line stretches to the door: a glass case full of banana and coconut pies slathered in fresh whipped cream. The savory pies are just okay. But the sweet pies—especially the macadamia nut chocolate praline—are intergalactic. For breakfast, the outstanding seared ahi Benedict come with pesto, watercress, avocado, and local eggs. At lunch, oversized sandwiches come in tempting combinations like the Ham'n—a hot and juicy mess of Duroc ham, island pesto, melted Jarlsberg cheese, and apricot-tomato jam on buttered rye bread. Housemade buns and condiments like local *poha* berry mustard and Maui pineapple chutney mean even hot dogs ($7.50) are a treat; Leoda's potato buns and American Kobe beef elevate burgers ($12–$14). Leoda's belongs to the Star Noodle, Old Lahaina Luau, and Aloha Mixed Plate restaurant family—a crew that knows how to please. The eatery's bright decor pays homage to Maui's bygone plantation days.

820 Olowalu Village Rd. (off of Honoapiilani Hwy), Lahaina. www.leodas.com. © **808/662-3600.** Hot breakfast items $7–$20; main courses $8–$16. Daily 7am–8pm.

Penne Pasta Café ★ ITALIAN/MEDITERRANEAN   This casual, indoor-outdoor spot on a side street features delicious Southern Italian and Mediterranean cuisine. It's a sit-down meal at takeout prices: Order at the counter, and the pasta, flatbreads, sandwiches, or salads (try the Niçoise) will be brought to your table. The penne puttanesca, oven-roasted butternut squash, and lamb osso buco (Wed-night special) are wonderful. Meatballs feature Maui Cattle Co. grass-fed beef, while chef-owner Juan Gomez occasionally draws from his Hispanic roots to create silky flan for dessert. Wine (from $8 a glass) and beer are available, too.

180 Dickenson St., Lahaina. www.pennepastacafe.net © 808/661-6633. Main courses $9–$18. Daily 11am–9:30pm.

Star Noodle ★★ NOODLES/FUSION This hip noodle house at the top of Lahaina's industrial park offers a deceivingly simple menu of noodles and share plates. The hapa ramen, with its smoky pork and spicy miso broth, is guaranteed to be unlike any you've had before. Each dish is a gourmet twist on a local favorite; the Lahaina fried soup isn't soup at all but thick and chewy house-made noodles tossed with ground pork and bean sprouts. The ahi avo is a divine mix of fresh red tuna and buttery avocado swimming in a pool of lemon-pressed olive oil and spiked with sambal. With its long communal table, Shepard Fairey artwork, and glamorous washrooms, this casual eatery has an urban feel. From the window seats you can catch a hint of an ocean view—just enough to remind you that you're still in Hawaii.

286 Kupuohi St., Lahaina. www.starnoodle.com. © 808/667-5400. Main courses $10–$18. Daily 10:30am–10pm.

Sunrise Café ★ CAFE For a bargain lunch or breakfast, follow the surfers to this hole-in-the-wall located just off Front Street. (The address says Front St., but it's really off of Market, across from the library.) The kitchen turns out tasty breakfast burritos, a lox Benedict with home-fried potatoes, and decent sandwiches, mango barbecued chicken among them. Service can be slow, but the prices can't be beat in this neighborhood. Eat in the covered patio out back or take it to go and picnic in the adjoining park. It's tough to find a parking spot nearby (and you can't park at the library), but you'll probably want a brisk walk after eating here anyway.

693A Front St., Lahaina. © 808/661-8558. Breakfast $7–$14; lunch $8–$11. No credit cards. Daily breakfast 6am–3pm, lunch 11:30am–3pm.

EAT LIKE A local

Are you the type of visitor who feels you haven't "experienced" a destination unless you've hit the restaurants where the local residents eat? Then sign up for **Tour da Food** ★★★ (www.tourdafood. com; © 808/242-8383). Pastry chef, cookbook author, and food writer/publicist Bonnie Friedman takes foodies off the tourist path to discover culinary treasures—from snack shacks to restaurants to markets and manufacturers—in either Wailuku or Upcountry Maui. Along the way she shares tidbits about the culture and the people creating the delicious food. Prices begin at $425 per couple, which includes transportation from Heritage Gardens Kepaniwai Park in Wailuku, lunch, snacks, dessert, a bag of goodies to take home, and Bonnie's personal list of under-the-radar eating places. *Tip:* Book this tour early in your trip, so you have time to follow Bonnie's terrific suggestions of places to eat on Maui.

Kaanapali

EXPENSIVE

Japengo ★★★ SUSHI/PACIFIC RIM   The open-air dining room hanging over the Hyatt pool is divided into multiple private nooks, evoking the feel of a Japanese teahouse—one that also happens to witness spectacular sunsets. Superb Japanese-influenced entrees and inspired sushi, sashimi, and hand rolls deservedly keep Japengo at the top of local best-of lists. Depending on what the fishermen reeled in that day, the *moriawase,* or chef's platter ($35 or $65), may include vibrant red tuna, translucent slivers of Big Island *hirame* (flounder), poached local abalone, creamy wedges of *uni* (sea urchin), or raw New Caledonia prawn. The sushi wizards at the bar beautifully garnish this bounty with nests of peppery daikon and aromatic shiso leaves. Delicious vegetable sides—kabocha pumpkin with fried garlic, asparagus in Thai sweet chili sauce, and lavender-honey stir-fry corn—originate on nearby Simpli-Fresh farm.

At the Hyatt Regency Maui Resort, 200 Nohea Kai Dr., Kaanapali. http://kaanapali resort.com/japengo. © **808/661-1234.** Main courses $24–$69, sushi rolls $16–$24. Restaurant and sushi bar daily 5:30–9:30pm; lounge daily 5–10pm; happy hour 5–6pm.

Roy's ★★ HAWAII REGIONAL CUISINE   Roy Yamaguchi, the James Beard award–winning chef and one of the pioneers of Hawaii Regional Cuisine, has largely divested himself from Roy's restaurants outside of Hawaii to focus on his home-state holdings. On Maui that would be this dining room next to the Kaanapali Golf Course and Wailea's **Humble Market Kitchin** (p. 115). At dinner, main courses fall into the very expensive category (most above $45), like Roy's signature misoyaki butterfish ($48), although some are less pricey, like the honey-mustard-glazed beef short ribs ($40). Breakfast has some downright affordable options, although you may want to spring for a Benedict with blackened ahi or crispy crab cake ($24), or avocado toast with sous vide egg ($16); at lunch, sandwiches ($15–21) offer ingredients such as grilled kalbi ribs, grilled cheese with candied bacon, and grass-fed beef meatloaf. The restaurant also serves a bar menu from 2 to 5pm that features the "canoe for two," an appetizer platter of baby-back ribs, ahi poke, pork and shrimp lumpia, chicken potstickers, and skewered shrimp ($38). *Tip:* Two words: chocolate soufflé. It takes 20 minutes to prepare, so let your waiter know you want it in advance. And when it arrives, wait a moment for it to cool—don't burn your tongue on the hot lava chocolate!

2290 Kaanapali Pkwy., Kaanapali. www.royshawaii.com/roys-kaanapali.html. © **808/669-6999.** Main courses $8–$24 breakfast, $17–$22 lunch, $31–$69 dinner. Daily breakfast 6–10:30am; lunch 11am–2pm; bar menu 2–5pm; dinner 4:30–9:30pm.

Son'z Steakhouse ★ STEAK/SEAFOOD   Descend a palatial staircase for dinner at Son'z, where tables overlook a lagoon with white and black swans gliding by. This is classy digs for a steakhouse; imagine Ruth's Chris with extra flavor and a fairy-tale atmosphere. Chef Geno Sarmiento knows how to prepare protein; his filet mignon is on point with "Mauishire" steak sauce, as are the slow-braised prime short ribs. Seafood options include catch of the day inspired by sibling restaurant **Nick's Fishmarket** (p. 114), with Molokai sweet potato hash browns, and delectable shrimp scampi with baked potato ravioli, mushrooms, and cherry tomatoes. Most sides are sold separately, with choices like grilled asparagus, four-cheese gnocchi, and the loaded baked potato, a decadent spud cooked low and slow (200° for 4 hr.) and sinfully stuffed with mascarpone, bacon bits, truffle butter, chives, and Parmesan. Finish with fudge lava cake, its warm, oozing center melding perfectly with haupia (coconut pudding) ice cream and fresh berries.

At the Hyatt Regency Maui Resort, 200 Nohea Kai Dr., Kaanapali. www.sonzsteakhouse. com. ✆ **808/667-4506.** Main courses $30–$64. Daily 5–9:30pm.

MODERATE

Duke's Beach House ★ PACIFIC RIM There are few more beautiful places to enjoy breakfast than here, facing Kahekili Beach (also known as North Kaanapali Beach). This restaurant mimics an open-air plantation home, decorated with memorabilia chronicling the life of world-famous Hawaiian surfer Duke Kahanamoku. It's part of the T S Restaurants family, which includes Kimo's, Hula Grill, and Leilani's on Maui, Keoki's Paradise on Kauai, and Duke's in Waikiki—among others. Although you can order the massive signature hula pie for dessert, the rest of the menu reflects a less formulaic approach. Lunch offers a kicky Korean fish bowl and steak street tacos along with crowd-pleasing burgers and fish and chips, while dinner features sustainable fresh catches, perhaps steamed in banana leaves with sake ginger sauce or sautéed in a crust of macadamia nuts, Parmesan, and panko. The gracious sea-breeze-kissed locale, including the handsome Ohia Bar, and the kitchen's commitment to serving locally raised beef, eggs, and vegetables are also pluses. Add to that live music during dinner and the daily "aloha hour" (3–5pm).

At Honua Kai Resort & Spa, 130 Kai Malina Pkwy. www.dukesmaui.com. ✆ **808/662-2900.** Main courses $13–$19 breakfast, $14–$26 brunch, $16–$19 lunch, $18–$46 dinner. Daily breakfast 7:30am–11am; Sat–Sun brunch and daily lunch 11am–3pm; dinner 4:45–9:30pm.

Leilani's on the Beach ★★ STEAK/SEAFOOD Another outpost of the T S Restaurants empire, Leilani's showcases sustainable seafood and local produce, sourcing from some 40 Maui farms. Try the taro hummus with Kumu Farms crudités and taro chips or the ahi poke with avocado for starters, and for a main, the lemongrass miso-glazed salmon with chilled noodle salad or citrus-soy glazed *huli huli* (barbecued) chicken with pork char sui fried rice. The **Beachside Grill**—with tables just off Kaanapali Beach—features a separate, more casual menu. Here you can people-watch while snacking on Cajun-rubbed fish tacos or a Korean fried chicken sandwich and tossing back a hibiscus Paloma. In lieu of T S' trademark hula pie, finish with the lighter but still satisfying passionfruit Pono Pie made with Hana breadfruit, Kula strawberries, and gluten-free nut crust.

At Whalers Village, 2435 Kaanapali Pkwy., Kaanapali. www.leilanis.com. © **808/661-4495.** Reservations suggested for dinner. Beachside Grill lunch and dinner main courses $16–$25; Leilani's dinner main courses $19–$51. Beachside Grill daily 11am–10:30pm (bar till 11pm). Leilani's daily 4:45–9:30pm.

INEXPENSIVE

Whalers Village, 2435 Kaanapali Pkwy. in Kaanapali (www.whalersvillage. com/restaurants.htm), has a branch of Lahaina's **Choice Health Bar** (p. 100) open 8am to 9:30pm, as well as the restaurants mentioned above and coffee, shave ice, and ice cream outlets. The lower-level food court includes a casual version of Chef Joey Macadangdang's Filipino-inspired **Joey's Kitchen** in Napili (p. 106), open daily 8am–9pm (www.joeyskitchenhimaui.com; © **808/868-4474**), and budget- and family-friendly **Nikki's Pizza** (© **808/667-0333**), open daily 7am–9pm, which serves breakfast all day. With courtyard seating, the food court makes an inexpensive, handy stop for shoppers and Kaanapali beachgoers.

Castaway Café ★ AMERICAN   Hidden away in the Aston Maui Kaanapali Villas, this little cafe sits right on Kahekili Beach—privy to perfect views and salty breezes. Chef Lyndon Honda and the Cohn Restaurant group breathed new life into this local favorite, long famous for its Saturday-night prime rib special, with casual fare like the ahi BLT sandwich with wasabi aioli on focaccia, fish tacos, and an array of burgers available all day. Dinner plates (from 4pm) include a daily fresh catch and 10-ounce grilled rib-eye ($28). Enjoy live music on the lanai 4 to 7pm Wednesday to Friday, or an extra-relaxing breakfast any day of the week, when the choices are tough—avocado toast with two eggs or Meyer lemon ricotta pancakes with lilikoi puree? Kalua pork in huevos rancheros or a breakfast burrito?

In the Aston Maui Kaanapali Villas, 45 Kai Ala Dr., Kaanapali. www.castawaycafe.com. © **808/661-9091.** Main courses $11–$15 breakfast; $12–$24 lunch; $12–$28 dinner. Daily breakfast 7:30am–11:30am, lunch 11:30am–9pm, dinner 4–9pm.

CJ's Deli & Diner ★ AMERICAN/DELI   Need a break from resort prices? Head to this happening eatery just off of Honoapiilani Highway in Kaanapali, where most entrees are under $12. The atmosphere is colorful and slightly chaotic, with a huge billboard menu that spans the back wall, shelves stuffed with souvenirs and brochures, and a . . . basketball hoop? Practice your free throws while debating over breakfast options: cheese omelet, Norwegian smoked salmon bagel, or French toast made with Hawaiian sweet bread. Lunch ranges from cold or grilled sandwiches to fish and chips, mochiko chicken, and mango-glazed barbecue ribs. The ample kids menu includes happy-face pancakes and **"lizard toes and squid-eyes" soup.** If you're heading out to Hana or up to Haleakala, stop by for a box lunch. Toppings are

MAKE TIME FOR tiki

While the dining at Kaanapali Beach Hotel (p. 52) may not be dazzling, you'd be missing out on some of the best free entertainment on Maui if you skipped dinner at the hotel's casual outdoor **Tiki Grill,** open daily 11:30am to 8pm, or a tropical cocktail at the adjacent thatched-roof **Tiki Bar,** open daily 10am to 10pm. That's because the large stage next to them hosts nightly music and hula from 6 to 9pm, often with brightly costumed groups of dancers from local *halau* (hula schools). Although the performances are first-rate, the vibe is relaxed, in authentic backyard Hawaiian style. The Hawaii Regional Cuisine at the more formal indoor-outdoor **Tiki Terrace** restaurant can be uneven, but its Sunday champagne brunch ($48 adults, $25 6–12) is popular with locals and visitors for the sheer vastness of its options; reservations are recommended. At dinner, the Native Hawaiian plate ($25 chicken, $26 fish) takes inspiration from the pre-Western contact diet that was low in fat and sodium; it's a little bland and starchy, with grilled bananas, taro, sweet potatoes, and poi along with a steamed protein. Nevertheless, serving such fare in the employee cafeteria for many years now has had a positive impact on staff health.

packed separately so sandwiches don't get soggy. You can even order online for a to-go pickup.

At the Fairway Shops at Kaanapali, 2580 Kekaa Dr. (just off the Honoapiilani Hwy.), Kaanapali. www.cjsmaui.com. © **808/667-0968.** Breakfast main courses $8–$13; lunch items $10–$17; Hana Lunch Box $14. Daily breakfast 7am–1pm, lunch/dinner 11am–8pm.

Honokowai, Kahana & Napili

Note: You'll find the following restaurants on the "Hotels & Restaurants from Kapalua to Honokowai" map on p. 55.

EXPENSIVE

Sea House Restaurant ★ PACIFIC RIM A bit dated, this oceanfront restaurant at the Napili Kai Beach Resort is a throwback to earlier days, but the view here can't be beat. Breakfast is lovely under the umbrellas outside, overlooking serene Napili Bay. The oven-baked Crater pancake is a special treat, made with custard batter. Sunset is a good time to come, too; sit at the **Whale Watcher's Bar** and order classic cocktails and poke nachos. The happy hour menu (2–4:30pm) is a terrific bargain, with delicious, filling appetizers like Kula onion soup, coconut shrimp, seared ahi, and balsamic glazed brussels sprouts just $6 to $8. Early-bird diners (5:30–6pm) will appreciate the three-course special for $38: salad, tropical dessert, and choice of macadamia nut–crusted fish, filet mignon, or shrimp scampi. The wine list is reasonable by resort standards, too.

At the Napili Kai Beach Resort, 5900 Honoapiilani Hwy. www.napilikai.com. © **808/669-1500.** Main courses $9–$16 breakfast, $12–$20 lunch, $21–$44 dinner. Daily breakfast 7am–2pm, lunch 9am–2pm, dinner 5:30–9pm, happy hour 2–4:30pm.

MODERATE

Joey's Kitchen ★★ FILIPINO/PLATE LUNCH   Joey Macadangdang ran the kitchen at Roy's for many years, winning award after award for his inventive gourmet cuisine. Now he's got two restaurants of his own: an ultra-casual spot in the Whalers Village food court (p. 104) and this slightly fancier eatery in Napili, where Joey and his wife will personally take care of you. If you've never tried Filipino food before, this is your place. Get the savory pork adobo plate, or seafood *sinigang*—a hot and sour medley of fish, clams, and shrimp. You'll find familiar favorites, too—fried Brussels sprouts, fish and chips—and enticing Hawaiian seafood specials such as ahi salad with octopus and pan-seared *shutome* (swordfish) with shiitake mushroom risotto.

In Napili Plaza Shopping Center, 5095 Napilihau St., Napili. www.joeyskitchenhimaui. com. ⓒ **808/214-5590.** Daily 11am–2pm and 4–9pm. Entrees $9–$39.

Maui Brewing Co. ★ BREWPUB   Maui's uber-popular microbrewery has expanded to Oahu, but the home is where the heart is. The Kahana brewpub offers beer flights at the bar and excellent pub fare—much of it beer-battered, and some of it unique to Hawaii, like fried *ulu* (breadfruit) wedges or kalua pork flatbread. You can try limited-release brews here, along with the company's standards: Bikini Blonde Ale, Big Swell IPA, Pineapple Mana, and a rich and chocolatey coconut porter. Note the cute lamps made from miniature kegs. This eco-friendly, community-minded business regularly donates a portion of its sales to the Maui Forest Bird Recovery Project. The Kihei tasting room features a rotation of food trucks: Teddy's Burgers and Aloha Thai Fusion are regulars.

At the Kahana Gateway Shopping Center, 4405 Honoapiilani Hwy. www.mauibrewing co.com. ⓒ **808/669-3474.** Also at 605 Lipoa Pkwy., Kihei. ⓒ **808/213-3002** ext. 105. Main courses $12–$23. Daily 11am–10pm, happy hour 3:30–5:30pm.

INEXPENSIVE

Maui Tacos ★ MEXICAN   Many years ago, Mark Ellman launched this restaurant chain, dedicated to Mexican food with "Mauitude." Now it has locations as far away as Minnesota. Ellman has since moved on, but his successors' relatively healthful take on fast food will satisfy a hungry belly. Menu choices include fish tacos, chimichangas, and "surf burritos," loaded with charbroiled chicken or slow-cooked Hawaiian pork, black beans, rice, and salsa. Other locations are at Kamaole Beach Center, 2411 S. Kihei Rd., Kihei (ⓒ **808/879-5005**); Piilani Village, 225 Piikea Ave., Kihei (ⓒ **808/875-9340**); 58 Hookele St., Kahului (ⓒ **808/793-3932**);Queen Kaahumanu Center, 275 W. Kaahumanu Ave., Kahului (ⓒ **808/871-7726**).

At Napili Plaza, 5095 Napilihau St., Lahaina. ⓒ **808/665-0222.** All items $5–$12. Mon–Sat 9am–9pm; Sun 9am–8pm.

Pizza Paradiso Mediterranean Grill ★ ITALIAN/MEDITERRANEAN The pledge on the wall at this Honokowai hot spot—to use organic, local ingredients wherever possible and treat employees like family—gives a hint to the quality of food here. The large-ish menu includes gourmet and gluten-free pizzas with terrific toppings (barbecue chicken, smoked Gouda, cilantro), chicken shawarma, lamb gyros, kabobs, pastas, and more. The kitchen makes its own meatballs, out of grass-fed Maui Cattle Company beef, and its own sauces and dressings. But save room for dessert. The tiramisu is an award-winner, and the locally made coconut gelato should be.

At the Honokowai Marketplace, 3350 Lower Honoapiilani Rd., Kaanapali. www.pizza paradiso.com. © **808/667-2929.** Main courses $9–$17; pizzas $17–$27. Daily 10am–9pm.

Slappy Cakes ★ BREAKFAST The concept for this family favorite is certainly fun—make your own pancakes on tabletop griddles—but the food is actually pretty good, too, with everything made from scratch, minimal processed foods, and biscuits baked in house. While kids will enjoy choosing which batter to use (choices include chocolate, buttermilk, gluten-free/vegan, strawberry shortcake) and which "fixins" and toppings to fancy up their flapjacks (mango, papaya, peanut butter chips, etc.), adults will appreciate the quality cocktails with Maui-distilled Ocean Vodka, housemade syrups, and fresh ingredients. Country fried steak, hearty egg scrambles, candied bacon, and breakfast burrito add protein to the menu; wash it down with Maui coffee. *Note:* The staff can also cook pancakes for you.

In Honokowai Marketplace, 3350 Lower Honoapiilani Rd., Lahaina. www.slappycakes maui.com. © **808/419-6600.** Daily 7am–1pm. Pancake stack $10 (additional toppings/ fixins charge), breakfast plates $14–$18.

Kapalua

Note: You'll find the following restaurants on the "Hotels & Restaurants from Kapalua to Honokowai" map on p. 55. In addition to the listings below, check for inexpensive plate lunches, pizza, burgers, burgers, and deli sandwiches at **Honolua Store** (http://honoluastore.com; © **808/668-9105**), near the entrance to Kapalua Resort at 502 Office Road, Lahaina. The deli is open daily from 6am to 7pm, with breakfast items served from 6 to 10:30am (some till 5pm). Prices at the **Burger Shack** (http://burgershackkapalua.com; © **808/669-6200**), on the west side of D.T. Fleming Beach, fall firmly in the moderate category, but its mouthwatering burgers (Maui Cattle Co. beef, slow-roasted pork, seared mahi or black bean; $17–$24) and decadent shakes ($10–$12) can fuel an entire day at the beach. It's open daily 11am to 4pm.

VERY EXPENSIVE

Cane & Canoe ★ PACIFIC RIM Tables spill out from under a pointed roof styled like a traditional Hawaiian canoe house. On the oceanfront side of the intimate Montage Kapalua Bay, Cane & Canoe offers a striking view of Molokai across the resort's terraced pools, and solid interpretations of surf ("canoe") and turf ("cane"), at prices in keeping with the ultra-luxurious resort setting. Seafood offers the most opportunities to go local, like togarashi-crusted ahi with Kula corn puree, edamame succotash, grilled baby romaine, and papaya mustard. Sides like lobster mac & cheese and miso-glazed grilled asparagus are family-sized, and worth adding to the hefty tab. Sunday brunch features a Bloody Mary bar and live jazz, with main courses like shrimp and grits and chicken and waffles expanding the already ample temptations of the daily breakfast menu—don't miss the buttermilk malasadas with lavender-lilikoi butter.

At Montage Kapalua Bay, 1 Bay Dr., Lahaina. www.montagehotels.com/kapaluabay/dining/cane-and-canoe. ℂ **808/662-6681.** Reservations recommended. Main courses $18–$24 breakfast, $32–$68 dinner, $18–$31 Sun brunch. Mon–Sat 7–11am and 5–9pm; Sun 7am–noon and 5–9pm.

Merriman's Kapalua ★★★ PACIFIC RIM   James Beard award–winning chef Peter Merriman, who helped launch the Hawaii Regional Cuisine movement in the 1990s, has namesake restaurants on Oahu, the Big Island, and Kauai, but none in such a picturesque location as this, the end of a rocky point with views of Lanai and Molokai. He continues to champion the farm-to-table concept here, serving butter-poached Keahole lobster with local corn and grilled Kahua Ranch lamb with garlic whipped potatoes and chili pepper green beans. You can't go wrong with one of his original preparations, like the wok-charred ahi sashimi or the Waialua chocolate purse, a delicate, plump wonton oozing with warm chocolate from Oahu. Come before sunset to soak in the sensational scenery. If twilight tables are booked, come anyway and enjoy a handcrafted mai tai with *lilikoi* foam on the large patio out on the point; live music (5:30–8:30pm nightly) adds to the atmosphere. It's an exceedingly romantic spot; don't be surprised if you see a "Just Maui'd" couple stroll by or witness a neighboring diner propose. Sunday brunch is elegant, too, with live music (10:30am–1:30pm) and more moderate prices. The spicy red chili ramen with pork belly and a poached egg is a welcome hangover cure.

1 Bay Club Place, Kapalua. www.merrimanshawaii.com. ℂ **808/669-6400.** Reservations recommended. Main courses $14–$28 brunch, $31–$68 dinner. Daily 4:30–9pm; bar menu daily 3–9pm; Sun brunch 9:30am–1:30pm.

EXPENSIVE

Banyan Tree ★★ PACIFIC RIM   This gorgeous open-air dining room on the grounds of the Ritz-Carlton, Kapalua, was undergoing major renovations at press time, with plans for reopening with an all-new menu before 2020. In the interim, the culinary team was trying out new dishes and cocktails at its Hook & Knife popup in the resort's **Ulana** restaurant, normally open for breakfast only. Hopefully standouts like the chunky Hawaiian seafood chowder and artful desserts will appear on the new Banyan Tree menu; the views and service are sure to be as rewarding as ever.

At the Ritz-Carlton, Kapalua, 1 Ritz-Carlton Dr., Lahaina. www.ritzcarlton.com/kapalua. ℂ **808/665-7096.** Reservations recommended. Dinner main courses $29–$65. Daily 5–9pm.

MODERATE

Plantation House Restaurant ★★ PACIFIC RIM   Although Chef Jojo Vasquez left in 2018 to helm the kitchen at Maui Brewing Co., the former chef's multicultural approach still applies at this dramatic destination for breakfast, lunch, or dinner, sitting amid lush golf greens with panoramic ocean views. Kona kampachi and Kauai prawns benefit from a Thai curry with snowpeas and lotus root, while Hawaiian ahi appears in Japanese style: *katsu* with baby bok choy, shiitake mushrooms, and a wasabi reduction. The "comfort food" half of the menu offers not only a ribsticking beef ragu fettucine but also a cauliflower steak. At breakfast, enjoy a bowl of flawlessly ripe tropical fruit or choose from "Six Degrees of Benediction," a half-dozen Benedicts made with such delicacies as Korean style pork belly, roasted Maui vegetables (superb), or seared ahi with wasabi hollandaise. Lunch is less intriguing, but the adoboloco fried chicken sandwich remains as a shoutout to Vasquez' Filipino heritage; it also appears on the limited grill menu, which bridges lunch and dinner with savory if pricey fare like ahi poke tacos, a bacon cheese burger, and baby-back ribs ($19–$23).

At the Kapalua Golf Club Plantation Course, 2000 Plantation Club Dr., Kapalua. www. theplantationhouse.com. ✆ **808/669-6299.** Reservations recommended. Main courses $7–$18 breakfast, $17–$21 lunch, $28–$44 dinner. Daily breakfast and lunch 8am–3pm, grill menu 3–5:30pm, dinner 5:30–9pm.

Sansei Seafood Restaurant & Sushi Bar ★★ PACIFIC RIM/SUSHI
With chef-owner D.K. Kodama's creative take on sushi rolls (mango and crab salad handrolls with Thai chili sauce and panko-crusted ahi sashimi rolls among them), Sansei's scores high with adventurous diners. But expertly sliced sashimi platters and straightforward gobo rolls will accommodate even the pickiest sushi snobs. Small and big plates are meant for sharing, though you'll fight over the last bites of misoyaki butterfish. The heavenly Dungeness crab ramen features an aromatic truffle broth flecked with cilantro, Thai basil, and jalapeños. For dessert, most people go for tempura-fried ice cream or the Granny Smith apple tart with homemade caramel sauce. *Tip:* Thursday and Friday nights, a rousing karaoke session erupts at the bar from 10pm to 1am, and sushi is 50% off. At the second location in Kihei Town Center, Kihei (✆ **808/ 879-0004**), sushi is 50% off on Sunday and Monday from 5 to 6:30pm.

600 Office Rd., Kapalua. www.sanseihawaii.com/kapalua. ✆ **808/669-6286.** Reservations recommended. Main courses $17–$41; sushi rolls $7–$17. Daily 5:30–10pm; Thurs–Fri late-night menu 10pm–1am.

Taverna ★★ ITALIAN Longtime Kapalua Chris Kaiwi (a former managing partner of Plantation House and Pineapple Grill) and his Italian-Swiss chef Roger Stettler pride themselves on "urban drinks and Italian eats," and Taverna delivers on both. Order one of the housemade pastas—tagliatelle with stewed tomato and octopus or casarecce with blue swimmer crab and spinach—and a salad with local veggies , or go big with a hearty cioppino or slow-braised Chianti beef short rib with Hamakua mushrooms. The new lunch menu includes margherita or sausage pizza by the slice ($6), burgers with local beef and housemade buns, fresh fish tacos, chicken panini, and the signature house lasagna.

2000 Village Rd., Kapalua. www.tavernamaui.com. ✆ **808/667-2426.** Main courses $16–$21 lunch, $23–$39 dinner, $12–$20 weekend brunch. Daily 2:30–5pm (happy hour and midafternoon menu) and 5:30–9pm; Mon–Fri 11am–2:30pm; Sat–Sun brunch 10am–2pm.

SOUTH MAUI

South Maui, like West Maui, is a popular visitor area, offering a range of restaurants. Some of Maui's top chefs and dining experiences can be found here, as well as affordable delis and diners. Starting in Kihei, the prices are more reasonable than that in the affluent Wailea Resort.

Kihei/Maalaea

Kihei has two **Maui Tacos**: at Kamaole Beach Center, 2411 S. Kihei Rd. (© **808/ 879-5005**), and at Piilani Village Shopping Center, 247 Piikea Ave. (© **808/ 875-9340**)

MODERATE

Cafe O'Lei Kihei ★ STEAK/SEAFOOD   Over the years, chefs Michael and Dana Pastula have opened multiple Cafe O'Lei restaurants across Maui. Every one has been a winner, and this one is nicest of all. The open, airy dining room is inviting, with hardwood floors, tables separated by sheer curtains, a big circular bar in the center of the restaurant, and a sushi bar and brick oven in back. The food is delicious and a bargain to boot. Call ahead for a midday table— locals flood this place during their lunch break. For dinner, the Maui onion soup (baked in the wood-burning oven) is a savory treat with fresh thyme and brandy. The *togarashi* (chili) and sesame-seared ahi with ginger butter sauce and wasabi aioli over steamed rice is as good as you'll find at fancier restaurants, here for nearly half the price. This is a great place to bring a group—the diverse menu offers something for everyone, from prime rib to sushi and even pizza with gluten-free crusts. *Note:* If you like Cafe O' Lei, you'll want to check out **Ami Ami** ★ (© **808/875-7522**), its nearby sibling in the Maui Coast Hotel, 2259 S. Kihei Rd. Ami Ami serves well-priced dishes such as kalua pork hash and eggs ($11) and bananas Foster pancakes ($9) daily from 7 to 11am, and an international menu of seafood, steak, and pasta ($15–$29) from 5 to 9pm.

In Rainbow Mall, 2439 S. Kihei Rd., Kihei. www.cafeoleirestaurants.com. © **808/891- 1368.** Reservations recommended. Main courses $9–$17 lunch, $19–$32 dinner. Daily 10:30am–3:30pm and 4:30–9:30pm.

Monsoon India ★ INDIAN   If there's one thing Maui could use more of, it's Indian flavors. Thank goodness for Monsoon India, a humble restaurant at the north edge of Kihei. The chicken korma here is creamy and fragrant, the chana masala spicy and satisfying. Even the simple dal curry is delightful. With tables that overlook Maalaea Bay, this serene spot is lovely just before sunset— particularly during winter when whales are jumping. You can also order a vegetarian "tiffin" picnic for two in stacked metal containers for $35 (plus $30 refundable deposit.) *Note:* The open-air dining room is closed when it rains. Monsoon's new crosstown rival, **Kamana Kitchen,** in Kihei Town Shopping Center, 1881 S. Kihei Rd. (www.kamanakitchen.com; © **808/879-7888**), is also worth a visit, especially for its Sunday lunch buffet 11am to 3pm.

In the Menehune Shores Bldg., 760 S. Kihei Rd., Kihei. www.monsoonindiamaui.com. © **808/875-6666.** Main courses $17–$28. Daily 5–9pm; Wed–Sun 11:30am–2pm.

Restaurants in South Maui

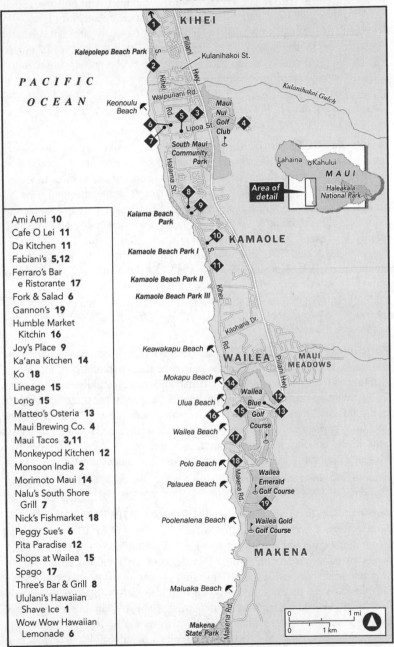

KIHEI

Kalepolepo Beach Park

Kulanihakoi St.

Filani

Kihei Hwy.

Kulanihakoi Gulch

PACIFIC

OCEAN

Keonoulu Beach

Waipuilani Rd.

S. Kihei Rd.

Lipoa St.

Maui Nui Golf Club

South Maui Community Park

Halama St.

Kalama Beach Park

Kamaole Beach Park I

KAMAOLE

S. Kihei Rd.

Kamaole Beach Park II

Kamaole Beach Park III

Kilohana Dr.

Keawakapu Beach

Piilani Hwy.

WAILEA

MAUI MEADOWS

Mokapu Beach

Wailea Blue Golf Course

Ulua Beach

Wailea Beach

Polo Beach

Makena Rd.

Wailea Emerald Golf Course

Palauea Beach

Poolenalena Beach

Wailea Gold Golf Course

MAKENA

Maluaka Beach

Makena Rd.

Makena State Park

Lahaina Kahului

Area of detail

MAUI

Haleakala National Park

0   1 mi
0   1 km

Ami Ami **10**
Cafe O Lei **11**
Da Kitchen **11**
Fabiani's **5,12**
Ferraro's Bar e Ristorante **17**
Fork & Salad **6**
Gannon's **19**
Humble Market Kitchin **16**
Joy's Place **9**
Ka'ana Kitchen **14**
Ko **18**
Lineage **15**
Long **15**
Matteo's Osteria **13**
Maui Brewing Co. **4**
Maui Tacos **3,11**
Monkeypod Kitchen **12**
Monsoon India **2**
Morimoto Maui **14**
Nalu's South Shore Grill **7**
Nick's Fishmarket **18**
Peggy Sue's **6**
Pita Paradise **12**
Shops at Wailea **15**
Spago **17**
Three's Bar & Grill **8**
Ululani's Hawaiian Shave Ice **1**
Wow Wow Hawaiian Lemonade **6**

INEXPENSIVE

Joy's Place ★ HEALTHY DELI Nourish yourself with nutritious, delicious meals at this small cafe, where the emphasis is on healthful living. For breakfast, rev your engine with an açai bowl or a still-warm spelt muffin. Soups are made daily, and sandwiches are huge, with thick slices of nitrate-free turkey piled onto sprouted grain bread—or, if you prefer, packed into a collard-green wrap. Most ingredients are organic.

In the Island Surf Bldg., 1993 S. Kihei Rd. (entrance on Auhana St.), Kihei. www.joys placemauihawaii.com. ℂ **808/879-9258.** All items under $12. Mon–Fri 7:30am–4pm; Sat 7:30am–2pm.

Nalu's South Shore Grill ★ AMERICAN Casual, noisy, and a lot of fun, this restaurant fills an important niche in Kihei. Order at the counter from a wide range of menu items—everything from chicken and waffles to a commendable Cubano sandwich. It's a great place to bring the family or big groups. Extra touches show that the owners care about customer satisfaction, from friendly and attentive service and a choice of flavored waters to terrific nightly live music, including a Saturday dinner show with local rock stars Barry Flanagan and Eric Gilliom and a Wednesday dinner show with Hawaiian music star Amy Hanaialii Gilliom. It's $25 for the show only and $55 for show plus a three-course meal. Reservations required.

1280 S. Kihei Rd. (in Azeka's II), Kihei. www.nalusmaui.com. ℂ **808/891-8650.** Main courses $10–$13 breakfast, $9–$17 lunch/dinner. Daily breakfast 8:30am–2:30pm, lunch/dinner 11am–9:30pm.

Peggy Sue's ★ AMERICAN This 1950s-style diner has oodles of charm and is a swell place to spring for the best chocolate malt on the island. You'll also find sodas, shakes, floats, egg creams, milkshakes, and Roselani gourmet ice cream. Old-fashioned soda-shop stools, an ELVIS PRESLEY BOULEVARD sign, and jukeboxes on every Formica table serve as a backdrop for the famous burgers made with Maui beef, brushed with teriyaki sauce and served with all the goodies. Turkey, seafood, or vegan patties are also options; the fries are great, too. Classic cars fill the lot for a Saturday show from 6 to 9pm.

In Azeka Place II Shopping Center, 1279 S. Kihei Rd., Kihei. ℂ **808/214-6786.** Burgers $12–$16; plate lunches $14–$16. Sun–Thurs 11am–9pm; Fri–Sat 11am–10pm.

Three's Bar & Grill ★★ PACIFIC RIM/SOUTHWESTERN In 2009, culinary-school and surfing buddies Travis Morrin, Cody Christopher, and Jaron Blosser figured a catering company would allow them time to catch waves in between kitchen duties. But demand for their varied cuisines—Southwestern, Pacific Rim, and Hawaiian—soon prompted them to open a full-blown causal restaurant, not too far from the surf, with affordable breakfast, lunch, and dinner options. Panko-crusted ahi roll (among a huge sushi menu), kalua pork quesadilla, and Hawaiian-style ribs represent satisfying signature dishes, with hot chocolate lava cake a popular finisher. Surfboards, naturally, greet you at the door, with impressive wave photography in the lounge and oil paintings by local artists in the dining room; a large monkeypod tree shades the pleasant outdoor patio. *Note:* The chefs' spinoff in Kihei, the somewhat healthier-themed **Fork & Salad** ★ in Azeka Shopping Center, 1278 S. Kihei Rd. (https://forkandsaladmaui.com; ✆ **808/793-3256**), has also won acclaim, recently sprouting a second location in Kahului.

In Kihei Kalama Village, 1945 S. Kihei Rd., Kihei. http://threesbarandgrill.com. ✆ **808/ 879-3133.** Main courses $9–$18 breakfast, $14–$20 lunch, $16–$36 dinner. Mon–Fri 8:30–11am, Sat–Sun 8am–11am; daily lunch 11am–4pm; dinner 5–10pm; happy hour 3–6pm and 9–10pm.

Wow Wow Hawaiian Lemonade ★ CAFE/JUICE BAR   The cashiers at this permanent lemonade stand are a testament to their product: sweet, wholesome, and helpful. Choose from an array of fresh-squeezed lime- and lemonades made with local honey, strawberry, *lilikoi*, watermelon, dragonfruit, mint, and basil. Purchase a custom Mason jar (complete with cozy and a reusable straw), and your future drinks are discounted. Trust us, you'll want to return as often as possible. The açai and pitaya bowls are enormous and generously loaded with goodies: coconut custard, cacao, bee pollen, taro, and apple bananas. Smoothies have similar ingredients, blended with sprouted almond or coconut milk.

In Azeka Shopping Center, 1279 S. Kihei Rd., Kihei. www.wowwowhawaiianlemonade. com. ✆ **808/344-0319.** All items under $12. Daily 8am–4pm.

Wailea

Note: You'll find the restaurants in this section on the "Restaurants in South Maui" map (p. 111). Most resort restaurants offer free valet parking with validation.

The **Shops at Wailea** (www.theshopsatwailea.com), with a sprawling location off 3750 Wailea Alanui Dr. between the Grand Wailea Resort and Wailea Beach Resort, offers 1 hour of free parking, or 4 hours with a validated $25 purchase. That's more than enough to visit one of its several chain restaurants and cafes, such as **Ruth's Chris Steak House, Tommy Bahama, Honolulu Coffee Company, Cheeseburger Island Style, and Lappert's Ice Cream.** More memorable dining can be found in the open-air mall at **Lineage** ★★★ and **Longhi's** ★ (see below); for drinking and late-night noshing, pop into the **Pint & Cork** ★ (www.thepintandcork.com; ✆ **808/727-2038**), a kid-friendly tavern that serves sturdy pub grub and an impressive bevy of alcoholic beverages from 11am to 2am daily.

VERY EXPENSIVE

Morimoto Maui ★★★ JAPANESE/PERUVIAN   Iron Chef Masaharu Morimoto's poolside, oceanview restaurant is sedate and spare, directing all of the attention to the culinary fireworks. The immaculate kitchen houses a space-age freezer full of fish bought at auction, and a rice polisher that ensures that every grain is perfect. The tasting menu starts with Morimoto-san's signature appetizer, the toro tartare ($29). Balanced on ice, it's edible artwork. A tilted rectangle offers up a delectable smear of minced Kindai bluefin tuna, accented by colorful stripes of condiments: black nori paste, wasabi, crème fraîche, Maui onion, and tiny yellow rice crackers. A chilled Japanese mountain peach serves as a palate cleanser. The chef's tribute to Maui features locally caught opakapaka (pink snapper) in Thai curry with *pohole* fern, plump mussels, and sushi rice, topped with grilled bananas that balance the curry's heat. Everything is indulgent here, including a *chawanmushi* (Japanese custard) flavored with foie gras and topped with slivered duck breast. Try the multi-course *omakase,* the chef's tasting menu ($140 per person), to experience the widest variety. The decadent lunch features flatbreads, sushi, Asian-inspired sandwiches, and many of the items served at dinner.

At the Andaz Maui, 3550 Wailea Alanui Dr., Wailea. www.maui.andaz.hyatt.com. ℂ **808/ 573-1234.** Main courses $19–$39 lunch, $36–$95 dinner. Daily 11:30am–2pm and 5:30–9pm; sushi (at the bar) 2–5pm.

Nick's Fishmarket Maui ★★ SEAFOOD   It's hard to beat the fantasy setting on the south Maui shoreline: Here's the place to bring your sweetie to enjoy the moon rise and the sweet smell of the stephanotis growing on the terrace. Fans love this classic seafood restaurant, which sticks to the tried and true, with just a few culinary innovations here and there. The menu features great fresh seafood like Nick's iconic cioppino, Hawaiian spiny lobster tail, Moroccan spiced salmon with a Hana avocado relish, and scallops and braised pork belly adobo with a rich risotto. Non-fish lovers will appreciate the large steaks and subtly updated dishes like roasted chicken breast with Italian sausage, goat cheese, and polenta, or the rack of lamb with a jalapeño-mint vinaigrette and Maui pineapple jam.

At the Fairmont Kea Lani Maui, 4100 Wailea Alanui Dr., Wailea. www.nicksfishmarket maui.com. ℂ **808/879-7224.** Reservations recommended. Main courses $29–$65. Daily 5:30–9:30pm.

Spago ★★★ ASIAN FUSION/NEW AMERICAN   At Wolfgang Puck's restaurant off the posh lobby of the Four Seasons, dishes are flavorful but light—not burdened by heavy sauces. If the chef tried to remove the ahi sesame-miso cones from the menu, fans would probably riot. This appetizer is perfection: bright red spicy ahi spooned into a crunchy, sweet, and nutty cone and topped with flying fish roe. The Thai coconut soup with kaffir lime and Keahole lobster is a gourmet version of the traditional staple—and it excels on every level. The Chinois lamb chops are worth the steep price tag. During truffle season, fragrant shavings of black or white truffles can be added to your dish. Seating hangs over the elegant pool with Pacific views (book tables no later than 5:45pm for best views), and the bartenders pour handcrafted libations with clever names like Pins and Needles (Hendrick's gin, rosemary, lemon, and cucumber) and Grin and Bare It (Tanqueray gin, lychee, and shiso).

At the Four Seasons Resort Maui at Wailea, 3900 Wailea Alanui Dr., Wailea. https:// wolfgangpuck.com/dining/spago-maui. ℂ **808/879-2999.** Reservations recommended. Main courses $39–$135. Daily 5:30–9:30pm. Bar with appetizers daily 5–11pm.

EXPENSIVE

Ferraro's Bar e Ristorante ★★ ITALIAN   The stunning location—overlooking Wailea Beach with an unobstructed view of the West Maui Mountains—sets the stage for a romantic (if pricey) repast, whether you dine beneath sun-splashed umbrellas by day or the starry sky at night. For lunch, indulge your inner celebrity: Sip a Prosecco or pineapple mojito and snack on a Kona lobster melt or tartufo pizza with Hamakua mushrooms pulled from the wood-burning oven. As the sun sinks into the Pacific, the atmosphere transforms. Live classical music (Tues–Sat 6:30–9:30pm) casts a spell over the terraced dining area. The breadbaskets are sumptuous, freshly baked with flecks of olive. You have your choice of two sea salts to season your meal, should you so desire. The entrees are not particularly adventurous—papardelle with lamb shank ragú, or seared ahi with white beans—but they are flawless. The desserts, which change often, are creative and worth every calorie.

At the Four Seasons Resort Maui at Wailea, 3900 Wailea Alanui Dr., Wailea. www.fourseasons.com/maui/dining. ℂ **808/874-8000.** Reservations recommended. Main courses $19–$28 lunch, $34–$52 dinner. Daily 11:30am–4pm and 5:30–9pm; bar 11am–9pm.

Gannon's ★★ HAWAII REGIONAL AMERICAN   This clubhouse on the Wailea Gold golf course has spectacular views in every direction, as well as the gourmet-style comfort food of award-winning chef Bev Gannon—the culinary force behind **Haliimaile General Store** (p. 119). For lunch, linger over the Haiku caprese with pistachio pesto or the fish tacos with taro flour tortillas, fresh catch, blackened shrimp, feta, and mole sauce. At night, when the view isn't a lure, it's fun to sit at the sparkly **Red Bar** and nibble on lobster spring rolls or kung pao calamari. Handcrafted cocktails include the refreshing Wailea Spritz (Aperol and Prosecco with a dash of passionfruit puree) or the Road to Hana (Maui Ocean organic vodka with guava and ginger liqueurs, soda, and mint.)

At the Wailea Gold Golf Course, 100 Wailea Golf Club Dr., Wailea. www.gannonsrestaurant.com. ℂ **808/875-8080.** Reservations recommended for dinner. Main courses $14–$28 lunch, $26–$42 dinner. Daily 11am–3pm and 5–9pm; happy hour 3–8pm.

Humble Market Kitchin ★★ HAWAII REGIONAL   For once, the ocean views live up to the food, and not the other way around. With Humble Market Kitchin, celebrity chef Roy Yamaguchi pays tribute to summers spent volunteering in his grandfather's general store. Opened in late 2016 as part of the Wailea Beach Resort's $100-million renovation, the restaurant serves up reimagined Hawaiian comfort foods: poke (raw, seasoned fish), misoyaki butterfish with forbidden rice, and ramen loaded with pork belly, dumplings, a sous vide egg, and lip-smacking sesame broth. Wander around the menu sampling the steamed dumplings, crispy chicken wings, and Szechuan babyback ribs just as if you were a teen snacking at your favorite grandpa's counter—only in this instance, "grandpa" is one of Hawaii's greatest chefs. Breakfast is a lavish affair here, with Hawaiian sweet-bread French toast slathered in whipped maple butter and *lilikoi* syrup—or, for the health-conscious, avocado toast on Blue Door sourdough.

At the Wailea Beach Resort, 3700 Wailea Alanui Dr., Wailea. www.hmkmaui.com. ✆ **808/879-4655.** Reservations recommended. Main courses $16–$25 breakfast, $34 breakfast buffet ($17 ages 12 and under), $22–$57 dinner. Daily 6:30–11am and 5–11pm.

Ka'ana Kitchen ★★★ HAWAII REGIONAL   You can hardly tell where the dining room ends and the kitchen begins in this bright, open restaurant. Sit ringside where you can watch Executive Chef Isaac Bancaco (or one of his talented team members) in action. Start off with a hand-mixed cocktail and the grilled octopus: fat chunks of tender meat tossed with frisée, watercress, and goat cheese. The ahi tataki is beautiful: ruby-red tuna, heirloom tomato, and fresh burrata topped with black salt and nasturtium petals. Don't be thrown by Bancaco's grid menu. Treat it like a gourmet bingo card; every combo is a winner. Bitters & Bites ($125) pairs a three-course meal with cocktails made with your choice of spirit; reserve at least 24 hours in advance for the 6pm-only seating. Breakfasts here are among the island's best, with local poached eggs, Molokai sweet potatoes, and creative bento boxes packed with fried rice and pickled vegetables. The $47 buffet grants you access to the kitchen's novel chilled countertops, which are stocked with every delicacy and fresh juice you could imagine.

At the Andaz Maui, 3550 Wailea Alanui Dr., Wailea. www.hyatt.com/en-US/hotel/hawaii/andaz-maui-at-wailea-resort/oggaw. ✆ **808/573-1234.** $49 breakfast buffet; main courses (a la carte) $21–$33 breakfast, $25–$57 dinner. Daily breakfast 6:30–11am and dinner 5:30–9pm.

Ko ★★★ HAWAII REGIONAL   Executive Chef Tylun Pang pays tribute to Maui's plantation heritage by incorporating the cuisines of the sugarcane fields' labor force—Hawaiian, Filipino, Portuguese, Korean, Puerto Rican, Chinese, and Japanese—into gourmet dishes with elegant presentations. The "ahi on the rock" appetizer features glistening squares of garnet-hued tuna accompanied by a hot rock on which to sear them; once done, dunk it in the delicious orange-ginger miso sauce. Other starter options include Pang's family recipe for Filipino *lumpia* (spring roll with green papaya, chicken, and mushroom, accompanied by a spicy sauce), Portuguese bean soup, and Kobe beef poke. Lobster tempura, ti-leaf-wrapped and steamed island fresh catch, and ginger hoisin BBQ pork chop with Chinese sausage fried rice tempt at dinner, but note that many entrees veer into the very expensive realm (over $45). Lunch isn't a bargain either, but it's delicious nonetheless—try the grilled ahi sandwich, kimchee fried rice, or island shrimp saimin (another Pang family recipe, with bone broth, char siu pork, noodles, and egg.)

At the Fairmont Kea Lani, 4100 Wailea Alanui Dr., Wailea. www.korestaurant.com. ✆ **808/875-2210.** Reservations recommended. Main courses $21–$28 lunch, $28–$62 dinner. Daily 11:30am–2:30pm and 5–9pm; bar 11am–10pm, happy hour 3–5pm.

Lineage ★★★ MODERN ISLAND   *Top Chef* fan favorite and Hilo native Sheldon Simeon has a long history on the Maui culinary scene, but he didn't have a restaurant of his own until he opened the humble but playful, lunch-only *Tin Roof* (p.91) in Kahului in 2016. In late 2018, he expanded his reach, geographically and artistically, with the dinner-only Lineage in the Shops at Wailea. Paying homage to his hometown and the local tradition of family feasts, Simeon maintains his playfulness but elevates his style with assurance. A cart with his interpretations of favorite local snacks—including spiced boiled peanuts, *pipikaula* (beef jerky) with Korean *kochujang* sauce, and a garden-vegetable poke—cruises the cozy dining room; you can also order appetizers like adobo-spiced *chicharon* (Filipino fried pork skins) and Bottom of the Plate Lunch—shaved cabbage with smoked beef fat, kalbi dressing, and mayo. For mains, the cold ginger chicken with green onion pesto or pork and peas (a family recipe) will please less adventurous diners, but I love the smoky sweetness of the squid luau (charred octopus in creamed taro leaf with coconut candy). Couples or small groups can order the whole huli huli roasted chicken ($65), or the beef shank and short-rib Lauya combo ($70). "Filipino cereal" wins the prize for the most inventive dessert on the island: a mix of crackers, milk, and avocado, it's Simeon's take on the breakfast cereal of childhood friends. *Note:* The full dinner menu is also available at the bar. Walk-ins are welcomed, but it's best to reserve (via OpenTable) when you can.

At the Shops at Wailea, 3750 Wailea Alanui Dr., Wailea. www.lineagemaui.com. ⓒ **808/879-8800.** Reservations recommended. Main courses $21–$28 lunch, $28–$62 dinner. Daily 5–11pm (last seating 10pm).

Longhi's ★ ITALIAN/SEAFOOD   Breakfast, lunch, and the bar are the enduring attractions of this breezy restaurant in the Shops at Wailea. The largely Italian-driven dinner menu—eggplant Parmigiana, seafood linguine, ahi au poivre—isn't disappointing, just rather pricey, although it does come with divine cheesy jalapeño pizza bread baked in-house. At breakfast, the lobster eggs Benedict ($25) is especially sumptuous, served on thick slices of grilled Italian bread; you can also order lobster in a three-egg omelet for the same price. Slightly less decadent is a healthful juice like the Green Destiny (cucumber, kale, celery, mint, watermelon, citrus, and ginger). For your French-press coffee, you have the choice of several Maui-grown beans from Kaana-pali and Kipahulu. Lunchtime sandwiches—Maui beef hamburger on brioche, or the open-face ahi tuna melt—are solid choices, too. At the bar, a tropical martini with coconut vodka or a li hing mui rim pairs well with happy hour specials ($8–$10) such as ahi fish tacos or an island ceviche with monchong and avocado. *Note:* There's also a Longhi's (the original in this family-owned chain) in Lahaina, as well as on Oahu.

At the Shops at Wailea, 3750 Wailea Alanui Dr., Wailea. www.longhis.com. ⓒ **808/891-8883.** Main courses $11–$25 breakfast, $14–$45 lunch, $20–$50 dinner. Daily 8am–9:30pm, happy hour 3–6pm. In Old Lahaina Center: 888 Front St., Lahaina. ⓒ **808/667-2288.** Mon–Fri 8am–10pm; Sat–Sun 7:30am–10pm. Daily happy hour 3–5pm.

MODERATE

Fabiani's ★ ITALIAN At the top of Wailea, this little bistro serves the most affordable breakfast, lunch, and dinner in the neighborhood. Come here early in your stay because you'll want to return. The Italian-born chef turns out tasty pastas and pizzas for literally half the price of spots down the road. Sate your hunger with Chef Lorenzo's meat lasagna—a rich medley of sausage, ground beef, pork, marinara, and béchamel. Make your own thin-crust Italian-style pizza with an array of gourmet toppings—a selection you won't find elsewhere on island—including mascarpone, Kalamata olives, shrimp, and pancetta. Gluten-free crusts are available for an extra $4. The bakery offers tempting French macaroons: pistachio and caramel sea salt, among others. A second location in Kihei (95 E. Lipoa St.; ⓒ **808/874-0888**) is open daily for breakfast (7–11am), lunch (11am–4pm), and dinner (4–9:30pm).

In the Wailea Gateway Plaza, 34 Wailea Gateway Pl., Wailea. www.fabianis.com. ⓒ **808/874-1234.** Main courses $18–$37; pizza $13–$18. Daily 4–9pm; happy hour 4–6pm.

Matteo's Osteria ★★ ITALIAN/SEAFOOD Although Wailea is hardly lacking in Italian eateries, it'd be a shame to miss this gracious restaurant and wine bar, nearly hidden in a small shopping strip just below the Residence Inn. Some 30 wines, mostly from Italy and Northern California, are available by the glass, while the 200-plus list of wines by the bottle includes rare Amarone, Barolo, and other Italian varietals from amiable chef-owner Matteo Mistura's personal collection. But you don't have to be an oenophile to appreciate the chef's deft blend of Italian cuisine and local ingredients, especially fresh fish. His poke Italiano adds black-ink rice chips, fennel, and cucumber foam to the more traditional ahi tuna and avocado, while Maui Cattle Co. beef, a tomato ragu, and homemade pasta anchor the lasagna. The catch of the day comes adorned with heirloom cherry tomatoes, Carnaroli risotto cake, mushroom trifolati, and an artichoke-thyme puree. For lighter eaters, Chef Matteo's salads can't be beat. The lounge offers wonderful happy-hour specials, all $8 apiece, from Italian and tropical cocktails to 5-oz. wine pours, along with savory items such as fried calamari, potato-pesto pizza, and kale quinoa salad with ricotta salata and pumpkin seeds.

161 Wailea Ike Pl., Wailea. www.matteosmaui.com. ⓒ **808/891-8466.** Main courses $26–$42; pizzas $18–$22. Daily 5–9:30pm; happy hour Mon–Fri 3–5pm, Sat–Sun 4–5pm.

Monkeypod Kitchen ★★ AMERICAN/LOCAL CUISINE Celebrated chef Peter Merriman's more casual outpost spotlights local, organic produce, pasture-raised beef, and sustainably caught fish—all of which translate here to better-tasting food. Pull up a seat at the lively bar here and enjoy *saimin* (soup with locally made noodles), bulgogi pork tacos, or Waipoli greens with beet and chèvre. The expansive drink menu is among the island's best—offering everything from fresh coconut water, kombucha, and "shrubs" (soda or juice with fresh muddled herbs) to award-winning handcrafted cocktails (especially the passionfruit foam-topped mai tai). The dessert menu is less inspired; the cream pies are only so-so. There's live music at 1, 4, and 7pm daily. *Note:* A second location at the Whalers Village shopping mall in Kaanapali serves the same fare, with similar entertainment.

In Wailea Gateway Center, 10 Wailea Gateway Place, Wailea. (C) **808/891-2322.** Also in Whalers Village, 2435 Kaanapali Pkwy., Kaanapali. (C) **808/878-6763.** www.monkeypod kitchen.com. Main courses $17–$41. Daily 10:30am–11pm; happy hour 3–5:30pm and 9–11pm.

Pita Paradise ★ GREEK/MEDITERRANEAN For fresh, flavorful Greek food cooked to order and served with creamy tzatziki sauce and rice pilaf, head to this oasis in Wailea. Owner Johnny Arabatzis, Jr., catches his own fish, which he prepares with dill scallionaise and roasted red peppers. The lamb in the gyros is free-range and the pita bread housemade; the latter provides the crust for a filling chicken Parmesan. Salads are vast, and even better with the grilled catch of the day. A trickling fountain serenades the tables in the courtyard, which sometimes hosts live music and belly dancers. The baklava ice cream cake is exquisite—though definitcly enough to share. The 7-inch "pitza's" at happy hour make a great snack to tide one over between meals.

In Wailea Gateway Center, 34 Wailea Ike Dr., Wailea. www.pitaparadisehawaii.com. (C) **808/879-7177.** Main courses $15–$27 lunch, $18–$34 dinner. Daily 11am–9:30pm; happy hour 3–6pm.

Haliimaile & Pukalani (on the Way to Upcountry Maui)

Away from the beaches, the Upcountry Maui area is generally a residential area that offers excellent dining opportunities. Here's your chance to sample Maui's top food without the resort areas' marked-up prices. If you're in a hurry going down or up the slopes of Haleakala, stop by **Pukalani Superette** ★, 15 Makawao Ave., Pukalani (http://pukalanisuperette.com; (C) **808/572-7616**), a long-running family-owned grocery that also prepares hot and cold island-style fare daily, including chili chicken and chow fun noodles. Order from the deli counter or pick up a ready-to-go bento box; it's open Monday to Saturday 5:30am to 9pm and Sunday 7am to 8pm.

EXPENSIVE

Haliimaile General Store ★★ HAWAII REGIONAL/AMERICAN Bev Gannon, one of the pioneering chefs of Hawaii Regional Cuisine, brought her gourmet comfort food to this renovated plantation store in rural Haliimaile in 1988. It was a gamble then; now it's one of the island's most beloved restaurants. Menu items reflect island cuisine with hints of Texas, from which Gannon hails, and most lunch items are moderately priced. Smoky baby-back pork ribs ($18) come with Asian slaw, while the brie and grape quesadilla ($14) includes cilantro-macadamia-nut pesto and sweet pea guacamole. At dinner, it's best to stick to one rich item like the coconut seafood curry ($38) or the crispy roast half duck ($36) rather than ordering several to share. That rule does not apply to the sashimi Napoleon, however. The creamy wasabi vinaigrette that the waiter pours atop your stack of ahi tartare, smoked salmon, and wonton chips is rich but worth the indulgence. Sound ricochets in this vintage camp store, with its polished wooden floors, high ceilings, and open kitchen. It's quieter in the back room, which is worth exploring anyway for its rotating exhibit of paintings by top local artists. Vegetarians: Ask for the extensive vegetarian dinner menu.

900 Haliimaile Rd., Haliimaile. www.hgsmaui.com. © **808/572-2666.** Reservations recommended. Main courses $14–$28 lunch, $29–$44 dinner. Mon–Fri 11am–2:30pm; daily 5–9pm.

Makawao
MODERATE
Casanova Italian Restaurant & Deli ★ ITALIAN   This upcountry institution serves wonderful Italian fare at a sit-down restaurant and an attached cozy deli. The deli serves simple breakfasts (omelets with fresh mozzarella, and buttermilk muffins and bagels loaded with lox and capers) and terrific sandwiches for lunch. Try the New York meatball on a baguette, or the goat cheese and eggplant on focaccia. The deli's outdoor barstool seating makes a great perch for observing the Makawao traffic—always entertaining. The restaurant proper opens for lunch and serves a range of pastas and pizzas baked in a brick oven, and tables are set with white linens. At dinner, snack on freshly baked focaccia with olive oil and balsamic vinegar while waiting for your entree; the truffle ravioli with sage sauce, with plump housemade pillows of spinach and cheese, is exceptional. Pizza is served until at least 10pm, and on many nights of the week the dance floor erupts to the sounds of live salsa or reggae music or visiting DJs—dinner earns you free admission. Check the website for the entertainment calendar.

1188 Makawao Ave., Makawao. www.casanovamaui.com. © **808/572-0220.** Reservations recommended for dinner. Restaurant: Lunch items $12–$26; dinner main courses $14–$46. Mon–Tues and Thurs–Sat lunch 11:30am–2pm; daily dinner 5–9:30pm. Dancing Wed, Fri–Sat 10pm–1:30am. Deli: Breakfast Mon–Sat 7:30–11am, Sun 8:30–11am; lunch Mon–Sat 7:30am–5:30pm, Sun 8:30am–5:30pm.

Market Fresh Bistro ★ GLOBAL/MEDITERRANEAN   At this off-the-beaten-path bistro, Chef Justin Pardo steadfastly adheres to the locavore ethic: Nearly everything he serves is grown within a few miles of the kitchen. Because of this, the menu changes daily. Salads are exceptional here, with slivered rainbow radishes, heirloom carrots, and greens picked literally that morning. Past entrees have included Kupaa Farm taro-crusted fish with asparagus in fennel-saffron tomato jus, and lamb ragout atop 2-inch-wide pasta ribbons. Breakfasts in the shaded courtyard will transport you to the French countryside: Thick slices of wheat toast slathered in house-made *lilikoi* (passionfruit) jam accompany omelets stuffed with goat cheese, mushrooms, and pesto. The high-quality ingredients are fresh off the farm, and you can taste it. On Thursday night, the team serves prix-fixe farm dinners, seven courses for $75 (more with wine pairing), with occasional tapas and wine tastings instead.

3620 Baldwin Ave., Makawao. www.marketfreshbistro.com © **808/572-4877.** Reservations recommended for dinner. Breakfast $10–$13; lunch $10–$15; dinner $28–$34. Tues–Sat 9–11am and 11:30am–3pm; Sun 9am–2pm; Thurs prix-fixe 6–8:30pm.

INEXPENSIVE

T. Komoda Store and Bakery ★ BAKERY   The coveted cream puffs (filled with vanilla or mocha cream) are just one of the temptations at this century-old family bakery. Stick donuts encrusted with macadamia nuts, Chantilly cakes, guava *malasadas*, fruit pies, and butter rolls keep loyal customers coming back. Old-timers know to arrive before noon or miss out. Bring cash and note the odd business hours.

3674 Baldwin Ave., Makawao. © **808/572-7261.** Pastries $1–$2, pies and cakes $8–$15. Mon, Tues, Thurs, Fri 7am–4pm; Sat 7am–2pm.

Kula (at the Base of Haleakala National Park)
MODERATE

Kula Bistro ★★ HAWAII REGIONAL/AMERICAN   Longtime high-end caterer Luciano Zanon, who grew up working a family-owned trattoria in Venice, returned to his roots with wife Chantal by opening this casual bistro in 2012. If you can pull your eyes away from the dessert and pastry case, at breakfast you'll find expertly executed eggs Benedict and frittata, plus local favorites like loco moco (eggs/beef patty/rice/gravy) and fried rice with eggs. The lunch and dinner menu reflects European techniques and island ingredients, from the calamari steak with lemon beurre blanc to the grilled mahi sandwich with pesto aoli, kalua pork panini, and crowd-pleasers like pasta, pizza, and prime rib. Alcohol is bring your own, with no corkage fee.

4566 Lower Kula Rd., Kula. www.kulabistro.com. © **808/871-2960.** Main courses $10–$18 breakfast, $15–$48 lunch and dinner; $16–$23 pizza. Mon–Sat 7:30am–10:30am; daily 11am–8pm.

La Provence ★★ BAKERY/FRENCH/PIZZA   Hidden away up in Kula is a family-owned French bakery that's worth driving across the island for. It's also worth overlooking the service, which can be slow and inconsistent. Every item stashed in the bakery case is exquisite. Arrive well before noon or risk watching the last almond croissants and mango blueberry scones float out the door without you. Dine in the garden courtyard beside cyclists who've worked up appetites circumnavigating the island. The crepes, filled with Kula vegetables and goat cheese or salmon and spinach, have a secret addictive ingredient: *béchamel* sauce. Eggs Benedict are served with perfect roasted potatoes and wild greens drizzled in a transcendent *lilikoi* balsamic dressing. For lunch, try the marvelous duck confit salad or roast chicken sandwich with melted Brie. For dinner, the filet mignon in puff pastry and lamb chops with peppercorn sauce are standouts. Bring cash; there isn't an ATM for miles and they don't take credit cards.

3158 Lower Kula Hwy., Kula. www.laprovencemaui.com. ℂ **808/878-1313.** Main courses $11–$13 breakfast (crepes $4–$13), $11–$13 lunch, $26–$32 dinner. Cash or check only. Wed–Fri 8:30–11am and 11:30am–2pm; Wed–Sun 5–9pm, brunch Sat–Sun 9am–2pm.

INEXPENSIVE

Grandma's Coffee House ★ COFFEEHOUSE/AMERICAN   Alfred Franco's grandmother started growing and roasting coffee in remote and charming Keokea back in 1918, when she was 16 years old. Five generations later, this family-run cafe is still fueled by homegrown Haleakala beans and frequented by local *paniolo* (cowboys). Line up at the busy counter for espresso, home-baked pastries, hot oatmeal, scrambled eggs, or, on Sundays, a variety of eggs Benedict served on a cornmeal waffle. Rotating lunch specials include spinach lasagna, teriyaki chicken, and beef stew. Sit out on the scenic lanai where the air is always the perfect temperature and listen to a Hawaiian guitarist serenade his bygone sweethearts. Pick up a few lemon squares and a slice of pumpkin bread to go.

9232 Kula Hwy. (Hwy. 37), Keokea. www.grandmascoffee.com. ℂ **808/878-2140.** Most items under $10. Daily 7am–5pm.

Kula Sandalwoods Cafe ★ AMERICAN   Chef Eleanor Loui Worth, a graduate of the Culinary Institute of America, makes hollandaise sauce every morning from fresh upcountry egg yolks, sweet butter, and Meyer lemons, which her family grows in the yard above the cafe. This is Kula cuisine, with produce from the backyard and everything made from scratch, including French toast with home-baked Portuguese sweet bread, hotcakes with fresh fruit, open-faced country omelets, hamburgers drenched in a special cheese sauce made with grated sharp cheddar, a killer kalua-pork sandwich, a grilled ono sandwich, and an outstanding veggie burger. Dine in the gazebo or on the terrace, with dazzling views in all directions—including, in the spring, a yard dusted with lavender jacaranda flowers and a hillside ablaze with fields of orange *akulikuli* blossoms.

15427 Haleakala Hwy. (Hwy. 377), Kula. www.kulasandalwoods.com. ℂ **808/878-3523.** Main courses $9–$15 breakfast, $8–$15 lunch. Mon–Fri 7:30am–3pm; Sun 7:30–noon.

EAST MAUI: ON THE ROAD TO HANA

The residential areas on the road to Hana range from the eclectic eateries in Paia to the gourmet cuisine at Colleen's in the Haiku Cannery to Mama's Fish House, which serves excellent fresh fish (at astronomical prices) in the oceanside community of Kuau.

Paia

MODERATE

Charley's Restaurant ★ AMERICAN   Named for Charley P. Woofer, a spotted Great Dane, this North Shore institution serves food and music to the masses. The downtown Paia hangout does double duty as a power-breakfast fuel station for windsurfers and an after-dark saloon with live music and DJs. It's a decent place to grab a bite before heading out to Hana. For breakfast, you'll find the standards: omelets, pancakes, biscuits and gravy. Lunch is half-pound burgers made from locally raised beef, fish and chicken sandwiches, salads, and pizza. Dinner is grilled fish and steak—hearty, but nothing exciting. Sushi chef Tom Kamijo spices it up a bit with his **sushi bar** (Tues–Sat 5–10pm), serving small plates, bowls, sashimi, and maki rolls, like the Fireball—spicy tuna and pickled radish.

142 Hana Hwy., Paia. www.charleysmaui.com. ⓒ **808/579-8085.** Main courses $10–$26 breakfast, $15–$20 lunch, $13–$38 dinner. Daily 7am–10pm.

Flatbread & Company ★★ PIZZA   This family-friendly Paia outpost embraces a locavore philosophy. The hand-colored menus highlight the best Maui farmers have to offer, particularly where the inventive daily *carne* and veggie specials are concerned. You can watch the chefs hand-toss organic dough, dress it with high-quality toppings—local goat cheese, macadamia-nut pesto, slow-roasted kalua pork, or homemade, nitrate-free sausage—and shovel it into the wood-burning clay oven that serves as the restaurant's magical hearth. Salads come sprinkled with grated green papaya and dressing so delicious that everyone clamors for the recipe. Tuesdays are charity night: $3.50 of each flatbread sold benefits a local cause.

89 Baldwin Ave., Paia. www.flatbreadcompany.com. ⓒ **808/579-9999.** Reservations recommended. Entrees $14–$25. Daily 11am–10pm.

Milagros Food Company ★ SOUTHWESTERN   Milagros has gained a following with its great home-style cooking, upbeat atmosphere, and highly touted margaritas. Sit outdoors and watch the parade of Willie Nelson look-alikes ambling by as you tuck into the ahi creation of the evening. The kitchen turns out Tex-Mex dishes with Maui flair, such as blackened mahi-mahi tacos with salsa, cheese, fresh guacamole, and sweet chili sauce (sounds strange perhaps, but tastes great). You can also order Anaheim chili enchiladas, fajitas with sautéed vegetables finished in achiote glaze, a variety of burgers, and giant salads. Happy hour deals include $5 margaritas and mai tais, $4 Mexican beer (can and draft), and $6 food specials.

3 Baldwin Ave., Paia. www.milagrosfoodcompany.com. ⓒ **808/579-8755.** All-day items $12–$20; dinner main courses $15–$23. Daily 11am–10pm; happy hour 3–6pm.

INEXPENSIVE

Cafe des Amis ★★ CREPES/MEDITERRANEAN/INDIAN   This sweet, eclectic restaurant serves crepes, curries, and Mediterranean platters that are fresh, tasty, and easy on the wallet. Savory crepes like the bacon, brie, and avocado combo come with organic local greens and a dollop of sour cream; sweet fillings include Maui cane sugar with lime and a decadent apple cheese-cake. The curries aren't exactly Indian, but they are delicious. Wraps come with cucumber raita; bowls with mango, tomato, and extra-hot habañero chutney on the side. The coconut shrimp curry is a fragrant blend of ginger, garlic, cinnamon, cilantro, and Bengal spices; the slow-cooked organic chicken curry has a creamy, tomato-y base. Excellent espresso is found here, along with some stiff *lilikoi* margaritas. Musicians often play beneath the twinkling lights in the courtyard seating area.

42 Baldwin Ave., Paia. www.cdamaui.com. © **808/579-6323.** Crepes $5–$13; all-day main courses $6–$18. Breakfast daily 8:30am–noon; all-day menu 8:30am–9pm; happy hour 4–6pm.

Paia Bay Coffee & Bar ★★ CAFE   Tucked behind the San Lorenzo swimsuit shop, this garden coffee shop is Paia's best-kept secret. Pop in for an expertly brewed espresso and a fresh-baked croissant or slice of banana bread and you'll see locals networking in shady corners over cappuccinos. The menu is a bit more sophisticated than that of your typical cafe, with a focus on local and sustainable. In addition to the standard bagel and lox, the kitchen turns out organic scrambled eggs and sandwiches garnished with brie, sliced green apple, microgreens, tomato, and black-pepper herb mayo. The vegan bagel is delicious—topped with roasted red peppers, local avocado, tomato, and pesto. The baristas are genuinely friendly and make everything with care here. New owners have added happy hour and dinner service, with shareable starters and tasty craft cocktails, like the lychee martini and mango mojito, as well as live music. Fun theme nights include Wahine Wednesdays, when all staff and entertainment are women.

115 Hana Hwy., Paia. www.paiabaycoffee.com. © **808/579-9125.** Breakfast and lunch items $10–$13; dinner main courses $10–$15. Daily breakfast 7am–4pm, dinner 4–8pm; happy hour 4–6pm.

Paia Fish Market ★ SEAFOOD   At the corner of Baldwin Avenue and Hana Highway in Paia, this busy fish market, founded in 1989, must maintain its own fleet of fishing boats. How else to explain how the cooks can dish out filet after giant fresh filet for little more than it would cost to buy the same at the grocery? Order the fish tacos or the fish sandwich—a giant slab of perfectly grilled ahi, opah, or opakapaka laid out on a bun with coleslaw and grated cheese is extra satisfying after a briny day at the beach. *Note:* Prices are mostly the same at lunch and dinner, but with larger portions for some dinner items. Also in Lahaina at 632 Front St. (across from the Banyan Tree), © **808/662-3456,** and in Kihei at 1913 S. Kihei Rd. (across from Kalama Park), © **808/874-8888.**

100 Hana Hwy., Paia. www.paiafishmarket.com. © **808/579-3111.** Main courses $9–$20. Daily 11am–9:30pm.

Haiku

MODERATE

Colleen's at the Cannery ★ ECLECTIC   This go-to spot for Haiku residents serves an excellent breakfast, lunch, and dinner in a casual yet classy setting. Slide into a booth beside world-famous surfers, yoga teachers, and inspirational speakers: Maui's local celebrities. Wake up with an omelet stuffed with portobello mushroom and goat cheese, accompanied by organic chai or a spicy Bloody Mary, depending on your mood. For lunch, the roasted eggplant sandwich is served warm, with sun-dried tomatoes, carrots, and melted Muenster cheese. Hearty burgers are made from Maui Cattle Company beef, and pizzas are loaded with creative toppings. For dinner, the local fish specials are spot-on, rivaling some of the island's pricier restaurants—but service can be frustratingly inattentive here. Happy hour takes the edge off, though, with $4 beer and a slice of pizza with beer for $6.50. The dessert case contains some treasures, including extra-rich espresso brownies and sweetly tart *lilikoi* (passionfruit) bars.

At the Haiku Cannery Marketplace, 810 Haiku Rd., Haiku. www.colleensinhaiku.com. © 808/575-9211. Reservations not accepted. Main courses $7–$15 breakfast, $7–$17 lunch, $13–$30 dinner. Breakfast Mon–Fri 6–11am, Sat–Sun 6–11:30am; lunch Mon–Fri 11am–3:30pm, Sat–Sun 11:45am–3:30pm; dinner daily 5–9:30pm; happy hour daily 3:30–5:30pm.

Nuka ★★ SUSHI   Sushi chef Hiro Takanashi smiles from behind the bar as he turns out beautiful specialty rolls loaded with sprouts, pea shoots, avocado, and glistening red tuna. The garden-fresh ingredients served at this compact sushi restaurant reflect its rural Haiku address, but the stylish decor suggests somewhere more cosmopolitan. Start with a side of house pickles or *kinpira gobo*—a salty, sweet, and sour mix of slivered burdock root. Then proceed to the sushi menu for excellent nigiri, sashimi, and rolls. Not up for sushi? The wonderful Nuka bowls—your choice of protein piled atop fresh herbs, crushed peanuts, sesame lime dressing, rice, and veggies—are deeply nourishing. At lunch, burgers with Maui beef or chopped fresh catch are also an option. For dessert, try the house-made black sesame ice cream. *Tip:* Nuka doesn't take reservations and is often packed; plan to eat early (before 6pm) or late (after 7:30pm) to avoid crowds.

780 Haiku Rd., Haiku. www.nukamaui.com. © 808/575-2939. Reservations not accepted. Main courses lunch $8–$21, dinner $8–$38. Daily 4:30–10pm; Mon–Fri 10:30–2:30.

Elsewhere on the Road to Hana

VERY EXPENSIVE

Mama's Fish House ★★★ SEAFOOD   Overlooking idyllic Kuau Cove on Maui's North Shore, this island institution is the realization of a South Pacific fantasy. Though pricey, a meal at Mama's is a complete experience.

Recapture the grace of early Hawaii when feasts lasted for days beneath the swaying palms. Wander through the landscaped grounds down to the restaurant, where smiling servers wear Polynesian prints and flowers behind their ears. The dining room features curved *lauhala*-lined ceilings, lavish arrangements of tropical flowers, and windows open wide to let the ocean breezes in. Start your repast with the coconut ceviche or the marvelous beef Polynesian— a garlicky mix of seared-steak morsels, tomatoes, and onion served in a papaya half. The menu lists the names of the anglers who reeled in the day's catch; you can order ono "caught by Keith Nakamura along the 40-fathom ledge near Hana" or deepwater ahi seared with coconut and lime. As a finale, the Tahitian Pearl dessert is almost too stunning to eat: a shiny chocolate ganache sphere filled with *lilikoi* crème, set in an edible pastry clamshell. Everything is perfect, from the refreshing, umbrella-topped cocktails to the almond-scented hand towels passed around before dessert. Squares of creamy coconut *haupia* are delivered with your bill. The menu (including high prices) is the same at lunch and dinner; you might be able to squeeze in for lunch without a reservation; otherwise, book tables well in advance, especially for dinner and weekends.

799 Poho Place, just off the Hana Hwy., Kuau. www.mamasfishhouse.com. © **808/579-8488.** Reservations strongly recommended. Main courses $44–$95. Daily 11am–9pm (last seating).

INEXPENSIVE

Kuau Store ★ DELI   Decorated with vintage maps of Maui, this is one of my favorite spots on the North Shore for breakfast or lunch to go. The handsome convenience store and deli offers gourmet breakfast paninis, smoothies with all kinds of extras, fresh juices, kombucha on tap, shoyu chicken plate lunches, and pulled pork sandwiches. Inside the deli case you'll find quinoa salads and four types of *poke*. The espresso counter is built out of repurposed wood from the mart that was here before. The logo hats behind the register make great souvenirs. For an easy entrance and exit, park on the side street under the bright mural featuring surfers, sharks, and owls.

701 Hana Hwy., Paia. www.kuaustore.com. © **808/579-8844.** Deli items $5–$12. Daily 6:30am–7pm.

THE END OF THE ROAD IN EAST MAUI: HANA

The quaint Hawaiian village of Hana offers visitors a trip back to Maui's yesteryear. Unfortunately, the town does not offer very many sit-down dining options—just the expensive dining room at Travaasa Hana (the town's only resort hotel) and the moderately priced Hana Ranch Restaurant that Travaasa Hana owns and operates across the street. At lunchtime, simple food trucks and other roadside fare, such as **Pranee's Thai Food** ★ (500 Uakea Rd.; ℂ **808/419-1533**), offer lower prices but not necessarily faster service. Make sure you have snacks in your car when you arrive in Hana.

EXPENSIVE

The Preserve Kitchen + Bar ★ AMERICAN/PACIFIC RIM Hana's only fine-dining restaurant has always struggled to assert itself, but the new chef, Bella Toland, seems up to the challenge. Half-French, half-Filipina, Toland worked for Wolfgang in Las Vegas and Wailea before finding this bewitching spot with its luxurious lanai overlooking the ocean and Kauiki Hill. Her menu showcases Hana-grown ingredients, including exotic tropical fruits from Ono Organic Farms, and Hawaiian seafood, in preparations such as pan-roasted fish served with locally foraged *pohole* ferns and a green papaya salad. Service is friendly but can be slow; try to dine on Monday, Wednesday, or Thursday, when outstanding Hawaiian musicians play, accompanied by a graceful hula dancer. High prices reflect the remote location as well as the upscale resort setting, while lunch and dinner portions do not reflect the oversize portions typical elsewhere. Value-seekers should hit the local food trucks instead.

At Travaasa Hana, 5031 Hana Hwy., Hana. www.travaasa.com/hana. ℂ **808/248-8211.** Main courses $15–$25 breakfast; $17–$32 lunch; $19–$45 dinner. Daily breakfast 7:30–10:30am, lunch 11am–2pm, dinner 5–9pm.

MODERATE

Hana Ranch Restaurant ★ AMERICAN Dining options are slim in Hana after 3pm, so you might find yourself hungry with nowhere else to eat. Owned and operated by Travaasa Hana, the Hana Ranch Restaurant is the informal, in-town alternative to the hotel's dining room for lunch or dinner, serving casual fare (burgers, grilled sandwiches, fish tacos, ribs, etc.) for slightly more than you'd pay elsewhere on Maui; adjust your expectations accordingly and you'll be satisfied. The service is friendly (if slow) and portions are large. Seating is at indoor tables or one of two outdoor pavilions that offer distant ocean views.

2 Mill St. (off Hana Hwy.), Hana. ℂ **808/270-5280.** Main courses $17–$32. Daily 11am–9pm.

INEXPENSIVE

Barefoot Café ★ SNACK SHOP/CAFE Place your order for simple homespun fare at the window and eat at picnic tables facing picturesque Hana Bay. This cash-only cafe is the spot for an unpretentious East Maui breakfast: Choose from Benedicts, fried rice, eggs, and fresh baked goods. Although lunch and dinner (kalbi beef, saimin) are less inspired, this is still an affordable alternative to the nearby resort restaurants.

At Hana Bay Beach Park, 1632 Keawa Pl., Hana. ℂ **808/446-5519.** Breakfast items $5–$10; lunch items $6–$16. Cash only. Daily 7–10am and 11am–5pm.

Huli Huli Chicken at Koki ★ PLATE LUNCH/BBQ   This roadside shack just past Koki Beach might be the best place to eat in Hana—but it's not really a restaurant and we can't vouch that it will be open when you arrive; the chicken typically runs out before the end of the day. Huli huli chicken is a mouthwatering Hawaiian version of barbecue. "Huli" means "turn" as in, turn over the flame. Place your order for chicken, pork, or ribs, served plate lunch–style with potato mac salad, rice, and green salad. Then park yourself at the picnic table facing scenic little Alau Island and count your blessings.

Just past Koki Beach Park on Haneoo Rd., Hana. Lunch items under $18. Daily 10am–6pm.

EXPLORING
MAUI

After you soak up rays for a day or two on the beach, Maui's many other attractions may start to beckon. The drive up majestic Haleakala can be as fascinating as the lunar crater at its summit, especially if you visit one of the unique farms or quaint towns en route. The road to Hana is also as much about the journey as the destination, with roadside stands, scenic overlooks, and waterfall hikes encouraging you to make a day or more of the drive. Lahaina's watering holes are the modern successors of saloons from its colorful whaling days, while the remains of its more serene history as a royal Hawaiian compound peek around every corner.

Maui's unique natural and human history provide much to explore. Eons of volcanic activity brought Maui's mountains out of the sea, while eons of erosion by wind, rain, and waves carved into them spectacular gullies, valleys, and beaches. Accidental migrations of flora and fauna that then evolved undisturbed for thousands of years led to distinctive life forms found nowhere else.

More than a millennium ago, the first intentional migrations began, by determined Polynesian voyagers who left the Marquesas Islands and headed some 2,100 nautical miles north in outrigger sailing canoes, guided by stars, waves, and seabirds. Western contact, initiated by Capt. James Cook in fall of 1778, eventually led to the arrival of whalers and missionaries from New England; in the late 18th and 19th centuries, plantation workers from China, Japan, Okinawa, Korea, the Philippines, the Azores, and Puerto Rico followed, creating today's rich cultural stew.

Divided by geographical area, here are highlights of sights and attractions to discover. You'll find additional listings of beaches and detailed descriptions of hiking trails in chapter 7.

Tip: If you're a history buff, buy a **"Passport to the Past"** for $10 and gain admission to Maui's four best museums: the Baldwin Home and Wo Hing Museum in Lahaina, Hale Hoikeike (Bailey House Museum) in Wailuku, and the Alexander & Baldwin Sugar Museum in Puunene. The passport is sold at each of these locations.

MAUI'S TOP SIGHTS & ATTRACTIONS

- Haleakala National Park (p. 154)
- Hana (p. 169)
- Iao Valley (p. 134)
- Lahaina (p. 135)
- Maui Ocean Center (p. 149)
- National Tropical Botanical Garden (p. 168)
- Ocean Organic Farm & Distillery (p. 152)
- Surfing Goat Dairy (p. 152)
- Maui Tropical Plantation (p. 132)

CENTRAL MAUI

Central Maui isn't exactly tourist central; this is where most residents live. You'll most likely land here and head directly to a resort area. However, there are more than a few sights worth checking out en route or before your return to the airport.

Kahului

Under the airport flight path, next to Maui's busiest intersection and across from Costco and Kmart in Kahului's business park, is a most unlikely place: the **Kanaha Pond Wildlife Sanctuary.** From the parking lot for this former royal fishpond, now a tranquil, 235-acre refuge for native birds, a 50-foot paved trail leads to a shade shelter and lookout. About 200 of the remaining 2,000 black-neck Hawaiian stilts (*ae'o*) nest here, along with similarly endangered Hawaiian ducks (*koloa*) and coots (*'alae*). Migrating shorebirds and nene, the endemic Hawaiian goose, also find a haven here. For a quieter, more natural-looking wildlife preserve, visit the **Kealia Pond National Wildlife Refuge,** in Kihei (p. 150).

Off Haleakala Highway Extension (Hwy. 36A) across from Triangle Square, between Hanakai and Koloa sts., Kahului. Open sunup to sundown. Free.

Maui Nui Botanical Garden ★ GARDEN   This garden is a living treasure box of native Hawaiian coastal species and plants brought here by Polynesian voyagers in their seafaring canoes. Stroll beneath the shade of the *hala* and breadfruit trees while taking a self-guided audio tour. You'll learn how the first Hawaiians made everything from medicine to musical instruments out of plants and trees. You can also take a docent-led tour ($10) by reservation only; they're offered 10am weekdays when available. If the garden happens to be hosting a lei-making or *kapa*-dyeing workshop while you're on the island, don't miss it. *Tip:* Saturday is free admission.

150 Kanaloa Ave., Kahului. www.mnbg.org. © **808/249-2798**. $5 adults, free for seniors and children 12 and under, and free to all on Sat; guided tours $10 per person, by reservation only, 10am weekdays. 8am–4pm Mon–Sat.

FLYING HIGH: helicopter rides

Some of Maui's most spectacular scenery—3,000-foot-tall waterfalls thundering away in the chiseled heart of the West Maui Mountains, for example—can only be seen from the air.

The first chopper pilots in Hawaii were good ol' boys on their way back from Vietnam—hard-flying, hard-drinking cowboys who cared more about the ride than the scenery. But not anymore. Today's pilots, like the ones at Blue Hawaiian (see below), are an interesting hybrid: part Hawaii historian, part DJ, part tour guide, and part amusement-ride operator. As you soar through the clouds, you'll learn about the island's flora, fauna, history, and culture.

Among the many helicopter-tour operators on Maui, the best is **Blue Hawaiian Helicopters ★★★**, at Kahului Airport (www.bluehawaiian.com; ✆ **800/745-BLUE** [2583] or 808/871-1107), which can escort you on one of their two types of helicopters: A-star or Eco-Star. Both are good, but the latter is worth the extra cash for its bucket seats (raised in the rear) and wraparound windows. Tours range from 50 to 90 minutes. If you take the 50-minute flight that includes Molokai, you'll spend more time over water, with not quite as much to see. The 65-minute Complete Island Tour is the best value, especially if it's been raining and the waterfalls are gushing. After exploring West Maui, your pilot will flirt at the edges of Haleakala National Park so you can peer into the crater's paint-box colors, and then zip over Oprah's organic farm in Kula. For literally over-the-top experiences, book the Maui Spectacular, which includes an exclusive landing at Ulupalakua Ranch for a 20-minute refreshment break, or one of the Heli-Ranch experiences that land at Piiholo Ranch for a 2-hour horseback ride (see "Horseback Riding" in chapter 7, p. 219). **Tip:** Seats in the back can actually be better for photos, since you can press your camera up to the window. Wear plain, dark colors so your clothing doesn't reflect off the glass. Flight times range from 50 to 90 minutes and cost $259 to $429, including taxes (Kahului Heliport parking $5–$7).

Puunene

This town, located in the middle of the central Maui plains, is nearly gone. Once a thriving sugar-plantation town with hundreds of homes, a school, a shopping area, and a community center, Puunene is little more than a post office and a museum today. The Hawaiian Commercial & Sugar Co., owner of the land, slowly phased out the rental plantation housing to open up more land to plant sugar but, unable to compete with foreign sugar producers, harvested its last crop in 2016 and shut down what was the one remaining sugar mill in Hawaii. Although employees mourned the loss of jobs, a number of Maui residents were delighted, citing the potential health threats from burning cane during harvest time each year. Native Hawaiian groups are now seeking restoration of the water diverted years ago from streams that fed their taro fields, before the fallow land is turned into housing.

Alexander & Baldwin Sugar Museum MUSEUM   This former sugar-mill superintendent's home has been converted into a museum that tells the story of sugar in Hawaii. Exhibits explain how workers of a variety of ethnic backgrounds grew, harvested, and milled sugarcane—back-breaking toil that also relied on innovative engineering. An eye-opening display shows how Samuel Alexander and Henry Baldwin managed to acquire huge chunks of land from the Kingdom of Hawaii, then fought to gain access to water on the other side of the island, making sugarcane an economically viable crop. Allow about half an hour to enjoy the museum, and don't forget to stop for plantation-themed sweets in the gift shop.

3957 Hansen Rd.. at Puunene Ave. (Hwy. 350) www.sugarmuseum.com. © **808/871-8058.** Admission $7 adults; $5 seniors; $2 children 6–12; free for children 5 and under. Daily 9:30am–4pm.

Waikapu

Across the sugarcane fields from Puunene, and about 3 miles south of Wailuku on the Honoapiilani Highway (Hwy. 30), lies the tiny, one-street village of Waikapu, which has a singular attraction well worth checking out.

Relive Maui's past by taking a 45-minute narrated tram ride around fields of pineapple, sugarcane, papaya, plus many more exotic fruits and flowers, at **Maui Tropical Plantation ★★**, 1670 Honoapiilani Hwy. (www.mauitropical plantation.com; © **800/451-6805** or 808/244-7643), a real working plantation open daily from 7am to 9pm. The grounds are fantastically landscaped with tropical plants and sculptures made from repurposed sugarcane-harvesting equipment. Its **Mill House ★★** restaurant and bar offers exceptional, inventive cuisine and cocktails from 11am to 9pm (www.millhouse.com, © **808/270-0333**). There are also nifty boutiques, an organic farmstand, a coffee shop, and a zipline course (see "Ziplining" in chapter 7, p. 221.) Admission is free; the tram tours, which include fruit tasting and a 15-minute stop at a tiki hut for a coconut husking and opening demonstration, are $20 for adults and $10 for kids 3 to 12. They start at 10am and leave hourly till 4pm. *Tip:* Do your tram ride before dining or shopping for produce; your tram ticket is good for 10% off at the Mill House, Kumu Farms Stand, and Mill House Roasting Co.

Wailuku

This historic gateway to **Iao Valley** (see below) is worth a visit, if only for a brief stop at the Bailey House Museum, two historic *heiau* (temples), and some terrific shopping and dining.

Hale Hoikeike (Bailey House) ★ MUSEUM Missionary and sugar planter Edward Bailey's 1833 home—an architectural hybrid of stones laid by Hawaiian craftsmen and timbers joined in a display of Yankee ingenuity—is a treasure trove of Hawaiiana. Inside, you'll find an eclectic collection, from precontact artifacts like precious feather lei, *kapa* (barkcloth) samples, a wooden spear so large it defies believability, dog-tooth necklaces, and a collection of gemlike Hawaiian tree-snail shells, to latter-day relics like Duke Kahanamoku's 1919 redwood surfboard and a koa-wood table given to President Ulysses S. Grant, who had to refuse it because he couldn't accept gifts

POWERFUL plantations

Pineapples once grew on huge farms in Hawaii, and coffee and macadamia nuts are still big business. But bigger than them all were the once-dominant sugar plantations. Sugar was Hawaii's claim to fame long before the tourists arrived, with the first plantation opening in 1835. At one time, more than 240,000 acres of sugarcane were under cultivation. But a little less than a century and a half later, sugar went bust—the victim of cheaper labor and cheaper shipping costs elsewhere. In the late 1970s Hawaii produced nearly 1.2 billion tons of sugar; the last commercial harvest in the islands was in 2016 at Puunene, Maui. Though most of the former fields of cane have given way to resorts and golf courses, their impact on Hawaiian culture should not be underestimated.

Plantation Life Low wages. Abusive overseers. Poor conditions. For plantation workers, these things were all part of the job. The immigrant laborers who built sugar into Hawaii's primary industry were generally treated like indentured servants. They signed binding contracts that required they pay off the cost of their transportation to the islands and their living expenses. Their paltry wages (41¢ per day in 1841) were quickly eaten up by exorbitant rates charged by the company store. However, from this disparaging past Hawaii's labor unions arose after World War II (some say because Hawaii's boys went out and saw that the rest of the world was not under the iron rule of plantations). Today, nearly 80 years later, Hawaii is still a strong labor union state.

A song popular with sugar plantation laborers at the turn of the 19th century summed up their lot in life.

Sure a Poor Man (Pua Mana No)
I labored on a sugar plantation
Growing sugarcane
My back ached, my sweat poured,
All for nothing.
I fell in debt at the plantation store.
I fell in debt at the plantation store.
And remained a poor man.

Plantations & Politics Many of Hawaii's first white families were missionaries who "came to do good and stayed to do well," as the local saying goes. Five prominent families, dubbed the Big Five, saw in sugar the potential for major profits, and they wasted no time in making sure their stranglehold on the industry was secure. From the beginning, the U.S. was the predominant beneficiary of all that sweetness. Just one problem: Hawaii was independent, which meant there were trade tariffs to be paid. No matter—white businessmen simply banded together to push through "reforms" that gave them more and more power. Sanford Dole, the son of missionaries, was an advisor to Queen Liliuokalani, but he was also interested in promoting the cause of his family's plantations. He helped lead the 1893 U.S. Marine-backed coup that overthrew the monarchy, then got himself named president of Hawaii from 1894 to 1900, and served as provisional governor after the U.S. annexed the islands.

—By Linda Barth

from foreign countries. Bailey's exquisite landscapes, painted from 1866 to 1896, decorate the rock walls of one room, capturing on canvas a Maui that exists only in memory. This is the largest public display of Hawaiiana in Maui County; the gift store, while compact, also yields treasures.

2375-A Main St. www.mauimuseum.org. ℂ **808/244-3326.** Admission $7 adults; $5 seniors; $2 children 7–12; free for children 6 and under. Mon–Sat 10am–4pm.

Halekii-Pihanai Heiau State Monument ★ HISTORIC SITE   These two *heiau,* or temples, built in 1240 from stones carried up from the Iao Stream below, sit on a hill with a commanding view of central Maui and Haleakala. Kahekili, the last chief of Maui, lived here. After the bloody battle at Iao Stream, Kamehameha I reportedly came to the temple here to pay homage to the war god, Ku, with a human sacrifice. Halekii ("House of Images") is made of stone walls with a flat grassy top, whereas Pihanakalani ("Gathering Place of Supernatural Beings") is a pyramid-shaped mount of stones. If you sit quietly nearby (never walk on any heiau—it's considered disrespectful), you'll see that the view alone explains why this spot was chosen. You'll need to walk up the entrance road to the 10-acre park, which is closed to vehicles.

Off Hea Pl., near the intersection of Kuhio Road and Waiehu Beach Road (Hwy. 340.) http://dlnr.hawaii.gov/dsp/parks/maui/halekii-pihana-heiau-state-monument. Daily 7:45am–4:30pm.

Iao Valley ★★★

A couple of miles north of Wailuku, where the little plantation houses stop and the road climbs ever higher, Maui's true nature begins to reveal itself. The transition from suburban sprawl to raw nature is so abrupt that most people who drive up into the valley don't realize they're suddenly in a rainforest. The walls of the canyon begin to close around them, and a 2,250-foot-high needle-like rock pricks gray clouds scudding across the blue sky. The moist, cool air and the shade are a welcome comfort after the hot tropic sun. This is Iao (pronounced *E*-ow) Valley, an eroded volcanic caldera in the West Maui Mountains whose great nature, history, and beauty have been enjoyed by millions of people from around the world for more than a century.

Iao ("Supreme Light") Valley is 10 miles long and encompasses 4,000 acres. The head of the valley is a broad circular amphitheater where four major streams converge into Iao Stream. At the back of the amphitheater is rain-drenched Puu Kukui, the West Maui Mountains' highest point. This peaceful valley, full of tropical plants, rainbows, waterfalls, swimming holes, and hiking trails, is a place of solitude, reflection, and escape for residents and visitors alike.

To get here from Wailuku, take Main Street to Iao Valley Road to the entrance to **Iao Valley State Monument ★★★**. Two paved walkways loop into the massive green amphitheater, across the bridge of Iao Stream, and along the stream itself. A leisurely stroll on the short paved lookout trail that climbs 200 feet will allow you to enjoy lovely views of the Iao Needle and the lush vegetation, including an ethnobotanical garden along the stream, accessed by an equally short paved loop. Others often proceed beyond the state park border and take two trails deeper into the valley, but the trails enter private land, and NO TRESPASSING signs are posted.

The feature known as **Iao Needle** is an erosional remnant consisting of basalt dikes. This phallic rock juts an impressive 2,250 feet above sea level; ancient Hawaiians were apparently less impressed, giving it the unflattering name of Kuka'emoku, "broken excrement."

Youngsters play in **Iao Stream,** a peaceful brook that belies its bloody history. In 1790, King Kamehameha the Great and his men engaged in the battle of Iao Valley to gain control of Maui. When the battle ended, so many bodies blocked Iao Stream that the battle site was named Kepaniwai, or "damming of the waters." An architectural park of Hawaiian, Japanese, Chinese, Filipino, Portuguese, and New England–style houses stands in harmony by Iao Stream in **the Heritage Gardens at Kepaniwai Park,** a county-managed park (hwww.mauicounty.gov/facilities) that serves as a good picnic spot, with plenty of tables and benches. *Note:* Damaged by flooding in 2016, the nearby **Hawaii Nature Center** (https://hawaiinaturecenter.org, ℂ **808/244-6500**) is no longer open to the public for drop-in visits, but offers school group tours, birthday parties, and summer nature camps.

WHEN TO GO Park hours are 7am to 7pm daily, and the entrance fee is $5 per car for visitors. Go early in the morning or late in the afternoon when the sun's rays slant into the valley and create a mystical mood. You can bring a picnic and spend the day, but be prepared at any time for one of the frequent tropical cloudbursts that soak the valley and swell both waterfalls and streams. For updated info, visit http://dlnr.hawaii.gov/dsp/parks/maui/iao-valley-state-monument or contact the state parks' Maui office at ℂ **808/984-8109.**

LAHAINA & WEST MAUI
Olowalu

Most people drive right by Olowalu, on the Honoapiilani Highway (Hwy. 30) 5 miles south of Lahaina; there's little to mark the spot but a small general store, a restaurant, and a fruit stand. Olowalu ("Many Hills") was the scene of a bloody massacre in 1790. The Hawaiians stole a skiff from the USS *Eleanora,* took it back to shore here, and burned it for its iron parts. The captain of the ship, Simon Metcalf, was furious and tricked the Hawaiians into sailing out in their canoes to trade with the ship. As the canoes approached, he mowed them down with his cannons, killing 100 people and wounding many others.

Known for its underwater coral gardens, Olowalu has great snorkeling around **mile marker 14,** where there is a turtle-cleaning station about 150 to 225 feet out from shore. Turtles line up here to have cleaner wrasses (small bony fish) pick off small parasites.

Historic Lahaina

Located between the West Maui Mountains and the deep azure ocean offshore, Lahaina stands out as one of the few places in Hawaii that has managed to preserve its 19th-century heritage while still accommodating 21st-century guests.

In ancient times, powerful chiefs and kings ruled this hot, dry, oceanside village. Legend has it that a powerful *moo* (lizard goddess) dwelt in a moat surrounding a palace here. At the turn of the 19th century, after King Kamehameha united the Hawaiian Islands, he made Lahaina the royal capital—which it remained until 1845, when Kamehameha III moved the capital to the larger port of Honolulu.

In the 1840s, the whaling industry was at its peak: Hundreds of ships called into Lahaina every year. The streets were filled with sailors 24 hours a day. Even Herman Melville, who later wrote *Moby-Dick,* visited Lahaina.

Just 20 years later, the whaling industry was waning, and sugar had taken over the town. The Pioneer Sugar Mill Co. reigned in Lahaina for the next 100 years.

Today, the drunken and derelict whalers who wandered through Lahaina's streets in search of grog, dance halls, and brothels have been replaced by hordes of tourists crowding into the small mile-long main section of town in search of boutiques, art galleries, and chic gourmet eateries. The action revolves around the town's giant, century-old banyan tree and busy recreational harbor. Lahaina is rife with tourist traps, but you can still find plenty of authentic history here. It's also a great place to stay; accommodations include a few old hotels (such as the Pioneer Inn on the harbor, built in 1901), quaint bed-and-breakfasts, and a handful of oceanfront condos.

See chapter 7 for details on the various cruises and outfitters operating out of Lahaina.

Baldwin Home Museum ★ MUSEUM   The oldest house in Lahaina, this coral-and-rock structure was built in 1834 by Rev. Dwight Baldwin, a doctor with the fourth company of American missionaries to sail to Hawaii. Like many missionaries, he came to Hawaii to do good—including inoculating residents with a smallpox vaccine to protect them during an epidemic in 1853—while also doing very well for himself. After 17 years of service, Baldwin was granted 2,600 acres in Kapalua for farming and grazing. His ranch manager experimented with growing a South American fruit that Hawaiians called *hala-kahiki,* or pineapple, on a 4-acre plot; the rest is history. The house looks as if Baldwin has just stepped out to tend to a sick neighbor down the street. On Fridays, you'll really feel you've stepped into history on a **candlelit twilight tour,** offered on the half-hour from dusk till 8pm.

Next door is the **Masters' Reading Room,** Maui's oldest surviving building; admission is included with Baldwin Home admission, as is the **Wo Hing Museum**, see below). Built in 1834 of coral and stone, this became visiting sea captains' favorite hangout once the missionaries closed down all of Lahaina's grog shops and banned prostitution. By 1844, when hotels and bars started reopening, it lost its appeal. It's now the headquarters of the **Lahaina Restoration Foundation,** a plucky band of historians who try to keep this

town alive and antique at the same time. Stop in and pick up a self-guided walking-tour map, which will take you to Lahaina's most historic sites. You can also pick up the **Passport to the Past** ($10) here; it includes admission to the Baldwin Home, Wo Hing and Alexander & Baldwin Sugar museums, and Hale Hoikeike (the Bailey House Museum).

120 Dickenson St. (at Front St.). www.lahainarestoration.org/baldwin-home-museum. (*) **808/661-3262.** Admission $7 adults; $5 seniors/military; free for children 12 and under. Sat–Thurs 10am–4pm; Fri 10am–8:30pm.

Banyan Tree ★★★ NATURAL ATTRACTION   Of all the banyan trees in Hawaii, this is the greatest—so big that you can't get it all in your camera's viewfinder. Imported from India, it was only 8 feet tall when it was planted in 1873 by Maui sheriff William O. Smith to mark the 50th anniversary of Lahaina's first Christian mission. Now it's more than 60 feet tall and a quarter-mile in circumference, and covers nearly 2 acres—the length of a city block—in the former Courthouse Square, now appropriately called Lahaina Court

Banyan Park. Its aerial roots have formed 15 additional trunks, whose branches are now home to hundreds of mynah birds. They make quite the clatter at nightfall—avoid walking under them.

Front Street at Canal Street. www.mauicounty.gov/facilities/Facility/Details/125.

Hale Pai ★ MUSEUM   When the missionaries arrived in Hawaii in 1820 to spread the word of God, they found the Hawaiians had no written language. They quickly rectified the situation by converting the Hawaiian sounds into a written language. Creating reading material took a bit longer. In 1831, they also founded the Lahainaluna Seminary, the oldest American school west of the Rockies, and 3 years later installed a printing press for educational materials that would assist them on their mission. The missionaries also taught students how to set type, bind books, and literally print money. In 1834, the press printed the first newspaper west of the Rockies, the Hawaiian-language weekly *Ka Lama Hawaii*. Today, Lahainaluna is the public high school for the children of West Maui, and the two-room timber and coral mortar building built for the press in 1837 is Hale Pai, a printing museum and archive that includes a book of Hawaiian myths printed in 1838 and a sample of the Hawaiian Kingdom's paper currency.

Lahainaluna High School Campus, 980 Lahainaluna Rd. (at the top of the mountain). www.lahainarestoration.org/hale-pai-museum. ℭ **808/662-0560.** Free admission. Mon–Wed 10am–4pm, or by appointment.

Lahaina Heritage Museum ★ MUSEUM   Located on the second floor of the old Lahaina Courthouse, this museum presents the history, culture, and environment of Lahaina, from precontact Hawaii (which once called this town Lele) through the missionary, whaling, and plantation eras to the beginnings of modern tourism and the Hawaiian Islands Humpback Whale National Sanctuary. In addition to ever-changing exhibits, there are videos, live demonstrations by cultural artisans, "touch and feel" displays, and interactive exhibits.

648 Wharf St. www.lahainarestoration.org/lahaina-heritage-museum. ℭ **808/661-3262.** Free admission. Daily 9am–5pm.

Lahaina Jodo Mission ★ TEMPLE   This site has long been held sacred. The Hawaiians called it Puunoa Point, which means "the hill freed from taboo." Once a small village named Mala (garden), this peaceful place became a haven for Japanese immigrants, who came to Hawaii in 1868 as laborers for the sugarcane plantations. They eventually built a small wooden temple to worship here. In 1968, on the 100th anniversary of Japanese presence in Hawaii, a Great Buddha statue (some 12 ft. high and weighing 3½ tons) was brought here from Japan. The immaculate grounds also contain a replica of the original wooden temple (destroyed by fire in 1968) and a 90-foot-tall, three-tiered pagoda, which holds the ashes of deceased worshippers.

12 Ala Moana St. (off Front St., near the Mala Wharf). http://hawaiijodoshu.org/lahaina-jodo-mission/. ℭ **808/661-4304.** Free admission. Daily during daylight hours.

Malu Ulu Olele Park ★ PARK   At first glance, this Front Street park appears to be only a hot, dry baseball field bracketed by tennis and basketball courts. But actually it's sacred ground; a royal compound stood here more than 100 years ago, now buried under tons of red dirt and sand. Here, Prince Kauikeaouli, who ascended the throne as King Kamehameha III when he was only 10, lived with the love of his life, his sister, Princess Nahienaena. Missionaries took a dim view of incest, which was acceptable to Hawaiian nobles in order to preserve the royal bloodline. Torn between love for her brother and the new Christian morality, Nahienaena grew despondent and died at the age of 21. King Kamehameha III, who reigned for 29 years—longer than any other Hawaiian monarch—presided over Hawaii as it went from kingdom to constitutional monarchy, and as power over the islands began to shift from island nobles to missionaries, merchants, and sugar planters. Kamehameha died in 1854 at the age of 39. In 1918, his royal compound, containing a mausoleum and artifacts of the kingdom, was demolished and covered with dirt to create a 4.7-acre public park (including restrooms). Tellingly, the latest incarnation of the first church on Maui, **Waiola Church** (535 Wainee St.; www.waiolachurch.org; ℂ **808/661-4349**), built in 1823 and rebuilt many times over the years, still borders the former compound; its Sunday services include a mix of Hawaiian and English language and hymns.

Front and Shaw sts. www.mauicounty.gov/Facilities/Facility/Details/132.

Plantation Museum ★ MUSEUM   Tucked away on the second floor of the Wharf Cinema Center, this compact exhibition space celebrates Maui's more than 150 years of colorful plantation history and the diverse communities that contributed to it. You'll learn about family life, festivals, and traditions as well as the tools and innovations that made sugar and pineapple such big business.

658 Front St. http://thewharfcinemacenter.com/plantation-museum. ℂ **808/661-3282.** Free. Daily 9am–6pm.

Wo Hing Museum & Cookhouse ★★ HISTORIC SITE   Sandwiched between souvenir shops and restaurants on Front Street, this ornate 1912 building once served as a fraternal and social meeting hall for Lahaina's Chinese immigrants, brought to Hawaii to work in the sugarcane fields. Today it houses fascinating Asian artifacts, artwork, and a lovely shrine in the altar room upstairs. In the front yard stands a bust of Chinese revolutionary Dr. Sun Yat-Sen, who spent more than 7 years on Maui at the turn of the last century. Beside the temple is a rustic cookhouse where you can watch some of Thomas Edison's first movies, filmed here in Hawaii. The footage of *paniolo* (cowboys) wrangling steer onto ships offshore and Honolulu circa 1898 is mesmerizing. Wo Hing hosts Lunar New Year and kite-making festivals that are catnip for kids.

858 Front St. www.lahainarestoration.org/wo-hing-museum. ℂ **808/661-3262.** $7 adults; $5 seniors/military; free for children 12 and under (includes entry to Baldwin House Museum; see above). Daily 10am–4pm.

WALKING TOUR: **HISTORIC LAHAINA**

START:	**Front and Dickenson streets.**
FINISH:	**Same location.**
TIME:	**About an hour.**
BEST TIME:	**Monday–Friday, 10am–3pm (go earlier to avoid heat)**

Back when "there was no God west of the Horn," Lahaina was the capital of Hawaii and the Pacific's wildest port. Today it's a milder version of its old self—mostly a hustle-bustle of whale art, timeshares, and "Just Got Lei'd" T-shirts. If you look hard, however, you'll still find the historic port town the early whalers loved, filled with the kind of history that inspired James Michener to write his best-selling epic novel *Hawaii*.

Members of the Lahaina Restoration Foundation have worked for decades to preserve Lahaina's past. They have labeled a number of historic sites with brown-and-white markers; below, I provide explanations of the significance of each site as you walk through Lahaina's past.

Begin your tour at the:

1 Master's Reading Room

This coral-and-stone building looks just as it did in 1834, when Rev. William Richards and Rev. E. Spaulding convinced the whaling-ship captains that they needed a place for the ships' masters and captains, many of whom traveled with their families, to stay while they were ashore. The bottom floor was used as a storage area for the mission; the top floor, from which you could see the ships at anchor in the harbor, was for the visiting ships' officers.

Next door is the:

2 Baldwin Home Museum

Harvard-educated physician Rev. Dwight Baldwin, with his wife of just a few weeks, sailed to Hawaii from New England in 1830. Baldwin was first assigned to a church in Waimea, on the Big Island, and then to Lahaina's Wainee Church (now Wailoa Church) in 1838. He and his family lived in this house until 1871. The Baldwin Home and the Master's Reading Room are the oldest standing buildings in Lahaina, made from thick walls of coral and hand-milled timber. Baldwin also ran his medical office and his missionary activities out of this house. (See "Baldwin Home Museum," p. 136, for hours and admission.)

On the other side of the Baldwin Home Museum is the former site of the:

3 Richards House

The open field is empty today, but it once held the home of Lahaina's first Protestant missionary, Rev. William Richards. Richards went on to

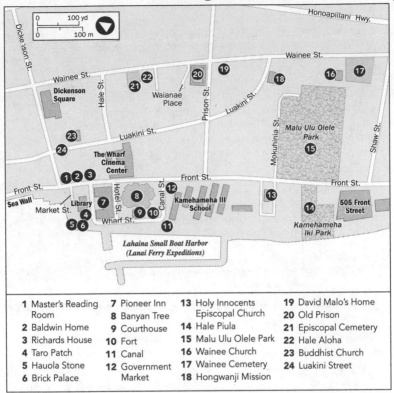

1 Master's Reading Room	**7** Pioneer Inn	**13** Holy Innocents Episcopal Church	**19** David Malo's Home
2 Baldwin Home	**8** Banyan Tree	**14** Hale Piula	**20** Old Prison
3 Richards House	**9** Courthouse	**15** Malu Ulu Olele Park	**21** Episcopal Cemetery
4 Taro Patch	**10** Fort	**16** Wainee Church	**22** Hale Aloha
5 Hauola Stone	**11** Canal	**17** Wainee Cemetery	**23** Buddhist Church
6 Brick Palace	**12** Government Market	**18** Hongwanji Mission	**24** Luakini Street

become the chaplain, teacher, and translator to Kamehameha III. He was also instrumental in drafting Hawaii's constitution and acted as the king's envoy to the United States and England, seeking recognition of Hawaii as an independent nation. After his death in 1847, he was buried in the Wainee Church cemetery.

From here, cross Front Street and walk toward the ocean, with the Lahaina Public Library on your right and the green Pioneer Inn on your left, until you see the:

4 Taro Patch

The lawn in front of the Lahaina Public Library was once a taro patch stretching back to the Baldwin home. The taro plant remains a staple of the Hawaiian diet: The root is used to make poi, and the leaves are used in cooking. At one time Lahaina looked like a Venice of the tropics, with streams, ponds, and waterways flooding the taro fields. As the population of the town grew, the water was siphoned off for drinking.

WHERE TO park FREE—OR NEXT TO FREE— IN LAHAINA

Lahaina is the worst place on Maui for parking. The town was created and filled with shops, restaurants, and historic sites before the throngs of tourists (and their cars) invaded. Street parking is hit-or-miss. You can either drive around the block for hours looking for a free place to park on the street or park in one of the nearly 20 paid parking lots. If you're staying in Kaanapali, it may be easier and cheaper to take the Outlets of Maui shuttle ($3) or, for guests at a Westin or Sheraton property on the resort, a free shuttle to downtown Lahaina. Maui Bus also has frequent service between the Wharf Cinema Center and Kaanapali, Napili, and Kapalua to the north, and Maalaea to the south; it's $2 one-way, or $4 for an all-day pass.

But if you really need to drive, you can get free or discounted parking with validated purchases at four lots. Three are within a block of the intersection of Papalaua and Wainee streets. The largest is the Outlets of Maui lot, the next in size is the Lahaina Center, across the street; both allow 2 hours free with a purchase from one of their respective stores (4 hours at Outlets of Maui with purchase from Ruth's Chris Steak House or Pi Artisan Pizza). The smallest is the Lahaina Square lot at Wainee Street, which offers 2 free hours for customers with validated purchase. Customers of the Wharf Cinema Center, located on Front Street, can also get a discount by parking in the large lot at the rear of the shopping center; it's between Dickenson and Hale streets, with entrances off Wainee and Luakini streets.

Walk away from the Lahaina Harbor toward the edge of the lawn, where you'll see the:

5 Hauola Stone

Hawaiians believed that certain stones placed in sacred places had the power to heal. *Kahuna* (priests) of medicine used stones like this to help cure illnesses.

Turn around and walk back toward the Pioneer Inn; look for the concrete depression in the ground, which is all that's left of the:

6 Brick Palace

This structure was begun in 1798 as the first Western-style building in Hawaii. King Kamehameha I had this 20×40-foot, two-story brick structure built for his wife, Queen Kaahumanu (who is said to have preferred a grass-thatched house nearby). Inside, the walls were constructed of wood and the windows were glazed glass. Kamehameha I lived here from 1801 to 1802, when he was building his war canoe, *Peleleu,* and preparing to invade Kauai. A handmade stone sea wall surrounded the palace to protect it from the surf. The building stood for 70 years. In addition to being a royal compound, it was also used as a meetinghouse, storeroom, and warehouse.

7 Pioneer Inn

Lahaina's first hotel was the scene of some wild parties at the start of the 20th century. George Freeland, of the Royal Canadian Mounted Police, tracked a criminal to Lahaina and then fell in love with the town. He built the hotel in 1901 but soon discovered that Lahaina didn't get a lot of visitors. To make ends meet, Freeland built a movie theater, which was wildly successful. The Pioneer Inn remained the only hotel in all of west Maui until the 1950s. You can still stay at this restored building, now managed as a Best Western (p. 44), or enjoy live music in its historic saloon 5:30 to 8pm Tuesdays and Thursdays.

From the Pioneer Inn, cross Hotel Street and walk along Wharf Street, which borders the harbor. On your left is the:

8 Banyan Tree
Planted in 1873, this tree has witnessed decades of luau, dances, concerts, private chats, public rallies, and resting sojourners under its mighty boughs, now home to hundreds of roosting mynahs at night. It's hard to believe that this huge tree was only 8 feet tall when it was planted here (see "Banyan Tree," p. 137, for details.)

Continue along Wharf Street. Near the edge of the park is the:

9 Courthouse
In 1858, a violent windstorm destroyed about 20 buildings in Lahaina, including Hale Piula, which served as the courthouse and palace of King Kamehameha III. It was rebuilt immediately, using the stones from the previous building. It served not only as courthouse, but also as custom house, post office, tax collector's office, and government offices. Upstairs on the second floor is the **Lahaina Heritage Museum ★**, with exhibits on the history and culture of Lahaina (free admission; open daily 9am–5pm).

Continue down Wharf Street to Canal Street. On the corner are the remains of the:

10 Fort
This structure once covered an acre and had 20-foot-high walls. In 1830, some whalers fired a few cannonballs into Lahaina in protest of Rev. William Richards' meddling in their affairs. (Richards had convinced Gov. Hoapili to create a law forbidding the women of Lahaina from swimming out to greet the whaling ships.) In response to this threat, the fort was constructed from 1831 to 1832 with coral blocks taken from the ocean. As a further show of strength, cannons were placed along the waterfront, where they remain today. Historical accounts seem to scoff at the "fort," saying it appeared to be more for show than for force. It was later used as a prison, until it was finally torn down in the 1850s; its stones were used for construction of the new prison, **Hale Paahao** (see stop 20, below).

Cross Canal Street to the:

11 Canal
Unlike Honolulu, Lahaina has no natural deep-water harbor. Whalers would anchor in deep water offshore, then board smaller boats (which they used to chase down and harpoon whales) to make the passage over

the reef to shore. When the surf was up, coming ashore could be dangerous. In the 1840s, the U.S. consular representative recommended digging a canal from one of the freshwater streams that ran through Lahaina and charging a fee to the whalers who wanted to obtain fresh water. In 1913, the canal was filled in to construct Canal Street.

Up Canal Street is the:

12 Government Market

A few years after the canal was built, the government built a thatched marketplace with stalls for Hawaiians to sell goods to the sailors. Merchants quickly took advantage of this marketplace and erected drinking establishments, grog shops, and other pastimes of interest nearby. Within a few years, this entire area became known as "Rotten Row."

Make a right onto Front Street and continue down the street, past Kamehameha III Elementary School. Across from the park is:

13 Holy Innocents Episcopal Church

When the Episcopal missionaries first came to Lahaina in 1862, they built a church across the street from the current structure. In 1909, the church moved to its present site, which was once a thatched house built for the daughter of King Kamehameha I. The present structure, built in 1927, features unique paintings of a Hawaiian Madonna and birds and plants endemic to Hawaii, executed by Delos Blackmar in 1940.

Continue down Front Street, and at the next open field, look for the white stones by the ocean, marking the former site of the "iron-roofed house" called:

14 Hale Piula

In the 1830s, a two-story stone building with a large surrounding courtyard was built for King Kamehameha III. However, the king preferred sleeping in a small thatched hut nearby, so the structure was never really completed. In the 1840s, Kamehameha moved his capital to Honolulu and wasn't using Hale Piula, so it became the local courthouse. The windstorm of 1858, which destroyed the courthouse on Wharf Street (see stop 9, above), also destroyed the iron-roofed house. The stones from Hale Piula were used to rebuild the courthouse on Wharf Street.

Continue down Front Street; across from the 505 Front Street complex is:

15 Malu Ulu Olele Park

This spot sacred to Hawaiians is now the site of a park and ball field. This used to be a village, Mokuhinia, with a sacred pond that was the home of a *moo* (a spirit in the form of a lizard), which the royal family honored as their personal guardian spirit. In the middle of the pond was a small island, Mokuula, home to Maui's top chiefs. After conquering Maui, Kamehameha I claimed this sacred spot as his own; he and his two sons, Kamehameha II and III, lived here when they were in Lahaina. In 1918, in the spirit of progress, the pond was drained and the ground leveled for a park.

Make a left onto Shaw Street and then another left onto Wainee Street. On the left side, just past the cemetery, is:

16 Wainee Church

This was the first stone church built in Hawaii (1828–32). At one time the church could seat some 3,000 people, albeit tightly packed together, complete with "calabash spittoons" for the tobacco-chewing Hawaiian chiefs and the ship captains. That structure didn't last long—the 1858 windstorm that destroyed several buildings in Lahaina also blew the roof off the original church, knocked over the belfry, and picked up the church's bell and deposited it 100 feet away. The structure was rebuilt, but that too was destroyed—this time by Hawaiians protesting the 1894 overthrow of the monarchy. Again the church was rebuilt, and again it was destroyed—by fire in 1947. The next incarnation of the church was destroyed by yet another windstorm in 1951. The current church, named Wailoa, has been standing since 1953. Be sure to walk around to the back of the church: The row of palm trees on the ocean side includes some of the oldest in Lahaina.

Wander next door to the first Christian cemetery in Hawaii:

17 Wainee Cemetery

Established in 1823, this cemetery tells a fascinating story of old Hawaii, with graves of Hawaiian chiefs, commoners, sailors, and missionaries and their families (infant mortality was high then). Enter this ground with respect, because Hawaiians consider it sacred—many members of the royal family are buried here, including Queen Keopuolani, who was the wife of King Kamehameha I, mother of kings Kamehameha II and III, and the first Hawaiian baptized as a Protestant. Among the other graves are those of Rev. William Richards (the first missionary in Lahaina) and Princess Nahienaena (sister of kings Kamehameha II and III).

Continue down Wainee Street to the corner of Luakini Street and the:

18 Hongwanji Mission

The temple was originally built in 1910 by members of Lahaina's Buddhist sect. The current building was constructed in 1927, housing a temple and language school. The public is welcome to attend the New Year's Eve celebration, Buddha's birthday in April (see "Maui County Calendar of Events," p. 20), and O Bon Memorial Services in August.

Continue down Wainee Street. Just before the intersection with Prison Street, look for the historical marker for:

19 David Malo's Home

Although no longer standing, the house that once stood here was the home of Hawaii's first scholar, philosopher, and well-known author, educated at Lahainaluna School. Malo's book on ancient Hawaiian culture, *Hawaiian Antiquities,* is considered *the* source on Hawaiiana today.

His alma mater celebrates David Malo Day every year in April in recognition of his contributions to Hawaii.

Cross Prison Street. On the corner of Prison and Wainee is the:

20 Old Prison

The Hawaiians called the prison Hale Paahao (Stuck in Irons House). Sailors who refused to return to their boats at sunset used to be arrested and taken to the old fort (see stop 10, above). In 1851, however, the fort physician told the government that sleeping on the ground at night made the prisoners ill, costing the government quite a bit of money to treat them—so the Kingdom of Hawaii used the prisoners to build a prison from the coral block of the old fort. Most prisoners here had terms of a year or less (those with longer terms were shipped off to Honolulu) and were convicted of crimes like deserting ship, being drunk, or working on Sunday. Today, the grounds of the prison have a much more congenial atmosphere and are rented out to community groups for parties.

Continue down Wainee Street, just past Waianae Place, to the small:

21 Episcopal Cemetery

This burial ground tells another story in Hawaii's history. During the reign of King Kamehameha IV, his wife, Queen Emma, formed close ties with British royalty. She encouraged Hawaiians to join the Anglican Church after asking the Archbishop of Canterbury to form a church in Hawaii. This cemetery contains the burial sites of many of those early Anglicans.

Next door is:

22 Hale Aloha

This "house of love" was built in 1858 by Hawaiians in "commemoration of God's causing Lahaina to escape the smallpox," while it decimated Oahu in 1853, carrying off 5,000 to 6,000 souls. The building served as a church and school until the turn of the 20th century, when it fell into disrepair. It is no longer standing, but artifacts remain.

Turn left onto Hale Street and then right onto Luakini Street to the:

23 Buddhist Church

This green wooden Shingon Buddhist temple is very typical of myriad Buddhist churches that sprang up all over the island when the Japanese laborers were brought to work in the sugarcane fields. Some of the churches were little more than elaborate false "temple" fronts on existing buildings.

On the side of Village Galleries, on the corner of Luakini and Dickenson streets, is the historical marker for:

24 Luakini Street

"Luakini" translates as a *heiau* (temple) where the ruling chiefs prayed and where human sacrifices were made. This street received its unforgettable name after serving as the route for the funeral procession of

Princess Nahienaena, sister of kings Kamehameha II and III. The princess was a victim of the rapid changes in Hawaiian culture. A convert to Protestantism, she had fallen in love with her brother, Kamehameha III. Just 20 years earlier, their relationship would have been nurtured in order to preserve the purity of the royal bloodlines. The missionaries, however, frowned on brother and sister marrying. In August 1836, the couple had a son, who lived only a few short hours. Nahienaena never recovered and died in December of that same year (the king was said to mourn her death for years, frequently visiting her grave at the Wainee Cemetery; see stop 17, above). The route of her funeral procession through the breadfruit and koa trees to the cemetery became known as "Luakini," in reference to the gods "sacrificing" the beloved princess.

Turn left on Dickenson and walk down to Front Street, where you'll be back at the starting point.

A Whale of a Place in Kaanapali

Farther north along the West Maui coast is Hawaii's first master-planned destination resort, Kaanapali. Along nearly 3 miles of sun-kissed golden beach, pricey midrise hotels are linked by a landscaped parkway and a beachfront walking path. Golf greens wrap around the slope between beachfront and hillside properties. Convenience is a factor here: Numerous restaurants are easy to reach on foot or by resort shuttle, as is **Whalers Village** shopping mall, an oceanfront shopping center with excellent restaurants and casual dining. Shuttles also go to Lahaina (see above), 3 miles to the south, for shopping, dining, entertainment, and boat tours, although some leave right from the beach in front of Kaanapali Beach Hotel. Kaanapali is popular with groups and families—and especially teenagers, who like all the action.

The Scenic Route from West Maui to Central Maui: The Kahekili Highway

The usual road from West Maui to Wailuku is the Honoapiilani Highway (Hwy. 30), which runs along the coast and then turns inland at Maalaea. But those in search of a back-to-nature driving experience should go the other way, along the **Kahekili Highway (Hwy. 340)** ★. (*Highway* is a bit of a euphemism for this paved but somewhat precarious narrow road; check your rental-car agreement before you head out—some companies don't allow their cars on this road. If it is raining or has been raining, skip this road entirely because of potential mud and rock slides.) The road is named after a fierce 18th-century Maui king who built houses from the skulls of his enemies.

You'll start out on the Honoapiilani Highway (Hwy. 30), which becomes the Kahekili Highway (Hwy. 340) after Honokohau, at the northernmost tip of the island. Around this point are **Honolua Bay** ★ and **Mokuleia Bay** ★, designated Marine Life Conservation Areas—meaning that the taking of fish, shells, or anything else here is prohibited.

From this point, the quality of the road deteriorates, and you may share the way with roosters, goats, cows, and dogs, not to mention oncoming cars and trucks that suddenly pop out of blind curves. The narrow road weaves along for the next 20 miles, following an ancient Hawaiian coastal footpath to Honokohau Bay, at the island's northernmost tip, past blowholes, sea stacks, seabird rookeries, and the imposing 636-foot Kahakuloa headland. These are photo opportunities from heaven: steep ravines, rolling pastoral hills, tumbling waterfalls, exploding blowholes, crashing surf, jagged lava coastlines, and a tiny Hawaiian village straight off a postcard.

Just before **mile marker 20,** look for a small turnoff on the *mauka* (*mowkah*, meaning toward the mountain) side of the road, just before the guardrail starts. Park here and walk across the road, and on your left you'll see a spouting **blowhole.** Stay well clear of the blowhole, where waves have swept the unwary out to sea. In winter, this is an excellent spot to look for whales.

On the *mauka* side, you'll pass high cliffs, deep valleys dotted with plantation houses, cattle grazing on green plateaus, old wooden churches, taro fields, and houses hung with fishing nets. It's slow going (you often have to inch past oncoming traffic on what feels like a one-lane track) but a spectacular drive.

About 3 miles farther along the road, you'll come to a wide turnoff providing another great photo op: a view of the jagged coastline down to the crashing surf.

Less than half a mile farther along, just before **mile marker 16,** look for the POHAKU KANI sign, marking the huge 6×6-foot **bell-shaped stone.** To "ring" the bell, look on the side facing Kahakuloa for the deep indentations, and strike the stone with another rock.

Along the route, nestled in a crevice between two steep hills, is the picturesque village of **Kahakuloa ★** ("The Tall Hau Tree"), with a dozen weatherworn houses, a church with a red-tile roof, and vivid green taro patches. From the northern side of the village, you can look back at the great view of Kahakuloa, the dark boulder beach, and the 636-foot Kahakuloa Head rising in the background. Between mile markers 12 and 13, stop in at the wooden roadside stand known as **Julia's Best Banana Bread** for world-famous warm, sweet loaves and coconut candy.

Artists' studios are nestled into the cliffs and hill at various points along the drive. One noteworthy stop is on the east side of Kahakuloa Head, **Karen Lei's Gallery & Gift Shop,** formerly called Kaukini Gallery (www.karenleis gallery.com; (✆ **808/244-3371**). The gallery features work by more than two dozen local artists, with lots of gifts and crafts to buy in all price ranges. (You may also want to stop here to use one of the few restrooms along the drive.)

Note: Check for road closures before heading out, especially if it's been raining heavily. Call Maui County at ✆ **808/270-7845.** Don't try this road in reverse; it's even more harrowing driving on the ocean side from Wailuku to Mokuleia Bay.

SOUTH MAUI

Maalaea

At the bend in the Honoapiilani Highway (Hwy. 30), Maalaea Bay runs along the south side of the isthmus between the West Maui Mountains and Haleakala. This is the windiest area on Maui: Tradewinds blowing between the two mountains are funneled across the isthmus, and by the time they reach Maalaea, gusts of 25 to 30 mph are not uncommon.

This creates ideal conditions for **windsurfers** out in Maalaea Bay. Surfers are also seen just outside the small boat harbor in Maalaea, which has one of the fastest breaks in the state.

Maui Ocean Center ★★★ AQUARIUM   This 5-acre facility houses the largest aquarium in the state and features one of Hawaii's largest predators: the tiger shark. Exhibits are geared toward the residents of Hawaii's ocean waters. As you walk past the three dozen or so tanks and numerous exhibits, you'll slowly descend from the "beach" to the deepest part of the ocean without ever getting wet. Start at the surge pool, where you'll see shallow-water marine life like spiny urchins and cauliflower coral; then move on to the reef tanks, turtle pool, touch pool (with starfish and urchins), and eagle-ray pool before reaching the star of the show: the 100-foot-long, 600,000-gallon main tank featuring tiger, gray, and white-tip sharks, as well as tuna, surgeonfish, triggerfish, and numerous others. The walkway tunnels right through the tank, so you'll be surrounded on three sides by marine creatures. Juvenile scalloped hammerhead sharks swim in another exhibit, while the **Shark Dive Maui Program** (Mon, Wed, and Fri; $199 per certified diver) allows certified scuba divers to plunge into the aquarium with sharks, stingrays, and tropical fish while friends and family watch from the other side of the glass. Fish-loving kids can book a sleepover in the aquarium, staying up into the wee hours to watch glowing jellies and other nocturnal animals. *Tip:* In peak seasons, buy your tickets online to avoid waiting in admission lines. Also check online for special discounts and packages.

At the Maalaea Harbor Village, 192 Maalaea Rd. (the triangle btw. Honoapiilani Hwy. and Maalaea Rd.). www.mauioceancenter.com. ☎ **808/270-7000.** $30 adults; $27 seniors; $20 children 4–12; free for children 3 and younger. Daily 9am–5pm.

Kihei

Capt. George Vancouver "discovered" Kihei in 1778, when it was only a collection of fishermen's grass shacks on the hot, dry, dusty coast (hard to believe, eh?). A **totem pole** stands today where he's believed to have landed, across from the Aston Maui Lu Resort, 575 S. Kihei Rd. Vancouver sailed on to what later became British Columbia, where a great international city, harbor, and massive island now bear his name. In an interesting twist, Kihei's sandy beach parks and the moderately priced condo developments lining them are particularly popular with Canadian visitors, a prime source of snowbirds in winter. Restaurants and nightlife are also more abundant and affordable here.

West of the junction of Piilani Highway (Hwy. 31) and Mokulele Highway (Hwy. 350) is **Kealia Pond National Wildlife Refuge** (www.fws.gov/ kealiapond; ✆ **808/875-1582**), a 700-acre U.S. Fish and Wildlife wetland preserve where endangered Hawaiian stilts, coots, and ducks hang out and splash. These picturesque ponds work two ways: as bird preserves and as sedimentation basins that keep the coral reefs from silting from runoff. You can take a self-guided tour along a boardwalk dotted with interpretive signs and shade shelters, through sand dunes, and around ponds to Maalaea Harbor. The boardwalk starts at the outlet of Kealia Pond on the ocean side of North Kihei Road (near mile marker 2 on Piilani Hwy.). Among the Hawaiian water birds seen here are the black-crowned high heron, Hawaiian coot, Hawaiian duck, and Hawaiian stilt. There are also shorebirds like sanderling, Pacific golden plover, ruddy turnstone, and wandering tattler. From July to December, the hawksbill turtle comes ashore here to lay her eggs. October through March, rangers offer guided bird walks at 9am Tuesday and family-friendly educational presentations, guided walks, and children's crafts from 9am to 2pm the third Saturday of the month. *Tip:* If you're bypassing Kihei, take the Piilani Highway (Hwy. 31), which parallels strip-mall-laden South Kihei Road, and avoid the hassle of stoplights and traffic.

Visitor Center entrance near mile marker 6 on Maui Veterans Hwy. (Hwy. 311). Boardwalk entrance near mile marker 2 on Piilani Hwy. www.fws.gov/kealiapond. ✆ **808/875-1582.** Free admission. Visitor Center: Mon 11am–3pm and Tues–Fri 9am–3pm; refuge Mon–Fri 7:30am–4pm; boardwalk daily 6am–7pm.

Wailea

The dividing line between arid Kihei and artificially green Wailea is distinct. Wailea once had the same kiawe-strewn, dusty landscape as Kihei until Alexander & Baldwin Inc. (of sugarcane fame) began developing a resort here in the 1970s (after piping water from the other side of the island to the desert terrain of Wailea). Today, the manicured 1,450 acres of this affluent resort stand out like an oasis along the normally dry leeward coast.

The best way to explore this golden resort coast is to rise with the sun and head for Wailea's 1½-mile **coastal nature trail** ★, stretching between the Fairmont Kea Lani Maui and the thorny *kiawe* thicket just beyond Marriott's Wailea Beach Resort. It's a great morning walk on a serpentine path that meanders uphill and down past native plants, old Hawaiian habitats, and a billion dollars' worth of luxury hotels. You can pick up the trail at any of the resorts or from clearly marked SHORELINE ACCESS points along the coast. The best time to go is early morning; joggers clog the trail by midmorning and beachgoers take over later on. As the path crosses several bold black-lava points, it affords vistas of islands and ocean. Benches allow you to pause and contemplate the view across Alalakeiki Channel, where you may see whales in season, to rosy Kahoolawe. Sunset is another good time to hit the trail.

Makena

A few miles south of Wailea, the manicured coast changes over to the wilderness of Makena (abundance). In the 1800s, cattle were driven down the slope from upland ranches and loaded onto boats that waited to take them to market. Now **Makena Landing ★★** is a beach park with boat-launching facilities, showers, toilets, and picnic tables. It's great for snorkeling and for launching kayaks bound for La Pérouse Bay and Ahihi-Kinau Natural Preserve. You may spot a half-dozen turtles or more hauled out at the edge of its cove, but please keep a respectful distance and do not disturb them—it's against the law.

From the landing, go south on Makena Road; on the right is **Keawalai Congregational Church** (www.keawalai.org; ℂ **808/879-5557**), built in 1855 with walls 3 feet thick. Surrounded by ti leaves, which by Hawaiian custom provide protection, and built of lava rock with coral used as mortar, this Protestant church sits on its own cove with a gold-sand beach. It always attracts a Sunday crowd for its 7:30am and 10am Hawaiian-language services. Take time to wander through the cemetery; you'll see some tombstones with a ceramic picture of the deceased on them, which is an old custom.

A little farther south on the coast is **La Pérouse Monument ★**, a pyramid of lava rocks that marks the spot where French explorer Adm. Comte de la Pérouse set foot on Maui in 1786. The first Westerner to "discover" the island, he described the "burning climate" of the leeward coast, observed several fishing villages near Kihei, and sailed on into oblivion, never to be seen again. To get here, drive south past **Makena State Park ★★★**, home to popular beaches and Puu Olai cinder cone, to Ahihi Bay, where the road turns to gravel. Just beyond this is **Ahihi-Kinau Natural Reserve ★★**, 1,238 acres of rare anchialine ponds and hardened lava fields from the last eruption of Haleakala, now thought to have occurred between 1480 and 1600. Go another 2 miles along the coast to **La Pérouse Bay;** the monument to its namesake sits amid a clearing in black lava at the end of the dirt road.

The rocky coastline and sometimes rough seas contribute to the lack of appeal for water activities here, and much of the marine reserve area is closed. **Hiking** opportunities, however, are excellent. Bring plenty of water and sun protection, and wear hiking boots that can withstand walking on lava. From La Pérouse Bay, you can pick up the old King's Highway (Hoapili Trail), which at one time circled the island. Walk along the sandy beach at La Pérouse and look for the trail indentation in the lava, which leads down to the lighthouse at the tip of Cape Hanamanioa, about .75-mile round trip. Or you can continue on the rugged trail as it climbs up the hill for 2 miles, then ventures back toward the ocean, where there are quite a few old Hawaiian home foundations and rocky coral beaches.

UPCOUNTRY MAUI

Come upcountry and discover a different side of Maui: On the slopes of Haleakala, cowboys, farmers, and other country people make their homes in

MAUI FARMS: stop & smell the lavender

Idyllic farms abound across Maui. Many open their doors to visitors and have terrific island-grown products for purchase. To spend the day farm-hopping, join Marilyn Jansen Lopes and her husband, Rick, who grew up in the plantation town of Haliimaile. These sweet, knowledgeable guides of **Maui Country Farm Tours** ★★ (www.mauicountryfarmtours. com; ☎ 808/283-9131) offer an overview of Valley Isle agriculture and regale guests with anecdotes and extra treats along the way. They share their love of Maui and provide historic background on the island's sugar mills, coffee plantations, family farms, and vineyards. Tours in 12-seat, air-conditioned buses start at $175, last 5½ to 6½ hours, and include lunch. The **Halfway to Hana** tour features tropical fruit tasting and waterfall dips when weather allows.

If you want to explore Maui's upcountry farms on your own, here are a few recommended stops to visit at your leisure:

o **Surfing Goat Dairy** ★★ (3651 Omaopio Rd., Kula; www.surfing goatdairy.com; ☎ 808/878-2870; Mon–Sat 9am–5pm, Sun 9am–2pm): Take a detour on wild Omaopio Road to meet the frisky kids at the

sweet, off-the-beaten-path. When you spot the surfboard nailed to the tree, you'll know you're close. Some 140 dairy goats blissfully graze the 42 acres and contribute the milk for 24 different cheeses, which are made every day. Casual 20-minute farm tours are $12 adults and $8 for kids. Book in advance if you want to help with "evening" chores—feeding goats in the pasture and milking mama goats by hand (Mon–Sat 3pm; $20 adults, $15 children). Cheese aficionados should also book ahead for a **Grand Dairy Tour** ($49 adults, $39 children 3–12): 2 hours of cheese-making and sampling the farm's award-winning chèvre, quarks, and truffles. Be sure to buy a bar or two of goat-milk soap.

o **Ocean Organic Vodka** ★★ (4051 Omaopio Rd., Kula; www.ocean vodka.com; ☎ 808/877-0009): Never heard of a vodka farm? Neither had I until Ocean Organic opened just below Surfing Goat Dairy. Sustainably harvested organic sugarcane is blended with deep ocean mineral water to make fine-quality liquor. See how it's done at this solar-powered distillery halfway

serene, neighborly communities like **Makawao** and **Kula,** a world away from the bustling beach resorts. Quaint B&Bs and a rustic lodge host a few visitors here, but even if you can't spare a day or two in the cool upcountry air, there are some sights that are worth a look on your way to or from the crater in the national park. Shoppers and gallery hoppers might want to spend more time here; see chapter 8 for details. For a map of this area, turn to the "Upcountry Hotels & Restaurants" map on p. 75.

On the slopes of Haleakala, Maui's farmers have been producing vegetables since the 1800s. In fact, during the gold rush in California, the Hawaiian farmers in Kula shipped so many potatoes that it was nicknamed Nu Kaleponi, a sort of pidgin Hawaiian pronunciation of "New California." In the late 1800s, Portuguese and Chinese immigrants, who had fulfilled their labor contracts with the sugarcane companies, moved to this area, drawn by the rural up the leeward slope of Haleakala. (The views alone are worth the price of admission.) Fun and informative tours are $12 a person (ages 12 and up). Lunch ($27 adults, $15 ages 20 and under) can be added with 24-hour advance notice. Those 21 and over can sample various spirits (and vodka-filled truffles!) and take home a souvenir shot glass. It's open daily 9:30am to 5pm.

o **Alii Kula Lavender** ★★ (1100 Waipoli Rd., Kula; www.aliikula lavender.com; ℂ **808/878-3004**): Stop and smell the lavender at this gorgeous property set high up on the leeward slope of Haleakala. On the 30-minute walking tour (five tours daily; $12 with advance reservation), you can sniff multiple varieties of lavender and tropical flowers and leave with a fragrant bouquet. The store is chock-full of great culinary products (lavender seasonings, honey, jelly, and teas) and bath and body goodies (the salve is a lifesaver). General admission is $3; lunches and/or treasure hunts for kids can be arranged with 24-hour notice. *Tip:* Although different varieties of lavender bloom here throughout the year, the purple

blossoms are at their peak in July and August.

o **O'o Farm** ★★★ (651 Waipoli Rd., Kula; www.oofarm.com; ℂ **808/667-4341**): Also on Waipoli Road, this farm hosts scrumptious "seed-to-cup" breakfast coffee tours and gourmet lunches. It's a pure delight to stroll through the 8½-acre citrus and coffee orchard and biodynamic farm, which was planted to supply the owners' West Maui restaurants: Pacifico, Feast at Lele, and Aina Gourmet Market. For breakfast, you'll pick your own coffee beans, learn how ripe cherries become drinkable roasts, and then settle under the vine-covered canopy for a feast prepared by chef Daniel Eskelsen in an outdoor wood-burning oven. He makes similar magic happen at lunch, a BYOB meal following a farm tour where you harvest the ingredients. The focaccia with Hawaiian sea salt is worth the price of admission all by itself. Both tours cost $64 adults ($32 children 5–12)—well worth it if you make this your main meal of the day. Bring sun protection, a light jacket, walking shoes, and your camera. The views from this elevation are stellar.

agricultural lifestyle. That lifestyle continues today, among the fancy gentlemen's farms that have sprung up in the past 3 decades. Kula farmers still grow its well-known onions, along with lettuce, tomatoes, carrots, cauliflower, cabbage, and persimmons. It is also a major source of cut flowers for the state: Most of Hawaii's proteas, as well as nearly all the carnations used in leis, come from Kula.

To experience a bit of the history of Kula, turn off the Kula Highway (Hwy. 37) onto Lower Kula Road. Well before the turnoff, you'll see a white octagonal building with a silver roof, the **Holy Ghost Catholic Church** (https://kulacatholiccommunity.org; ℂ **808/878-1091**). Hawaii's only eight-sided church, it was built between 1884 and 1897 by Portuguese immigrants. Open daily 8am to 6pm, it's worth a stop to see the hand-carved altar and works of art for the Stations of the Cross, with inscriptions in Portuguese.

Kula Botanical Garden ★ PARK/GARDEN   Take a self-guided, informative, leisurely stroll through this 5-acre garden of more than 700 native and exotic plants—including three unique collections of orchids, proteas, and bromeliads. It offers a good overview of Hawaii's exotic flora in one small, cool place, plus a few nifty fauna in its aviary.

Hwy. 377, south of Haleakala Crater Rd. (Hwy. 378), ½ mile from Hwy. 37. www.kula botanicalgarden.com. ✆ **808/878-1715.** Admission $10 adults; $3 children 6–12; free for children 5 and under. Daily 8am–4pm.

MauiWine (Tedeschi Vineyards) ★★ VINEYARD/WINERY   On the southern shoulder of Haleakala is **Ulupalakua Ranch,** a 20,000-acre spread once owned by the legendary sea captain James Makee, celebrated in the Hawaiian song and dance "Hula O Makee." Wounded in a Honolulu waterfront brawl in 1843, Makee moved to Maui and bought Ulupalakua. He renamed it Rose Ranch, planted sugar as a cash crop, and grew rich. Still in operation, the ranch is now home to Maui's only winery, established in 1974 by Napa vintner Emil Tedeschi, who began growing California and European grapes here and produces serious still and sparkling wines, plus a whimsical white wine made with pineapple juice. The grounds are the perfect place for a picnic, provided you purchase takeout deli fare at the Ulupalakua Ranch Store & Grill across the street (outside food is not allowed). Settle under the sprawling camphor tree, pop the cork on a blanc de blanc, and toast your good fortune. There's a charge for tasting a flight of five wines ($12–$14), but the twice-daily half-hour tours of the grounds are free. Three times a week the staff offers 40-minute historic tasting tours in the Old Jail, a stone building that was once Makee's private office, with more select wines to sample. *Tip:* Try to arrive before the late-afternoon bus tours returning from Hana, whose passengers can suddenly crowd the tasting room.

Across from the winery are the remains of the three smokestacks of the **Makee Sugar Mill,** built in 1878. You may do a double take at the people lounging on the front porch. On closer inspection you'll see that they are not "people," but the work of Maui artist Reems Mitchell, who carved the mannequins on the front porch of the Ulupalakua Ranch Store: a Filipino with his fighting cock, a cowboy, a farmhand, and a sea captain, all representing the people of Maui's history.

14815 Piilani Hwy., Kula. www.mauiwine.com. ✆ **808/878-6058.** Free. Half-hour tastings daily 10am–5pm ($12–$14 for flight of 5 wines). Old Jail tastings Fri–Sun 11:15am ($40). Tasting room open daily 10am–5:30pm. Free tours daily 10:30am and 1:30pm.

HALEAKALA NATIONAL PARK ★★★

At once forbidding and compelling, Haleakala ("House of the Sun") National Park is Maui's main natural attraction. More than 1.3 million people a year ascend the 10,023-foot-high mountain to peer down into the crater of the world's largest dormant volcano. (Haleakala is officially considered active,

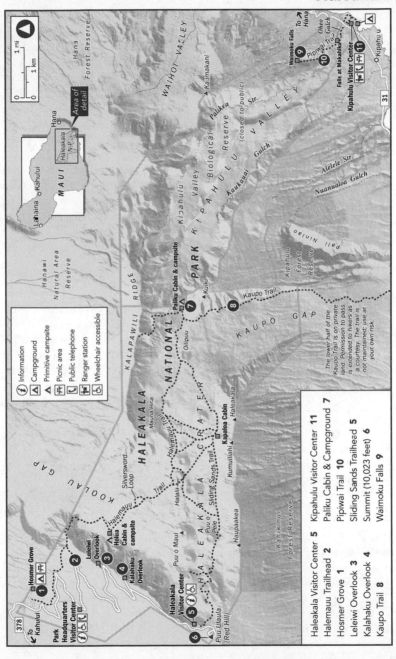

Haleakala Visitor Center **5**
Halemauu Trailhead **2**
Hosmer Grove **1**
Leleiwi Overlook **3**
Kalahaku Overlook **4**
Kaupo Trail **8**

Kipahulu Visitor Center **11**
Paliku Cabin & Campground **7**
Pipiwai Trail **10**
Sliding Sands Trailhead **5**
Summit (10,023 feet) **6**
Waimoku Falls **9**

even though it has not rumbled since 1600, according to the latest research.) That crater could hold Manhattan: It's 3,000 feet deep, 7½ miles long by 2½ miles wide, and encompasses 19 square miles.

The Hawaiians recognize the mountain as a sacred site. Ancient chants tell of Pele, the volcano goddess, and one of her siblings doing battle on the crater floor where Kawilinau (formerly called "Bottomless Pit") now stands. Commoners in ancient Hawaii didn't spend much time here, though. The only people allowed into this sacred area were the *kahuna* (priests), who took their apprentices to live for periods of time in this intensely spiritual place. Today, modern Hawaiian cultural practitioners greet the day here with chanting. New Agers also revere Haleakala as one of the earth's powerful energy points, while the U.S. Air Force maintains an observatory and research lab up here.

But there's more to do here than simply stare into a big black hole: Just going up the mountain is an experience in itself. Where else on the planet can you climb from sea level to 10,000 feet in just 37 miles, or a 2-hour drive? The snaky road passes through big, puffy cumulus clouds to offer magnificent views of the isthmus of Maui, the West Maui Mountains, and the Pacific Ocean.

Impressions

There are few enough places in the world that belong entirely to themselves. The human passion to carry all things everywhere, so that every place is home, seems well on its way to homogenizing our planet, save for the odd unreachable corner. Haleakala crater is one of those corners.

—Barbara Kingsolver, in the New York Times

Many drive up to the summit in predawn darkness to watch the **sunrise over Haleakala;** writer Mark Twain called it "the sublimest spectacle" of his life—one reason reservations are now required (see p. 160 in this chapter). Others visit the summit at dawn, then head just outside the park to coast down the 37-mile road with special brakes (see "Biking" in Chapter 7). Hardy adventurers hike and camp inside the crater's wilderness (see "Hiking & Camping," in chapter 7). Those bound for the interior should bring their survival gear, for the terrain is raw, rugged, and punishing—not unlike the moon. Haleakala's interior is one of the world's quietest places—so silent that it exceeds the technical capacity of microphones.

Just the Facts

Haleakala National Park extends from the summit of Mount Haleakala into the crater, down the volcano's southeast flank to Maui's eastern coast, beyond Hana. There are actually two separate and distinct destinations within the park: **Haleakala Summit** and the **Kipahulu** coastal district (see "Tropical Haleakala: Oheo Gulch at Kipahulu," p. 174). The summit gets all the publicity, but Kipahulu draws crowds, too—it's lush, green, and tropical, and home to Oheo Gulch (formerly known as Seven Sacred Pools). No road links the summit and the coast; you have to approach them separately, and you need at least a day to see each place.

WHEN TO GO   At the 10,023-foot summit, weather changes fast. With windchill, temperatures can be freezing any time of year. Summer can be dry and warm; winter can be wet, windy, and cold. Before you go, get current weather conditions from the park (www.prh.noaa.gov/hnl; ✆ **808/572-4400**) or the **National Weather Service** (✆ **866/944-5025**, option 4).

From sunrise to noon, the light is weak, but the view is usually free of clouds. The best time for photos is in the afternoon, when the sun lights the crater and clouds are few. Go on full-moon nights for spectacular viewing. However, even when the forecast is promising, the weather at Haleakala can change in an instant—be prepared.

ACCESS POINTS   **Haleakala Summit** is 37 miles, or a 1½- to 2-hour drive, from Kahului. To get here, take Hwy. 37 to Hwy. 377 to Hwy. 378. For details on the drive, see "The Drive to the Summit," below. Pukalani is the last town for water, food, and gas.

The **Kipahulu** section of Haleakala National Park is on Maui's east end near Hana, 60 miles from Kahului on Hwy. 36 (Hana Hwy.). Due to traffic and road conditions, plan on 4 hours for the one-way drive from Kahului. For complete information, see "Driving the Road to Hana," later in this chapter. Hana is the only nearby town for services, water, gas, food, and overnight lodging; some facilities may not be open after dark.

At both entrances to the park, the admission fee is $12 per person arriving by foot or bicycle, or $25 per car, good for 3 days of unlimited entry to either area.

INFORMATION, VISITOR CENTERS, & RANGER PROGRAMS   For information before you go, contact Haleakala National Park, (www.nps.gov/hale; ✆ 808/572-4400).

One mile from the park entrance, at 7,000 feet, is the **Headquarters Visitor Center**, open daily from 8am to 4pm. Stop here to pick up information on park programs and activities, get camping permits, and, occasionally, see a nene (Hawaiian goose)—one or more are often here to greet visitors. Restrooms and drinking water are available 24 hours a day.

The **Haleakala Visitor Center,** open daily from sunrise to noon, is near the summit, 11 miles past the park entrance. It offers a panoramic view of the volcanic landscape, with photos identifying the various features, and exhibits that explain the area's history, ecology, geology, and volcanology. Park staff members are often on hand to answer questions. Restrooms and water are available 24 hours a day.

Rangers offer excellent, informative, and free half-hour talks at 11am daily outside the Haleakala Visitor Center and at 3pm daily outside the Headquarters Visitor Center. The first 20 people who show up can take an hourlong guided walk with a ranger through Hosmer's Grove; meet in the parking lot 15 minutes before the hikes start at 9am Monday, Wednesday, and Friday. For more challenging hikes, meet a ranger at the trailhead of Keoneheehee ("Sliding Sands") Trail at 8:45am Saturday for a 2- to 3-mile hike, or Halemauu Trail at 8:45am Sunday for a 2.2-mile hike. These hikes begin at 9am and are

Dominating the east side of Maui is the 10,000-foot summit of Mount Haleakala, long recognized by Hawaiians as a sacred site. The volcano and its surrounding wilderness, extending down the volcano's southeast flank to Maui's eastern coast, offer spectacular treats for the senses. At the summit, you'll encounter dry alpine air, multihued volcanic landscapes, dramatic mists and clouds, and views of three other islands on a clear day; near the sea, the lush green of a subtropical rainforest takes over. You'll find freshwater pools, towering ohia and koa trees, ginger and ti plants, kukui (candlenut), mango, guava, and bamboo.

The "House of the Sun"

According to ancient legend, Haleakala got its name from a clever trick that the demigod Maui pulled on the sun. Maui's mother, the goddess Hina, complained one day that the sun sped across the sky so quickly that her kapa cloth couldn't dry. Maui, known as a trickster, devised a plan. The next morning he went to the top of the great mountain and waited for the sun to poke its head above the horizon. Quickly, Maui lassoed the sun, bringing its path across the sky to an abrupt halt. The sun begged Maui to let go, and Maui said he would on one condition: that the sun slow its trip across the sky to give the island more sunlight. The sun assented. In honor of this agreement, the Hawaiians call the mountain Haleakala, or "House of the Sun." To this day, the top of Haleakala has about 15 minutes more sunlight than the communities on the coastline below.

The Lay of the Land

Scientists believe that the Haleakala volcano began its growth on the ocean floor about 2 million years ago, as magma from below the Pacific Ocean floor erupted through cracks in the Pacific Plate. The volcano has erupted numerous times over the past 10,000 years. Though the most recent eruption is thought to have

limited to the first 12 people to arrive. Wear sturdy hiking shoes, sunglasses, and sunscreen and bring water, snacks, and a raincoat.

For information on hiking and camping, including cabins and campgrounds in the wilderness itself, see "Hiking & Camping," p. 203.

The Drive to the Summit

If you look on a Maui map, almost in the middle of the part that resembles a torso, you'll see a black wiggly line. That's **Hwy. 378,** also known as **Haleakala Crater Road**—one of the fastest-ascending roads in the world. This grand corniche has at least 33 switchbacks; passes through numerous climate zones; goes under, in, and out of clouds; takes you past rare silversword plants and waddling Hawaiian geese, and offers a view through clear, thin air that extends for more than 100 miles.

Going to the summit takes 1½ to 2 hours from Kahului. No matter where you start out, you'll follow Hwy. 37 (Haleakala Hwy.) to Pukalani, where you'll pick up Hwy. 377 (which is also Haleakala Hwy.), and follow that to Hwy. 378. Along the way, expect fog, rain, and wind. You may encounter stray cattle and downhill bicyclists. Fill up your gas tank before you go—Pukalani, 27 miles below the summit, is the last stop for fuel. Along the way, expect fog, rain, and occurred about 1600, Haleakala is still considered an active volcano. You'll pass through as many ecological zones on a 2-hour drive from the humid coast to the harsh summit of the mountain as you would on a journey from Mexico to Canada, and the temperature can vary 30 degrees from sea level to summit. Haleakala was designated an International Biosphere Reserve in 1980 and is home to more endangered species than any other national park in the U.S. Among the rare birds and animals you may see here:

○ **Nene** (Hawaiian goose) *[Branta sandwichensis]:* A relative of the Canada goose, the nene is Hawaii's state bird, standing about 2 feet high with a black head and yellow cheeks. The wild nene on Haleakala number fewer than 250, and the species remains endangered.

○ **'U'au** (Hawaiian petrel) *[Pterodroma sandwichensis]:* These large, dark-grey-brown and white birds travel as far as Alaska and Japan on 2-week feeding trips. Their status is listed as vulnerable; it's estimated that fewer than 1,000 birds are nesting on the Haleakala crater.

○ **Kike koa** (Maui parrotbill) *[Pseudonestor xanthophrys]:* One of Hawaii's rarest birds, currently listed on the endangered list, has an olive-green body and yellow chest. Its strong, hooked, parrotlike bill is used to pry chunks of koa bark as it searches for food.

○ **'Akohekohe** (Crested honeycreeper) *[Palmeria dolei]:* Listed as a critically endangered species, this bird is native only to a 22-square-mile area on the northeastern slope of Haleakala. It has primarily black plumage, with bright orange surrounding the eyes and nape, and a furl of white feathers sprouting over the beak.

wind. Be on the lookout for downhill bicyclists, stray cattle, and the endangered native geese, whose dark gray forms blend in with the pavement.

There are no facilities beyond the ranger stations, and no concessions in the park, so bring your own food and water. Consider a stop en route for the bento boxes and deli fare at **Pukalani Superette** (15 Makawao Ave., Pukalani, www.pukalanisuperette.com; © **808/572-7616**). If you plan to hike, bring even more water and snacks. Also take a jacket or a blanket, especially if you go up for sunrise or sunset. As you go up the slopes, the temperature drops about 3° every 1,000 feet, so the temperature at the top can be 30° cooler than it was at sea level.

Remember, you're entering a high-altitude wilderness area. Some people get dizzy due to the lack of oxygen; you might also suffer lightheadedness, shortness of breath, nausea, severe headaches, flatulence, or dehydration. People with asthma, pregnant women, heavy smokers, and those with heart conditions should be especially careful in the rarefied air.

At the **park entrance,** you'll pay an entrance fee of $25 per car or $20 per motorcycle ($12 for pedestrian or bicyclist). It's good for 3 days and includes access to the Kipahulu District on the east side of the island. Immediately after the park entrance, take a left turn into **Hosmer Grove.** A small campground

You need reservations to view sunrise from the summit. The National Park Service limits how many cars can access the summit between 3 and 7am. Book your spot up to 60 days in advance at **www.recreation.gov.** A fee of $1.50 (on top of the park entrance fee) applies. You'll need to show your reservation receipt and photo I.D. to enter the park.

Watching the sun's first golden rays break through the clouds *is* spectacular, though I recommend sunset instead. It's equally beautiful—and warmer! Plus, you're more likely to explore the rest of the park when you're not sleep-deprived and hungry for breakfast. Full-moon nights can be ethereal, too. No matter when you go, realize that weather is extreme at the summit, ranging from blazing sun to sudden snow flurries. As you ascend the slopes, the temperature drops about 3 degrees every 1,000 feet (305m), so the top can be 30 degrees cooler than it was at sea level. But it's the alpine wind that really stings. Come prepared with warm layers and raingear. For sunrise, bring every warm thing you can swaddle yourself with—blankets and sleeping bags included! And remember, glorious views aren't guaranteed; the summit may be misty or overcast at any time of day. Before you head up the mountain, get current weather conditions from the park (𝄐 **808/572-4400**) or the **National Weather Service** (𝄐 **866/944-5025,** option 4).

abuts a beautiful evergreen forest. During Hawaii's territorial days, forester Ralph Hosmer planted experimental groves, hoping to launch a timber industry. It failed, but a few of his sweet-smelling cedars and pines remain. Birders should make a beeline here. A half-mile loop trail snakes from the parking lot through the evergreens to a picturesque gulch, where rare **Hawaiian honeycreepers** flit above native *'ohi'a* and **sandalwood trees.** The charismatic birds are best spotted in the early morning hours.

About a mile from the entrance, at 7,000 feet, is **Haleakala National Park Headquarters** (𝄐 **808/572-4400**), open daily from 8am to 4pm. Stop here to pick up park information and camping permits, use the restroom, fill your water bottle, and purchase park swag. Keep an eye out for the native Hawaiian goose. With its black face, buff cheeks, and partially webbed feet, the gray-brown *nene* looks like its cousin, the Canada goose; but the Hawaiian bird doesn't migrate and prefers lava beds to lakes. *Nene* once flourished throughout Hawaii, but habitat destruction and introduced predators (rats, cats, dogs, and mongooses) nearly caused their extinction. By 1951, there were only 30 left. The Boy Scouts helped reintroduce captive-raised birds into the park. The species remains endangered, but is now protected as Hawaii's state bird.

Beyond headquarters are **two scenic overlooks** on the way to the summit; stop at Leleiwi on the way up and Kalahaku on the way back down, if only to get out, stretch, and get accustomed to the heights. Take a deep breath, look around, and pop your ears. If you feel dizzy or drowsy, or get a sudden headache, consider turning around and going back down.

Leleiwi Overlook ★ is just beyond mile marker 17. From the parking area, a short trail leads you to a panoramic view of the lunarlike crater. When the clouds are low and the sun is in the right place, usually around sunset, you may experience a phenomenon known as a "Brocken Spectre"—you can see a reflection of your shadow, ringed by a rainbow, in the clouds below. It's an optical illusion caused by a rare combination of sun, shadow, and fog that occurs in only two other places on the planet: Scotland and Germany.

Continue on to the **Haleakala Visitor Center,** open daily at sunrise to noon. It offers panoramic views, with photos identifying the various features, and exhibits that explain the area's history, ecology, geology, and volcanology. Park staff members are often on hand to answer questions. Restrooms and water are available 24 hours a day. The actual summit is a little farther on, at **Puu Ulaula Overlook** (also known as Red Hill), the volcano's highest point, where you'll see Haleakala Observatories' cluster of buildings—known unofficially as **Science City.** The Puu Ulaula Overlook, with its glass-enclosed windbreak, is a prime viewing spot, crowded with shivering folks at sunrise. It's also the best place to see a rare **silversword.** This botanical wonder is the punk of the plant world—like a spaccy artichoke with attitude. Silverswords grow only in Hawaii, take from 4 to 30 years to bloom, and then, usually between May and October, send up a 1- to 6-foot stalk covered in multitudes of reddish, sunflower-like blooms. Don't walk too close to silversword plants, as footfalls can damage their roots.

Two miles farther along is **Kalahaku Overlook ★**. On a clear day, you can gaze across the Alenuihaha Channel to the island of Hawaii, where the summit of Mauna Kea often wears a mantle of snow.

Tip: Be sure to put your car in low gear when driving back down the mountain on the Haleakala Crater Road. That way, you won't destroy the brakes by riding them the whole way down.

THE ROAD TO HANA ★★★

Top down, sunscreen on, radio tuned to a little Hawaiian music on a Maui morning: It's time to head out to Hana along the Hana Highway (Hwy. 36), a wiggle of a road that runs along Maui's northeastern shore. The drive takes at least 3-plus hours from Lahaina or Kihei—but give yourself plenty of time and don't rush. Going to Hana is about the journey, not the destination.

GO WITH THE friends

The Friends of Haleakala National Park is a volunteer organization that leads 3-day service trips into the crater's wilderness. Backpack into the heart of Haleakala, spend a few hours pulling weeds or painting cabins, and gain a deeper appreciation for this magnificent terrain in the company of like-minded volunteers. Trip leaders take care of renting the cabins and supervising rides and meals—which can be hard to do from afar. The trip is free, though you will pitch in for shared meals. Be prepared for 4 to 10 miles of hiking in inclement weather. Sign up at www.fhnp.org.

There are wilder roads, steeper roads, and more dangerous roads, but in all of Hawaii, no road is more celebrated than this one. It winds 50 miles past taro patches, magnificent seascapes, waterfall pools, botanical gardens, and verdant rainforests, and ends at one of Hawaii's most beautiful tropical places.

The outside world discovered the little village of Hana in 1926, when pickax-wielding convicts carved a narrow road out of the cliff's edge. Often subject to landslides and washouts, the mud-and-gravel track was paved in 1962, when tourist traffic began to increase; it now sees around 1,000 cars and dozens of vans a day. That translates to half a million people a year, which is way too many. Go at the wrong time, and you'll be stuck in a bumper-to-bumper rental-car parade. Peak traffic hours are midmorning and midafternoon year-round, especially on weekends.

In the rush to "do" Hana in a day, most visitors spin around town in 10 minutes and wonder what all the fuss is about. It takes time to soak up the serene magic of Hana, play in the waterfalls, sniff the rain-misted gingers, hike through clattering bamboo forests, and merge with the tension-dissolving scenery. Stay overnight if you can, and meander back in a day or two. If you really must do the Hana Highway in a day, go just before sunrise and return after sunset.

Tips: Practice aloha. Yield at one-lane bridges; letting four to six waiting cars a time go before you is typical. Wave at oncoming motorists, let the big guys in 4×4s have the right of way—you're not in a hurry, after all! If the guy behind you blinks his lights, let him pass. Unless you're rounding a blind curve, don't honk your horn—in Hawaii, it's considered rude. *Safety note:* Be aware of the weather when hiking in streams. Flash floods happen frequently in this area. *Do not attempt to cross rising stream waters.* In the words of the Emergency Weather Forecast System: "Turn around. Don't drown."

Guided tours: One more problem with driving the road to Hana? If you're the driver, you'll only catch glimpses of what your passengers are oohing and aahing about. Instead, you're likely to be white-knuckling around some of the blind curves or feeling pressure to speed up from (understandably) impatient local commuters. So for those who can afford it, I strongly recommend taking a guided tour with a small group, or even privately. **Temptation Tours** (www.temptationtours.com; © **808/877-8888** or 800/817-1234) uses eight-passenger luxury vans with captain's chairs and full-length windows on each side so everyone can relish the views. State-certified guides provide expert but not overly chatty commentary; tours ($219–$344) include a dip in a waterfall pool or swimming at a beach, with options for picnicking, sit-down dining, a cave tour, or an equally scenic return via helicopter.

Tip: Book directly for a 15% discount.

But for the adventurous and budget-minded:

THE JOURNEY BEGINS IN PAIA   Before you start out, fill up on fuel. Paia is the last place for gas until you get to Hana, 54 bridges and 617 hairpin turns down the road. Or is it 56 bridges and 620 turns, as others report?

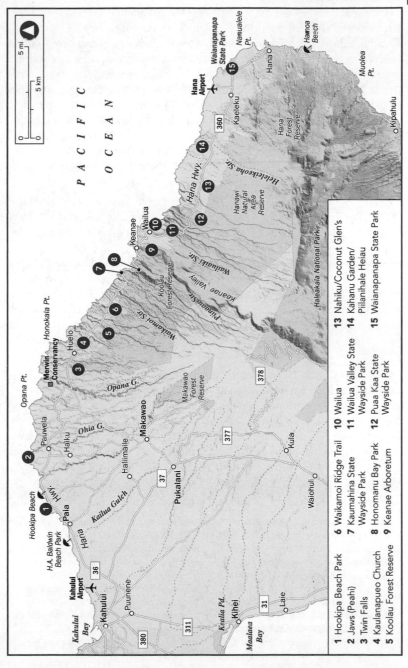

PACIFIC OCEAN

Kahului Bay

Maalaea Bay

1 Hookipa Beach Park
2 Jaws (Peahi)
3 Twin Falls
4 Kaulanapueo Church
5 Koolau Forest Reserve

6 Waikamoi Ridge Trail
7 Kaumahina State Wayside Park
8 Honomanu Bay Park
9 Keanae Arboretum

10 Wailua
11 Wailua Valley State Wayside Park
12 Puaa Kaa State Wayside Park

13 Nahiku/Coconut Glen's
14 Kahanu Garden/ Piilanihale Heiau
15 Waianapanapa State Park

Personally, I've always lost count long before I get there, but it's fun to see how many you can tally en route.

Paia ★★ was once a thriving sugar-mill town. The skeletal mill is still here, but in the 1950s the bulk of the population (10,000 in its heyday) shifted to Kahului. Like so many former plantation towns, Paia nearly foundered, but its beachfront charm lured hippies, followed by adrenaline-seeking windsurfers and, most recently, young families. The town has proven its adaptability. Now trendy boutiques and eateries occupy the old ma-and-pa establishments. Plan to get here early, around 7am, when **Charley's** ★, 142 Hana Hwy. (www.charleysmaui.com ☎ **808/579-8085**), opens. Enjoy a big, hearty breakfast for a reasonable price or continue down the road to the little town of **Kuau.** A rainbow fence made of surfboards announces **Kuau Store** ★ (www.facebook.com/kuaustoremaui; ☎ **808/579-8844**), a great stop for smoothies, breakfast panini, poke, and snacks, although parking can be tight.

WINDSURFER WATCHING Just before mile marker 9 is **Hookipa Beach Park** ★★★, where top-ranked windsurfers come to test themselves against thunderous surf and forceful wind. On nearly every windy day after noon (the board surfers have the waves in the morning), you can watch dozens of windsurfers twirling and dancing in the wind like colored butterflies. To watch them, do not stop on the highway, but go past the park and turn left at the entrance on the far side of the beach. Park on the high grassy bluff or drive down to the sandy beach and park alongside the pavilion. **Green sea turtles** haul out to rest on the east end of the beach. Go spy on them, but stay a respectful distance (at least 10 ft.) away. Facilities include restrooms, a shower, picnic tables, and a barbecue area; food trucks operate on the bluff.

IN JAWS COUNTRY Past Hookipa Beach, the road winds down into **Maliko Gulch.** Big-wave surfers use the boat ramp here to launch jet skis and head out to **Jaws,** one of the world's biggest surf breaks a few coves over. The cliffs above the break gave it its Hawaiian name, **Peahi**; the English nickname is because the waves, which can rise to 60 feet, will chew you up. You'll have to content yourself with watching videos later of the expert tow-in surfers at

The Poet's Garden

Pulitzer Prize–winning poet, antiwar activist, and environmentalist W.S. Merwin, who died in 2019 at the age of 91, left a special legacy at his beloved Maui home: a **botanical garden in Peahi** with more than 2,740 palm trees in nearly 900 different varieties. It took decades to restore the denuded land—former pineapple fields—along the road to Hana. The 18.8-acre palm garden is managed by the **Merwin Conservancy,** which offers monthly 3-hour hiking tours. Available by reservation only, the hikes include informal botanical and historical discussion, poetry readings, and time for quiet reflection—all in the spirit of the garden's founder. Tours are free, but donations are welcome; check the schedule and sign up online at **merwinconservancy.org**. To reach the garden, turn off the Hana Highway past the turnoff to the town of Haiku.

Jaws, though, because the land in front of the break is not open to the public. Continue instead on the Hana Highway, passing through the rural area of **Haiku** for the next few miles; here banana patches and guava trees litter their sweet fruit onto the street.

At mile marker 16, the curves begin, one right after another. Slow down and enjoy the view of fern-covered hills and plunging valleys punctuated by mango and kukui trees. After mile marker 16, the road is still called the Hana Highway, but the number changes from Highway 36 to Highway 360, and the mile markers go back to 0.

TWIN FALLS   Not far beyond mile marker 2, you'll see a large fruit stand on the *mauka* (mountain) side of the road—most likely surrounded by lots of cars. This is **Twin Falls** (www.twinfallsmaui.net; ✆ **808/463-1275**), a privately owned piece of paradise with more waterfalls than anyone can count. A gravel footpath leads to the first waterfall pool. Continue up the mountain path to find many more. Swimming is safe as long as it's not raining and you don't have open wounds. (Bacterial infections aren't uncommon.) Be respectful of the residents and pack out your trash.

From here on out, there's a waterfall (and one-lane bridge) around nearly every turn in the road, so drive slowly and be prepared to stop and yield to oncoming traffic.

HIDDEN HUELO   Just before mile marker 4 on a blind curve, look for a double row of mailboxes on the left side by a pay phone. Down the road lies a hidden Hawaii of an earlier time, where an indescribable sense of serenity prevails. Hemmed in by Waipo and Hoalua bays is the remote community of **Huelo ★**, which means "tail end, last." This fertile area once supported a population of 75,000; today only a few hundred live among the scattered homes and vacation rentals here.

The only reason Huelo is even marked is the historic 1853 **Kaulanapueo Church.** Reminiscent of New England architecture, this coral-and-cement church, topped with a plantation-green steeple and a gray tin roof, is still in use, although services are held just once or twice a month. It still has the same austere interior of 1853: straight-backed benches, a no-nonsense platform for the minister, and no distractions on the walls to tempt you from paying attention to the sermon. Next to the church is a small graveyard, a personal history of this village in concrete and stone.

KOOLAU FOREST RESERVE   After Huelo, the vegetation seems more lush, as though Mother Nature had poured Miracle-Gro on everything. This is the edge of the **Koolau Forest Reserve.** *Koolau* means "windward," and this certainly is one of the greatest examples of a lush windward area: The coastline here gets about 60 to 80 inches of rain a year, as well as runoff from the 200 to 300 inches that falls from farther up the mountain. You'll see trees laden with guavas, as well as mangoes, java plums, and avocados the size of softballs. The spiny, long-leafed plants are *hala* trees, which the Hawaiians used for weaving baskets, mats, and even canoe sails. From here on out, there's a waterfall (and a one-lane bridge) around nearly every turn in the road, so drive slowly and be prepared to stop and yield to oncoming cars.

WILD CURVES   About a half-mile after mile marker 6, there's a sharp U-curve in the road, going uphill. The road is super narrow here, with a brick wall on one side and virtually no maneuvering room. Sound your horn at the start of the U-curve to let approaching cars know you're coming. Take the curve slowly.

Just before mile marker 7, a forest of waving **bamboo** takes over the right-hand side of the road. To the left, you'll see a stand of **rainbow eucalyptus trees,** recognizable by their multicolored trunks. Drivers are often tempted to pull over here, but there isn't any shoulder. Continue on; you'll find many more beautiful trees to gawk at down the road.

A GREAT FAMILY HIKE   At mile marker 9, there's a small state wayside area with restrooms, picnic tables, and a barbecue area. The sign says KOOLAU FOREST RESERVE, but the real attraction here is the **Waikamoi Ridge Trail ★,** a great family hike that wanders on a clearly marked path, has a very gentle slope (easy enough for toddlers and grandparents) and scenic vistas, and has lots of interesting vegetation (which is marked with signs). The start of the trail is just behind the QUIET: TREES AT WORK sign. The .75-mile loop is just the right amount of time to stretch your legs and be ready to get back in the car and head to Hana.

CAN'T-MISS PHOTO OPS   Just past mile marker 12 is the **Kaumahina State Wayside Park ★** (*kaumahina* means "moon rise"). This is not only a good pit stop (restrooms are available) and a wonderful place for a picnic (with tables and a barbecue area), but also a great vista point. The view of the rugged coastline makes an excellent shot—you can see all the way down to the jutting Keanae Peninsula.

Another mile and a couple of bends in the road, and you'll enter the Honomanu Valley, with its beautiful bay. To get to the **Honomanu Bay County Beach Park ★,** look for the turnoff on your left, just after mile marker 14, located at a point in the road where you begin your ascent up the other side of the valley. The rutted dirt-and-cinder road takes you down to the rocky black-sand beach. There are no facilities here. Because of the strong rip currents offshore, swimming is best in the stream inland from the ocean. You'll consider the drive down worthwhile as you stand on the beach, well away from the ocean, and turn to look back on the steep cliffs covered with vegetation.

KEANAE PENINSULA   Below mile marker 17, the vintage Hawaiian village of **Keanae ★★** stands out against the Pacific like a place time forgot. Here, on an old lava flow graced by an 1860 stone church and swaying palms, is one of the few remaining coastal enclaves of Native Hawaiians. They still grow taro in patches and pound it into poi, the staple of the old Hawaiian diet. And they still pluck *opihi* (limpet) from tide pools along the jagged coast and cast throw nets at schools of fish.

The turnoff to the Keanae Peninsula is on the left, just after **Keanae Arboretum** (see below). The road passes by farms as it hugs the peninsula. Where the road bends, there's a small beach where fishermen gather to catch dinner. A quarter-mile farther is the **Keanae Congregational Church** (www.hcucc. org/keanae-congregational-church; © **808/248-8031**), built in 1860 of lava rocks and coral mortar, standing in stark contrast to the green fields surrounding it. Beside the church is a small beachfront park, with false kamani trees against a backdrop of black lava and a roiling turquoise sea.

To experience untouched Hawaii, follow the road until it ends. Park by the white fence and, if ocean conditions permit, take the short 5-minute walk along the shoreline over the black lava. Continue along the footpath through the tall California grass to the black rocky beach, separating the freshwater stream, **Pinaau,** which winds back into the Keanae Peninsula, nearly cutting it off from the rest of Maui. This is an excellent place for a picnic and a swim in the cool waters of the stream, in calm conditions. There are no facilities here, so be sure you carry everything out with you and use restrooms before you arrive. As you make your way back, notice the white PVC pipes sticking out of the rocks—they're fishing pole holders for fishermen, usually hoping to catch ulua. Before you leave the hamlet, pick up a loaf of still-warm banana bread from **Aunty Sandy's** (10 Keanae Rd.).

Closer to the highway, **Keanae Arboretum** showcases Hawaii's botanical world in three ways: native forest, introduced forest, and traditional Hawaiian plants, food, and medicine. You can swim in the pools of Piinaau Stream or press on along a mile-long trail into Keanae Valley, where a lovely tropical rainforest waits at the end. Had enough foliage for one day? This is the prime spot to turn around.

ANOTHER PHOTO OP: KEANAE LOOKOUT Just past mile marker 17 is a wide spot on the ocean side of the road, where you can see the entire Keanae Peninsula's checkerboard pattern of green taro fields and its ocean boundary etched in black lava. Keanae was the result of a postscript eruption of Haleakala, which flowed through the Koolau Gap and down Keanae Valley and added this geological punctuation to the rugged coastline.

FRUIT & FLOWER STANDS Around mile marker 18, the road widens; you'll start to see numerous small stands selling fruit or flowers. I recommend stopping at **Uncle Harry's** (© **808/633-3129**), which you'll find just after the Keanae School around mile marker 18. His family sells a variety of fruits and juices, coffee, kalua pork tacos, and banana bread daily from 10am to 3pm.

WAILUA Just after Uncle Harry's, look for Wailua Road on the left. If you have time for a detour, this road will take you down through the hamlet of homes and churches of Wailua, which also contains a shrine depicting what the community calls a "miracle." Behind the pink **St. Gabriel's Church** is the smaller, blue-and-white **Coral Miracle Church,** home of the **Our Lady of Fatima Shrine.** According to legend, in 1860 the men of this village were building a church by diving for coral to make the stone. But the coral offshore was in deep water and the men could only come up with a few pieces at a time, making the construction of the church an arduous project. A freak storm hit the area and deposited the coral from the deep on a nearby beach. The Hawaiians gathered what they needed and completed the church. After the church was completed, another freak storm hit the area and swept all the remaining coral on the beach back out to sea.

If you look back at Haleakala from here, on your left you can see the spectacular, near-vertical **Waikani Falls.** On the remainder of the dead-end road is an eclectic collection of old and modern homes. Turning around at the road's end is very difficult—and some residents resent tourist incursions—so I suggest you just turn around at the church and head back for the Hana Highway.

Back on the Hana Highway, just before mile marker 19, is the **Wailua Valley State Wayside Park ★** (*wailua* means "two waters"), on the right side of the road. Climb up the stairs for a view of the Keanae Valley, waterfalls, and Wailua Peninsula. On a really clear day, you can see up the mountain to the Koolau Gap.

For a better view of the Wailua Peninsula, continue down the road about ¼ mile. There's a pull-off area with parking on the left (ocean side).

PUAA KAA STATE WAYSIDE PARK   Don't skip this small park, a half-mile past mile marker 22. Park on the left side of the highway, by the restrooms, then cross the road to explore the jade green waterfall pool. Break out your picnic lunch here at the shaded tables. Practice saying the park's name, pronounced pooh-*ahh*-ahh kahh-*ahh,* which means "rolling pig."

NAHIKU   For the world's best dessert (only a slight exaggeration), continue on to this old Hawaiian community near mile marker 27.5 (yes, half-mile markers come into play in this wild territory). You'll see the rainbow-splashed sign on the right for **Coconut Glen's ★★** (www.coconutglens.com; ⓒ **808/248-4876**). Pull over and indulge in some truly splendid ice cream—organic and vegan, made with coconut milk. Scoops of chocolate chili, *lilikoi* (passionfruit), and honey macadamia nut ice cream are served in coconut bowls, with coconut chips as spoons. Open daily 11am to 5pm, this whimsical stand oozes with aloha. From here, you're only 20 minutes from Hana.

KAHANU GARDEN & PIILANIHALE HEIAU ★★★   To see one of Hawaii's most impressive archaeological sites, take a detour off of Hana Highway down Ulaino Road. The **National Tropical Botanical Garden** maintains the world's largest breadfruit collection here—including novel varieties collected from every tropical corner of the globe. Ancient Hawaiian history comes alive when you walk through the manicured canoe garden and first glimpse the monumental 3-acre Piilanihale *heaiu* (temple). Built 800 years ago from stacked rocks hand-carried from miles away, it is a testament to the great chiefdoms of the past. Gaze in wonder at the 50-foot retaining wall and thatched canoe *hale* (house). Imagine steering a war canoe onto the wave-swept shore, where today you might spy a snoozing Hawaiian monk seal. Take time to soak in the site's *mana* (spiritual power). Admission is $10; 2-hour guided tours are $25 (650 Ulaino Rd., Hana; www.ntbg.org; © **808/248-8912**).

HANA AIRPORT After mile marker 31, a small sign points to the Hana Airport, down Alalele Road on the left. Commuter airline Mokulele (www. mokulele.com; © **866/260-7070 or** 808/495-4188) offers flights twice a day from Kahului to Hana and back. *Be warned:* Flights are not timed well for connecting to mainland flights, and there is no public transportation or public taxi service in Hana (plus poor cellphone service makes ride-hailing services problematic.) However, **Travaasa Hana, Maui** (p. 81), offers guests free airport shuttle service and has a few rental cars and Jeeps available ($90–$150 daily, $450–$750 weekly), through a partnership with Enterprise; those not staying at the hotel are welcome to rent them too. Contact the Travaasa concierge directly at © **808/359-2401**.

WAIANAPANAPA STATE PARK ★★ At mile marker 32, just on the outskirts of Hana, shiny black-sand **Waianapanapa Beach** appears like a vivid dream, with bright-green jungle foliage on three sides and cobalt-blue water lapping at its feet. The 120-acre park on an ancient lava flow includes sea cliffs, lava tubes, arches, and the beach, plus a dozen rustic cabins. It also provides tent camping, picnic pavilions, restrooms, showers, drinking water, and hiking trails. If you're interested in staying here, see "Hiking & Camping" as well as "Beaches" in chapter 7.

THE END OF THE ROAD: HEAVENLY HANA ★★

Green, tropical Hana, which some call heavenly, is a destination all its own, a small coastal village in a rainforest inhabited by 1,235 people, many with Native Hawaiian ancestry. The last unspoiled Hawaiian town on Maui is, oddly enough, the home of Maui's first resort, which opened in 1946. Beautiful Hana enjoys more than 90 inches of rain a year—more than enough to keep the scenery lush. Banyans, bamboo, breadfruit trees—everything seems larger than life, especially the flowers, like wild ginger and plumeria. Several roadside stands offer exotic blooms for $5 a bunch. As the signs say, just PUT MONEY IN BOX. It's the Hana honor system. The best farm stand of the bunch is **Hana Farms ★★**, 2910 Hana Hwy. (www.hanafarms.com; © **808/248-7371**), a full-blown local market and farm-to-table food truck.

A Look at the Past

The Hana coast is rich in Hawaiian history and the scene of many turning points in Hawaiian culture. The ancient chants tell of rulers like the 15th-century **Piilani,** who united the island of Maui and built fishponds, irrigation fields, paved roads, and the massive **Piilanihale Heiau ★★**, which still stands today in **Kahanu Garden ★★★**, part of the National Tropical Botanical

Garden system (see "Outdoor Activities," p. 173). Piilani's sons and grandson finished the *heiau* and built the first road to Hana from West Maui, not only along the coast, but also up the Kaupo Gap and through Haleakala Crater. For information on visiting the garden, see "Hiking" under "Outdoor Activities," chapter 7.

In 1849, the cantankerous sea captain **George Wilfong** brought commerce to this isolated village when he started the first sugar plantation on some 60 acres. Because his harsh personality and set demands for plantation work did not sit well with the Hawaiians, Wilfong brought in the first Chinese immigrants to work his fields.

In 1864, two Danish brothers, **August** and **Oscar Unna,** contributed to the growth of the local sugar industry when they established the Hana Plantation. Four years later they brought in Japanese immigrants to labor in the fields.

By the turn of the 20th century, sugar wasn't the only crop booming in greater Hana (there were some six plantations in the area): Rubber was being commercially grown in Nahiku, wheat in Kaupo, and pineapple in Kipahulu.

In the 1920s and 1930s, several self-sufficient towns lined the coast, each with its own general store, school, and churches; some had movie theaters as well. Hana had all of the above plus some 15 stores, a pool hall, and several restaurants.

One can only guess what those towns would have been like today if not for the huge tsunami that hit the state on April 1, 1946. The damage along the East Maui coast was catastrophic: The Keanae Peninsula was swept clear except for its stone church; Hamoa was totally wiped out, accounting for 10 of the 14 deaths on Maui; and many houses disappeared.

After World War II, the labor movement became a powerful force in Hawaii. **C. Brewer,** owner of the largest sugar plantation in Hana, decided to shut down his operation instead of fighting the labor union. The closure of the plantation meant not only the loss of thousands of jobs, but also the loss of plantation-supplied homes and the entire plantation lifestyle. Thankfully, **Paul I. Fagan,** an entrepreneur from San Francisco who had purchased the Hana Sugar Co. from the Unna brothers in the 1930s, became the town's guardian angel.

Fagan wanted to retire here, so he focused his business acumen on the tiny town with big problems. Recognizing that sugar was no longer economically feasible, he looked at the community and saw other opportunities. He bought 14,000 acres of land in Hana, stripped it of sugarcane, planted grass, and shipped in cattle from his ranch on Molokai.

Next he did something that was years ahead of his time: He thought tourism might have a future in Hana, so he established an inn in 1946 that later became the **Hotel Hana-Maui,** now called the **Travaasa Hana** (p. 81). Fagan also pulled off a public relations coup: He brought the entire San Francisco Seals baseball team (which he happened to own) to Hana for spring training, and, more important, he brought out the sportswriters as well. The writers loved

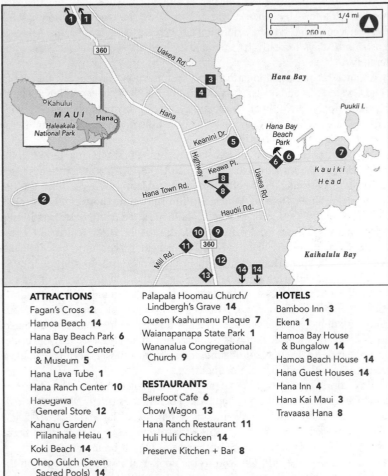

ATTRACTIONS
Fagan's Cross **2**
Hamoa Beach **14**
Hana Bay Beach Park **6**
Hana Cultural Center
& Museum **5**
Hana Lava Tube **1**
Hana Ranch Center **10**
Hasegawa
General Store **12**
Kahanu Garden/
Piilanihale Heiau **1**
Koki Beach **14**
Oheo Gulch (Seven
Sacred Pools) **14**

Palapala Hoomau Church/
Lindbergh's Grave **14**
Queen Kaahumanu Plaque **7**
Waianapanapa State Park **1**
Wananalua Congregational
Church **9**

RESTAURANTS
Barefoot Cafe **6**
Chow Wagon **13**
Hana Ranch Restaurant **11**
Huli Huli Chicken **14**
Preserve Kitchen + Bar **8**

HOTELS
Bamboo Inn **3**
Ekena **1**
Hamoa Bay House
& Bungalow **14**
Hamoa Beach House **14**
Hana Guest Houses **14**
Hana Inn **4**
Hana Kai Maui **3**
Travaasa Hana **8**

Hana and wrote glowing reports about the town; one even gave the town a nickname that stuck: "Heavenly Hana."

In 1962, the state paved Hana Highway. By the 1970s, tourists not only had "discovered" Maui, but also were willing to make the long trek out to Hana.

The biggest change to the local lifestyle came in December 1977, when television finally arrived—after a local cable operator spent 6 months laying cable over cinder cones, mountain streams, and cavernous gulches from one side of the island to the other. Some 125 homes tuned in to the tube—and the rural Hawaiian community was never the same.

Seeing the Sights

Most visitors zip through Hana, perhaps taking a quick look out their car windows at a few sights before buzzing on down the road. They might think they've seen Hana, but they definitely haven't experienced Hana. Allow at least 2 or 3 days to really let this land of legends show you its beauty and serenity.

Another recommendation: See Hana's attractions, especially the pools, ponds, waterfalls, and hikes, early in the day. You'll have them all to yourself. The day-trippers arrive in Hana around 11am and stay until about 4pm; that's when the area is overrun with hundreds of people in a hurry, who want to see everything in just a few hours.

As you enter Hana, the road splits about ½ mile past mile marker 33, at the police station. Both roads will take you to Hana, but the lower road, Uakea Road, is more scenic. Just before you get to Hana Bay, you'll see the old wood-frame **Hana District Police Station and Courthouse,** built in 1871 and the size of a Yankee one-room schoolhouse; the courthouse is still used occasionally for minor local matters. Next door is the **Hana Cultural Center & Museum ★,** 4974 Uakea Rd. (www.hanaculturalcenter.org; © 808/248-8622), usually open Monday through Friday from 10am to 4pm, with a $3 donation requested. This small building has an excellent collection of Hawaiian quilts, artifacts, books, and photos. Also on the grounds are **Kauhale O Hana,** composed of four *hale* (houses) for living, meeting, cooking, and canoe building or canoe storage. A sign notes that in pre-Western-contact times, a favorite male cousin was often sacrificed and buried under the center post of a hale to give the building *mana*, or spiritual power. Fortunately, these are replicas—no human sacrifice required.

Kitty-corner from the cultural center is the entrance to **Hana Bay ★★.** You can drive right down to the pier and park. There are restrooms, showers, picnic tables, barbecue areas, and even a snack bar here. The 386-foot, red-faced cinder cone beside the bay is **Kauiki Head,** the scene of numerous fierce battles in ancient Hawaii and the birthplace of Queen Kaahumanu in 1768. A short 5-minute walk will take you to the spot. You might see people on the trail along the hill on the wharf side, which leads through ironwood trees, but don't try to follow them unless you're willing to risk a broken limb in a remote area with limited medical services. The trail to a small cove with a beach of eroded red cinders (admittedly very photogenic), is very narrow, crumbling, and slippery, particularly after rainfall, which is common in Hana; visitors have been severely injured here falling onto lava rocks.

Instead, head to the center of town by leaving Hana Bay, crossing Uakea Road, and driving up Keawa Place; turn left on Hana Highway, and on the corner will be **Travaasa Hana,** a now-luxurious hotel resort that was formerly the Hotel Hana-Maui, established by a San Francisco entrepreneur named Paul Fagan in 1946. On the green hills above Travaasa Hana stands a 30-foot-high white cross made of lava rock. Citizens erected the cross in memory of

Fagan, who founded not only the hotel but Hana Ranch and helped keep the town alive. The memorial went up 2 years after his death in 1960. The hike up to **Fagan's Cross** provides a gorgeous view of the Hana coast, especially at sunset, when Fagan himself liked to climb this hill (see "Hiking and Camping" in chapter 7 for details).

Back on the Hana Highway, just past Hauoli Road, is the majestic **Wananalua Congregational Church.** It's listed on the National Register of Historic Places not only because of its age (it was built in 1838–42 using coral stones), but also because of its location, atop an old Hawaiian *heiau.*

Just past the church, on the right side of Hana Highway, is the turnoff to the **Hana Ranch Center,** the commercial center for Hana, with a post office, bank, general store, the Hana Ranch Stables, and a restaurant and snack bar. But the real shopping experience is across the Hana Highway at the **Hasegawa General Store ★★** (p. 232), a Maui institution, which carries oodles of merchandise from fine French wines to fishing line and name-brand clothing, plus everything you need for a picnic or a gourmet meal. Buy a T-shirt or bumper sticker and check out the machete display above the office window. This is also the place to find out what's going on in Hana: The bulletin board at the entrance has fliers and handwritten notes advertising everything from fundraising activities to classes to community-wide events. Don't miss this unique store.

Outdoor Activities

Hana is one of the best areas on Maui for ocean activities; it also boasts a wealth of nature hikes, remote places to explore on horseback, waterfalls to discover, and even lava tubes to investigate; see chapter 7, "Fun On and Off the Beach."

Above all, don't miss **Kahanu Garden ★★★**, owned and operated by the **National Tropical Botanical Garden** (650 Ulaino Rd., https://ntbg.org/gardens/kahanu; ✆ **808/248-8912**). Admission is $10 for adults and free for children 12 and under. The garden is open weekdays from 10am to 4pm and 9am to 2pm Saturdays and holidays. Allow an hour and a half for the self-guided tour. Be sure to wear comfortable walking shoes and long pants, and bring mosquito repellent, a hat for shade, and water. Guided tours (offered by reservation only) start at 11am Monday to Saturday and cost $25 per person (free children 12 and under). Many of the guides hail from Hana and share stories of ancient Hawaii and cultural traditions as well as botanical knowledge.

The 122 acres here encompass plant collections from the Pacific Islands, concentrating on plants of value to the people of Polynesia, Micronesia, and Melanesia. Kahanu Garden contains the largest known collection of breadfruit cultivars from more than 17 Pacific Island groups and Indonesia, the Philippines, and the Seychelles. Interpretive signs line a walking trail.

The most intriguing draw here is **Piilanihale Heiau** (see "A Look at the Past," earlier in this chapter), a national historical landmark. Believed to be the largest such temple in Polynesia, it measures 341×415 feet, and it was built in a unique terrace design not seen anywhere else in Hawaii. The walls are 50 feet tall and 8 to 10 feet thick. Historians believe that Piilani's two sons and his grandson completed the mammoth temple, which was dedicated to war, sometime in the 1500s, 3 centuries after work began on it. The heiau had become completely covered by plants by 1974, when Hana Ranch and local families donated the land it sits on and some 60 surrounding acres to the National Tropical Botanical Garden, which agreed to restore the temple and provide public access. Stonemasons from Hana used traditional methods to restack fallen terrace walls, finishing their work in 1999.

If you have time to visit one beach on East Maui, make it **Hamoa Beach ★★★**. Viewed from above, this half-moon-shaped, gray-sand beach is vision of paradise. The wide stretch of sand (a mix of coral and lava) is three football fields long and sits below 30-foot black-lava sea cliffs. Swells on this unprotected beach break offshore and roll in, making it a popular surfing and bodysurfing area. Hamoa is often swept by powerful rip currents, so take care; the typically calm left side is best for snorkeling in summer. The beach shares some of its facilities with Travaasa Hana resort, but there are showers and restrooms for non-guests. Parking is limited to on-street parallel parking (if you're staying at Travaasa, take advantage of its free shuttle.)

Access is from the looping Haneoo Road, which intersects the Hana Highway (Hwy. 360) 1.7 miles south of Travaasa Hana and hugs the coast before curving uphill again above Hamoa Beach. Haneoo Road intersects the highway again less than a half-mile farther.

Just Beyond Hana
OHEO GULCH AT KIPAHULU ★★★

If you're thinking about heading out to the so-called Seven Sacred Pools, west of Hana at the Kipahulu end of Haleakala National Park, let's clear this up right now: There are *more* than seven pools—about 24, actually—and *all* water in Hawaii is considered sacred. It's a PR campaign spun out of control into contemporary myth. Folks here call the attraction by its rightful name, **Oheo Gulch ★★★**, and visitors sometimes refer to it as Kipahulu, which is actually the name of the area where Oheo Gulch is located. No matter what you call it, it's a beautiful sight. The dazzling series of pools and cataracts cascading into the sea is so popular that it has its own roadside parking lot. Keep in mind that the pools are often closed because of the danger of flash flooding, rockfall, and water quality. Be sure to comply with any signs posted by the park service, which recommends against swimming in the pools in general; people have been swept out to sea, crushed by rocks, or have fallen from ledges. *Note:* The sky can be sunny near the coast, but floodwaters from Kipahulu Valley can cause the pools to rise 4 feet in less than 10 minutes.

Even though Oheo is part of Haleakala National Park, you cannot drive here from the summit. Starting from Hana, you'll head another 10 miles farther west along the sinuous Hana Highway (Hwy. 31) to the park's **Kipahulu District** (www.nps.gov/hale/planyourvisit/kipahulu.htm; © **808/248-7375**) The visitor center, which has restrooms, a water bottle refilling station, gift shop, safety information, and exhibits, is open 9am to 5pm daily. Rangers offer a weekly guided hike of Pipiwai Trail, which leads to two waterfalls, at 10am Sundays; book no more than 1 week in advance by calling © **808/248-7375.** For details on hiking and camping here, see "Hiking & Camping," chapter 7.

LINDBERGH'S GRAVE

A mile past Oheo Gulch, off a marked dirt road on the ocean side of the Hana Highway, is **Palapala Hoomau Congregational Church** ★ (http://palapala hoomau.org), built in 1857 of limestone coral with a green-timbered roof and small steeple. Although its charming design includes a glass painting of a Polynesian Jesus in a royal feather cape on the rear window, it's better known as the home of **Lindbergh's Grave.** First to fly solo across the Atlantic Ocean, in 1927, Charles A. Lindbergh suffered the death of his 20-month-old son in a notorious kidnapping case 5 years later. In the late 1960s, he found peace in the Pacific, settling in Hana, where he eventually died of cancer in 1974. The famous aviator is buried under river stones in the small cemetery, shaded by a Java plum tree. His tombstone is engraved with his favorite words from Psalm 1939: "IF I TAKE THE WINGS OF THE MORNING AND DWELL IN THE UTTERMOST PARTS OF THE SEA."

EVEN FARTHER AROUND THE BEND

Be careful, as portions of the road here are unpaved all the way to the fishing village of **Kaupo.** It narrows to one lane at times, wandering in and out of valleys with sharp rock walls and blind bends hugging the ocean cliffs (tap your horn gently to warn oncoming traffic, although there isn't much of it.) You may encounter wild pigs and stray cows. About 6 miles and 60 minutes from Oheo Gulch, you'll see windswept **Huialoha Congregationalist "Circuit" Church** (www.huialohachurchkaupo.org), originally constructed in 1859 and most recently restored in 2015. Across from the church and down the road a bit is the **Kaupo Store** (© **808/248-8054**), which marks the center of the ranching community of Kaupo. Store hours are officially Monday through Saturday from 10am to 5pm, but in this arid cattle country, posted hours often prove meaningless. The Kaupo Store is the last of the Soon family stores, which at one time stretched from Kaupo to Keanae. Service isn't exactly known for being warm, and you'll be expected to tip to use the restroom, even if you purchase a cold drink or (not particularly fresh) snack. Still, as the only such oasis en route to Ulupalakua, it's worth a couple of dollars, especially if you enjoy perusing vintage cameras, clocks, and other antiques from the Soons' collection.

From the Kaupo Store, the landscape turns into barren, dry desert. In the lee of Haleakala, this area gets little rain. Between mile markers 29 and 30, look for the ancient lava flow that created an arch as it rolled down Haleakala. Keep an eye peeled for cattle—this is open-range country. Eventually the road will wind uphill, and suddenly the forest and greenery of Ulupalakua will come into sight.

There are no phones or services from Kaupo until you reach **Ulupalakua Ranch** (p. 154), which has a winery and a general store. Just 5½ miles past Ulupalakua is **Ching's Store** (9212 Kula Hwy., ℭ **808/878-1556**), which sells gas and groceries from 7:30am to 6:30pm daily.

From here, you're about 30 minutes from Kahului, 40 minutes to Kihei, and an hour to Lahaina.

FUN ON & OFF THE BEACH

The sun, sand, and sea may have drawn you to Maui, but there's also a world of wonder to explore in the green valleys, forested mountains, and rugged lava landscapes. This chapter covers the best of the island's outdoor activities, from golfing, snorkeling, or hiking on your own to exciting guided adventures on land or sea (and sometimes above and below them). It's fine just to relax on one of the top beaches mentioned here, but you'll be missing out on some of Maui's magic if you don't take at least one foray into the rest of its great outdoors.

BEACHES

Although its nickname is the Valley Isle, Maui's crowning jewels may well be its more than 80 accessible beaches, from black-sand beaches peppered with white coral to powdery golden ones, from intimate coves to impossibly long stretches of sand. What follows is a personal selection of the finest of Maui's beaches, appealing to a variety of interests and activities, including safety, provided reasonable caution is exercised. The ocean safety mantra "When in doubt, don't go out" is wise to remember here; if you're a novice swimmer, consider visiting one of Maui's nine beaches with year-round lifeguards (noted below). You'll find current ocean conditions and a map of lifeguarded conditions at **www.hawaiibeachsafety. com/maui**.

All beaches, even those fronted by exclusive resorts, are public property, and you are welcome to visit. Hawaii state law requires that all resorts, hotels, and even residential communities offer public right-of-way access to the beach. For a map of 48 notable beach and shoreline access points, see www.mauimapp.com/information/shoreline.htm.

Many beach access points also include parking, though not always in the supply to meet the demand; plan to get up early to nab a prime spot. And while you're not welcome to plop down on resort beach lounges, grab resort towels, or dip into resort pools or hot tubs, you're certainly free to rent snorkel gear, buy refreshments, or pay for any other services hotels offer oceanside.

West Maui

Beaches in this section are listed roughly north to south.

D.T. FLEMING BEACH PARK ★★

This broad, crescent-shaped beach, named after the man who started the commercial growing of pineapples on the Valley Isle, is a great place to take the family. Just north of the **Ritz-Carlton, Kapalua** (p. 59), it begins near at the 16th hole of the Kapalua golf course (Makaluapuna Point) and rolls around to the sea cliffs at the other side. Ironwood trees provide shade on land. Offshore, a shallow sandbar extends to the edge of the surf. The waters are generally good for swimming and snorkeling; sometimes, off on the right side near the sea cliffs, the waves build enough for body boarders and surfers to get a few good rides in. This park has lots of facilities: restrooms, showers, picnic tables, barbecue grills, and a paved parking lot. Be sure to stop at the Ritz's **Burger Shack ★** (daily 11am–4pm) at the beach's southern end for a craft beer, hearty burger, or tropical shake.

Note: On the west side of Makaluapuna Point is even less crowded **Oneloa Beach ★★**, nicknamed "Ironwood" for the nearby trees; the Kapalua Coastal Trail passes right by it, with 16 public parking spaces at the intersection of Lower Honoapiilani Road and Kapalua Place.

From D.T. Fleming, it's also just a 3-minute drive east via Honoapiilani Highway to a handful of parking spots on the left, just past mile marker 31. You'll then have to walk down about 80 cement steps to Mokuleia Bay and well-shaded **Slaughterhouse Beach ★**—named for a thankfully long-closed ranch facility—but the trek is worth it, especially in calm conditions (typically in summer) when you can snorkel with sea turtles. The pristine bay is part of a marine preserve with Honolua Bay (a surf contest site in winter), which lies around the point to the east. There are no facilities, though, so plan ahead.

KAPALUA BEACH ★★★

This beach cove is the stuff of dreams: a golden crescent bordered by two palm-studded points. The sandy bottom slopes gently to deep water at the bay mouth; the water's so clear that you can see it turn to green and then deep blue. Protected from strong winds and currents by the lava-rock promontories, Kapalua's calm waters are ideal for swimmers of all abilities. The bay is big enough to paddle a kayak around in without getting into the more challenging channel that separates Maui from Molokai. Fish hang out by the rocks, making it decent for snorkeling. The sandy strip isn't so wide that you burn your feet getting in or out of the water, and it's edged by a shady path and cool lawns. Access the beach via a small tunnel beside **Merriman's** restaurant (p. 108). Parking is limited to about 30 spaces in a small lot off Lower Honoapiilani Road by **Napili Kai Beach Resort** (p. 53). so arrive early. Facilities include showers, restrooms, lifeguards, a rental shack, and plenty of shade. *Note:* You can also park here and walk through Napili Kai to **Napili Bay ★★**, another attractive golden crescent beach that has good swimming and

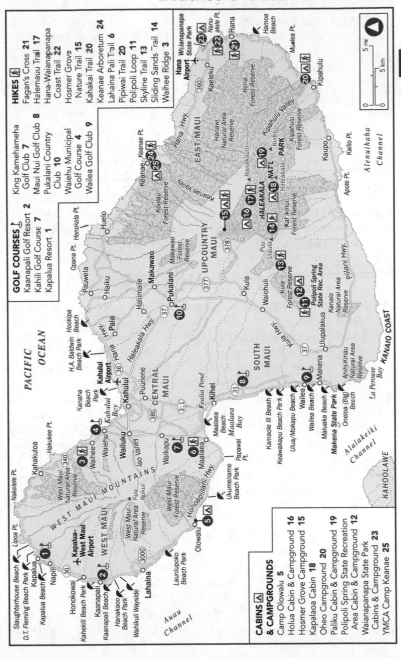

HIKES

Fagan's Cross **21**
Halemauu Trail **17**
Hana-Waianapanapa Coast Trail **22**
Hosmer Grove Nature Trail **15**
Kahakai Trail **20**
Keanae Arboretum **24**
Lahaina Pali Trail **6**
Pipiwai Trail **20**
Polipoli Loop **11**
Skyline Trail **13**
Sliding Sands Trail **14**
Waihee Ridge **3**

GOLF COURSES

King Kamehameha Golf Club **7**
Maui Nui Golf Club **8**
Pukalani Country Club **10**
Waiehu Municipal Golf Course **4**
Wailea Golf Club **9**

Kaanapali Golf Resort **2**
Kahili Golf Course **7**
Kapalua Resort **1**

CABINS & CAMPGROUNDS

Camp Olowalu **5**
Holua Cabin & Campground **16**
Hosmer Grove Campground **15**
Kapalaoa Cabin **18**
Oheo Campground **20**
Paliku Cabin & Campground **19**
Polipoli Spring State Recreation Area Cabin & Campground **12**
Waianapanapa State Park Cabins & Campground **23**
YMCA Camp Keanae **25**

snorkeling in calm summer conditions and also tends to be more crowded, thanks to the condo resorts lining it.

KAHEKILI BEACH PARK ★★★

On the north side of Black Rock, this beach is often referred to as "North Kaanapali" or "Airport Beach"—before all the condos and timeshares on either side of the park, this area used to host an airstrip. This park gets top marks for everything: grassy lawn with a pavilion and palm trees, plenty of soft sand, and a vibrant coral reef a few fin-kicks from shore. Herbivorous fish (surgeonfish and rainbow-colored parrotfish) are off-limits to fishermen here, so the snorkeling is truly excellent. Facilities include picnic tables, barbecues, showers, restrooms, and parking. On a stretch of coast where parking is often a problem, this park with its big shady lot is a gem. Heading north on Honoapiilani Highway past the Kaanapali Resort, turn left onto Kai Ala Road (labeled Puukolii Road on the mountain side of the highway).

KAANAPALI BEACH ★★

Turn your back to the high-rise hotels and condos lining mile-long Kaanapali Beach, and you'll be dazzled by the multi-island view, especially at sunset. A paved beach walk links hotels and condos, open-air restaurants, and Whalers Village shopping center along the long stretch of light blond sand, shrunken in places by storms but still expansive enough to offer plenty of room to pitch a beach umbrella. In summertime, swimming is typically excellent, although you'll want to observe any warning flags if posted. In calm conditions, the best snorkeling is around **Black Rock** (known as Puu Kekaa in Hawaiian), in front of the **Sheraton Maui** (p. 51) at the beach's northern end. The water is clear, calm, and populated with clouds of tropical fish. You might even swim with a turtle or two; I've also seen a spotted eagle ray and a Hawaiian monk seal cruising the area. Various beach-activity vendors line up in front of the hotels, offering nearly every type of water activity and equipment, so no worries if you need snorkel gear or a stand-up paddleboard to ply the waters. *Note:* If the kiosks aren't renting due to high waves or strong currents, follow their lead and stay out of the water. Locals may know how to navigate stiff shorebreak on a boogie board, but less-experienced visitors have been seriously injured here during rough conditions.

Facilities include outdoor showers, but restrooms and parking are a problem. Blue SHORELINE ACCESS signs mark the very limited public access parking lots off Kaanapali Parkway, which intersects with Honoapiilani Highway. You'll see them near the southern parking lot of the **Hyatt Regency Maui** (p. 50), between Whalers Village and the **Westin Maui** (p. 51) , and just south of the Sheraton. Unofficially, you can park in the Whalers Village paid parking structure, which posts "NO BEACH ACCESS" signs but doesn't appear to enforce it; just be sure to buy something in one of the stores or dine at one of its great restaurants. You'll not only get validation to offset any parking free, you'll earn beach karma points.

Frustrated in your hunt for parking? Get back on the highway and head instead to nearby **Kahekili** or **Hanakaoo** beach parks (see below)—you can even walk from the latter to Kaanapali if you're really motivated.

HANAKAOO BEACH PARK ★★

Connected to Kaanapali Beach in a narrow stretch south of the **Hyatt Regency Maui** (p. 50), this slightly rockier, slimmer beach draws a big local crowd on weekends—and no wonder: It boasts easy parking (well, at least on weekdays), plus showers, restrooms, barbecues, covered picnic tables, and a lifeguard tower. Outrigger canoe clubs practice here, leading to its modern nickname, Canoe Beach; its Hawaiian name means "Digging Stick Bay." Bodysurfers dig the shorebreak here. Entrance is on the oceanside of Honoapiilani Highway, near mile marker 23, about a half-mile north of the Lahaina Civic Center.

WAHIKULI WAYSIDE PARK ★

About 1 mile south of Hanakaoo Beach Park, this small stretch of sand with a larger green lawn between Lahaina and Kaanapali is one of Lahaina's most popular beach parks. It's packed on weekends, but during the week it's a great place for swimming, snorkeling (watch for turtles), sunbathing, and picnics. Facilities include paved parking (73 marked spaces and 33 unmarked), restrooms, showers, and 30 small covered pavilions with picnic tables and barbecue grills. There are two entrances, both off Honoapiilani Highway near Leialii Parkway.

LAUNIUPOKO BEACH PARK ★★

Families with children will love this small park off Honoapiilani Highway, just south of Lahaina. A large wading pool for kids fronts the shady park, with giant boulders protecting the wading area from the surf outside. Just to the left is a small sandy beach with good swimming when conditions are right. Offshore, the waves are occasionally big enough for surfing; you may spot beginning surfers taking lessons or outrigger surf canoes. The view from the park is one of the best: You can see the islands of Kahoolawe and Lanai. Facilities include a paved 40-space parking lot, plus 50 spaces across the highway, one restroom and shower, 16 picnic tables, and 10 barbecue grills. It's popular for local gatherings, and crowded on weekends.

South Maui

Wailea's beaches may seem off-limits, hidden from plain view as they are by an intimidating wall of luxury resorts, but all are open to the public. Look for the shoreline access signs along Wailea Alanui Drive, the resort's main boulevard. Fortunately, Kihei makes the hunt for beach parking much easier.

KAMAOLE III BEACH PARK ★

Three beach parks—**Kamaole I, II, and III**—stand like golden jewels in the front yard of suburban Kihei. They're popular with local residents and visitors alike because they're easily accessible. On weekends, they're jam-packed with picnickers, swimmers, and snorkelers.

The most popular, Kamaole III, nicknamed "Kam-3," is the biggest of the three beaches, with wide pockets of gold sand. It's the only one with a children's playground and a grassy lawn that meets the sand. Swimming is generally safe here, but scattered lava rocks are toe-stubbers at the waterline. Both the north and the south shores are rocky fingers with a surge big enough to attract fish and snorkelers; the winter waves appeal to bodysurfers. Kam-3 is also a wonderful place to watch the sunset. Facilities include restrooms, showers, picnic tables, barbecue grills, and lifeguards. There's plenty of parking on South Kihei Road, south of Keonekai Road and across from the Maui Parkshore condos.

KEAWAKAPU BEACH PARK ★★

You can't see this mile-long beauty from the road, so keep an eye out for the blue shoreline-access signs as you head toward Wailea on South Kihei Road. The long expanse of soft, white-gold sand has more than enough room for the scores of people who come here to stroll and swim. Clear, aquamarine waves tumble to shore—just the right size for gentle riding, with or without a board. During winter, mama whales come in close to give birth and teach their calves the finer points of whale acrobatics. Dip your head underwater to eavesdrop on the humpbacks' songs. At any time of year, gorge yourself on phenomenal sunsets. The beach has three separate entrances: The first is an unpaved lot just past the Mana Kai Maui hotel, the second is a shady paved lot at the corner of South Kihei Road and Kilohana Drive (cross the street to the beach), and the third is a large lot at the terminus of South Kihei Road. Facilities include restrooms (at the third entrance only), showers, and parking.

ULUA/MOKAPU BEACHES ★★

The twin beaches of Ulua and Mokapu, separated by a rocky point, are popular with sunbathers, snorkelers, and scuba divers alike. Some of Wailea's best snorkeling is found on the adjoining reef. The ocean bottom is shallow and gently slopes down to deeper waters, making swimming generally safe. In high season (Christmas–Mar and June–Aug), the sand may be carpeted with beach towels and packed with sunbathers like sardines in cocoa butter. Facilities include showers, restrooms, and a 71-space parking lot. Beach equipment can be rented at the nearby Wailea Ocean Activity Center. Look for the blue shoreline access sign at Halealii Place off Wailea Alanui Drive near the Wailea Beach Marriott Resort & Spa. You can also access the beaches from the 1½-mile **Wailea Beach Path**.

WAILEA BEACH ★

The fancy resorts that claim this gold-sand crescent as their front yard put out plenty of umbrellas and beach chairs, but don't be afraid to stake your own claim to a piece of the broad sand or the magnificent view of Kahoolawe and Lanai and the tiny crescent of Molokini, probably the most popular diving and snorkeling spot in these parts. You'll also be able to ogle humpback whales in season (Dec–Mar) and iridescent sunsets. Facilities include restrooms, outdoor showers, and limited free parking at the blue shoreline access sign, on Wailea Alanui Drive, the main drag of this resort.

MALUAKA BEACH ★★

For a less crowded beach experience, head south. Development falls off dramatically as you travel toward Makena and its wild, dry countryside of thorny *kiawe* trees. Maluaka Beach is notable for its beauty and its views of Molokini Crater, the offshore islet, and Kahoolawe, the so-called target island (it was used as a bombing target from 1945 until the early 1990s). This golden, sandy crescent has a large grassy knoll on one end, but little shade, so bring your own umbrella. Sea turtles will often swim alongside you here (remember: look but don't touch or approach). The waters around Makena Landing, at the north end of the bay, are particularly good for snorkeling. Facilities include restrooms, showers, picnic tables, and parking. From Makena Alanui, turn right on Makena Road, and head down to the shore.

MAKENA STATE PARK (BIG BEACH) ★★★

One of the most popular beaches on Maui, the "Big Beach" in Makena State Park, also called Makena Beach, is so vast it never feels crowded. Ancient Hawaiians named it Oneloa, or "Long Sand": It's more than 100 feet wide and stretches out 3,300 feet from Puu Olai, the 360-foot cinder cone on its north end (where the snorkeling is good) to its southern rocky point. The golden sand is luxuriant, deep, and soft, but the shorebreak is steep and powerful. Many a visitor has broken an arm—or worse—in the surf here. If you're an inexperienced swimmer, better to watch the pros shred waves on skimboards. Facilities include portable toilets, but there's plenty of parking and lifeguards at the first two entrances off Makena Alanui Road, heading south from Wailea, plus a food truck at the first one. Dolphins often frequent these waters, and nearly every afternoon a heavy cloud rolls in, providing welcome relief from the sun.

If you clamber up Puu Olai, you'll find **Little Beach** ★ on the other side, a small crescent of sand where assorted nudists work on their all-over tans in defiance of the law. The shoreline doesn't drop off quite so steeply here, and bodysurfing is terrific—no pun intended. About 3¾ miles south of the **Grand Wailea Resort** (p. 72), before you reach the first paved entrance to the park, a dirt road leads to small, well-shaded **Oneuli Beach** ★, whose name means "dark sand" in Hawaiian. The black sand beach, formed with the help of eroding Puu Olai, is best for snorkeling or turtle-spotting.

Note: The park is open daily 6am to 6pm.

Upcountry & East Maui
H.A. BALDWIN BEACH PARK ★★
Named for a sugarcane mogul who represented territorial Hawaii in Congress in the 1920s, this beach park off the Hana Highway between Spreckelsville

and Paia draws lots of Maui families, as well as fishermen, yoga enthusiasts, and boogie boarders. The far ends of the beach are safest for swimming: "the cove" in the lee of the rocks at the north end, and "baby beach" at the south end, where an exposed reef creates a natural sandy swimming pool—often with a current that's fun to swim against. Facilities include a pavilion with picnic tables, barbecue grills, restrooms, showers, a semipaved parking area, a soccer field, and lifeguards. The park is busy on weekends and late afternoons; mornings and weekdays are much quieter. Heading east on Hana Highway, turn left at the soccer field just before reaching Paia.

HOOKIPA BEACH PARK ★★★

Hookipa means "hospitality," and this sandy beach on Maui's north shore certainly rolls out the red carpet for waveriders. Two miles past Paia on the Hana Highway, it's among the world's top spots for windsurfing and kiting—thanks to tradewinds that kick up whitecaps offshore. Hookipa offers no less than five surf breaks, and daring watermen and -women paddle out to carve waves up to 25 feet tall. Voyeurs are welcome as well; the clifftop parking lot has a bird's-eye view. On flat days, snorkelers explore the reef's treasure trove of marine life: Gentle garden eels wave below the surface. Sea turtles hunt for jellyfish and haul out by the dozens to nap on the sand at the eastern end of the beach. More than once, a rare Hawaiian monk seal has popped ashore during a surf contest. Facilities include restrooms, showers, pavilions, picnic tables, barbecue grills, and parking.

WAIANAPANAPA STATE PARK ★

Four miles before Hana, off the Hana Highway, is this 120-acre beach park, which takes its name from the legend of the Waianapanapa Cave. Chief Kaakea, a jealous and cruel man, suspected his wife, Popoalaea, of having an affair. Popoalaea left her husband and hid herself in a chamber of the Waianapanapa Cave. A few days later, when Kaakea was passing by the cave, the shadow of a servant gave away Popoalaea's hiding place, and Kaakea killed her. During certain times of the year, the water in the tide pool turns red, commemorating Popoalaea's death. (Scientists claim, less imaginatively, that the water turns red from the presence of small red shrimp.)

Safety Tip

Be sure to see the "Health & Safety" section in chapter 12 before setting out on your Maui adventures. You'll find useful information on hiking, camping, and ocean safety, plus how to avoid seasickness and sunburn, and what to do should you get stung by a jellyfish.

With jet-black sand, a cave pool, sea arches, blowholes, and historic *hala* groves, the park offers many less morbid fascinations. Listen to the lava boulders wash up in the foamy surf. Swim with caution; the sea here is churned by strong waves and rip currents. Watch the seabirds circle the offshore islet. Follow moss-covered stone steps through the tunnel of *hau* branches and dare yourself to plunge into the chilly freshwater cave. These are experiences that will make a deep impression on your psyche. Waianapanapa offers wonderful shoreline hikes and picnicking spots; you can follow the coastal trail for a long distance in both directions from the parking lot.

Weekdays are generally a better bet for fewer fellow travelers, but bring insect repellent, since mosquitoes are always plentiful. Facilities include picnic tables, barbecue grills, restrooms, showers, tent sites, and 12 cabins (p. 207).

HAMOA BEACH ★★

This half-moon-shaped, gray-sand beach (a mix of coral and lava) in a truly tropical setting is a favorite among sunbathers seeking rest and refuge. James Michener called it "a beach so perfectly formed that I wonder at its comparative obscurity." The 100-foot-wide beach is three football fields long and sits below 30-foot black-lava sea cliffs. Surf on this unprotected beach breaks offshore and rolls in, making it a popular surfing and bodysurfing area. Hamoa is often swept by powerful rip currents, so be careful. The calm left side is best for snorkeling in summer. The beach shares some of its facilities with Travaasa Hana resort, but there are showers and restrooms for nonguests. Parking is limited. Look for the Hamoa Beach turnoff from Hana Highway.

WATERSPORTS

The watersports options on Maui are mind-boggling—from lazy snorkeling to high-energy kitesurfing and everything in between. Colorful, fish-filled reefs are easily accessible, often from a sandy beach.

You'll find rental gear and ocean toys all over the island. Most seaside hotels and resorts are stocked with watersports equipment (complimentary or rentals), from snorkels to kayaks to Hobies. **Snorkel Bob's** (www.snorkelbob. com) rents snorkel gear, boogie boards, wetsuits, and more at seven locations convenient to visitors: 1217 Front St., Lahaina (✆ **808/661-4421**); Napili Village, 5425 C Lower Honoapiilani Hwy., Lahaina (✆ **808/669-9603**); Kahana Gateway Center, 4405 Honoapiilani Hwy., Lahaina (✆ **808/334-0245**); Honokowai Market Place, 3350 Lower Honoapiilani Hwy., Lahaina (✆ **808/667-9999**); Azeka Place II, 1279 S. Kihei Rd., #310, Kihei (✆ **808/875-6188**); Kamaole Beach Center, 2411 S. Kihei Rd., Kihei (✆ **808/879-7449**); 100 Wailea Ike Dr., Kihei (✆ **808/874-0011**). All locations are open daily from 8am to 5pm, including Christmas Day. If you're island hopping, you can rent from a Snorkel Bob's location on one island and return equipment to a location on another.

Boss Frog's Dive, Surf, and Bike Shops (www.bossfrog.com) has eight locations for snorkel, boogie board, longboard, and stand-up paddleboard rentals and other gear, including these locations: 150 Lahainaluna Rd. in Lahaina (✆ **808/661-3333**); 3636 Lower Honoapiilani Rd. in Kaanapali

(© **808/665-1200**); Napili Plaza, 5095 Napilihau St. in Napili (© **808/669-4949**); and 1215 S. Kihei Rd. (© **808/891-0077**), 1770 S. Kihei Rd. (© **808/874-5225**), and Dolphin Plaza, 2395 S. Kihei Rd. (© **808/875-4477**) in Kihei. Their $30 weekly snorkel rentals are the best deal.

Boating & Sailing

The best views of Maui and its sister islands, not to mention its marine life, are from the ocean. Half-day and daylong cruises abound not only from the historic harbor in Lahaina, where rowdy whalers once came to call, but also from Maalaea Harbor, boat ramps in Kihei and Makena, and even straight from the beach in Kaanapali.

You'll need a boat to visit the crescent-shaped islet **Molokini,** one of the best snorkel and scuba spots in Hawaii, where more than 250 species of fish frolic in water with up to 150 feet of visibility. Coral Gardens in Olowalu and Turtle Landing near Makena Landing are also worthy destinations novices will want to reach by watercraft. Trips to the island of **Lanai** (see chapter 10) are also popular for a day of snorkeling. Wear a swimsuit and bring a towel, reef-safe sunscreen, and a hat on a snorkel cruise; everything else is usually included. If you'd like to go a little deeper than snorkeling allows, consider trying **SNUBA,** a shallow-water diving system in which you are connected by a 20-foot air hose to an air tank that floats on a raft at the water's surface. Most of these snorkel boats offer it for an additional cost; it's usually around $60 for a half-hour or so. No certification is required for SNUBA. For fishing charters, see "Sport Fishing," below.

Maui Classic Charters ★ TOUR Maui Classic Charters offers morning and afternoon **snorkel cruises to Molokini** on *Four Winds II,* a 55-foot, double-deck power catamaran with waterslide. Online rates for the 5-hour morning sail to Molokini Crater alone are $95 for adults, $65 for children 3 to 12, including continental breakfast and barbecue lunch. The 3½-hour afternoon sail is a steal at $52 ($38 for children), although the captain has a choice of only visiting Coral Gardens instead. All *Four Winds* trips include complimentary beer, wine, and soda; fresh-baked cookies; snorkeling gear and instructions. Those hoping to catch sight of dolphins should book a trip on the state-of-the-art catamaran *Maui Magic;* its 5½-hour morning sail includes Molokini and an additional "Captain's Choice" snorkeling site (most likely Turtle Town). It costs $110 ($80 children) and includes all the amenities of the *Four Winds II* morning cruise. Private charters are also available.

Maalaea Harbor, slip 55 and slip 80. www.mauicharters.com. © **800/736-5740** or 808/879-8188. Prices vary depending on cruise; add $10 to fares not booked online.

Pacific Whale Foundation ★★ TOUR This not-for-profit foundation supports its whale research, public education, and conservation programs by offering **whale-watch cruises, wild dolphin encounters,** and **snorkel tours,** some to Molokini, Honolua Bay, and Lanai. Numerous daily trips are offered out of both Lahaina and Maalaea harbors. Two special tours include the **Island Rhythms Sunset Cruise** ($85 adults, $45 children 3–12) with Marty Dread, a jammin' island-style reggae artist, and the **Sunset and Celestial Cruise** ($69 adults, $45 children) with Harriet Witt, a wonderful astronomer and storyteller who highlights stars significant to Hawaiian culture, including those used in traditional star-based navigation.

Lahaina Ocean Store, 612 Front St., Lahaina. **Maalaea Ocean Store,** the Shops at Maalaea Harbor, 300 Maalaea Rd., Wailuku. www.pacificwhale.org. © **800/942-5311** or 808/249-8811. Trips from $38 adults, $25 children 5–12, free for 1 child 4 and under per adult; snorkeling cruises from $69 adults, $50 children 7–12.

Scotch Mist Sailing Charters ★★ TOUR The *Scotch Mist II,* an exceptionally swift, 50-foot Santa Cruz sailboat, offers intimate, exhilarating 4-hour **snorkel-sail cruises,** limited to 25 passengers. You'll visit the glittering outer reefs at Olowalu or another West Maui site offering optimal snorkeling that day. Rates ($112 ages 13 and up, $55 kids 5–12) include breakfast (homemade bread and other treats), post-snorkeling lunch (sandwich wraps, fruit, chips, and cookies), beverages, gear, and instruction. The adults-only champagne sunset cruises ($71) are an elegant, gorgeous way to end the day, especially during winter when they double as a whale watch. *Note:* No children under 5 allowed unless the whole boat is chartered.

Lahaina Harbor, slip 2. www.scotchmistsailingcharters.com. © **808/661-0386.** Prices vary depending on cruise, starting at $60.

Kai Kanani ★★★ TOUR For more than 3 decades, this Native Hawaiian family-owned company has been South Maui's premier tour-boat operator. Moored off Maluaka Beach in Makena (meaning you launch right from the beach), the luxury catamaran *Kai Kanani* has only 3 short miles to cross to Molokini. With a 6:15am departure, its 3-hour **sunrise snorkel** ($198 adults, $161 children 2–12) allows you to appreciate the multihued marine life of Molokini Crater before any other boats arrive, then enjoy a gourmet breakfast (frittatas, breakfast sliders, yogurt parfaits with Maui strawberries). There's also a 9:45am departure, with a similarly appetizing lunch, and **sunset** and **whale-watching cruises.** A Mercedes shuttle from select Wailea resorts is available for an additional $15 per person. *Note:* Kai Kanani adds the standard 4.166% tax plus 3.361% mooring fee on all fares.

34 Wailea Gateway Center, Kihei. www.kaikanani.com. © **808/879-7218.** Prices vary by cruise, starting at $89.

Trilogy Excursions ★★★ TOUR Trilogy offers my favorite **snorkel-sail trips** from West Maui. The family-run company prioritizes environmental stewardship—along with ensuring that you have a stellar marine adventure. Hop aboard one of Trilogy's fleet of custom-built catamarans, 55 to 64 feet long, for the 9-mile **Maui-to-Lanai sail** from Lahaina Harbor to Hulopoe Marine Preserve and a fun-filled day of sailing and snorkeling. This is the only cruise that offers a personalized ground tour of the island and the only one with rights to take you to Hulopoe Beach. The 8-hour day trip costs $220 for adults, $189 ages 13 to 18, and $120 for kids 3 to 12.

Trilogy also offers **snorkel-sail trips to Molokini.** This half-day trip leaves from Maalaea Harbor and costs $140 for adults, $125 for teens, and $85 for kids 3 to 12. These are among the most expensive sail-snorkel cruises on Maui, but they're worth every penny. The crews are fun and knowledgeable, and the boats are comfortable and well-equipped. All trips include breakfast (Mom's homemade cinnamon buns) and a very good barbecue lunch (onboard on the half-day trip; on land on the Lanai trip). During winter, 2-hour **whale watches** depart conveniently right from the sand on Kaanapali Beach ($60 adults, $50 teens, $35 children); Trilogy also offers whale-watching from Lahaina (same rate) and Maalaea ($89 adults, $75 teens, $50 children).

The **Captain's Sunset Dinner Sail** is a romantic adults-only adventure. Couples enjoy a four-course feast (with choice of steak, fish, chicken, or vegetarian entree) at private, candlelit tables, complete with handcrafted cocktails, Prosecco, and cozy blankets ($135 per person).

www.sailtrilogy.com. (C) **888/225-MAUI** (6284) or 808/874-5649. Prices and departure points vary depending on cruise.

DAY CRUISES TO LANAI

You can visit the island of Lanai by booking a trip with **Trilogy** (see above) or by taking the **Expeditions** passenger ferry (www.go-lanai.com; (C) **800/695-2624** or 808/661-3756) from Lahaina. It runs five times a day, 365 days a year, departing Lahaina at 6:45 and 9:15am, and 12:45, 3:15, and 5:45pm. The return ferry from Lanai's Manele Bay leaves at 8 and 10:30am, and at 2, 4:30, and 6:45pm. The 9-mile channel crossing takes between 45 minutes and an hour, depending on sea conditions. Tickets cost $30 adults, $20 children 2 to 11 each way; reservations are strongly recommended. During winter, the trip doubles as a whale watch; dolphins may frolic in the ferry's wake year-round. You can walk from the harbor to Hulopoe Beach, but if you want to explore the island further, you'll have to rent a car (if available) or book a tour. See p. 289 in chapter 11 for details.

Body Boarding (Boogie Boarding) & Bodysurfing

Bodysurfing—riding the waves without a board, becoming one with the rolling water—is a way of life in Hawaii. Some bodysurfers just rely on their hands to ride the waves; others use hand boards (flat, paddlelike gloves). For additional maneuverability, try a boogie board or body board (also known as belly boards or *paipo* boards). These 3-foot-long boards support the upper part of your body and are easy to carry and very maneuverable in the water. Both bodysurfing and body boarding require a pair of open-heeled swim fins to help propel you through the water.

Baldwin Beach, just outside of Paia, has great bodysurfing waves nearly year-round. In winter, Maui's best bodysurfing spot is **Mokuleia Beach,**

FANTASY ISLAND: maui mermaids

One of Maui's most unusual water activities allows wanna-be mermaids and mermen to experience swimming in a sleek, colorful tail while also learning about ocean conservation. The lifeguard-certified marine naturalists of **Hawaii Mermaid Adventures** (www.hawaii mermaidadventures.com; *C* **808/ 495-8919**) will teach children, men, and women how to swim "Little Mermaid"–style at a West or South Maui beach, and share tips for protecting marine life along with mermaid lore. The lessons cost $199 for a single student, $139 per student for two or more, and include digital souvenir photos captured by instructors' underwater GoPro cameras. You can also buy a tail to take home with you. **Note:** Students must weigh between 50 and 210 pounds.

known locally as Slaughterhouse because of the cattle slaughterhouse that once stood here, not because of the waves—although they are definitely for expert bodysurfers only. Storms from the south bring fair bodysurfing conditions and great boogie boarding to the lee side of Maui: **Oneloa Beach (Big Beach)** in Makena is for experts only, while **Ulua Beach** and **Kamaole III Beach Park** in Kihei, and **Kapalua Beach** are all good choices.

Ocean Kayaking

Gliding silently over the water, propelled by a paddle, seeing Maui (and perhaps a humpback whale, dolphin, or sea turtle) from the water the way the early Hawaiians did is what ocean kayaking is all about. But be aware that winds can whip up by midmorning, and strong currents have whisked the unwary far out in channels. It's best to take at least one kayak tour before launching out on your own, and don't even consider going out on your own if you've never kayaked in the ocean before.

Fortunately, numerous companies launch kayak tours from South and West Maui beaches. Some are definitely better than others—the difference being the personal attention from the guides and their level of experience. Kayaking can be a slog if you have to keep up with your guide, rather than paddle alongside someone who shares local knowledge. My favorite operator, **Hawaiian Paddle Sports ★★★** (www.hawaiianpaddlesports.com; *C* **808/875-4848**) launches trips from Makena Landing, Olowalu, and (June–Aug only) D. T. Fleming Beach. The 3-hour tours are pricy but private—only you or your party will be on the trip, and all include snorkeling, digital photos, and snacks. Rates for Makena and Olowalu trips are $249 for a single participant, $159 per person for two to four guests, or $139 for 5 or more guests; the D. T. Fleming tour, which heads to Honolua Bay, costs $159 for one to six guests (not recommended for children under 12, due to paddling into the wind). Expert kayakers only may opt for the **Molokini Crater Challenge,** a 3½-mile paddle from Makena Landing that starts before dawn and includes snorkeling inside the crater before the flotilla of large tour boats arrive. The 3- to 4-hour tour

($249 for one person, $199 each for two or more) may include a paddle around the massive back wall of the crater if conditions permit

On all tours, you will get a wildlife adventure like no other, with a knowledgeable, friendly personal guide ready to point out snowflake eels hiding in the coral, guide you to hidden caverns, and shoot photos of you swimming with sea turtles. Owner Timothy Lara hires similarly trained guides for his other eco-friendly company, **Maui Kayak Adventures** ★★★, which also offers group tours ($89 per person) and private tours ($159 per person, two-person minimum) in Olowalu and Makena. Similar, summer-only Honolua Bay tours for ages 12 and up cost $159 per person for groups or $199 per person for private tours (www.mauikayakadventures.com; ✆ **808/442-6465**).

Aloha Kayaks Maui ★★ (www.alohakayaksmaui.com; ✆ **808/270-3318**) is also excellent and more affordable, with multi-party trips starting at $85 per person ($60 children 5–9), with a max of eight people. Professional, informative, and eco-aware guides lead 3- and 4-hour trips that launch from Makena Landing (secluded coves with underwater arches and caves) or Olowalu (vibrant coral reefs and possible manta ray sightings). During whale season, guides can steer you towards the gentle giants for a once-in-a-lifetime encounter. Private trips are also available, starting at $139 per person ($99 ages 5 to 9).

Also consider a kayak tour with one of the friendly watermen working for **Hawaiian Ocean Sports** ★★ (www.hawaiianoceansports.com; ✆ **808/633-2800**), a Native Hawaiian–owned company that encourages guides to share their cultural knowledge as well as marine experience. Tours depart Wailea Beach or Ukumehame Beach (near mile marker 12 off Honoapiilani Hwy., between Olowalu and Maalaea) and run 1 to 3 hours, with **snorkeling** and **whale-watching options** ($75–$149).

Outrigger Canoeing

Outrigger canoes are much revered in Hawaiian culture, and several hotels—among them, the Fairmont Kea Lani Maui and the Andaz Maui—offer this wonderful cultural activity right off the beach. If you want to give paddling a try, expect to work as a team with five other paddlers. Your guide and steersman will show you how to haul the sleek boat into the water, properly enter and exit the boat, and paddle for maximum efficiency. These days, you're also likely to learn some of the rich cultural elements involving canoeing, from the traditional call-and-response chant canoe builders used while carrying koa trees down from the forest to the Hawaiian words for the paddling commands.

Hawaiian Paddle Sports ★★★ TOUR   For an intimate adventure on the great blue, book an outrigger canoe trip with Hawaiian Paddle Sports. Learn how to paddle in sync with your family or friends, just as the ancient Polynesians did when colonizing these islands. You'll visit some of Maui's very best snorkel spots: Makena Landing, the outer reef at Olowalu, or (June–Aug only) Honolua Bay. The owner, Tim Lara, is one of the best in the business, brimming with knowledge about the island's culture, history, and marine life. When turtles, whales, manta rays, or monk seals surface alongside your canoe, you'll feel like a *National Geographic* explorer. And you'll have the pictures to prove it. Lara's guides are whizzes with a GoPro camera; after the trip they'll send you under- and above-water shots guaranteed to dazzle your friends. Experienced paddlers can book the **Molokini Outrigger Challenge** for 9 miles of paddling that includes a quick dip at the crater (and less cultural commentary). If you're feeling sporty, book the 2-hour **canoe surfing trip** ★★★ on a shorter four-person canoe and race down the face of breaking waves. Hawaiian Paddle Sports also offers kayak tours and surf and SUP instruction.

Departs from various locations. www.hawaiianpaddlesports.com. ✆ **808/442-6436.** Makena, Olowalu, Honolua tours $159 per person. Molokini Challenge $199 per person, 2-person min. Canoe surfing $249 for 1 guest, $159 per person for 2–3 guests, or $129 for 4 or more guests willing to rotate.

Hawaiian Outrigger Experience ★★★ TOUR   The most culturally oriented and authentically Hawaiian outrigger canoe tours launch from Wailea Beach Park, thanks to this Native Hawaiian–owned company. It's part of the **Hawaiian Ocean Sports** family created by Kevin Hoke, a second-generation "beach boy" and grandson of a hula master. On the hour-long **Hawaiian Culture and Turtle Tour,** you'll learn to chant an *oli* and hear about the history and legends of Hawaii while paddling to the typically turtle-laden waters off Wailea Point ($89 per person). While no turtles were spotted on the day I paddled, I still loved being out on the water with my knowledgeable guide, proud of his heritage—including family members whose portraits are displayed on the canoe's sleep prow—and full of genuine aloha. A 90-minute **snorkel tour** ($119) lasts 90 minutes, with time in the abundant coral gardens close to shore. In winter (Dec–Apr), the 90-minute **whale-watching tour** ($119) goes in search of humpback whales, with beautiful island and mountain backdrops guaranteed. Tours are open to ages 5 and older. *Note:* Bring a dry-bag to protect your phone or camera.

Wailea Beach Park, off Wailea Alanui Dr. btwn. Grand Wailea and the Four Seasons Resort Maui, Wailea. www.hawaiianoutriggerexperience.com. ✆ **808/633-2800.** Tours $89–$119. Book outrigger canoe tour and receive 25% off other Hawaiian Ocean Sports activities (hawaiianoceansports.com; same telephone).

Ocean Rafting

If you're semi-adventurous and looking for a wetter, wilder experience, try ocean rafting. The inflatable rafts typically hold 6 to 30 passengers, while tours usually include snorkeling and coastal cruising. Pregnant women and people with back problems are advised to avoid—as are those who might wish to use bathroom facilities other than the ocean. During winter, these maneuverable boats offer exciting whale-watching tours.

   Captain Steve's Rafting Excursions ★★ (www.captainsteves.com; ✆ **808/667-5565**) offers 7-hour snorkel trips from **Mala Wharf** in Lahaina to the waters around **Lanai** (you don't actually land on the island). **Dolphin sightings** are almost guaranteed on these action-packed excursions. Discounted online rates of $135 for adults and $95 for children 5 to 12 include continental breakfast, deli-style lunch, and snorkel gear, with wetsuits, flotation devices, and life jackets available upon request.

Hawaii Ocean Rafting ★ (www.hawaiioceanrafting.com; ⓒ **808/661-7238**), which operates out of Lahaina Harbor, also zips out towards **Lanai.** The best deal is the 4½-hour morning tour ($85 adults, $72 children 5–12); it includes three snorkeling stops and time spent watching for dolphins, plus continental breakfast and midmorning snacks. Check for online discounts.

Maui Reef Adventures ★★★ (www.mauireefadventures.com; ⓒ **808/244-7333**) operates out of Maalaea Harbor, convenient for those staying in Kihei and Wailea. *Ocean Freedom*, its 41-foot Navatek seating 30, zips over to Molokini Crater (allowing a snorkel on the backside) and Makena Landing's Turtle Town on 4-hour morning tours Tuesday through Saturday ($129 ages 5 and older, including continental breakfast and lunch).

One of the few ways to see the sea caves, coral reefs, and frequent pods of dolphins along the untrammeled **Kanaio coast** south of Makena, inaccessible by car, is with **Blue Water Rafting** ★★ (www.bluewaterrafting.com; ⓒ **808/ 879-8238**). The 4-hour **Kanaio Coast** tours with snorkeling ($115 adults, $94 children 4–12) rely on swift, rigid-hulled 24-passenger rafts with canopies and include lunch. A 5½-hour version ($140 adults, $115 children) includes snorkeling in La Perouse Bay and at Molokini Crater, while a 2-hour **Molokini Express** waits for the crowds to thin out before dashing over for snorkeling ($57 adults, $47 children; drinks included).

Parasailing

Soar high above the crowds (at around 400 ft.) for a bird's-eye view of Maui. This ocean adventure sport, which is something of a cross between skydiving and water-skiing, involves sailing through the air, suspended under a large parachute attached by a towline to a speedboat. Keep in mind, though, that parasailing tours don't run during whale season, which is roughly December through mid-May (just to be safe; that's later than whale-watch cruises are offered).

I recommend **UFO Parasailing** (ⓒ **800/FLY-4-UFO** [359-4836] or 808/ 661-7-UFO [7836]; www.ufoparasail.net), which picks you up at Kaanapali Beach near Whalers Village. UFO departs on hourlong parasail trips daily from 9am to 4pm, and occasionally earlier. The cost is $89 for the standard flight of 7 minutes of airtime at 800 feet, $99 for a 10-minute ride at 1,200 feet. You can go up alone or with a friend; observers may accompany you for $49, with trips limited to eight passengers. No experience is necessary, but participants must be at least 5 years old and weigh at least 160 pounds to fly alone.

Scuba Diving

Some people come to Maui for the sole purpose of plunging into the tropical Pacific and exploring the underwater world. You can see the great variety of tropical marine life (more than 100 endemic species found nowhere else on the planet), explore sea caves, and swim with green sea turtles and perhaps even a Hawaiian monk seal in the clear tropical waters off the island. I recommend going early in the morning. The tradewinds often rough up the seas in the afternoon, so most dive operators schedule early-morning dives that end at noon, and then take the rest of the day off.

Unsure about scuba diving? Take an introductory dive: Most operators offer no-experience-necessary dives, ranging from $119 to $150. You can learn from this glimpse into the sea world whether diving is for you.

Most divers start with **Molokini** (see "Snorkeling," below). In addition to the popular basin, experienced divers can explore the crater's dramatic **back wall ★★★**, which plunges 350 feet and is frequented by larger marine animals and schools of rare butterflyfish. Other top sites include **Mala Wharf,** the **St. Anthony** (a sunken longliner), and **Five Graves** at Makena Landing. Don't be scared off by the latter's ominous name—it's a magical spot with sea caves and arches.

Ed Robinson's Diving Adventures ★★ DIVE COMPANY   Ed Robinson, a widely published underwater photographer, offers specialized charters for small groups aboard the *Sea Spirit.* Two-tank dives are $145 ($168 with all the gear); more experienced divers will want to book the two-tank adventure dive (Sun and Fri; same price) or an all-day, three-tank adventure dive offered on Tuesdays ($190, $213 with gear). The check-in for the dive is at 165 Halekuai St. in Kihei, while the boat departs from the Kihei Boat Ramp, 2988 S. Kihei Rd., just south of Kamaole Beach Park 3.

165 Halekuai St., Kihei. www.mauiscuba.com. (C) **808/879-3584.**

Maui Dreams Dive Company ★★★ DIVE COMPANY   Run by husband-and-wife team Rachel and Don Domingo, this is the best full-service dive operation on the island. Stop in at their South Maui shop, and you might just end up scuba-certified ($299 for a 2-day course). The skilled dive masters and instructors are so fun that they make every aspect of getting geared up to go underwater enjoyable. You don't need certification for an intro shore dive at Ulua Beach ($99), but you do for a two-tank adventure to **Molokini** aboard the *Maui Diamond II* ($159 with gear, $139 without). Captain Don regales his passengers with jokes, snacks, and local trivia. Rachel has a knack for finding camouflaged **frogfish** on the reef. Even experienced divers will be dazzled by the **guided scooter dives** ($139–$169). The rideable rockets allow you to zip along the ocean's floor and visit sunken **World War II wrecks,** caves, and turtle-cleaning stations.

1993 S. Kihei Rd. (at Auhana St.), Kihei. www.mauidreamsdiveco.com. (C) **808/874-5332.**

AN EXPERT SHARES HIS SECRETS: maui's best dives

Ed Robinson, of **Ed Robinson's Diving Adventures** (see above), knows Maui's best dives. Here are some of his favorites:

Hawaiian Reef   This area off the Kihei-Wailea Coast is so named because it hosts a good cross section of Hawaiian topography and marine life. Diving to depths of 85 feet, you'll see everything from lava formations and coral reef to sand and rubble, plus a diverse range of both shallow- and deep-water creatures. It's clear why this area was so popular with ancient Hawaiian fishermen: Large helmet shells, a healthy garden of antler coral heads, and big schools of snapper are common.

Third Tank   Located off Makena Beach at 80 feet, this World War II tank is one of the most picturesque artificial reefs you're likely to see around Maui. It acts like a fish magnet: Because it's the only large solid object in the area, any fish or invertebrate looking for a safe home comes here. Surrounding the tank is a cloak of schooling snappers and goatfish just waiting for a photographer with a wide-angle lens. Despite its small size, Third Tank is loaded with more marine life per square inch than any site off Maui.

Molokini Crater   The backside of the crater is always done as a live boat-drift dive. The vertical wall plummets from more than 150 feet above sea level to around 250 feet below. Looking down to unseen depths gives you a feeling for the vastness of the open ocean. Pelagic fish and sharks are often sighted, and living coral perches on the wall, which is home to lobsters, crabs, and a number of photogenic black-coral trees at 50 feet.

There are actually two great dive sites around Molokini Crater. Named after

common chub or rudderfish, **Enenue Side** gently slopes from the surface to about 60 feet and then drops rapidly to deeper waters. The shallower area is an easy dive, with lots of tame butterflyfish. Enenue Side is often done as a live boat-drift dive to extend the range of the tour. Diving depths vary. Divers usually do a 50-foot dive, but on occasion advanced divers drop to the 130-foot level to visit the rare boarfish and the shark condos.

Almost every kind of fish found in Hawaii can be seen in the crystalline waters of **Reef's End.** It's an extension of the rim of the crater, which runs for about 600 feet underwater, barely breaking the surface. Reef's End is shallow enough for novice snorkelers and exciting enough for experienced divers. The end and outside of this shoal drop off in dramatic terraces to beyond diving range. In deeper waters, there are shark ledges at varying depths and dozens of eels, including moray, dragon, snowflake, and garden eels. The reef is covered with cauliflower coral; in bright sunlight, it's one of the most dramatic underwater scenes in Hawaii.

La Pérouse Pinnacle   In the middle of scenic La Pérouse Bay, site of Haleakala's most recent lava flow, is a pinnacle rising from the 60-foot bottom to about 10 feet below the surface. Getting to the dive site is half the fun: The scenery above water is as exciting as that below the surface. Underwater, you'll enjoy a very diversified dive. Clouds of damselfish and triggerfish will greet you on the surface. Divers can approach even the timid bird wrasse. There are more porcupine puffers here than anywhere else, as well as schools of goatfish and fields of healthy finger coral. La Pérouse is good for snorkeling and long, shallow second dives.

Mike Severns Diving ★★★ DIVE COMPANY   For personalized diving tours on a 38-foot Munson/Hammerhead boat (with a freshwater shower), call Pauline Fiene at Mike Severns Diving. She and her fellow dive masters lead trips for a maximum of 12 people, divided into two groups of six. Exploring the underwater world is educational and fun with Fiene, a biologist who has authored several spectacular marine-photography books and leads dives during **coral spawning** events. She's particularly knowledgeable about nudibranchs, two of which have been named for her, *Hallaxa paulinae* and *Hypselodoris paulinae.* Two-tank dives are $159, including equipment rental, or $139 if you bring all your own equipment. Experienced divers can rent underwater digital cameras ($40, including a photo CD or uploading your images to a web-hosting site) and tag along behind the pro photographers. Trips depart from Kihei Boat Ramp, 2988 S. Kihei Rd., just south of Kamaole Beach Park 3.

www.mikesevernsdiving.com. © **808/879-6596.**

Maui Dive Shop ★ (www.mauidiveshop.com), Maui's largest diving retailer, offers everything from rentals to scuba-diving instruction to dive-boat charters, including a twice-weekly West Maui dive with guaranteed **manta ray sightings** ($130). Stop by one of its retail locations (see below)for a free copy of the 40-page *Maui Dive & Surf Magazine,* which includes maps to the 20 best shoreline and offshore dives and snorkel sites, each ranked for beginner, intermediate, or advanced snorkelers/divers, with detailed information. Maui Dive Shop has branches in Kihei at Azeka Place II Shopping Center, 1455 S. Kihei Rd. (© **808/879-3388**), and the Shops at Wailea, 3750 Wailea Alanui Rd. (© **808/875-9904**). Its *Maka Koa* dive boat is moored at Maalea Harbor.

Snorkeling

Snorkeling is a prime attraction of Maui—and almost anyone can do it. All you need are fins, a mask, a snorkel, and some basic swimming skills. Floating over underwater worlds through colorful clouds of tropical fish is like a dream. In many places all you have to do is wade into the water—avoiding walking or touching on live coral, of course—and look down. If you've never snorkeled before, most resorts and excursion boats offer instruction, but it's plenty easy to figure out for yourself. Mornings are best; blustery trade winds kick in around noon.

Some snorkeling tips: Always go with a buddy. Look up every once in a while to see where you are, how far offshore you are, and whether there's any boat traffic. Don't touch anything; not only can you damage coral, but camouflaged fish and shells with poisonous spines can also damage you. Always check with a dive shop, lifeguards, and others on the beach about the area in which you plan to snorkel: Are there any dangerous conditions you should know about? What are the current surf, tide, and weather conditions? If you're not a good swimmer, wear a life jacket or another flotation device, which you can rent at most places offering watersports gear.

Snorkel Bob's ★ (www.snorkelbob.com) or **Boss Frog's Dive and Surf Shops** (www.bossfrog.com) will rent you everything you need; see p. 185 and 186 for their locations. Also see "Maui Dive Shop," above, for a free booklet on great snorkeling sites.

West Maui's best snorkeling spots include **Black Rock (Puu Kekaa)** at the northern end of Kaanapali Beach, in front of the Sheraton; **Kahekili Beach**, just beyond Black Rock; and **Olowalu,** around mile marker 14 of Honoapi-iilani Hwy., where turtles line up to have cleaner wrasses pick off small parasites at a "cleaning station" about 150 to 225 feet from shore. In South Maui, the rocky points around **Ulua** and **Mokapu** beaches in Wailea offer the most marine life.

Three **truly terrific snorkel spots** are difficult to get to but rewarding—they're home to Hawaii's tropical marine life at its best:

Ahihi-Kinau Natural Preserve ★★ NATURAL ATTRACTION   This 2,000-acre state natural area reserve in the lee of Cape Kinau, on Maui's rugged south coast, is home to bejeweled Ahihi Bay. It was here that Haleakala spilled its last red-hot lava into the sea, so the entrance to the ocean is sharp and rocky. Ease into the water to see brilliant corals and abundant fish. Fishing is strictly forbidden, and the fish know it; they're everywhere in this series of rocky coves and black-lava tide pools. To get here, drive south of Makena and watch for signs. A state naturalist is often onsite to offer advice. *Note:* The Hawaii Department of Land and Natural Resources has indefinitely restricted access to portions of the popular and heavily used preserve. The first mile of the coastline at its northern end is open 5:30am to 7pm. Visit dlnr.hawaii.gov/ecosystems/nars/maui for details.

Honolua Bay ★★★ NATURAL ATTRACTION   The snorkeling in this wide, secluded bay is worth the drive out to West Maui's far corner. Spectacular coral formations glitter beneath the surface. Turtles, rays, and a variety of snappers and goatfish cruise along beside you. In the crevices are eels, lobster, and rainbow-hued fish. Dolphins sometimes come here to rest. Follow Honoa-piilani Highway past Kapalua to mile marker 32. Follow the dirt trail down through the dense forest to the sea (make sure to leave nothing in your car; break-ins have happened in this remote area.)

Molokini ★★★ NATURAL ATTRACTION   A sunken crater that sits like a crescent moon fallen from the sky, almost midway between Maui and the uninhabited island of Kahoolawe, Molokini stands like a scoop against the tide. This offshore site is very popular, thanks to astounding visibility (you can often peer down 100 ft. or more) and an abundance of marine life, from manta rays to clouds of yellow butterflyfish. On its concave side, Molokini serves as a natural sanctuary and preserve for tropical fish; the back "wall" is an exciting place to snorkel or dive as well. Molokini is accessible only by boat, and snorkelers commute here daily in a fleet of dive boats. See "Boating," above,

FUN ON & OFF THE BEACH | Watersports

7

for outfitters that can take you here. Expect crowds, unless you arrive early via a sunrise cruise or speedy raft.

If you'd like to head over to Lanai for a day of snorkeling in its pristine waters, see "Day Cruises to Lanai," earlier in this chapter.

SNORKEL TOURS

In addition to the excellent snorkel tours listed under "Boating," "Ocean Kayaking," "Ocean Rafting," and "Outrigger Canoeing," above, consider a snorkel-sail tour on the *Pride of Maui* from Maalaea Harbor. It offers 5-hour **snorkel cruises to Molokini** stops at Turtle Town in Makena; the online rate is $99 for ages 13 and up and $69 for children 3 to 12. Rates include continental breakfast, barbecue lunch, beverages and open bar, gear, and instruction. Other snorkeling options include an afternoon Turtle Town cruise ($59 adults, $49 children) and seasonal 3-hour whale-watching cruises that include 1 hour of snorkeling ($59 adults, $49 children). *Note:* Add $10 per fare if not booking online.

Maalaea Harbor. ℂ **877/TO-PRIDE** [867-7433] or 808/242-0955. www.prideofmaui.com. Prices vary depending on cruise.

Sport Fishing

Marlin (as big as 1,200 lb.), tuna, ono, and mahimahi await the baited hook in Maui's coastal and channel waters. No license is required for saltwater fishing; just book a sport-fishing vessel out of Lahaina or Maalaea harbor. Most charter boats that troll for big-game fish carry a maximum of six passengers. You can walk the docks, inspect boats, and talk to captains and crews, or book through your hotel's activities desk or through **Sportfish Hawaii** (below).

Shop around: Prices vary widely depending on the boat, the crowd, and the captain. A shared boat for a half-day of fishing starts at $169; a shared full day of fishing starts at around $279. A half-day exclusive (you get the entire boat) starts at $950; a full-day exclusive starts at $1,399. Also, many boat captains tag and release marlin or keep the fish for themselves (sorry, that's Hawaii style). If you want to eat your mahimahi for dinner or have your marlin mounted, tell the captain before you go.

The best way to reserve a sport-fishing charter is through the experts; **Sportfish Hawaii** ★ (www.sportfishhawaii.com; ℂ **877/388-1376**) books boats on all the major Hawaiian islands. These fishing vessels have been inspected and must meet rigorous criteria to guarantee that you'll have a great time. Prices start at $1,399 for a full-day exclusive charter (meaning you, plus five friends, get the entire boat to yourself); it's $699 for a half-day exclusive. **Bottom-fishing** trips for delicious snappers run $165 per adult; you'll share the boat with up to nine other anglers.

Submarine Dives

Plunging 100 feet below the surface of the sea in a state-of-the-art, high-tech submarine is a great way to experience Maui's magnificent underwater world, especially if you're not a swimmer. **Atlantis Adventures** ★, 658 Front St., Lahaina (www.atlantisadventures.com; ⓒ **800/548-6262** or 808/667-2224), offers trips out of Lahaina Harbor every hour on the hour from 9am to 2pm; prices are $104 for adults and $38 for children 11 and under (children must be at least 3 ft. tall). Book on the website and receive a free child ticket for each paying adult. Allow 2 hours for this underwater adventure, which navigates around the artificial reef created by the *Carthaginian,* a replica of a 19th-century supply boat that was deliberately sunk in 2005—much to the delight of the coral and fish who now call it home. *Warning:* Even though each passenger has a porthole, this is not a good choice if you're claustrophobic, for obvious reasons.

Surfing & Stand-up Paddling (SUP)

The ancient Hawaiian sport of *hee nalu* (wave sliding), better known as **surfing,** is probably the sport most people picture when they think of the islands. If you want to learn to surf, the best beginners' spots are **Charley Young Cove** in Kihei (South Kihei Road at Iliili Road, near the far southern end of Kalama Beach Park), the break in front of **505 Front Street** mall in Lahaina, and several breaks along Honoapiilani Highway, including **Ukumehame Beach Park,** about 3 miles south of Olowalu. The first two are the most convenient, with surf schools nearby. The breaks along Honoapiilani Highway tend to be longer, wider, and less crowded—perfect if you're confident enough to go solo. Do the reefs a favor, though, and wear reef-safe sunscreen or a long-sleeved rashguard.

During summer, gentle swells roll in long and slow along the South Shore. It's the best time to practice your stance on a longboard. During winter, the North Shore becomes the playground for adrenaline junkies who drop in on thundering waves 30 feet tall and higher. If you want to watch, head to **Hookipa Beach** (p. 184) or **Honolua Bay** (p. 196) where you can view the action from a cliff above.

Hydrofoiling or foil surfing, which involves attaching a hydrodynamic fin to a surfboard, allows riders to take advantage of both big waves and marginal surf, but requires some training. Alan Cadiz's **Hawaiian Sailboarding Techniques** (www.hstwindsurfing.com; ⓒ **808/871-5423**) gives 2-hour lessons for $299, with two-way headsets, helmet, and life jacket among the gear included, at **Kanaha Beach Park** near the airport in Kahului.

Stand-up paddling (SUP) is one of Hawaii's oldest and newest ocean sports. Practiced by ancient Hawaiian kings, it's now back in fashion. You can SUP just about anywhere you can surf—and more, since you don't need a swell to get going, just a wide board and paddle, strong arms, and some balance. (And if you lack the latter two, willingness will make up for it.) Gliding over the fish-filled reefs with an unobstructed view of the islands on the horizon is a topnotch experience. For novices, the same cautions as with ocean kayaking apply: Potentially strong winds and currents make it best to take a lesson and/or guided tour before heading out on your own.

Virtually every hotel beach kiosk rents SUP boards, and many rent surfboards as well, although board conditions may vary due to high-volume use and inexpert handling. More experienced wave riders will prefer to choose from a wide range of surf and stand-up paddle boards (as well as windsurfing gear) for rent from **Maui Windsurf Company,** 22 Hana Hwy., Kahului (www.mauiwindsurfcompany.com; ℂ **808/877-4816**). Surfboards run $15 a day, $97 per week; SUP boards $29 a day, $187 per week; optional insurance is $11 per day. Closer to the West Maui resorts, **Maui Surf Clinics,** 505 Front St., Lahaina (www.mauisurfclinics.com; ℂ **808/244-7873**), rents beginner and high-performance surfboards for $25 to $30 a day, $140 per week; and SUP boards for $40 a day.

SURF LESSONS

Hawaiian Paddle Sports ★★★   Exercising surf etiquette and protecting the reef as much as finding the right stance and reading the waves are part of this eco-friendly company's surfing curriculum. The 2-hour lessons for beginning and intermediate surfers take place in West Maui, wherever that day's guide feels the conditions are best for you. Lessons are all private, $199 for an individual or $139 for a group (more than four will receive a second instructor). Your instructor will send you digital photos later in the day. www.hawaiianpaddlesports.com. ℂ **808/442-6436.**

Maui Surfer Girls ★★★   Despite its name, MSG offers coed surf and SUP instruction for groms and Betties alike—meaning men, women, and children. Owner Dustin Tester is a big-wave surf pioneer; she's among the first women to charge "Jaws," one of the planet's biggest breaks, and her commitment to helping others shred waves is inspirational. (She even coached her dog Luna to hang ten alongside her.) Personalized 2-hour lessons at Ukumehame Beach Park with Tester or her teammates are $89 for groups (minimum age 10), $130 semi-private (your own party, for up to four students; minimum age 9), and $185 for private lesson (minimum age 5). Couples wishing to mark a special occasion can book a package with a photographer and bottle of sparkling wine or cider ($350 per couple). But MSG's best offering is the **weeklong surf camp.** If you've got a teen girl who dreams of growing gills, sign her up for 7 saltwater-soaked days full of watersports, camaraderie, healthy food, island adventures, and campfire counsel ($2,375); women ages 18 and up can share similar experiences at their own surf camps ($1,950). The oceanfront **Camp Olowalu** (p. 205) serves as headquarters for a transformational experience. www.mauisurfergirls.com. ℂ **808/201-6879.**

Maui Stand Up Paddle Boarding ★★   Get up on a board and "walk on water" with a private SUP lesson or guided tour ($199 for one person, $139 for two or more). Adventures start out with an overview of paddling techniques on shore, then you'll launch into the water at Makena Landing, Olowalu, or Kapalua Bay for 2 salty hours. (Wear a water-friendly hat and sunglasses.) During whale season, you might be surprised by the exhalation of a mighty humpback nearby. Your instructor will snap digital action shots of you and deliver them by day's end. The company also rents NAISH inflatable boards for $55 per day, with free pickup at its Kihei headquarters or delivered to you for $75.

27-B Halekaui St. Kihei. www.mauistanduppaddleboarding.com. © **808/568-0151.**

Maui Surf Clinics ★　One of Maui's oldest surf schools is just steps away from the reliable break at 505 Front Street. Paddle out to the swell and your instructor will cheer you on as you hang ten for the first time. It's $85 per person for a 2-hour group lesson; private classes are $170, and semiprivate are $105 to $135 per person, depending on the number of students. Standard lessons are for ages 9 and up; children as young as 4 can take a 1-hour lesson for $100. SUP lessons are available for the same rates for ages 9 and up, but there's no option for younger children. All instructors are lifeguard certified.

505 Front St., Suite 224B, Lahaina. www.mauisurfclinics.com. © **808/244-7873.**

Zack Howard Surf ★★　Zack is a lifelong waterman who will help you stand up and surf—even on your very first wave. Sharing his skills and passions are fellow instructors Sarah Howard (his wife) and Tyler Larronde, two Maui natives who grew up into world-class surfers, and California-raised elite longboarder Shawn Thompson. While most surf schools take newbies out into the crowded breaks at Charley Young in Kihei or the Lahaina Breakwall, Zack and company steer beginning students into the surf at Ukumehame, a gentle, consistent rolling break alongside Honoapiilani Highway. They also help intermediate surfers sharpen their skills at world-famous Hookipa. In between swells, you'll receive tips on how to improve your stance and technique. Group lessons for three or more run $100 per person for 1½ hours. Two people can book the same class for $260, while a private lesson costs $220.

www.zackhowardsurf.com. © **808/214-7766.**

SUP TOURS

For those with some paddling experience, **Maui Stand Up Paddleboarding** ★★ (see above) offers SUP tours of crystal waters above intricate coral formations for the same rates as lessons: $199 private, $139 for your group of two to five (larger groups pay the same rate, accompanied by a second guide). **Hawaiian Paddle Sports** ★★★ (see above) combines lessons with tours by certified naturalist guides in 2-hour forays of Makena's "Turtle Town," Oluwalu, Olowalu, and Kapalua Bay, although exact locations vary based on conditions. The private classes/tours cost $199 for one, $139 for two to four, with a second instructor for larger groups.

Whale-Watching

Every winter, pods of North Pacific humpback whales make the 3,000-mile swim from the chilly waters of Alaska to bask in Maui's summery shallows, fluking, spy-hopping, spouting, and having an all-around swell time.

The humpback is the star of the annual whale-watching season, which usually begins in December or January and lasts until early April. Although the number of sightings has declined in recent years, for unknown reasons, it's believed that about 11,000 whales still make the annual migration to Hawaiian waters, including the remote Northwestern Hawaiian Islands, a chain of rocky islets and atolls stretching towards Midway. In 1992, some of the waters around the state were designated the **Hawaiian Islands Humpback Whale National Marine Sanctuary** (hawaiihumpbackwhale.noaa.gov), the country's first federal single-species sanctuary.

These are massive marine mammals—adults grow to about 45 feet long and weigh a hefty 40 tons—and seeing them leap out of the sea or perfect their tail slap is mesmerizing. You can hear them sing underwater, too: Just duck your head a foot below the surface and listen for creaks, groans, and otherworldly serenades.

WHALE-WATCHING FROM SHORE Just look out to sea anytime during the winter months. There's no best time of day, but it seems that when the sea is glassy and there's no wind, the whales appear. Others claim the opposite: that whales are most active when the water is pocked with whitecaps.

Good whale-watching spots on Maui include:

o **MCGREGOR POINT** On the way to Lahaina, this scenic lookout at the Hwy. 30 mile marker 9 (just before you get to the Lahaina Tunnel) is a good spot to scan for whales. A Pacific Whale Foundation docent is usually on hand in season with brochures and binoculars, although sometimes the whales are only yards away. Parking is very limited, and be careful exiting or reentering the highway, as accidents have happened here.

o **OLOWALU REEF** Along the straight part of Honoapiilani Highway, between McGregor Point and Olowalu, you'll sometimes see whales leap out of the water. Their appearance can bring traffic to a screeching halt: People have abandoned their cars to run down to the sea to watch, causing a major traffic jam. If you want to stop, pull off the road so others can pass.

o **WAILEA BEACH MARRIOTT RESORT & SPA** Along the Wailea Coastal Walk, stop at this resort to look for whales through the telescope installed as a public service by the Hawaii Islands Humpback Whale National Marine Sanctuary.

WHALE-WATCHING BY KAYAK & RAFT ★★ In winter, any kayak tour becomes a whale-watching tour. I also recommend viewing humpback whales from a maneuverable, high-speed raft, which can bring you close to more distant cetaceans while still remaining at a safe distance. **Capt. Steve's**

Rafting Excursions (www.captainsteves.com; © 808/667-5565) offers 2-hour whale-watching excursions out of Lahaina Harbor (from $55 adults, $45 children 5–12). *Tip:* Save $10 by booking the early-bird adventure, which leaves at 7:30am. The only rafting company in Maalaea Harbor, and therefore more convenient for Kihei and Wailea visitors, **Maui Reef Adventures** (www.mauireefadventures.com; © 808/244-7333) takes its sturdy, speedy 30-passenger raft on whale-watching excursions at 11:30am Tuesday and Friday ($55 ages 5 and older).

WHALE-WATCHING CRUISES Just about all of Hawaii's snorkel and dive boats become whale-watching boats in season; some of them even carry professional naturalists onboard (so you'll know what you're seeing) and drop hydrophones in the water (so you can better hear the whales' songs). For options, see "Boating," earlier in this section.

Windsurfing and Kitesurfing

Maui has Hawaii's best windsurfing beaches. In winter, windsurfers from around the world flock to the town of **Paia** to ride the waves; **Hookipa Beach ★★★**, known all over the globe for its brisk winds and excellent waves, is the site of several world championship contests. **Kanaha Beach,** west of Kahului Airport, also has dependable winds. When the winds turn northerly, **North Kihei** is the place to be (some days, you can even spot whales in the distance behind the windsurfers). **Ohukai Park,** the first beach as you enter South Kihei Road from the northern end, has good winds, plus parking, a long strip of grass to assemble your gear, and easy access to the water.

EQUIPMENT RENTALS & LESSONS **Hawaiian Sailboarding Techniques,** 425 Koloa St., Kahului (www.hstwindsurfing.com; © 808/871-5423), offers windsurfing rentals and 2½-hour lessons from $99 at Kanaha Beach early in the morning before the breeze gets too strong for beginners. Founder Alan Cadiz also helped inaugurate kitesurfing on the island decades ago; private introductory 3-hour lessons are $225 per person, including equipment. **Maui Windsurf Company,** 22 Hana Hwy., Kahului (www.mauiwindsurf company.com; © 808/877-4816), offers complete equipment rental (Goya boards, sails, rig harnesses, and roof racks) from $59, plus 2½-hour group lessons from $99 and private instruction at $99 per hour.

DAILY WIND & SURF CONDITIONS For reports on wind and surf conditions, call Hi-Tech's **Wind & Surf Report** at © 808/877-3611, ext. 2.

SURF VAN Since most windsurf gear won't fit into a typical rental car, check with **Aloha Rent-a-Car/Al West's Maui Vans** (www.mauivans.com; © 808/877-0090) about renting a newish (or old) van. It runs a shuttle from the airport to its rental facility 5 minutes away in Kahului. Older vans start at $149 per week; the newest Ford E-150 and Doge Ram cargo vans start at $399 per week. Rates included ice cooler, beach chairs, beach mats, child's seat, beach toys, and hose to wash your gear at the beach.

HIKING & CAMPING

Despite the high-rise hotels and condos lining Kaanapali and the sprawling resorts of Wailea, much of Maui remains largely untouched by human hands—and can only be explored by foot. Those interested in seeing the backcountry—dotted with pristine waterfalls, remote wilderness trails, and quiet, meditative settings—should head for Haleakala's upcountry or the tropical Hana Coast. For detailed information and directions to 18 trails maintained by the state's Department of Land and Natural Resources as part of the **Na Ala Hele Trail System**, including those mentioned below, see https://hawaiitrails.hawaii.gov.

Like hiking, camping on Maui can be wet, cold, and rainy, or hot, dry, and windy—often all on the same day. If you're heading for Haleakala, remember that U.S. astronauts trained for the moon inside the volcano: Bring survival gear. Don't forget raingear, especially if you're bound for Waianapanapa.

RENTING GEAR   To avoid the hassle, and possible airline baggage fees, of bringing camping equipment with you, rent your gear on island—just make sure you reserve it in advance. There are no walk-up rentals available on Maui, although guests at **Camp Olowalu** (see below) may rent a limited number of tents and some equipment for use onsite.

Maui Camping Company (www.mauicampingcompany.com; ℂ **808/762-1168**) offers three kinds of camping kits, from basic to "glamping," all with inflatable mattresses, sleeping bags, pillows, four-person tent, and other essentials, starting at $100 for 1 to 3 days, $150 for the week. Prices are based on two campers, but you can add extra sleeping gear for $10 to $15 per person, or upgrade to a six-person tent for an extra $10 per kit. Backpacking kits, which include a lightweight two-person tent, sleeping bag, pillow, pad, kitchen kit, and headlamp, among other items, run $150 for 1 to 3 days or $200/week; add an extra backpack, sleeping bag, and pad for $50. Excursion kits ($100 for 1 to 3 days, $150/week) are perfect for ferrying over to Lanai or flying to another island, and can even be mailed back (box provided) if you're not returning to Maui. Add-on rentals range from trekking poles ($15–$20) to Yeti coolers ($30–$40) and even ukuleles ($15–$20) and guitars ($20–$25). Maui Camping Company doesn't have a storefront, but uses **Adventure Sports Maui,** 400 Hana Hwy., Kahului (www.adventuresportsmaui.com; ℂ **808/877-7443**), for pickups and dropoffs.

In Kihei, **Maui Camping King** (www.mauicampingking.com; ℂ **808/214-0714**) offers similar rentals of conveniently bundled camping gear and cooking kits from its second-story headquarters at Ohukai Plaza, 357 Huku Lii St. Call for prices.

TIPS ON SAFE HIKING & CAMPING   Water might be everywhere in Hawaii, but it more than likely isn't safe to drink. Most stream water must be treated because cattle, pigs, and goats have probably contaminated the water upstream. The Department of Health continually warns campers of bacterium leptospirosis, which is found in freshwater streams throughout the state and enters the body through breaks in the skin or through the mucous membranes. It produces flulike symptoms and can be fatal. Make sure that your drinking water is safe by vigorously boiling it, or if boiling is not an option, use tablets with hydroperiodide; portable water filters will not screen out bacterium leptospirosis. Firewood isn't always available, so it's a good idea to carry a small, light backpacking stove, which you can use both to boil water and cook meals.

Remember, the island is not crime-free: Never leave your valuables (wallet, laptop, and so on) unprotected. Carry a day pack if you have a campsite, and never camp alone. Some more do's and don'ts: Do bury personal waste away from streams. Don't eat unknown fruit. Do carry your trash out. And don't forget there is very little twilight in Maui when the sun sets—it gets dark quickly. See "Health & Safety" in chapter 11 for more safety tips.

GUIDED HIKES   If you'd like a knowledgeable guide to accompany you on a hike, call **Maui Hiking Safaris** ★ (www.mauihikingsafaris.com; © **888/445-3963** or 808/573-0168). Owner Randy Warner takes visitors on half- and full-day hikes into valleys, rainforests, and coastal areas. Randy's been hiking around Maui since 1981 and is wise in the ways of Hawaiian history, native flora and fauna, and volcanology. His rates are $69 to $89 for a half-day and $120 to $169 for a full day, which include day packs, rain parkas, snacks, water, and, on full-day hikes, sandwiches. Hikes are limited to eight clients, with a minimum of two; larger families and groups may book private tours.

Maui's oldest hiking-guide company, **Hike Maui** ★ (www.hikemaui.com; © **866/324-6284** or 808/879-5270) is headed by Ken Schmitt, who pioneered guided hikes on the Valley Isle. Hike Maui offers a variety of East Maui waterfall and rainforest hikes ($95–$210) and a 7-hr. Haleakala Crater hike ($190), along with hikes that include ziplining ($229) or kayaking and snorkeling ($179). *Note:* Book online for a 10% discount.

Campsites

YMCA Camp Keanae ★★   Halfway to Hana, on a grassy oceanview bluff above the secluded Keanae Peninsula, this well-run YMCA facility offers a variety of accommodations. All guests can enjoy the covered firepit and outdoor seating, large grass field, and gymnasium with basketball/volleyball court. **Tent or van campers** have access to bathhouses with hot showers, an ice machine, and charcoal grills; they pay $25 a night for a solo traveler or $40 for a family of two adults and minor children—but they also have access to a beautiful site perched along the cliff's edge. Guests in seven **cabins and bunk rooms,** which have electricity and sleep 12 to 60 in twin-size bunks, share access to the same facilities; they pay $30 a night per person for ages 5 and older. Two **suites** offer more privacy, beds and futons with linens, covered lanais, and kitchenettes, although bathrooms are still in the communal bathhouses; they also require a 2-night minimum. Off the back of the gym, the King Suite, which sleeps four, costs $150 plus $25 cleaning fee per night (so 2 nights runs $350); the Ohana Suite, which sleeps eight, costs $300 plus $25 cleaning fee per night. Two two-bedroom **cottage units** in an oceanview duplex each have one queen bed, two twin beds, a private bathroom with shower/tubs, bed and bath linens, a full kitchen, and a furnished lanai; just bring food and toiletries. These run $180 to $210 a night, plus nightly $25 cleaning fee, with a 2-night minimum.

At mile marker 16.5 on Hwy. 360 (Road to Hana), Keanae. https://ymcacampkeanae.org. ⓒ **808/248-8355.** Unspecified number of tent and camper van sites and 11 cabin, bunkroom, suites, and cottages. Tents and camper vans: $25 single, $40 family (two adults and minor children). Cabins and bunk rooms (sleeping 12 to 60): $30 per person ages 5 and older. King Suite (sleeps 4): $150 plus $25 cleaning fee nightly, 2-night minimum. Ohana Suite (sleeps 8): $300 plus nightly $25 cleaning fee; 2-night minimum. Cottages: $180 for four people, $210 for five, plus nightly $25 cleaning fee; 2-night minimum.

Camp Olowalu ★ Halfway to Lahaina on the Honoapiilani Highway, this campground abuts one of the island's best coral reefs. It's perfect for snorkeling and (during winter) whale-watching. (You can hear the whales slap their fins against the sea's surface at night—a magical experience.) The 35 tent sites are $20 with access to flush toilets, enclosed outdoor showers, and picnic tables. The six mountain-view "tentalows" have two or four twin beds (which can be made up into one or two king beds) with linens, Adirondack chairs, and private outdoor showers. They're close to the highway, but still cheapish at $80 per night ($95 during holiday season). Large groups can rent the six A-frame cabins, each with six cots (but no linens) and access to private bathrooms, showers, and a kitchen. The music and noise curfew is 9:30pm, but bring earplugs in any case. *Note:* All accommodations incur the state's 4.166% sales tax, but tentalows and cabins are also subject to the 10.25% transient accommodations tax. **Guided kayak/snorkeling tours** are available here (www.kayakolowalu.com; $65 adults, $45 children 7–12).

800 Olowalu Village Rd., Lahaina (off Honoapiilani Hwy.). www.campolowalu.com. ⓒ **808/661-4303.** 6 cabins, 6 tentalows, 35 tent sites. Tent sites: $20 per night adults ($5 per night children 9–17), 6 person maximum per site. Tentalows (2-night minimum): $95 for 2 persons or $150 for 4 persons, plus up to 2 children on cots ($20 per cot). Cabins: $750–$1,100 for all 6 cabins (sleeps 36; 2-night minimum).

Haleakala National Park ★★★ This stunning national park offers a variety of options for campers throughout its diverse landscape: **car camping** at Hosmer Grove halfway up the summit or at Oheo Gulch in Kipahulu; **pitching a tent** in the central Haleakala wilderness; or cozying up in one of the crater's **historic cabins.** Car and tent camping are free (aside from the $25 park entrance fee). No permit is required, but there's a 3-night limit. The cabins cost a flat $75, whether you rent them for 1 or 12 people.

Hosmer Grove, located at 6,800 feet, is a small, open grassy area surrounded by forest and frequented by native Hawaiian honeycreepers. Trees protect campers from the winds, but nights still get very cold; sometimes there's even ice on the ground up here. Bring an insulated sleeping bag, a mat to put under it, and layered clothing. Still, this is an ideal spot to spend the night if you want to see the Haleakala sunrise. Come up the day before, enjoy the park, take a day hike, and then turn in early; after sunrise, enjoy the sound of native birds on the self-guided nature trail. Facilities include a covered pavilion with picnic tables and grills, chemical toilets, and drinking water; sites are first come, first served, and are limited to 50 people.

On the other side of the island, **Kipahulu Campground** is in the Kipahulu section of Haleakala National Park. You can set up your temporary home at a first-come, first-served drive-in campground with tent sites for up to 100 people near the ocean. *Tip:* Get here early in the day to snag one of the secluded oceanfront sites under a shady *hala* tree. The campground has picnic tables, barbecue grills, and chemical toilets—but no potable water, so bring your own. Bring a tent as well—it rains 75 inches a year here. Call the **Kipahulu Ranger Station** (© 808/248-7375) for local weather updates.

Inside the volcano are two **wilderness tent-camping** areas: **Holua,** in shrubland just off the Halemauu Trail, 3.7 miles from its trailhead; and **Paliku,** near the Kaupo Gap at the lush, foggy, and often rainy eastern end of the valley, 10.4 miles from the Halemauu trailhead. Both are well over 6,000 feet in elevation and chilly at night. Facilities are limited to pit toilets and nonpotable catchment water, which must be treated before drinking. Water at Holua is limited, especially in summer. No open fires are allowed inside the volcano, so bring a stove if you plan to cook. Tent camping is restricted to the signed area and is not allowed in the horse pasture or the inviting grassy lawn in front of the cabins. Permits are issued at park headquarters daily from 8am to 3pm on a first-come, first-served basis on the day you plan to camp; bring a photo ID. Occupancy is limited to 25 people in each campground (groups may be no larger than 12 persons each).

Also inside the volcano are three **wilderness cabins** built in 1937 by the Civilian Conservation Corps. Each has 12 padded bunks (bring your own bedding), a table, chairs, cooking utensils, a two-burner propane stove, and a woodburning stove with firewood kept in an outside locker; pit toilets and nonpotable water (filter or treat before drinking) are nearby. The cabins are spaced so that each one is a nice hike from the next: **Holua** cabin is 3.7 miles down the zigzagging Halemauu Trail, **Kapalaoa** cabin is 5½ miles down the Sliding Sands (Keoneheehee) Trail, and **Paliku** cabin is the farthest, at 9.3 miles down Sliding Sands and across the moonscape to the crater's eastern end. In spring and summer, the endangered *'ua'u* (Hawaiian dark-rumped petrel) can be heard yipping and chortling on their way back home to their cliffside burrows. You can reserve cabins up to 6 months in advance on the park's reservation website (www.recreation.gov; © 877/444-6777). You're limited to 2 nights in one cabin and 3 nights total in the wilderness each month. *Note:* All wilderness campers must watch a 10-minute orientation video at the park's visitor center.

Haleakala National Park, at top of Crater Rd., and at Kipahulu Visitor Center, 12 miles past Hana on Hana Hwy. www.nps.gov/hale. ☎ **808/572-4400.** 3 cabins, 100-plus tent sites. $75 flat rate for cabins; tent campers free (aside from $25 park entrance fee). Cabins by reservation only.

Polipoli Spring State Recreation Area ★

High up on the slope of Haleakala, at 6,200 feet in elevation, this state park has a network of trails that winds through conifer forests similar to those of the Pacific Northwest. It's frequently cold and foggy here—be prepared for extra-chilly nights—but on clear days the views of Maui and its neighbor islands are spectacular. One eight-bunk cabin is available for $90; it has a cold shower and a gas stove but no electricity or drinking water (bring your own). The cabin can't be booked online; you can reserve by phone and must pick up and return keys to the state parks office in Wailuku. Tent-campers can pitch on the grass nearby, reserve on the website, and print out their permit, which must be displayed. No fires are allowed. *Note:* The park is only accessible by 4WD vehicles. Hikers should wear bright clothing due to the presence of year-round pig hunters and seasonal bird hunters.

9¾ miles up Waipoli Rd., off Kekaulike (Hwy 377); 4WD vehicle required. By reservation only: c/o State Parks Division, 54 S. High St., Room 101, Wailuku. www.dlnr.hawaii.gov/dsp/camping-lodging/maui. ☎ **808/984-8109.** 1 cabin. $90 per night (sleeps 8). $18 for 1st tent-camper (ages 2 and older), $3 for additional campers; $30 maximum per night, 5-night maximum.

Waianapanapa State Park ★★

The 12 rustic cabins tucked in the *hala* (pandanus) groves of Waianapanapa State Park are one of the best lodging deals on Maui. Each cabin has three sets of twin bunk beds (sleeping six total), bathroom with shower, kitchen (two-burner electric hot plate, microwave, and refrigerator), and a large lanai where you can while away the hours watching rainstorms roll in from sea. Cabins #5 and #6 are closest to the water. They've recently been spiffed up, but they're still frequented by geckos and are fairly spartan; bring your own linens, towels, dishes, cookware, and eating utensils. You can also pitch a tent above the black-sand beach on Pailoa Bay, with undesignated sites for up to 60 permit holders available, or park a camper van at one of six designated sites. Watch the sun rise out of the ocean and beat the crowds to the beach. There's an on-site caretaker, along with restrooms, showers, picnic tables, shoreline hiking trails, and historic sites. Bring raingear and mosquito protection—this is the rainforest, after all. Reserve online and print out your permit, which must be displayed. *Note:* Check in after 2pm, check out by 10am.

End of Waianapanapa Rd., off Hana Hwy. By reservation only: http://dlnr.hawaii.gov/dsp/parks/maui/waianapanapa-state-park. ☎ **808/984-8109.** 12 cabins. $90 per cabin per night (sleeps up to 6), 2-night minimum (unless only a single night is available). $18 for 1st tent-camper or camper-van user ages 2 and older, $3 for additional campers; $30 maximum per site, 5-night maximum.

A Word of Warning about the Weather

The weather at nearly 10,000 feet can change suddenly and without warning. Come prepared for cold, high winds, rain, and even snow in winter. Temperatures can range from 77°F (25°C) down to 26°F (–3°C), and high winds (which make it feel even colder) are frequent.

Rainfall varies from 40 inches a year on the west end of the crater to more than 200 inches on the eastern side. Bring boots, waterproof gear, warm clothes, extra layers, and lots of sunscreen—the sun shines very brightly up here.

Hiking in Haleakala National Park ★★★

For complete coverage of the national park, see "Haleakala National Park," p. 205.

WILDERNESS HIKES: SLIDING SANDS (KEONEHEEHEE) & HALEMAUU TRAILS

Hiking into Maui's dormant volcano is unforgettable. The terrain inside the wilderness area of the volcano, which includes burnt-red cinder cones, jet-black lava flows, and spiky silverswords, is stark but beautiful. Inside the crater are some 27 miles of hiking trails, two camping sites, and three cabins.

Entrance is $25 per car, valid for 3 days. Rangers lead **free guided nature walks** during the week and **free guided hikes** on weekends, which are a wonderful way to learn about the unique flora and distinctive geology here. For all hikes, you'll want to wear sturdy hiking boots, sunscreen, sunglasses, and a hat, and bring snacks, plenty of water, and a rain poncho or jacket—the sun, wind, and rain can all be intense here. Since hikes and other programs are subject to change, check the latest schedule at www.nps.gov/hale or call © **(808) 572-4400.**

Avid hikers should try to stay at least 1 night in the park; 2 or 3 nights will allow you even more time to explore the fascinating interior of the volcano (see "Campsites," above, for details on the cabins and campgrounds in the wilderness area of the valley). The best route includes two trails: into the crater along **Sliding Sands (Keoneheehee) Trail ★★**, which begins on the rim at 9,800 feet and descends 9.2 miles to Paliku at 6,380 feet, and back out along the 10.3-mile **Halemauu Trail ★**. You can also cross over from the Sliding Sands Trail to Halemauu at several earlier points in the crater, creating an 11.2-mile hike.

The descending and ascending trails aren't loops; the trailheads are miles (and several thousand feet in elevation) apart, so you'll need to make advance transportation arrangements to get back to your car, which you'll leave at the beginning of the hike, about a 30- to 45-minute drive from where the Halemauu Trail ends. You either arrange with someone to pick you up, leave your car at Halemauu and hitchhike to Sliding Stands to start your hike (recommended by the park service, which has designated a "hiker pickup" area), or hook up with other people doing the same thing and drop off one car at each trailhead. Before you set out, stop at park headquarters to get camping and hiking updates.

The trailhead for Sliding Sands is well marked, and the trail is easy to follow over lava flows and cinders. As you descend, look around: The view is breathtaking. In the afternoon, waves of clouds flow into the Kaupo and Koolau gaps. Vegetation is sparse to nonexistent at the top, but the closer you get to the crater floor, the more growth you'll see: bracken ferns, pili grass, shrubs, even flowers. On the floor, the trail travels across rough lava flows, passing by rare silversword plants, volcanic vents, and multicolored cinder cones.

The Halemauu Trail goes over red and black lava and past vegetation such as evening primrose as it begins its ascent up the crater wall. Occasionally, riders on horseback use this trail as an entry and exit from the park. The proper etiquette is to step aside and stand quietly next to the trail as the horses pass.

Note: Some campers and hikers exit the park at Paliku through the Kaupo Gap—8.6 miles to the remote Piilani Highway. The first 3.7 miles of the Kaupo Trail are within park boundaries, but the remainder is not—and isn't maintained, so the park service recommends against it.

DAY HIKES FROM THE MAIN ENTRANCE

In addition to the difficult hike into the crater, the park has a few shorter and easier options. Anyone can take a ½-mile walk down the **Hosmer Grove Nature Trail ★** at 6,750 feet elevation, about a mile below the Headquarters Visitor Center, where native honeycreepers flit about the forest and native shrubland. At 8,840 feet, the ½-mile round-trip trail to the **Leleiwi Overlook ★** starts across the road from the parking lot and leads to a panorama of cinder cones and cliffs that are home to nesting seabirds between March and October. Next to the Haleakala Visitor Center at 9,740 feet, the .4-mile round-trip **Pa Kaoao Trail ★★** ascends a small cinder cone for views of ancient rock-wall shelters and the crater.

At the opposite end of the parking lot, you can start down **Sliding Sands Trail ★★** for a mile or two to get a hint of what lies ahead; be aware that even this short hike can be exhausting at the high altitude. The crater floor is 3.9 miles down the Sliding Sands Trail; it typically takes hikers twice as long to ascend as to descend, so plan accordingly. A good day hike is **Halemauu Trail ★★** from its trailhead at 7,990 feet to Holua Cabin and back, an 8-mile, half-day trip, but you can also just hike the first 1.1 miles on a rocky path to a crater overlook, or continue on another quarter-mile to a land bridge nicknamed the Rainbow Bridge.

HIKING AT KIPAHULU (NEAR HANA)

You'll need to drive or bicycle 12 curving miles from Hana to the lush and rainy enclave of Kipahulu; it's not accessible from the summit. The entry fee is $25 a car, the same as for the summit atop Haleakala, and valid for 3 days. *Note:* Your receipt for summit entry is valid here, and vice-versa. Check in at the ranger station before you begin your hike; the staff can inform you of current conditions, especially the risk of flash flooding along streams and in Oheo Gulch, and share other knowledge of the area.

There are three hikes you can take here. The first is a short, easy ½-mile loop along the **Kuloa Point Trail ★★,** named for the windy bluff overlooking **Oheo Gulch.** The clearly marked path leaves the visitor center and leads toward the ocean along a flat, grassy peninsula, passing the Pools of Oheo and a Hawaiian cultural demonstration area. The tumbling pools are above and below a bridge; the best for swimming are usually above the bridge, although all are frequently closed because of hazardous conditions (and the park recommends against swimming here in general).

From Kuloa Point, the **Kahakai Trail ★** extends a half-mile along the coast to the Kipahulu Campground, offering views of the ocean and ancient archaeological sites.

The third hike, **the Pipiwai Trail,** is for the hardier. Although just a 4-mile round-trip, the trail is steep and you'll want to stop and take plenty of pictures, so allow 3 hours. Take water and snacks, and wear hiking boots and insect repellent. This walk will pass two magnificent waterfalls, the 181-foot **Maka-hiku Falls ★★** and the even bigger 400-foot **Waimoku Falls ★★,** with boardwalks and footbridges along the way. The trail starts at the ranger station, where you'll walk uphill for ½ mile to a fenced overlook at the thundering Makahiku Falls. If you're tired, you can turn around here, but press on if you can. At about 1 mile in, the trail winds through a bamboo forest, which creates natural wind chimes when the breezes are blowing. Another mile farther, after a total gain of 800 feet in elevation, you'll arrive at majestic, cliff-hugging Waimoku Falls. You're not allowed to stand underneath it, since debris can hurtle down just as easily as the misty waters, but the view is tremendous all the same. *Note:* Rangers at Kipahulu conduct a guided Pipiwai Trail hike by reservation only at 10am Sundays. Reserve up to a week before by calling ℱ **808/248-7375.**

Polipoli Spring State Recreation Area ★

At this state recreation area, part of the 21,000-acre Kula and Kahikinui Forest Reserve on the slope of Haleakala, it's hard to believe that you're in Hawaii. First of all, it's cold, even in summer, because the loop is up at 5,300 to 6,200 feet elevation. Second, this former forest of native koa, ohia, and mamane trees, which was overlogged in the 1800s, was reforested in the 1930s with introduced species: pine, Monterey cypress, ash, sugi, red alder, redwood, and several varieties of eucalyptus. The shade of today's towering trees helps keep temperatures cool and contributes to the sometimes eerie ambience.

SKYLINE TRAIL ★★

This is some hike—strenuous but worth every step. It's 6.8 miles, down and then back up, with a dazzling 100-mile view of the islands dotting the blue Pacific, plus the West Maui Mountains, which seem like a separate island.

The trail is located just outside Haleakala National Park at Polipoli Spring State Recreation Area, but you access it by going through the national park to the summit. It starts just beyond the Puu Ulaula summit building on the south side of Science City and follows the southwest rift zone of Haleakala from its lunarlike cinder cones to a cool redwood grove. The trail drops 2,600 feet into the 12,000-acre Kahikinui Forest Reserve. Plan on 8 hours; bring water and gear for extreme weather (wind, rain, and sun).

POLIPOLI LOOP ★

Follow the Skyline Trail to its terminus, and you'll reach the state recreation area. Alternately, you can drive straight there (4-wheel-drive recommended), and embark on several cool-weather hikes. The **Polipoli Loop** is an easy 3½-mile hike that takes about 3 hours. To get here, take the Haleakala Highway (Hwy. 37) to Keokea and turn right onto Hwy. 337; after less than a half-mile, turn on Waipoli Road, which climbs swiftly. After 10 miles, Waipoli Road ends at the Polipoli Spring State Recreation Area campground. The well-marked trailhead is next to the parking lot, near a stand of Monterey cypress. In clear weather, the tree-lined trail offers the best view of the island; I've been there during pea-soup-thick fog, when it was downright spooky.

The Polipoli Loop is really a network of three trails: **Haleakala Ridge Trail, Plum Trail,** and **Redwood Trail.** After ½ mile of meandering through groves of eucalyptus, blackwood, swamp mahogany, and hybrid cypress, you'll join the Haleakala Ridge Trail, which, about a mile in, joins with the Plum Trail (named for the plums that ripen in June–July). This trail passes through massive redwoods and by an old Conservation Corps bunkhouse and a rundown cabin before joining up with the Redwood Trail, which climbs through Mexican pine, tropical ash, Port Orford cedar, and, of course, redwood.

Because pig hunters come to this area year-round, with bird hunting allowed on weekends from roughly October to April, it's a smart idea to wear bright clothing when hiking here, and to dress warmly.

Hiking in Hana ★★

Hana-Waianapanapa Coast Trail ★★   This is an easy 6-mile hike through Waianapanapa State Park, where vine-laced cliffs frame a black-sand beach. Allow 4 hours to walk along the relatively flat trail, which parallels the sea, along lava cliffs and a forest of hala trees. The best time to take the hike is either early morning or late afternoon, when the light on the lava and surf makes for great photos. Midday is the worst time; not only is it hot (lava intensifies the heat), but no shade or potable water is available. There's no formal trailhead; join the route at any point along the Waianapanapa Campground and go in either direction.

Along the trail, you'll see remains of an ancient *heiau* (temple), stands of *hala* (pandanus trees), caves, a blowhole, and a remarkable plant, *naupaka,* that flourishes along the beach. Upon close inspection, you'll see that naupaka has only half blossoms; according to Hawaiian legend, a similar plant living in the mountains has the other half of the blossoms. As the story goes, they represent star-crossed lovers, one banished to the mountains and the other to the sea.

Fagan's Cross ★★   This 3-mile hike to the cross erected in memory of Paul Fagan, the founder of Hana Ranch and Hotel Hana Maui (now the Travaasa Hana Resort), offers spectacular views of the Hana Coast, particularly at sunset. The uphill trail starts across Hana Highway from the Travaasa Hana resort. Enter the pastures at your own risk; they're often occupied by glaring bulls and cows with new calves. Watch your step as you ascend this steep hill on a jeep trail across open pastures to the cross and the breathtaking view.

Keanae Arboretum ★

About 33 miles from Kahului along the Hana Highway, just after the YMCA Camp Keanae (and just before the turnoff to the Keanae Peninsula), is an easy walk through the Keanae Arboretum. The 6-acre arboretum features both native and introduced plants, maintained by the Hawaii Department of Land and Natural Resources. Allow 1 to 2 hours, longer if you take time out to swim. Take raingear and mosquito repellent (and leave nothing in your rental car—break-ins have happened here).

To park, look for the pullouts between mile markers 16 and 17 on the Hana Highway. Walk along the fairly flat jeep road to the entrance. For ½ mile, you will pass by plants introduced to Hawaii (rainbow eucalyptus, torch ginger, pomelo, banana, papaya, hibiscus, and more), all with identifying tags. Next is a taro patch showing the different varieties that Hawaiians used as their staple crop. After the taro, a 1-mile, unmaintained trail leads through a Hawaiian rainforest, crisscrossing a stream along the way. You'll see a few shallow swimming holes; be careful entering and exiting them—the rocks can be slippery—and avoid altogether if it's been raining; flash floods are a potential danger.

Lahaina Pali Trail ★

Unless you're very hardy, you'll want to drop off a vehicle at the western end of this trail, 5.5 miles one way, or have someone meet you there. But it's not too much of a sacrifice for those who wait, since they're at Ukumehame Beach, which has picnic tables overlooking the sandy beach (and convenient portable toilets). The eastern trailhead lies at a gravel parking lot .2 miles south of the intersection of Honoapiilani Highway (Hwy. 30) and Kihei Road (Hwy. 310), on the right side of the road if coming from Kihei.

The well-signed trail doesn't look like much at first; you pass through dry scrubland and kiawe before starting to cross a series of gullies as you ascend Kealaloloa Ridge and the **Lahalna Pali** (the Hawaiian word for "cliff"). Turn left on unpaved McGregor Point Road and follow to stone steps leading to the highest point of the trail, 1,600 feet, and a pasture with sweeping views of Kahoolawe, Molokini, and Haleakala. Cross the gravel access road past wind turbines—a line of white windmills incongruously marching downslope and visible from points far south—and carefully make your way over and around the three switchbacks of Manawainui Gulch.

Five more gulches, some deep, some shallow, await until the trail flattens out above the Lahaina Tunnel, where you can also spy Lanai and Lahaina. The trail follows the coast until a right turn onto an old cliff road, which leads to the final descent into Manawaipueo Gulch and the Ukumehame parking area. You may spot whales along the way, so consider bringing binoculars along with lots of water, sunglasses, and a hat—there's almost no shade.

Waihee Ridge ★

This strenuous 5-mile round-trip hike, with a 1,500-foot climb, offers spectacular views of the valleys of the West Maui Mountains. Allow 3 to 4 hours for the ascent and descent. Pack a lunch, carry lots of water, and pick a dry day, as this area is very wet. There's a picnic table at the summit with great views. Native apapane, a red-breasted bird with black wing and tails, flit among the tufted ohia blossoms in the forest canopy, while below them native amau and hapuu ferns unfurl their fronds.

To get here from Wailuku, turn north on Market Street, which becomes the Kahekili Highway (Hwy. 340) and passes through Waihee. Go just over 2½ winding, often steep miles from the Waihee Elementary School and, after passing Mendes Ranch, look for the turnoff at Boy Scouts' Camp Maluhia on the left. Turn into the camp and drive nearly a mile to the trailhead on the jeep road. About ⅓ mile in, there will be another gate, marking the entrance to the West Maui Forest Reserve. A foot trail, kept in good shape by the Department of Land and Natural Resources, begins here, leading through kukui, guava, Cook pines, and eucalyptus before reaching a bench overlooking a waterfall along Makamakaole Stream. Catch you breath before climbing to the top of the ridge, **Lanilili Peak**, which at 2,563 feet offers panoramic vistas of green gulches, cleft ridges, and Wailuku—providing it's not too misty.

GOLF

Renowned as the longtime host of PGA's Tournament of Champions, Maui could entice anyone to take up the sport, given its spectacular links from north to south. Most are open to the public, and there's even a stunning municipal course that offers 18 holes along a white sand beach for under $65.

Be forewarned; the tradewinds pick up in the afternoon and can seriously alter your game, especially between 10am and 2pm, when winds of 10 to 15 mph are the norm. Play two to three clubs up or down to compensate for the wind factor. I also recommend bringing extra balls—the rough is thicker here and the wind will pick your ball up and drop it in very unappealing places (like water hazards).

If your heart is set on playing on a resort course, book at least a week in advance. Greens fees are pricey, but for the ardent golfer on a tight budget, consider playing in the afternoon, when discounted twilight rates are in effect. There's no guarantee you'll get 18 holes in, especially in winter when it's dark by 6pm, but you'll have an opportunity to experience these world-famous courses at half the usual fee.

Greens fees include use of cart except where noted. Be sure to check online for aeration and maintenance schedules; many courses close for a week in April, May, June, or September.

Stand-by Golf (www.hawaiistandbygolf.com; ✆ 888/645-2665) offers savings off greens fees at Kaanapali, Wailea Golf Club's Gold and Emerald courses, Kahili, and Pukalani golf courses. **Golf Club Rentals** (www.maui clubrentals.com; ✆ 808/665-0800) has custom-built clubs for men, women, and juniors (both right- and left-handed) with rates that include free pickup and delivery: $25 a day for a set of steel clubs, $30 for graphite.

Central Maui

Although not part of posh resorts, courses in this area feature equally beautiful scenery—and often much better rates, making them worth the 30- to 40-minute drive from Kihei or Lahaina, and just a few minutes longer from Kaanapali or Wailea.

King Kamehameha Golf Club ★★ This private club seems to float on its perch 700 feet up the West Maui Mountains, across from Haleakala, with no condos or other development hemming it in. It also boasts the only golf clubhouse designed by Frank Lloyd Wright, a striking, 74,000-square-foot terraced facility; a tiered course designed by Ted Robinson, Sr., in 1991 (and refreshed 14 years later by his son) with bicoastal ocean views, waterfalls, and other water features; and a unique "Guest for a Day" offer that allows visitors to play the links for $249 ($209 if you're a member of another club with reciprocal privileges). There's a limited amount of tee times for guests, restricted to before 8am or after 11am; book 1 month out (the earliest possible) for best availability, using the website's request form.

2500 Honoapiilani Hwy. (Hwy. 30), Wailuku. www.kamehamehagolf.com. ✆ 808/249-0033. One-time "Guest for a Day" greens fees $249 ($209 for members of club with reciprocal privileges); must be booked in advance using form on website. Club rentals $59 (reserve at same time as tee time). From intersection of Honoapiilani Hwy. and Kihei Rd. (Hwy. 310) near Maalaea, head 1.4 mile north to entrance on left.

Kahili Golf Course ★ This popular, public partner to the private King Kamehameha Golf Club in the West Maui Mountains near Waikapu shares similar breathtaking ocean and valley views on a 6,572-yard, par 72 course designed by Robin Nelson and Rodney Wright. Shifts in elevation, doglegs, a lake, and creek bed provide intriguing challenges for all levels of golfers. Check online for current "dynamic" pricing (often higher than standard rates below) and special offers, some including breakfast or lunch at Kahili Restaurant, that bring overall costs down.

2500 Honoapiilani Hwy. (Hwy. 30), Wailuku. www.kahiligolf.com. ℂ **808/242-4653.** Standard greens fees $109, twilight rates (after noon) $95, nine holes $59 (twilight $45), juniors $55 (free for play with adult after 3pm), replay $45 (same day nine holes, $29). Nonplaying riders $35. Travelers package (green fees, club rentals, glove, two sleeves of balls) $175, "ohana" play (two adults and two juniors after 2pm) $125. Club rentals $55 ($20 juniors 12 and younger), shoes $10. From intersection of Honoapiilani Hwy. and Kihei Road (Hwy. 310) near Maalaea, head 1.4mi north to entrance on left.

Waiehu Municipal Golf Course This public, oceanside par-72 golf course is like playing two different courses: The first 9 holes, built in 1930, are set along the dramatic coastline, while the back 9 holes, added in 1966, head toward the mountains. It's a fun course that probably won't challenge your handicap. The one hazard here is the wind, which can rip off the ocean and play havoc with your ball. The only hole that can raise your blood pressure is the 511-yard, par-5 4th hole, which is very narrow and very long. Facilities include a snack bar, lighted driving range, practice greens, club rentals, and a clubhouse. Because this is a public course, the greens fees are low—but getting a tee time is tough.

200 Halewaiu Rd., Waiehu. www.mauicounty.gov/90/Golf-Course. ℂ **808/243-7400.** Greens fees $58 weekday, $63 weekend; twilight rates (after 2pm) half-price. Juniors $2 weekday, $3 weekend. Cart $21. Club rentals $25. From the intersection of Kahekili Hwy. (Hwy. 340) and Waiehu Beach Rd. (Hwy. 3400) in Wailuku, follow Kahekili Hwy. 1.2 miles north to Waihee Ball Park and turn right on Halewaiu Rd. Follow ½ mile to pro shop.

West Maui

Note: Avid golfers staying in West Maui will want to consider a hop to Lanai to experience **The Challenge at Manele Bay** ★★★, a Jack Nicklaus–designed oceanfront course with gorgeous views and challenging holes, including one with a 200-yard tee shot across the ocean. A special package includes round-trip ferry ride from Lahaina, shuttle to and from the harbor, continental breakfast, and greens fees, for $575; book through **Expeditions** ferry (http://go-lanai.com/lanai_golf; ℂ **800/695-2624**). For more details on the course, see p. 306 in Chapter 11, "Lanai."

Kaanapali Golf Resort ★ Both courses at Kaanapali will challenge golfers, from high-handicappers to near-pros. The par-72, 6,305-yard **Royal Kaanapali (North) Course** is a true Robert Trent Jones, Sr., design: It has an abundance of wide bunkers; several long, stretched-out tees; and the largest, most contoured greens on Maui. The tricky 18th hole (par-4, 435-yard) has a water hazard on the approach to the green. The par-72, 6,250-yard **Kai Kaanapali (South) Course** is an Arthur Jack Snyder design; although shorter than the North Course, it requires more accuracy on the narrow, hilly fairways. It also has a water hazard on its final hole, so don't tally up your scorecard until you sink the final putt. Facilities include a driving range and putting course. Celebrated chef Roy Yamaguchi, one of the founders of the Hawaii Regional Cuisine movement, operates the clubhouse restaurant, **Roy's ★★**. Families with nongolfers and soccer fans may also enjoy **footgolf,** a nine-hole loop on the Kai Course with its own holes (in the rough, to protect the greens) in which you attempt to kick a soccer ball to make par. It's available after 4pm for $15 per player, with optional cart and ball rental.

2290 Kaanapali Pkwy., Lahaina (1st building on right after left turn off Hwy. 30 into Kaanapali Resort.) www.kaanapaligolfcourses.com. ✆ **866/454-4653** or 808/661-3691. Greens fees: **Royal Kaanapali Course** $255 ($179 for Kaanapali guests), twilight rates (starting at 1pm) $149, super twilight rates (offered seasonally, starting at 3pm) $109, junior (ages 7–17) $75; **Kai Kaanapali Course** $205 ($139 for Kaanapali guests), twilight rates (starting at 1pm) $99, super twilight rates $79, juniors $55. Nonplaying riders (both courses) $30, after 1pm $15. Same-day replay $49. Club rentals $55–$85, after 1pm $25–$35. Shoe rentals $10. *Note:* Greens fees may be higher online due to "dynamic" pricing. In summer (June–Aug), juniors play free with paying adult on Kai course; junior rates drop to $49 on Royal Course before 3pm, free after 3pm.

Kapalua Resort ★★★　The views from these two championship courses are worth the greens fees alone. The par-72, 6,761-yard **Bay Course** was designed by Arnold Palmer and Ed Seay. This course is a bit forgiving, with its wide fairways; the greens, however, are difficult to read. The oft-photographed 5th plays over a small ocean cove; even the pros have trouble with this rocky par-3, 205-yard hole. The **Plantation Course,** site of the annual PGA Tournament of Champions, is a Ben Crenshaw/Bill Coore design that was undergoing enhancements set to debut in late 2019. The 6,547-yard, par-73 course along a rolling hillside is excellent for developing your low shots and precise chipping. Facilities for both courses include locker rooms, a driving range, and great dining. Sharpen your skills at the attached golf academy, which offers half-day golf school, private lessons, club fittings, and special clinics for beginners; check online for special packages.

2000 Plantation Dr., ocean side of Hwy. 30, in the Kapalua Resort, Lahaina. https://golfat kapalua.com. ✆ **877/527-2582** or 808/669-8044. Greens fees: **Bay Course** $229 ($209 for resort guests), twilight rates (starting at 1pm) $169, late afternoon/extended nine-hole rate (starting at 3:30pm, Dec 20–Mar 31) $149, junior $149, replay $99; **Plantation Course** $329 ($299 for guests), twilight rates $249, late afternoon/extended nine-hole rate $199, junior $199, replay $119. Juniors play free on both courses with paid adult after 2:30pm. Nonplaying riders $49. Club rentals $79 ($59 after 1pm), shoes $19.

South Maui

Maui Nui Golf Club ★   The name has changed (formerly Elleair), but the Kihei course is the same forgiving, beautiful playground. Unspooling across the foothills of Haleakala, it's just high enough to afford spectacular ocean vistas from every hole. *One caveat:* Go in the morning. Not only is it cooler, but (more important) it's also less windy. In the afternoon, the winds bluster down Haleakala with gusto. It's a fun course to play, with some challenging holes; the par-5 2nd hole is a virtual minefield of bunkers, and the par-5 8th hole shoots over a swale and then uphill. For better exercise, try the "Walk About Golf" option—cartless play after 3:30pm daily for $79 single, $139 couple. Walking without play is $20. Amenities include a driving range, pro shop, lessons, and **Sunsets Bar & Grill.**

470 Lipoa Pkwy., Kihei. www.mauinuigolfclub.com. ℂ **808/874-0777.** "Dynamic" greens fees typically $99 7:30–11am; $48–$89 after 11am. Club rentals $40–$60. Check website for specials and off-season rates.

Wailea Golf Club ★★   You'll have three courses to choose from at Wailea. The **Blue Course,** a par-72, 6,758-yard course designed by Arthur Jack Snyder and dotted with bunkers and water hazards, is for duffers and pros alike. The wide fairways appeal to beginners, while the undulating terrain makes it a course everyone can enjoy. More challenging is the par-72, 7,078-yard championship **Gold Course,** designed by Robert Trent Jones, Jr., with narrow fairways and several tricky dogleg holes, not to mention such natural hazards as lava-rock walls. The **Emerald Course,** also designed by Trent Jones, Jr., is Wailea's most scenic, with tropical landscaping and a player-friendly design. Sunday mornings are the least crowded. Facilities include a golf training facility, two pro shops, locker rooms, and two restaurants: **Gannon's** ★★, by Bev Gannon (another Hawaii Regional Cuisine cofounder), and **Mulligan's** ★, a popular Irish pub.

Blue Course: 100 Wailea Ike Dr., Wailea. www.waileagolf.com. ℂ **808/879-2530.** Emerald and Gold courses: 100 Wailea Golf Club Dr., Wailea. ℂ **888/328-MAUI [6284]** or 808/875-7450. Blue Course greens fees: $209 ($189 for Maui resort guests), $179 Wailea resort guests), $149 after noon, $115 after 2pm; juniors (ages 7–17) $115 before 10am, $85 after 10am, free with playing adult after 3pm; nine holes $95 after 10am, $80 after noon ($60 and $50 for juniors). Gold Course and Emerald Course greens fees: $250 ($225 for Maui resort guests, $209 for Wailea Resort guests), $175 after noon, $119 after 3:30pm; juniors $95 after 10am, $55 after 3pm (free with playing adult). Nonplaying riders $35. Club rentals $60–$150. Shoes $25. Check website for specials and unlimited passes.

Upcountry Maui

Pukalani Country Club   This cool par-72, 6,962-yard course at 1,100 feet offers a break from the resorts' high greens fees, and it's really fun to play. The 3rd hole offers golfers two options: a tough (especially into the wind) iron shot from the tee, across a gully (yuck!) to the green, or a shot down the side of the gully across a second green into sand traps below. (Most people choose to shoot down the side of the gully; it's actually easier than shooting across a ravine.) High handicappers will love this course, and more experienced players can make it more challenging by playing from the back tees. Facilities include practice areas, lockers, a pro shop, and a restaurant.

360 Pukalani St., Pukalani. www.pukalanigolf.com. ⓒ **808/572-1314.** Greens fees for 18 holes (including cart) $89, $69 11am–1pm, $39 1–2:30pm, $29 after 2:30pm. Check online for visitor specials. Club rentals $45 before 1pm, $30 after 1pm. Nonplaying riders $25. Take the Hana Hwy. (Hwy. 36) to Haleakala Hwy. (Hwy. 37) to the Pukalani exit; turn right onto Pukalani St. and go two blocks.

OTHER OUTDOOR ACTIVITIES

Biking

It's not even close to dawn, but here you are, rubbing your eyes awake, riding in a van up the long, dark road to the top of Maui's dormant volcano. It's colder than you ever thought possible for a tropical island. The air is thin. The place is crowded, packed with people. You stomp your chilly feet while you wait, sipping hot coffee. Then comes the sun, exploding over the yawning Haleakala Crater, which is big enough to swallow Manhattan whole—it's a mystical moment you won't soon forget. Now you know why Hawaiians named the crater the House of the Sun. But there's no time to linger: You're you about to cruise down a 10,000-foot volcano on a bicycle.

Several companies offer the opportunity to coast down Haleakala on a basic cruiser bike to the shore, some 37 miles of descent. It can be quite a thrilling experience—but one that should be approached with caution. Despite what various companies claim about their safety record, people have been injured and killed participating in this activity. If you do choose to go, pay close attention to the safety briefing. Bike tours aren't allowed in Haleakala National Park, so your van will take you to the summit first, and then drop you off just outside of the park. You'll descend through multiple climates and ecosystems, past eucalyptus groves and flower-filled gulches. But bear in mind: The roads are steep and curvy without designated bike lanes and little to no shoulder. During winter and the rainy season, conditions can be particularly harsh; you'll be saran-wrapped in raingear. Temperatures at the summit can drop below freezing and 40-mph winds howl, so wear warm layers whatever the season.

Maui's oldest downhill company is **Maui Downhill** (www.mauidownhill. com; ⓒ **808/871-2155**), which offers sunrise bike tours, including breakfast and lunch stops (not hosted), starting at $189 (substantial discounts online). Be prepared for a 3am departure! **Mountain Riders Bike Tours** (www.mountain riders.com; ⓒ **800/706-7700**) offers sunrise rides for $180 and midday trips for $160 (discounted if booked online). If you want to avoid the crowds and go down the mountain at your own pace (rather than in a choo-choo train of other bikers), call **Haleakala Bike Company** (www.bikemaui.com; 𝒞 **808/ 575-9575**). After assessing your skill, they'll outfit you with the latest gear and shuttle you up Haleakala. They also offer Haleakala sunrise tours sans bike—a decent option for folks who might feel too sleepy to pedal or drive.

Note: Not all tours begin with a visit to the summit; be sure to confirm if you want that to be part of your experience. After making sure you are secure on the bike, the staff will typically let you ride down by yourself at your own pace.

RENTALS

Maui offers dynamic terrain for serious and amateur cyclists. If you've got the chops to pedal *up* Haleakala, the pros at **Maui Cyclery** ★★★ (99 Hana Hwy., Paia; www.gocyclingmaui.com; 𝒞 **808/579-9009**) can outfit you and provide a support vehicle. Tour de France athletes launch their Maui training sessions from this full-service Paia bike shop, which rents top-of-the-line carbon-fiber Scott and Felt road bikes ($65 $85 a day) and hybrid Scott bikes ($30 a day) and offers a range of guided tours; it also rents car racks for $5. Shop owner Donny Arnoult hosts 6-day cycling camps and sponsors the annual **Cycle to the Sun contest** (www.cycletothesun.com), when riders travel from around the globe to tackle the 10,023-foot volcano on two wheels.

If **mountain biking** is more your style, hit up Moose at **Krank Cycles** ★★★ (1120 Makawao Ave., Makawao; www.krankmaui.com; 𝒞 **808/572-2299**) for a tricked-out bike ($60–$115 per day) and directions to the Makawao Forest trails. For easier riding, Krank also offers e-bikes ($69 a day) and beach cruisers ($45–$60) that include delivery to your door.

Maui County has produced a **full-color map** of the island with various cycling routes, information on road suitability, climate, mileage, elevation changes, bike shops, and safety tips. It's available at most bike shops. You can also download it from the webpage of **South Maui Bicycles** (1993 S. Kihei Rd., Kihei; www.southmauibicycles.com; 𝒞 **808/874-0068**), which rents high-performance Trek road bikes ($30–$60 per day, $130–$250 per week), hybrid city bikes ($22 per day, $99 per week), and e-bikes ($60 per day, $250 per week).

Horseback Riding

Home to generations of *paniolo* (cowboys), Maui offers spectacular horse rides through rugged ranchlands and into tropical forests. I recommend **Piiholo Ranch Adventures** ★★★ in Makawao (www.piiholo.com; 𝒞 **808/740-0727**). This 800-acre, working cattle ranch owned by the *kama'aina* (long-time resident) Baldwin family offers a variety of horseback adventures to suit your ability. Among them, the 2- to 3-hour private rides meander through the misty, flowering slopes of Haleakala with stops for snacks or picnic lunches (starting at $229). You can even play "Cowboy for a Day" and learn how to round up cattle ($349). For a truly special occasion, book the

Heli Ranch Experience (starting at $3,340 for two people): A limo delivers you to the Kahului heliport, where you board one of Blue Hawaiian's Eco-Star helicopters and fly a breathtaking route over Haleakala's craters and Hana's waterfalls to a private ranch cabin. After a pastries and coffee, a 2-hour horseback ride leads through pastures and woods to the immaculate stables, where an SUV limo awaits to return you to Kahului. The ranch also hosts a zipline (see Ziplining, p. 221).

Another multigeneration family of Maui horsemen runs **Mendes Ranch Trail Rides** ★★ (www.mendesranch.com; ✆ **808/871-5222**) on 3,000-acre Mendes Ranch above Wailuku. This working cowboy ranch is impossibly picturesque, with waterfalls, palm trees, coral-sand beaches, lagoons, tide pools, a rain forest, and its own volcanic peak (more than a mile high). Your guides, bonafide wranglers, will take you from the edge of the rain forest out to the sea and even teach you to lasso. They'll field questions and point out native flora, but generally just let you soak up Maui's natural splendor in golden silence. Experienced riders can run their horses. A 1½-hour morning or afternoon ride costs $135; contact **Sunshine Helicopters** (✆ **808/871-0722**) for pricing and availability of a package that includes a 30-minute helicopter ride over the West Maui Mountains. The ranch entrance is at 3530 Kahekili Hwy., 6¼ miles past Wailuku.

Spelunking

Don't miss the opportunity to see how the Hawaiian Islands were made by exploring a million-year-old underground lava tube/cave. After more than 10 years of leading scuba tours through underwater caves around Hawaii, Chuck Thorne discovered some caves on land that he wanted to show visitors. When the land surrounding the largest cave on Maui went on the market in 1996, Chuck snapped it up and created an attraction called **Hana Lava Tube** ★★ (www.mauicave.com; ✆ **808/248-7308**). You can take a self-guided, 40-minute tour for just $12 (free for kids 5 and under) between 10:30am and 4pm daily. Those who prefer to stay above ground can wander through Thorne's botanical maze created from red ti plants, and all can picnic afterward in the pleasant shelter overlooking the maze.

If you want to combine caving with a tour of Hana, contact **Temptation Tours** (www.temptationtours.com; ✆ **808/877-8888**). Its Cave Quest option costs $239, which covers a 1-hour cave tour of the enormous Kaeleku lava tube, an air-conditioned van tour from your hotel to Hana (eight passengers maximum), continental breakfast, a beachside picnic lunch, and a stop for a swim at a waterfall or beach.

Tennis & Pickleball

Maui's public tennis courts are free and available from daylight to sunset (a few are even lit until 10pm for night play). For a complete list of public courts, call **Maui County Parks and Recreation** (✆ **808/270-7383**) or visit www.co.maui.hi.us/facilities.aspx. Courts are available on a first-come, first-served basis; when someone's waiting, limit your play to 45 minutes. Most convenient for visitors:

- **Napili:** Two courts in Napili Park, Honoapiilani Hwy. at Maiha St.
- **Lahaina:** Nine lighted courts east of **Lahaina Civic Center**, 1840 Honoapiilani Hwy. (mountain side), next to the Lahaina Post Office.
- **Kihei:** Four courts in **Kalama Park** (② 808/879-4364), 1900 South Kihei Rd., and six courts in **Waipuilani Park** (② 808/879-4364) on West Waipuilani Rd., behind the Maui Sunset condos.
- **Hana:** Two courts in the **Hana Community Center and Ballpark** (② 808/248-7022), 5091 Uakea Rd.

Private tennis courts are also available at several resorts and hotels on the island (see chapter 4, "Where to Stay," p. 39). On the Kapalua Resort, the **Kapalua Tennis Garden** (www.golfatkapalua.com/tennis_garden; ② 808/662-7730) has 10 oceanview courts in five tiered pairs lined with trees; they're home to the **Kapalua Open,** which features the largest purse in the state, held on Labor Day weekend. The rest of the year, court rentals are $25 per person per hour. Weekly court passes ($80 single, $150 double, $175 family) come with perks that include free racket and rentals (otherwise $15 per day), free Drop-in Doubles (normally $25 per person, offered 3pm Mon and Wed, and 2pm Sat), and discounts on daily morning clinics (typically $45 per person), ball machines, and pro shop merchandise. At press time, the Tennis Garden was still planning to add pickleball courts.

The **Wailea Tennis Club,** 131 Wailea Ike Place (www.waileatennis.com; ② 808/879-1958), has 11 Sportsmaster courts as well as several new **pickleball courts**. Tennis court fees are $25 per player, pickleball courts $15 per player, both for 90 minutes of play. Reservations may be made up to a week in advance. Tennis racket rentals are $10 per day, pickleball paddles $5 per day (including a ball).

Ziplining

Ziplines have spread across Hawaii almost as fast as zipline riders whisk along the steel cables to which they're safely tethered. One reason ziplines took off so quickly: It's an eco-friendly activity that helps landowners preserve open space. The views are typically dazzling, although more easily photographed from the landings between the rides; most providers rent GoPros you can attach to your helmet—a smart alternative to dropping your cellphone into a steep ravine while you try to video your ride.

Note: Ziplines have minimum ages (typically 7–10) and minimum and maximum weight limits; check online for your providers' specific requirements, including clothing. All require closed-toe shoes; some suggest lightweight long pants and jackets, especially in cooler areas. Reserve early, especially for larger groups, since tours are typically limited to 12 people or fewer. Don't forget to bring $10 to $20 per person to tip your guide, based on the length of the tour and their helpfulness.

Flyin' Hawaiian Ziplines ★★★ Although you check in at Maui Tropical Plantation, this course is not to be confused with the tamer one for novices also on-site. Instead, you'll start with a 4x4 drive into Waikapu Valley in the West Maui Mountains before zipping across nine valleys and 11 ridges—a 4- to 5-hour journey with eight ziplines covering 2½ miles of rainforest and arid scrubland. The longest is a whopper at 3,600 feet, and all have panoramic views of coastline and mountains. Along the way you'll do some short hikes and learn about Native Hawaiian culture and the indigenous ecosystem, helping with the latter's restoration by watering thirsty plants. At the end in Maalaea, an air-conditioned van shuttles you back to Maui Tropical Plantation. Tours depart at 7am, 10am, and 1pm daily.

At Maui Tropical Plantation, 1670 Honoapiilani Hwy. (Hwy. 30), Wailuku. www.flyin hawaiianzipline.com. © **808/463-5786**. Tours $185.

Kapalua Ziplines ★★ Couples and the intrepid will gravitate to this aerial attraction, which offers Maui's longest all-dual-zipline course—even zips totaling 9,750 feet over former pineapple fields and deep green gullies with intoxicating views of the brilliant blue ocean and the ridges of Molokai. Whether you're doing the five-, six-, or seven-zip tour, you'll also cross the island's longest and tallest suspension bridge, a 360-foot-long, 200-foot-high span over Kaopala Stream. All tours include a ride on a Polaris ATV and a souvenir water bottle; the seven-zip tour, which lasts about 3½ hours, includes some short trail hikes with scenic overlooks and commentary on the cultural heritage and ecology of the area.

500 Office Rd. (in Kapalua Resort), Lahaina. www.kapaluaziplines.com. © **808/756-9147**. Tours $180–$210.

Maui Zipline ★ For those without a lot of time, or possibly nerve, a 2-hour tour on this entry-level course over the flowering gardens, orchards, and fields above Maui Tropical Plantation is just the ticket. It's also the most family-friendly, since it's open to children as young as 5 (weighing at least 45 lb.) and the five ziplines are all side by side. The last flies over a lagoon, where non-zipping parties can also observe the fun. Tours typically go out at least three times a day, at 10am, 12:30pm, and 3pm, and more often in peak periods. You're in a great spot for lunch or a shave ice afterwards.

At Maui Tropical Plantation, 1670 Honoapiilani Hwy. (Hwy. 30), Wailuku. https://maui tropicalplantation.com/maui-zip-lines. © **800/451-6805**. Tours $110.

Piiholo Ranch Adventures ★★ Explore this family ranch in the Makawao forest from above—flying through the eucalyptus canopy on up to seven ziplines. Those who'd rather walk than zip can accompany participants on the standard tours, which have four or five lines (the latter including one that's 2,800 feet long), for $25. The treetop version keeps zippers in the canopy with access to an aerial bridge, tree platforms, and two treehouses. Several times a month, typically on a weekday, Piiholo offers a zipline/waterfall hike combo, an all-day option that includes a drive along the Hana Hwy. to short hikes, led by a naturalist, to two nearby waterfalls for a refreshing dip. Children ages 8 to 12 may zip free with paying adult on select tours; call for details.

799 Piiholo Rd., Makawao. www.piiholozipline.com. © **808/572-1717.** Zipline-only tours $140–$165. Treetop tours with 6 or 7 ziplines $135–$145. Zip/waterfall combo $229.

Skyline EcoAdventures ★ Go on, let out a wild holler as you soar above a rainforest gulch or through a eucalyptus grove. Pioneers of this internationally popular activity, the Skyline owners brought the first ziplines to the U.S. and launched them from their home, right here on Maui. Skyline has two courses, one with ocean and island views in Kaanapali and the other in a forest halfway up Haleakala. Both are fast and fun, the guides are savvy and safety-conscious, and the scenery breathtaking. Kaanapali's eight-line tour lasts approximately 3½ hours and its 11-line tour about 4 hours; Haleakala's five-line tour takes about 90 minutes. This eco-conscious company is also carbon-neutral and donates thousands of dollars to local environmental agencies. *Tip:* Book online to save $10 off for adults and $50 off for children 8 to 13.

Haleakala location, 2½ miles up Haleakala Hwy., Makawao. www.zipline.com. © **808/269-7180.** Tours $120. Kaanapali location: In the Fairway Shops, 2580 Kekaa Dr. #122, Lahaina. © **808/662-1500.** Tours $170–$190.

SHOPPING MAUI

Maui's best shopping is found in the small, independent boutiques and galleries scattered around the island—particularly in Makawao and Paia, towns appealing to both visitors and residents. (If you're in the market for a bikini, there's no better spot than the intersection of Baldwin Ave. and Hana Hwy. on Maui's North Shore.) The two upscale resort shopping malls, the **Shops at Wailea** in South Maui and **Whalers Village** in Kaanapali, have everything from Louis Vuitton to Gap—plus a handful of local designers. If you're looking for that perfect souvenir, consider visiting one of Maui's farms or farmer's markets, most of which offer fantastic value-added products. Take home Kaanapali coffee, Kula lavender spice rub, Ocean Vodka (p. 152), Maui Gold pineapple, and other tasty treats.

Don't be afraid to stop by a table on the side of the road to purchase some fresh fruit, dried fish, wooden carvings, or handmade shell jewelry; you'll also find arts and crafts vendors in rotation at hotel lobbies, luau grounds, and regular evening art festivals in Lahaina and Wailuku. "Talking story," local-style, is part of the appeal.

THE ESSENTIALS   **Major shopping centers** are open Monday through Saturday from 9:30am to 9pm and Sunday from 10am to 5pm. The United States has no value-added tax (VAT) or other indirect tax at the national level. The **state general excise tax (GET)** can vary in Hawaii due to county surcharges; on Maui, it's 4.166% on all purchases. Keep in mind that mainland-bound passengers cannot take home most fresh fruit, plants, or seeds (including some leis) unless they are **sealed and labeled as permitted for transport**—you cannot seal and pack them yourself.

CENTRAL MAUI
Kahului

Kahului's shopping is concentrated in two malls:

THE MAUI MALL   Home to **Whole Foods Market, T.J. Maxx,** and **Tasaka Guri Guri**—the latter the decades-old purveyor of inimitable icy treats that are neither ice cream nor shave ice, but something in between—plus Kahului's largest movie theater, a 12-screen megaplex that features mainly current releases. This mall also has a large **Longs Drugs**, a Hawaii institution selling great stashes of local food treats, Hello Kitty Hawaii–themed items, beach mats, etc., as well as items typically found in its mainland counterparts in the CVS chain. 70 E. Kaahumanu Ave. www. mauimall.com. © **808/877-8952.**

QUEEN KAAHUMANU CENTER A 7-minute drive from the Kahului Airport, this mall also has a Longs in its two levels of shops, restaurants, and theaters. It covers the bases, from arts and crafts to **Macy's** and mall standards like **Forever 21, Victoria's Secret,** and **Local Motion** (surf- and beachwear). Maui-based vendors include handbag maker **Happy Wahine,** jeweler **Kanilehua,** and **Hoomana Hawaii Polynesian Boutique,** which stocks well-priced, locally designed women's clothing and accessories. **Maui Friends of the Library** (www.mfol.org; © **808/877-2509**) runs a new and used bookstore that is an excellent source for Hawaii reading material; it also has locations in Puunene and at the Wharf Cinema Center in Lahaina. Like Tasaka Guri Guri, **Camellia Seed Shop** (© **808/877-5714**) is a throwback to plantation days when locals enjoyed sweet-and-sour treats made from pickled plum seeds, including mango, guava peel, and red ginger. Give them a try! 275 Kaahumanu Ave. www.queenkaahumanucenter.com. © **808/877-3369.**

Maui Swap Meet ★ Admission to this colorful maze of booths and tables is just 50¢ (free for shoppers 12 and under). The Maui Swap Meet in held in the Maui Community College's parking lot every Saturday from 7am to 1pm. Vendors come from across the island to lay out their treasures: fresh fruits and vegetables from Kula and Keanae, orchids, jewelry, ceramics, clothing, household items, homemade jams, and baked goods. It's fun to stroll around and "talk story" with the farmers, artists, and crafters. At Maui Community College in an area bounded by Kahului Beach Rd. and Wahine Pio Ave. (access via Wahine Pio Ave.). www.mauiexposition.com. © **808/244-3100.**

Wailuku

Wailuku's vintage architecture, antiques shops, and mom-and-pop eateries imbue the town with charm. You won't find any plastic aloha in Wailuku; in fact, this is the best place to buy authentic souvenirs.

Stores stay open late the first Friday of each month, with live music and entertainment from 6 to 9pm along Market Street.

Hale Hoikeike (Bailey House) Museum Shop ★ The small gift shop at the entrance of this wonderful museum offers a trove of authoritative Hawaiiana, from hand-sewn feather hatbands to traditional Hawaiian games, music, and limited-edition books. Make sure to stroll through the gracious gardens and view Edward Bailey's paintings of early Maui. At the very least, take time to appreciate the massive koa outrigger canoe displayed outside. Hale Hoikeike (Bailey House) Museum, 2375-A Main St. www.mauimuseum.org. © **808/244-3326.**

Bird of Paradise Unique Antiques ★   Come here for old Matson liner menus, vintage aloha shirts, silk kimonos, and anything nostalgic that happens to be Hawaiian. Owner Joe Myhand collects everything from 1940s rattan furniture to Depression-era glass and lilting Hawaiian music on vinyl or cassette. 56 N. Market St. ℂ **808/242-7699.**

Native Intelligence ★★★   This wonderful shop feels like a museum or gallery—only you can take the marvelous artifacts home with you. From the rich monkeypod wood floors to the collection of finely woven *lauhala* hats, shopping here is a feast for the senses. The store's owners, hula expert Kaponoai Molitau and wife, Jenny, are committed to supporting indigenous Hawaiian artisans, who come here both to shop and stock the shelves with artwork of the highest craftsmanship. Browse the truly Hawaiian keepsakes and gifts: locally designed Kealopiko clothing silkscreened with Hawaiian proverbs, *kukui* nut spinning tops, soaps scented with native herbs, and *lei o manu*—fierce war clubs fringed with shark teeth. You can also buy bags of fresh poi and the island's most precious leis, made of feathers, shells, or fragrant flowers. 1980 Market St., #2. www.native-intel.com. ℂ **808/242-2421.**

WEST MAUI

Lahaina

Lahaina's merchants and art galleries go all out from 7 to 10pm every Friday, when **Art Night** ★ brings an extra measure of hospitality and community spirit. The Art Night openings are usually marked with live entertainment and refreshments, plus a livelier-than-usual street scene. A free walking map of participating galleries is available at the **Lahaina Visitor Center** in the Old Lahaina Courthouse, 648 Wharf St., #101, Lahaina (www.visitlahaina.com; ℂ **808/667-9175**).

Across from the seawall on Front Street, you'll find the **Outlets of Maui,** 900 Front St. (www.outletsofmaui.com; ℂ **808/667-9216**). There's plenty of free validated parking and easy access to more than two dozen outlet shops, including **Calvin Klein, Coach, Banana Republic, Adidas, Kay Jewelers; Maui Sunglass** sells locally designed Maui Jim polarized specs. At the northern end of Lahaina town, what was formerly a big, belching pineapple cannery is maze of shops and restaurants known as the **Lahaina Cannery Mall,** 1221 Honoapiilani Hwy. (www.lahainacannerymall.com; ℂ **808/661-5304**). The air-conditioned building holds a **Longs Drugs,** a 24-hour **Safeway** for groceries, an **ABC store** (a ubiquitous souvenir and convenience shop), plus more intriguing independent stores like **IPU Island Crafts** and **Maui Art A La Carte.**

Honolua Surf ★   Gear up for a day on the water at this local franchise named for one of Maui's best surf breaks. You'll find cute beach cover-ups, rash guards, bikinis and surf trunks, sweatshirts, sandals, hats and even duffle bags to carry it all. www.honoluasurf.com. Lahaina: 845 Front St., ℂ **808/661-18848;**

also 754 Front St., ℂ **808/667-1863;** Lahaina Cannery Mall, 1221 Honoapiilani Hwy., ℂ **808/661-5777.** Kaanapali: At Whalers Village, 2345 Kaanapali Pkwy. ℂ **808/661-1778.** Kihei: 2411 S. Kihei Rd. ℂ **808/874-0999.** Wailea: At Shops of Wailea, 3750 Wailea Alanui. ℂ **808/891-8229.** Paia: 115 Hana Hwy. ℂ **808/579-9593.**

Lahaina Arts Society Galleries ★★ Since 1967, the Lahaina Arts Society has been promoting the excellent work of local artists. The society's two galleries inhabit the Old Lahaina Courthouse, the historic building that sits between Lahaina harbor and the giant banyan tree in the center of town. In addition to hosting changing monthly exhibits, the galleries are jam-packed with paintings, photography, ceramics, jewelry, and more. The artists host "Art in the Park" fairs several times each month in the shade of the sprawling banyan tree (check the website for dates). 648 Wharf St. www.lahainaarts.com. ℂ **808/661-0111.**

Lahaina Galleries ★ Sea creatures sculpted from bronze and wood greet you at the entrance of this Front Street haven for art. Whether you fancy Robert Bissell's whimsical portraits of elephants swarmed by monarch butterflies, Guy Buffet's Parisian cafe scenes, or Dario Campanile's provocative still lifes, this gallery has an artist and aesthetic for you. The knowledgeable staff is helpful and not prone to the high-pressured sales pitches of some nearby galleries. Lahaina: 736 Front St. www.lahainagalleries.com. ℂ **808/856-3080.** Also at the Shops at Wailea, 3750 Wailea Alanui. ℂ **808/874-8583.**

Mahina ★★ Fashionable young women make a beeline for Mahina for wardrobe staples: feminine mini and maxi dresses, strappy shoes, clutches with pineapple prints, and gold bangles decorated with puka shells. Reasonable prices make it easy to rock tropical glamour at the beach or bar. www.shopmahina.com. Lahaina: 335 Keawe St. ℂ 808/661-0383. Kaanapali: At Whalers Village, 2345 Kaanapali Pkwy. ℂ 808/793-2231. Kihei: 1913 S. Kihei Rd. ℂ **808/879-3453.** Wailea: At Shops at Wailea, 3750 Wailea Alanui Dr. ℂ **808/868-4717.** Paia: 23 Baldwin Ave. ℂ **808/579-9131.**

Maui Hands ★★ This collective of more than 300 artists has several consignment shops/galleries around the island, each teeming with handcrafted treasures by local artisans. You'll find Niihau shell necklaces, vivid paintings of local beaches and tropical flowers, carved koa bowls and rocking chairs, screen-printed textiles, and one-of-a-kind souvenirs for every budget. The artists are on hand and happy to discuss their work. www.mauihands.com. Lahaina: 612 Front St. ℂ **808/667-9898.** Paia: 84 Hana Hwy. ℂ **808/579-9245.** Makawao: 1169 Makawao. ℂ **808/572-2008.** Kaanapali: In the Hyatt Regency, 200 Nohea Kai Dr., Kaanapali. ℂ **808/667-7997.**

Kaanapali

WHALERS VILLAGE ★★ Right on Kaanapali Beach, this open-air mall offers everything from **Louis Vuitton** to **Tommy Bahama,** with a few island designers in the mix. Find classy aloha wear from Honolulu's **Tori Richard**

(www.toririchard.com; © **808/667-7762**) and matching mother-daughter batik clothing from Maui's **Blue Ginger** (www.blueginger.com; © **808/667-5793**). The **Totally Hawaiian Gift Gallery** (www.totallyhawaiian.com; © **808/667-4070**) carries Niihau shell jewelry, Norfolk pine bowls, and Hawaiian quilt kits, while you'll find smaller koa wood items like pens, jewelry, and photo frames among the art gallery-worthy wooden tables and bedframes at **Martin & MacArthur** (martinandmacarthur.com; © **808/667-7422**). The Honolulu-based chain **Na Hoku** jewelers (www.nahoku.com; © **808/667-5411**) offers stellar island-inspired sparkles and watches. In contrast to most Maui shops, stores here remain open until 10pm. Sate your hunger at **Monkeypod Kitchen** (p. 118), **Leilani's on the Beach** (p. 103), or, hidden in the otherwise unimpressive food court, **Joey's Kitchen** (p. 106). Parking is unfortunately expensive (and prohibited to beachgoers, though it's not clear how they monitor this; be sure to get a parking validation with purchase). 2435 Kaanapali Pkwy. www.whalersvillage.com. © **808/661-4567.**

Honokowai, Kahana & Napili

Those driving north of Kaanapali toward Kapalua will notice the **Honokowai Marketplace,** on Lower Honoapiilani Road, only minutes before the Kapalua Airport. It houses a couple of restaurants and coffee shops, a dry cleaner, the flagship **Times Supermarket,** and a few clothing stores.

Kapalua

Village Galleries ★★ This well-regarded gallery showcases the finest regional artists in a small space inside the Ritz-Carlton lobby, with a branch in Lahaina, too. View Pegge Hopper's iconic Hawaiian women, George Allan's luminous oil landscapes, and Betty Hay Freeland's colorful local scenes. Three-dimensional pieces include gemstone-quality Niihau shell leis, hand-blown glass sculptures, and delicately turned bowls of Norfolk pine. www.villagegalleriesmaui.com. Kapalua: At the Ritz-Carlton Kapalua, 1 Ritz-Carlton Dr. © **808/669-1800.** Lahaina: 120 Dickenson St. © 808/661-4402.

SOUTH MAUI
Kihei

Kihei is one long stretch of strip malls. Most of the shopping is concentrated in the **Azeka Place Shopping Center,** 1280 South Kihei Rd. (www.azeka shoppingcenter.com; © **808/588-9532**), which has stores on both the *makai* (ocean) and *mauka* (mountain) sides of the road; the mountain side is also known as Azeka Place II, 1279 South Kihei Rd. Offerings include simple but popular restaurants like **Nalu's South Shore Grill** (p. 112), stores for everyday needs (including **Ace Hardware**), and a few specialty boutiques like **Maui Quilt Shop** (mauiquiltshop.com; © **808/874-8050**), which not only sells tropical-themed quilts but also patterns, fabrics, and kits to try Hawaii's signature style of stitchery yourself.

Wailea

SHOPS AT WAILEA ★★ This elegant high-end mall mainly features luxury brands (**Prada, Tiffany & Co., Gucci**), but some less well-known gems are hidden amid the complex's 50-odd shops. **Martin & MacArthur** (martinandmacarthur.com; ✆ **808/891-8844**) sells luminous, curly koa bowls and keepsake boxes—or you could bring home a beautiful handmade Hawaiian musical instrument from **Mele Ukulele** (www.meleukulele.com; ✆ **808/879-6353**). The mall is home to several good restaurants—including "Top Chef" fan favorite Sheldon Simeon's **Lineage** (p. 116) and the **Island Gourmet Markets** (✆ **808/874-5055**)—that offer affordable options for breakfast and lunch: everything from pastries to sushi, burgers, sandwiches, and gelato. 3750 Wailea Alanui. www.theshopsatwailea.com. ✆ **808/891-6770**.

UPCOUNTRY MAUI

Makawao has several gorgeous boutiques and galleries to browse, plus a small grocery. **Rodeo General Store,** 3661 Baldwin Ave. (✆ **808/572-1868**) offers ready-made items, dry goods, kombucha, housemade bread, local produce, and other fresh items, along with an excellent deli. A temperature-controlled cave at the back of the store houses a superior wine selection. Fuel up with stick donuts from one of Maui's oldest and most beloved mom-and-pop shops, **T. Komoda Store & Bakery** (see p. 121).

Altitude ★★ Owner and Frenchwoman Jeannine deRoode is every bit as stylish and charming as her boutique, which offers an array of classy, contemporary clothing, jewelry, and handbags. This is the place to find wardrobe staples that will last a lifetime. 3620 Baldwin Ave. ✆ **808/573-4733**.

Driftwood ★★ One-stop shopping for a glamorous life: Browse the shelves for baby-soft suede boots, booty-bearing bikinis, swoon-worthy photo books, and dangly crystal earrings that will draw second looks as you cross Makawao Avenue, a surprisingly fashionable address. Candles, pottery, edibles, and Maui-made shrubs (cocktail mixers) are also on hand for your entertaining needs. 1152 Makawao Ave. www.driftwoodmaui.com. ✆ **808/573-1152**.

Homme by Nature ★★ The well-dressed (and well-heeled) man will want to check out the au courant surf wear, tasteful Hawaiian shirts, graphic tees, designer sunglasses, and other clothing and accessories in Desiree and Marco Daniele's carefully curated boutique. 3643 Baldwin Ave. ✆ **808/572-3456**.

Hot Island Glassblowing Studio & Gallery ★★ Watch glass blowers transform molten glass into artwork in this Makawao Courtyard studio. If you didn't witness it happening, you might not believe that the kaleidoscopic vases and charismatic marine animals were truly made out of the fragile, fiery-hot medium. Several artists show their work here; prices range from $25 for pretty plumeria dishes to over $4,000 for sculptural pieces. In the middle range ($190–$420) are Chris Richards' luminescent jellyfish floating in glass and Chris Lowry's petal-patterned "Chris-anthemum" bowls ($500). 3620 Baldwin Ave. www.hotislandglass.com. © **808/572-4527.**

Hui Noeau Visual Arts Center ★★   On the wonderfully leafy grounds of Kaluanui Estate, which you can wander through on your own or via a guided tour (Mon and Wed 10am; $12), is the gift shop of this marvelous gallery in the former Baldwin Family home, built in 1917. The Hui is a hub for local art and education, and many inspired artists contribute their work to the shop here. Browse the shelves for whimsical jewelry, paintings, woodblock prints, children's toys, and much more. 2841 Baldwin Ave. www.huinoeau.com. © **808/572-6560.**

The Mercantile ★★   Every texture in this boutique is sumptuous, from the cashmere sweaters to the tooled leather belts. In addition to upscale men and women's clothing, you'll find Spiritual Gangster yoga wear, Jurlique organic body products, Maui-made Rue Belle gemstone jewelry, and an assortment of French soaps and luxurious linens. 3673 Baldwin Ave. © **808/572-1407.**

Viewpoints Gallery ★★   Tucked into in Makawao Courtyard, this small gallery features the museum-quality work of 40 established Maui artists. The front half is dedicated to revolving solo shows and invitational exhibits—always worth a look. The gallery's back half features works by collective artists: luminous oils by George Allan (an island resident since 1973), evocative watercolor landscapes by Diana Lehr, and stylized ceramic serving dishes and vases by Christina Cowan. 3620 Baldwin Ave. www.viewpointsgallerymaui.com. © **808/572-5979.**

Fresh Flowers in Kula

Like anthuriums on the Big Island, proteas are a Maui trademark and an abundant crop on Haleakala's rich volcanic slopes. They also travel well, dry beautifully, and can be shipped worldwide with ease. **Proteas of Hawaii,** 15200 Haleakala Hwy., Kula (www.proteasofhawaii.com; © **808/878-2533,** ext. 210), located next door to the Kula Lodge, is a reliable source of this exotic flower.

EAST MAUI

Paia

Maui Crafts Guild ★★   On the corner of Hana Highway and Baldwin Avenue, this artists' collective features distinctive, high-quality crafts. For over 3 decades, the guild's dozen or so artists have been fashioning exquisite works out of ceramic, glass, wood, mixed media, and natural fibers. Look for the shell-adorned silver jewelry by Gaby Dunn, the intricate woven artwork by Maui native Fiama von Schuetz, and Debra Lumpkins' traditional Japanese *gyotaku*, colorful prints made by rubbing tropical fish in ink. (She uses the fresh catch of her spearfisher husband and nontoxic ink, so the fish can be eaten afterward.) 120 Hana Hwy. www.mauicraftsguild.com. ⓒ **808/579-9697.**

Pearl ★★ This chic housewares shop supplies everything necessary for beach cottage living: Turkish spa towels, vintage hardware, embroidered cover-ups, and Indonesian furnishings. Stylish shop owner Malia Vandervoort collects treasures from around the globe that match her soulful, simple aesthetic. Among her best-selling items, Annie Fischer's handpainted, made-in-Maui pillows capture the hypnotic colors of Baldwin Beach just down the road. 71 Baldwin Ave. www.pearlbutik.com. ⓒ **808/579-8899.**

Wings ★ Founded by besties Samantha Howard and Melody Torres shortly after they graduated from the University of Hawaii, Wings relies on local designers and seamstresses for its whimsical, sustainable clothing (made with organic or recycled fabrics, nontoxic dyes, and the like). You'll find one-of-a-kind pieces (boyfriend flannels with crochet patches and repurposed kimonos) and screen tees, tanks, and hoodies with clever logos—everything a young or young-at-heart lady needs to rule the beach like a queen. 69 Hana Hwy. www.wingshawaiishop.com. ⓒ **808/579-3110.**

Hana

Hana Coast Gallery ★★★ Hidden away in the posh Travaasa Hana resort, this critically acclaimed, 3,000-square-foot gallery is a cultural experience to savor. You won't find pandering sunsets or jumping dolphins here. Known for its quality curatorship and commitment to Hawaiian culture, this art haven is almost entirely devoted to Hawaii artists. Among the stellar Maui artists represented are *plein air* painter Michael Clements, master carver Keola LeVan Sequeira, and Melissa Chimera, whose massive botanical

---

Maui's North Shore Is Bikini Central

Paia has a half-dozen boutiques dedicated to Maui women's sun-kissed beach uniform, the bikini. And that's not all; many of the other shops lining Baldwin Avenue and Hana Highway also sell swimwear. Head to this North Shore beach town for everything from Brazilian thongs to full-figured, mix-and-match-your-own suits. The best of the bunch are **Maui Girl,** 12 Baldwin Ave. (www.maui-girl.com; ⓒ **808/579-9266**), featuring local designer Debbie Kowalski Wilson's swimwear (popularized in *Sports Illustrated* photo shoots);

LeTarte, 24 Baldwin Ave. (www.letarte swimwear.com; ⓒ **808/579-6022**), the flagship store for Maui designer (and professional windsurfer) Lisa Letarte Cabrinha's line of cute swimsuits and slinky resort wear; **Pakaloha,** 120 Hana Hwy. (www.pakalohamaui.com; ⓒ **808/ 579-8882**), which offers expert fitting advice and also has a Lahaina storefront at 815 Front St. (ⓒ **808/661-6888**); and **San Lorenzo,** 115 Hana Hwy. (www. sanlorenzobikinis.com; ⓒ **808/873-7972**), which fuses South American flair with Hawaiian style.

canvases feature endemic Hawaiian flowers. If you're considering buying a koa wood bowl or piece of furniture, look here first; you'd be hard-pressed to find a better selection under one roof. At the Travaasa Hana. www.hanacoast.com. © **808/248-8636.**

Hasegawa General Store ★ This family-run, tin-roofed mercantile has been serving the Hana community since 1910, its eclectic wares even inspiring a popular song recorded in 1961 and occasionally covered today. Harkening back to the days when stores like these were islanders' sole shopping outlet, the store is packed with books and music, fishing poles, Hana-grown coffee, diapers, fridge magnets, garden tools, fresh vegetables, dry goods, and ice cream. Check out the assortment of machetes above the office window. If you're so inclined, buying a Hasegawa T-shirt or baseball cap will prove you were here. It's opened 7am to 7pm daily, which is the Hana version of a 24-hour store. 5165 Hana Hwy. © **808/248-8231.**

NIGHTLIFE

While a lively luau is a must for any first-time visitor to the islands, Maui's nightlife comes in as many hues as a rainbow's. Nationally and regionally renowned performers in all genres of music, theater, and dance appear regularly at the Maui Arts & Cultural Center; clubs in resort areas and local communities feature blues, rock, and karaoke, not to mention native Hawaiian music; hotel bars offer innovative mixology with sunset chasers, while cognoscenti of craft brews and fine wine can confidently imbibe in several venues. Magic shows and luaus offer family-friendly fun, while a night under the stars—whether watching a movie or simply taking a romantic stroll—makes a splendid end to any day.

THE PERFORMING ARTS

Concert & Theater Venues

Iao Theater ★★   This beautifully renovated vintage theater in Wailuku, built in 1928 in the Spanish Mission style, has been home to the **Maui OnStage** community theater company since 1984. Shows range from locally written productions to well-known plays and musicals—think Gilbert & Sullivan or "Mamma Mia"—and free "one night only" performances. An intriguing assortment of edgier acts appear at the annual Maui Fringe Theater Festival, typically the third weekend in January. The **Maui Chamber Orchestra** (www.mauichamberorchestra.org) also regularly plays here. 68 N. Market St. ✆ **808/242-6969** for box office and program information. www.mauionstage.com.

Maui Arts & Cultural Center ★★★   Commonly referred to as the MACC (pronounced "mack"), this $32-million compound in Kahului attracts an exceptional lineup of artists and events throughout the year. Its **A&B Amphitheater,** which can host more than 4,000 patrons, presents diverse big-name draws such as Pearl Jam, Jimmy Buffett, and Ziggy Marley (reggae is a always a big draw) and the annual Maui Brewers Festival, the MACC's popular annual fundraiser. Home to the **Maui Pops Orchestra** (http://mauipops.org), the MACC's state-of-the-art, 1,200-seat **Castle Theater** also boasts an impressive variety of acts, such as ukulele sensation Jake Shimabukuro, the American Indian Dance Theatre, author David

Sedaris, and comedian George Lopez. Top Hawaiian musicians and other local talent typically perform in the center's 250-seat **McCoy Studio Theater.** Go early to a show in the Castle Theater to browse the rotating art exhibitions in the expertly lit **Schaefer International Gallery,** which is also open Tuesday to Sunday 10am to 5pm, and during some intermissions. 1 Cameron Way (near the intersection of Kahului Beach Rd. and Wahinepio Ave.), Kahului. www. mauiarts.org. ✆ **808/242-7469.**

ProArts Playhouse ★ Those reeling from sticker shock for South Maui luaus and prices in general will appreciate the reasonably priced tickets ($15–$26) of this talented community theater, which offers plays and musicals by established playwrights like Terrence McNalley and Christopher Durang. *Bonus:* You can choose your seats in the tiered, 200-seat playhouse in Kihei's Azeka Shopping Center when buying online. The troupe also rents out its space to comedy groups and other artists. 1280 S. Kihei Rd. (near Taco Bell in Azeka Shopping Center), Kahului. www.proartsmaui.com. ✆ **808/242-7469.**

luau, **MAUI STYLE**

Most of the larger hotels in Maui's major resorts offer luaus on a regular basis. You'll pay about $80 to $120 to attend one, but don't expect it to be a home-grown affair prepared in the traditional Hawaiian way. There are, however, commercial luaus that capture the romance and spirit of the luau with quality food and entertainment.

Maui's best choice for families is indisputably the nightly **Old Lahaina Luau** ★★★ (www.oldlahainaluau.com; ✆ **800/248-5828** or 808/667-1998). Located just ocean-side of the Lahaina Cannery, the Old Lahaina Luau maintains its high standards in food and entertainment—and enjoys an oceanfront setting that is peerless. Local craftspeople display their wares only a few feet from the ocean. Seating is provided on cushions at low tables for those who wish to dine much as the traditional Hawaiians did, but there are tables and chairs for everyone else. The 3-hour program has no fire dancing, but you won't miss it (for that, go to the romantic **Feast at Lele,** p. 94, or the energetic **Drums of the Pacific Luau** at the Hyatt Regency Maui

Resort & Spa, p. 50). The Old Lahaina Luau offers a healthy balance of entertainment, showmanship, authentic, high-quality food, educational value, and sheer romantic beauty (no watered-down mai tais either; these are the real thing).

The luau begins at sunset and features Tahitian and Hawaiian entertainment, including powerful hula *kahiko* (ancient hula), hula *auana* (modern hula), and an intelligent narrative on the dance's rocky course of survival into modern times. The food, served from an open-air thatched structure, is as much Pacific Rim as authentically Hawaiian: *imu*-roasted kalua pig, seasonal fresh fish, guava-marinated chicken and shredded chicken with ginger and rice bean noodles ("chicken long rice"), grilled steak, a vegan/gluten-free taro/sweet potato/tofu patty, lomilomi salmon, poi, tuna and octopus poke, Hawaiian sweet potato, sautéed vegetables, fried rice, and taro leaves with coconut milk. The cost is $125 for adults, $78 for children ages 3 to 12 (free for younger children not needing a seat).

For information on all of Maui's luaus, go to **www.mauihawaiiluau.com.**

Long-Running Shows

At press time, the venerable multimedia, Hawaiian-themed extravaganza known as **Ulalena** ★★★ (www.ulalena.com) was still seeking new ownership after a rent dispute over the 680-seat **Maui Theatre** on Lahaina's Front Street forced the show to close. Check the website for possible updates.

Free Range Comedy ★   Nearly every Saturday night, you'll find this flock of six to eight improv artists spinning hilarity out of audience suggestions in fast-paced shows lasting an hour to 90 minutes. The venues alternate among South, Central and North Maui: the **ProArts Playhouse** in Kihei (see above); **Maui Coffee Attic** in Wailuku (59 Kanoa St.; www.mauicoffeeattic. com; ℂ **808/250-9555**); and the **Temple of Peace** in Haiku (575 Haiku Rd.; www.templeofpeacemaui.com; ℂ **808/575-5220**). Performances typically start at 7:30pm, with tickets just $10. Check weekly schedule at www.mauifree rangecomedy.com

Masters of Hawaiian Slack Key Guitar ★★★   Virtuosos of slack key guitar—named for Hawaiian guitarists' technique of loosening strings (or "keys") to produce unique, richly resonant tunings—perform Wednesday nights at the Napili Kai Beach Resort's indoor amphitheater, the Aloha Pavilion. Slack key also involves nimble finger-picking and often *leo nahenahe*— gentle, sweet vocals, sometimes including falsetto—in songs inspired by Hawaiian legends, landscapes, and love. Host George Kahumoku, Jr., now a senior scion of a revered Hawaiian musical dynasty, introduces a different slack key master every week. Not only is there incredible Hawaiian music and singing, but George and his guests also "talk story" about old Hawaii, music, and local culture, sharing insights and lore you might otherwise never encounter. For a leisurely, well-spent evening, take advantage of the ticket option ($95) that includes dinner at the resort's nearby **Sea House Restaurant.** Napili Kai Beach Resort, 5900 Lower Honoapiilani Rd., Lahaina. www.slackkey.com. ℂ **888/669-3858.** Tickets $38 advance, $45 at the door; $95 with 5pm dinner (advance purchase only). Performances Wed 7:30pm (doors open 6:45pm).

Warren & Annabelle's ★★   This magic/comedy cocktail show with twice-nightly seatings stars illusionist Warren Gibson and "Annabelle," a ghost from the 1800s who plays the grand piano (even taking requests from the audience), as Gibson dazzles you with his sleight-of-hand magic. (*Note:* Similarly entertaining guest magicians fill in when Gibson's away; he lists his replacements on a schedule posted online.) Appetizers, desserts, and cocktails are available first, either as a package or a la carte, accompanied by ghostly music in "Annabelle's parlor," and followed by the interactive show in a 78-seat theater. You must be 21 or older (with ID) to attend; book tickets during peak periods in advance. 900 Front St., Lahaina. www.warrenandannabelles.com. ℂ **808/667-6244.** Tickets $69 show only; $120 for show, appetizers, two cocktails, and dessert, incl. gratuity. Performances Mon–Sat 5 and 7:30pm.

Free Hula Shows

If you're put off by the price of the typical luau, take advantage of one of the island's free evening hula shows by Maui *halau hula* (hula schools.)

In West Maui, the lower-level courtyard of **Whalers Village** (2435 Kaanapali Pkwy., Lahaina; www.whalersvillage.com; *𝄞* **808/661-4567**) hosts hourlong shows of traditional hula by Halau Hula Malani O Kapehe at 7pm Wednesday and Saturday. After a warm day, it's a treat to cool down at the air-conditioned **Lahaina Cannery Mall** (1221 Honoapiilani Hwy., Lahaina, https://lahainacannerymall.com; *𝄞* **808/661-5304**), which presents free 1-hour shows at 7pm Wednesday, as well as 1pm weekends.

In South Maui, the **Shops at Wailea** (3750 Wailea Alanui Dr., Wailea; www.theshopsatwailea.com; *𝄞* **808/891-6770**) showcases Polynesian dance, including hula, at 5:30pm Tuesday and Thursday. *Note:* The first hour of parking is free; three more hours can be validated with $25 purchase.

THE BAR & MUSIC SCENE

Nightlife in Maui begins at sunset, when all eyes turn westward to see how the day will end. And what better way to take it all in than over cocktails? With its view of Molokai to the northwest and Lanai to the west, Kaanapali and West Maui boast panoramic vistas unique to this island. In South Maui's resort areas of Kihei and Wailea, the island of Kahoolawe and the crescent-shaped atoll of Molokini islet are visible on the horizon, while the West Maui Mountains look like an entirely separate island. No matter what your vantage point, you are likely to be treated to an astonishing view.

Of course, you won't need brilliant sunsets if the talent onstage shines equally bright. If **Amy Hanaialii Gilliom, Kealii Reichel,** or **Willie K** are playing anywhere on their native island, don't miss them; they're among the finest Hawaiian musicians around today. Same with **Hapa,** a first-rate band comprised of **Barry Flanagan** and rotating guests. You'll find them performing in some of the clubs and restaurants listed below; keep in mind that most resort lobby lounges offer evening music and occasional hula.

West Maui

In Kapalua, ogle Molokai and Lanai to the tune of live acoustic music during the daily happy hour from 3 to 5pm at the open-air **Point Lounge at Merriman's** (1 Bay Club Pl., Lahaina; www.merrimanshawaii.com/kapalua; *𝄞* **808/669-6400**); bring a light jacket to stay after dark. For late-night revelry, **Sansei Seafood Restaurant & Sushi Bar** (600 Office Rd., Kapalua; www.sansei hawaii.com; *𝄞* **808/669-6286**) has karaoke Thursday and Friday from 10pm to 1am—when you can also enjoy 50% off sushi and appetizers. The original **Maui Brewing Company** brewpub in Kahana Gateway Center (4405 Honoapiilani Hwy., Lahaina; www.mbcrestaurants.com; *𝄞* **808/669-3474**) is open 10am to 11pm daily, with $1 off beer during happy hour (daily 3:30–5:30pm).

In Kaanapali, park at Whalers Village and head for **Leilani's on the Beach** (www.leilanis.com; © 808/661-4495) or **Hula Grill** (www.hulagrill.com; © 808/667-6636), next to each other on the beach. Both have busy, upbeat bars and tables bordering the sand. These are happy places for great people-watching, gazing over at Lanai, and enjoying mai tais and margaritas. Hula Grill's Barefoot Bar appetizer menu is a cut above. Leilani's has live music and happy-hour specials Monday and Wednesday through Friday from 3 to 5pm, while at Hula Grill the happy hour starts at 2:30pm daily, with live music and often hula from 2pm to 9pm Monday to Saturday (starting at 11am on Aloha Fri).

Now, Lahaina: It's a sunset lover's nirvana, lined with restaurants that have elevated mai tais to an art form. Fleetwood Mac cofounder Mick Fleetwood runs the multistory **Fleetwood's on Front Street** (744 Front St.; www. fleetwoodsonfrontst.com; © 808/669-6425) and often drops in to jam with other entertainers. There's live music on the main stage on Sunday to Wednesday from 6 to 9pm and Thursday to Saturday 7 to 10pm; in the main bar Saturday to Thursday 2:30 to 5:30pm; and on the breezy rooftop nightly from 7 to 9pm (with dinner service) and Aloha Friday from 2 to 4pm. Don't miss one of the daily sunset ceremonies (5:45pm) on the roof; a Hawaiian *kumu* alternates with a Scottish bagpiper except on Saturdays, when both appear. The rooftop also hosts live music during weekend brunch from noon to 2pm, including the ace Hawaiian-pop duo of **Eric Gilliom** and **Barry Flanagan** (of Hapa), who perform most Sundays.

The historic saloon at the **Pioneer Inn,** 658 Wharf St., Lahaina (www.pioneer innmaui.com; © 808/661-3636), offers a variety of live music Tuesday and Thursday nights 5:30 to 8pm. At **Cheeseburger in Paradise** (811 Front St.; www.cheeseburgerland.com; © 808/661-4855), both music and patrons come in high volume; contemporary and classic rock bands perform daily from 5:30 to 9:30pm. Happy hour runs 3 to 6pm and 9pm to closing, while margaritas are just $2 on Monday. Just down the road, the Monday-to-Saturday evening lineup at **Kimo's** (www.kimosmaui.com; © 808/661-4811), part of the restaurant group that includes Hula Grill and Leilani's on the Beach, includes jazz, Hawaiian, and jazz-inflected Hawaiian music by Maui-based artists.

South Maui

Inspired by her Hawaiian grandmother's career as a vocalist and hula performer in New York's Hawaiian Room, jazzy Hawaiian songbird **Amy Hana-ialii Gilliom** presents a dinner show on Wednesdays at 7:30pm at **Nalu's South Shore Bar & Grill,** in Azeka Shopping Center (1280 S. Kihei Rd., Kihei; www.nalusmaui.com; © 808/891-8650). Talented brother **Eric Gilliom** plays with **Barry Flanagan** in a dinner show at Nalu's every Saturday at 7:30pm.

Craft-brew lovers will want to check out **Maui Brewing Company**'s newest brewpub (605 Lipoa Pkwy., Kihei; ww.mbcrestaurants.com; © 808/201-2337), which has 36 specialty beers on tap and daily live music. The daily happy hour is 3:30 to 5:30pm and 9:30 to 11pm, and includes $10 pizzas, $1 off house beers and $3 off cocktails.

Also in Kihei, **Kahale's Beach Club** (36 Keala Pl. ✆ **808/875-7711**) proudly dubs itself "Maui's oldest dive bar," offering live bands nightly and the island's longest happy hour (10am–5pm). Across from Kalama Park, **Haui's Life's a Beach** (1913 S. Kihei Rd.; www.mauibars.com; ✆ **808/891-8010**) hosts karaoke Sunday to Thursday at 9pm and live music at 9:30pm on weekends. As with its Kapalua counterpart, **Sansei Seafood Restaurant & Sushi Bar**, in Kihei Town Center (1881 South Kihei Rd.; www.sanseihawaii.com; ✆ **808/879-0004**), serves up karaoke 10pm to 1am Thursday to Saturday, along with 50% off sushi and appetizers. Move to the groove at **South Shore Tiki Lounge** in Kihei Kalama Village (1913-J South Kihei Rd.; www.southshoretikilounge.com; ✆ **808/874-6444**), where DJs spin music for dancing from 10pm to 1:30am nightly; live acts perform 4 to 6pm daily.

In Wailea, Maui's answer to Jimi Hendrix, **Willie K** performs a weekly dinner show at 6:30pm Wednesday at **Mulligan's on the Blue** (100 Kaukahi St., Wailea; www.mulligansontheblue.com; ✆ **808/874-1131** [restaurant] and ✆ **808/280-8288** [show reservations]). Mulligan's, which proudly proclaims itself "Maui's only Irish pub," also presents live Irish music every Sunday at 7pm, magic (6:30pm) and comedy (9pm) on Tuesdays, and country music the first Friday of the month.

Mixology mavens will feel at home in the Lobby Lounge of the **Four Seasons Maui Resort Wailea** (see p. 71), which also offers hula at sunset, live music from 5:30 to 11pm, and delicious sushi, along with a gorgeous sunset view. At the **Fairmont Kea Lani** (see p. 70), **Luana Lounge** boasts similar sunset vistas, unique cocktails, and live music 7 to 10pm nightly; happy hour runs 8 to 10pm. For alcohol-free entertainment, head to the **Shops at Wailea** (3750 Wailea Alanui Dr., Wailea; www.theshopsatwailea.com; ✆ **808/891-6770**) for

WATCH FOR THE green flash

If you're gathered in a crowd on Maui watching a sunset, you may hear someone call out: "Green flash!" If you're lucky, you may get to see it yourself.

The romantic version of the story is the green flash happens when the sun kisses the ocean good night (honeymooners love this version). The scientific version is not quite as dreamy: Light bends as it goes around the curve of the earth. When the sun dips beneath the horizon, it is at the far end of the spectrum. So this refraction of the sun's light, coupled with the atmosphere on the extreme angle of the sunset on the horizon, causes only the color green to be seen in the color spectrum just before the light disappears.

Here's how to view the green flash: First, it has to be a clear day, with no clouds or haze on the horizon. Second, the sun has to set on the ocean (if it sets behind an island, you won't see the flash). Keep checking the sun as it drops (try not to look directly into the sun; just glance at it to assess its position). If the conditions are ideal, just as the sun drops into the blue water, a "flash" or laserlike beam of green will appear to shoot out and spread along the horizon for an instant.

free 90-minute concerts by some of Hawaii's award-winning vocalists; the shows begin at 5:30pm on Wednesdays.

Central Maui, Upcountry and Paia

In Waikapu, the **Maui Tropical Plantation**, 1670 Honoapiilani Hwy. (www.mauitropicalplantation.com; ℂ 808/270-0333), is a lushly landscaped venue for outdoor movies, parties, and live entertainment; check the website for upcoming events. Enjoy West Maui mountain views from its **Mill House** restaurant and bar, where happy hour runs from 2 to 5pm daily.

The bustling **Kahului Ale House,** 355 E. Kamehameha Ave., Kahului (www.mauimall.com/store/kahului-ale-house; tel] 808/877-0001), is more of a sports bar, with 35 high-definition TVs and 16 beers on tap, but offers *pau hana* (end of workday) live music daily, along with a huge menu. In Wailuku, **Wai Bar**, 45 North Market St. (www.waibarmaui.com; ℂ 808/214-9829), is a gay-friendly oasis with frequent DJs and live music, including jazz on the first Fridays of the month.

In Paia, **Charley's Restaurant & Saloon,** 142 Hana Hwy. (www.charleysmaui.com; ℂ 808/579-8085), has been around since 1969, but gained renown once Willie Nelson started dropping by a few decades ago. Today it features an eclectic selection of live music, from country to reggae to rock 'n' roll Tuesday to Saturday. Check website for showtimes.

Upcountry in Makawao, the party never ends at the popular Italian restaurant **Casanova**, 1188 Makawao Ave. (www.casanovamaui.com; ℂ 808/572-0220). If a big-name mainland band is resting up on Maui following a sold-out concert on Oahu, you may find its members setting up for an impromptu night here. DJs take over on Wednesday (ladies' night); on Friday and Saturday, live music and dancing starts between 9:30 and 10pm most nights and continues to 1:30am. Sunday afternoon concerts start at 3pm. Expect blues, hip-hop, rock 'n' roll, reggae, jazz, and Hawaiian. Elvin Bishop, the local duo Hapa, Los Lobos, and others have taken Casanova's stage. The cover is usually $10 to $20.

Hana

If you need another excuse to spend a night in Hana beyond avoiding the rigors of driving the road there and back in one day, the **Preserve Restaurant & Bar** at Travaasa Hotel Hana (see p. 81) has one ready for you. Sweet-voiced musicians and graceful dancers share the traditions of *kanikapila* (jamming) and

9

NIGHTLIFE | The Bar & Music Scene

THE BEST PLACE IN THE WORLD TO SEE A movie

Imagine lounging on a comfy beach chair on the island of Maui watching the stars come out in the night sky. As soon as it gets dark enough, the biggest outdoor screen you've ever seen comes to life with a film premiere. This has to be the best place in the entire world to watch movies.

If you're headed to Maui in June, plan your travel dates around the **Maui Film Festival** (www.mauifilmfestival.com; ℂ 808/579-9244), which always starts the Wednesday before Father's Day. This is an event you won't want to miss. The 5-day festival features nightly films in the "Celestial Cinema," an under-the-stars, open-air "outdoor theater" on the Wailea Gold & Emerald Golf Course, lit by the moon and powered by the sun (thanks to its capture of solar energy). The event features premieres and special advance screenings on a 50-foot-wide screen in Dolby Digital Surround Sound, as well as in-person appearances of A-list film luminaries. The festival organizer, director and film producer Barry Rivers, selects "life-affirming" films that often become box office hits. As Rivers puts it, the festival offers "rising stars, shooting stars, movie stars, all under the stars."

In addition to the 5 days and nights of films and filmmaker panels, the festival includes free "Toes in the Sand" screenings at the beach, movies at the MACC (see p. 233), a Taste of Chocolate night, a Taste of Wailea (with Maui's top chefs creating exquisite culinary masterpieces), and a closing-night dance

hula in the open-air bar overlooking the ocean from 6 to 8pm Monday, Wednesday, and Thursday.

MOVIES

The 12-screen Regal movie megaplex at the **Maui Mall,** 70 E. Kaahumanu Ave. (ℂ **808/871-6684**), in Kahului, features current releases and modern stadium-style seating. In June, the not-to-be-missed **Maui Film Festival ★★★** (see "The Best Place in the World to See a Movie," below) puts on nights of cinema under the stars in Wailea and at the MACC .

Check websites or local newspapers to see what's playing at the other theaters around the island: the somewhat scruffy, six-screen **Consolidated Kaahumanu Theatres,** at the Kaahumanu Center, 275 W. Kaahumana Ave., Kahului (www.consolidatedtheatres.com/kaahumanu; ℂ **808/873-3137**); the newly posh **Regency Theatres Kihei Cinemas,** which has four screens at 1819 S. Kihei Rd., in Kukui Mall, Kihei (https://regencymovies.com; ℂ **808/874-8624**); and the three-screen **Regal Wharf Cinema Center,** 658 Front St., Lahaina (http://thewharfcinemacenter.com; ℂ **808/249-2222**). The latter offers 2 hours of parking validation for patrons in the lot behind the cinema on Luakini St.

Families will appreciate the free outdoor movies in the lower courtyard at **Whalers Village,** 2435 Kaanapali Pkwy., Lahaina (www.whalersvillage.com; ℂ **808/661-4567**); screenings start 15 minutes after sunset Tuesday and Thursday. Bring a blanket or chair for comfortable seating.

MOLOKAI, THE MOST HAWAIIAN ISLE

"Don't try to change Molokai. Let Molokai change you." That's the mantra on this least developed of the major Hawaiian Islands. No luxury hotels, no stoplights, and "no rush" are points of pride for locals, nearly half of whom are of Native Hawaiian descent. The island welcomes adventure travelers, spiritual pilgrims, and all who appreciate its untrammeled beauty and unhurried ways.

Known as "the child of the moon" in Native Hawaiian lore, Molokai remains a place apart, luminous yet largely inaccessible to the casual visitor. Tourism, and modern conveniences in general, have only a small footprint here, and although the island is just 38 miles long by 10 miles wide, it takes time to see what it has to offer. As the sign at the airport reads: ALOHA, SLOW DOWN, THIS IS MOLOKAI.

Patience and planning reward travelers with a compass of superlatives. The world's tallest sea cliffs stand on the North Shore; on the South Shore, historic fishponds line the state's longest fringing reef. The island's most ancient settlement sits within gorgeous Halawa Valley on the East End, while the West End offers one of the most impressive stretches of golden sand in Hawaii, the more than 2-mile-long (and often empty) Papohaku.

The percentage of people of Native Hawaiian decent is also higher on Molokai than on the other major islands. This slipper-shaped island is the birthplace of hula and the ancient science of aquaculture. An aura of ancient mysticism clings to the land here, and the old ways still govern life. The residents survive by fishing and hunting wild pigs and axis deer on the range. Some folks still catch fish for dinner by throwing nets and trolling the reef.

Many have maintained or revived Hawaiian traditions such as growing taro, managing fishponds, and staging games for Makahiki, the winter festival. "Sustainability" isn't a buzzword here but a way of life, and one that eyes modern innovations with caution—many islanders are fiercely opposed to growth.

Residents and visitors alike take inspiration from the stories of Father Damien and others who cared for the suffering exiles of Kalaupapa. Once a natural prison for those diagnosed with leprosy, the remote North Shore peninsula is now a national historical park with very limited access but profound appeal—much like Molokai itself.

FROMMER'S FAVORITE MOLOKAI EXPERIENCES

o **Venturing into the Garden of Eden:** Drive the 30 miles along Molokai's East End (p. 247). Take your time. Stop to smell the flowers and pick guavas by the side of the road. Pull over for a swim. Wave at every car you pass and every person you see. At the end of the road, stand on the beach at Halawa Valley and see Hawaii as it must have looked in A.D. 650, when the first people arrived on the islands. Book a cultural tour (p. 266) to go into the lush depths of the valley, learn about its history and traditions, and swim in a waterfall pool.

o **Celebrating the Ancient Hula:** Hula is the heartbeat of Hawaiian culture, and Molokai is its birthplace. Although most visitors to Hawaii only glimpse a bit of traditional hula during commercial luaus, it's possible to immerse yourself in its origins here once a year, typically the last weekend in May. That's when Molokai celebrates the birth of the hula at its Ka Hula Piko Festival (www.kahulapiko.com), a daylong affair featuring dance, music, food, and crafts.

o **Strolling the Sands at Papohaku:** Go early, when the tropical sun isn't so fierce, and stroll this 3-mile stretch of unspoiled golden sand on Molokai's West End. It's one of the longest beaches in Hawaii. The big surf and riptides make swimming often risky, but Papohaku is perfect for walking, beachcombing, and, in the evening, picnicking and sunset watching.

o **Traveling Back in Time on the Pepeopae Trail:** This awesome hike takes you through the Kamakou Reserve and back a few million years in time. Along the misty trail (actually a boardwalk across the bog), expect close encounters of the botanical kind: mosses, sedges, violets, lichens, and knee-high ancient ohia. You'll need a four-wheel-drive vehicle and dry weather to make it to the trailhead, and ideally a spot on one of the Nature Conservancy's seven guided hikes a year (p. 264) to appreciate what you're seeing.

o **Soaking in the Warm Waters off Sandy Beach:** On the East End, about 20 miles outside Kaunakakai—just before the road starts to climb to Halawa Valley—lies a small pocket of white sand known as Sandy Beach (p. 271). Submerging yourself here in the warm, calm waters (an outer reef protects the cove) is a sensuous experience par excellence.

Molokai

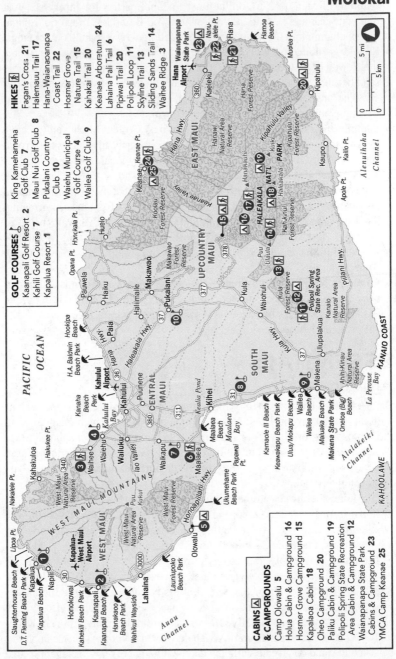

o **Snorkeling Among Clouds of Butterfly Fish:** The calm waters off Murphy (Kumimi) Beach (p. 270), on the East End, are perfect for snorkelers. Just don your gear and head to the reef, where you'll find lots of exotic tropical fish, including long-nosed butterfly fish, saddle wrasses, and convict tangs.

o **Kayaking Along the North Shore:** For expert and hardy kayakers, this is the Hawaii of your dreams: waterfalls thundering down sheer cliffs, remote sand beaches, miles of tropical vegetation, and the wind whispering in your ear. The only time to go is in summer, especially August to September, when the powerful waves tend to settle down.

o **Sampling the Local Brew and Music:** Stop by Coffees of Hawaii (p. 258), in Kualapuu, for a fresh cup of java made from beans that were grown across the road and twice-weekly jam sessions by local musicians.

o **Tasting Aloha at a Macadamia Nut Farm:** It could be the owners, Tuddie and Kammy Purdy, and their friendly disposition that make the macadamia nuts here taste so good. Or it could be their years of practice in growing, harvesting, and shelling them on their 1½-acre farm. Either way, they produce a perfect crop. See how they do it on a short, free tour of Purdy's All-Natural Macadamia Nut Farm (p. 259), in Hoolehua, just a nut's throw from the airport.

o **Posting a Nut:** Why send a picturesque postcard to your friends and family back home when you can send a coconut? The Hoolehua Post Office (p. 259) will supply the coconuts if you'll supply the postage fee of $15 to $20, weight dependent.

ESSENTIALS

Arriving

BY PLANE Unless you're flying to the island as part of a Kalaupapa charter tour, you'll arrive in **Hoolehua** (airport code: MKK), which many just call the Molokai Airport. It's about 7½ miles from the center of Kaunakakai town. *Note:* Make sure to book your flight for daylight hours and get a window seat. The views of Molokai from above are outstanding, no matter which way you approach the island.

Hawaiian Airlines (www.hawaiianairlines.com; (⌀ **800/367-5320**) services Molokai from Honolulu, Oahu, via its subsidiary, Ohana by Hawaiian. The twin-engine turboprops, which feature splashy designs by Sig Zane and carry 48 passengers, make the 28-minute hop several times a day.

The visuals are doubly impressive from the single-engine, nine-seat aircraft of **Mokulele Airlines** (www.mokuleleairlines.com; (⌀ **866/260-7070** or 808/270-8767 outside the U.S.), which offers nonstop, 35-minute flights service from Honolulu more than a dozen times a day. Mokulele also flies to Molokai nonstop from Maui, five times a day from the main airport in Kahului (OGG) and once daily from tiny Kapalua (JHM). *Note:* At check-in, you'll be asked to stand on a scale with any carry-on luggage. Only the agent is able to see the results, but those who weigh more than 350 pounds are not allowed to fly. Keep your shoes on—there are no security screenings.

Makani Kai Air (www.makanikaiair.com; *©* **808/834-1111**) also flies nine-seaters to Molokai from Oahu and Kahului, Maui, for a flat fee of $50 (plus $20 per checked bag, in line with other airlines' baggage fees). In addition, the small airline offers tour packages to Kalaupapa National Historical Park from Honolulu and Kahului. Flights are met by **Damien Tours**—the only way visitors, who must be at least 16 years old, are allowed inside the national historical park. Don't book Kalaupapa flights independently. See page 266.

Note: Important to consider if you're booking connecting flights: On Oahu, Makani Air departs from a private terminal on the perimeter of the Honolulu airport. Mokulele operates from the commuter terminal (now called Terminal 3) and Ohana by Hawaiian from the interisland terminal (now Terminal 2). From Kahului, Maui, Makani Air and Mokulele both depart from small commuter terminals within walking distance of the main airports. The Maui commuter terminal has its own convenient parking lot.

Visitor Information

Molokai Visitors Association (www.gohawaii.com/molokai; *©* **808/553-5221**) offers a wealth of information on its website and friendly advice at its airport booth. The *Molokai Dispatch* (www.themolokaidispatch.com), the island's weekly newspaper, covers local issues and special events of interest to visitors; pick up a free copy, published Wednesdays, for the island's current dining specials and entertainment. Some of the practical information on **VisitMolokai.com** (slogan: "EVERYTHING ABOUT MOLOKAI, BY FOLKS WHO LIVE ON MOLOKAI") is outdated, but the website still has a useful events calendar, sightseeing tips, photos, and insights. These sources all maintain regularly updated Facebook pages, too.

The Island in Brief

Only 38 miles from end to end and just 10 miles wide, Molokai stands like a big green wedge in the blue Pacific. It has an east side, a west side, a back side, and a top side. This long, narrow island is like yin and yang: One side is dry scrublands; the other is a lush, green, tropical Eden. Three volcanic eruptions formed Molokai; the last produced the island's "thumb"—a peninsula jutting out of the steep cliffs of the north shore, like a punctuation mark on the island's geological story.

KAUNAKAKAI ★

On the red-dirt southern plain, where most of the island's 7,350 residents live, the rustic village of **Kaunakakai** ★ looks like a plantation town from the 1930s, only with newer-model trucks. Mile marker 0, in the center of town, divides the island into east and west. Kaunakakai is the closest thing Molokai has to a business district. Nearly every restaurant, store, and community facility on the island lies within a few blocks of one another. You'll find a public library with a great Hawaiian history section, the two gas stations, and two family-owned grocery stores, **Friendly Market** and **Misaki's Market; Kanemitsu's Bakery & Coffee Shop** is renowned for its hot bread available most evenings, but also produces delicious loaves, doughnuts, and other pastries daily. At the end of Wharf Road is **Kaunakakai Wharf,** a picturesque place to fish, photograph, and just hang out. The state's longest pier serves fishing boats, outrigger canoes, and kids enjoying a dip in the ocean. Other than Saturday mornings, when it seems as if the entire island turns out for the farmer's market, it's easy to find a parking space among the pickup trucks.

CENTRAL UPLANDS & NORTH SHORE ★★

Upland from Kaunakakai, the land tilts skyward and turns green, with scented plumeria in yards and glossy coffee trees all in a row, until it blooms into a true forest—and then abruptly ends at a great precipice, falling 3,250 feet to the sea. The green sea cliffs are creased with five V-shaped crevices so deep that light is seldom seen (to paraphrase a Hawaiian poet). The north coast is a remote, forbidding place, with a solitary peninsula—**Kalaupapa National Historical Park ★★★**—where generations of people diagnosed with leprosy (now called Hansen's disease) were exiled. This region is easy on the eyes but difficult to visit. It lies at a cool elevation, and frequent rain squalls blow in from the ocean. In summer the ocean is calm, providing great opportunities for kayaking, fishing, and swimming, but during the rest of the year, giant waves come rolling onto the shores.

The forest grows denser and the air cooler as Kalae Highway (Hwy. 470) passes the island's lone golf course and ends at **Palaau State Park ★★**, known for its phallic rock and dramatic overlook of Kalaupapa, some 1,700 feet below. To the east stand the world's tallest sea cliffs, 3,600 to 3,900 feet, which bracket the North Shore's cascading waterfalls, lush valleys, and dramatic islets, all virtually inaccessible. Fishing charters, helicopter tours from Maui, and, in summer, a strenuous kayak trip can bring them within closer view.

THE WEST END ★

This end of the island, once home to **Molokai Ranch** (closed in 2008), is miles of stark, dry terrain, bordered by some of the most beautiful white-sand beaches in Hawaii, most famously the nearly 3-mile-long **Papohaku Beach ★★★**. The plantation-era village of **Maunaloa** at the end of the Maunaloa Highway (Hwy. 460) remains a virtual ghost town, and the decaying buildings of Kaluakoi Hotel (closed in 2001), above **Kepuhi Beach ★★**, look like a set from *Lost*. Summer is the best time to explore the shoreline here, although the crash of winter waves provides a convenient sleep aid for inhabitants of the three still-open condo developments on the overgrown **Kaluakoi** resort. Look out for axis deer when driving here at night; wild turkeys rule the roost by day. The West End is dry, dry, dry. It hardly ever rains, but when it does (usually in the winter), expect a downpour and lots of red mud.

THE EAST END ★★★

The area east of Kaunakakai is lush, green, and tropical, with golden pocket beaches and a handful of cottages and condos that are popular with thrifty travelers. With this voluptuous landscape comes rain. However, most storms are brief (15-min.) affairs. Winter is Hawaii's rainy season, so expect more rain from January to March, but even then, the storms usually are brief, and the sun comes back out.

From Kaunakakai, the two-lane King Kamehameha V Highway (Hwy. 450) heads 27 miles east past coastal fishponds and sculpted hillsides to **Halawa Valley.** This stunning, culturally significant enclave is only accessible by guided tour, though anyone may drive to the road's end and explore **Halawa Beach Park ★★**. Before the road makes its final dip to the valley, pull over for a distant view of 500-foot **Hipuapua Falls** and 250-foot, two-tiered **Mooula Falls** (also known as Moaula Falls). Before you arrive, though, you'll pass pocket beaches, a mom-and-pop grocery/take-out counter, two churches built by St. Damien (see "The Saints of Molokai," p. 257), and picturesque **Puu O Hoku,** a working cattle ranch and biodynamic farm that also serves as a reserve for nene, the endangered state bird. Stop here for local honey and fresh produce. This is the rainier half of the island, with more frequent showers January through March, but be careful: The sun still blazes here, too.

GETTING AROUND

Getting around Molokai isn't easy without a rental car, which you should reserve as early as possible. During special events and holiday weekends, rental agencies run out of vehicles. Stay alert to invasive axis deer darting onto the highway, especially at night.

BY CAR   The international chain **Alamo Rent a Car** (www.alamo.com; © 888/826-6893) has both an office and cars at the airport in Hoolehua. The office of **Molokai Car Rental** (www.molokaicars.com; © 808/336-0670) may be in Kaunakakai, where owner Amanda Schonely also sells her unique shell-decorated caps and island jewelry, but she's happy to leave a serviceable car (or minivan) for you at the airport or ferry dock, with the keys inside. If you're renting for a week or longer, consider reserving a lightly used but perfectly adequate car, van, or SUV from **Mobettah Car Rentals** (www.mobettah carrentals.com; © 808/308-9566). The company will drop vehicles at the airport, or you can pick up your rental at its office 2 miles west on the Maunaloa Highway. If you are staying 3 weeks or longer, Clare Mawae of **Molokai Outdoors** (www.molokai-outdoors; © 877/553-4477 or 808/633-8700) can also arrange reasonable car rentals.

BY TAXI   Per state law, taxis charge $3 a mile plus a "drop charge" of $3.50, or about $32 from the airport to the Hotel Molokai in Kaunakakai and $42 to a West End condo. Try to arrange rides a day or two in advance, either with the friendly folks at **Hele Mai Taxi** (www.molokaitaxi.com; © 808/336-0967) or **Midnight Taxi** (© 808/658-1410).

BY BUS   The nonprofit **Maui Economic Opportunity, Inc.** (www.meoinc. org; 🕿 808/877-7651) provides free daytime shuttle bus service between Kaunakakai and the East End, Hoolehua/Kualapuu, and Maunaloa/Kaluakoi, running six times daily Monday to Friday. It's designed for rural residents but open to all; if you're feeling adventurous, check out the online schedule (click "Programs & Services," and then follow the drop-down links, starting with "Transportation").

[FastFACTS] MOLOKAI

Note: All addresses are in Kaunakakai unless otherwise noted.

ATMs/Banks   Both **Bank of Hawaii,** 20 Ala Malama Ave. (www.boh.com; 🕿 808/553-3273), and **American Savings Bank,** 40 Ala Malama Ave. (www.asb hawaii.com; 🕿 808/553-8391), have 24-hour ATMs.

Cellphones   Good luck getting service here. The island has a few cellphone towers, but the signal is weak island-wide. Kaunakakai tends to have the best reception.

Dentists/Doctors   The **Molokai Community Health Center,** 30 Oki Place (www.molokaichc.org; 🕿 808/553-5038), provides dental services Monday through Thursday from 7am to 5pm and medical services weekdays from 7am to 5pm.

Emergencies   Call 🕿 **911** in life-threatening circumstances. Otherwise, contact the **police** at 🕿 **808/553-5355** or the **fire department** at 🕿 **808/553-5601.**

Hospital   Molokai General Hospital, 280 Homeolu Place (www.molokaigeneral hospital.org; 🕿 **808/553-5331**), has 15 beds, a 24-hour emergency room open daily, and an outpatient clinic open weekdays 7am to 5:30pm.

Internet Access   **Molokai Public Library,** 15 Ala Malama Ave. (www.libraries hawaii.org; 🕿 **808/553-1765**), offers free Wi-Fi and computers by reservation. **Hotel Molokai** and several restaurants also offer free, semi-reliable Wi-Fi.

Pharmacy   A Kaunakakai fixture since 1935, the family-run **Molokai Drugs,** 28 Kamoi St. (www.molokai drugs.com; 🕿 **808/553-5790**), carries everything from greeting cards to hospital-grade equipment and is open weekdays 8:45am to 5:45pm and Saturday 8:45am to 2pm.

Post Office   The **central office** at 120 Ala Malama Ave. is open weekdays 9am to 3:30pm and 9 to 11am Saturday. The **Hoolehua branch,** just off Farrington Avenue (Hwy. 480) at 69-2 Puupeelua Ave., offers the popular "Post-a-Nut" service (p. 259); it's open 8:30am to noon and 12:30 to 4pm weekdays. Closest to the West End condos is the Maunaloa branch, open Mondays 9:30am to 1:30pm.

WHERE TO STAY

Molokai is Hawaii's most affordable island, especially for hotels—there's only one, and it's not particularly luxurious. Most visitors stay in modern condo units or vacation cottages with kitchens, which can save a bundle on dining costs, while hardy souls pitch their own tent at the beach or in the cool upland forest (see "Hiking & Camping," earlier in this chapter).

I've listed my top picks below; for additional options, **Molokai Vacation Properties** ★★ (www.molokai-vacation-rental.net; 🕿 800/367-2984 or

808/553-8334) can help you navigate what's available. The agents represent only licensed and legal rentals, most of them oceanfront and all guaranteed to be clean and fully equipped. You can book online, but it's best to contact the office directly to identify the most suitable unit for your needs. Their customer service is excellent.

You'll find more (though not necessarily licensed) properties online at VRBO.com, Airbnb.com, and other rental websites. Maui County, of which Molokai is a part, is actively working to shut down unlicensed rentals, so to avoid unpleasant surprises during your stay, it's best to book licensed properties only. Licensed listings will include the owners' state tax ID and/or its permit number; you can also find a list of currently permitted properties online at www.mauicounty.gov/1377/Short-Term-Rentals.

Note: Taxes of 14.42% will be added to your hotel bill. Parking is free. See the map "Restaurants & Hotels on Molokai" for locations of the following accommodations.

Kaunakakai

Note: Some travelers may appreciate the convenience of a condo at **Molokai Shores,** 1 mile east of town, with many units managed by Molokai Vacation Properties (see above) or **Castle Resorts** (www.castleresorts.com; ✆ 877/367-1912). I find the complex lacks the resort ambience and privacy found farther out on the East or West End, while the compact units (510–663 sq. ft.) can be noisy and hot.

MODERATE

Hotel Molokai ★   The free earplugs on the nightstands give away the downside of this charmingly retro collection of Polynesian-style A-frames and a single-story wing: Some rooms suffer from traffic noise. Also, as with most lodgings on the South Side, the beach isn't good for swimming—the water is shallow and murky, although coconut palms arch invitingly over the shoreline. The upsides: Sunset and sunrise views from the small but attractive pool or hammocks are outstanding, the staff is friendly, and the remodeled rooms are cool in both senses of the word, thanks to big ceiling fans; and more and more rooms even have air-conditioning units (read room details before booking to avoid sweaty disappointment). All have microwaves, mini fridges, and coffeemakers, but since most are a petite 228 square feet, it's better to spring for one of the deluxe second-floor rooms (432 sq. ft.) with kitchenettes. Families can take advantage of suites with a king-size bed downstairs and twin beds in a loft. Under new management since late 2017, the oceanfront restaurant **Hiro's Ohana Grill** (see p. 253) features a locally sourced, deliciously island-style menu and live Hawaiian music nightly.

1300 Kamehameha V Hwy. (Hwy. 450), 2 miles east of Kaunakakai. www.hotelmolokai. com. ✆ **877/553-5347** or 808/553-5347. 40 units (14 timeshares). $120–$395 double. Daily resort fee $10 (includes Wi-Fi, snorkel and beach gear, DVD library). Rollaway $25 (not permitted in all rooms); free crib. Airport shuttle $25. **Amenities:** Restaurant, bar; coin laundry; gift shop; pool; activity desk; free Wi-Fi.

INEXPENSIVE

Kahakai Hale ★★★ There are only two licensed bed-and-breakfasts on Molokai, but this would be the pick of any crop. Owned and managed by Mike and Yvette Carlton, who also operate the West End vacation rental **Hale Kamaluhia** (see p. 250), Kahakai Hale is a bright, cheery, and immaculate two-bedroom, 1-bath cottage, just 200 feet from the water and 1 mile east of One Alii Beach Park. While it's too shallow to swim in the former fishpond, you can borrow one of the provided kayaks or stand-up paddleboards to explore offshore. The contemporary furnishings—no dated rattan or sagging couches here—exude breezy beach style. One bedroom has a queen, the other two twins (which can be pushed together to form a king), but it's well-priced even if only one couple is staying.

10 Hoolu Pl. (off Hwy. 450), Kaunakakai. www.halekamahulia.com, www.vrbo.com/1044414. © **808/829-3719.** $125–$140 double, $15 per extra person (maximum four), $95 cleaning fee.

The West End

All the properties described here fall under the inexpensive to moderate categories; summer rates are often, though not always, cheaper than the winter "snowbird" season. *Note:* Keep in mind that there's limited shopping out here; you'll want to stock up groceries and supplies in Kaunakakai before heading to your condo.

Kaluakoi Resort ★★ Developed and managed separately, these three condo complexes near Maunaloa have much in common. Negatives include a remote location, varying quality of furnishings and decor, and a slightly haunted ambience thanks to the shuttered hotel next door. Positives: easy access to Kepuhi and other West End beaches (see "Beaches," p. 268), large lanais, and serene silence—I didn't even hear the crow of wild roosters on my last visit. Built in 1983, the 120-unit, two-story **Ke Nani Kai** ★★ (50 Kepuhi Place) is set back farthest from Kepuhi Beach but boasts the nicest pool and the only hot tub and tennis courts of the bunch; units are two-bedroom, two-bathroom (880–990 sq. ft.) or one-bedroom, one-bathroom (680 ft.). One of the best of the eight managed by Molokai Vacation properties is **No. 237**, an oceanview end unit on the second floor with a roomy sundeck, handsome light wood floors, a queen bed, two twin beds, and living-room futon ($135–$175, plus $130 in one-time cleaning and booking fees). **Hale Kamaluhia,** an independently managed, attractively furnished, and spotlessly maintained one-bedroom unit on Ke Nani Kai's top floor, offers sweeping beach views and its own washer-dryer for just $130 a night, plus one-time $115 cleaning and condo fees.

Built in 1978, the diverse condos of **Kepuhi Beach Villas** ★ (255 Kepuhi Beach) are closest to the sand, with a generous oceanview pool on the grounds of the abandoned Kaluakoi Hotel. The 148 units are spread among two-story buildings with shared laundry facilities (and thin walls), and eight duplex "cottages" with individual washer/dryers; the largest units have a ground floor (642 sq. ft.) with a master bedroom and bathroom, and a small loft (which can get hot in summer) with a second bedroom and bathroom. **Cottage 2B**, perhaps the nicest of the 11 units managed here by Molokai Vacation Properties, features that floorplan in a setting as close to the waves as you can get; watch surfers ride breaks from its large shaded lanai. Palm-accented furnishings include a queen in the downstairs bedroom, two twin beds in the loft, and a living-room sleeper sofa; a washer-dryer is in the downstairs bathroom ($200 –$250, plus $155 in cleaning and booking fees). Paul and Stacy Cook manage **Hale Maluhia** here; it's a smartly updated, 300-sq.-ft. studio, including granite kitchen and bathroom counters, queen bed, and a leather couch that unfolds into a twin bed ($95–$105, plus $75 cleaning fee).

Nearly hidden in tropical foliage, the 78-unit **Paniolo Hale** ★ (100 Lio Place) means "cowboy house," and the large screened lanais and wooden floors give it a hint of the Old West. Built in 1980, the 21 two-story buildings come in a host of floor plans, from studios (548 sq. ft.) to two-bedroom, two-bathroom units (1,398 sq. ft.), some with lofts and sleeping quarters in the living room. Of the half-dozen managed by Molokai Vacation Properties, **studio I2** has the best ocean view, with the roomy lanai making you feel that much closer; it's also just a few steps to the pool and barbecue area ($125–$155, plus one-time $115 cleaning and booking fees.)

Kaluakoi Resort, off Kaluakoi Road, Maunaloa. 346 units. Reservations for select units c/o Molokai Vacation Properties: www.molokai-vacation-rental.com. ✆ **800/367-2984** or 808/553-8334. $120–$250 condo; 10% discount for stays of a week or more. $75–$125 cleaning fee. 3- to 7-night minimum. **Hale Kamaluhia** (in Ke Nani Kai): www. halekamaluhia.com. ✆ **808/829-3719.** $130 double, $95 cleaning fee, $20 condo fee. 2-night minimum. **Hale Maluhia** (in Kepuhi Beach Villas): www.hale-maluhia.com. ✆ **864/616-2247.** $95–$105, $75 cleaning fee. **Amenities:** Barbecues; Jacuzzi; pools; tennis courts (Ke Nani Kai only); Wi-Fi (varies by unit).

The East End

Puu O Hoku Ranch ★★★ Its name means "hill of stars," which accurately describes this 14,000-acre working cattle ranch and biodynamic farm on a cloudless night. You'll stay in one of two 1930s-era cottages, thoughtfully decorated with Hawaiian and Balinese furnishings. The two-bedroom, two-bathroom **Sunrise Cottage** offers a panoramic view, while the one-bedroom, one-bathroom **Sugar Mill Cottage,** named for the nearby remains of a mill, hides just above **Murphy (Kumimi) Beach** ★★ (p. 270). Only ranch guests have access to its numerous hiking trails, which pass ocean bluffs, an ancient and sacred kukui grove, and a nursery for nene, the endangered state bird. The cottages' farm-style kitchens are perfect for taking advantage of the ranch's freshly harvested venison, its organic beef, and produce, too; ask about deliveries when making reservations. *Note:* Groups (a minimum of 14 people) should inquire about the possibility of booking the handsome 11-room lodge, which comes with a private pool, yoga deck, and fireplace; it was unavailable at press time, but has previously been rented for $185 per person a night, including meals.

Main entrance off Kamehameha V Hwy. (Hwy. 450) at mile marker 25, before descent into Halawa Beach Park. https://puuohoku.com. © 808/558-8109. 2 units. **Sunrise Cottage:** $275 for up to 4, $195 cleaning fee. **Sugar Mill Cottage:** $250 double, $30 extra person (maximum 4), $175 cleaning fee. Both units: 7th night free, 2-night minimum. **Amenities:** Store (Mon–Fri 9am–5pm); free Wi-Fi hotspot (at ranch office).

Dunbar Beachfront Cottages ★★ This is one of the most peaceful, comfortable, and elegant properties on Molokai's East End, and the setting is simply stunning. Each of these green-and-white plantation-style cottages (2 of them) sits on its own secluded beach (good for swimming)—you'll feel like you're on your own private island. Perfect for a family, units sleep four with two bedrooms (one with twin beds), one bathroom, a full kitchen, washer and dryer, 25-inch flatscreen TV with DVD player, Wi-Fi, ceiling fans, tropical furniture, a large furnished deck (perfect for whale-watching in winter), and views of Maui, Lanai, and Kahoolawe across the channel. The family-friendly Pauwalu cottage is at ocean level, with a queen-size bed in the master and an ancient fishpond out front. The Puunana cottage has a king-size bed in its master bedroom and sits one flight of stairs above the beach.

9750 Kamehameha V Hwy. (Hwy. 450), past mile marker 18, Kainalu. www.molokaibeach frontcottages.com. © 800/673-0520 or 808/558-8153. 2 cottages (each sleeps 4). $210, $90 cleaning fee. 3-night minimum. No credit cards. **Amenities:** BBQ with picnic table, free Wi-Fi.

Wavecrest Resort ★★ Halfway to Halawa Valley from Kaunakakai, this three-story condo complex on 6 green acres is a clean and convenient home base. Your best bet is Building A, the closest to the ocean; Molokai Vacation Properties' 10 listings here include the third-floor A310, a beauty with koa-style pergo floors, a king bed in the bedroom, and a deluxe kitchen with stainless steel appliances, plus a washer/dryer combo ($125–$150 a night, plus one-time cleaning and booking fees of $115). Top floors in general offer the best views of Maui, Lanai, and uninhabited Kahoolawe, but keep in mind that the resort has no elevators (or air-conditioning). Bottom-floor units aren't bad, as they open straight to the grass and plumeria trees. Bedroom windows face the parking lot, so you'll hear traffic. The units are mostly one-bedroom, one-bath, but some two-bedroom floorplans can accommodate up to six (with a sleeper sofa in the living room); all are individually owned and decorated; scrutinize photos and amenity lists closely. The gated pool and cabana with barbecues are well-maintained, and the front desk has free tennis equipment to use on its two courts.

7148 Kamehameha V Hwy. (Hwy. 450), 13 miles east of Kaunakakai. 128 total units. Reservations for select units c/o Molokai Vacation Properties: www.molokai-vacation-rental.com. © 800/367-2984 or 808/553-8334. $120–$200 condo; 10% discount for stays of a week or more. $75–$100 cleaning fee, $30 booking fee. 3- to 7-night minimum. **Amenities:** Barbecues; coin laundry; pool; tennis courts; Wi-Fi (varies by unit).

WHERE TO EAT ON MOLOKAI

Gourmands looking for fine dining will be disappointed on Molokai, but with a little strategizing you can eat well; just be prepared for a little bit of sticker shock. If you're planning on cooking most of your meals—a wise idea if you are staying any distance from Kaunakakai—see p. 254 for where to stock up before heading out to your accommodations. Most restaurants and groceries are only open Monday through Saturday, although more are starting to offer limited Sunday hours.

Kaunakakai

Modern innovations often take a while to reach Molokai, but the island can now boast two food trucks. The **Ono Fish and Shrimp Truck** ★★ parks outside of Molokai Fish and Dive, 53 Ala Malama Ave., with a few outdoor seats available; try its garlic shrimp, fresh poke, or fish tacos with mango salsa ($12–$13, including soda). **A Taste of Molokai** ★★ near Friendly Market Center at 82 Ala Malama Ave. (✆ **808/658-9164**), serves acai bowls ($7–$12) for breakfast and delectable fresh poke bowls ($8–$12) for lunch.

There are also two appealing sit-down, though still casual, restaurants in or just outside of town. At **Hotel Molokai** (p. 249), the seaside **Hiro's Ohana Grill** ★★ (www.facebook.com/HirosOhanaGrillLLC; ✆ **808/660-3400**), is a family affair, with several generations stepping in to serve island-style dishes with flair. The locally sourced fish entrees and poke, fresh pesto chicken sandwiches, and bananas lumpia Foster dessert have won diners' devotion. Specials like the $10 brioche-bun hamburger dinner and Sunday brunch buffet ($35 adults, $17.50 children 5–12) featuring slow-roasted top sirloin, lightly battered mahimahi, and an omelet station, among other items, also keep patrons coming back. It's open for lunch and dinner daily, 11am to 9pm, and fills up early on Friday afternoons when local musicians perform.

Besides Hiro's, **Paddlers' Restaurant and Bar** ★★ (see "Molokai Nightlife," below) is the only other restaurant in town that serves alcohol (including draft beer), which used to explain its popularity when it was still called Paddlers' Inn. But since chef Kainoa Turner reopened and renamed the restaurant in 2017, its multicultural, pan-Asian-fusion menu has become the star of the show. The eclectic entrees ($14–$29) include gourmet pastas and burgers on brioche buns, mochiko chicken with peanut satay, *camarones ala diabla* (sauteed garlic shrimp in chipotle cream sauce), kalbi short ribs, and pork chop schnitzel. It's open 10am to 9pm Monday to Saturday.

For even more casual dining, Kaukanakai has a half-dozen solid options. On the corner of Highway 450 and Ala Malama Avenue, **Molokai Burger** ★ (www.molokaiburger.com; ✆ **808/553-3533**) offers burgers ($4–$10) and dinner plates ($9–$17) such as fried chicken, salmon, or kalbi ribs. It's open Monday to Saturday until 9pm, with egg dishes and pancakes ($3–$10) available

GROCERIES, MARKETS & edibles

Nearly every storefront in Kaunakakai sells groceries of some sort, but you may need to visit several to stock up on specialty items. Most stores close by 6:30 or 8:30pm. Note that grocery shopping is very limited outside of Kaunakakai.

KAUNAKAKAI

- Start at **Friendly Market Center,** 90 Ala Malama Ave. (📞 **808/553-5595**), a compact supermarket with a variety of dry goods and a small produce section. *Note:* It's closed Sundays.

- A few doors down, **Misaki's Grocery Store** (78 Ala Malama Ave.; 📞 **808/553-5505**) features fresh poke (seasoned, raw fish) and a few more vegetables among its wares; its Sunday hours are 9am to noon.

- Across the street, tiny **C. Pascua Store,** 109 Ala Malama Ave. (📞 **808/553-5443**), stays open till 10pm daily. It often has ripe fruit and jumbo frozen prawns farm-raised on Oahu.

- Pair your prawns from C. Pascua Store with a crisp Sauvignon Blanc from **Molokai Wines N Spirits,** 77 Ala Malama Ave. (📞 **808/553-5009**). Aside from an excellent array of adult beverages, it also has gourmet cheeses and crackers.

- For organic and health-food brands, head to the **Planter Box,** 145 Puali St. (📞 **808/560-0010**).

- **Molokai Minimart,** 35 Mohala St. (📞 **808/553-4447**), is one of the few stores that stays open late, until 11pm daily.

- At the **Saturday morning farmer's market ★★★** in Kaunakakai (8am–noon), vendors sell homegrown fruits and vegetables, along with arts, crafts, and prepared foods. Another farm stand is a little farther out: **Kumu Farms ★★**, 9 Hua Ai

Road, 1 mile south of Highway 460, near the airport (https://kumufarms. com; 📞 **808/351-3326**), is famed for its luscious, GMO-free papayas. It also sells organic herbs, vegetables, pesto, banana bread, and other treats. It's open Tuesday through Friday 9am to 4pm.

THE WEST END

- The **Maunaloa General Store ★**, 200 Maunaloa Hwy., Maunaloa (📞 **808/552-2346**), has staples and occasional plate lunches for sale; it's open Monday to Saturday 9am to 6pm, Sunday 9am to noon.

- Thirsty beachgoers will be glad to discover **A Touch of Molokai** (📞 **808/552-0133**), inside the otherwise-empty Kaluakoi Hotel. It's open 9am to 5pm daily, with snacks, sodas, and microwaveable fare.

The East End

- On the East End, the "Goods" (convenience store) half of **Manae Goods & Grindz ★,** 8615 Kamehameha V Hwy., Pukoo, near mile marker 16 (📞 **808/558-8498**), is open weekdays 6:30am to 6pm, weekends 7:30am to 4:30pm.

- At mile marker 25, the **Puu O Hoku Ranch Store ★★** (https:// puuohoku.com; 📞 **888/573-7775**) sells organic produce, honey, fresh herbs, frozen awa, and free-range organic beef—all produced at the ranch.

Central Uplands

- **Kualapuu Market,** 311 Farrington Rd. (Hwy. 480) at Uwao Street, Kualapuu (📞 **808/567-6243**), is handy for picking up a ready-to-grill steak or bottle of wine, among other food and sundries (Mon–Sat 8:30am–6pm).

7 to 10:30am Saturday and free Wi-Fi. Next door, **Molokai Pizza Cafe ★**, 15 Kaunakakai Place, off Wharf Road (*℗* **808/553-3288**), serves standard pizza, salads, and burgers in a 1950s diner setting and is one of the few places that stays open late (until 11pm Fri–Sat, otherwise 10pm); it takes cash only.

Locals flock to **Maka's Korner ★**, 35 Mohala St. (*℗* **808/553-8058**) for plate lunches (try the mahimahi) and more burgers, best enjoyed to go. It has a handful of outdoor tables (beware of flies) with counter service for breakfast, lunch, and dinner weekdays (breakfast and lunch only weekends). One plus: It's open from 7am to a relatively late 9pm weekdays, with weekend hours 8am to 2pm. The same family owns **Molokai Minimart** (p. 254) and the newer **Hula Bean Cafe** along the same shopping strip. The latter is open 6am to 5pm Monday to Saturday and 8am to 5pm Sunday, a real boon to visitors. While the espresso bar at **Coffees of Hawaii** remains under a years-long renovation, this is the best (and apparently the only) place to get your macchiatos and lattes; fortunately, they're quite tasty, as are the smoothies and breakfast paninis.

The quaint **Store House ★**, 145 Puali St. (*℗* **808/553-5222**), has an array of tropical lemonades, smoothies, pastries, salads, and sandwiches (check the specials). It's a great place to stock up before heading out on an East End adventure. It's open 7am to 5pm weekdays and 9am to 5pm on weekends.

Sweets lovers have many temptations. At **Kamoi Snack-n-Go ★**, 28 Kamoi St. (*℗* **808/553-3742**), choose from more than 31 flavors of Dave's Hawaiian Ice Cream from Honolulu, including local favorites such as *kulolo* (taro-coconut custard), *haupia* (coconut pudding), and *ube* (purple yam). You can't miss the lime-green storefront of **Kanemitsu's Bakery ★★**, 79 Ala Malama Ave. (*℗* **808/553-5585**), a throwback to the 1960s that churns out pies, pastries, and cookies as well as sweet and savory breads (see "The Hot-Bread Run," p. 280). During breakfast and lunch hours, the attached restaurant (with retro orange booths under a hand-painted map of Molokai) serves typical American fare with local touches, such as kimchi fried rice with eggs ($9) and local organic papaya (for just $1).

Elsewhere on the Island

Outside of Kaunakakai, the **Kualapuu Cookhouse ★**, 102 Farrington Rd. and Uwao Street, Kualapuu (*℗* **808/567-9655**), serves gourmet and diner-style dishes. Entrees ($11–$33) include seafood specials such as spicy crusted ahi with lime cilantro sauce or sauteed ono with lilikoi-butter white reduction sauce and a Thursday prime-rib special that's a local favorite. Breakfast and lunch menus are less ambitious but still tasty; sit amid cheery plantation-style decor inside the small cottage dining room or at covered picnic tables outside. Don't be in a rush, though; as the menu says, "If you're in a hurry, you're on the wrong island." The cash-only restaurant is open Monday 7am to 2pm, Tuesday to Saturday 7am to 8pm, and Sunday 9am to 2pm and is BYOB.

On the East End, the takeout counter at **Manae Goods & Grindz,** 8615 Kamehameha V Hwy., Pukoo, near mile marker 16 (*℗* **808/558-8498**), is the

Flying a Kite (p. 280)   You can get a guaranteed-to-fly kite at the **Big Wind Kite Factory** (www.facebook.com/bigwindkites; © **808/552-2364**) in Maunaloa, where kite designer Jonathan Socher offers free kite-flying classes to kids, who learn how to make their kites soar, swoop, and, most important, stay in the air for more than 5 minutes.

Spending the Day at Murphy (Kumimi) Beach Park (p. 270)   Just beyond Waialua on the East End is this small wayside park that's perfect for kids. You'll find safe swimming conditions, plenty of shade from the ironwood trees, and small pavilions with picnic tables and barbecue grills.

area's lone dining option. Smiling faces serve simple fare—tuna sandwiches, shrimp or beef burgers, and acai bowls for breakfast—through the counter window. It's open from 6:30am to 6pm weekdays and 7:30am to 4:30pm weekends.

For food on the West End, see "Groceries, Markets & Edibles," above.

EXPLORING MOLOKAI

Note: You'll find the following attractions on the "Molokai" map (p. 243). For the "topside" churches associated with Father Damien, see "The Saints of Molokai" (p. 257).

KAUNAKAKAI
Kapuaiwa Coconut Grove/Kiowea Park ★ HISTORIC SITE/PARK Planted in the 1860s by King Kamehameha V (born Prince Lot of Kapuaiwa), this royal grove of around 1,000 coconut trees (some sadly now dead and frondless) on 10 oceanfront acres is off-limits to visitors, for safety and preservation reasons, but still presents a side-of-the-road photo op. Across the highway stands Church Row: seven churches, each of a different denomination—clear evidence of the missionary impact on Hawaii.

Ocean side of Maunaloa Hwy. (Hwy. 460), 2 miles west of Kaunakakai.

Molokai Plumerias ★★ FARM   Hundreds of plumeria trees produce fragrant yellow, pink, and scarlet blooms virtually year-round here, just off the main highway between the airport and town. Drop in to purchase a lei or make a weekday appointment for an informative blossom-gathering tour that ends with a lesson on how to string your own lei. The perfume is intoxicating.

1342 Maunaloa Hwy. (Hwy. 460), 2½ miles west of Kaunakakai. www.molokaiplumerias.com. © **808/553-3391.** Tours $25 (Mon–Fri by appointment).

The North Coast
Even if you don't get a chance to see Hawaii's most dramatic coast in its entirety—not many people do—you shouldn't miss the opportunity to

glimpse it from the **Kalaupapa Lookout** at Palaau State Park. On the way, there are a few diversions (arranged here in geographical order).

CENTRAL UPLANDS & NORTH SHORE

Akaula Cat Garden ★ ANIMAL SHELTER   You're bound to see homeless (not necessarily feral) cats on the island, but thanks to this leafy, indoor-outdoor shelter—the only animal sanctuary on the island, and welcoming to visitors—more of the island's felines stand a chance of finding homes. Founder Carol Gartland enlists the help of students at neighboring Akaula School to care for some 75 cats, and will even pay the costs of flying a kitty home with you, should you be so smitten.

Next to Akaula School, 900 Kalae Hwy. (Hwy. 470), just south of Farrington Rd., Kualapuu. www.akaulacatgarden.org. ✆ **808/658-0398.** Open by appointment.

THE saints OF MOLOKAI

Tiny Molokai can claim two saints canonized by the Roman Catholic church in recent years, both revered for years of devotion to the outcasts of Kalaupapa (see "Tragedy & Inspiration: Kalaupapa National Historical Park," below). Born in Belgium as Joseph de Veuster, **Father Damien** moved to Hawai'i in 1864, building churches around the islands until 1873, when he answered a call to serve in the island's infamous leper colony (a now-discouraged term). He tended the sick, rebuilt St. Philomena's church, and pleaded with church and state officials for better care for the exiles, the earliest of whom had been thrown overboard and left to fend for themselves. Damien himself ultimately died of Hansen's disease, as leprosy is now known, in Kalaupapa in 1889. Caring for him at the end was **Mother Marianne,** who came to Hawai'i with a group of nuns from New York in 1883. She spent 30 years serving the Kalaupapa community, before dying in 1918 at age 80, without contracting the disease. (It's only communicable to a small percentage of people.)

You'll see many images of both saints in Kalaupapa as well as "topside" (the exiles' nickname for the rest of Molokai).

Three topside churches are worth peeking into: in Kaunakakai, the modernist, concrete **St. Damien Church** ★ (115 Ala Malama Ave.) features four lovely mosaics depicting scenes from Damien's life. Inside, you'll find a life-size wooden sculpture of the eponymous saint, canonized in 2009. Turn around to see the large banners bearing his photograph and one of Marianne, canonized in 2012. Next door, the parish office offers exhibits on both saints (open Tues–Fri 9am–noon).

Ten miles east of Kaunakakai, on the ocean side of Highway 450, **St. Joseph** ★★ is a diminutive wood-frame church built by Damien in 1876. A lava-rock statue of the sainted Belgian priest stands in the little cemetery by the newer, 7-foot marble sculpture of Brother Joseph Dutton, a Civil War veteran and former alcoholic inspired by Damien to serve at Kalaupapa for 45 years, until his death in 1931. Four miles east, set back from the large cross on the mountain side of the highway, is the larger but still picturesque **Our Lady of Seven Sorrows** ★, the first church Damien built on Molokai outside Kalaupapa. Inside both East End churches hang colorful iconic portraits of the saints by local artist Linda Johnston.

Coffees of Hawaii ★ FARM   Molokai's coffee farm includes a gift shop where you can buy bags (and cups) of Muleskinner coffee, coffee-related souvenirs, and upscale local art, as well as a few snacks. (At press time, a larger espresso bar had been "under renovation" for several years.) The real attraction? The twice-weekly morning jam sessions held on the building's wide front porch, with a view of coffee trees across the road. Every Tuesday and Friday from 10am to noon, visiting musicians (some of the best in Hawaii) join *kupuna* (seniors) in unrehearsed but stellar performances.

1630 Farrington Ave. (Hwy. 480), off Hwy. 470, Kualapuu. www.coffeesofhawaii.com (online sales only). ☏ **877/322-3276** or 808/567-9490.

Molokai Museum and Cultural Center ★ MUSEUM/HISTORIC SITE   En route to the California Gold Rush in 1849, Rudolph W. Meyer (a German surveyor) came to Molokai, married the Hawaiian chiefess Kalama, and began to operate a small sugar plantation near his home. Now on the National Register of Historic Places, this restored 1878 sugar mill, with its century-old steam engine, copper clarifiers, and redwood evaporating pan (all in working order), is the last of its kind in Hawaii. The museum has a large gift shop of local arts and crafts (look for *lilikoi* butter) and eclectic exhibits from petroglyphs to plantation-era furnishings. Lining the walls are poignant portraits of Kalaupapa residents.

Kalaupapa's historic buildings are the subject of one of two 10-minute videos shown on a TV; the other focuses on the ingenuity of the mill. Walk a few yards uphill from the museum (the Meyers' former home) to see the barn-like mill and outdoor pit where circling mules once powered cane-crushing machinery. Sadly, a rent dispute between the Meyer family trust and the long-time operators of the **mule ride to Kalaupapa** (see "Kalaupapa Tours," p. 266), whose stables and trailhead are on Meyer land, escalated in 2018 to questions of which family's Hawaiian heritage gives them the most property rights. Kalama's descendants seemed to have the upper hand when they evicted the "muleskinning" Sproat family in 2018 and chained the gate at the trailhead, but the latter eventually found alternative stables and at press time had resumed operations.

West side of Kalae Hwy. (Hwy. 470), near mile marker 4 (just past turnoff for the Iron-wood Hills Golf Course), Kalae. ☏ **808/567-6436.** $5 adults; $1 children and students. Mon–Sat 10am–2pm.

Palaau State Park ★ PARK   This 234-acre piney-woods park, 8 miles out of Kaunakakai, doesn't look like much until you get out of the car and take a hike, which literally puts you between a rock and a hard place. Go right, and you end up on the edge of Molokai's magnificent sea cliffs, with its panoramic view of Kalaupapa; go left, and you come face to face with a stone phallus.

If you have no plans to scale the cliffs on foot (see "Hiking & Camping," later in this chapter), the **Kalaupapa Lookout** ★★★ is the only place from which to see the former place of exile without paying for a helicopter or plane ride (see "Tragedy & Inspiration: Kalaupapa National Historical Park," below). The trail is marked, and historic photos and interpretive signs will explain what you're seeing.

It's airy and cool in the ironwood forest, where camping is free at the designated state campground. You'll need a permit from the **Department of Land and Natural Resources of Parks** (https://camping.ehawaii.gov; ✆ **808/984-8109**). Not many people seem to camp here, probably because of the legend associated with the **Phallic Rock** ★, known in Hawaiian as Kauleonanahoa. Six feet high and pointed at an angle that means business, Molokai's famous Phallic Rock is a legendary fertility tool: According to Hawaiian legend, a woman who wishes to become pregnant need only spend the night near the rock and, *voilà!* (Treat this cultural site with respect, as signs urge.) *Note:* There are restrooms near the overlook and at a small pavilion on the left before the parking lot, but no potable water.

Phallic Rock lies at the end of a well-worn uphill path that passes an ironwood grove and several other rocks that vaguely resemble sexual body parts. No mistaking the big guy, though. Supposedly, it belonged to Nanahoa, a demigod who quarreled with his wife, Kawahuna, over a pretty girl. In the tussle, Kawahuna was thrown over the cliff, and both husband and wife were turned to stone. (Kauleonanahoa means "the penis of Nanahoa.") Of all the phallic rocks in Hawaii and the Pacific, this is the one to see.

At the northern end of Kalae Hwy. (Hwy. 470), Palaau. https://dlnr.hawaii.gov/dsp/parks/molokai/palaau-state-park. ✆ **808/567-6923.** Free admission.

Post-A-Nut ★ ICON   The postal workers here will help you say "Aloha" to friends back home with a Molokai coconut. Just write a message on the coconut with a felt-tip pen, and they'll send it via U.S. mail. Coconuts are free, but postage averages $12 to $20 for a smaller, mainland-bound coconut. The post office mails out about 3,000 per year, usually decorated with colorful stamps.

Hoolehua Post Office, 69-2 Puupeelua Ave. (Hwy. 480), near Maunaloa Hwy. (Hwy. 460). ✆ **808/567-6144.** Mon–Fri 8:30am–noon and 12:30–4:30pm.

Purdy's All-Natural Macadamia Nut Farm ★ FARM   Hawaiian homesteaders Kammy and Tuddie Purdy offer free tours in the shade of their macadamia nut orchard, planted more than a century ago. Tuddie is a wealth of information and aloha. After an educational spin around the family farm, he'll ply you with samples of delicious nuts—raw, salted, or air-dried—and macadamia blossom honey. Whatever you can't stuff in your suitcase can be shipped home.

4 Lihi Pali Ave., above Molokai High School, Hoolehua. www.molokai-aloha.com/macnuts. ✆ **808/567-6601.** Mon–Fri 9:30am–3:30pm and Sat 10am–2pm; Sun and holidays by appointment.

TRAGEDY & INSPIRATION: KALAUPAPA NATIONAL HISTORICAL PARK ★★★

Kalaupapa, an old tongue of lava that sticks out to form a peninsula, became infamous because of the inhumanity to those with a formerly incurable and often disfiguring communicable disease, then called leprosy.

Today leprosy is known as Hansen's disease, after Dr. Gerhard Hansen of Norway, who discovered the germ that caused it in 1873. But for centuries those who contracted the disease, or who appeared to have a similar condition, bore the stigma of being called "lepers," carrying biblical undertones of impurity and intensifying their shame and shunning. *Note:* Hawaii's state legislature banned the use of "leprosy" for this affliction in 1981, while the use of "lepers" and "leper colony" have also long been discouraged by Kalaupapa residents, park officials, and medical authorities. (While I avoid that wording here, you may see them in historical contexts.)

King Kamehameha V sent the first group with Hansen's disease—nine men and three women—into exile on this lonely shore, at the base of forbidding natural ramparts, on January 6, 1866. By 1874, more than 11,000 people had been dispatched to die in one of the world's most beautiful—and lonely— places. They called Kalaupapa "The Place of the Living Dead."

Hansen's disease is actually one of the world's least contagious diseases. The Centers for Disease Control notes that 95% of the world's population has natural immunity to it. Further, it's transmitted only by direct, repetitive contact over a long period of time to the germ that causes it, *Mycobacterium leprae,* which attacks the nerves, skin, and eyes, and is found mainly, but not exclusively, in tropical regions. U.S. scientists found the first effective treatments for the disease in the 1940s, eventually leading to the end of mandatory isolation at Kalaupapa in 1969.

But before science intervened, there was Father Damien. Born to wealth in Belgium as Joseph de Veuster, he traded a life of excess for a life of service in Hawaii, taking the name Damien at his ordination in Honolulu in 1864. After working for 8 years on Hawaii Island, where he became fluent in Hawaiian, he volunteered to care for the afflicted at Kalaupapa when no others would do so. Horrified by the conditions he saw upon his arrival in 1873, Father Damien went to work building houses and schools, and expanding a church, giving hope and restoring dignity to many residents.

Known to share a bowl of *poi* or even his pipe with his flock, as well as tend to their sores and bandages, Damien himself contracted Hansen's disease after 12 years in Kalaupapa. He died there on April 15, 1889, at age 49, tenderly cared for by two Americans, his tireless colleague Mother Marianne Cope (see "The Saints of Molokai," p. 257) and equally selfless assistant Brother Joseph Dutton. Mother Marianne helped move the settlement from the rainy Kalawao side of the peninsula to the drier Kalaupapa side after Damien's death.

Originally buried at Kalaupapa, then reinterred in Belgium, Damien was canonized as a saint by the Catholic Church in 2009. A relic from his remains—one of his hands, a symbol of service—was taken to churches around the islands to celebrate his sainthood before being returned to his gravesite in Kalaupapa.

This small peninsula is also the final resting place of more than 8,000 souls who suffered from Hansen's disease, the majority of them Native Hawaiians. Among them was the self-sacrificing Jonathan Hawaii Napela, a Mormon leader who arrived the same year Damien did, in 1873, when his wife Kitty was exiled to Kalaupapa. He also ministered to the community before eventually dying from the disesase.

Park workers and volunteers have helped restore several cemeteries, sorted by religious affiliation—Catholic, Protestant, Buddhist—of those who died here. But so many are buried in unmarked graves that no accurate census of the dead exists; efforts are underway to create a memorial listing as many names as possible of those who died here.

The Kalaupapa peninsula, originally known as Makanalua, is also one of Hawaii's richest archaeological preserves, with sites that date from A.D. 1000. Since 1980 it has been a National Historical Park (www.nps.gov/kala; © 808/567-6802), with unique arrangements for the remaining residents. After their exile ended in 1965, about 60 former patients chose to stay in the tidy village, where statues of angels stand in the yards of whitewashed houses; today only a few are still alive, with the future use of the historic site under debate.

For now, just 100 people a day, age 16 and older, may visit, and then only by reservation with a tour operator who can arrange the necessary permits (see "Organized Tours," p. 266). Visitors must arrive on foot, by mule, or by plane—there's no road, and access by water is not allowed—but the trek is well worth the effort. Hikers and mule riders may descend in a light mist and be rewarded by rainbows soaring above the sea cliffs, while passengers on prop planes land at a tiny airstrip near the Pacific's tallest lighthouse. The tours, led by guides with companies owned by former patients, visit a number of buildings and ruins on both sides of the peninsula. While you won't see any residents, you'll sense the spirits of those who preceded them in this lonely, tragic, but beautiful place.

Kalaupapa. www.nps.gov/kala. © **808/567-6802.** Access restricted to ages 16 and older on guided tours only, Mon–Sat. Kalaupapa Trail starts on east side of Kalae Hwy. (behind gate marked No TRESPASSING). All packages from **Kekaula Tours** (https:// muleride.com; © **808/567-6088**) include permit, tour, and picnic lunch: hiking, $79; mule ride, $209 ($199 military); flying from "topside," $249; flying from Honolulu or Kahului, Maui, $349. **Damien Tours** (www.damientoursllc.com; © **808/567-6171**) also leads tours for $60, meeting hikers or those arriving by plane at the trailhead.

10

MOLOKAI | Exploring Molokai

The West End
MAUNALOA
The 1920s-era pineapple-plantation town of Maunaloa has become a virtual ghost town ever since the Molokai Ranch closed all of its operations in 2008 (including a restaurant, lodge and beach bungalows, gas station, and the island's only movie theater). The only draws now are the plantation-inspired architecture and friendly staff of the welcoming **Maunaloa General Store** (p. 254) and the charmingly eclectic **Big Wind Kite Factory & Plantation Gallery** (p. 280).

ON THE NORTHWEST SHORE: MOOMOMI DUNES
Undisturbed for centuries, the Moomomi Dunes, on Molokai's northwest shore, are a unique treasure chest of great scientific value. The area may look like just a pile of sand as you fly over on the final approach to Hoolehua Airport, but Moomomi Dunes is much more than that. Archaeologists have found adz quarries, ancient Hawaiian burial sites, and shelter caves; botanists have identified five endangered plant species; and marine biologists are finding evidence that endangered green sea turtles are coming out from the waters once again to lay eggs here. The greatest discovery, however, belongs to Smithsonian Institute ornithologists, who have found bones of prehistoric birds—some of them flightless—that existed nowhere else on earth.

Accessible by rough four-wheel-drive jeep trails that thread downhill to the shore, this wild coast is buffeted by strong afternoon breezes. It's hot, dry, and windy, so take water, sunscreen, and a windbreaker; be cautious as you hike or drive, since there's no cellphone service. At Kawaaloa Bay, a 20-minute walk to the west, is a broad golden beach that you can have all to yourself. (*Warning:* Due to the forceful currents and shorebreak, stay out of the water, especially in winter.) Within the dunes, there's a 920-acre preserve administered by the **Nature Conservancy of Hawaii.** It offers free monthly guided hikes from March to October, with advance signup required; call ℂ **808/553-5236,** ext. 6581, or e-mail hike_molokai@tnc.org for an exact schedule and details. The guided hikes are free, but donations are welcome. Stop by the Nature Conservancy office, 23 Pueo Pl. in Kualapuu, between 8am and 3pm weekdays for maps and directions.

To get to the dunes, take Hwy. 460 (Maunaloa Hwy.) from Kaunakakai; turn right onto Hwy. 470, and follow it to Kualapuu. At Kualapuu, turn left on Hwy. 480 and go through Hoolehua Village; it's 3 miles to the bay. If it's been raining on the north shore, do not attempt this drive—you may get stuck with no way to call for a tow.

The East End
The East End is a cool and inviting green place that's worth a drive to the end of King Kamehameha V Highway (Hwy. 450).

ILIILIOPAE HEIAU

A trek through a mango grove followed by an uphill walk through a kiawe forest and java plums leads to Iliiliopae, a *heiau luakini* (sacrificial temple) that looks like something right out of *Indiana Jones.* A huge rectangle of stone made of 90 million rocks, this temple of doom stands across a dry streambed under cloud-laced Kaunolu, the 4,970-foot island summit, and overlooks the ruins of the once-important village of Mapulehu and four ancient fishponds.

As one of Hawaii's most powerful *heiau,* Iliiliopae attracted *kahuna* (priests) from all over the islands. They came to learn the rules of human sacrifice at this university of sacred rites. Contrary to Hollywood's version, historians say that the victims here were always men, not young virgins, and that they were strangled, not thrown into a volcano, while priests sat on lauhala mats watching silently.

This is the biggest, oldest, and most famous *heiau* on Molokai, and one of the largest in all of Hawaii. The massive 22-foot-high stone altar is dedicated to Lono, the Hawaiian god of fertility. The *heiau* resonates with *mana* (power) strong enough to lean on. Legend says Iliiliopae was built in a single night by a thousand men who passed rocks hand over hand through the Wailau Valley from the other side of the island; in exchange for the *ili'ili* (rock), each received an *'opae* (shrimp). Others say it was built by *menehune,* mythic elves who accomplished Herculean feats.

Iliiliopae stands on private property, but at press time the owners were working on a waiver for visitors to sign so their insurance company will officially permit hikers. If you plan to visit, please park on a highway pullout, stay on the trail, and be respectful—no standing on the temple, moving or stacking stones, or leaving litter behind, please. Look for the sign saying "heiau" on the mountain side of King Kamehameha V Highway (Hwy. 450), near mile marker 15, and follow the signs once you pass through the gate.

KAMAKOU PRESERVE

It's hard to believe, but close to the nearly mile-high summit here, it rains more than 80 inches a year—enough to qualify as a rain forest. The Molokai Forest, as it was historically known, is the source of 60% of Molokai's water. Nearly 3,000 acres, from the summit to the lowland forests of eucalyptus and pine, are now held by the Nature Conservancy, which has identified 219 Hawaiian plants that grow here exclusively. The preserve is also the last stand of the endangered *olomao* (Molokai thrush) and *kawawahie* (Molokai creeper).

To get to the preserve, you'll need a four-wheel-drive vehicle and dry weather. From Kaunakakai, take Hwy. 460 west for 3½ miles and turn right before the Maunawainui Bridge onto the unmarked Molokai Forest Reserve Road (sorry, there aren't any road signs). The pavement ends at the cemetery; continue on the dirt road for about 45 minutes to Waikolu Lookout Campground; from here, you can venture into the wilderness preserve on foot across a boardwalk on a 1½-hour hike (see "The Pepeopae Trail," p. 275). For more information, or to sign up for one of the free monthly guided hikes March through October, contact the **Nature Conservancy** (www.nature.org or e-mail hike_molokai@tnc.org; ℂ **808/553-5236,** ext. 6581). You can also stop by the Nature Conservancy office, 23 Pueo Pl. in Kualapuu, between 8am and 3pm weekdays for maps and directions. As with Moomomi Dunes, you'll want to avoid the forest preserve if it's been raining; the dirt road turns even more treacherous.

EN ROUTE TO HALAWA VALLEY

No visit to Molokai is complete without at least a passing glance at the island's **ancient fishponds,** a singular achievement in Pacific aquaculture. With their hunger for fresh fish and lack of ice and refrigeration, Hawaiians perfected aquaculture in A.D. 1400, before Christopher Columbus "discovered" America. They built gated, U-shaped stone and coral walls on the shore with *makaha* (sluice gates) to catch fish on the incoming tide; smaller fish could enter but were trapped as they grew larger. The result: a constant, ready supply of fresh fish.

The ponds, which stretch for 20 miles along Molokai's south shore and are visible from Kamehameha V Highway (Hwy. 450), offer insight into the island's ancient population. It took something like a thousand people to tend a single fishpond, and more than 60 ponds once existed on this coast. Some are silted in by red-dirt runoff from south-coast gulches; others are in use by folks who raise fish and seaweed.

The largest, 54-acre **Keawa Nui Pond,** is surrounded by a 3-foot-high, 2,000-foot-long stone wall. The 15th-century **Alii Fish Pond,** reserved for kings, is visible through the coconut groves at One Alii Beach Park (p. 269). From the road, you can see **Kalokoeli Pond,** 6 miles east of Kaunakakai on the highway. Visitors can join community workdays organized by **Ka Honua Momona** (www.kahonuamomona.org; ℂ **808/553-8353**) to restore Alii Fishpond and Kalokoeli Pond, about 3½ miles apart. The workdays typically take place the third Saturday of each month.

Our Lady of Seven Sorrows Church ★ CHURCH   One of four Catholic churches and chapels built by St. Damien on "topside" Molokai (two no longer survive), this was the first outside Kalaupapa, built in 1874. The narrow white building, 22 feet wide by 44 feet long, features a bright red roof and quaint steeple. Rebuilt in 1960 while keeping its original dimensions and styling, the west-facing church boasts a large wooden cross in its yard and large sign by the road, both hard to miss. For a closer look, park in the church lot (except on Sun mornings, when Mass is held at 7am).

8300 King Kamehameha V Hwy. (Hwy. 450), Kaluahaa, across the highway from Niaupala Fishpond.

St. Joseph's Church ★ CHURCH   On the ocean side of the highway, this little 1876 wood-frame Catholic church is one of four St. Damien built "topside" on Molokai. Restored in 1971, the church stands beside a seaside

MOLOKAI   Exploring Molokai

HALAWA VALLEY: A hike BACK IN HISTORY

"There are things on Molokai, sacred things, that you may not be able to see or may not hear, but they are there. As Hawaiians, we respect these things." says Pilipo Solatorio, born and raised in Halawa Valley. He was just 6 when the 1946 tsunami barreled into the valley, by then settled by Hawaiians for some 1,300 years, and still lives there today.

If people are going to "like Molokai," Solatorio feels it is important that they learn about the history and culture; these are part of the secret of appreciating the island. "I see my role as educating people, outsiders, on our culture, our history," he said of the cultural hikes he and his son Greg lead on their family property in Halawa Valley. "To really appreciate Molokai, you need to understand and know things so that you are *pono*, you are right with the land and don't disrespect the culture. Then, then you see the real Molokai."

One of only two Halawa families who offer guided hikes into the valley, which is otherwise closed to visitors, the Solatorios begin their tours at the county park pavilion with a history of the valley, a discussion of the Hawaiian culture, and a display of the fruits, trees, and other flora you will see in Halawa. Along the intermediate-level hike, 3.4 miles round-trip, they will stop to point out historical and cultural aspects, chanting in Hawaiian before entering a sacred *heiau* (temple) area. At 250-foot **Moolua Falls,** visitors can swim in the brisk pool water, weather permitting.

The cost for the 4-hour tour is $60, minimum of two, with advance bookings required (http://halawavalleymolokai.com; © **808/542-1855**). Your feet will get wet and or muddy, so wear appropriate closed-toe shoes (no "slippahs" or sandals). Bring insect repellent, water, a snack or lunch, and a swimsuit with towel if you plan to swim. Don't forget your camera.

Note: If you venture away from the county park and into the valley on your own, you are trespassing and can be prosecuted.

cemetery, where a lei-bedecked Damien statue of lava rock serenely surveys the gravestones. Although it's no longer in regular use, doors are typically not locked, and you're welcome to peer inside.

King Kamehameha V Hwy. (Hwy. 450), Kamalo, just after mile marker 10.

Smith Bronte Landing Site ★ HISTORIC SITE   In 1927, Charles Lindbergh soloed across the Atlantic Ocean in a plane called *The Spirit of St. Louis* and became an American hero. That same year, Ernie Smith and Emory B. Bronte took off from Oakland, CA, on July 14, in a single-engine Travel Air aircraft named *The City of Oakland,* and headed across the Pacific Ocean for Honolulu, 2,397 miles away. The next day, after running out of fuel, they crash-landed upside down in a kiawe thicket on Molokai, but emerged unhurt to become the first civilians to fly to Hawaii from the U.S. mainland. The 25-hour, 2-minute flight landed Smith and Bronte a place in aviation history—and billing on a roadside marker on Molokai. *Note:* Once you've read this entry, there's no reason to stop here; it's also on private property.

King Kamehameha V Hwy. (Hwy. 450), at mile marker 11, on the makai (ocean) side.

HALAWA VALLEY ★

Of the five great valleys of Molokai, only Halawa—with its two waterfalls, golden beach, sleepy lagoon, great surf, and offshore island—is easily accessible. The trail through fertile Halawa Valley leading to the 250-foot Moaula Falls passes through private property, however, requiring you to book one of the tours offered here to avoid confrontations, trespassing citations, or other serious hassles (see "Halawa Valley: A Hike Back in History," on p. 265).

You can spend a day at the county beach park (described under "Beaches," below), but do not venture into the valley on your own. In a kind of 21st-century *kapu,* the private landowners in the valley, worried about slip-and-fall lawsuits and inadvertent or intentional destruction of cultural resources, have posted NO TRESPASSING signs on their properties.

To get to Halawa Valley, drive north from Kaunakakai on Hwy. 450 for 30 miles along the coast to the end of the road, which descends into the valley past the tiny, green-planked **Ierusalema Hou Church**. If you'd just like a glimpse of the valley on your way to the beach, there's a scenic overlook along the road: After Puu O Hoku Ranch at mile marker 25, the narrow two-lane road widens at a hairpin curve, and you'll find the overlook on your right; it's 2 miles more to the valley floor.

10 Organized Tours

Although Molokai attracts (and rewards) independent travelers, a few guided tours are essential—they're the only way to see the island's most awe-inspiring sights up close.

BIRDING TOURS Arleone Dibben-Young will chauffer you to the island's unpredictably great birding spots: suburban wetlands, a wastewater treatment plant, mangrove-fringed mudflats, and a softball field, where a rare seabird likes to hang out on the diamond. Not only can Dibben-Young reliably call the rare kioea (bristle-thighed curlew), she has a permit to shelter endangered nene (Hawaiian geese) at her home. Even non-birders will get a kick out of her tremendous humor and passion for Hawaiian avifauna. Contact **Ahupuaa Natives ★★** (© 808/553-5992) for early-morning excursions, typically at high tide. Tours cost $60 per hour, per person, with 1½ hours minimum.

KALAUPAPA TOURS The only way to explore the spectacular, haunting Kalaupapa peninsula is on a guided tour led by one of two companies owned by former patients or their surviving families. **Damien Tours ★★★** (www.damientoursllc.com; © 808/567-6171) is the original, founded in 1966. Its folksy guides drive a vintage school bus to the original graves of Father Damien and Mother Marianne (see "The Saints of Molokai," p. 257); St. Philomena Church, where the Belgian priest carved holes in the floor so patients could discreetly spit during services; a resident-owned snack shop and government bookstore (bring cash; no large bills); and a small museum with heart-rending photos and artifacts, such as a spoon reshaped for a disfigured hand.

Lunch is an oceanside picnic at Kalawao, overlooking rocky islets under towering sea cliffs. Restricted to ages 16 and older, the tour costs $60, with limited space. *Note:* To take this tour, you must either be able to hike down and up the punishingly steep, 3½-mile Kalaupapa Trail, or if arriving by plane, walk a half-mile from the airport runway to the trail. You must book the tour in advance; you can be cited for descending the trail on your own or arriving by plane without tour reservations. For regularly scheduled flights to Kalaupapa, contact **Makani Kai Air** (www.makanikaiair.com; ✆ **808/834-1111**).

The guided mule ride, operated by Kalaupapa Rare Adventures but better known as **Molokai Mule Ride** (https://muleride.com; ✆ **808/567-6088**), shut down temporarily in 2018 during an ongoing rent dispute with the owners of the stables and land near the trailhead. But they have since resumed the rides led by "mule skinners," or guides, with the mules arriving at the trailhead by trailer. Hold on tight, but trust your mule as it descends the stony steps and 26 switchbacks of the trail; it's physically challenging for some to lean back in the saddle going down and forward going up the trail, which has an elevation gain of 1,700 feet. In general, going up is a little less daunting, and less jolting—you can tell the mules smell the barn. Frail or out-of-shape travelers may prefer the flight option; there's a 250-pound weight limit for riders and the park's minimum age of 16 for visitors also applies.

Mule rides are met by the two white vans of **Kekaula Tours** (same contact details as the Molokai Mule Ride, above), which shuttle visitors to all the significant sites on the peninsula, including a picnic stop. The all-day (8:15am–3pm) mule ride costs $209 ($199 military with ID), including the park tour, light lunch, bottled water, and a souvenir certificate. Kekaula Tours provides the same amenities in packages for hikers ($79) and air passengers ($149 from the "topside" airport in Hoolehua, $349 from Honolulu or Kahului, Maui).

Mokulele Airlines (www.mokuleleairlines; ✆ **808/495-4188**) can also arrange tour packages with charter flights from Hoolehua or other islands.

Note: A newer tour operator, **Father Damien Tours** (www.fatherdamientours.com; ✆ **808/349-3006**), offers more expensive hiking and flying options, including a round-trip from Kona for $598, but has received negative reviews on social media for frequent cancellations. Don't confuse this newer tour with the original Damien Tours (see above), created by Gloria Marks and her late husband, a former Kalaupapa patient; although its bus ride may be bumpy, it has a reputation for reliability and integrity in sharing Kalaupapa's poignant legacy.

HALAWA VALLEY TOURS   On the East End, a guided tour or authorized escort is required to go beyond Halawa Beach Park into breathtakingly beautiful Halawa Valley, home to the island's earliest settlement and 250-foot Mooula Falls. **Pilipo and Greg Solatorio**'s 4-hour, culturally focused tours start with traditional Hawaiian protocol and are the most renowned (see "A Hike Back in History" on p. 265 for details). **Kalani Pruet** will pair Halawa

Valley tours ($40 adults, $20 children) with a visit to his flower farm (www. molokaiflowers.com; ℘ **808/542-1855**; Tues–Sat 10am–4pm, Sun by appointment; e-mail him several days in advance at kuleanaworkcenter@yahoo.com or leave a voicemail—the phone line is on Oahu, since there's no signal in Halawa Valley, but is monitored by his wife).

Note: The valley is privately owned—trespassers may be prosecuted, and almost certainly hassled, if caught.

WHALE-WATCHING TOURS If you're on island in winter (Dec–Mar), don't miss the chance to see humpback whales from Alaska frolic in island waters, often with clingy calves in tow, or boisterous pods of males competing for a female's attention. Though you may spot whales spouting or breaching from the shore, a whale-watching cruise from Kaunakakai skirts the fringing reef to provide front-row seats. Veteran outfitter **Molokai Fish & Dive** (www. molokaifishanddive.com; ℘ **808/553-5926**) offers 2- to 3-hour tours ($79 adults, $45 children 6–12) on *Ama Lua*, a comfortable 31-foot, double-hulled power catamaran, or *Coral Queen*, a 38-foot, two-level dive boat. **Molokai Ocean Tours** (www.molokaioceantours.com; ℘ **808/553-3290**) also leads humpback-spotting hunts on *Manu Eleele*, its 40-foot power catamaran with cushy leather seats; its tours costs $75 for adults, $60 for children 12 and under (minimum of two adults, maximum six passengers). Whale sighting is guaranteed January 15 to March 31; all tours include coffee, bottled water, and a Molokai souvenir. Veteran captain Mike Holmes of **Fun Hogs Sports Fishing** (www.molokaifishing.com; ℘ **808/336-0047**) also takes passengers out in whale season for daily 2-hour sessions ($70, four-person minimum) on his sturdy Force 27 flybridge powerboat, *Ahi*.

VAN TOURS If your time on the island is tight—as in a day trip from Maui or Oahu—I also recommend a van tour with an affable local guide who will pick you up and drop you off at the airport. **Molokai Outdoors** (www. molokai-outdoors.com; ℘ **877/553-4477** or 808/633-8700) offers the 7- to 8-hour **Island Tour** ($165), covering Halawa Valley Lookout on the East End to Kaunakakai, the Kalaupapa Lookout, and Coffees of Hawaii with lunch included. You'll need a minimum of four passengers to book, however, unless you pay $180 to upgrade to a private tour. Stops on the West End can be arranged in advance, while owner Clare Mawae can also create charter tours of 2 hours or more.

BEACHES

With imposing sea cliffs on one side and vast fishponds on the other, Molokai has little room for beaches along its 106-mile coast. Still, a big gold-sand beach flourishes on the West End, and you'll find tiny pocket beaches on the East End. The emptiness of Molokai's beaches is both a blessing and a curse: The seclusion means no lifeguards on any of the beaches, and only a few with any facilities. (Cell signal may also be spotty or nonexistent, so if traveling on your own, let someone know where you're headed.) To locate these beaches, see the "Molokai" map (p. 243).

Kaunakakai

ONE ALII BEACH PARK

This thin strip of sand, once reserved for the *alii* (chiefs), is the oldest public beach park on Molokai. Local kids swim off the wharf, but if you just want to dip your feet in the water, head 3 miles east along the Kamehameha V Highway to the sandy shore of **One Alii Beach Park ★**. Pronounced *"o-nay ah-lee-ee,"* it has a thin strip of golden *one* (sand) once reserved for the *ali'i* (high chiefs). Although the water is too shallow and murky for swimming, the spacious park is a picnic spot and draws many families on weekends. Facilities include outdoor showers, picnic areas, and restrooms; tent camping allowed with permit (see "Camping" on p. 276).

The West End

KEPUHI BEACH ★★, MAKE HORSE BEACH ★, AND KAWAKIU BEACH ★

Much of the shoreline here is for sightseeing only, thanks to dangerous currents and fierce surf—especially in winter. But solitude, sunsets, and clear-day vistas of Diamond Head on Oahu across the 26-mile Kaiwi Channel make it worth the trek. From Kaunakakai, take Maunaloa Highway (Hwy. 460) almost 15 miles west, turn right on Kaluakoi Road, and drive 4½ miles until you see the sign on your right pointing to Ke Nani Kai; turn right for public beach access parking at the end of the road. Walk past the eerily decaying, closed hotel to gold-sand **Kepuhi Beach ★★**, and watch surfers navigate the rocky break. A 15-minute walk north along the bluff leads to the Pohaku Mauliuli cinder cone, which shares its name with two sandy coves better known as **Make Horse Beach ★**, pronounced *"mah-kay"* and meaning "dead horse" (don't ask). You can snorkel and explore the tide pools in calm conditions, but do keep an eye on the waves. Hiking another mile north on a rugged dirt road leads to the lovely white crescent of **Kawakiu Beach ★**, the original launch site of the Molokai-to-Oahu outrigger canoe race. It's relatively safe in summer, but be wary when the surf is up.

PAPOHAKU BEACH ★★★

Over 2 miles long and 300 feet wide, gold-sand Papohaku Beach is one of the biggest in Hawaii (17-mile-long Polihale Beach on Kauai is the longest). It's great for walking, beachcombing, picnics, and sunset watching year-round. The big surf and riptides make swimming risky except in summer, when the waters are calmer. Go early in the day, when the tropic sun is less fierce and the winds are calm. The beach is so vast that you may never see another soul. County facilities—restrooms, water, picnic, and campsites (see "Camping" on

p. 276)—are at the northern end, a third of a mile past Kaluakoi Road's inter-section with Pa Loa Loop Road (a shortcut back to upper Kaluakoi Road).

DIXIE MARU (KAPUKAHEHU) BEACH ★★★

Cozy Dixie Maru Beach's Hawaiian name is Kapukahehu, but locals gave it this nickname after a Japanese boat with that moniker shipwrecked nearby. Popular with families in summer, this sheltered cove is the island's best, safest spot to swim, but it has no facilities. From Papohaku Beach, follow Kaluakoi Road 1¾ miles south to the T at Pohakuloa Road; turn right and head another 1¾ miles. Just before the road ends, turn seaward at the beach access sign. Park in the small lot and follow a short downhill path.

HALE O LONO ★

Technically on the South Shore, this set of narrow sandy beaches and adjacent harbor lie at the end of a 7-mile unpaved road from Maunaloa, so it feels like an excursion to the West End to get here. Named for an ancient temple to Lono, the Hawaiian god of fertility, agriculture, and peace (among other aspects), today's "house of Lono" is also the start of annual outrigger canoe and other paddling races across the rough Kaiwi Channel to Oahu, a 41-mile journey. It's dangerous to swim here in winter, and even when conditions appear calm, the rocky and often shallow ocean floor may mean it's still not conducive to swimming or snorkeling. But you may enjoy the solitude—and the sight of spouting whales in winter. Fisherman may sometimes keep you company, too. From Maunaloa, follow Hwy. 460 past Mokio Street and take the first dirt road on your right. Drive carefully nearly 7 miles downhill to a fork and take the left branch to the beach park; the last part of the road is now paved. No facilities.

The East End

HALAWA BEACH PARK ★★

At the narrow end of the winding highway, 28 miles east of Kaunakakai, lies **Halawa Beach Park ★★**, a beautiful black-sand beach with a palm-fringed lagoon, a wave-lashed island offshore, and a distant view of the West Maui Mountains across the Pailolo Channel. Tucked between sea cliffs, the wide, rocky bay is beautiful but not safe for swimming. Behind it, the gray-sand cove adjacent to the river is a serene option for those willing to ford the stream (avoid this during winter or after heavy rains). Look back into Halawa Valley (accessible only via cultural tours; see p. 267) for distant waterfall views. A picnic pavilion has restrooms, a shower, and water tap; it's 100 yards from the shore, across from **Ierusalema Hou,** a tiny green church built in 1948.

MURPHY BEACH PARK (KUMIMI BEACH PARK)

In 1970, the Molokai Jaycees wanted to create a sandy beach park with a good swimming area for the children of the East End. They chose a section known as Kumimi Beach, which was owned by the Puu O Hoku Ranch. The beach was a dump—literally. The ranch owner, George Murphy, gave his permission to use the site as a park, and the Jaycees cleaned it up and built three small pavilions, with picnic tables and barbecue grills. Officially, the park is called the George Murphy Beach Park (or just Murphy Beach Park), but some old-timers still call it Kumimi Beach, and, just to make things really confusing, some people call it Jaycees Park.

The small park is shaded by ironwood trees lining a white-sand beach. This is generally a very safe swimming area, and on calm days snorkeling and diving are great outside the reef. Fishermen also come here to look for papio and other fish. From Kaunakakai, take Hwy. 450 east to mile marker 20.

SANDY BEACH ★

Molokai's most popular swimming beach—ideal for families with small kids—is a roadside pocket of gold sand partially protected by a reef, with a great view of Maui and Lanai. Don't go out in high surf, though, and be aware there may be strong currents on the right side. You'll find it off the King Kamehameha V Highway (Hwy. 450) between mile markers 21 and 22; it's the last sandy beach before the road heads uphill.

WATERSPORTS

The miles-long, untrammeled South Shore reef is home to curious turtles and Hawaiian monk seals, billowing eagle and manta rays, and giant bouquets of colorful fish, but because it lies a half-mile or more offshore, it's easiest to explore via watercraft of some kind. Surfers, stand-up paddleboarders, and boogie boarders can find waves to entertain themselves, just as sport fishers have numerous near-shore and deep-sea options; since conditions are variable by day as well as by season, consult one of the Kaunakakai-based outfitters below before venturing out.

Diving, Fishing & Snorkeling

While boat captains on other islands usually specialize in one or more excursions, Molokai's handful of commercial seafarers tend to offer diving, snorkeling, sport-fishing, sunset cruises, whale-watching, or whatever will keep them out in the uncrowded waters of the South Shore. In winter, book early to avoid disappointment—these tour boats also tend to be much smaller than those on Maui or Oahu. *Note:* Bring snorkel gear if not booking a tour or staying in lodgings that offer some; there's no place to rent any on the island.

Owner, captain, and certified dive master Tim Forsberg of **Molokai Fish & Dive,** 61 Ala Malama Ave. (www.molokaifishanddive.com; ℭ **808/553-5926**), carefully selects the day's best South Shore sites for its **snorkel tours** ($79 standard) and two-tank **scuba dives** ($145) aboard one of two Coast Guard–inspected boats: the comfy, 38-foot Delta dive boat *Coral Princess* and the twin-hulled, 31-foot power catamaran *Ama Lua.* When conditions permit, Forsberg offers three-tank dives ($295) along the remote North Shore. You can also take an introductory dive ($210) or lessons (call for price). Half-day

MOLOKAI'S BEST snorkel SPOTS

Most Molokai beaches are too dangerous for snorkeling in winter, when storms that sweep down from Alaska generate big waves and strong currents. From mid-September to April, stick to **Murphy Beach Park** (also known as Kumimi Beach Park) on the East End. In summer, roughly May to mid-September, the Pacific Ocean turns into a flat lake, and the whole west coast of Molokai opens up for snorkeling. Captain Mike Holmes of **Fun Hogs Sport Fishing** (see above) says the best spots are as follows:

Kawakiu, Make Horse, and Ilio Point (West End)   These are all special places seldom seen by travelers, or even some residents. You can reach **Make Horse** and **Kawakiu** beaches (p. 269) on foot, and Ilio Point after a hot, dusty ride in a four-wheel-drive vehicle, but it may be easier to go by sea. See "Diving, Fishing & Snorkeling," above, for snorkel tours and charters. It's about 2 miles as the crow flies from Make Horse to Ilio

Point. Stay out of the water when conditions are rough and always snorkel with a buddy.

Dixie Maru (Kapukahehu) Beach (West End)   This gold-sand family beach is well-protected, and the reef is close and shallow. The name Dixie Maru comes from a 1920s Japanese fishing boat stranded off the rocky shore. One of the Molokai Ranch cowboys hung the wrecked boat's nameplate on a gate by Kapukahehu Beach, and the name stuck. To get here, take Kaluakoi Road to the end of the pavement, and then take the footpath 300 feet to the beach. *Note:* Erosion has been threatening the reef here, but at press time the community was planning to take action.

Murphy (Kumimi) Beach Park ★ (East End)   This beach is located between mile markers 20 and 21 off Kamehameha V Highway. The reef here is easily reachable, and the waters tend to be calm year-round.

deep-sea fishing charters start at $695. All kinds of dive and fishing gear, along with snacks and gifts, are for rent or sale at the downtown headquarters.

November through June, **Molokai Ocean Tours,** 40 Ala Malama Ave., above American Savings Bank (www.molokaioceantours.com; © **808/553-3290**), uses its two six-passenger power catamarans to offer 4-hour **troll fishing** ($650 for the boat up to six people) and a half-day **deep-sea fishing charter** (call for current rates). Its **snorkel tours** ($75 adults, $60 children 10 and younger) include a **SNUBA** option that allows up to two people at a time to dive 30 feet, using hoses connected to a special mouthpiece. Charter sunset cruises with appetizers and water for two to six passengers ($460–$510) are also a possibility.

Among several other charter operators, Tim Brunnert of **Captain T's Charters** (www.captaintcharters.com; © **808/336-1055** or 808/552-0390) books 2- to 3-hour **snorkel, sunset,** and **sightseeing cruises** ($75, 4-person minimum) on the comfortable 31-foot *Hapa Girl*. You can also book a **fishing charter** to hunt for ono, mahimahi, marlin, and other deep-sea fish for $450 to $850 for 4 to 8 hours for the entire boat; he'll filet and package your catch to take home to grill. Captain Tim is also a certified divemaster.

Captain Mike Holmes of **Fun Hogs Sport Fishing** (http://molokaifishing. com; *℗*808/336-0047) trolls for massive Pacific blue marlin, yellowfin and skipjack tuna, mahimahi and ono (wahoo) along the ledges and in deep waters around Molokai in the *Ahi*, a twin-engine flybridge sportfisherman built in Hilo. Book the entire boat (six-passenger maximum) from $450 for 4 hours to $750 for 8 hours.

While you can also charter his 24-foot power catamaran for light-tackle and deep-sea sport fishing, Captain Clay of **Hallelujah Hou Fishing** (www. hallelujahhoufishing.com; *℗* **808/336-1870**) specializes in catch-and-release fishing for Molokai's enormous bonefish from a skiff in the shallow flats. An advocate for sustainability, Captain Clay is also a longtime resident and minister who considers fishing here "almost a spiritual journey." The 4- to 6-hour bonefishing trips cost $600 for one to two anglers, plus $150 for extra anglers, up to four.

Experienced mariner Capt. Joe Reich searches for pelagic fish—marlin, yellowfin tuna, mahimahi, etc.—in the triangle formed by south Molokai, Lanai, and the Penguin Bank, the coral beds of an underwater shield volcano west of Molokai. His **Alyce C Sportfishing** (www.alycecsportfishing.com; *℗* **808/ 558-8377**) operates out of Kaunakakai Harbor; call for current rates.

For **whale-watching tours** (Dec–Mar), see "Organized Tours" on p. 266.

Paddle Sports

During the summer months, when the waters on the North Shore are calm, Molokai offers some of the most spectacular kayaking in Hawaii, but you must be expert level and very hardy. Fortunately, the reef-protected South Shore offers year-round opportunities for less experienced paddlers, whether on stand-up paddleboards (SUP) or in kayaks or outrigger canoes. Strong winds make it imperative, though, that you arrange for a pickup when traveling downwind, or book a tour to be safe. *Note:* If not taking a tour, you'll have to bring your own gear or see if your lodgings will provide some; there are no longer any rentals on the island. One outfitter now focuses on group excursions, while the other says too many visitors got themselves into trouble while stand-up paddling independently.

For groups of four or more, **Molokai Outdoors** ★★ (www.molokai-outdoors. com; *℗* **877/553-4477** or 808/633-8700) leads fantastic downwind **kayak** and **stand-up-paddleboard reef tours**, which range from 5 to 8 miles, depending on your experience level ($90 adults, $47 children). Owner and former world champion windsurfer Clare Seeger Mawae occasionally guides the tours, which can be packaged with a mini island van tour (for an additional $166 for adults, $87 for children); see "Organized Tours," p. 266, for a description of the island tours. Mawae can help experienced paddlers arrange a self-guided North Shore kayak excursion that starts in Halawa Valley, including gear and pickup by boat.

If you want to experience the ancient sport of **outrigger canoe paddling,** visit the **Waakapaemua Canoe Club** (molokaiwaa@gmail.com; © **808/553-8018**) at Kaunakakai Wharf on Thursday morning at 7:15am sharp. You can jump into a six-person boat and participate in the club's weekly practice. First come, first paddle! Bring a $25 cash donation to help support the youth teams. Custom bookings are available for parties of four or more.

Surfing, Bodyboarding & Bodysurfing

Molokai isn't a place to learn to surf—the currents and waves may be too strong for beginners—but experienced riders can enjoy good, uncrowded breaks depending on the time of year and the wave conditions. Be sure to show courtesy to the local surfers.

Surfers and bodyboarders have a long paddle out to the break beyond the reef at **Kaunakakai Wharf,** but the summer swell (May–Sept) seems to make it worth it, judging by the numbers in the water. On the West End, almost as many surfers head to **Kepuhi Beach** (p. 269) in front of the old Kaluakoi Hotel for an adventurous break nicknamed Sheraton's, after the former hotel operator; the surf is a little gentler at nearby **Dixie Maru** (p. 270). You'll find less competition, but more rugged conditions, at **Hale O Lono** (p. 270). On the East End, you may find the right conditions at **Waialua Beach,** a narrow, rocky-bottomed, reef-fringed beach near Hwy. 450's mile marker 18 (before you get to Murphy/Kumimi Beach). Or keep going to **Halawa Beach Park** (p. 270) at the end of the road, where winter surf attracts experienced wave riders.

Molokai has only three beaches that offer good waves for bodyboarding and bodysurfing: **Papohaku** (p. 269), Kepuhi, and Halawa. Even these beaches are only for experienced bodysurfers, though, due to the strength of the rip currents and undertows.

For rentals, head to **Beach Break** (www.bigwindkites.com/beachbreak; © **808/567-6091**), conveniently located between the airport and Kaunakakai at the corner of highways 460 and 470 (Holomua Junction). You can't miss its rainbow fence made of surfboards. Inside, owner, photographer, and avid surfer Zack Socher rents surfboards ($24–$30 daily/$120–$150 weekly), bodyboards ($10/$35), and fins ($5/$21). Check out the bright array of bikinis, board shorts, "slippahs," T-shirts, and sarongs, too. Socher dispenses free coffee and advice on surf spots during store hours, Monday through Saturday 10am to 4pm. You can also buy surfboards, bodyboards, and related clothing and gear in Kaunakakai at **Malama Surf Shop,** 93 Ala Malama Ave. (www.facebook.com/malamasurfshop; © **808/553-3399**).

HIKING & CAMPING

With most land privately held, the only real hiking opportunities on Molokai are the Kalaupapa Trail (permit and tour required; see p. 266), Halawa Valley by guided tour (see p. 267), or in two hard-to-access Nature Conservancy preserves (below). *Note:* Do not attempt to follow pig or hunting trails on your own through the mountains or rainforest. The slippery soil, loose volcanic rocks, and steep gulches hold pitfalls for even experienced hikers. In 2018, a man honeymooning on the island fell to his death while trying to follow a trail he'd spotted near the East End's Pia Gulch.

Hiking Pepeopae Trail & Moomomi Dunes

For spectacularly unique views of Molokai, the Nature Conservancy of Hawaii offers **monthly guided hikes** ★★★ March through October into two of the island's most fragile landscapes: the windswept dunes in the 920-acre **Moomomi Preserve** (p. 262) on the northwest shore, and the cloud-ringed forest of the island's highest mountain, part of the 2,774-acre **Kamakou Preserve** (p. 263) on the island's East End.

Just 8½ miles northwest of Hoolehua, Moomomi is the most intact beach and sand dune area in the main Hawaiian islands, harboring jewel-like endemic plants, nesting green sea turtles, and fossils of now-extinct flightless birds.

Towering over the island's eastern half, 4,970-foot Kamakou provides 60% of the fresh water on Molokai and shelter for rare native species, such as happy-faced spiders and deep-throated lobelias. Molokai's most awesome hike is the **Pepeopae Trail** ★★, which takes you back a few million years. On the cloud-draped trail (actually a boardwalk across the bog), you'll see mosses, sedges, native violets, knee-high ancient ohia, and lichens that evolved in total isolation over eons. Eerie intermittent mists blowing in and out will give you an idea of this island at its creation. The 3-mile round-trip trail leads to a view of pristine Pelekunu Valley on the North Shore.

Hikes are free (donations welcome), but the number of participants is limited. Hikes usually take place on Saturdays, but the conservancy website (www.nature.org/hawaii) doesn't always specify the dates. To confirm dates and availability, e-mail hike_molokai@tnc.org, or call the field office (© **808/553-5236**; weekdays 8am–3pm).

It's possible to access the preserves on your own, but you'll need a rugged four-wheel-drive (4WD) vehicle, dry roads, and clear weather. Check in first at the field office, just north of Kaunakakai in Molokai Industrial Park, 23 Pueo Place, off Ulili Street near Highway 460. Ask for directions and current conditions of the red-dirt road that leads to the trailhead. In the case of Moomomi, you'll also need to get a pass for the locked gate. Clean your shoes and gear before visiting the preserves to avoid bringing in invasive species, and drive cautiously—a tow job from these remote areas can easily cost $1,000.

Hiking to Kalaupapa ★★

This hike to the site of Molokai's infamous place of exile (see "Tragedy & Inspiration: Kalaupapa National Historical Park," p. 260) is like going down a switchback staircase with what seems like a million steps. You don't always see the breathtaking view because you're too busy watching your step. It's easier going down (surprise!)—in about an hour, you'll go 2½ miles, from 2,000 feet to sea level. The trip up sometimes takes twice as long. The trailhead starts on the mauka (inland) side of Hwy. 470. *Note:* You must have a permit and reservation for a tour (see "Kalaupapa Tours," p. 266) before you go, as well as be at least 16 years or older, by order of the state health department. Wear good hiking boots or sneakers, bring lots of water and a snack, and carry a rain poncho.

Hiking the East End

The 3.4-mile round-trip hike through verdant, history-filled **Halawa Valley,** which leads to the 250-foot Mooula Falls and its bracingly cool pool at the bottom, may only be undertaken as part of a guided tour (see "Halawa Valley Tours," p. 267). The cost and effort are well worth it, however, to absorb the beauty and heritage of this special place. **Puu O Hoku Ranch** (see "Where to Stay," p. 248) also boasts a variety of trails, but they are only open to guests.

Camping

All campgrounds are for tents only, and permits for county and state sites must be purchased in advance. You'll have to bring your own equipment or plan to buy it on the island, as there are no rentals, although you can buy some in Kaunakakai's variety stores.

AT THE BEACH

County Campgrounds ★ The family-friendly **One Alii Beach Park** (p. 269) provides restrooms, barbecues, outdoor showers, drinking water, picnic tables, and electricity; **Papohaku Beach Park ★★** (p. 269), one of the best year-round places to camp on Molokai, has the same, minus electricity and plus plenty of sharp *kiawe* thorns. Basic groceries are available in Maunaloa, 6 miles away, and snacks and sundries at the Kaluakoi Resort, 1 mile away (see "Shopping," p. 278), but plan to bring all supplies with you. *Note:* The NO CAMPING signs near the Papohaku parking lot apply only to the lawn to the right of the restrooms.

Permits $10 adults, $6 minors Mon–Thurs, $20 adults, $12 minors Fri–Sun and holidays (discounts for state residents). 3-night maximum. Available in person 8am–1pm and 2:30–4pm weekdays at the Maui County parks office, Mitchell Pauole Community Center, 90 Ainoa St., Kaunakakai, 96748. ☎ **808/553-3204.** To purchase by mail, download the form at www.mauicounty.gov/410/Park-Permits and mail to the parks office with check and self-addressed, stamped envelope.

IN THE FOREST

State Campgrounds ★★ The state manages two campgrounds at high, often misty elevations: **Palaau State Park ★★** (p. 258), where the ironwood forest is airy and cool, and remote **Waikolu Overlook** in the rain forest of the Molokai Forest Reserve. Both have restroom and picnic facilities, but no drinking water or barbecues; Waikolu Overlook also has a covered pavilion. Palaau is home to the Kalaupapa Lookout, the best vantage point for seeing the national historical park if you're not hiking. *Note:* Waikolu is spectacular, but requires a 4WD vehicle to drive 10 miles up mostly unpaved road starting from an unmarked intersection with Maunaloa Highway (Hwy. 460) near mile marker 4; do not attempt in muddy or rainy conditions (see "Hiking Pepeopae Trail," above). If the area is not covered in clouds, you'll be rewarded with views of the pristine Waikolu Valley and the Pacific, and be that much closer to the **Kamakou Preserve ★★★** (p. 263).

Permits $18 per campsite (up to 6 persons), $3 per additional person (kids 2 and under free). 5-night maximum. ℂ **808/984-8100.** Available online at http://dlnr.hawaii.gov/dsp/camping-lodging/molokai.

OTHER OUTDOOR ACTIVITIES

Bicycling

With lightly used roads, Molokai is a great place to explore by bicycle, especially on the East End, where sandy coves invite you to pull off the road for a quick dip. The only way to rent a bike is from friendly Phillip Kikukawa at **Molokai Bicycle,** 80 Mohala St., Kaunakakai (www.bikehawaii.com/molokaibicycle; ℂ **808/553-3931**), which offers mountain, road, and hybrid bike rentals for $25 to $32 a day, or $95 to $130 a week, including a helmet and lock. Because Phillip is a schoolteacher, the store is open only Wednesday (3–6pm) and Saturday (9am–2pm); call to set up an appointment for other hours. Dropoff and pickup in or near Kaunakakai is free, with charges for runs to the airport ($20 each way/$30 round-trip) or Kaluakoi Resort and Wavecrest condos ($25 each way).

Golf

Take a swing back into golf history at **Ironwood Hills Golf Course** (ℂ **808/567-6000**). Built in 1929 by the Del Monte Plantation for its executives, the nine-hole, undulating course with uneven fairways lies a half-mile down an unpaved road off Highway 470 in Kalae, between Coffees of Hawaii in Kualapuu and the Kalaupapa Lookout. Gorgeous mountain and ocean views, some filtered by tree growth, also compensate for the challenging course, maintained by local residents since its pro moved off-island in recent years. Greens fees are $20 for 9 holes; club rentals are $10.

Tennis

The only public tennis courts on Molokai are located at the **Mitchell Pauole Center,** in Kaunakakai (ℂ **808/553-3204**). Both are lit for night play (you switch on the lights yourself) and are available free on a first-come, first-served basis, with a 45-minute time limit if someone is waiting. The vacation rental condos at **Ke Nani Kai** on the West End (p. 250) and **Wavecrest** on the

East End (p. 252) offer courts for use of their guests only. Bring your own rackets and balls.

SHOPPING

For a small island, Molokai has a surprising number of intriguing gift stores and catchall mom-and-pop shops. Most are closed on Sunday, though, so plan your souvenir shopping accordingly.

Kaunakakai

The eclectic **Kalele Bookstore& Divine Expressions** ★★★, 64 Ala Malama Ave. (www.molokaispirit.com; ℂ **808/553-5112**), is a great place to start your Molokai vacation. Enjoy a free cup of coffee while you ogle the feather lei, shell necklaces, and earrings made with *kapa* (traditional bark fabric), then peruse the excellent collection of new and used books (including many rare Hawaiian titles), locally made artwork, and children's games.

The artist cooperative **Molokai Art From the Heart** ★★, also at 64 Ala Malama Ave. (http://molokaigallery.com; ℂ **808/553-8018**), features works by some 150 artists, virtually all from Molokai. **Something For Everybody** ★, 40 Ala Malama Ave. (www.allthingsmolokai.com; ℂ **808/553-3299**) will print custom T-shirts or trucker hats to commemorate your trip, in addition to selling locally designed clothes for all ages, accessories, and items for the home. **Imports Gift Shop** ★★, 82 Ala Malama Ave. (https://molokaiimports. com; ℂ **808/553-5734**), carries a huge array of aloha and surf wear, jewelry, Hawaiian quilts, body lotions, and other gifts—just be aware, as the name implies, that much of the inventory is not made on Molokai.

Next to Molokai Pizza in the Huina Center, **Makana Nui Hawaiian Gift Shop** ★★, 15 Kaunakakai Pl. (www.facebook.com/makananuimolokai; ℂ **808/553-8158**), offers Hawaiian and Polynesian jewelry, sarongs, clothing, jewelry, gourd bowls, and other small home decor. Owner Denise Taueetia used to run the estimable Denise's Gifts in Kualapuu before moving to town.

The island's only pharmacy, the venerable **Molokai Drugs** ★, 28 Kamoi St. (www.molokaidrugs.com; ℂ **808/553-5790**), also holds a cache of cute souvenirs and sundries, including greeting cards and gift wrap. T-shirts with original island-inspired designs, hats, aloha shirts, sporting goods, and various souvenirs can be found at **Molokai Fish & Dive** ★★, 53 Ala Malama St. (www.molokaifishanddive.com; ℂ **808/553-5926**); it's one of the rare birds open Sunday. In addition to surfboards and swimwear, **Malama Surf Shop**, 93 Ala Malama Ave. (www.facebook.com/malamasurfshop; ℂ **808/553-3399**), carries cute shave-ice-themed "hydroflasks" (reusable water bottles) and the local Hulalei line of pretty shell and silver jewelry.

Make sure to hit the **Saturday morning farmer's market** ★★★ (8am–noon) in downtown Kaunakakai; among the aunties sitting on the sidewalk with giant papaya and other produce, you'll find a dozen vendors of island arts and crafts, clothing, and specialty foods such as local vanilla extract.

Elsewhere on the Island

Don't speed past **Hoolmua Junction** at the intersection of highways 460 and 470 on the way to Kualapuu. The entrepreneurial ladies at **Kupu Ae ★★★** (www.kupuaemolokai.com; ℂ **808/646-1504**) design and handcraft beautiful silkscreens and batiks—scarves, sarongs, pillows, wall hangings and more— each with deep Hawaiian meaning. You'll also find lovely jewelry, soaps, and art supplies. (A small selection of their exquisite wares are also sold at Aunty's Leis shop at the Hoolehua airport.) Next door, the **Beach Break ★★** sporting goods store and gift shop (www.bigwindkites.com/beachbreak; ℂ **808/567-6091**) sells nearly everything you need for fun in the sun, plus top-quality ukuleles, cards, books, children's items, home decor, women's clothing in natural fabrics, and large-format prints of owner Zack Socher's impressive photos from around the island.

The "plantation store" at **Coffees of Hawaii ★**, 1630 Farrington Ave., Kualapuu (www.coffeesofhawaii.com; ℂ **808/567-9490**), has seen better days as a gift shop, but you can still sample the local Muleskinner and Malulani roasted beans here and buy bags to take home as well as a few souvenirs. Tucked behind Coffees of Hawaii, the **Molokai Arts Center ★** (www.molokai artscenter.com; ℂ **808/567-9696**) is an active hub for local ceramicists and you can buy beautiful handmade bowls, chimes, and mugs for decent prices. Park on Hula Street and follow the signs.

North of Kualapuu, near mile marker 4 of the Kalae Hwy. (Hwy. 470), is the **Molokai Museum Gift Shop ★★** (ℂ **808/567-6436**), a trove of crafts,

MOLOKAI SALT: THE perfect MOLOKAI SOUVENIR

It's small, it's easy to pack and take back home, and it's made only on Molokai: Molokai salt. The **Hawaii Kai Corporation** (www.hawaiikaico.com) has two product lines featuring Molokai salt, the gourmet **Soul of the Sea** and the **Palm Island Premium.** Soul of the Sea salt is hand-harvested from some of the cleanest ocean water in the state, hand-processed and hand-packed on Molokai. It comes in three varietals: Papohaku White, Kilauea Black, and Haleakala Red. Palm Island Gourmet is Molokai salt with trace minerals restored; it comes in White Silver, Red Gold, or Black Lava. The dozen varieties of local sea salts from **Pacifica Hawaii** (www.pacifica hawaii.com) also make ideal gifts. Saltmaster Nancy Gove evaporates seawater in elevated pans at the front of her home in Kaunakakai and then infuses colors and flavors via ingredients such as local red clay, Kauai-made rum, and Maui sugar. You'll find both brands of Molokai salt in local stores.

fabrics, cookbooks, quilt sets, and other gift items. There's also a modest selection of cards, T-shirts, coloring books, and, at Christmas, handmade ornaments made of lauhala and koa. Its hours are limited, like the museum's, to Monday to Saturday 10am to 2pm.

On the West End, Zack Socher's parents, Jonathan and Daphne, own the colorful **Big Wind Kite Factory & Plantation Gallery ★★**, 120 Maunaloa Hwy., Maunaloa (www.bigwindkites.com; ℂ **808/552-2364**), chock-full of Balinese furnishings, stone and shell jewelry, Kalaupapa memoirs, and other books on Molokai. Test-fly one of the handmade Big Wind kites at the nearby park. **A Touch of Molokai ★** overlooks the pool at the closed Kaluakoi Hotel, 1121 Kaluakoi Rd., Maunaloa (ℂ **808/552-0133**). It carries a small sampling of apparel, crafts, and souvenirs of its Kaunakakai motherhouse, **Molokai Imports Gift Shop** (see p. 278).

ENTERTAINMENT & NIGHTLIFE

The few choices for evening entertainment at least mean a lively crowd is guaranteed wherever you go. **Paddlers Restaurant and Bar,** on the ocean side of Highway 450 at 10 Mohala St. (www.paddlersrestaurant.com; ℂ **808/553-3300**), is the island's primary watering hole as well as one of its top restaurants. Happy-hour specials, such as $2 Primo beer, are available Monday to Saturday 2 to 5pm (the restaurant is closed Sun.) The spacious indoor-outdoor restaurant and bar also hosts live music—predominantly local acts in various genres—and dancing most nights. A group of ukulele-strumming aunties and uncles, Na Kupuna Molokai ("the elders of Molokai") play sweet Hawaiian music on Fridays from 4 to 6pm.

Most nights of the week, Hawaiian music enlivens **Hiro's Ohana Grill,** the oceanfront/poolside bar and restaurant at Hotel Molokai (p. 249); some of Hawaii's most famous entertainers have appeared on its stage opposite the pool. On Thursdays, live music (plus the prime rib) draws patrons to **Kualapuu Cookhouse** (p. 255). Finally, while it's not nightlife, per se, the twice-weekly **kanikapila** (jam session) at **Coffees of Hawaii,** 1630 Farrington

---

The Hot-Bread Run

Whenever people on Molokai mention "hot bread," they're talking about the hot-bread run at **Kanemitsu's Bakery and Restaurant** (see p. 255), the surreal late-night ritual for die-hard bread lovers. Those in the know line up at the bakery's back door (79 Ala Malama St.; look for the sign that says HOT BREAD in the alley behind the bakery) beginning at 8pm, when the bread is whisked hot out of the oven and into waiting hands. You can order your fresh bread with butter, jelly, cinnamon, or cream cheese ($7.50–$9.75), and the bakers will cut the hot loaves down the middle and slather on the works so it melts in the bread. The cream-cheese-and-jelly bread makes a fine substitute for dessert.

ancient CELEBRATIONS

If possible, time your trip to coincide with **Ka Hula Piko** ★★★ (www.kahulapiko.com), an intimate celebration of the ancient art of hula. Over 3 days, hula practitioners offer powerful chants and dance, not as performance but as gifts to their ancestors. This hula is unlike anything you'll see elsewhere: dances mimicking mythological turtles, honoring the work of taro farmers, and proclaiming ancient prophecies. The island-wide festivities typically occur in late May and early June, wrapping up with an all-day *ho'olaule'a* (festival) during which visiting hula troupes from as far as Japan and Europe share their skills.

The annual **Ka Molokai Makahiki** ★★★ (www.molokaievents.com) is another not-to-miss event. Islanders celebrate the rainy season—a time of peace and prosperity in ancient Hawaii—with traditional crafts, hula, chanting, games, and competitions. All of Molokai gathers for the daylong event, held on a Saturday in January at the Mitchell Pauole Center in Kaunakakai.

Hwy. (www.coffeesofhawaii.com; © **808/567-9490**), is definitely worth attending. The senior musicians of Na Kupuna Molokai (see above) fill the broad lanai, playing American and Hawaiian standards. Don't miss it: Tuesday and Friday mornings from 10am to noon.

LANAI

Lanai is changing—but not in the way many expected. Some presumed that Silicon Valley billionaire Larry Ellison would bring unwanted hustle and bustle to the former Pineapple Isle, known for its sleepy, small-town feel, when he bought 98% of its 141 square miles in 2012. Instead, he thinned the already low number of visitors by closing the island's three hotels for prolonged renovations and substantially hiking prices when they reopened. Ellison also shut down one of two interisland airlines with regular flights to Lanai; most visitors now arrive by ferry from Maui.

With fewer guests patronizing the mom-and-pop boutiques and restaurants of tiny Lanai City, pop. 3,100, some on Lanai are feeling squeezed out. But Ellison's largesse has also funded restoration of cultural heritage sites and community resources. Longtime locals—many descended from former Dole pineapple plantation workers—are determined to hold onto their low-key lifestyle, too. So while you may only be able to afford a day trip, it's still worth the effort: There's really no other place like Lanai.

Lanai (pronounced "Lah-*nigh*-ee"), the nation's biggest defunct pineapple patch, now claims to be one of the world's top tropical destinations. It's a bold claim because so little is here; Lanai has even fewer dining and accommodations choices than Molokai. There are no stoplights and barely 30 miles of paved road. This almost-virgin island is unspoiled by what passes for progress, except for a tiny 1920s-era plantation village—and, of course, the luxury Four Seasons Resort Lanai, where ocean-view rooms easily run $1,000 a night.

As soon as you arrive on Lanai, you'll feel the small-town coziness. Locals wave to every car and stop on the street to "talk story" with their friends. Hunting, fishing, and working in the garden are considered priorities in life, and leaving your keys in the car's ignition is standard practice.

For generations, Lanai was little more than a small village, owned and operated by the pineapple company, surrounded by acres of pineapple fields. The few visitors to the island were either relatives of the residents or occasional weekend hunters. Life in the 1960s was pretty much the same as in the 1930s. But all that

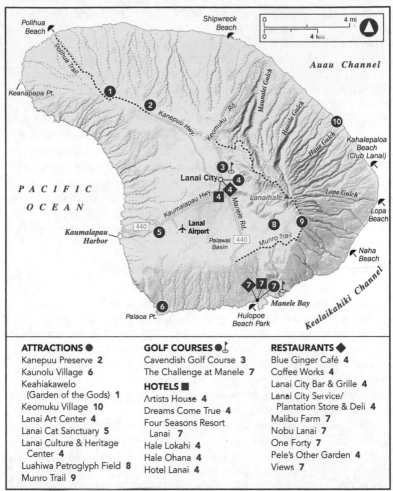

Polihua Beach
Shipwreck Beach
0   4 mi
0   4 km
Keanapapa Pt.
Auau Channel
Polihua Trail
Kanepuu Hwy.
Keomuku Rd.
Maunalei Gulch
Hauola Gulch
Haua Gulch
10
Kahalepaloa Beach (Club Lanai)
PACIFIC OCEAN
Lanai City
3
4
4
4
Lanaihale
Lopa Gulch
Lopa Beach
Kaumalapau Hwy.
Manele Rd.
Kaumalapau Harbor
440
5
Lanai Airport
Palawai Basin
440
Munro Trail
8
9
Naha Beach
7 7 7
Manele Bay
6
Palaoa Pt.
Hulopoe Beach Park
Kealaikahiki Channel

ATTRACTIONS ●	GOLF COURSES ●⛳	RESTAURANTS ◆
Kanepuu Preserve **2**	Cavendish Golf Course **3**	Blue Ginger Café **4**
Kaunolu Village **6**	The Challenge at Manele **7**	Coffee Works **4**
Keahiakawelo (Garden of the Gods) **1**	**HOTELS** ■	Lanai City Bar & Grille **4**
Keomuku Village **10**	Artists House **4**	Lanai City Service/ Plantation Store & Deli **4**
Lanai Art Center **4**	Dreams Come True **4**	Malibu Farm **7**
Lanai Cat Sanctuary **5**	Four Seasons Resort Lanai **7**	Nobu Lanai **7**
Lanai Culture & Heritage Center **4**	Hale Lokahi **4**	One Forty **7**
Luahiwa Petroglyph Field **8**	Hale Ohana **4**	Pele's Other Garden **4**
Munro Trail **9**	Hotel Lanai **4**	Views **7**

changed in 1990, when the Lodge at Koele, a 102-room hotel resembling an opulent English Tudor mansion, opened its doors, followed a year later by the 250-room Manele Bay, a Mediterranean-style luxury resort overlooking Hulopoe Bay. Overnight the isolated island was transformed: Corporate jets streamed into tiny Lanai Airport, former plantation workers were retrained in the art of serving gourmet meals, and the population of 2,500 swelled with transient visitors and outsiders coming to work in the island's new hospitality industry. Microsoft billionaire Bill Gates chose the island for his lavish wedding, booking all of its hotel rooms to fend off the press—and uncomplicated

Lanai officially went on the map as a vacation spot for the rich and powerful. No wonder Oracle founder and America's Cup yachtsman Larry Ellison snapped it up for reportedly a mere $300 million when Castle & Cooke owner David Murdock put it on the market in 2012.

Despite the hurdles of high costs and limited transport that Ellison's ownership has created for today's visitors, this island is also still a place where people come for beauty, quiet, solitude, and an experience with nature. They also come for the wealth of activities: snorkeling and swimming in the marine preserve known as Hulopoe Bay, hiking on 100 miles of remote trails, talking story with the friendly locals, and beachcombing and whale-watching along stretches of otherwise deserted sand. For the adventurous, there's horseback riding in the forest, scuba diving in caves, playing golf on a course with stunning ocean views, or renting a four-wheel-drive vehicle for the day and discovering wild plains where spotted deer run free.

The real Lanai is a multifaceted place that's so much more than its luxury resorts—and it's the traveler who comes to discover the island's natural wonders, local lifestyle, and other inherent joys who is bound to have the most genuine island experience.

The Pineapple Island's Unusual Past

This old shield volcano in the rain shadow of Maui has a history of resisting change in a big way. Early Polynesians, fierce Hawaiian kings, European explorers, 20th-century farmers—the island has seen them all and sent most of them packing, empty-handed and broken. The ancient Hawaiians believed that the island was haunted by spirits so wily and vicious that no human could survive here. People didn't settle here until around A.D. 1400. Remnants of ancient Hawaiian villages, temples, fishponds, and petroglyphs decorate the Lanai landscape. King Kamehameha spent his summers here at a cliffside palace overlooking the sunny southern coast.

But those spirits never really went away, it seems. In 1778, the king of the Big Island, Kalaniopuu, invaded Lanai in what was called "the war of loose bowels." His men slaughtered every warrior, cut down trees, and set fire to all that was left except a bitter fern whose roots gave them all dysentery.

The island's arid terrain was once native forest—patches of which persist on the 3,366-foot summit of **Lanaihale**—along with native birds, insects, and jewel-like tree snails. But the 1800s brought foreign ambitions and foreign strife to Hawaii: Disease took more than half of the native people, and Western commerce supplanted the islanders' subsistence culture. Exotic pests such as rats, mosquitos, and feral goats and cattle decimated the native ecosystem and the island's watershed.

In 1802, Wu Tsin made the first attempt to harvest a crop on the island, but he ultimately abandoned his sugarcane fields and went away. Charles Gay acquired 600 acres at public auction to experiment with pineapple as a crop, but a 3-year drought left him bankrupt. Others tried in vain to grow cotton, sisal, and sugar beets; they started a dairy and a piggery and raised sheep for wool. But all enterprises failed, mostly for lack of water.

Harry Baldwin, a missionary's grandson, was the first to succeed on Lanai. He bought Lanai for $588,000 in 1917, developed a 20-mile water pipeline between Koele and Manele, and sold the island 5 years later to Jim Dole for $1.1 million.

Dole planted and irrigated 18,000 acres of pineapple, built Lanai City, blasted out a harbor, and turned the island into a fancy fruit plantation. For 70 years, the island was essentially one big pineapple patch. Acres of prickly fields surrounded a tiny grid of workers' homes. Life continued pretty much unchanged into the 1980s.

Even Dole was ultimately vanquished, however: Cheaper pineapple production in Asia brought an end to Lanai's heyday. In 1985, self-made billionaire David Murdock acquired the island in a merger (well, 98% of it anyway; the remaining 2% is owned by the government or longtime Lanai families). Murdock built two grand hotels, and almost overnight, the plain, red-dirt pineapple plantation became one of the world's top travel destinations, with luxury residences lining the resorts' golf courses. He also created a large solar farm on the island's south side. Murdock's grand maneuver to replace agriculture with tourism never proved quite lucrative enough, however. In 2012, after years of six-figure losses, he sold his share of the island to the eight-richest person in the world, Larry Ellison.

The software tycoon made important moves to appeal to the tiny, tight-knit community. He reopened the movie theater and the public swimming pool, closed for a decade. He built ball courts so that student athletes finally had somewhere to practice. He formed Pulama Lanai, a company tasked with directing the island's future, and hired a Lanai native to run its chief operating office. Ellison's ambitious plans include everything from sustainable agriculture (including a hydroponic farm) to another über-exclusive resort on Lanai's pristine eastern shore. Longtime residents who have lived through several island makeovers appreciate the improvements, but worry that local businesses will be unable to compete with Ellison's focus on luxury, not to mention unlimited wealth. A popular family-owned poke restaurant, for example, closed its doors when Ellison's nearby grocery store opened a poke bar with markedly lower prices.

Although visitors will find an island still in flux, Lanai has plenty of timeless charms to capture a traveler's imagination, from wild dolphins jumping at Hulopoe Beach to mysterious petroglyphs reflecting ancient Hawaiian ways. The cool, misty uplands of Koele and sprawling, fallow fields where the ocean shimmers in the distance resemble nowhere else in Hawaii, although they may remind you of forests and moors across the sea. In many places, the island looks just like the old plantation-era photographs you can see at the Lanai Culture and Heritage Center. The back-breaking work may be gone, but the unassuming spirit and resilience of its laborers lives on.

FROMMER'S FAVORITE LANAI EXPERIENCES

o **Snorkeling at Hulopoe Beach:** Tropical fish create an underwater kaleido-scope in the clear waters off one of Hawaii's best beach parks, which also boasts tide pools teeming with sea life. A pod of spinner dolphins often swims into the bay to catch up on daytime rest, while migratory humpback whales sometimes shelter here in winter.

o **Visiting the "Garden of the Gods":** The boulder-strewn, raw-earth, rust-colored landscape 7 miles northwest of Lanai City offers impressive views across the channel to Molokai. Nicknamed for a Colorado attraction with a similar lunar landscape, this area has a Hawaiian name, Keahiakawelo ("the fire of Kawelo"), that better reflects the eerie legend of how it became bar-ren; see p. 297.

o **Traversing the Munro Trail:** The vistas atop Lanaihale, the 3,366-foot volcano that formed Lanai, are also stunning, but you don't have to hike the full 12 miles of the Munro Trail to enjoy the cool forest or glimpses of Maui and Molokai; you can hike just a few miles to the first lookout. The hardy will want to carry on, though, and if conditions are dry enough, a four-wheel-drive vehicle makes it easy to circle the rim and return to town. See p. 298.

o **Exploring by Four-Wheel-Drive:** With only 30 miles of paved roads, four-wheel-drive Jeeps, SUVs, and pickup trucks are the vehicles of choice for islanders. Though rentals can be pricey, you'll want one, too, to check out Lanai's deserted beaches, historic village sites, and rugged canyons. Before you go, download the **Lanai Guide app** (www.lanaiguideapp.org), devel-oped by the Lanai Culture & Heritage Center, to appreciate the natural and cultural treasures you'll discover on the way.

o **Camping by the Beach:** The privately managed, pristine campground at Hulopoe Beach Park offers ideal conditions, if you're willing to bring your gear with you. After a cookout under the stars, fall asleep to the sound of waves rolling on the shore, then wake to birdsong and the chance to explore Hulopoe's crystalline waters. See p. 293.

o **Watching the Whales at Polihua Beach:** This windswept beach on the unpopulated, untrammeled north side of the island serves as a scenic view-point to watch for whales in winter. You'll need a four-wheel-drive vehicle, and a little gumption, to get here, but you'll likely have it to yourself—unless one of the nesting turtles it's named for makes an appearance. See p. 301.

o **Enjoying a Stroll, Dinner, and a Movie Near Dole Park:** Go local with a walk through the lofty Cook pines lining Dole Park in Lanai City, followed by dinner at one of the town's casual restaurants and a movie in its restored 1926 cinema, Hale Keaka Lanai Theater (p. 309). If you're in town on the fifth Friday of the month, you'll also be able to browse craft and food tables, listen to live music, and enjoy the festive, kid-friendly vibe of one of the evening Fifth Friday Town Parties (p. 308)

o **Petting Cats in an Outdoor Sanctuary:** If you love felines, and perhaps saving endangered birds as well, a visit to the innovative, open-air Lanai Cat Sanctuary is a must. No appointment is necessary; you can even pack a picnic to enjoy more time with your purring companions. See p. 298.

ORIENTATION

Arriving

BY PLANE   Public flights to Lanai Airport (LNY) are extremely limited. Hawaiian Airlines' **Ohana by Hawaiian** interisland service (www.hawaiian airlines.com; ✆ **800/367-5320**) includes flights to Lanai from Honolulu on comfortable, 48-seat turboprop planes.

Guests of the Four Seasons Resort Lanai may also book private flights on **Lanai Air** (✆ **833/486-8397**), starting at $500 for two people, one way, from Honolulu, Maui (Kahului), or Hawaii Island (Kona), aboard luxurious 10-passenger Pilatus PC-12 aircraft. All guests traveling to or from the Four Seasons via Honolulu can take advantage of the hotel's private guest lounge on the second floor of Terminal 2.

Mokulele Airlines (www.mokuleleairlines.com; ✆ **866/260-7070**), which actually provides the service for Lanai Air, also offers charter flights from Maui on its 9-passenger Cessna Grand Caravan planes.

The flight from Honolulu to Lanai's tiny but surprisingly modern airport in Palawai Basin, once the world's largest pineapple plantation, takes just 25 minutes. From the airport, it's about 10 minutes by car to Lanai City and 25 minutes to Manele Bay.

BY BOAT   A round-trip on **Expeditions Lahaina/Lanai Passenger Ferry** (http://go-lanai.com; ✆ **800/695-2624** or on Maui 808/661-3756) takes you between Maui and Lanai for $30 adults and $20 children ages 2 to 11 each way. The ferry runs five times a day, 365 days a year, between Lahaina (on Maui) and Lanai's Manele Bay harbor. The 9-mile channel crossing takes approximately an hour, depending on sea conditions. Reservations are strongly recommended; call or book online. Two checked bags and one carry-on may be brought on board for free; fees apply for excess baggage and bulky items such as bicycles and surfboards over 7 feet long. *Bonus:* During the winter months, taking the ferry amounts to a free whale-watch, while spinner dolphins may accompany the ship anytime.

Four Seasons Resort Lanai guests who feel the need for speed (and have $1,600 to spare) charter private passage with **Lanai Ocean Sports** (✆ **808/866-8256**) aboard *Lanai Five*. The six-person 48-foot inflatable can zip along at 50mph; on a calm day you'll cross the channel separating Maui and Lanai in just 20 minutes.

Visitor Information

The **Maui Visitors and Convention Bureau,** 1727 Wili Pa Loop, Wailuku, Maui (www.gohawaii.com/lanai; © **800/525-6284** or 808/244-3530) provides information on Lanai. You can download a travel planning brochure from the website, or request one be mailed to you.

The Island in Brief

Inhabited Lanai is divided into two regions: Lanai City, up on the mountain where the weather is cool and misty, and Manele, on the sunny southwestern coast where the weather is hot and dry.

Lanai City (pop. 3,200) sits at the heart of the island at 1,645 feet above sea level. It's the only place on Lanai that offers services (gas and groceries), and the airport is just outside of town. Built in 1924, this plantation village is a tidy grid of quaint tin-roofed cottages in bright pastels, with backyard gardens of banana, passionfruit, and papaya. Many of the residents are Filipino immigrants who once toiled in Lanai's pineapple fields. Their humble homes, now worth $450,000 or more (for a 1,500-sq.-ft. home, built in 1935, on a 6,000-sq.-ft. lot), are excellent examples of historic preservation; the whole town looks like it's been kept under a bell jar.

Around **Dole Park,** a charming village square lined with towering Norfolk and Cook pines, plantation buildings house general stores, a post office (where people stop to chat), two banks, a half-dozen restaurants, an art gallery, an art center, a few boutiques, and a coffee shop that easily outshines any Starbucks. The historic one-room police station displays a "jail" consisting of three padlocked, outhouse-size cells as a throwback to earlier times. The new station—a block away, with regulation-size jail cells—probably sees just as little action.

Just up the road from Dole Park is the former Four Seasons Lodge at Koele, a stately resort owned by tech billionaire Larry Ellison that was still undergoing $75 million in renovations at press time. It's expected to reopen as the **Koele Wellness Experience,** featuring new spa and fitness facilities, such as a yoga pavilion, and an "Adventure Center" with ziplines, a giant swing, tightropes, and other activities on two holes of the former Koele golf course.

Manele is directly downhill—comprising Manele Bay (with its small boat harbor, where the ferry docks), dreamy Hulopoe Beach, and the island's

THERE'S AN app FOR THAT

The Lanai Culture & Heritage Center (see below) partnered with Pulama Lanai to create a great new tool for exploring the island. The **Lanai Guide** is both a website, www.lanaiguideapp.org, and a GPS-enabled app that directs you to historic sites and trails, replete with detailed maps, old photos, aerial videos, and chants. Download the app for free on the website or from iTunes.

primary bastion of extravagance, the **Four Seasons Resort Lanai.** You'll see more of "typical" Hawaii here—sandy beach, swaying palms, and superlative sunsets—plus the towering landmark of Lanai, **Puu Pehe,** also known as Sweetheart Rock.

[FastFACTS] LANAI

Doctors & Dentists For over-the-counter prescriptions and vaccines, head to **Rainbow Pharmacy,** right by Dole Park, 431 7th St., Lanai City (www.rainbowpharmacy.com; © 808/565-9332). If you need a doctor, contact the **Straub Lanai Family Health Center** (www.hawaiipacifichealth.org/straub; © 808/565-6423) or the **Lanai Community Hospital**

(© 808/565-8450; www.mauihealthsystem.org/lanai-hospital), both at 628 7th St., Lanai City. The **Hawaii Dental Clinic**, 730 Lanai Ave., Suite 101, Lanai City (www.hawaiidentalclinic.com; © 808/565-6418), offers full services from 8am to 6pm Monday to Saturday.

Emergencies In case of emergencies, call the

police, fire department, or ambulance services at © **911,** or the **Poison Control Center** at © 800/222-1222. For non-emergencies, call the **police** at © 808/565-6428.

Weather For both land and sea conditions, visit the **National Weather Service** website (www.prh.noaa.gov) and type "Lanai, HI," in the search box.

GETTING AROUND

The island has little infrastructure, so you'll need to plan your transportation in advance. **Rabaca's Limousine Service** (© 808/565-6670) will retrieve you from the airport or harbor for $10 per person (bring cash, exact change if possible). Guests at the **Four Seasons Resort Lanai** (www.fourseasons.com/lanai; © 808/565-2000) will be retrieved by a complimentary shuttle bus or can hire a private SUV ($215 per vehicle from the airport or $85 from the ferry, for up to four passengers). If you're camping at Hulopoe Beach, you can walk over from the harbor—a 5-minute stroll. Farmer and local newspaper publisher **Alberta de Jetley** also runs the island's lone taxi service, with drivers who can double as impromptu tour guides. It's best to arrange all rides in advance, however (© 808/649-0808.)

Once you've arrived at your lodging, it's entirely possible to enjoy Lanai without getting behind the wheel. Lanai City is easily walkable and if you're staying at the Four Seasons, you'll hardly want to stray from the luxurious property. But if you plan to explore the island's remote shores or forested summit (which I highly recommend) on your own, you'll need a four-wheel-drive (4WD) vehicle for at least a day.

Reserve your ride *far in advance;* cars are in short supply here. On top of that, gas is expensive on Lanai—upward of $4 a gallon—and off-road vehicles get lousy mileage. Spending $40 to $50 per day on gas isn't unheard of. *Tip:* Rent only for the day (or days) you want to explore the island's hinterlands. Keep in mind that rainy weather makes many roads impassable. Check with your rental agent to see which roads are open—and whether renting that day is worth your money.

At press time, the island's lone national-brand rental car agency, Dollar, had just closed its doors—and Lanai's only public towing service. In its place, local artist Judi Riley opened **808 Day Trip** (https://808daytrip.com; ℂ **808/ 649-0664**), which offers two types of cars, both for paved-road use only: five-door hatchbacks ($149 a day) and five-door sport-utility vehicles ($199 a day). Pick up the car at the harbor, airport, or in town.

Guests of the **Four Seasons** (see above) can rent four-door, fully loaded Jeep Wranglers for $150 to $225 per 24 hours, including gas, directly from the hotel's Adventure Center; Toyota Land Cruisers and 4Runners, better suited to paved roads, are also available. **Adventure Lanai Island Club** (http://jeeplanai.net; ℂ 800/565-7373; call for pricing) rents two- and four-door Jeep Wranglers that can be delivered to you at the airport, ferry, or lodging; they can also provide advice on which unpaved roads and trails are passable. The Club also rents out adventure gear such as kayaks, mountain bikes, and surfboards, which it can deliver with your Jeep and the appropriate roof racks, and leads off-road excursions; contact for current pricing.

If you'd rather leave the driving to someone else, **Rabaca's Limousine Service** (see above) is a terrific option for a short romp around the island. Knowledgeable local drivers will navigate the rough roads for you, visiting Shipwreck Beach, Keahiakawelo, and even Keomoku Village in roomy Suburbans. Trips run 3½ hours and cost $80 per person (minimum two guests). If you've got a larger group, Rabaca's will chauffer the lot of you around in a six-person SUV for $110 per hour. Fifteen-passenger vans go for $150 per hour; they stay on paved roads.

Whether or not you rent a car, sooner or later you'll find yourself at the **Lanai Plantation Store,** 1036 Lanai Ave. (ℂ **808/565-7227 ext. 3**). Get directions, maps, and the local gossip at this all-in-one grocery, gourmet deli, gas station, rental-car agency, and souvenir shop. It's also a good place to fill your water jugs: A reverse-osmosis water dispenser is just out front. *Note:* It's only open 8am to 4pm weekdays and noon to 10pm weekends.

WHERE TO STAY

The reopening of the Four Seasons Lodge at Koele as the spa-focused, 94-room **Koele Wellness Center** was still eagerly anticipated at this writing; prices are expected to rise substantially from its former incarnation as an English-style hunting lodge amid the misty pines. Keep an eye on www.fourseasons.com/lanai for updates.

In the meantime, choices on Lanai are fairly limited. You can go for broke at the luxurious Four Seasons Resort overlooking Hulopoe Bay or one of the nearby homes along the golf course for a minimum 30-day rental. You can also book a more moderately priced stay in "the village," as residents call Lanai City, with a room at the boutique Hotel Lanai or a short-term vacation rental in a former plantation cottage. The cheapest (though not actually cheap) option: Camp at Hulopoe Beach Park for $80 a night.

Platforms such as VRBO and Airbnb offer plenty of vacation rentals; to avoid legal conflicts, look for the county license number in the listings. Maui County also lists permitted rentals at www.mauicounty.gov/1377.

Don't forget when calculating lodging costs that hotel and state taxes will add 14.42% to your bill.

Very Expensive

Four Seasons Resort Lanai ★★★ A conch shell's trumpeting call announces your arrival at this oceanfront retreat, where everyone magically knows your name—even the computer screen in your bathroom mirror. Every inch of this opulent oasis reflects the latest in tech-savvy luxury, from the wristband room keys to the Toto toilets. Service is impeccable: The concierge texts you when dolphins or whales appear in the bay. Beach attendants set up umbrellas in the sand for you, spritz you with Evian, and deliver popsicles.

Guest rooms are large and luxurious, with blackout shades that you can control with a flick of your hand. Suites have Japanese cedar tubs and views that stretch on forever. The resort's two wings overlook Hulopoe Beach and are lushly landscaped with waterfalls, koi-filled lotus ponds, and artwork tucked into every corner. Rare Polynesian artifacts purchased from the Bishop Museum decorate the main lobby's lower level, which is home to two fantastic restaurants: **Nobu Lanai ★★★** and **One Forty ★★★**. Other amenities include a first-rate adventure center, a chic sports bar, adults-only and family pools, and an 1,100-square-foot yoga pavilion with free classes, including aerial yoga, and a killer ocean view (*Namaste!*). Inspired by indigenous healing traditions, the resort's **Hawanawana Spa** offers traditional *lomi lomi* Hawaiian massages, seaweed body wraps, facials, and salon services in serene treatment rooms. Guests have free access to the spa facility's saunas and steam rooms. The "Kids for All Seasons" childcare activities are excellent, but you'll probably have trouble pulling your youngsters away from the beach and tide pools. Animal lover Larry Ellison gets credit for agreeing to provide long-term housing for rescued exotic birds, who have their own caretaker, large aviaries, and daily outings at the beach.

1 Manele Bay Rd., Lanai City. www.fourseasons.com/lanai. © **800/321-4666** or 808/ 565-2000. 168 rooms, 45 suites. Doubles from $875 garden view, $1,000 ocean view; suites from $2,000 garden view, $2,325 ocean view. **Amenities:** 5 restaurants; bar with live music; babysitting; children's program; concierge; fitness center w/classes; golf at Jack Nicklaus–designed Challenge at Manele; whirlpools; 2 pools; room service; full spa; 3 tennis courts; watersports equipment; Wi-Fi (free or premium for $20/day).

Expensive

Tucked in a quiet neighborhood, the exceptionally private, well-landscaped two-bedroom, two-bath **Artists House ★★**, 1243 Queens St., Lanai City (www.airbnb.com/rooms/17501056), sleeps six and was lovingly renovated by longtime Lanai artist Jordanne Weinstein before she moved to Maui. Her bright paintings of pineapples adorn the well-insulated walls, the kitchen gleams with stainless-steel and granite counters, and the master bath includes a leafy outdoor shower. It's $389 a night, plus a $175 cleaning fee; inquire with the property manager about car rentals.

Moderate

In addition to the choices listed below, consider a licensed vacation-home rental, especially if you're traveling with children or other couples. **Hale Ohana ★★,** 1344 Fraser Ave., Lanai City (www.vrbo.com/268485ha), is a smartly renovated two-bedroom, 1½-bath cottage with bamboo floors, modern bathrooms and kitchen appliances, flatscreen TVs, and Wi-Fi; rates are $250 a night for up to 5 people, plus a $100 cleaning fee. Families and groups will also appreciate the beautifully updated three-bedroom, two-bath **Hale Lokahi ★★**, 1346 Houston St., Lanai City (www.vrbo.com/1189259), which has a nautical theme and comes with Wi-Fi, Netflix, Xbox, and a DVD player to keep you entertained on rainy days. Nightly rates run $290 to $325, plus a $150 cleaning fee.

Hotel Lanai ★   Also part of Larry Ellison's empire, this plantation-era hotel in the heart of town underwent significant renovations in 2018, changing out the quaint decor and outdated fixtures for modern style and comforts, including flatscreen TVs, phones, air-conditioning, and bidet-style toilets. Two holdovers from the plantation era: Guest rooms are small and noise travels (so adding TVs may not have been the best idea). Still, it's a relative bargain compared with the Four Seasons. The popular lanai units are slightly larger than the garden units and share a furnished deck that faces Dole Park. (At press time, the one-bedroom cottage in the rear had yet to reopen, but it boasts the added amenities of a private yard, living room with TV, and a bathtub; it's also the only unit that can accommodate more than two people.) All of Lanai City is within walking distance. The in-house restaurant, **Lanai City Bar & Grille ★★,** is not only an excellent dining choice but a lively social spot where visitors mingle with locals in the bar, talking or playing the ukulele long into the night. *Tip:* Room rates are cheaper on weekdays.

828 Lanai Ave., Lanai City. www.hotellanai.com. ✆ **800/795-7211** or 808/565-7211. 10 units, 1 cottage. $250–$300 garden rooms, $300–$350 lanai rooms; cottage rates not yet determined. Rates include continental breakfast. Free parking. **Amenities:** Restaurant; bar; access to golf course; complimentary beach equipment; nearby tennis courts; free Wi-Fi.

Inexpensive

Dreams Come True ★★   Susan and Michael Hunter have operated this bed-and-breakfast in the heart of Lanai City for more than 35 years, although sadly they may have put it up for sale by the time you read this. The nicely renovated 1925 plantation house is roomy and quaint, with four bedrooms, four bathrooms, and a backyard orchard of papaya, banana, and avocado trees. Among the many perks: marble bathrooms, fresh *lilikoi* juice served with the delicious breakfast each morning, and proprietors who raised four children here and love the island.

1168 Lanai Ave., Lanai City. https://dreamscometruelanai.com ℂ **808/565-6961** or 808/565-7211. 4 rooms, or entire house. Double $161; $644 entire house, plus $100 cleaning fee. Rates include full breakfast. **Amenities:** Laundry; barbecue; free Wi-Fi.

Camping at Hulopoe Beach Park ★★★

There is only one legal place to camp on Lanai, but it's a beauty. **Hulopoe Beach Park** (www.lanai96763.com/information; ℂ **808/215-1107**) has eight campsites on the shady grass lawn fronting this idyllic white-sand beach. Facilities include restrooms, showers, barbecues, and picnic tables; bring an air mattress or sleeping pad along with a tent and the rest of your gear. You can buy food, ice, and other basic supplies a half-mile away at the harbor, or pony up for a meal at the nearby Four Seasons. To request a first-come, first-served permit, e-mail info@lanaibeachpark.com at least 72 hours in advance. (*Note:* National holiday windows—Thanksgiving, Christmas, Fourth of July, etc.—are reserved for residents.) You'll pay an $80 permit fee, which covers four people for 3 nights. Payment is by credit card only, paid on arrival.

WHERE TO EAT

Lanai offers dining experiences on two ends of the spectrum, from humble mom-and-pop eateries to world-class culinary adventures, although both are few in number. Expect to pay more here than on the larger islands, because of transportation costs; and posh resort restaurants require especially deep pockets. Lanai can claim a food truck, though: **Anuenue Juice Truck ★**, selling fresh cold-pressed juices, smoothies, acai and pitaya bowls. It's parked by Lanai High and Elementary School, 555 Fraser Ave., weekday afternoons and by Dole Park 8am to noon Saturday, during the weekly **Lanai Market Place** (see "Shopping," p. 307).

Note: You'll find the restaurants reviewed in this chapter on the map on p. 283.

Very Expensive

Nobu Lanai ★★★ JAPANESE   What does Lanai have in common with New York, Milan, Budapest, and Mexico City? All have a Nobu restaurant—a measure of how fun a place is, according to pop star Madonna. The best way to experience this epicurean phenomenon is to order the *omakase*—the chef's tasting menu—for $195 (all diners in your party must order it). Some dishes are found only on Lanai, and all are as delicious as they are artful: the smoked Wagyu gyoza with jalapeño miso, the immaculate plates of nigiri sushi, and the ahi avocado salad with greens grown at Alberta de Jetley's farm up the road. A teppanyaki tasting menu—15 courses for $250—is available at one of the two teppan tables. The wine and cocktail list is topnotch, including exclusive Hokusetu sake and a sassy caipirinha with Pisco, fresh lime, ginger beer, and sprigs of shiso. The resident sake master can recommend the right pairing; you can also learn the subtleties of a dry *onigorishi* and a dynamic *daiginjo* at 4pm tastings on Sundays.

At the Four Seasons Resort Lanai, 1 Manele Bay Rd., Lanai City. www.noburestaurants. com/lanai/dining. © **808/565-2832.** Sushi rolls $8–$22, main courses $19–$58; 15-course tasting menu $195. Daily 6–9pm.

One Forty ★★★ BREAKFAST/STEAK & SEAFOOD   Named for the number of miles in the radius in which the restaurant tries to source most of its ingredients (i.e., within the state of Hawaii), this restaurant shines day and night. The over-the-top **breakfast buffet** ($55) rivals the best in Hawaii, while the view overlooking Manele Bay ain't bad either. Besides the mandatory platters of ripe tropical fruit, "make-your-own" omelet and smoothie stations, cheese, and charcuterie found at other resort buffets, One Forty offers four types of sausages, brioche French toast, gourmet breakfast burritos, dim sum, congee malted waffles, and a machine cranking out hot *malasadas* (Portuguese doughnut holes), among other delicacies. For a fall-of-Rome level of decadence, order the Petrossian salmon ($98); it comes with organic scrambled eggs, avocado, and Tsar Imperial caviar (of course). Dinner is equally sumptuous. Look for the Lanai rack of venison, a hearty 15-oz. portion with goat cheese and plum tart ($72), or Maine lobster, actually reared in the deep, chilly ocean waters off Keahole on the Big Island, and served with crispy garlic and roasted corn ($72). For $28, you can also add a Keahole lobster tail to any entree, including the cuts of Wagyu beef ($59–$74) and vegetarian dishes such as the Penang red curry ($42). Order the chocolate soufflé early; it takes 20 minutes to bake but is worth every second of the wait.

At the Four Seasons Resort Lanai, 1 Manele Bay Rd., Lanai City. www.fourseasons.com/ lanai/dining. © **808/565-2290.** Breakfast main courses $16–$33; buffet $55; dinner $32–$95. Daily 6:30–11am and 5:30–9pm.

Moderate

Lanai City Bar & Grille ★★ AMERICAN   This Lanai mainstay has three comfortable dining areas to choose from: the bright and lovely dining room, the bar with large-screen TVs and couchlike chairs, and the outdoor patio where Hawaiian musicians croon under the stars. Local venison is the star of executive chef Joel Harrington's menu, which also features fresh seafood and farm-sourced pasta, burgers, and specialty cocktails; save room for the bananas Foster bread pudding. The service is friendly if a tad slow. Bring a jacket if you want to sit outside by the firepits and soak up the friendly Lanai ambience and fantastic live music.

At the Hotel Lanai, 828 Lanai Ave., Lanai City. https://lanaicitybarandgrille.com. © **808/565-7212.** Main courses $18–$34. Tues–Thurs 5–10pm; Fri–Sat 5–11pm; Sun 10am–3pm.

Malibu Farm ★ AMERICAN   The Lanai outpost of Swedish chef Helene Henderson's organic, farm-focused Malibu Farm Pier Cafe in Southern California, the Four Seasons' poolside restaurant—open for lunch and cocktail hour only—offers the healthful/comfort fare favored by the Hollywood set. If you skipped breakfast, start with an acai bowl or fried egg sandwich with Havarti cheese and bacon; for lunch, black quinoa and white rice accompany the local fish sandwich, while one of the seven salads pairs burrata and papaya. At dusk, pull up a seat at the bar for a craft cocktail and watch the sun melt into the sea.

At the Four Seasons Resort Lanai, 1 Manele Bay Rd., Lanai City. www.fourseasons.com/lanai/dining. © **808/565-2092.** Main courses $18–$34. Daily 11am–5pm; cocktails 5–6pm.

Inexpensive

Blue Ginger Cafe ★ COFFEE SHOP   With its cheery curtains and oilcloth-covered tables, this humble eatery welcomes residents and locals alike in for eggs and Spam (a beloved breakfast meat in Hawaii), epic plates of fried rice, fried chicken katsu, grilled mahi-mahi sandwiches and burgers, and decent egg/tuna/chicken-salad sandwiches on homemade bread. The kitchen staff bakes all of its own breads and pastries, so burgers and sandwiches taste especially fresh. Hot out of the oven, the blueberry turnovers, cinnamon buns, and cookies are local favorites; come at noon for the day's fresh bread.

409 Seventh St. (at Ilima St.), Lanai City. www.bluegingercafelanai.com. © **808/565-6363.** Breakfast and lunch items under $17; dinner main courses under $18. Cash only. Thurs–Mon 6am–8pm; Tues–Wed 6am–2pm.

Coffee Works ★ COFFEEHOUSE   A block from Dole Park, this cozy coffeehouse churns out excellent espresso drinks, plus "small kine" breakfast and lunch items: amply loaded lox and bagels, acai bowls, ice cream, quesadillas, and sandwiches. The renovated plantation home is the perfect place to fuel up in the morning. It's also Lanai City's local watering hole—expect to see your waiter from dinner last night chatting away with the shuttle driver on the wide wooden deck. As you wait for your cappuccino, browse the gift items opposite the counter: T-shirts to prove you were here, tea infusers and pots, and island coffee beans.

604 Ilima St. (at Sixth St.), Lanai City. www.coffeeworkshawaii.com. © **808/565-6962.** Most items under $15. Mon–Fri 7am–4pm; Sat 8am–3pm; Sun 8am–noon.

Lanai City Service/Plantation Store & Deli ★ DELI   The island's sole gas station includes a souvenir shop and deli with tasty sandwiches and a few hot items. It's more gourmet than you might expect: Grilled cheese features Boursin, Swiss, provolone, and avocado, while the crab-cake special hoagie comes with wasabi black-pepper mayo. Check the Lanai City Service Facebook page for daily specials and plan to picnic elsewhere; this is a gas station, after all.

1036 Lanai Ave., Lanai City. © **808/565-7227.** Lunch items $5–$11. Deli open daily 6am–4pm; gas station and store till 10pm.

Pele's Other Garden ★ DELI/BISTRO   The checkered floor and vanity license plates decorating the walls set an upbeat tone at this casual bistro in a cheery yellow cottage. For lunch, dig into an avocado and feta wrap or an Italian hoagie. Cheese lovers will melt over the thin-crusted four-cheese pizza—a gooey medley of mozzarella, Parmesan, feta, and provolone. During happy hour, nosh on onion rings, coconut shrimp, and similar snacks at one of Lanai City's two bars. Enjoy cocktails, wine by the glass, or one of the dozen brews on tap (just $5). The atmosphere grows a bit more romantic after sundown, with white linens on tables and twinkle lights over outdoor seating.

811 Houston St., Lanai City. https://pelesothergarden.com. © **808/565-9628.** Main courses $11–$17 lunch, $17–$20 dinner; pizza from $11. Lunch Mon–Fri 11am–2pm; happy hour Mon–Sat 4:30–6:30pm; dinner Mon–Sat 5–8pm.

EXPLORING LANAI

You'll need an off-road vehicle to reach most of the sights listed below. Four-wheel-drive rentals on Lanai are expensive—but worth it for a day or two of adventure. For details on vehicle rentals, see "Getting Around," above.

Your first stop on Lanai (perhaps after baptizing yourself at Hulopoe Beach) should be the **Lanai Culture & Heritage Center** ★★, 730 Lanai Ave. (www.lanaichc.org; © **808/565-7177**), located in the heart of town. Orient yourself to the island's cultural and natural history at this tiny, well-curated museum. Learn how indigenous Hawaiians navigated thousands of miles of Pacific Ocean, see relics of the Dole plantation years, and get directions to the island's petroglyph fields. Even better, ask the docents to recount local legends passed down in their families. It's open weekdays 8:30am to 3:30pm; admission is free, but donations are greatly appreciated.

Note: You'll find the following attractions on the map on p. 283.

Kanepuu Preserve ★

This ancient grove on Lanai's western plateau is the island's last remaining dryland forest, containing 48 native species. A self-guided hike allows visitors to see the rare trees and shrubs, including sandalwood, that once covered the dry lowlands of all the main Hawaiian Islands. Elsewhere these species have succumbed to axis deer, agriculture, and "progress." The botanical marvels

ESPECIALLY FOR kids

Exploring Hulopoe Tide Pools

(p. 301) An entire world of marine life lives in the tide pools on the eastern side of Hulopoe Bay. Everything in the water, including the tiny fish, is small—kid size. After examining the wonders of the tide pool, check out the larger swimming holes in the lava rock, perfect for children.

Hunting for Petroglyphs

(p. 299) The Luahiwa Petroglyph Field, located just outside Lanai City, is spread out over a 3-acre site. Make it a game: Whoever finds the most petroglyphs gets ice cream from the Pine Isle Market.

Listening to Storytellers Check with the **Lanai Public and School Library,** 555 Fraser Ave. (near Fifth St.), in town (www.librarieshawaii.org/branch/lanai-public-and-school-library; ✆ **808/565-7920**), to see if any storytelling or other children's activities are scheduled. The events are usually free and

open to everyone. Storytelling for preschoolers is usually held on Friday at 10am, and "Game Day Fun" (playing board and card games) for age 8 and up is on Wednesday at 1:30pm. Lego building for all ages takes place Thursday at 5pm.

Playing with Clay The **Lanai Art Center** (p. 299) by Dole Park offers hourlong classes each Wednesday at 1:30pm that teach kids the basics of working with clay. Your child can create a ceramic souvenir and gain some creative skills for a drop-in fee of $5.

Cuddling the Kitties As long your kids aren't allergic, they'll love romping with the hundreds of furry felines in the open-air, nonprofit **Lanai Cat Sanctuary** (p. 298) near the airport. It's open daily and free, although donations are very welcome.

growing within this 590-acre reserve include *olopua* (Hawaiian olive), *lama* (Hawaiian ebony), and *ma'o hau hele* (a Hawaiian hibiscus), among others. Kanepuu is easily reached via 4WD. Head west from Koele on Polihua Road; in about 1¾ miles, you'll see the fenced area on the left.

Keahiakawelo (Garden of the Gods) ★★★

A four-wheel-drive dirt road leads out of Lanai City, through fallow pineapple fields, past the Kanepuu Preserve (see above) to Keahiakawelo. The rugged beauty of this place is punctuated by boulders strewn by volcanic forces and sculpted by the elements into varying shapes and colors—brilliant reds, oranges, ochers, and yellows.

Modern visitors nicknamed this otherworldly landscape "the Garden of the Gods," but its ancient Hawaiian name, Ke-ahi-a-kawelo, means "the fire of Kawelo." According to legend, it's the site of a sorcerers' battle. Kawelo, a powerful *kahuna* (priest), noticed that the people and animals of Lanai were falling ill. He traced their sickness to smoke coming from the neighboring island of Molokai, visible from Keahiakawelo. There, an ill-intentioned priest, Lanikaula, sat chanting over a fire. Kawelo started a fire of his own, here at Keahiakawelo, and tossed some of Lanikaula's excrement into the flames.

Abandoned and feral cats used to roam freely around the island, unless someone called animal control, which promptly euthanized them. Lanai City resident Kathy Carroll decided there must be a better way to care for these creatures and cajoled Castle & Cooke, then the island's owners, into donating 3 acres near the airport for the island's first shelter, now known as the **Lanai Cat Sanctuary** ★★★ (1 Kaupili Rd., https://lanaicatsanctuary.org; 📞 **808/ 215-9066**). Deer netting, wooden pallets, and baskets allowed for the first simple but effective open-air housing, which also serves to protect the island's rare native and migratory birds from predation. Today the cleverly arranged, brightly painted compound hosts more than 600 "Lanai lions"; senior cats and those needing medical care are lovingly tended in separate areas. You're welcome to drop by, free of charge, any day of the week between 10am and 3pm to pet and play with the healthy, spayed and neutered felines. Sporting gleaming ginger, gray, tuxedo and tabby coats, the cats love to perch on visitors' laps. **Rabaca's Limousine** (p. 289) will shuttle you here for $10 from the harbor, airport or hotels. **Lost on Lanai** (https://lostonlanai.com; 📞 **888/716-6366**) can arrange round-trip ferry tickets from Lahaina and transportation to and from the sanctuary for $85 adults, $65 children ages 2 to 11. The temptation will be to take a cat back with you—which can certainly be arranged—but the nonprofit sanctuary also gratefully accepts donations, including funds to "adopt in place."

The smoke turned purple, Lanikaula perished, and health and prosperity returned to Lanai.

Take the dusty, bumpy drive out to Keahiakewalo early in the morning or just before sunset, when the light casts eerie shadows on the mysterious lava formations. Drive west from Koele on Polihua Road; in about 2 miles, you'll see a hand-painted sign pointing left down a one-lane, red-dirt road through a *kiawe* forest to the large stone sign. Don't stack rocks or otherwise disturb this interesting site; please leave everything as you found it.

Munro Trail ★

In the first golden rays of dawn, when owls swoop silently over the abandoned pineapple fields, take a peek at **Mount Lanaihale,** the 3,366-foot summit of Lanai. If it's clear, hop into a 4×4 and head for the Munro Trail, the narrow, winding ridge trail that runs across Lanai's razorback spine to its peak. From here, you may get a rare treat: On a clear day, you can see most of the main islands in the Hawaiian chain.

But if it's raining, forget it. On rainy days, the Munro Trail becomes slick and boggy with major washouts. Rainy-day excursions often end with a rental jeep on the hook of a tow truck—and a $500 tow charge. You could even slide off into a major gulch and never be found, so don't try it. But in late August and September, when tradewinds stop blowing and the air over the islands stalls in what's called a *kona* condition, Mount Lanaihale's suddenly visible summit becomes an irresistible attraction.

Look for a red-dirt road off Manele Road (Hwy. 440), about 5 miles south of Lanai City; turn left and head up the ridgeline. No sign marks the peak, so you'll have to keep an eye out. Look for a wide spot in the road and a clearing that falls sharply to the sea. From here you can also see silver domes of Space City atop the summit of Haleakala on Maui; Puu Moaulanui, the summit of arid Kahoolawe; the tiny crescent of Molokini; and, looming above the clouds, Mauna Kea on Hawaii Island. At another clearing farther along the thickly forested ridge, all of Molokai, including the 4,961-foot summit of Kamakou and the faint outline of Oahu (more than 30 miles across the sea), are visible. For details on hiking the trail, see "Hiking" on p. 306.

Luahiwa Petroglyph Field ★★

Lanai is second only to the Big Island in its wealth of prehistoric rock art, but you'll have to search a little to find it. Some of the best examples are on the outskirts of Lanai City, on a hillside site known as Luahiwa Petroglyph Field. The characters incised on 13 boulders in this grassy 3-acre knoll include a running man, a canoe, turtles, and curly-tailed dogs (a latter-day wag put a leash on one).

To get here, take Manele Road from Lanai City toward Hulopoe Beach. About 2 miles out of town, you'll see a pump house on the left. Look up on the hillside for a cluster of dark boulders—the petroglyphs are there, but you'll have to zigzag to get to them. Two dirt roads lead off of Manele Road, on either side of the pump house. Take the first one, which leads straight toward the hillside. After about 1 mile, you'll come to a fork. Head right. Drive for another ½ mile. At the first V in the road, take a sharp left and double back the way you came, this time on an upper road. After about ¼ mile; you'll come to the large cluster of boulders on the right. It's just a short walk up the cliffs (wear walking or hiking shoes) to the petroglyphs. Exit the same way you came. Go between 3pm and sunset for ideal viewing and photo ops. Don't touch the petroglyphs or climb on the rocks; these cultural resources are very fragile.

Rainy-Day Fun: Lanai Art Center

A perfect activity for a rainy day in Lanai City is a class at the **Lanai Art Center,** 339 Seventh St., in the center of town. Top artists from across Hawaii frequently visit this homegrown art program and teach a variety of classes, including *raku* (Japanese pottery), silk printing, silk screening, creating your own design on the islander wrap known as a pareo, and watercolor drawing, among other crafts. The cost for the 2- to 3-hour classes is usually in the $25-to-$70 range (materials are extra). For information, call ℂ **808/565-7503** or visit www.lanaiart.org.

Kaunolu Village ★★

Out on Lanai's nearly vertical, Gibraltar-like sea cliffs is an old royal compound and fishing village. Now a national historic landmark and one of Hawaii's most treasured ruins, it's believed to have been inhabited by King Kamehameha the Great and hundreds of his closest followers about 200 years ago.

It's a hot, dry 3-mile 4×4 drive from Lanai City to Kaunolu, but the mini-expedition is worth it. Take plenty of water, don a hat for protection against the sun, and wear sturdy shoes. Signs explain the sacred site's importance. Ruins of 86 house platforms and 35 stone shelters have been identified on both sides of Kaunolu Gulch. The residential complex also includes the **Halulu Heiau temple,** named after a mythical man-eating bird. The king's royal retreat is thought to have stood on the eastern edge of Kaunolu Gulch, overlooking the rocky shore facing **Kahekili's Leap.** Chiefs leapt from the 62-foot-high perch as a show of bravado. Nearby are **burial caves,** a **fishing shrine,** a **lookout tower,** and warrior-like stick figures—**petroglyphs**—carved on boulders. Just offshore stands the distinctive rock formation of **Shark Fin Rock,** a popular dive spot that teems with bright tropical fish and, frequently, sharks.

off the tourist trail: EASTSIDE LANAI

If you've got good weather and a trusty 4×4 vehicle, go find adventure on Lanai's untamed east side. Bring snacks and extra water; there are no facilities out here and cell service is scarce. Follow Keomoku Road for 8 miles to the coast. Here the road turns to dirt, mud, or sand; proceed with caution. Head left to find **Shipwreck Beach** and the **Kukui Point petroglyphs** (p. 302).

Venture right to explore a string of empty beaches and abandoned villages, including **Keomoku**—about 5¾ miles down the rough-and-tumble dirt road. This former ranching and fishing community of 2,000 was home to the first non-Hawaiian settlement on Lanai. A ghost town since the mid-1950s, it dried up after droughts killed off the Maunalei Sugar Company. Check out **Ka Lanakila,** a sweetly restored church that dates back to 1903.

Continue another 2 miles to the deserted remains of **Club Lanai,** where day-trippers used to arrive by boat from Maui, seen from the quiet shore. A lonely pier stretches into the Pacific from a golden-sand beach populated by coconut palms, a few gazebos, and an empty bar floating in a lagoon. You can pretend you're on the set of *Gilligan's Island* or *Lost* here. This secluded area's Hawaiian name, **Kahalepaloa,** means "whale ivory house." Historians speculate that the teeth and bones of a sperm whale—rare in these waters—once washed ashore here. If you have time, press on to **Lopa Beach** (good for surfing, not for swimming), home to one of Lanai's four ancient fishponds. The road ends at **Naha Beach,** home to another fishpond and surf break. Return the way you came, carefully, and take any trash with you.

From Lanai City, take Kaumalapau Highway (Hwy. 440) past the airport. Look for a carved boulder on the left side of the road. Turn left onto a dirt road (Kaupili Rd.) and drive east until you see another carved boulder. Turn right, toward the ocean. *Tip:* On your way out, turn right to continue on Kaupili Road. It meets with Hulopoe Drive, a shortcut to Manele Bay.

BEACHES

If you like big, wide, empty, gold-sand beaches and crystal-clear, cobalt-blue water full of bright tropical fish—and who doesn't?—go to Lanai. With 18 miles of sandy shoreline, Lanai has some of Hawaii's least crowded and most interesting beaches. Relax on the sand with a Tommy Bahama backpack beach chair rented for $10 from **808 Day Trip** (www.808daytrip.com; © **808/649-0664**). *Note:* For descriptions of the east side's **Kahalepaloa, Lopa** and **Naha** beaches, see "Off the Tourist Trail," p. 300.

Hulopoe Beach ★★★

Hulopoe is one of the loveliest beaches in all of Hawaii. Palm-fringed golden sand is bordered by black-lava fingers, which protect swimmers from ocean currents. The bay at the foot of the Four Seasons Resort Lanai is a protected marine preserve, with schools of colorful fish, spinner dolphins, and humpback whales that cruise by in winter and often stop to put on a show. The water is perfect for snorkeling, swimming, or just lolling about; the water temperature is usually in the mid-70s (mid-20s Celsius). Swells kick up slightly in winter. Hulopoe is also Lanai's premier beach park, with a grassy lawn, picnic tables, barbecue grills, restrooms, showers, and ample parking. You can camp here, too (p. 293).

HULOPOE'S TIDE POOLS ★★ Some of the best **tide pools** in Hawaii are found along the east side of Hulopoe Bay. These submerged pockets of lava rock are full of strange creatures such as asteroids (sea stars) and holothurians (sea cucumbers), not to mention spaghetti worms, barber pole shrimp, and Hawaii's favorite local delicacy, the *opihi,* a tasty morsel also known as the limpet. Youngsters enjoy swimming in the enlarged tide pool at the eastern edge of the bay. *A few tips:* When you explore tide pools, do so at low tide. Never turn your back on the waves. Wear tennis shoes or reef walkers, as wet rocks are slippery. Collecting specimens in this marine preserve is forbidden, so don't take any souvenirs home.

Polihua Beach ★

According to legend, a mythical sea turtle once hauled herself out of the water to lay her eggs in the deep sand at Polihua, or "egg nest." This deserted beach lies at the end of Polihua Road, a 4-mile Jeep trail. When it isn't windy, this huge, empty stretch on Lanai's northwestern shore is ideal for beachcombing, fishing, or indulging fantasies of being marooned on a desert island. When the wind *is* blowing, beware—you'll be sandblasted. Look for treasures in the flotsam and (during winter months) whales on the horizon. There are no facilities except fishermen's huts and driftwood shelters. Bring water and sunscreen. Strong currents and undertow make the water here unsafe for swimming.

Shipwreck Beach ★★

This 8-mile-long windswept strand on Lanai's northeastern shore—named for the rusty ship *Liberty* abandoned on the coral reef, and actually several beaches—is a sailor's nightmare and a beachcomber's dream. The strong currents yield all sorts of sea debris, from hand-blown glass fishing floats and paper nautilus shells to lots of junk. Shipwreck isn't good for swimming, but it's a great place to spot whales from December to April, when Hawaiian humpbacks cruise in from Alaska. The road to the beach is paved most of the way, but you really need a four-wheel-drive to get down here. At the end of the road, you'll find a trail that leads about 200 yards inland to the **Kukui Point petroglyphs;** follow the stacked rock *ahu* (altars) to the large boulders. Respect this historic site by not adding anything to it or taking anything away. Most important, *do not* touch the petroglyphs; they're very fragile, so just take photos.

WATERSPORTS

Because Lanai lacks major development and experiences very little rainfall/runoff, it typically boasts Hawaii's best water clarity. The coast is washed clean daily by strong sea currents, which can wash you away, too, if you aren't careful where you jump in. Most of the aquatic adventures—swimming, snorkeling, scuba diving—are centered on the somewhat protected west coast, particularly around Hulopoe Bay. Spinner dolphins often cruise this coast, traveling in large pods and leaping from the water to twirl midair. Green sea turtles, humpback whales, and monk seals make appearances, too. For surf breaks, head to the untamed east shore.

Boat trips—along with most island activities—can be booked at the Four Seasons' **Adventure Center** (1 Manele Bay Rd., Lanai City; ✆ **808/565-2072**). Its watersports vendor, **Lanai Ocean Sports** (www.lanaioceansports.com; ✆ **808/866-8256**), offers sailing and snorkeling tours aboard the decked-out 49-foot catamaran *Lanai* and chartered adventures on *Lanai 5*, a 48-foot rigid-hull inflatable that can seat six. Keep in mind that during "festive season" (mid-Dec through the first week of Jan), the boats are fully committed to Four Seasons guests.

Kayaking

Lanai's south and west coastlines offer spectacular vistas: dramatic sea cliffs punctuated by hidden caves, quiet coves, and mysterious sea stacks. You can put kayaks in at **Manele** or **Kaumalapau Harbor**. Both are working harbors, but not very busy; Kaumalapau is closed, however, on barge days (typically Wed–Thurs). From Kaumalapau, paddle roughly two-and-a-half miles north to reach **Nanahoa**, a cluster of needle-like sea stacks. It's a picturesque lunch stop, with a shady cave and rocky apron to pull up onto for a landing. The snorkeling around these islets can be magical. Check weather conditions and currents before you go. You can rent kayaks and gear from **Lanai Adventure Club** (http://jeeplanai.net; ✆ **800/565-7373**). The Club also offers 4-hour guided tours from 8am to noon and 5-hour surf kayak safaris; call for pricing. **Lanai Surf School & Safari** (www.surfinglanai.com; ✆ **808/649-0739**) rents two-person kayaks for $80 for 24 hours.

Sailing & Whale-Watching

Every evening, **Lanai Ocean Sports** (see above) offers a **2-hour sunset sail.** Cruise past sea cliffs and unspoiled coastline while spinner dolphins and flying fish dart ahead of the bow. You'll arrive at Puu Pehe, Sweetheart Rock, just in time for the best sunset shots. The trip costs $125 ($135 for those who aren't guests of the Four Seasons), inclusive of appetizers, open bar, and Dramamine for those who suffer from seasickness.

During whale season (Dec–Mar), Hawaiian humpback whales put on impressive shows, breaching, slapping their pectoral fins, and singing complex melodies underwater. You can view them from just about any spot on Lanai, particularly on the eastside, looking toward Maui. To witness whales up close, hop aboard Lanai Ocean Sports' catamaran for a **2-hour whale-spotting tour.** Scan the horizon for the massive marine mammals, which are almost guaranteed to surface nearby with gusty exhalations. The captain and crew are certified naturalists who make each trip educational. The cost and amenities are the same as the sunset sails.

Snorkeling Tours

To snorkel on your own, simply strap on a mask and head out from **Hulopoe Beach,** provided conditions are calm. The marine-life conservation area is Lanai's best snorkeling spot; fish are abundant in the bay and marine mammals regularly swim by. Try the lava-rock points at either end of the beach and around the tide pools. *Note:* Four Seasons' beachside stand offers complimentary gear, including prescription masks, for guests.

Venture farther afield with **Lanai Ocean Sports** (see above) aboard their 49-foot sailing catamaran. The captains will steer you alongside the island's dramatic southern coast to a site near the Kaunolu lighthouse. The **3-hour snorkel trips** cost $169 for Four Seasons guests ($175 for non-resort guests), with discounts for children 3 to 11; ages 2 and under are free. Offered Tuesday, Thursday, and Saturday, the excursion includes sandwiches, cookies, cocktails, and local microbrews. Help yourself to one of two standup paddleboards onboard and organic sunscreen.

Scuba Diving

Two of Hawaii's best-known dive spots are found in Lanai's clear waters, just off the south shore: **Cathedrals I** and **II**, so named because the sun lights up an underwater grotto like a magnificent church. Green sea turtles (and the occasional hawksbill) bob among the sunny-hued butterflyfish while harlequin shrimp and octopus hide among lava-tube caverns. **Shark Fin Rock** (see above) also teems with coral and a rainbow collection of reef fish. Sadly, the on-island scuba options have shrunk over the years. **Lanai Ocean Sports** (see above) is your best bet. It offers a two-tank dive ($249) every Monday, Wednesday, and Friday; it's certified divers only, so make sure you bring your PADI or NAU card. Pool and intro one-tank dives for Four Seasons guests are offered on request, but be sure to book well in advance. See Maui's "Scuba Diving" section (p. 193) for more options on exploring Lanai's underwater treasures.

Sport Fishing

Sport fishers can charter *Lanai Five*, a 48-foot rigid-hull inflatable from **Lanai Ocean Sports** (see above), for $240 per person, maximum of six people (at least one must be a Four Seasons guest). Request well in advance.

Surfing/Stand-up Paddleboarding (SUP)

If you've ever wanted to learn how to surf, let instructor and surfing champion Nick Palumbo take you on a 4WD surfing safari to a secluded surf spot on the island's rugged eastside. The Lanai native will have you up and riding the waves in no time. His **Lanai Surf School & Surf Safari** ★★ (www.lanaisurf safari.com; ✆ **808/649-0739**) offers 5-hour surf safaris, which include four-wheel-drive transportation to Lopa Beach, refreshments, and "a really good time." The adventures cost $200 per person, minimum of two guests. He also offers stand-up paddleboarding (SUP) lessons at Hulopoe Beach, 2 hours for $100. Already experienced on the waves? The Surf School rents soft-tops surfboards ($6/24 hr.), paddleboards ($50/hr.), and, for shallow-water action, boogie boards and skim boards ($25/24 hr.). **808 Day Trip** (www.808daytrip. com; ✆ **808/649-0664**) rents paddleboards for cruising off Hulopoe Beach for $50 an hour.

OTHER OUTDOOR ACTIVITIES

The **Adventure Center** (www.fourseasons.com/lanai/adventure; ✆ **808/565-2072**) at the **Four Seasons Lanai** (see p. 291) can book an assortment of activities for the general public as well as guests: sporting clays, off-road tours, horseback rides, and more. Located next door to the resort's tennis courts, it's open from 6am to 6pm. *Note:* Except for the sporting clays, nonguests may book activities no more than 24 hours in advance.

Archery & Sporting Clays

Sharpen your shooting skills in two different modes at the **Lanai Archery and Shooting Range**, booked through the Four Seasons **Adventure Center** (see above). Both sharpshooters and novices will enjoy the 14-station shooting clay course in the Lanai uplands, zipping from station to station beneath the whispering ironwood trees in their own golf cart. Each target mimics the movement of a different bird or rabbit; shots grow increasingly difficult as the course progresses. Private lessons start at $125 per person, or $225 per couple, for 1 hour, with options for experienced shooters. Aspiring archers can aim at 3D animal targets or traditional paper bulls-eye's ($75 for 1 hr., $125 for 2 hr.). Wear closed-toe shoes and bring a jacket.

ATV Tours

The Four Seasons' **Adventure Center** (see above) offers the Cadillac version of this excursion. Slide on a sleek helmet, balaclava, and goggles, and mount your Polaris Razor 1000; the off-road suspension is so smooth you'll hardly notice the boulders. Local guides will chauffeur you into the forested uplands above Palawai Basin where you'll explore an ancient agricultural temple, view petroglyphs, and dodge spotted deer. Wear long pants, closed-toed shoes, a jacket, and clothes that can handle dirt. Two-hour tours leave twice daily at 9am and 1:30pm and cost $247.50 for one, $395 per couple. Private guided sunrise tours, which greet dawn at the Naha Lookout, are also available (2 hr. for $375, $495 per couple; and 3 hr. for $425 single, $545 couple). Four Seasons guests can also preorder breakfast for an additional fee.

Biking

The relatively car-free paved roads around Lanai City are ideal for cyclists, but note that biking from the harbor up to Lanai City or down to Shipwrecks and back requires excellent fitness; you'll also have to bring your own bicycle. The Four Seasons **Adventure Center** (see above) rents mountain bikes, but only to guests; a half-day is $30, full day $50.

Golf

Cavendish Golf Course ★   This quirky par-36, 9-hole public course lacks not only a clubhouse and club pros, but also tee times, scorecards, and club rentals. To play, just show up, put a donation into the little wooden box next to the first tee, and hit away. The 3,071-yard, E. B. Cavendish–designed course was built by the Dole plantation in 1947 for its employees. The greens are a bit bumpy, but the views of Lanai are great and the temperatures usually quite mild. You'll need to bring your own clubs; you can't rent them from the Four Seasons golf shop to use here.

Off of Kaunaoa Dr. in Koele. Greens fees by donation.

The Challenge at Manele ★★★   Designed by Jack Nicklaus, this target-style, desert-links course is one of the most challenging courses in the state. Check out some of the course rules: NO RETRIEVING GOLF BALLS FROM THE 150-FOOT CLIFFS ON THE OCEAN HOLES 12, 13, OR 17, and ALL WHALES, AXIS DEER, AND OTHER WILD ANIMALS ARE CONSIDERED IMMOVABLE OBSTRUCTIONS. That's just a hint of the unique experience you'll have on this starkly beautiful oceanfront course, which is routed among lava outcroppings, archaeological sites, and *kiawe* groves. The five sets of staggered tees pose a challenge to everyone from the casual golfer to the pro. The staff hands out complimentary Bloody Marys and screwdrivers to those who partake, and carts come with Bluetooth, so you can stream your own music. *Fun fact:* Bill and Melinda Gates tied the knot at the 12th hole's tee box. The clubhouse's **Views** restaurant is a destination in its own right. Other facilities include a pro shop, rentals, practice area, lockers, and showers.

Next to the Four Seasons Resort Lanai. www.fourseasons.com/lanai. ℂ **808/565-2222.** Greens fees $495 ($350 for hotel guests) adults; $275 ($175 hotel guests) juniors ages 17 and under; replay $100. Club rentals $85 per day (juniors $25).

Horseback Riding

Get a taste of the *paniolo* (cowboy) life on a horseback tour. Sign up for an upland trail ride at the **Four Seasons' Adventure Center** (see above), where you'll catch a shuttle up to Koele and meet your steed. On horseback, you'll meander through guava groves and past ironwood trees; catch glimpses of spotted deer, wild turkeys, and quail; and end with panoramic views of Maui and Lanai. The trails are dusty and rain is frequent; wear clothes you don't mind getting dirty and bring a light jacket. Long pants and closed-toe shoes are required. Daily tours start at 9am, 11am, and 1pm, last 1½ hours, and cost $165 per person. Private rides are available for $220 per person per hour.

Even if you don't book a ride, you may want to visit the stables to "Meet the Minis." Visitors who drop by around lunchtime can help groom the 12 miniature horses and four donkeys; the Four Seasons can arrange a shuttle for hotel guests.

Hiking

For more information on these trails and others, such as the 1-mile **Kealia-Kapu Kaunolu Trail** near the ancient village of Kaunolu (p. 300), visit the **Lanai Culture & Heritage Center website** (www.lanaichc.org) and download its free Lanai Guide app. The **Four Seasons' Adventure Center** (see above) can provide maps for its new **Pohakuloa Gulch** hiking trail near the Manele resort and for **Koloiki Ridge** (see below) near the former Lodge at Koele.

KAPIHAA TRAIL   An old fisherman's trail starts at Manele Bay and snakes along the scenic coastline, passing historic village sites with interpretive signs. This easy, 1-mile round-trip hike will expose you to Lanai's unique geography, cultural heritage, and many unusual native Hawaiian coastal plants.

KOLOIKI RIDGE HIKE The leisurely 2-hour self-guided hike starts behind the former Lodge at Koele and takes you on a 5-mile loop through stands of Norfolk Island pines, into Hulopoe Valley, past wild ginger, and up to Koloiki Ridge, with its panoramic view of Maunalei and Naio gulches and the islands of Molokai and Maui in the distance. Go in the morning; by afternoon, the clouds usually roll in, marring visibility at the top and increasing your chance of being caught in a downpour. It's considered moderate, with some uphill and downhill hiking; it overlaps with the Munro Trail (see below) along a dirt road from here.

MUNRO TRAIL This tough, 11-mile (round-trip) uphill climb through groves of Norfolk pines is a lung-buster, but if you reach the top, you'll be rewarded with a breathtaking view of Molokai, Maui, Kahoolawe, and Hawaii Island. Figure on 7 hours. The trail begins at Lanai Cemetery (interesting in its own right) along Keomoku Road (Hwy. 440) and follows Lanai's ancient caldera rim, ending up at the island's highest point, **Lanaihale.** Go in the morning for the best visibility. After 4 miles, you'll get a view of Lanai City. The weary retrace their steps from here, while the more determined go the last 1.25 miles to the top. Diehards head down Lanai's steep south-crater rim to join the highway leading to Manele Bay.

PUU PEHE Skirt along Hulopoe Bay to scale the cliff on its southern edge (it's a gentle slope, not a steep climb). This 20-minute hike leads above the turquoise-gray waters to the dramatic point overlooking Puu Pehe, or Sweetheart's Rock. The picturesque islet rises 80 feet from the sea and is home to nesting seabirds. Look closely and you'll see an *'ahu,* altar of rocks at the top. According to legend, a young Lanai warrior hid his beautiful wife in a sea cave at the base of the cliffs here. One day a storm flooded the cave and she drowned. Grief-stricken, her beloved climbed the sheer face of the islet, carrying her body. He buried her, then jumped to his death in the pounding surf below.

Tennis

Three public courts, lit for night play, are available in Lanai City at no charge; call ✆ **808/565-6979** for reservations. If you're staying at the Four Seasons (p. 291), you can take advantage of the upgraded "tennis garden," with its two Plexi-Pave cushion courts and Har-Tru green clay court—the same used by the pros. Court access comes with complimentary use of Prince rackets, balls, and bottled water—even shoes if you need them.

SHOPPING

Lanai has limited shopping, but you can find some gems here. A stroll around Dole Park will yield original artwork, clothing, and souvenirs, and the Four Seasons has well-curated boutiques. Just remember that groceries are delivered only once a week (Thurs is barge day); plan your shopping accordingly.

Shops are typically open from 9am to 6pm Monday to Saturday, with more limited hours on Sunday. *Note:* The **Fifth Friday Lanai** events, from 5:30 to 8pm on the fifth Friday of each month, attract a good variety of local artisans.

Art

Lanai Art Center ★★ Established in 1989, the Lanai Art Center showcases works by island residents, including evocative watercolor paintings of local landmarks, silkscreened clothing, and jewelry. Often, the artists are at work in back. The center also offers painting parties and reasonably priced workshops; artists offer instruction on everything from *raku* (Japanese pottery) to silk printing, lei-making, and *gyotaku* (printing a real fish on your own T-shirt). 339 Seventh St., Lanai City. www.lanaiart.org. ✆ **808/565-7503.**

Mike Carroll Gallery ★★★ Oil painter Mike Carroll left a successful 22-year career as a professional artist in Chicago for a distinctly slower pace on Lanai a year after visiting here in 2000. Today, his gorgeous, color-saturated interpretations of local life and landscapes fill the walls of his gallery, which also sells original work by top Maui and Lanai artists. Sales of Carroll's charming "Cats in Paradise" oils, prints, and photos help support the ingenious **Lanai Cat Sanctuary** (p. 298), which wife Kathy Carroll founded. 443 Seventh St., Lanai City. www.mikecarrollgallery.com. ✆ **808/565-7122.**

Edibles & Grocery Staples

Pine Isle Market ★ The Honda family has operated this grocery since 1949 (though its sign says "est. 1951.") Three doors down from Richard's (below), it carries everything that its competition doesn't; a visit to both will net you a fine haul. Pine Isle specializes in locally caught fresh fish, but you can also find ice cream, canned goods, fresh herbs, toys, diapers, paint, and other essentials. Take a spin through the fishing section to ogle every imaginable lure. The market is open Monday to Saturday 8am to 7pm and Sunday 8am to 5pm. 356 Eighth St., Lanai City. ✆ **808/565-6488.**

Richard's Market ★★ Since 1949, this family grocery has been the go-to for dry goods, frozen meats and vegetables, liquor, paper products, cosmetics, utensils, and other miscellany. After a major makeover, courtesy of Larry Ellison and Pulama Lanai, it now resembles a miniature Whole Foods with an array of fancy chocolates and fine wines, along with aloha shirts, foldup *lauhala* mats, and poke (raw seasoned fish) at the fish counter. Don't faint when you see that milk costs $9 a gallon; that's the price of paradise. Open daily 6am to 10pm. 434 Eighth St., Lanai City. ✆ **808/565-3781.**

Lanai Market Place ★ From 8am to noon-ish each Saturday, the southeast corner of Dole Park turns into a farmer's market. Lanai residents bring their homegrown fruits and vegetables, freshly baked pastries, plate lunches, and handicrafts to sell. If you want one of Juanita's scrumptious pork flautas with a dollop of hot sauce, get here early. Other treats include fresh pressed juices from the Anuenue Juice Truck and fantastic Thai summer rolls.

Gifts & Souvenirs

In addition to the Lanai City shops below, adults will find elegant splurges on swimwear, jewelry, and housewares at the **Makamae** and **Pilina** boutiques in the Four Seasons Resort Lanai (p. 291); the resort's sundries store **Mua Loa** carries cute children's items and beach gear.

The Local Gentry ★★ Jenna (Gentry) Majkus manages to outfit her small but wonderful boutique with every wardrobe essential, from fancy lingerie to stylish chapeaux, for the whole family, plus accessories and gifts, including Maui Jim sunglasses. 363 Seventh St., Lanai City. ✆ **808/565-9130.**

Rainbow Pharmacy ★★ Like so many island institutions, this pharmacy plays dual roles. It's not just a place to fill your prescription or stock up on earplugs and sunburn gel; you'll also find quality locally made souvenirs here (including coin purses and clutches crafted with vintage Hawaiian fabric by Lanai native Cory Labang). From the counter in back, you can order an assortment of medicinal Chinese teas and—surprise—shave ice. 431 Seventh St., Lanai City. ✆ **808/565-9332.**

LANAI NIGHTLIFE

The Four Seasons and Hotel Lanai are the island's two mainstays for nightlife. Before sunset, head to **Malibu Farm** at the **Four Seasons Resort Lanai,** 1 Manele Bay Rd. (www.fourseasons.com/lanai; ✆ **808/565-2093**), for cocktails; after dark, you can shoot pool in the resort's **Sports Bar & Grill.** The heated outdoor patio at **Lanai City Bar & Grille** ★★, part of the Hotel Lanai, 828 Lanai Ave. (www.opentable.com/lanai-city-grille; ✆ **808/565-7212**), lets you enjoy jam sessions by local musicians under the stars; karaoke may be a weekly event by the time you read this. Bring a jacket if you plan to sit outside, just in case you're not close to a firepit or heat lamp.

Another fun option is the wonderfully renovated Lanai Theater, also named **Hale Keaka** ★ (www.lanai96763.com/showtimes; 456 Seventh St., Lanai City). Built in 1926, this iconic landmark shared films, live plays, and musical performances with the community for 80 years. A $4-million renovation in 2015 kept the vintage feel but added air-conditioning, digital sound, two stages and screens, cushy seats, and more. Two films—an adult and a children's selection—change weekly. The box office opens 1 hour prior to the start of each movie; tickets are $10 adults, $9 seniors and students, $7 children ages 3 to 11. And because it's Lanai, you'll find *furikake* and shoyu among the complimentary popcorn condiments.

Occasionally, special events will bring in a few more nightlife options. Some of Hawaii's best musicians arrive to show their support for Lanai during the annual **Pineapple Festival** (www.lanaipineapplefestival.com), generally the first weekend in July (see "Maui County Calendar of Events," p. 20). The **Aloha Festival** (www.alohafestivals.com) takes place at the end of September or during the first week in October, and the **Christmas Festival** is held on the first Saturday in December. For details on these festivals, contact the **Lanai Visitors Bureau,** c/o Maui Visitors Bureau (www.gohawaii.com/lanai; © **800/947-4774** or 808/565-7600).

PLANNING
YOUR TRIP TO
MAUI

Maui may be a paradise in many respects, but it's not Disneyland: For optimum enjoyment and safety, you do need to plan ahead and take reasonable precautions once you're on the island. While travelers from the U.S. mainland should have no problems navigating their way around the Valley Isle, all visitors should take note of local customs, such as removing one's shoes before entering a residence, and be aware that the forces of nature, especially the ocean, demand special respect.

GETTING THERE & GETTING AROUND

Getting to Maui

BY PLANE

If you think of the island of Maui as the shape of a head and shoulders of a person, you'll probably arrive at its neck, at **Kahului Airport** (OGG). If you're headed for Lanai (LNY), you'll usually need to connect through Honolulu (HNL); Molokai (MKK) has air service from both Kahului and Honolulu.

Try to avoid a layover in Honolulu if possible, since it can add several hours to your travel time. Many airlines offer nonstop flights to Maui from the mainland U.S., including **Hawaiian Airlines** (www.hawaiianair.com; ✆ 800/367-5320), **Alaska Airlines** (www.alaskaair.com; ✆ 800/252/7522), **United Airlines** (www.united.com; ✆ 800/241-6522), **Delta Air Lines** (www.delta.com; ✆ 800/221-1212), **American Airlines** (www.aa.com; ✆ 800/882-8880), and **Southwest Airlines** (www.southwest.com; ✆ 800/435-9792). The only international flights to Maui originate in Canada. **Air Canada** (www.aircanada.com; ✆ 888/247-2262) has daily service from Vancouver and Calgary, Alberta; **WestJet** (www.

westjet.com; ✆ **888/937-8538**) flies daily from Vancouver, with seasonal service from Calgary and Edmonton, Alberta, from December to April.

Other major carriers stop in Honolulu, where you'll typically catch an interisland flight to Maui on **Hawaiian.** The carrier also offers daily nonstop flights to Kahului from Kauai (LIH) and Hawaii Island's Kona (KOA) and Hilo (ITO) airports, in case you plan to island-hop. Hawaiian's **Ohana by Hawaiian** subsidiary also flies to Lanai and Molokai from Honolulu.

Commuter service **Mokulele Airlines** (www.mokuleleairlines.com; ✆ **866/260-7070**) flies from Honolulu to Kahului and Maui's two other, significantly smaller airports. If you're staying in Lahaina or Kaanapali, you might consider flying in or out of **Kapalua–West Maui Airport** (JHM). From this tiny airstrip, it's only a 10- to 15-minute drive to most hotels in West Maui, as opposed to an hour or more from Kahului. Same story with **Hana Airport** (HNM): Flying directly here will save you a challenging 3-hour drive. However, rental-car pickup at either Kapalua or Hana airports is very limited.

From Kahului, Mokulele also flies several times a day to Molokai and to two airports on the Big Island: the small commuter airfield at Kamuela (MUE) and the much busier Kona, near the main resorts. Mokulele also offers charter flights to Lanai. Check-in is a breeze: no security lines (unless leaving from Honolulu). You'll be weighed, ushered onto the tarmac, and welcomed aboard a nine-seat Cessna. The plane flies low, and the views between the islands are outstanding.

If you want to continue your travels in the Pacific or Asia, the short hop to Honolulu will connect you to nonstop flights to Japan, South Korea, China, the Philippines, Australia, New Zealand, Fiji, Samoa, or Tahiti.

ARRIVING AT THE AIRPORT

If there's a long wait at baggage claim, step over to the state-operated **Visitor Information Center,** where you can ask about island activities and pick up brochures and the latest issue of *This Week Maui,* which features great regional maps of the islands. After collecting your bags from the poky carousels, turn right at the exit and walk to the rental-car shuttle pickup area, and wait in line (often breezy and hot) for the appropriate shuttle van to take you a half-mile away to the rental-car lots. (All major rental companies have branches at Kahului; see "Getting Around Maui," below.)

If you're not renting a car, the cheapest way to exit the airport is the **Maui Bus** (www.mauicounty.gov/bus; ✆ **808/871-4838**). For $2, it will deposit you at any one of the island's major towns. Simply cross the street at baggage claim and wait under the awning. Unfortunately, bus stops are far and few between, so you'll end up lugging your suitcase a long way to your destination. A much more convenient option is **Roberts Hawaii Express Shuttle** (www.airportshuttlehawaii.com/shuttles/maui; ✆ **866/898-2523** or

If you're looking for a taste of several islands, consider a cruise ship. Several lines regularly visit Hawaii; two in stark contrast to each other are **Norwegian Cruise Line** (www.ncl.com; $\mathcal{C}$ **800/327-7030**) and **Adventure Smith Explorations** (www.AdventureSmith Explorations.com; $\mathcal{C}$ **800/728-2875**). Norwegian's 2,240-passenger *Pride of America* circles the islands weekly, launching from Honolulu and calling in Kahului, Hilo and Kailua-Kona on Hawaii, and Nawiliwili Harbor on Kauai before returning to Oahu. Prices range from $1,329 to $4,100 per person. Adventure Smith Explorations' 145-foot *Safari Explorer* holds just 36 passengers in 18 staterooms. Its 8-day cruises start on Molokai and visit Lanai and West Maui before ending on Hawaii Island. Rates run from $5,200 to $8,400 per person. The disadvantage of a cruise is that you won't be able to see any of the islands in depth, although both ships offer a variety of intriguing excursions; the advantage is that your island-hopping won't involve repacking or time in airport security lines.

808/439-8800), which offers curb-to-curb service in a shared van or small bus and easy online booking. Plan to pay $24 (one-way) to Wailea and $34 to Kaanapali. **SpeediShuttle Maui** (www.speedishuttle.com; $\mathcal{C}$ **877/242-5777**) offers one-way, shared van service from the Kahului airport, ranging from $45 to Wailea to $62 to Kaanapali; it also offers shared van rides from the Kapalua airport (e.g., $11 to Kaanapali.) Book 24 hours in advance. ***Bonus:*** You can request a **fresh flower lei greeting** for an added fee.

Taxis usually cost 30% more than the shuttles—except when you're traveling with a large party, in which case they're a deal. **West Maui Taxi** (www. westmauitaxi.com; $\mathcal{C}$ **888/661-4545**), for example, will drive up to six people from Kahului Airport to Kaanapali for $80. ***Note:*** **Ride-sharing services** Lyft and Uber are now authorized to make airport pickups and dropoffs at an area that had yet to be designated at press time.

If possible, avoid landing on Maui between 3 and 6pm, when the working stiffs on Maui are "*pau* work" (finished with work) and traffic near the airport often backs up.

AGRICULTURAL SCREENING AT THE AIRPORTS

When you leave, baggage and passengers bound for the mainland must be screened by agricultural officials. Officials will confiscate local produce, like avocados, bananas, and mangoes, in the name of fruit-fly control. Pineapples, coconuts, and papayas inspected and certified for export; boxed flowers; most leis without seeds; and processed foods (macadamia nuts, coffee, dried fruit, and the like) will pass. You'll need to pack jams or honey in checked bags if they exceed 3 ounces, or wait to buy them at a post-security gift shop.

Getting Around Maui

BY CAR

To rent a car in Hawaii, you must be at least 25 years of age and have a valid driver's license and credit card. *Note:* If you're visiting from abroad and plan to rent a car, keep in mind that foreign driver's licenses are usually recognized in the U.S., but you should get an international one if your home license is not in English.

The simplest way to see Maui is by rental car; public transit is very limited. All of the major car-rental firms—including Alamo, Avis, Budget, Dollar, Enterprise, Hertz, National, and Thrifty—have agencies on Maui. If you're traveling with a large group or bulky sports gear, you can rent older vans, mini-vans and SUVs, as well as sedans, from **Aloha Rent-a-Car** (www.aloha rentacar.com; ℡ **888/4562-5642** or 808/877-4477); rates include two beach chairs and a cooler. (For more driving tips, see "Insurance," p. 315, and "Driving Rules," p. 315.) Book well in advance for holiday periods.

Maui has only a handful of major roads, and you can expect a traffic jam or two heading into Kihei, Lahaina, or Paia during morning and evening rush hours. In general, the roads hug the coastlines; one zigzags up to Haleakala's summit. When asking locals for directions don't bother using highway numbers; residents know the routes by name only.

Traffic advisory: Be alert on the Honoapiilani Highway (Hwy. 30) en route to Lahaina. South of the Lahaina "bypass" (Hwy. 3000, now the only connection from Olowalu to Lahaina), drivers ogling whales in the channel between Maui and Lanai often slam on the brakes and cause major tie-ups and accidents. This is the main road connecting the west side to the rest of the island; if an accident, rockslide, flooding, or other road hazard occurs, traffic can back up for 1 to 8 hours (no joke). So before you set off, check with Maui County for road-closure advisories (www.co.maui.hi.us; ℡ **808/986-1200**). The most up-to-date info can be found on its Twitter feed (@CountyofMaui) or that of a local news agency (@MauiNow).

BY MOTORCYCLE   Feel the wind on your face and smell the salt air as you tour the island on a Harley, available for rent from **Maui Motorcycle Co.,** 150 Dairy Rd., Kahului (www.mauimotorcycleco.com; ℡ **808/877-7433**); rentals start at $132 a day, including taxes and fees.

Stay off the Cellphone

Unless it's hands-free, talking or texting on a cellphone while driving on Maui is a big no-no. Fines range from $297 to $347. Your car must be completely stopped, the engine turned off and the car in a safe location on the side of a road or driveway to be able to use your cellphone without a headset or ear-piece.

BY TAXI   Because Maui's various destinations are so spread out, taxi service can be quite expensive and should be limited to travel within a neighborhood. **West Maui Taxi** (www.westmauitaxi.com; ℗ **888/661-4545**) offers 24-hour service island-wide, while **Kihei Wailea Taxi** (www.kiheitaxi.com; ℗ **808/298-1877**) serves South Maui. The metered rate is $3 per mile. **Ride-sharing services** Lyft and Uber offer competitive rates, but prices vary by demand.

BY BUS   The **Maui Bus** (www.mauicounty.gov/bus; ℗ **808/871-4838**) is a public/private partnership that provides affordable but sadly inconsistent public transit to various communities across the island. Expect hour waits between rides. Air-conditioned buses service 13 routes, including several that stop at the airport. All routes operate daily, including holidays. Suitcases (one per passenger) and bikes are allowed; surfboards are not. Fares are $2.

GASOLINE   Gas prices in Hawaii, always much higher than on the U.S. mainland, vary from island to island. At this writing, average prices for regular gas in Maui are about $4.49 per gallon (except in Hana, where gas is around $5). On Molokai gas is $5.19 and on Lanai gas is $5.49. *Note:* Taxes are already included in the printed price. Check **www.gasbuddy.com** to find the cheapest gas in your area.

INSURANCE   Hawaii is a no-fault state, which means that if you don't have collision-damage insurance, you are required to pay for all damages before you leave the state, whether or not the accident was your fault. Your personal car insurance may provide rental-car coverage; check before you leave home. You may want to bring your insurance identification card if you decline the optional loss and/or liability insurance, which can add $30 a day or more to your bill. Some credit card companies also provide collision-damage insurance for their customers; check with yours before you rent.

DRIVING RULES   Hawaii state law mandates that all car passengers must wear a **seat belt,** and all infants must be strapped into a car seat. You'll pay a $102 fine if you don't buckle up. **Pedestrians** always have the right of way, even if they're not in the crosswalk. You can turn **right on red** after a full and complete stop, unless otherwise posted.

ROAD MAPS   The best and most detailed maps for activities are published by **Franko Maps** (www.frankosmaps.com), which feature a host of island maps plus a terrific "reef creatures" guide for snorkelers curious about the fish they spot underwater. Rental car companies offer island guides with free road maps, as does the free, widely distributed *This Week Magazine* (www.this weekhawaii.com/maui). Be aware that limited or no cell service in remote areas can prevent access to online maps—although it's hard to get lost on an island with relatively few roads.

University of Hawaii Press maps for Maui, Molokai, and Lanai include a detailed network of island roads, large-scale insets of towns, historical and contemporary points of interest, parks, beaches, and hiking trails. If you can't find them in a bookstore near you, contact **University of Hawaii Press** (www. uhpress.hawaii.edu; © **888/UHPRESS** [847-7377]). For topographic and other maps of the islands, go to the **Hawaii Geographic Society** (https:// hawaii-geographic-society.business.site; © **808/782-3562**).

TIPS ON ACCOMMODATIONS

Maui offers all kinds of accommodations, from campsites, simple rooms in restored plantation homes, and small hotels to luxurious condo units and opulent suites in beachfront resorts. *Note:* The proliferation in vacation rentals in non-resort neighborhoods through platforms such as Airbnb and VRBO.com has led to community backlash and tighter regulations on where and how such lodgings may operate. Remember that units that register for licenses and pay local taxes (the General Excise Tax, or GET, and Transient Accommodations Tax, or TAT) contribute to services you'll enjoy while on island, too, so look for those fees in your bill.

Due to Maui's very strict no-smoking laws (see "Butting Out in Hawaii," p. 320), smoking is not allowed in public areas, and most vacation rentals and accommodations generally ban smoking in guest rooms, too. Hotels that do offer smoking areas and smoking-permitted rooms may not designate more than 20% of its rooms as such.

Types of Accommodations
HOTELS
On Maui, a "hotel" can indicate a wide range of options, from few or no on-site amenities to enough extras to qualify the place as a mini-resort. Generally, a hotel offers daily maid service and has a restaurant, laundry facilities, a pool, and a sundries/convenience-type shop. Top hotels also have activities desks, concierge and valet services, room service, business centers, bars and/or lounges, and perhaps a few more shops and shuttle services. Some hotels may be a short walk to the beach, rather than beachfront.

RESORTS
In Hawaii, a resort offers everything a hotel does—and more. You can expect direct beach access, with lounge chairs and beach gear rentals; pools and a hot tub; a spa and fitness center; restaurants, bars, and lounges; a 24-hour front desk; concierge, valet, and bellhop services; room service (often 24 hr.); an activities desk; tennis and golf onsite or nearby; ocean activities; a business center; kids' programs; and more. Don't be misled by a name, though—just because a place is called "ABC Resort" doesn't mean it actually *is* a resort. Make sure you're getting what you pay for. Note that many of the more high-end resorts and large hotels charge "resort fees"—ranging from around $15 a night to $40—covering incidentals like pool towels, local phone calls, even

parking. Before you book, check your hotel to see if it tacks on a resort fee—the daily charge adds up.

CONDOS

The roominess and convenience of a condo—which is usually a fully equipped, multiple-bedroom apartment—make this a great choice for families. Condominium properties on Maui generally consist of several apartments set in either a single high-rise or a cluster of low-rise units. Condos usually have amenities such as some maid service (ranging from daily to weekly; it may or may not be included in your rate), a pool, and an on-site front desk or a live-in property manager. Condos tend to be clustered in resort areas. There are some very high-end condos, but most are relatively affordable, especially if you're traveling in a group.

The advantages of a condo are privacy, space, and conveniences—which usually include a full kitchen, a washer and dryer, home entertainment system, and more. The downsides are typically the lack of an on-site restaurant and the density of the units; many often have minimum stays of 3 to 5 nights, or longer in holiday periods. Cleaning fees (for when you leave, not during your stay) can also considerably increase the cost.

BED & BREAKFASTS

Bed & breakfasts can be an affordable way to go or a splurge. As defined by county ordinance, they require the owner or a manager to live onsite, with no more than six bedrooms available for rental. Maui has a wide range of places that call themselves B&Bs: everything from a traditional B&B—several bedrooms in a home, with breakfast served in the morning—to what is essentially a vacation rental on an owner's property that comes with fixings for you to make your own breakfast. Make sure that the B&B you're booking matches your own mental picture.

Hosts are often happy to act as your own private concierge, but some prospective guests may balk at a set time for breakfast, few amenities (e.g. laundry facilities or phone), and generally no maid service. B&B owners typically require a minimum stay of 2 or 3 nights, and it's often a drive to the beach. (For a list of permitted B&Bs, see www.mauicounty.gov/DocumentCenter/View/11127/Permitted-Bed-Breakfast -List-9302018.)

VACATION RENTALS

This is another great choice for families and long-term stays. "Vacation rental" usually means that no one will be on the property where you're staying. The actual accommodations can range from an apartment to an entire fully equipped house. Generally, vacation rentals allow you to settle in and make yourself at home for a while. They have kitchen facilities (or at least a kitchenette), a phone (although landlines are disappearing), and Wi-Fi; TVs may have cable, streaming services, and/or DVD players.

Shoes off

On Maui, as elsewhere in Hawaii, it's customary to remove your shoes (including sandals or flip-flops, known here as "slippahs") before entering anyone's home. The same is true at most bed-and-breakfasts and vacation rentals; plan to stay elsewhere if you prefer to keep your shoes on.

The advantages of a vacation rental are complete privacy, your own kitchen (which can save you money on meals), and lots of conveniences. The disadvantages are a lack of an on-site property manager and generally no maid service; often a minimum stay is required (sometimes as much as a week). By county ordinance, short-term vacation rental homes (i.e., those rented less than 6 months) outside of the usual resort areas must have onsite parking and a manager who can arrive within 1 hour of being contacted by phone; ads, including online listings, must include the permit number (see www.mauicounty.gov/DocumentCenter/View/14762/Approved-Short-Term-Rental-Homes-List-9302018 for a list of permitted rentals).

GETTING MARRIED IN THE ISLANDS

In a state nicknamed for aloha, one of whose meanings is "love," some 6,300 weddings (including more than 300 same-sex couples) take place on Maui every year, with at least half involving travelers. It's no wonder: The beautiful sunsets and starry nights, the green mountains hovering above sun-kissed golden beaches, the warm air with caressing trade winds all inspire romance. Plus, after the ceremony, you're already on your honeymoon. And the members of your wedding party will most likely be delighted, since you've given them the perfect excuse for their own island vacation.

The booming wedding business has spawned more than 70 companies that can help you organize a long-distance event and stage an unforgettable wedding, Hawaiian-style or your style. However, you can also plan your own island wedding, even from afar, and not spend a fortune doing it.

The Paperwork

The state of Hawaii has some very minimal procedures for obtaining a marriage license or civil union. The first thing you should do is find a "performer," i.e., the officiating minister or judge, listed at **https://marriage.ehawaii.gov**, and confirm his or her availability. Then download and complete an application for a marriage license, which requires the name of the officiant and a fee of $65. Both parties must then present themselves in person to a marriage licensing agent: You can find a list of some local agents at http://health.hawaii.gov/vitalrecords/license-agents, or go to the office of the **Marriage License**

Office, State Department of Health Bldg., 54 S. High St., Wailuku (🕿 **808/984-8210;** open weekdays 8am–4pm). Licenses are valid for 30 days. *Note:* All licensing agents will give you a form to pass on to the officiant, which must be completed to receive a marriage certificate.

Both parties must be 18 years of age or older and not more closely related than first cousins. Anyone 16 to 17 years may wed with written consent of both parents, legal guardian, or judge of a family court; 15-year-olds can marry with written approval of both parents *and* a family court judge.

DOING IT YOURSELF

The marriage-licensing agents, who range from employees of the governor's satellite office in Kona to private individuals, are usually friendly, helpful people who can steer you to a nondenominational minister or marriage performer who's licensed by the state of Hawaii. These marriage performers are great sources of information for budget weddings. They usually know wonderful places to have a ceremony for free or for a nominal fee.

Be aware that state rules require permits for any "commercial activity" on the shoreline—and if you're paying anyone for any part of the wedding ceremony, such as photography or officiating, that's commercial activity. The use of chairs (except for people with disabilities) and other furniture is banned, and a certificate of liability insurance for $1,000,000 that includes the state of Hawaii as one of the insured required. The price for a permit is 10 cents per square foot, with a minimum fee of $20. You can find details at https://dlnr.hawaii.gov/ld/files/2013/07/Wiki-Permits-FAQ-1601.pdf or let a wedding planner do the work.

USING A WEDDING PLANNER

Wedding planners—many of whom are marriage-licensing agents as well—can arrange everything for you, from a small, private outdoor affair to a full-blown formal ceremony in a tropical setting. They charge anywhere from a couple hundred dollars to a small fortune—it all depends on what you want.

Planners on Maui include **Hawaii Weddings** (www.hawaiiweddings.com; 🕿 **808/366-0329**), **White Orchid Wedding** (www.whiteorchidwedding.com; 🕿 **800/240-9336**), **A Dream Wedding: Maui Style** (www.adreamwedding.net; 🕿 **800/743-2777** or 808/661-1777), and **Love Maui Weddings** (www.lovemauiweddings.com; 🕿 **800/793-2-WED** [2933] or 808/669-8787). In business since 1994, **Gay Hawaiian Weddings** (www.gayhawaiiwedding.com; 🕿 **808/891-1200**) offers a variety of religious, Hawaiian, and "spiritual but not religious" weddings, as well as civil union ceremonies; it's also gay-owned and -operated.

For more providers, check with the **Maui Visitors and Convention Bureau** (www.gohawaii.com/islands/maui/weddings; 🕿 **800/525-MAUI** [6284]). Many of the big resorts have their own coordinators on staff as well.

Butting Out in Hawaii

Hawaii has some of the country's strictest no-smoking laws, with fines ranging from $50 to $500. Smoking is not allowed in beaches or parks (as well as in their parking lots), nor is it permitted in public buildings, including restaurants, bars, retail stores, movie theaters, government offices, museums, and the like; there is also no smoking within 20 feet of a doorway, window, or ventilation intake (so no hanging around outside a bar to smoke—you must go 20 ft. away). Most hotels are either completely nonsmoking or limit smokers to a few outdoor areas, with no more than 20% of guest rooms allowed to be designated for smoking. On Maui, it's also illegal to smoke at a bus stop, or in a car with passengers 18 years or younger. For those who do smoke, please extinguish and discard your butts properly. Many parts of the island have easily ignited dry brush, while wildlife, including migratory seabirds and green sea turtles, may also be harmed by accidentally ingesting butts.

HEALTH & SAFETY

Hiking Safety

Especially since cell service isn't always available in remote areas, hikers should always let someone know where they're heading, when they're going, and when they plan to return; too many hikers get lost in Hawaii because they don't let others know their basic plans and they may not be able to dial ℂ 911 in case of emergency.

And make sure you know how strenuous the route and trail you will follow are—don't overestimate your ability.

Before you head out, always check weather conditions on Maui with the toll-free **National Weather Service** (ℂ 866/944-5025 or www.prh.noaa.gov). Do not hike if rain or a storm is predicted; flash floods are common in Hawaii. Hike with a pal, never alone. Plan to finish your hike at least an hour before sunset; because Hawaii is so close to the equator, it does not have a twilight period, and thus it gets dark quickly after the sun sets. Wear hiking boots, a sun hat, clothes to protect you from the sun and from getting scratches, and high-SPF sunscreen on all exposed areas of skin. Take plenty of water, a basic first-aid kit, a snack, and a bag to pack out what you pack in. Stay on the trail and watch your step; it's easy to slip off precipitous trails and into steep canyons.

Vog

As of this writing, Maui and the other Hawaiian islands have been enjoying clear air for months. But during the previous 35 years of eruptions from Kilauea volcano on Hawaii Island, a volcanic haze dubbed *vog* would intermittently travel over to Maui, especially when winds shifted from their usual patterns. Those with existing respiratory ailments might find them worse with prolonged exposure, but it's highly unlikely to cause you any harm in the course of your visit.

Ocean Safety

Because most people coming to Hawaii are unfamiliar with the ocean environment, they're often unaware of the natural hazards it holds. With just a few precautions, your ocean experience can be a safe and happy one. An excellent book is *All Stings Considered: First Aid and Medical Treatment of Hawaii's Marine Injuries,* by Craig Thomas and Susan Scott (University of Hawaii Press, 1997). New and used copies are available on Amazon.com.

Note: Although 40 species of sharks call Hawaii home, there are relatively few attacks, especially given the number of people in the water—three or four year, and rarely fatal. Here are the general rules for avoiding sharks: Don't swim at sunrise, at sunset, or where the water is murky due to stream runoff—sharks' preferred times and locale for feeding. And don't swim where there are bloody fish in the water, as sharks become aggressive around blood.

Some 90% of the world's population tends toward seasickness. The waters in Hawaii can range from as calm as glass to downright frightening (during storms); conditions usually fall somewhere in between. In general, expect rougher conditions in winter than in summer. If you've never been out on a

SAVE THE REEFS AND YOUR skin

The closer you are to the equator and the paler your skin, the likelier you are to develop malignant melanoma (deadly skin cancer) over the course of your life. Yet nobody is completely safe from the sun's harmful rays: All skin types and races can burn. Thus using sunscreen is just common sense.

Several sunscreen ingredients are associated with coral bleaching, however, which has devastating effects on marine life. Effective January 2021, Hawaii will enforce a ban on the sale or distribution of sunscreens with the ingredients oxybenzone and octinoxate, sometimes labeled benzophenone-3 or octyl methoxycinnamate, respectively. To ensure that your vacation won't be ruined by a painful sunburn, while still protecting the reefs, consider wearing the lightweight, close-fitting, long-sleeved garments known as "rash guards" when swimming or snorkeling. On land, wear a wide-brimmed hat and sunglasses.

For areas of skin that can't be covered or shaded, use a strong but "reef-friendly" sunscreen, which rely on zinc oxide or titanium dioxide to block harmful UVA and UVB rays; some even have tinting to offset the somewhat chalky residue. Keep infants under 6 months out of the sun completely, and slather older babies and children with reef-friendly sunscreen frequently.

If you do get a burn, aloe vera, cool compresses, cold baths, and benzocaine can help with the pain. Stay out of the sun until the burn is completely gone.

boat, or if you've been seasick in the past, you might want to heed the following suggestions:

○ The day before you go out on a boat, avoid alcohol; caffeine; citrus and other acidic juices; and greasy, spicy, or hard-to-digest foods.

○ Get a good night's sleep the night before.

○ Take or use whatever seasickness prevention works best for you—medication, an acupressure wristband, ginger-root tea or capsules, or any combination. But do it *before* **you board;** because once you've set sail, it's generally too late.

○ While you're on the boat, stay as low and as near the center of the boat as possible. Avoid the fumes (especially if it's a diesel boat); stay out in the fresh air and watch the horizon. Do not read.

○ If you start to feel queasy, drink clear fluids, like water, and eat something bland, such as a soda cracker.

The most common **stings** in Hawaii come from jellyfish, particularly Portuguese man-of-war and box jellyfish. Since the poisons they inject are very different, you need to treat each type of sting differently.

A bluish-purple floating bubble with a long tail, the **Portuguese man-of-war** is responsible for some 6,500 stings a year on Oahu alone, especially during prolonged periods of trade winds that blow them onto beaches. These stings, although painful and a nuisance, are rarely harmful; fewer than 1 in 1,000 requires medical treatment. The best prevention is to watch for these floating bubbles as you snorkel (look for the hanging tentacles below the surface). Get out of the water if anyone near you spots these jellyfish.

Reactions to stings range from mild burning and reddening to severe welts and blisters. *All Stings Considered* recommends the following treatment: First, pick off any visible tentacles with a gloved hand, a stick, or anything handy; then rinse the sting with salt water or fresh water and apply ice to prevent swelling and to help control pain. Avoid folk remedies like vinegar, baking soda, or urinating on the wound, which may actually cause further damage. Most Portuguese man-of-war stings will disappear by themselves within 15 to 20 minutes if you do nothing at all to treat them. Still, be sure to see a doctor if pain persists or you develop a rash or other symptoms.

Transparent, square-shaped **box jellyfish** are nearly impossible to see in the water. Fortunately, they seem to follow a monthly cycle: Eight to 10 days after the full moon, they appear in the waters on the leeward side of each island,

---

Everything You've Always Wanted to Know About Sharks

The Hawaii State Department of Land and Natural Resources offers a website, **http://dlnr.hawaii.gov/sharks**, that covers the biology, history, and culture of these carnivores. It also provides safety information and data on shark bites in Hawaii (about 3–4 a year, generally by tiger sharks in waters well offshore).

Maui County publishes an **Ocean Safety Guide** with maps to lifeguarded beaches and important tips on avoiding rip currents, sharks, and other hazards; look for it at the airport, where ocean safety videos now play above baggage carousels, or better yet, download it in advance at **www.mauicounty.gov/463/Ocean-Safety**. The most important reminders: Never turn your back on the ocean; swim with the current, never against it; and always talk to lifeguards about conditions before entering the water, or local beachgoers if lifeguards are not present. "When in doubt, don't go out" should be your mantra.

although less so on Maui than on Oahu, and hang around for about 3 days. Also, they seem to sting more in the morning hours, when they're on or near the surface.

The stings can cause anything from no visible marks to hivelike welts, blisters, and pain lasting from 10 minutes to 8 hours. *All Stings Considered* recommends the following treatment: First, pour regular household vinegar on the sting; this will stop additional burning. Do not rub the area. For pain, apply an ice pack. Seek additional medical treatment if you experience shortness of breath, weakness, palpitations, muscle cramps, or any other severe symptoms. Most box-jellyfish stings disappear by themselves without any treatment.

Most sea-related **punctures** come from stepping on or brushing against the needlelike spines of sea urchins (known locally as *wana*). Be careful when you're in the water; don't put your foot down (even if you have booties or fins on) if you can't clearly see the bottom. Waves can push you into *wana* in a surge zone in shallow water. The spines can even puncture a wet suit.

A sea urchin puncture can result in burning, aching, swelling, and discoloration (black or purple) around the area where the spines entered your skin. The best thing to do is to pull any protruding spines out. The body will absorb the spines within 24 hours to 3 weeks, or the remainder of the spines will work themselves out. Again, contrary to popular wisdom, do not urinate or pour vinegar on the embedded spines—this will not help.

All **cuts** obtained in the marine environment must be taken seriously because the high level of bacteria present in the water can quickly cause the cut to become infected. The best way to prevent cuts is to wear a wet suit, gloves, and reef shoes. Never touch coral; not only can you get cut, but you also can damage a living organism that may grow less than an inch per year.

The symptoms of a coral cut can range from a slight scratch to severe welts and blisters. *All Stings Considered* recommends gently pulling the edges of the skin open and removing any embedded coral or grains of sand with tweezers. Next, scrub the cut well with fresh water. If pressing a clean cloth against the wound doesn't stop the bleeding, or the edges of the injury are jagged or gaping, seek medical treatment.

[FastFACTS] MAUI

Agricultural Check
Known as "ag check," this airport screening of carry-on and checked baggage is separate from the security screening. Mainland-bound passengers cannot take home most fresh fruit, plants, or seeds (including some leis) unless they are sealed and labeled as permitted for transport—you cannot seal and pack them yourself.

Area Codes Hawaii's area code is 808; it applies to all islands.

Business Hours Most offices are generally open Monday through Friday from 9am to 5pm. Bank hours are Monday through Thursday from 8:30am to 4pm and Friday from 8:30am to 6pm; some banks are open on Saturday as well. Major shopping centers are open Monday through Saturday from 9:30am to 9pm and Sunday from 10am to 5pm.

Car Rental See "Getting Around Maui," earlier in this chapter.

Cellphones See "Mobile Phones," later in this section.

Crime See "Safety," later in this section.

Customs Since Hawaii is part of the U.S., regulations on what can be brought to the islands, other than agricultural products and live animals, only apply to international arrivals. Maui currently has international

nonstop flights only from Canada. *Note:* Flights both to and from Canada will clear U.S. Customs in Canada, not in Hawaii.

For information on what you're allowed to bring home from the U.S., contact one of the following agencies:

Canada: Canada Border Services Agency (www.cbsa-asfc.gc.ca; ℭ **800/461-9999** in Canada or 204/983-3500).

United Kingdom: HM Revenue & Customs (www.gov.uk/browse/abroad; ℭ **0300 200 3700** in the U.K. or +44 2920 501 261).

Australia: Australian Customs and Border Protection Service (www.customs.gov.au; ℭ **1300 363 263**).

New Zealand: New Zealand Customs Service (www.customs.govt.nz; ℭ **64 9 927 8036** outside of New Zealand, or 0800/428-786).

Dentists If you have dental problems, a nationwide referral service known as **1-800-DENTIST** (ℭ **800/336-8478**) will provide the name of a nearby dentist or clinic. Emergency dental care is available at **Hawaii Family Dental,** 1847 S. Kihei Rd., in Kihei Pacific Plaza, Kihei (ℭ **808/874-8401**); 95 Lono Ave., Ste. 210, Kahului (www.hawaiifamilydental.com; ℭ **808/856-4626**), or at **Aloha Lahaina Dentists,** 134 Luakini St. (in the Maui Medical

Group Bldg.), Lahaina (ℭ **808/661-4005**).

Doctors Urgent Care West Maui, located in the Fairway Shops, 2580 Kekaa Dr., Suite 111, Kaanapali (www.westmauidoctors.com; ℭ **808/667-9721**), is open 365 days a year; no appointment necessary. In Kihei, call **Urgent Care Maui,** 1325 S. Kihei Rd., Suite 103 (at Lipoa St., across from Times Market), Kihei (ℭ **808/879-7781**); it's open Monday to Saturday 7am to 9pm and Sunday 8am to 2pm.

Drinking Laws Beer, wine, and liquor are sold at grocery stores, convenience stores, and liquor stores from 6am to 11pm. In Maui County (Maui, Molokai, and Lanai), bars and nightclubs must close by 2am.

The legal age for purchase and consumption of alcoholic beverages is 21; proof of age is required and often requested at bars, nightclubs, and restaurants, so it's always a good idea to bring ID when you go out. Do not carry open containers of alcohol in your car or any public area that isn't zoned for alcohol consumption. The police can fine you on the spot. Don't even think about driving while intoxicated (the legal blood alcohol concentration limit for adults is .08%; for ages under 21, it's .02%.) You may lose your license, be fined, and face jail time, or all three.

Driving Rules See "Getting Around Maui," earlier in this chapter.

Electricity Like Canada, the United States uses 110 to 120 volts AC (60 cycles), compared to 220 to 240 volts AC (50 cycles) in most of Europe, Australia, and New Zealand. Downward converters that change 220–240 volts to 110–120 volts are difficult to find in the United States, so bring one with you.

Embassies & Consulates All embassies are located in the nation's capital, Washington, D.C.; many have consulates in Honolulu, the closest option to Maui. If your country isn't listed below, visit **https://travel-hawaii.com/hawaii_embassy_guide.html.**

The consulate of **Australia** is at 1000 Bishop St., Honolulu (https://usa.embassy.gov.au/honolulu; ✆ **808/529-8100**). The Australian consulate also provides services for residents and citizens of **Canada**.

The nearest consulate for **Ireland** is in San Francisco (www.consulateofireland sanfrancisco.org; ✆ **415/392-4214**).

The consulate of **New Zealand** is at 733 Bishop St., Honolulu (www.mfat.govt.nz/en/embassies; ✆ **808/675-5555**).

The nearest consulate of the **United Kingdom** providing services to British nationals visiting Hawaii is in Los Angeles (www.gov.uk/world/usa; ✆ **310/789-0031**, calling from the U.K. 020/7008-1500).

Emergencies Call ✆ **911** for police, fire, and ambulance service. District stations are located in Lahaina (✆ **800/661-4441**), Kihei (✆ **808/875-8190**), and Hana (✆ **808/248-8311**). For the **Poison Control Center,** call ✆ **800/222-1222.**

Family Travel Maui is paradise for children, with beaches and lawns to run on, water to splash in, and unusual sights to see. To locate attractions that are particularly child-friendly, check out the "Especially for Kids" boxes for suggested family activities.

The larger hotels and resorts offer **supervised programs** for children and can refer you to qualified **babysitters**. By state law, hotels can only accept children ages 5 and older in supervised activities programs, but they often accommodate younger kids by simply hiring babysitters to watch over them.

Baby's Away (www.babysaway.com; ✆ **800/942-9030** or 808/250-2733) rents cribs, strollers, highchairs, playpens, and infant seats. The staff will deliver whatever you need to wherever you're staying and pick it up when you're done.

Gasoline Please see "Getting Around Maui," earlier in this chapter.

Hospitals Maui Memorial Medical Center is the only acute-care hospital on the island; it's at 221 Mahalani, Wailuku (www.mauihealthsystem.org/maui-memorial;

✆ **808/244-9056**). East Maui's **Hana Community Health Center** is open Monday to Saturday at 4590 Hana Hwy (www.hana health.org; ✆ **808/248-8294**, after-hours physician 808/268-0688). In upcountry Maui, **Kula Hospital** offers urgent and limited emergency care at 100 Keokea Pl. (off of Kula Highway), Kula (www.mauihealth system.org/kula-hospital; ✆ **808/878-1221**).

Insurance Travel insurance is a good idea if you think for some reason you may be canceling your trip. It's cheaper than the cost of a no-penalty ticket, and it gives you the safety net if something comes up, enabling you to cancel or postpone your trip and still recover the costs.

For information on traveler's insurance, trip-cancellation insurance, and medical insurance while traveling, please visit www.frommers.com/planning.

Internet & Wi-Fi In 2018 the state began rolling out 1,000 free, public Wi-Fi hotspots on Maui (including the Hasegawa General Store), Oahu, Kauai, and Molokai. Many other places on Maui offer free Wi-Fi, including **Starbucks** (www.starbucks.com/store-locator), which has branches in Kahului, Wailuku, Pukalani, Lahaina, and Kihei. Most lodgings offer free Wi-Fi, although hotels may bundle it into a daily resort fee.

Branches of the **Hawaii State Public Library System** have computers with

Internet access. Maui has branches in Hana, Kahului, Kihei, Lahaina, and Makawao; for addresses and hours, check **www.libraries hawaii.org**. There is no charge for use of the computers, but you must have a Hawaii library card, which is free to Hawaii residents and members of the military. Visitors have a choice of two types of cards: a $25 nonresident card that is good for 5 years (and may be renewed for an additional $25) or a $10 visitor card that is good for 3 months and may be renewed for $10. Download an application from the website (click on "How Do I..."), complete it, and present with photo ID at any location.

Language As in the rest of the United States, English is spoken in Hawaii, but it helps to recognize common Hawaiian words (as in mahalo, or "thank you") and understand the basics of pronunciation for unfamiliar place or personal names. Hawaiian pidgin, a simplified English that includes loan words from Hawaiian, Chinese, Japanese, among other sources, has also contributed many words to common usage (e.g., "grindz" for food), but nonlocals are advised not to imitate it.

Legal Aid Generally, Hawaii has the same laws as the mainland United States. Nudity is illegal in Hawaii. There are *no* legal **nude beaches** (despite what you might see at Maui's Little

Beach, or read elsewhere). If you are nude on a beach (or anywhere) in Hawaii, you can be arrested.

Selling, owning, or using **marijuana** for recreational purposes is illegal. At press time, the state legislature was still trying to figure out how to register out-of-state patients and caregivers in the local medical cannabis registry program (http://health.hawaii.gov/medical cannabisregistry). For now, if you attempt to buy marijuana or light up, you can be arrested.

While driving, if you are pulled over for a minor infraction (such as speeding), never attempt to pay the fine directly to a police officer; this could be construed as attempted bribery, a much more serious crime. Pay fines by mail, online, or directly into the hands of the clerk of the court. If accused of a more serious offense, say and do nothing before consulting a lawyer. In the U.S., the burden is on the state to prove a person's guilt beyond a reasonable doubt, and everyone has the right to remain silent, whether he or she is suspected of a crime or actually arrested. Once arrested, a person can make one telephone call to a party of his or her choice. The international visitor should call his or her embassy or consulate.

LGBT Travelers Hawaii is known for its acceptance of all groups. The number of gay- or lesbian-specific accommodations on the

islands is limited, but most properties welcome gays and lesbians like any other travelers. The magazine **Out Traveler** includes features on Hawaii and listings on its website, www.outtraveler.com/hawaii.

Mail As of press time, domestic postage rates are 35¢ for a postcard and 55¢ for a letter. For international mail, a first-class letter of up to 1 ounce costs $1.15; a first-class postcard costs the same as a letter. For more information go to **www.usps.com**.

If you aren't sure what your address will be in the United States, mail can be sent to you, in your name, c/o General Delivery at the main post office of the city or region where you expect to be. (See www.usps.com for information on the nearest post office.) The addressee must pick up mail in person and must produce proof of identity (a driver's license or a passport, for example). Most post offices will hold mail for up to 1 month and are open Monday to Friday from 9am to 4pm; some are also open Saturday from 9am to noon.

Medical Requirements No inoculations or vaccinations are required for entry into the United States. For the latest information on vaccination requirements or disease outbreaks, visit the Travelers' Health webpage of the Centers for Disease Control and Prevention, wwwnc.cdc.gov/travel.

Mobile Phones Just because your cellphone works at home doesn't mean it'll will work everywhere in Hawaii. Before you get on the plane to Hawaii, check your wireless company's coverage map on its website. AT&T and Verizon have the widest coverage, but there are parts of Maui where coverage is not very good or nonexistent. If you need to stay in touch at a destination where you know your phone won't work, **rent** a phone that does from **InTouch USA** (http://intouchusa.us; ☏ **800/872-7626**).

Do *not* use your cellphone while you are driving unless in a completely hands-free mode. Strict laws with heavy fines (up to $347) are diligently enforced.

MONEY & COSTS

THE VALUE OF US$ VS. OTHER POPULAR CURRENCIES

US$	C$	£	€	A$	NZ$
1.00	1.32	0.79	0.88	1.36	1.44

Frommer's lists exact prices in the local currency. The currency conversions quoted above were correct at press time. However, rates fluctuate, so consult a currency exchange website such as www.xe.com to check up-to-the-minute rates.

ATMs (cashpoints) are everywhere in Maui—at banks, supermarkets, Longs Drugs, and in most resorts and shopping centers. The **Cirrus** (www.mastercard. com; ☏ **800/424-7787**) and **PLUS** (www.visa.com/ atmlocator; ☏ **800/843-7587**) networks span the country; you can find them even in remote regions. Go to your bank card's website to find ATM locations at your destination. Be sure you know your daily withdrawal limit before you depart.

Note: Many banks impose a fee every time you use a card at another bank's ATM, and that fee is often higher for international transactions (up to $5 or more) than for domestic ones (where they're rarely more than $3.50). In addition, the bank from which you withdraw cash may charge its own fee. Visitors from outside the U.S. should also find out whether their bank assesses a fee on charges incurred abroad.

Credit cards are accepted everywhere except some taxicabs, some small restaurants and bed-and-breakfasts, and most roadside stands.

Multicultural Travelers See "Embassies & Consulates" (p. 325), "Language" (p. 326), "Medical Requirements" (p. 326), "Money & Costs" (above), "Passports" (p. 328), and "Visas" (p. 331).

Newspapers, Magazines & Websites The island's daily newspaper is the *Maui News* (www. mauinews.com) while the alternative weekly paper is *Maui Time* (www.mauitime. com); you can find both on Facebook as well.

Publications for visitors include *This Week Maui* (www.thisweek.com), *Maui Visitor Magazine* (www. alohavisitorguides.com), and *101 Things to Do on Maui* (www.101thingstodo.com/ maui). **Maui Now** (www. mauinow.com) is an online portal with useful entertainment and dining news as well as local reports.

Packing Maui is very informal. Shorts, T-shirts, and sandals or tennis shoes will get you by at most restaurants and attractions; a casual dress or a polo or aloha shirt and khakis are fine even in the most expensive places. Aloha wear, which does not include T-shirts, is acceptable everywhere, so you may want to plan on buying an aloha shirt or a muumuu (a Hawaiian-style dress) while you're in the islands.

Bring T-shirts, shorts, long pants (for hiking or cool evenings), a couple of bathing suits, a long-sleeve coverup (to throw on at the

WHAT THINGS COST ON MAUI	$
Hamburger	6.00–12.00
Movie ticket (adult/child)	11.75/9.00
Taxi from Kahului Airport to Kaanapali	89.00
Fare for Atlantis Adventures submarine (adult/child)	119.00/38.00
Entry to Maui Ocean Center (adult/child)	30.00/20.00
Entry to Haleakala National Park	12.00/person or 25.00/car
Entry to Iao Valley State Park (nonresidents)	5.00 per car
Maui Tropical Plantation tram tour (adult/child)	20.00/10.00
Trilogy Sailing Trip to Lanai (adult/child)	218.42/120.36
Old Lahaina Luau (adult/child)	125/78.12
20-ounce soft drink at convenience store	3.00
16-ounce apple juice	4.00
Cup of coffee	3.00
Moderately priced three-course dinner without alcohol	50.00
Moderately priced hotel room (double)	225.00–300.00

beach when you've had enough sun for the day), tennis shoes, rubber water shoes or flip-flops, and hiking boots and good socks if you plan on hiking.

The tropical sun poses the greatest threat to anyone who ventures into the great outdoors, so be sure to pack a good pair of sunglasses, strong reef-safe sunscreen (see "Save the Reefs and Your Skin," p. 321), a light hat, and a reusable water bottle— you'll easily dehydrate in the tropical heat. Campers should bring water-purification tablets or devices.

One last thing: **It really can get cold on Maui.** If you plan to see the sunrise from the top of Maui's Haleakala Crater, take a warm jacket; an upcountry temperature of 40°F (4°C), even

in summer when it's 80°F (27°C) at the beach, is not uncommon. It's always a good idea to bring at least a windbreaker, a fleece pullover, or a light jacket. Rain showers can happen any time, but especially between November and March, so a waterproof poncho may come in handy.

Passports Travelers entering the U.S. are required to show a passport, but if you're coming to Maui, you will go through passport control and customs elsewhere. In Hawaii, only Honolulu and Kona airports have nonstop international flights from countries other than Canada, where U.S. passport control and customs takes place in Canadian airports.

Australia Australian Passport Information Service

(✆ **131 232;** www. passports.gov.au).

Canada Passport Program (✆ **800/567-6868;** www.cic. gc.ca).

Ireland Passport Service (✆ **353/1-671-1633;** www. foreignaffairs. gov.ie).

New Zealand Passport Office (✆ **0800/22-50-50** [in New Zealand] or 64/[4] 463-9360 [overseas]; www. passports.govt.nz).

United Kingdom Identity and Passport Service (✆ **0300/222-0000** [in the U.K.] or 44 [0] 300/222-0000 [overseas]; www.ips.gov.uk).

Petrol It's called gasoline, or gas, in the United States. Please see "Getting Around Maui," earlier in this chapter.

Police In an emergency, dial ✆ **911** for police. For nonemergencies, call the district station in Lahaina (© **808/661-4441**), Kihei (© **808/875-8190** or Hana (© **808/248-8311**). On Lanai, call © **808/244-6496;** on Molokai, call © **808/244-6311.**

Post Office   To find the nearest post office, visit www.usps.com and click on Mail & Ship. The branch at the Lahaina Civic Center, 1760 Honoapiilani Hwy., Lahaina, is closest to Kaanapali and Kapalua lodgings, while the one at 1254 S. Kihei Rd., Kihei, is closest to Kihei and Wailea lodgings; both have Saturday morning as well as weekday hours. Most branches are only open weekdays, between 9am and 4pm.

Safety   Although tourist areas are generally safe, visitors should always stay alert, even on laid-back Maui (and especially in resort and beach areas). Avoid deserted areas, especially at night. Don't go into any city park at night unless it's the site of an event that attracts a crowd. Generally speaking, you can feel safe in areas where there are many people and open establishments.

Common sense applies: Don't leave cameras, cellphones, laptops or other expensive gear unattended. Always keep your possessions in sight. Remember also that hotels are open to the public and that at a large property, security may not be able to screen everyone entering. Always lock your room door—don't assume that once inside

your hotel, you're automatically safe.

Break-ins of cars in unattended parking lots, especially at beaches and in remote areas, has become more common. Park in well-lighted and well-traveled areas, if possible. Never leave any packages or valuables visible in the car, or luggage in the trunk. When you arrive, drop your bags off at your lodgings before sightseeing; hotel bell desks will be happy to stow them before check-in or after check-out.

In the unlikely event someone attempts to rob you or steal your car while you are present, do not try to resist the thief or carjacker—report the incident to the police department immediately. The **Visitor Aloha Society of Hawaii** can also help in the aftermath of crime or misfortune; call © **808/926-8274** any time of day. It also offers tips for travelers at https://visitoralohasocietyofhawaii.org/traveler-informations.

Senior Travel   Always carry identification with proof of your age—it can really pay off. Discounts for seniors, up to 20%, are available at almost all of Maui's major attractions and occasionally at hotels and restaurants. Always ask when making hotel reservations or buying tickets.

The U.S. National Park Service offers an **America the Beautiful—National Park and Federal Recreational Lands Pass Lifetime Senior Pass**, which gives U.S. citizens or

residents 62 years or older lifetime entrance to all properties administered by the National Park Service (NPS)—national parks, monuments, historic sites, recreation areas, and wildlife refuges—for a one-time fee of $80 (plus $10 handling charge for online or mail-in orders). There's also a one-year option for $20 (plus $10 for handling.) The pass may be purchased in person at any NPS facility that charges an entrance fee, or online at https://store.usgs.gov/recreational-passes (download a mail-in application from https://store.usgs.gov/s3fs-public/senior_pass_application.pdf.) Besides free entry for the cardholder and companions in the same vehicle, the America the Beautiful Senior Pass offers a 50% discount on some federal-use fees charged for such facilities as camping, swimming, parking, boat launching, and tours. For more information, go to www.nps.gov/planyourvisit/passes.htm or call the United States Geological Survey (USGS), which issues the passes, at © **888/275-8747.**

Single Travelers   Traveling in Hawaii is very safe. See "Safety," above.

Smoking   Hawaii has some of the toughest anti-smoking laws in the United States. See the box "Butting Out in Hawaii" on p. 320.

Taxes   The United States has no value-added tax (VAT) or other indirect tax at the national level. The state general excise tax (GET) can vary in Hawaii due to county surcharges; on Maui, it's 4.166% on all purchases. The transient accommodations tax (TAX) is 10.25%; combined with GET, it means 14.416% will be added to your bill for hotel or other lodgings.

Telephones All calls to destinations on Maui are local calls; calls from Maui to another island via a landline are long-distance, so you must dial 1; then the Hawaii area code, 808; and then the phone number. (With cellphones now ubiquitous, interisland long-distance charges are rarely an issue.) Many convenience groceries and packaging services sell **prepaid calling cards.** The state has more public pay phones than most on the mainland; some even accept American Express, MasterCard, and Visa. **Local calls** made from most pay phones cost 50¢. **To make calls within the United States and to Canada,** dial 1 followed by the area code and the seven-digit number. **For other international calls,** dial 011 followed by the country code, the city code, and the number you are calling.

Calls to area codes **800, 888, 877,** and **866** are toll-free. However, calls to area codes **700** and **900** (chat lines, bulletin boards, "dating" services, and so on) can be expensive—charges of 95¢ to $3 or more per minute. Some numbers have minimum charges that can run $15 or more.

For **reversed-charge or collect calls,** and for person-to-person calls, dial the number 0 and then the area code and number; an operator will come on the line, and you should specify whether you are calling collect, person-to-person, or both. If your operator-assisted call is international, ask for the overseas operator.

For **directory assistance** ("Information"), dial 411 for local numbers and national numbers in the U.S. and Canada. For dedicated long-distance information, dial 1, then the appropriate area code plus 555-1212. There is a fee for the assistance.

Time The continental United States is divided into **four time zones:** Eastern Standard Time (EST), Central Standard Time (CST), Mountain Standard Time (MST), and Pacific Standard Time (PST). Alaska and Hawaii each have their own zone: Alaska Standard Time (AST) and Hawaii Standard Time (HST). For example, when it's 7am on Maui (HST), it's 9am in Los Angeles (PST), 10am in Denver (MST), 11am in Chicago (CST), noon in New York City (EST), 5pm in London (Greenwich Mean Time), and 2am the next day in Sydney.

Daylight Saving Time, which moves the clock 1 hour ahead of standard time, is in effect from 2am on the second Sunday in March to 2am on the first Sunday in November in most of the United States. **Hawaii does not observe Daylight Saving Time.**

Note: During Daylight Saving Time, Hawaii is 3 hours behind the West Coast and 6 hours behind the East Coast.

Tipping Especially in Hawaii, tips are a very important part of certain low-wage workers' income, and gratuities are the standard way of showing appreciation for services provided. (Tipping is certainly not compulsory if the service is poor!) In hotels, tip **bellhops** at least $2 per bag (more if you have a lot of luggage or very bulky bags), and tip **housekeepers** $2 to $5 per day depending on the size of the room (more if you've left a disaster area to clean up). Tip the **doorman** or **concierge** only if he or she has provided you with some specific service (for example, calling a cab for you or obtaining difficult-to-get theater tickets). Tip the **valet-parking attendant** $3 to $5 every time you get your car.

In restaurants, bars, and nightclubs, tip **service staff** and **bartenders** 15 to 20% of the check, and tip **valet-parking attendants** $3 to $5 per vehicle.

As for other service personnel, tip **cab drivers** 15% of the fare; tip **skycaps** at airports at least $2 per bag; and tip **hairdressers** and **barbers** 15 to 20%.

Toilets You won't find public toilets or "restrooms" on the streets in most U.S. cities, but they can be found in hotel lobbies, bars, restaurants, museums, department stores, and service stations. Large hotels and fast-food restaurants are often the best bet for clean facilities. Restaurants and bars in resorts or heavily visited areas may reserve their restrooms for patrons.

Travelers with Disabilities The **Hawaii State Department of Health** has compiled tips for travelers with disabilities, including equipment rentals and transportation options, for each of the main islands; find the tips for Maui at https://health.hawaii.gov/dcab/files/2018/07/Maui-2018.pdf. The **Hawaii Visitors Bureau** offers additional advice at www.gohawaii.com/trip-planning/accessibility. Travelers with disabilities are typically made to feel very welcome on Maui; federal law requires hotels and airlines to accommodate wheelchair users, while tour companies provide many special services. The only travel agency in Hawaii specializing in services for travelers with disabilities, **Access Aloha Travel** (www.accessalohatravel.com; © 800/480-1143), can book anything, including rental vans, accommodations, tours, cruises, airfare, and more.

VAT See "Taxes," above.

Visas The U.S. State Department has a **Visa Waiver Program (VWP)** allowing citizens of the following countries (at press time) to enter the United States without a visa for stays of up to 90 days: Andorra, Australia, Austria,

Belgium, Brunei, Chile, Czech Republic, Denmark, Estonia, Finland, France, Germany, Greece, Hungary, Iceland, Ireland, Italy, Japan, Latvia, Liechtenstein, Lithuania, Luxembourg, Malta, Monaco, Netherlands, New Zealand, Norway, Portugal, San Marino, Singapore, Slovakia, Slovenia, South Korea, Spain, Sweden, Switzerland, Taiwan, and the United Kingdom. Even though a visa isn't necessary, visitors from VWP countries must register online through the Electronic System for Travel Authorization (ESTA), https://esta.cbp.dhs.gov/esta/, before boarding a plane or a boat to the U.S. Travelers must complete the online application providing basic personal and travel eligibility information, which the Department of Homeland Security recommends doing at least 3 days before traveling. Authorizations will be valid for up to 2 years or until the traveler's passport expires, whichever comes first. Currently, there is a $14 fee for the online application. Existing ESTA registrations remain valid through their expiration dates. **Note:** Passports issued by a VWP country must be an **e-passport** for travelers to be eligible to enter the U.S. without a visa. Citizens of these nations also need to present a round-trip air or cruise ticket upon arrival. E-passports contain computer chips capable of storing biometric information, such

as the required digital photograph of the holder.

Citizens of countries not covered by the Visa Waiver Program must have (1) a valid e-passport that expires at least 6 months later than the scheduled end of their visit to the U.S.; and (2) a tourist visa. For more information, see **https://travel.state.gov/content/travel/en/us-visas.html**.

Visitor Information The **Maui Visitors Bureau**, which includes Molokai and Lanai, is at 1727 Wili Pa Loop, Wailuku, Maui (www.gohawaii.com; © **800/525-MAUI** [6284] or 808/244-3530).

Water The water in your hotel or at public drinking fountains is safe to drink, although it may have more chlorine than you like. To avoid bacterial disease such as leptospirosis, never drink water from streams or waterfalls without treating first, and avoid swimming in fresh water with open cuts.

Weather For the current weather, the Haleakala National Park weather, or marine and surf conditions, call the **National Weather Service's Hawaii forecast** (© **866/944-5025** or 808/944-3756) or visit weather.gov/hawaii and click on the island of Maui.

Wi-Fi See "Internet & Wi-Fi," earlier in this section.

Women Travelers Travel in Hawaii is very safe. Take the usual precautions you would in your hometown. See "Safety," above.

AIRLINE WEBSITES

Air Canada
www.aircanada.com

Alaska Airlines
www.alaskaair.com

American Airlines
www.aa.com

Delta Air Lines
www.delta.com

Hawaiian Airlines
www.hawaiianair.com

Mokulele Airlines
www.mokuleleairlines.com

Southwest Airlines
www.southwest.com

United Airlines
www.united.com

WestJet
www.westjet.com

Index

See also Accommodations and Restaurant indexes, below.

Restaurants

RESTAURANT INDEX

Map List

Photo Credits

Frommer's EasyGuide to Maui, 1st Edition

Published by
FROMMER MEDIA LLC

ISBN 978-1-62887-486-0 (paper), 978-1-62887-487-7 (e-book)

Editorial Director: Pauline Frommer
Editor: Alexis Lipsitz Flippin
Production Editor: Kelly Dobbs Henthorne
Cartographer: Liz Puhl
Page Compositor: Lissa Auciello Brogan
Photo Editor: Meghan Lamb
Assistant Photo Editor: Phil Vinke

For information on our other products or services, see www.frommers.com.

Frommer Media LLC also publishes its books in a variety of electronic formats. Some content that appears in print may not be available in electronic formats.

Manufactured in the United States

5   4   3   2   1

ABOUT THE AUTHOR

Jeanne Cooper writes frequently about Hawaii for the *San Francisco Chronicle*, where she previously worked as a travel editor, as well as for *Marin* magazine and HawaiiIslander.com. Her stories about the islands also have appeared in the *Houston Chronicle* and other newspapers, plus magazines such as *Southwest, Sunset, Modern Luxury Silicon Valley* and *Luxury Las Vegas*. Before helping relaunch Frommer's Hawaii, she contributed to guidebooks on San Francisco, Boston, and Washington, D.C., for several different publishers. Now living on Moku o Keawe, the Big Island, she was inspired to study hula by her mother, who learned to play ukulele and dance hula in pre-statehood Hawaii.

ABOUT THE FROMMER TRAVEL GUIDES

For most of the past 50 years, Frommer's has been the leading series of travel guides in North America, accounting for as many as 24% of all guidebooks sold. I think I know why.

Though we hope our books are entertaining, we nevertheless deal with travel in a serious fashion. Our guidebooks have never looked on such journeys as a mere recreation, but as a far more important human function, a time of learning and introspection, an essential part of a civilized life. We stress the culture, lifestyle, history, and beliefs of the destinations we cover, and urge our readers to seek out people and new ideas as the chief rewards of travel.

We have never shied from controversy. We have, from the beginning, encouraged our authors to be intensely judgmental, critical—both pro and con—in their comments, and wholly independent. Our only clients are our readers, and we have triggered the ire of countless prominent sorts, from a tourist newspaper we called "practically worthless" (it unsuccessfully sued us) to the many rip-offs we've condemned.

And because we believe that travel should be available to everyone regardless of their incomes, we have always been cost-conscious at every level of expenditure. Though we have broadened our recommendations beyond the budget category, we insist that every lodging we include be sensibly priced. We use every form of media to assist our readers, and are particularly proud of our feisty daily website, the award-winning Frommers.com.

I have high hopes for the future of Frommer's. May these guidebooks, in all the years ahead, continue to reflect the joy of travel and the freedom that travel represents. May they always pursue a cost-conscious path, so that people of all incomes can enjoy the rewards of travel. And may they create, for both the traveler and the persons among whom we travel, a community of friends, where all human beings live in harmony and peace.

Arthur Frommer